Plot Outlines of 100 Famous Novels

THE SECOND HUNDRED

Plot Outlines of 100 Famous Novels

THE SECOND HUNDRED

Edited by
LEWY OLFSON

Dolphin Books
Doubleday & Company, Inc.
Garden City, New York

The Dolphin Books edition is the first publication of
Plot Outlines of 100 Famous Novels: The Second Hundred

Dolphin Books edition: 1966

INTRODUCTION

One of the joys of the world of literature is its great wealth of fascinating novels. Yet, with the pace of life what it is today, many superb masterpieces of fiction remain little more than admired names to many people.

To provide a satisfying acquaintance with a large number of outstanding and representative novels from English, American, and other literatures, the publishers issued some time ago *Plot Outlines of 100 Famous Novels,* now called *Plot Outlines of 100 Famous Novels: The First Hundred.* The book gave pleasure to so many readers that it has seemed essential to bring to this audience a companion volume, presenting outlines of a hundred novels not included in the first book, but in all respects as famous, as absorbingly interesting, and as influential as those in the earlier volume.

Our book is therefore called *Plot Outlines of 100 Famous Novels: The Second Hundred.* It is in every sense a companion to the first book. For adequate coverage of novelists and their works, the two volumes must be considered together. Novelists all or most of whose best-known works are included in the first volume do not appear in this second book (as, for example, Hawthorne and Scott). Some novelists who can be more fully appreciated through a knowledge of certain of their novels which are not among those in the first book are represented again in *The Second Hundred* by other major works. Thus, many outstanding novelists of all periods will be found in both volumes. In addition to these, this new book introduces many important novelists whose works were not among those in *The First Hundred.* In this latter group are books by a number of quite recent American masters of fiction as well as a notable assembling of the great eighteenth-century English novelists, and a richly varied selection of outstanding works by great novelists of continental Europe and the Orient.

In arranging the plot outlines we have retained essentially the same plan as before, dividing the novels into English and Irish Novels, American Novels, French Novels, Russian

Novels, and Novels of Various Countries. However, within each category, we have placed the plot outlines in approximately chronological order instead of alphabetically. The chronological arrangement provides a quick glance at the broad coverage which the book achieves, as will be seen readily in the Table of Contents. For convenience in locating a specific work, an alphabetical Index of Authors and Titles will be found at the end of the book.

A valuable feature is the inclusion of biographical sketches of each of the novelists. Where a man or woman is represented by more than one work, the biographical sketch always precedes the first of that author given here. These sketches offer a glimpse of the author and background for the novel presented as a plot outline.

It is the editor's hope that *The Second Hundred* will bring as much enjoyment to readers and students as *The First Hundred* has; and that together they will prove constantly valuable as reference works, in addition to being friendly treasuries of stimulating, informative, and adventurous reading.

The editor wishes to acknowledge with thanks the invaluable help of Patricia L. White, Daniel Fields, and Lawrence W. Lamm of Copeland & Lamm, Inc., in the preparation of this book. And he owes a special debt of gratitude to William E. Dickinson of Croft Educational Services for his generous cooperation.

L. O.

ACKNOWLEDGMENTS

Esther Waters by George Moore: Herbert S. Stone & Company. *Chance* by Joseph Conrad: Doubleday & Company, Inc. *Heart of Darkness* by Joseph Conrad: Doubleday & Company, Inc. *The Secret Sharer* by Joseph Conrad: Doubleday & Company, Inc. *Zuleika Dobson* by Max Beerbohm: Dodd, Mead & Company. *The Old Wives' Tale* by Arnold Bennett: Doubleday & Company, Inc. *Of Human Bondage* by W. Somerset Maugham: Doubleday & Company, Inc. *A Portrait of the Artist as a Young Man* by James Joyce: The Viking Press. *The Crock of Gold* by James Stephens: The Macmillan Company. *Mrs. Dalloway* by Virginia Woolf: Harcourt, Brace & World, Inc. *Herself Surprised* by Joyce Cary: Grosset Dobson, Inc. *Point Counter Point* by Aldous Huxley: Harper & Row, Publishers. *Brave New World* by Aldous Huxley: Harper & Row, Publishers. *Lost Horizon* by James Hilton: William Morrow & Co., Inc. *Nineteen Eighty-Four* by George Orwell: Harcourt, Brace & World, Inc. *A Passage to India* by E. M. Forster: Harcourt, Brace & World, Inc. *The Heart of the Matter* by Graham Greene: The Viking Press. *The End of the Affair* by Graham Greene: The Viking Press. *Washington Square* by Henry James: Modern Library, Inc. *The Turn of the Screw* by Henry James: Heritage Press. *The Golden Bowl* by Henry James: Dell Publishing Co., Inc. *The Age of Innocence* by Edith Wharton: New American Library of World Literature. *Sister Carrie* by Theodore Dreiser: Harper & Row, Publishers. *Death Comes for the Archbishop* by Willa Cather: Alfred A. Knopf, Inc. *The Call of the Wild* by Jack London: The Macmillan Company. *Main Street* by Sinclair Lewis: Harcourt, Brace & World, Inc. *Babbitt* by Sinclair Lewis: Harcourt, Brace & World, Inc. *The Late George Apley* by John P. Marquand: Little, Brown and Company. *The Great Gatsby* by F. Scott Fitzgerald: Charles Scribner's Sons. *Tender Is the Night* by F. Scott Fitzgerald: Charles Scribner's Sons. *Sanctuary* by William Faulkner: Random House, Inc. *Light in August* by William Faulkner: Random House, Inc. *The Bridge of San Luis Rey* by Thornton Wilder: Pocket Books, Inc. *For Whom the Bell Tolls* by Ernest Hemingway: Charles Scribner's Sons. *The Old Man and the Sea* by Ernest Hemingway: Charles Scribner's Sons. *Gone With the Wind* by Margaret Mitchell: The Macmillan Company. *Look Homeward, Angel* by Thomas Wolfe: Charles Scribner's Sons. *The Grapes of Wrath* by John Steinbeck: The Viking Press. *Of Mice and Men* by John Steinbeck: The Viking Press. *All the King's Men* by Robert Penn Warren: Harcourt, Brace & World, Inc. *The*

Catcher in the Rye by J. D. Salinger: Little, Brown and Company. *The Princess of Cleves* by Mme. de Lafayette: New American Library of World Literature. *Manon Lescaut* by Abbé Prévost: Charles Scribner's Sons. *The Charterhouse of Parma* by Stendhal: Liveright Publishing Corp. *Salammbô* by Gustave Flaubert: E. P. Dutton & Co., Inc. *Around the World in Eighty Days* by Jules Verne: Dodd, Mead & Company. *Thaïs* by Anatole France: Fawcett World Library. *The Immoralist* by André Gide: Alfred A. Knopf, Inc. *The Counterfeiters* by André Gide: Alfred A. Knopf, Inc. *The Wanderer* by Alain-Fournier: Heritage Press. *The Little Prince* by Antoine de Saint-Exupéry: Harcourt, Brace & World, Inc. *Wind, Sand, and Stars* by Antoine de Saint-Exupéry: Reynal & Hitchcock. *The Stranger* by Albert Camus: Alfred A. Knopf, Inc. *The Plague* by Albert Camus: Alfred A. Knopf, Inc. *The Death of a Nobody* by Jules Romains: New American Library of World Literature. *Man's Fate* by André Malraux: Modern Library, Inc. *Dead Souls* by Nikolai Gogol: Penguin Books, Inc. *Virgin Soil* by Ivan Turgenev: E. P. Dutton & Co., Inc. *The Idiot* by Fyodor Dostoyevsky: Heritage Press. *War and Peace* by Leo Tolstoy: Bantam Books, Inc. *The Kreutzer Sonata* by Leo Tolstoy: Random House, Inc. *The Golden Ass* by Apuleius: The Crowell-Collier Publishing Co. *The Tale of Genji* by Lady Murasaki: Houghton Mifflin Company. *Dream of the Red Chamber* by Tsao Hsueh-chin: Twayne Publishers. *The Sorrows of Young Werther* by Johann Wolfgang von Goethe: New American Library of World Literature. *The Three-Cornered Hat* by Pedro Antonio de Alarcón: Barron's Educational Series, Inc. *The World's Illusion* by Jakob Wassermann: Harcourt, Brace & World, Inc. *The Magic Mountain* by Thomas Mann: Alfred A. Knopf, Inc. *Steppenwolf* by Hermann Hesse: Modern Library, Inc. *Kristin Lavransdatter* by Sigrid Undset: Alfred A. Knopf, Inc. *The Confessions of Zeno* by Italo Svevo: Alfred A. Knopf, Inc. *The Trial* by Franz Kafka: Alfred A. Knopf, Inc. *Darkness at Noon* by Arthur Koestler: The Macmillan Company. *Cry, the Beloved Country* by Alan Paton: Charles Scribner's Sons. *Ehrengard* by Isak Dinesen: Random House, Inc.

CONTENTS

AMERICAN NOVELS

FRENCH NOVELS

RUSSIAN NOVELS

NOVELS OF VARIOUS COUNTRIES

ENGLISH AND IRISH NOVELS

ROBINSON CRUSOE

Daniel Defoe

Daniel Defoe was born in London in 1660. He was educated as a member of a dissenting religious sect, and went into business in 1685. When his business failed, he received government posts from King William III, whose death meant the loss of these posts and Defoe's consequent full-time career as a journalist and pamphleteer. He began writing fiction in 1719, and in his work laid the foundation for the modern English novel. Defoe's works of fiction are characterized by first-person narrative of events, presented to the reader as actual fact in a journalistic style; they are perhaps the first realistically detailed fiction in English literature. Defoe never realized much money from his numerous writings, and was usually deeply in debt. He died under somewhat mysterious circumstances in London on April 26, 1731.

From his earliest youth, Robinson Crusoe, third son of a well-to-do merchant, has longed to go to sea. But when he reaches his teens, and presents this idea to his father, his parent always advises against it, urging instead that Robinson take up a more stable trade.

Finding himself, however, in the seaside port of Hull on an errand one day, young Crusoe is once again overwhelmed with wanderlust—and this time the call of the sea is too strong to be resisted. On an impulse, he signs on a vessel as a seaman. Much to his surprise and regret, he proves less able a sailor than he had hoped. The ship on which he sails encounters rough weather, and Robinson is very seasick. When the storm increases in intensity and the ship is wrecked, young Crusoe's sailing career almost ends before it has properly begun—but fortunately he and his mates are rescued.

Once again on dry land, Crusoe debates with himself whether he should return to his father's house and admit that he was not cut out for the sailor's life; but with the pride and impetuosity of youth, he decides once again on setting out to sea.

Robinson's second voyage is no more successful than the

first. This time his ship is attacked by marauding Moors, and he is taken their prisoner. It is only after several years of slavery that he is able to effect his escape in a longboat. He is rescued from the sea by an excellent Portuguese sea captain, who takes him to the Brazils. There Robinson settles down to a life of agriculture—his sailing days over forever, or so it would seem.

After four years as a farmer, during which he becomes a comparatively wealthy man, Crusoe sees an opportunity to make an even greater fortune by engaging in the slave trade. So it is that he sets out on a slaving mission to Guinea, sailing on September 1, 1658—exactly eight years to the day since he first set foot on a sailing vessel back in Hull, England.

Crusoe's dreadful luck at sea once again becomes apparent. The ship on which he sails encounters miserable weather, and early one morning she strikes sand and begins to break apart. He and his comrades scramble into one small boat, hoping that it will carry them to safety. But the boat is overturned, and, losing track of his fellows, Crusoe is carried along by the sea.

Tossed about by the turbulent waters, poor Crusoe despairs of his life—but for once, luck seems to be with him. Finding that the waves carry him closer and closer to land, he waits for his opportunity—then grabs for a jutting rock, and after much effort, pulls himself to shore, and drags himself onto a small strip of sandy beach where he lies exhausted.

When his strength begins to return, he searches about until he finds a supply of fresh water. His first thought, after slaking his thirst, is to collapse upon the ground and sleep—for every muscle and nerve in his body aches from the ordeal through which he has passed. But reasoning that wild animals might devour him as he sleeps, and that he therefore would have been spared a hideous death at sea only to meet with one more hideous on land, he climbs into a tree for safety. There he falls asleep, thus passing his first night on the deserted island which is to be his home for almost twenty-nine years.

For a deserted island it is, as Robinson ascertains the following day. Reasoning that the Lord must have placed him in this isolated situation for some purpose, he refuses to give way to despair, but sets his mind to the problem of survival and endurance with an intensity and purpose that surprises even himself.

As luck would have it, the wrecked ship on which he had sailed is washed ashore nearby, and from it Crusoe is able to salvage much that is to prove of value: lumber, victuals, sailors' clothes, arms, a carpenter's chest, a grindstone, nails and spikes, bullets, powder, bedding—all the portable items that he can manage he brings to his cove of safety in an extended series of trips. At last, the wrecked vessel is stripped —and Crusoe has accomplished his task none too soon, for shortly afterward a storm arises, destroying the ship and all that remains aboard.

Though his progress in all things is slow, owing to the inadequacy of his supplies and his own lack of skill, Crusoe works steadily each day, providing himself with what he considers the essentials for life, against such time as he shall be rescued. A tent, enclosed by a high fence, is his first major project, and when it is completed, he turns his attention to other necessary things. It takes him four whole days to make a chair—but though he keeps track of the time by cutting notches into a post each day as a sort of calendar, time itself has little meaning for him, and he is patient to accomplish things slowly and steadily.

And so the days slip into weeks, the weeks into months, the months into years. Before long, Crusoe ceases to think of possible rescue, and devotes all of his thought and energy to improving his island refuge. He breeds some tame creatures for food; he kills wild animals, using their skins to make clothes and an umbrella to protect him from the sun; he catches a parrot and teaches it to say his name. And, regularly, he finds time to pray, and with the passing of years he derives great sustenance from his faith in God.

After ten years of solitary life on his island, Robinson Crusoe is confronted with the idea of other human life: he finds the print of a man's naked foot in the sand. He is petrified, and worries about it for months, but when he sees no further evidence of human life, his fears begin to fade, and his life resumes its lonely but productive course.

It is only many years later—after a full twenty-three years on the island—that the matter of human life is again raised in his mind. He sees, at a distance, a group of savages beaching two canoes on the shore. He knows not what to make of them, but when he sees them depart with the rising of the tide, he is easy in his mind once again.

In May of his twenty-fourth year, he sees more signs of life—this time of civilized life. A ship is wrecked offshore, and Crusoe is beside himself with anxiety, hoping that some survivor or other will make his way to the island. But none do, and it is a lonely Robinson Crusoe who salvages supplies from the wrecked vessel when it is washed into his harbor.

At last, however, he is fated to meet another man. A group of savages, similar to those whom he had seen earlier, return to Crusoe's island—this time carrying with them two prisoners. The Englishman is horrified when he realizes that the men are cannibals, intent on feasting upon their poor captives. With great ingenuity he manages to rout the savages and free one of their captives, a handsome, strong young man who, in his gratitude to Crusoe, shows in sign language that he is determined to be Crusoe's slave forever.

Crusoe is both impressed with the dignity and gratitude of the savage, and touched by the fact that after so many years he has once again made personal contact with another human soul. He brings the savage back to his tent, feeds him and nurses him, and christens him Friday, in honor of the day on which the two met.

Friday proves to be an intelligent companion and a fast learner. The days that follow his arrival fly by quickly for Crusoe, who now is able to teach Friday to speak English, convert him to Christianity, and enjoy with him the companionship of which he has been so long deprived.

As time passes and Friday becomes more adept in English, Robinson Crusoe learns more and more of his story. His joy is unbounded when he discovers that seventeen white men, victims of some past shipwreck, have made their home with Friday's people. And though he says nothing to the savage, the idea begins to grow in Crusoe's mind of trying to make contact with these other men of his own kind.

One day, during Friday's third year on the island, the two men come upon another group of savages, these also about to feast upon two miserable prisoners. Working in close coordination, Robinson and Friday employ an ingenious strategy by which they manage to kill most of the cannibals, rout the rest, and rescue the two prisoners. One of these is a Spaniard;

the other—and this explains to Robinson the sudden flash of joy on Friday's face—is Friday's own father.

When the Spaniard and Friday's father have been nursed back to health, Crusoe announces his plan to meet the white men who have taken refuge with Friday's people. The men determine to wait another year, until sufficient food can be raised to supply these white men should contact be made.

Before the plan can be effected, however, the island is once again visited by a group of strangers. This time it is the crew of an English ship—and, watching through his spyglass, Crusoe realizes that he is witness to a mutiny. After much secret planning with his three comrades, Robinson contrives to take the mutineers prisoner. The coup is a success, and though some blood is shed, the British ship and all her crew fall at last to Robinson's control.

So it comes about that long after he has given up hope of ever seeing civilization again, Robinson Crusoe is enabled to leave his island home. He sets sail on December 19, 1686, after having spent twenty-eight years, two months, and nineteen days upon the island; and he arrives in England after an absence of thirty-five years.

His affairs in the Americas having been entrusted to a loyal and astute man, Crusoe discovers that he is now wealthy beyond his wildest imaginings. But he does not forget that isolated spot in the Atlantic where he spent the major part of his manhood. Indeed, he is one day to return to his island, and what he finds there amazes him beyond belief.

But that, as Robinson Crusoe himself observes, is another story. . . .

PAMELA

Samuel Richardson

Samuel Richardson was born in Derbyshire, England, in 1689, the son of a cabinetmaker. He was apprenticed to a London printer, and, after marrying his master's daughter, rose rapidly to become Printer of the Journals of the House of Commons and Law-Printer to the King. Friends of Richardson's who were booksellers and who knew of his facility at writing letters requested that he write a volume of model letters for the guidance of those who found it difficult to compose their own. Richardson undertook the task on

*the condition that the models would at the same time stress morality
and virtuous behavior. He became intrigued with the story possibilities of certain of his model letters from an imaginary father to his
daughter; he expanded these into a story, and the result, published
in 1740, was* Pamela: or Virtue Rewarded, *often called the first
English novel, and certainly the first novel in which character,
sensibility, and sentiment are the dominant themes. Pamela became, immediately after its publication, the most fashionable and
popular book in England; it was at the same time extravagantly
admired by the literati in England, France, and Germany, and
provoked, besides imitations, an extraordinary number of satires
(notably* Joseph Andrews) *and parodies that took issue with the
pious morality proposed by the author. Richardson wrote two other
novels, both in the epistolary (letter-writing) form, and from his
writings lived a life of comfort and respectability until his death
in 1761.*

Upon the death of the goodhearted, aristocratic mistress for
whom she has worked, fifteen-year-old Pamela Andrews is
distraught over her future prospects. Must she return to her
impoverished parents? Will she find a suitable position as
lady's maid elsewhere? Fortunately, her late mistress' son
and heir, the handsome Mr. B——, takes a personal interest
in Pamela; and the girl writes happily to her parents, telling
them that she will be allowed to stay in her present position,
and forwarding to them the six gold sovereigns which the
new master has given her for having served his late mother
so well.

The elder Andrewses reply with a letter of dire warning
to their daughter. They wonder if Pamela's naïve innocence
and extreme beauty will not make her prey to Mr. B——,
and they question the nobleman's motives. They caution
their daughter that Mr. B—— is probably planning an assault upon her virtue, and they remind her that they would
rather follow her body to the graveyard than learn that she
has surrendered that most precious jewel, her honor.

Pamela writes them a letter of reassurance, citing as evidence of her master's pure intent the fact that he would not
consent to Pamela's going to serve in the home of his own
sister, Lady Davers, for fear that the girl would be seduced
by his sister's nephew, Jackey. Surely there can be no better proof of her master's honorable intentions.

All too soon, however, Pamela has cause to wonder if perhaps her parents' warning was not justified, for the master takes liberties with her one day when he surprises her in the greenhouse. When Pamela confides the incident to the kindly, motherly housekeeper, Mrs. Jervis, however, the master insists that she has misinterpreted his behavior.

Soon, however, the master again gives evidence of desiring more freedom with his beautiful serving girl than ordinarily would prevail, and for her own protection, Pamela begins to sleep in Mrs. Jervis' room. But even this does not insure her against further overtures from the master, and soon there can be no doubt whatever that Mr. B____ has immoral designs on Pamela.

In desperation, the girl resolves to leave service and return to her parents, though they can ill afford to keep her. No sacrifice is too great, however, when it comes to preserving her honor. She prevails upon her master to give her permission to leave, and at last he sets a day for her departure. At this Pamela breathes a little easier—but she is still not safe from the impassioned advances of the master. (Once he even goes so far as to secrete himself in a closet in Mrs. Jervis' room while Pamela readies herself for bed. It is only the girl's being driven into a hysterical fit leading to unconsciousness that frightens the master sufficiently for him to abandon his forceful intent.)

At last the appointed day for her departure arrives; and to convince Pamela that he wishes her no ill (the master has all along insisted that he is innocent of any evil intent against the girl), Mr. B____ provides a carriage and coachman to take her to her parents' home. Too late, Pamela realizes that the coachman is acting under special orders from the master. Instead of taking her to the village where Goodman Andrews resides, he takes her to the country estate of Mr. B____, and there Pamela finds herself kept a prisoner in the house under the ever-watchful eye of the villainous housekeeper, Mrs. Jewkes.

Now there can be no doubt whatever of the role Mr. B____ intends for Pamela to play in his life. Even were he inclined to marry, he would never stoop so low as to marry a serving maid. He intends to make Pamela his mistress. At this realization, the virtuous girl is in a frenzy of despair; but miserable as her situation is, she cannot but shrink with horror at the contemplation of her loss of honesty, and she determines not to yield to her master under any circumstances.

With each passing day, Pamela sees more clearly how villainous her master is, and how fiendish are the plots which he concocts against her to insure her ultimate ruin. Mrs. Jewkes is under orders to keep Pamela in sight at all times, and whenever the girl is insolent or willful, Mrs. Jewkes beats her. The other servants of the place are equally her enemies, all of them being loyal to the orders of their master. Pamela's only consolation in this misery is the journal she keeps, in which she daily records the horror of her position, the fiendishness of her master's designs, and her determination to preserve her purity.

Pamela's one hope of salvation lies with the local parson, Mr. Williams, an impoverished clergyman whose future is entirely in Mr. B____'s hands. Mr. Williams alone is sympathetic to Pamela's plight; he alone shares her conviction that nothing is worse than for a maiden to surrender her honor; and the two are able to set up a clandestine correspondence, hiding their letters beneath a loose, moss-covered stone lying near a sunflower.

In her letters to him, Pamela begs Mr. Williams to make her case known to the nearby gentry, and to plead for their intercession in her behalf. This Mr. Williams does—though at great risk to his future happiness, for he knows that such behavior cannot help but become known to Mr. B____ and incur his wrath; but all of the nearby gentlemen are as morally dissolute as Mr. B____, and none will come to Pamela's aid —not even Mr. Peters, the minister of the local parish, whose career also rests on Mr. B____'s pleasure.

Mr. Williams at last confides to Pamela that her only hope of escaping seduction and ruin by Mr. B____ is to contrive an escape from the house, and to become Mrs. Williams. The young parson makes clear that he offers marriage not only to help Pamela out of her dishonorable predicament, but also because he has come to love her, having had such ample evidence of her purity and nobility of spirit.

This offer, however, repels Pamela, for she has no wish to marry anyone, but longs only to be allowed to return to the humble poverty of her parents' cottage, where she will be free to live a life of simple labor and do good works in accord with her religious faith.

Though Mr. B⸺ has not yet visited Pamela in her bucolic prison, he has been in frequent touch with her by mail, and his letters alternate between forceful threats and honeyed entreaties. But Pamela sees only too readily that each letter is merely a ruse designed to get her to surrender willingly that which she will *never* surrender.

By accident, a letter meant for Mrs. Jewkes falls into Pamela's hands, and from it she learns the full range of Mr. B⸺'s villainy. Not only is he determined to possess this beautiful serving maid, because of whom he is driven nearly mad with passion, but also he has discovered the correspondence between Pamela and Mr. Williams, and has for revenge had the innocent parson thrown into debtor's prison. He writes further that he is coming soon to Pamela, and that willingly or unwillingly, she will become his mistress.

Pamela then decides upon a desperate measure. Having obtained from Williams a key to the gate, she decides that she must escape now or never. Accordingly, she manages to slip through the bars of her bedroom window late one night, leap to the roof of the conservatory below, and from there jump to the ground. She is severely hurt in this escapade, but she drags herself on, her determination to preserve her virtue giving her strength against her pain. She manages to get to the gate, and there discovers, to her horror, that the fiendish Mrs. Jewkes has had the locks changed. Thus, her escape attempt comes to nought, and it is duly reported to Mr. B⸺ by Mrs. Jewkes.

At last, the dreaded day arrives, and Mr. B⸺ appears in person at the estate. He makes clear to Pamela that he will stop at nothing short of having his desire of her, but assures her that if she will consent to become his mistress willingly, he will settle a fortune upon her and allow her to live in ease and luxury. He warns her, further, that if she will not give freely what he asks under such munificent terms, he will seize what he wants by force, and Pamela will have nothing for her pains. But the girl will not yield, and as modestly and sincerely as possible she communicates to him that she cannot accept any terms if the price be her virtue.

Thus goaded beyond endurance, the hot-blooded Mr. B⸺ concocts yet another of his devilish schemes, and, with the connivance of Mrs. Jewkes, he one night surprises Pamela in her bed. Mrs. Jewkes holds the terrified girl's arms, so that she cannot move, and it seems clear that at last Mr. B_____ will achieve by force what he has been so long unable to achieve by words. But Pamela's horror is so great that it provokes one of her hysterical seizures. This frightens Mr. B_____ sufficiently to drive him from the room —indeed, he believes the girl is at the point of death—and again Pamela's virtue is saved.

Now the half-crazed master learns of the existence of Pamela's journals, in which she has recorded every word, every action, every thought of her long imprisonment, and he forces her to surrender the documents to him. The girl is beside herself with terror at this turn of events; for though her journals record her fight for her virtue in complete honesty, she knows that Mr. B_____ cannot be pleased by the impressions of him and his actions as she has recorded them.

The journals do not, however, have upon Mr. B_____ the effect feared by Pamela. Instead, her lucid prose and her utterly open sanctity move him deeply, and for the first time he realizes the horror of what he has tried to do to this girl. Regretfully—for he does not deny that he still desires her madly —he tells Pamela that she is free to return to her father's house, and that he will never again importune her with his base desires.

Pamela is overjoyed at this news, and reaffirms her long-standing feeling that but for this one evil and persistent idea of seizing her virtue, Mr. B_____ is the most goodhearted and virtuous man alive. Joyfully, she sets out for her parents' home.

When her journey is but a day completed, however, a horseman overtakes Pamela with a letter from Mr. B_____. In it, he tells her that he has fallen ill, and begs her to return to him. Convinced of his reformation, Pamela has not the heart to refuse his plaintive request, and she returns to the house where she had so lately been a prisoner.

Upon her return, Pamela goes to Mr. B_____ to ask his reason for sending for her. In a moving interview, the master confides his love, his admiration, his esteem of Pamela, and he asks her to become his wife. At this happy resolution to all her misery, Pamela is overjoyed, and plans are made for the wedding.

At first, the nearby gentry are not kindly disposed to this serving girl who is to become a great lady. But when they meet her, none can resist her beauty, her tact, her warmth, her open charm, and all fall under her sway. As the day of the wedding nears, Pamela finds herself accepted by such people as Lady Jones and Sir Simon Darnford—personages whom she well knows to be far above her own humble station.

Mr. B——, who is now truly reformed, proves himself to be the most admirable of men. There is nothing that he will not do to please his Pamela. She asks him, as evidence of his good heart and his kind intentions toward her, to forgive Mr. Williams, and restore him to wealth and happiness. This Mr. B—— consents to do. (Later, he is to grant similar requests of Pamela's on behalf of Mrs. Jervis and Mr. Longman, two of his servants who had befriended Pamela during her imprisonment and who, thereby incurring his wrath, had won their dismissals.) He also establishes her parents in a small estate of his at Kent, and provides them with a generous annual income.

The wedding takes place as planned, and Pamela is made the happiest of women. Mr. B—— proves to be all that any woman could ask for in a husband, and Pamela believes her griefs to be at an end. There is, however, one further trial in store for her.

Lady Davers, with her nephew Jackey, arrives, to inquire into rumors they have heard that Mr. B—— is keeping Pamela as his mistress. As luck would have it, when they arrive Mr. B—— himself is absent, having been called to attend at the bedside of a dying friend. Thus it happens that Pamela must receive the haughty Lady Davers by herself.

Although Mr. B—— has let his marriage be known among the local gentry, he has not yet announced it to society at large. Therefore, Lady Davers knows nothing of the change in Pamela's station—and the poor girl dares not enlighten her without having her husband's permission first to do so. Therefore Lady Davers is most insolent to the one-time serving maid who, she supposes, has become her brother's strumpet and who now behaves as though she were mistress of the manor and Lady Davers' equal. To all of this abusive raillery Pamela submits, but when Lady Davers at last strikes her, calling her an unprintable name, Pamela bursts out with the news that she is, indeed, Mrs. B——.

Lady Davers refuses to believe this, but eventually, after

Pamela has been subjected to great indignities, Mr. B——— himself arrives, and tells Lady Davers the truth. The aristocratic lady determines never to speak to Mr. B——— again. But at the insistence of the meek and humble Pamela, the brother and sister are reconciled, and Lady Davers admits that her brother has, indeed, married a beautiful, intelligent, and virtuous woman, albeit one of humble rank.

At last, Mr. B——— takes his bride back to town with him. As Pamela had feared, the gentry are at first reluctant to accept her. But no one, having met her, can resist Pamela's goodness, and soon she is accepted as an equal by the greatest ladies in the land.

She continues to prove her gracious qualities to her husband, who cannot be sufficiently grateful that he has so noble a wife. Perhaps typical of Pamela's greatness of character is her ready forgiveness of Mr. B——— when she learns that he has an illegitimate daughter, and her kind insistence that she, Pamela, become an "aunt" to the little girl, and give her the loving care that is suitable to the child of an aristocrat.

Thus does Pamela shine forth for all the world as an example of how no danger or distress can ever carry one beyond the care of Providence, and as a proof that meekness, purity, humility, and virtue will surely be rewarded.

JOSEPH ANDREWS

Henry Fielding

Henry Fielding was born on April 22, 1707, in Somerset, England. He studied at the University of Leiden, but left to write plays, which were produced in London with some success. When the number of theaters was limited by law in 1737, Fielding began to write novels. He had entered the bar, and eventually became a principal justice of the peace. Fielding had begun Joseph Andrews as a parody of Richardson's moralistic Pamela, but he soon found himself creating a new fictional genre in which characters were delineated against the broad background of English society by an author with an omniscient view of the proceedings. Fielding thus created the English novel as we know it. In the essays that are interwoven in his novel, Tom Jones, he provided the first critical theories of the novel, both as a literary art and as the most valid means of describing the complexities and events of human society.

Fielding's own life was troubled with poor health; he died in Lisbon, where he had gone for a cure, on October 8, 1754.

At the age of ten, Joseph Andrews, only son of Gaffar and Gammar Andrews and brother of that paragon Pamela (of whom Richardson has written the story), is apprenticed to Sir Thomas Booby. He becomes an excellent horseboy, and so pleases Lady Booby that he is raised to the station of her footman when he is seventeen.

While in service at the Boobys', Joseph falls under the kindly moral influence of the curate, Mr. Abraham Adams, who helps the young man form a chaste character. And when Joseph falls in love with the young serving girl, Fanny, it is Mr. Adams who convinces them that they will do well to wait a few years before marrying.

Shortly thereafter the Boobys remove to London, taking Joseph with them. In the great city Joseph becomes something of a dandy, and by the time he is twenty-one he is as handsome, charming, and altogether appealing a young man as one could hope for. But withal, he sacrifices none of the virtues and moral piety which form the basis of his chaste character. Indeed, it is his piety which shortly thereafter preserves Joseph from the amorous advances of Lady Booby, who, on the death of Lord Booby, reveals an inclination to alter the mistress-servant relationship. No sooner has Joseph fended off the lady, however, than he is assaulted by the lady's maid—the ugly, pretentious, middle-aged Mrs. Slipslop; but fortunately his virtue (and his naïveté) save him once again. He pays for his insistence on preserving his virtue, however, for the outraged Lady Booby discharges him.

Joseph sets out on foot for his old village, and after several comic adventures on the road, he is reunited with Mr. Adams, the curate, at an inn where further attempts on the lad's virtue are made by a serving wench—but to no avail. Joseph and the curate decide to travel together, and farther on their journey they fall in again with Mrs. Slipslop, with whom they meet a number of interesting travelers, one of the most important being an itinerant peddler who, by lending Adams some money, makes it possible for the travelers to pay their bill at the inn.

Mr. Adams, ever the absent-minded one, manages to separate himself from Joseph and the other travelers. While wan-

dering about the countryside trying to find his way, he rescues a young woman from the advances of a ruffianly
would-be ravisher. When Adams and the young woman are
discovered by a group of rustics standing by the ruffian's
prostrate form, however, they are assumed to be murderers.
The country folk bind them and lead them to the town justice; and as they walk, Adams discovers that the girl is none
other than Joseph's beloved, Fanny. The two are eventually
cleared, and together they make their way to a neighboring
inn—where they discover Joseph and Mrs. Slipslop. Here the
two young lovers are reunited, much to the dismay of Mrs.
Slipslop, who has not relinquished her amorous inclinations
toward the young footman. Mrs. Slipslop leaves in high dudg-
eon, and Joseph, Fanny, and Mr. Adams begin their journey
once more.

Traveling by foot across a heath one night, they stop at a
deserted cottage to ask if they may rest awhile. The house-
holder, one Mr. Wilson, is at first suspicious of them; but
when his fears are allayed, he and Mrs. Wilson make them
welcome. Wilson tells his life story—a fascinating account, including many trials and hard circumstances; but he concludes
that he and his wife of twenty years are now perfectly
content, their only grief being the loss of their eldest son,
who was stolen by gypsies at the age of three and has never
been heard of since.

Assured that Wilson will one day visit them in Adams'
parish, the three travelers take up their journey the next
morning, and, as usual, fall subject to further adventures
with the various people whom they meet. One of these is a
vicious squire, who pretends hospitality to them—but only
that he may have many practical jokes played on Adams. It
is the squire's intent to get Adams and Andrews drunk, and
then to satisfy his lust for the beautiful Fanny. This scheme
is foiled when Adams, sober in spite of many great draughts
of gin-and-beer, denounces the squire and takes his humble
companions away with him.

The next morning, however, the three travelers are overtaken at an inn by the squire's followers who, in spite of a
brave fight, manage to subdue Joseph and the curate and tie
them up, and then to abduct Fanny. Though Joseph and
Mr. Adams are helpless, all is not lost, for miraculously
Fanny's screams are heard by a passer-by who proves to be

Peter Pounce, long the head servant at Booby Hall. Recognizing Fanny, he quickly believes her tale and rescues her from the abductors, returns her to her lover at the inn, and insists that Adams accompany him in the carriage to Booby Hall, whither he too is bound, while Fanny and Joseph shall go on horseback.

As Pounce precedes his mistress, Lady Booby, by only a short time, the arrival at Booby Hall proves to be a mass homecoming. The lady turns first red and then white when she sees Joseph—her ardor not having cooled. But when, the next day in church, she hears the banns announced for him and Fanny, she rages with vengeance. Calling upon a crafty lawyer, she arranges to have Fanny and Joseph arrested and removed from the parish.

Shortly after she sets this scheme in motion, Lady Booby's nephew, the new Lord Booby, arrives at the ancestral home with his bride—who turns out to be Joseph's sister, Pamela. He is instrumental in obtaining the release of Fanny and Joseph from the trumped-up charges of Lawyer Scout. The elder Lady Booby, delighted at an excuse for a reconciliation with Joseph, welcomes him to her home again; but of course she remains adamant in her detestation for Fanny. Her first ruse to rid herself of the beautiful maiden having failed, Lady Booby tries another. She introduces Fanny to Beau Didapper, in the hope that the man's worldly attractions will lure Fanny from Joseph; but this too fails.

A sudden turn of events, however, seems to insure that the marriage between Joseph and Fanny will never take place. A traveling peddler—the same that had loaned Adams some money at an inn during the journey already described—arrives in the parish, and on hearing that it is the seat of Booby Hall, he makes a startling disclosure:

His common-law wife had, some years before, confessed on her deathbed that she had once traveled with a band of gypsies. While with them she had stolen an infant girl and left it with the servants at Booby Hall. This instance so closely parallels Fanny's own origins that more details are pressed for, whereupon the peddler recalls that his wife said she had stolen the child from a family named Andrews—a family that had another daughter by the unusual name of Pamela. Thus it turns out that Fanny is Joseph's own sister!

Unhappy, Joseph and Fanny pledge that if the tale be true, they will live together forever in platonic celibacy.

The day is saved, however, with the arrival of Gaffar and Gammar Andrews, for Gammar is able to explain that when she bore her second child (which she did while Gaffar was off in the army) she bore a daughter; but that the child had been stolen from its cradle by a band of passing gypsies, who had placed a male child in its stead. This male child was Joseph, whom Gammar had raised as her own, trusting to the Lord that someday her real child would be returned to her.

And when it is demonstrated that Joseph has on his breast a strawberry mark, it is clear that he, in fact, is the son of Mr. Wilson—who propitiously arrives at Booby Hall at this moment to be reunited with his long-lost child.

Thus, at last, Joseph and Fanny are married, and go to live with the Wilsons. Young Squire Booby insists on setting Mr. Adams up in much greater style than he has been accustomed to—much to the delight of Adams' wife and six children. And all ends happily—even for Lady Booby, who returns to London shortly after Joseph's wedding, and is soon receiving the attentions of a most handsome captain of the dragoons.

THE EXPEDITION OF HUMPHRY CLINKER

Tobias Smollett

Tobias Smollett was born in Dumbartonshire, Scotland, in 1721. In Glasgow he began the study of surgery, which he interrupted at the age of eighteen in order to bring a play he had written to London. He found no one interested in his play and took a position as surgeon's mate on a warship. He returned to London in 1744, set up practice as a surgeon, and began to write novels which made him an extremely successful author in his lifetime, although he did take up an inordinate amount of editing and translating to supplement his income. He is credited with expanding the diary or epistolary method, as he does in The Expedition of Humphry Clinker, so that the personalities of the characters become apparent and differentiated in their supposed entries. Smollett was also the first English novelist to write of contemporary trends and ideas in science, politics, the arts, and other fields with which men of his time were concerned. Smollett wrote Humphry Clinker, his last major work, near Leghorn on the coast of Italy, where he had settled for reasons of health. It was there that he died on September 17, 1771.

Through an extensive series of letters exchanged among various friends of differing social positions and intellectual attitudes, there has been preserved a panoramic view of life in the British Isles in the middle eighteenth century, as well as the particulars of the story of a family named Bramble.

Upon discovering the attachment his niece and ward, Lydia Melford, has formed with a handsome actor named Wilson, the goodhearted Squire Matthew Bramble determines to take her to Bath, in the hope that she will forget a romance fostered, he believes, only by her innocence. With them go the squire's maiden sister, Tabitha, a meddlesome, unpleasant, foolish spinster; and Lydia's patronizing young brother Jerry, just down from Cambridge.

Wilson, however, pursues Liddy to Bath, where, disguised as an old spectacle-seller, he makes himself known to her and again declares his love. Conscience-bound, however, she refuses any further commerce with him. Simultaneously, another love affair blossoms, as Aunt Tabby commences a flirtation with an out-at-the-elbows baronet, Sir Ulic Mackilligut. This is a short-lived romance, though, as he discovers her to be not as rich as he had thought; and on the interruption of her little love affair, Tabitha becomes more disagreeable than ever.

After a month at Bath, Bramble decides to go to London, so the entire menage moves on—bags, baggage, pets, and servants. On the road the party picks up a ragged youth of about twenty. Discovering that he is a penniless orphan, Bramble gives him some money. Whereupon Humphry Clinker—that is the lad's name—determines out of gratitude to follow Bramble and serve him the rest of his life. So Clinker joins the Bramble household as footman.

In London, Humphry proves to be a highly individual and excellent young man, combining the virtues of piety, simplicity, humility, and goodheartedness.

Mr. Martin, a handsome young man-about-town, falls in love with Liddy and pursues her; but she, ever true to her love for Wilson, disdains his overtures. Encouraged in his suit by Jerry and the squire, however, Martin declares himself, only to be misunderstood by Tabitha, who takes his proposal for herself. This dreadful error is set to rights at last, much to Tabby's embarrassment and consternation; and Lydia, confessing to her uncle that she loves Wilson yet, though she does not communicate with him, receives Bramble's permission to send Mr. Martin away.

No sooner is this comedy resolved when, upon false witness, Humphry is arrested as a highwayman, convicted, and sent to prison. Bramble, however, is convinced of Humphry's innocence, and resolves to do all he can to clear the young man and free him.

Jerry Melford, who is also convinced of Humphry's innocence, is told by a constable that the real thief is none other than Mr. Martin, whom the law has been watching for some time. Though until now Martin has been too clever to be caught, it seems only a matter of time before he will be brought to justice. This does Humphry little good, of course; but when Bramble goes to Clerkenwell Prison in an attempt to cheer him, he finds Clinker not only well composed, but happily preaching to his fellow inmates, a large number of whom he has converted to religion. Several days later, the false witness against Humphry is himself caught in a crime; and, the man originally robbed having been found and declaring Humphry not to be the man involved, Humphry is set free and returned to the Bramble family.

Setting forth on its travels once again, the entourage begins to journey north. On the road, some highwaymen are rumored to be near; and when Humphry goes to investigate, whom should he come upon but Edward Martin! Martin presents himself to the Brambles as a protector, and rides with them a way until they stop at an inn. From their conversation with him, Martin learns that both Jerry and the squire are familiar with his true calling. After he leaves the party, Martin sends a letter to Bramble confessing that he practices thievery only because he is unable to earn an honest living, and begging the squire to save him from the gallows by making an honest man of him and giving him a position in the Bramble household. He writes further that he will be in touch with the Brambles once again later in the journey, at which time he will expect an answer from the squire about this humble proposal.

The trip northward continues, and at every stop some new adventure meets the travelers. The people they encounter, the episodes they endure—all are of a hilarious nature. And, of course, Tabitha manages to have several more unrequited romances, among her lovers being one ridiculous elderly Scotchman, Obadiah Lismahago.

At Stockton, Mr. Martin once again appears. His situation having been changed by his extraordinary luck at cards, he now finds himself in command of a small fortune—but one which he is unable to use, as the justices keep such a close watch on him that they mistake each move he makes. It is determined, therefore, that with Squire Bramble's help he shall go to the East Indies, and there set himself up in an honest profession.

It is in the north country that love comes to Humphry Clinker, the object of his affection being Mrs. Winifred Jenkins, Aunt Tabby's maid. He has a rival in Dutton, Jerry's servant. But before the competition passes beyond the stage of minor fisticuffs, Dutton elopes with a pawnbroker's daughter, and Clinker once more has the field to himself.

Liddy's romance is also revived in the north country, by the appearance of a "Mr. Gordon"—who bears a singular resemblance to Mr. Wilson. But again she refuses to be false to her promise to her uncle, and she does not speak with him.

Traveling onward, the party once again encounters the ridiculous Lieutenant Lismahago. This time it appears that Aunt Tabby may have greater success with him, for he joins the party and confesses to the squire that he intends to press his suit upon the old woman.

Turning homeward, the travelers encounter further adventures. Liddy's Mr. Wilson is again seen—and again he disappears without making himself known.

Of even greater importance is the accident befalling Squire Bramble. His coach turns over in the river, and at great risk to himself, Humphry Clinker rescues the squire. Sopping wet, he is taken to the home of a nearby gentleman, Charles Dennison—with the whole party, of course, in his wake. Dennison instantly recognizes in Bramble the young man Matthew Lloyd, with whom he had been at college. Bramble explains that after leaving college, for reasons to do with his patrimony, he changed his name to Bramble, but that he is indeed the former Matthew Lloyd—whereupon Clinker, in a frenzy of disbelief, produces a letter signed by Lloyd in Matthew Bramble's own hand proving that Clinker is none other than Bramble's (actually Lloyd's) illegitimate son, Clinker being merely the name of the man to whom Humphry was apprenticed as a child. Already overwhelmed by the endless services shown him by Humphry, Bramble determines to recognize the young man and install him in the rank and position to which he is entitled.

Being prevailed upon by Dennison to stay awhile, the Brambles become his house guests, and learn his story. Imagine their surprise and delight when they discover that his only son is none other than the man who has been wooing Liddy under the name of Wilson and in the disguise of an actor. The Brambles are now reconciled to the match, and Lydia and her love are reunited.

The sojourn at the Dennisons' is capped by a triple wedding: that of Lydia to George Dennison, Tabitha to Lieutenant Lismahago, and Humphry, now called Clinker Lloyd, to Winifred Jenkins.

Young Jerry Melford, of course, is above such things as weddings and romance. And yet he cannot help but be susceptible to the charms of Liddy's dearest friend, Laetitia Willis, who attends the wedding as Liddy's maid-of-honor. And one wonders. . . .

TRISTRAM SHANDY

Laurence Sterne

Laurence Sterne was born in 1713 in Ireland, where his father, a minor officer in an English regiment, was stationed. He was educated at Cambridge, and upon his graduation in 1736 he became a clergyman in Yorkshire, where he lived comfortably for about twenty years. The first two volumes of Tristram Shandy, *Sterne's only novel, were published in 1759, and they created a literary sensation. The public and the literati were delighted, and Sterne, now a celebrity, announced his intention of continuing to work on the story of the Shandy family. The last volume of the novel appeared in 1767. Although one of the earliest novels in English,* Tristram Shandy *continues to this day to be one of the most unconventional. Sterne employed the stream-of-consciousness technique to record events and impressions as experienced subjectively by his characters. The text contained blank pages, black pages, diagrams, seemingly irrelevant punctuation, and many other devices which would now be called experimental or avant-garde;*

the use of a unified, coherent, and structured plot, moreover, was deliberately and plainly avoided. Sterne's last years, which saw his fame spreading over the continent of Europe, were troubled with ill-health. His last book, the delightful travel account, A Sentimental Journey Through France and Italy, treated only of France; Sterne died in 1768 before the Italian accounts were written.

This is the autobiography of one Tristram Shandy, gentleman. But unlike most autobiographies, this one begins before the author's birth; for Tristram believes it necessary that all of the influences upon his life be made clear to the reader. So before Tristram's birth is described, several other matters must be described first.

To start with, there is the inopportune conversation between his parents, Walter Shandy and the former Elizabeth Mollineaux, as they are in the act of begetting their son. That Mrs. Shandy should have asked her husband at such a crucial moment whether he had remembered to wind the clock seems to Tristram to have been a most inauspicious beginning for any life, and he attributes to it many of his own shortcomings.

The nuptial conversation leads into Tristram's description of the local midwife, and thence to a discussion of Parson Yorick and his horse. Then, following his own peculiar logical train, Tristram introduces into the text for the reader's edification a complete transcript of his mother's marriage articles.

One of the items in that document leads to the author's presenting a learned dissertation on the subject of prenatal baptism—all of it transcribed for the reader with utmost fidelity, in French!

The argument sets the stage for Tristram to introduce the local male midwife, Dr. Slop, and from him Tristram moves to an introduction of his beloved Uncle Toby Shandy.

Uncle Toby is the bachelor brother of Tristram's father, and the most goodhearted man in Christendom. He suffers from two tragedies—one spiritual, one physical. The spiritual affliction is his extreme sensitiveness to any mention of Aunt Dinah, a noble lady who had had the poor judgment to run off with a servant. The pathos of her story has never ceased to upset Toby. His physical tragedy resulted from a wound in the groin which he sustained at the siege of Namur. Ever since, Toby has remained a semi-invalid, waited upon by his faithful servant, James Butler (who, as Tristram explains at length, is called Corporal Trim).

The main joy, the main delight, indeed, the main purpose of Uncle Toby's life, is now his hobby—and a most unusual hobby it is. He and Corporal Trim have devoted themselves to constructing upon the grounds of the Shandy estates an enormous complex of forts and fortresses, duplicating in minute detail the terrain of all the major battles of the war, and there they re-enact each battle, each assault, and each siege. So devoted a rider of his hobby horse is Uncle Toby, that at every opportunity he launches into a detailed discussion of arms and armaments. But he is such a goodhearted soul, and so pitiable is the thought of the wound in his groin, that all who know him tolerate his whimsical devotion to his hobby.

Uncle Toby and Corporal Trim having left the stage temporarily, we are next presented with a sermon on the subject of conscience. This is followed by an extended discussion of the comparative virtues of being born head first as opposed to being born feet first; by the transcription in both Latin and English of a horrendous form of excommunication taken from the records of the Church of Rome; by the Preface to the autobiography itself; and by a description of the flirtation between Corporal Trim and the Widow Wadman's cook, Bridget, which results in the destruction of one of Uncle Toby's model bridges.

With all these descriptions and introductions and transcriptions, it happens that Tristram Shandy is born somewhere between chapters in the middle of Book Three—with a mashed nose.

Now, noses are a subject as interesting to Tristram's father as armaments are to Uncle Toby. Walter Shandy believes that the size of the nose is directly related to the quantity of the intellect. (We are treated to the reproduction of the monograph on the topic by the eminent Hafen Slawkenbergius.) Thus, Tristram's nose being mashed through Dr. Slop's carelessness is a major tragedy. And as if that were not bad enough, the newly born, nasally mutilated infant is misnamed Tristram, a name which Walter Shandy hates above all others. (The mistake is owing to the maid Susannah's inability to remember the chosen name, Trismegistus.)

This calamity is followed by a chapter (short) on sleep.

The next chapter (ten pages in length, the author tells us) is omitted altogether.

Next comes the description of a meeting among the clergymen Didius, Yorick, and Phutatorius, which is held to determine whether Tristram's name may be changed; but the question remains problematical, as the meeting turns to chaos when a hot roasted chestnut accidentally falls into the front of Phutatorius' breeches.

We are now at Book Five, which begins with a chapter on the topic of whiskers. The next few chapters are devoted to the news of the death of young master Bobby, Tristram's brother—probably the most casually recorded infant death in all of literature.

Then there are dissertations on education, on paternity, and on health (with other subjects scattered here and there along the way.) All this time, Tristram has been growing up offstage, as it were, and when Book Six begins, he is five years old.

It is determined that Tristram must have a tutor, and Master LeFever is proposed for the post by Uncle Toby. This, of course, occasions the lengthy description of LeFever's life: how his father was a soldier, how Uncle Toby met him and nursed him through illness, &c, &c, &c.

The LeFever story is followed by a recording of the momentous debates between Mr. and Mrs. Shandy concerning the ordering of young Tristram's first pair of breeches.

The author now returns to Uncle Toby and his hobby horse, and a complete description of the mock battles he and Corporal Trim engage in. Uncle Toby's joy is not to last, however, for the signing of the Peace of Utrecht makes further war games impossible. (Indeed, Uncle Toby regards the peace treaty as a personal affront.)

It seems that the old man will fall into a desolate melancholia, being thus deprived of his hobby—but at the last moment he is saved—*mirabile dictu*—by falling in love with gossipy Widow Wadman. (Several blank pages are here bound into the text, that the reader may sketch his own picture of her.)

Shortly thereafter, Book Seven begins, but as it is a sort of travelogue about France (with various religious observations and stories thrown in) we need not concern ourselves with it here, but may proceed directly to Book Eight, which, with Book Nine, completes the story of Uncle Toby (and indeed of Tristram Shandy) and contains, in addition, the interpolated story of the King of Bohemia and His Seven Castles.

The Widow Wadman, having long viewed Uncle Toby from afar as an object not altogether ineligible, at last determines upon a plan of assault. Using every known female wile, she stalks her prey until, with the greatest subtlety, she leads him to the point where he falls in love with her. (Simultaneously, her cook, Bridget, has been spending her time with Corporal Trim, and using *her* wiles to further her mistress' interest with Trim's master.)

Uncle Toby, realizing that he is in love, goes to Widow Wadman's to propose marriage to her. All seems to be going well until the widow begins to question him about the wound he sustained at the siege of Namur. Uncle Toby mistakes her intent, and goes to fetch a map of the battleground, to show her precisely where he was struck. But Bridget goes straight to the point with Corporal Trim, and makes clear that Widow Wadman seeks to know whether Uncle Toby's wound will interfere with conjugal activity.

So shocked are Trim and Toby by this vulgarity that they decamp from Widow Wadman's. And so Uncle Toby's romance and the autobiography of Tristram Shandy come to an end.

EMMA

Jane Austen

Jane Austen was born on December 16, 1775, in a Hampshire, England, village where her father was the rector. Never married, she lived with her family all her life and accompanied them when they changed residence. Her time was spent on domestic duties, writing, and, we may gather from the evidence of her novels, carefully observing the upper-middle-class provincial society to which she belonged. She referred to her writings as the work of a miniaturist, working on a small "bit of ivory with so fine a brush." She had no concern for the vast forces—aesthetic, philosophical, religious, political, technological, or economic—which were altering European civilization while she lived. The problems that arise in her six novels are those of social status, proper marriage, and inheritance of property. These Miss Austen writes of with an unerring ear for dialogue, with a devastating eye for the intricacies and foibles of human behavior, with a sense of structure and timing, and with a clarity and precision of style unmatched in the English novel of manners. Her novels were published anonymously, and recognition of her achievement did not come until some time after her death. She died in Winchester, where she is buried in the cathedral, on July 18, 1817.

Emma Woodhouse is the beautiful younger daughter of one of the most respected families in Highbury. Her mother having died during Emma's earliest childhood, and her sister Isabella having married John Knightley several years ago, Emma is mistress of the house, and the spoiled darling of her hypochondriacal father. (There is a nominal governess for Emma—Anne Taylor—but she too is completely under Emma's sway; and when she marries the good-natured Mr. Weston, Emma's life is left completely unsupervised, and she is free to indulge in whatever whims she desires.)

To amuse herself, Emma befriends a young girl named Harriet Smith. Of uncertain parentage and no fortune, Harriet's major recommendations are her good looks and even temper; but Emma, quick to distort the perception of reality to suit her own temperamental demands, decides that Harriet must be taken under her own wing and "made something of."

When the fine, upstanding farmer, Robert Martin, proposes to Harriet, Emma cleverly leads Harriet to believe that she is far above him; and Harriet, who idolizes Emma and is horrified to realize that if she were to marry Martin she must give up Emma's society, rejects the good farmer.

Emma determines that a suitable match for Harriet would be the vicar, Mr. Elton, and she decides to contrive as much as possible to bring the two of them together. She is warned of the folly of this enterprise by George Knightley, the bachelor brother-in-law of Isabella, and the only person who sees Emma as she really is and candidly reveals her faults to her. Knightley tells Emma that Elton is looking for a woman with rank and fortune, and that he will not look at Harriet, who would be happiest if she encouraged Robert Martin's advances. But Emma is convinced that she has a knack for matchmaking and that she is far more perceptive of peoples' feelings than Knightley; so she continues her little plans.

All seems to be going well in the drawing-on of Mr. Elton.

He spends much time in the company of Emma and Harriet, and seems to be showing toward Harriet all the signs of a lover. And, of course, it is no trouble at all for Emma to fan the flames of passion for Mr. Elton in the bosom of the impressionable Harriet. Mr. Knightley's black prediction, however, finally bears fruit; Elton proposes to Emma, and makes it clear that he has tolerated Harriet's company only so that he could press his suit on Emma. Horrified by this turn of events, Emma rejects Elton, and breaks the awful news to Harriet, who goes into the depths of despair. Emma's guilt over the harm she has done Harriet is in no way lightened when within a month Elton marries the vulgar and snobbish— but rich—Clara Hawkins. Emma is forced to concede that, in this affair at least, Knightley has been right and she wrong.

Emma's chance to make everything right with Harriet by providing her with a better husband than Elton arrives in the person of Frank Churchill, the handsome stepson of Emma's former governess, Anne Weston. Everyone in Highbury is charmed with the dashing good looks and easy, witty manner of this newcomer to the town—everyone, that is, except Knightley. He believes Frank Churchill to be superficial, spoiled, and wanting in human warmth. Emma defends Frank—but decides to be discreet about her plans for matching him with Harriet, and says nothing of them to Knightley.

Frank Churchill is indeed flirtatious—in that, Emma must concede to Knightley's view of him. He pays his attentions and flattering court to a number of ladies, being equally dashing and unserious with all: Mrs. Elton, Harriet, Emma, and Jane Fairfax—the last-named being the impoverished, beautiful niece of the town's silliest and most talkative woman, Miss Bates. Though Emma has always intensely disliked the quiet Jane Fairfax—Emma recognizes, in her secret heart, that Jane is a superior person, in every way what Emma herself would like to be—she appreciates Churchill's courtesies toward Jane as appropriately charitable to one in the girl's low position.

Where Churchill's heart really lies, it soon seems clear to Emma, is with herself. For a short while she wonders if she can really be falling in love with him; but when she discovers that she is not, she determines that he shall be Harriet's.

At a local ball, Harriet is cruelly snubbed by the malicious Eltons—who seem determined to punish the poor girl for having loved Mr. Elton before his marriage and without his consent—and Knightley lives up to his name by rescuing Harriet and being her partner for the evening. Noticing his kindness to her friend, Emma discovers her estimation of Knightley—whom she had always found cold—rising.

The next day, Harriet is again rescued—this time from a more serious adventure. She is set upon by a pack of gypsies, and only the opportune arrival upon the scene of Frank Churchill saves her from unknown terrors. Later, when Emma archly asks Harriet if she loves "a certain man who has saved her," she is gratified to note Harriet's blushes as the girl answers yes. Though Harriet never mentions Frank by name, Emma is quietly delighted to know that she is in love with the man Emma has picked for her. And, it appears, Frank Churchill is beginning to reciprocate. (To a casual observation by Knightley that Churchill seems to be far more interested in Jane Fairfax, Emma fairly hoots in derision, explaining to the imperceptive Knightley that Churchill is merely being kind to the orphan; indeed, Churchill and Emma have made several jokes together about the poor girl.)

Emma's triumph over Knightley is not long-lived, however. It soon is revealed that Churchill, who had known Jane in Weymouth, had become secretly engaged to her. They are as much in love now as ever, and all of Churchill's flatteries and flirtations were merely a screen behind which he hoped to hide the truth. Emma is distressed as to how to break the news to Harriet that yet another of the men she has proposed should have turned elsewhere.

Much to her surprise, Harriet is not the least upset by Churchill's engagement to Jane. When Emma asks incredulously if she has not loved the man, the surprised Harriet answers no: it is Knightley whom she has been worshiping. When she hears Knightley's name, Emma for the first time realizes that she, Emma Woodhouse, must marry him, and she makes this clear to Harriet.

At this, Harriet's heart again undergoes a minor fracture, and she travels to London to visit Emma's sister Isabella, in the hope that there she will overcome this amatory failure.

Fortunately for Emma, Knightley confesses that he has loved her all along. Emma now recognizes what a superficial person she has been in the past, and how much wiser

Knightley is in all things. She resolves to be a good wife to him, and they plan to be married.

In London, Harriet by chance encounters her long-rejected suitor, Robert Martin, and Emma is delighted to learn that he has again pressed his suit, and that this time Harriet has accepted him. Emma now recognizes Martin's true worth and suitability for Harriet—sentiments Knightley has voiced from the beginning—and she is delighted for her friend.

Thus, in the autumn, three couples are married by Elton, the vicar: Jane to Frank Churchill, Harriet to Robert Martin, and Emma to George Knightley.

NIGHTMARE ABBEY

Thomas Love Peacock

Thomas Love Peacock was born in 1785 in Dorsetshire, England. He was self-educated, and published his first work, a volume of poems, in 1804. He received a post in the East India Company in 1819, and by 1836 had risen to chief examiner. His short novels, although not widely popular, were the delight of the intellectuals of his generation. Peacock was thoroughly familiar with all the intellectual, spiritual, literary, economic, and philosophical currents of his time, and his cynical, skeptical attitude is apparent in the play of ideas and characters in his conversational and witty novels. Nightmare Abbey is one of Peacock's best and most typical novels, and one in which the author's favorite target, the Romantic movement, is deftly satirized. The characters are based on contemporary figures: Scythrop is Percy Shelley (Peacock's closest friend), and Stella is Mary Wollstonecraft Shelley, while Cypress and Flosky are caricatures, respectively, of Byron and Coleridge. Peacock wrote a total of seven novels; he retired from his government post in 1856 and died in England ten years later.

To Nightmare Abbey, ancestral castle of the widowed Christopher Glowry, Esq., comes young Scythrop Glowry. He has completed his studies at the university, where he has become every bit as morose a person as his venerable father. Scythrop has just been spurned by Miss Emily Girouette, and in his despair he finds Nightmare Abbey the perfect place to drown his sorrows in *Young Werther*. Spacious, dark, and silent, the mansion is surrounded by fens and marshes. It is the quintessence of Gothic lugubriousness, and here—surrounded only by the household servants (Raven the butler, Crow the steward, Skellet the valet, and Mattocks and Graves the grooms)—Scythrop intends to pass his days in lonely misery. He reads. He stalks the ramparts of the Abbey. He contructs a hidden passageway to his chamber. He writes a philosophical treatise—*Philosophical Gas; or, a Project for a General Illumination of the Human Mind*—which sells seven copies. He is happy, because he is miserable.

Scythrop is not to remain in solitude long, however, for his father, Mr. Glowry, returns to the Abbey, and soon there are in residence a number of house guests—most of them as melancholic as the Glowrys themselves. There is Mr. Flosky, a lachrymose and morbid litterateur of little note; the Reverend Mr. Larynx, an obliging and innocuous divine; and Mr. Toobad, Mr. Glowry's dearest friend, who maintains that though a happy day may yet come, in which the Evil One and his Powers shall be overthrown, such a day will not arrive "in our time."

To this party are added Mr. and Mrs. Hilary, relations (albeit distant ones) of Mr. Glowry, and their irrespressible, flirtatious niece and ward, Marionetta.

Paying little heed to the long philosphical discussions that occupy most of the residents of Nightmare Abbey, Marionetta immediately sets her cap for Scythrop—and much to his perturbation, he finds himself succumbing to the blandishments of this vivacious creature so unlike himself. Glowry makes clear his displeasure—he has arranged with Toobad that Scythrop shall marry Toobad's daughter Celinda (who is currently studying in Germany)—but this only makes Scythrop more determined in his love for Marionetta.

Convinced that the young man will change his mind once he sees Celinda, Toobad departs for London where he is to meet her, and old Glowry eagerly awaits their return. When Toobad does return, however, it is with bad news. His daughter has refused a match with a man she has never seen and has fled, leaving no trace.

Two more house guests arrive at Nightmare Abbey: Mr. Asterias, the famed ichthyologist, and his son Aquarias. They are in search of a mermaid (a species the existence of which they do not doubt), and have decided to search for one in the fens of Glowry's estate. Much to their delight they actually spot one—but she eludes them before they can catch her.

Shortly thereafter, Marionetta notices a distinct coolness toward her on the part of her beloved Scythrop. This, naturally enough, makes her melancholy—and her melancholia seems to flame Scythrop's interest. When his renewed interest in her revives her spirits, however, Scythrop again finds her somewhat less attractive.

Marionetta becomes convinced that some dark secret is preying on Scythrop's mind—but neither Mr. Listless nor Mr. Flosky is able to discover it to her. It is true that a ghost has been seen walking the ramparts at night, garbed in flowing white and a bloody turban—but Marionetta does not believe that this can be the cause of Scythrop's malaise.

As it happens, however, it *is* the ghost—or, rather, the person who has been mistaken for a ghost—that has brought perturbation to young Scythrop. On returning to his study the night that Mr. Asterias spotted the mermaid, he was surprised to find the self-same apparition made flesh, as it were. A young woman revealed herself to him. Refusing to tell Scythrop her name, she explained only that she was in desperate straits; that she required to be hidden from those who would pursue her; and that she had come to Scythrop because he had authored the philosophical work which had most drastically affected her thinking. Flattered beyond words, Scythrop secreted her in the passageway behind the moving panel in his chamber. After that, he passed many rapturous hours in the company of the mysterious lady (who called herself Stella), deep in philosophical conversation. (The lady is of so lugubrious a disposition, however, that he is grateful, on occasion, to refresh himself at the feet of the ever-cheerful Marionetta.)

As a relief from their own conversation, the house guests are treated to a brief visit from the pessimistic poet Mr. Cypress, a college friend of Scythrop's who has come to say farewell, as he is leaving England. The company is infinitely cheered by his brief visit; he is clearly far more unhappy and melancholic than any of them.

Shortly after Cypress' departure, Mr. Glowry happens to pass Scythrop's closed door and overhears within a female voice which he does not recognize. After pounding on the door, he is admitted by Scythrop, who denies everything. But at last the secret chamber is revealed, and so is the lady. Mr. Glowry lets slip in her presence mention of Scythrop's intended betrothal to Marionetta, at which "Stella" screams in despair. This brings the entire household to the tower apartment, and all are amazed to discover the Abbey ghost in person. The two who are the most surprised are Marionetta, who now understands what has been causing Scythrop lately to behave in such a strange manner toward her, and Mr. Toobad, who exclaims that "Stella" is his own daughter, Celinda.

At this, Glowry is delighted. Now, since they have fallen in love on their own, surely Scythrop and Celinda will be content to marry. Celinda refuses, however; haughtily she declares that Marionetta clearly has the prior claim on Scythrop, and she rejects him.

Marionetta, however, rejects Scythrop also, on the grounds that he has obviously transferred his affections to Celinda.

Within a matter of hours, all the visitors have left Nightmare Abbey, thoroughly shocked at Scythrop's scandalous behavior. As for that young man, he is beside himself with despair; whereas his problem had been deciding between Celinda and Marionetta, he now finds himself deserted by both. True to his melancholic posturing, he declares to his father that unless one of the two maidens relents, suicide is his only answer. Terrified, Glowry persuades Scythrop to wait a week; if, says the old man, he is not able to bring back one of the girls to Nightmare Abbey within seven days, Scythrop may then blow his own brains out.

Scythrop agrees, and the old man goes off posthaste for London, hoping to effect some stratagem with Celinda or Marionetta that will save Scythrop's life.

The first day, Scythrop regrets his bargain, and longs only to put a bullet through his own brain. The next day is sunshiny; he is pleased when Raven announces dinner. On the third evening, he puts a new flint in his pistol. On the fourth, he locks the pistol in a drawer—where he leaves it till the morning of the seventh day.

True to his word, Mr. Glowry returns on the seventh day—bringing neither Celinda nor Marionetta, but only a letter to Scythrop from each. The first is signed Celinda Flosky; the second, Marionetta Listless—both girls having found husbands at Nightmare Abbey.

Scythrop is beside himself with rage. He tears the letters to bits. He rails at the heavens against the fickleness of women. He storms. He curses. And then he and Mr. Glowry move toward the dining room. Nodding toward Raven the butler, Scythrop says, "Bring some Madeira."

A CHRISTMAS CAROL

Charles Dickens

Charles John Huffam Dickens was born at Landport, England, in 1812, the son of a low-salaried government clerk. When the elder Dickens was imprisoned for debt, the ten-year-old Charles went to work in a shoe-polish factory. His sporadic formal education ended when he was fifteen, whereupon he entered a successful journalistic career as a news and parliamentary reporter. His first literary efforts were short sketches signed with the pseudonym "Boz" and they were published in periodicals. The public and critical response was encouraging, and Dickens thereupon began the creation of a series of novels which have come to occupy a unique place in world literature. Dickens was the most widely read and admired novelist of his time, and if certain aspects of his work, notably his criticism of social conditions, are not particularly meaningful in the mid-twentieth century, there are many other qualities which have ensured his continuing popularity. He created a galaxy of characters so memorable that their names have often become generic for the qualities they represent, and he placed these characters in settings and situations which he had carefully observed (or even lived, as he drew a great deal of material from his own childhood). Dickens became wealthy from his writings and from reading tours in the United States. He died suddenly in the year 1870, and was buried in the Poets' Corner of Westminster Abbey.

Ebenezer Scrooge, surviving partner of Scrooge and Marley's, a successful London moneylending firm, hates Christmas. Convinced that Christmas is merely a plot concocted by the working classes to pick the pockets of their employers, he begrudges giving the day as a paid holiday to his clerk, Bob Cratchit; he shouts to his nephew, Fred, who has invited him to share his Christmas feast, that the holiday is a humbug; and to the men who come collecting Christmas alms for the poor, he exclaims: "Are there no prisons? Let them go there!"

He is a hated man, a lonely man; but what does Scrooge care? Nothing.

But a curious thing happens to Ebenezer Scrooge one Christmas Eve. Everywhere he goes in his rooms, he seems to see the face of his long-dead partner, Jacob Marley. "Humbug!" he mutters, trying to reassure himself, as he pulls the covers tight up over his head.

But it is not humbug. Soon he begins to hear the sound of chains . . . and then, the very ghost of Jacob Marley passes through the locked door and into Scrooge's bedchamber.

Marley's ghost tells Scrooge that he has come to warn him to change his ways, ere it be too late; and that his warning will take the form of three supernatural visitors: the Ghost of Christmas Past, the Ghost of Christmas Present, and the Ghost of Christmas Yet to Come.

When Marley disappears, Scrooge is tempted to think that he dreamed the entire episode. But suddenly the clock strikes one, and Scrooge finds that his bedchamber is being invaded by a curious figure: a man with the face of a child, but crowned with long, white hair. Clearly, this is the first of the three Spirits—the Ghost of Christmas Past. Placing his hand upon Scrooge's heart, the Spirit leads him through the chamber window, and out into the starry night.

Such visions of Scrooge's own past does the Spirit conjure up! They visit the school where Scrooge had been as a boy—and there, there is the boy Scrooge himself! It is the Christmas after Scrooge's father has had a change of heart, and has agreed to have the boy home for the holidays. Scrooge watches as his sister—long since dead, but now, strangely, alive as a little girl—comes to fetch him home. From there Scrooge and his guide pass to the home of young Scrooge—and the old man remembers the Christmas when, alone, he was kept company only by his friends from books, who had seemed to come to life. The next visit is to Old Fezziwig's, the shop in which Scrooge had been apprenticed as a young man. Here he witnesses another Christmas past, with the beaming Mrs. Fezziwig as jovial hostess, and young Scrooge himself, dancing and singing and happy as a lark. There is yet another Christmas past to witness, this one not so happy; for it was at this holiday time that Scrooge's fiancée had given him up, seeing in him the grasping man he was to become. One more Christmas—this time in the home of that same woman, now married to a happier man and surrounded by loving children such as Scrooge has never known.

When he has witnessed this last scene, and feels that he

can take no more, lo! the Spirit of Christmas Past is gone, and he is in his own bedchamber again.

Scrooge barely drifts off to sleep, when the clock strikes again: One. "Impossible!" he thinks, bolting up. But there, in the midst of the room, he sees another Spirit—the second one Marley had foretold: the Ghost of Christmas Present.

Once again, Scrooge flies through the night sky with his spirit companion, now to visit scenes of Christmas of the present day. As they pass through the sky, Scrooge sees below the happy bustling of men and women with gifts and marvelous Christmas foods in their arms, on their way to their homes, the homes of loved ones, or church. Then the Spirit indicates a window into which he wishes Scrooge to look. It is the home of Scrooge's underpaid clerk, Bob Cratchit. How Scrooge envies the little family! Though they are poor and humble, and the youngest child, Tiny Tim, is a cripple, they are full of joy and love and delight in one another and the day. Indeed, the only unhappy note is struck when his own name is proposed by Cratchit for the toast: "I give you Mr. Scrooge." By the way the faces fall, old Scrooge discovers how low the Cratchits hold him in their esteem. But Tiny Tim raises everyone's spirits by crying, "God bless us, every one!"

Leaving the Cratchits behind, the Spirit carries Scrooge to the poorest, darkest, meanest spots on earth; and in each, Christmas is being celebrated with reverence and with love.

Next they visit the home of Scrooge's nephew, Fred; and the old man hears Fred tell his guests how he pities his uncle, rich as he is, for his poverty in spirit.

Turning to his ghostly companion, Scrooge notices two childish faces—poor and suffering—peeking from the Spirit's robes. The Spirit explains that they represent the children of Man; the boy being Ignorance, and the girl, Want.

"Have they no refuge or resource?" asks Scrooge, touched.

"Are there no prisons?" torments the Spirit.

But before he can protest the mocking words, Scrooge finds himself back once more in his chamber, alone.

Now, as Marley's ghost has foretold, the bell strikes twelve —and the third Spirit appears, a draped and hooded phantom that speaks no word, but in awful silence leads Scrooge on the most frightening visits of all. For this is the Ghost of Christmas Yet to Come.

As they speed through the night, they hear a group of men below them talking of a man recently dead; and from their conversation, Scrooge knows that though the man has been rich, he has been hated. The next scene shows the dead man's charwoman, his laundress, and the undertaker—the only ones to honor his deathbed with their presence; but they have come to plunder, not to mourn. From thence they pass to the home of a poor young couple, and from their words Scrooge learns that the death of the hated man has brought them to the brink of misery, for he died without relenting of a harsh and unjust debt against them. The next scene is even more cruel for Scrooge to bear: it is the home of the Cratchits—but the chair by the fire is now empty, and the little crutch is without an owner. Deprived of proper care for want of money, Tiny Tim is dead.

There is one scene more: a wretched, neglected grave-yard. The specter points to one stone, and Scrooge knows that beneath it lies the man who has caused all this misery. As weeds have covered the stone, he has to trace the letters with his fingers; they spell—EBENEZER SCROOGE.

Shaken to the very fiber of his being at last, Scrooge begins to exhort the Spirit to change what he has seen. "Good Spirit," he pursues, as down upon the ground he falls before it, "your nature intercedes for me, and pities me. Assure me that I yet may change these shadows you have shown me, by an altered life. I will honor Christmas in my heart, and try to keep it all the year. I will live in the Past, Present, and the Future. Oh, tell me I may sponge away the writing on this stone."

But the Spirit is gone . . . and Scrooge is alone in his bedroom.

The Spirit is gone, but not the change that has come over Scrooge. "I *will* live in the Past, the Present, and the Future!" he exclaims. As the bells of Christmas Day begin to toll, Scrooge jumps into his clothes, for he has much to do, many wrongs to right, and many people of whom to ask forgiveness.

He is, indeed, a changed man from this time. He raises Bob Cratchit's salary; takes a kindly interest in his nephew, Fred; becomes a good and just man in his business—and, most important of all, sees to it that Tiny Tim has the best doctor possible, so that in time he may be cured.

He has no further intercourse with Spirits; and it is now

always said of him that he knows how to keep Christmas well, if any man alive possesses the knowledge. May that be truly said of us, and all of us! And so, as Tiny Tim observed, God bless us, every one!

GREAT EXPECTATIONS

Charles Dickens

The orphaned Philip Pirrip—called Pip—lives with his termagant sister, Mrs. Joe Gargery, and her husband, the kindly and loving blacksmith. Although he goes to the village school, where he learns more from a young girl called Biddy than he does from the ancient schoolmistress, Pip longs for nothing more than to be apprenticed one day to his dear brother-in-law.

Visiting his parents' graves one night, Pip is confronted by an escaped convict who threatens dire consequences unless the boy secretly fetches him some food and a file. Terrified, Pip obeys, and he lives in mortal fear that the theft from his sister's larder will be discovered. But shortly thereafter the convict is taken, and he declares that he himself has stolen food and a file from the blacksmith's house. Thus is Pip spared discovery.

Through the offices of Pip's distant relative, the hypocritical and canting Mr. Pumblechook, it is arranged that Pip will visit occasionally at Satis House, the greatest mansion in town. Satis House is owned by the strange Miss Havisham, an elderly spinster who was deserted on the night of her intended marriage by her unscrupulous fiancé, and who, ever since, has altered nothing: she still wears her wedding dress, now faded and tattered; her wedding cake lies moldering on a table; all clocks have been stopped at the hour of her desertion.

This partly mad Miss Havisham has a young adopted daughter, the beautiful Estella. It is to play cards with Estella that Pip has been sent for, but the haughty young girl treats Pip with nothing but scorn and contempt. Nonetheless, and in spite of the fact that he realizes Miss Havisham is raising Estella to torture men with her beauty and heartlessness, as a means of insuring her own revenge upon the sex, Pip falls desperately in love with Estella.

Pip is miserable with his lot now, although he is finally apprenticed to Joe Gargery, and he confides to Biddy that he longs to be a gentleman. (Biddy now lives with the Gargerys, and nurses Mrs. Joe, who has been in a state of shock since being attacked one night by an unknown man.) Biddy gives Pip sensible advice, but in his foolishness, Pip claims that she has a mean nature. For love of Estella, Pip wishes to become a gentleman.

Oddly enough, Pip soon gets his chance. A lawyer, Mr. Jaggers, tells Pip that an anonymous benefactor has given Pip great expectations. Pip is heir to a fortune, and is to be raised in London as a gentleman. He is never, however, to seek to know the name of his benefactor.

The fact that Pip has seen Jaggers several times at Satis House, and that the tutor proposed by Jaggers for him is one Herbert Pocket, a distant relative of Miss Havisham's whom Pip has also seen on one of his visits, leads Pip to believe that his benefactor is none other than Miss Havisham. This impression is confirmed by Miss Havisham's fond attitude toward him when he pays her a last visit before going to London.

Biddy and Joe give Pip a tearful goodbye, but though he loves them, he is already a bit ashamed of them. He is very aware of his own importance in his new clothes; and he is determined to become a true gentleman as quickly as possible. To this end he has an admirable tutor, young Herbert Pocket; and soon Pip and Herbert are leading as idle and carefree an existence as any two men about town. When debts begin accumulating, however, Pip's conscience bothers him for Herbert's sake, as Herbert cannot afford their mode of living. Pip arranges with Mr. Jaggers and his clerk, the kindly Wemmick, to provide a business opening for young Pocket. Though the money backing the venture is Pip's, its source is to be kept a mystery to Pocket.

By the time Pip comes of age, and comes into the annual sum of five hundred pounds, he is a polished young gentleman —though not particularly skilled or educated. Indeed, he is something of a snob, and his occasional meetings with the good but humble Joe and Biddy afford him extreme embarrassment.

Estella, too, has blossomed in gentility and polish, but Pip finds her as hard as ever. Indeed, she several times warns him that she has no heart, and will only bring him sorrow, but Pip does not care, and loves her as much as ever. When he discovers that she is seeing a good deal of a loathesome, callow youth of fortune named Drummle, however, he is revolted, and insists upon an interview at Satis House.

During the course of the interview, Miss Havisham realizes for the first time what a monster she has made of Estella. As for the girl, she rejects Pip for the last time, and assures him of her intention of marrying Drummle. Miss Havisham begs Pip's forgiveness, which he grants; and shortly thereafter, the old lady sets fire to herself accidentally, and dies. In her will, she cuts off all of her sponging and sycophantic relations, and leaves a large sum of money to Matthew Pocket, the one relative who had always ignored her. Pip had, just before her death, asked her to do something for Herbert Pocket's father, and he is gratified that Miss Havisham has done him this favor.

By this time, Pip no longer hopes for anything for himself from Miss Havisham, for he has learned who his benefactor really is: Abel Magwitch, now masquerading under the name of Provis—the convict Pip had helped in the churchyard many, many years before.

The discovery of the loathesome man to whom he owes everything overwhelms Pip with revulsion. But soon he comes to see things in perspective. He hears Magwitch's story—a sordid and unhappy enough one—and learns that the man has been hounded through life by a scoundrel called Compeyson. (Later, Pip discovers that this Compeyson is the same man who had jilted Miss Havisham years before and absconded with a fortune of her money.)

The one person who had ever shown Magwitch a real kindness (except for his long-missing wife and infant daughter) was Pip, and Magwitch says that he had promised himself that night in the graveyard that if he ever had anything, it should all go to Pip. Escaped from prison in Australia, he has become a fabulously wealthy man, and all of his fortune has been at Pip's disposal through Jaggers. Now Magwitch has come to England to see Pip with his own eyes, to see how happy he is; and this pathetic and wistful declaration wins Pip's heart. Knowing that Magwitch will be executed if found in England, Pip contrives to help him make his escape from the country by boat.

The plan is in the process of execution, but disaster overtakes Magwitch in the person of the evil demon, Compeyson, who has tracked Magwitch down and determines to see him dead. In a scuffle on the water, both men go down. Compeyson drowns, but Magwitch is taken prisoner. He is tried and sentenced to be executed. Though Pip is unable to save him, he is able to perform two last favors for Magwitch. One is to keep the convict in ignorance of the fact that his fortune is surrendered to the Crown, and that he dies leaving Pip penniless. Thus he preserves the old man's dream of having made a gentleman of the blacksmith's boy. The second favor is to reveal to Magwitch that his long-lost daughter is alive and well, and that Pip loves her—for Pip has learned that she is, indeed, none other than Estella.

With the death of the convict and the loss of his fortune, Pip finds himself a gentleman fit for nothing and deeply in debt. Joe Gargery—now married to the patient Biddy—pays Pip's creditors, and Pip realizes how heartless he has been to turn his back on his childhood friends. Pocket, now a partner in a commercial enterprise, never dreaming that Pip set him up in it, offers Pip a position as clerk in the company.

Several years later, through patient and diligent toil, Pip has worked himself up in the company; and when, inadvertently, Pocket discovers how much he is indebted to Pip, Pip is taken into partnership.

All these experiences have finally made a man of young Pip. He returns to the home of his childhood to visit Joe and Biddy, and while there, he meets the now-widowed Estella. She too has grown in character as the result of suffering. They recognize their mutual love, and agree never to part again.

PENDENNIS

William Makepeace Thackeray

William Makepeace Thackeray was born in Calcutta, India, in 1811, the son of a ranking colonial official. He was sent to England in 1815 and entered Cambridge at the age of eighteen. He left without taking a degree, began and abandoned the study of law,

*and settled in Paris in 1834 to study art. He returned to England,
married, and began contributing humorous pieces to periodicals.
The serialized publication of* Vanity Fair, *the first installment of
which appeared in 1846, immediately established him as one of
the foremost novelists of his day. He made a successful lecture tour
of America, and continued his writing and editing until his death
in 1863.*

*Pendennis, which appeared serially, is an autobiographical novel,
the theme being the eventual maturing of the hero and his acceptance of conventional bourgeois standards. As in all of Thackeray's novels, it is the author's acute perception of English middle-
class society and his talent for characterization which have assured*
Pendennis *its continuing literary fame.*

Arthur Pendennis is a brilliant, if spoiled, young man of little
means. Brought up in the country and pampered by his dot-
ing mother (his father is dead), waited upon and idolized
by his younger distant cousin Laura, who has been adopted
into the household, Pen is used to having his own way.

When he falls in love with a beautiful actress in the
nearby town of Clavering—Emily Fotheringay, ten years his
senior—Pen will hear nothing of his mother's horrified protests. In despair Mrs. Pendennis sends to London for her
brother-in-law, the sophisticated man-of-the-world Major
Pendennis, begging him to persuade Pen of the lad's foolishness. Too shrewd and too knowledgeable of human character
to make harsh demands or give strict orders to his young
nephew, Major Pendennis moves with subtlety. He communicates to Pen the glorious future he has planned for him—a
future that would be considerably dimmed by Pen's alliance
with Emily. Also, he reveals to Emily's father, the blustery
Irish soldier Captain Costigan, the truth that Pen has no
fortune. This information is enough to do the trick, and Pen
receives his dismissal from Miss Fotheringay. At first, he refuses to believe that he is rejected, but when Emily and her
father cut him dead in the street, Pen is forced to conclude
that the lady has been merely toying with him. To insure the
success of his efforts, Major Pendennis arranges for Miss
Fotheringay to be hired away from the theater in Clavering
by the London theatrical manager Dolphin.

Pen declares that he will die of a broken heart, but his
mother, his little cousin Laura, and his good friend Foker

(through whom he had first met the actress) save him from so dreadful a fate.

Pen now goes off with Foker to be educated at "Oxbridge." There his uncle's influence and connections continue to be of use to him, and he is soon initiated into the society of idle gentlemen and dandies. In spite of the fact that Mrs. Pendennis must scrimp to keep him in school—Pen's father having left no fortune—Pen continues to waste his time in frivolous entertainments, all the while making fun of the dull, stolid boys who do nothing but study. Much to his shame, Pen's innocent wildness has its price. He fails his examinations, while those whom he has ridiculed achieve honors. To add to his humiliation, his debts are paid for him by his gentle cousin Laura, and Pen returns home in disgrace.

As usual, Laura and his mother dote on him, but his chief fascination comes from Blanche Amory, the beautiful young woman newly resident at one of the local estates, Clavering Park. Blanche is the daughter by a first marriage of the kind and amusing Mrs. Clavering, whose husband, Sir Francis Clavering, a vulgar wastrel, seems to care little for his wife. The only people who can claim Sir Francis' attention are his small son and heir, Frank Clavering, and the mysterious Colonel Altamont. For reasons which none can fathom, Sir Francis seems to be under the influence of the evil Altamont, whose demands for money Sir Francis never turns aside, though he is himself in straitened circumstances.

Pen imagines himself in love with the beautiful Blanche, but his passion is only sporadically reciprocated. Whenever a handsomer face or richer person enters her vision, Blanche is only too ready to ignore Pen. Crushed by her heartless rebuffs, Pen condescends to propose marriage to his cousin Laura. She, however, now grown into a modest, attractive, and worthy young woman, spurns him. She tells Pen that she cannot marry him simply because his mother wishes it and he is willing to act charitably. Taken aback by her refusal of him, Pen (who has by this time passed his university examinations) determines to quit the countryside.

He goes to London, with the intention of studying law. There he lives with another Oxbridge graduate, George Warrington. London life, however, proves too much for Pen's resolve, and soon he has reverted to a life of idling and self-entertainment, similar to that which he had led when first

an undergraduate. While in London, Pen forms an attachment to the poorly-born Fanny Bolton, who comes to love him
truly; but he is not yet a real man, and ultimately he leaves
her, innocent but broken-hearted.

Pen is at last reduced again to near-poverty, but Warrington comes to his aid by helping Pen get a start as a writer. He
becomes a regular contributor to the *Pall Mall Gazette*, and
in time writes a popular novel. This success invokes his
uncle's pride in him, and Major Pendennis introduces Pen
into the best London society. While with his uncle in London,
Pen again meets the drunken Colonel Altamont, whom Major
Pendennis had known years before. Somehow Major Pendennis manages to get Altamont to arrange for Pen to have Sir
Francis Clavering's seat in Parliament; and, urging his nephew
to marry well, he induces Pen and Blanche, who comes with
a generous dowry, to become engaged.

Before the marriage can take place, however, Pen learns
the truth about the hold Altamont has on Clavering. Altamont is, in fact, Mrs. Clavering's first husband, Amory—the
father of Blanche. If the resultant illegality of the Clavering
marriage were to come to light, the fortune that is now
destined for little Frank Clavering would revert to Blanche.

Unwilling to share in any way the benefit of this blackened
fortune, Pen writes to Blanche that he will marry her only if
she turns her back on the family wealth. This idea is, to
Blanche, absurd; and Pen's old friend Foker, having become
wealthy through inheritance, is accepted by Blanche in his
place.

Having relinquished the offered seat in Parliament, Pen
returns home to find that, all along, he has really loved Laura.
He now proposes to her once more, and this time, as his
proposal is worthy of himself and of her, Laura accepts him.

Foker, having discovered the truth about Blanche's family,
and also that Blanche had all along concealed this knowledge
from him, rejects her, and ultimately the fickle beauty goes
to Europe where she marries a reputed Count. Fortunately
for the good Mrs. Clavering, it appears that her marriage to
Amory (alias Altamont) was never a legal union, and, as
a result, she truly is the wife of Sir Francis (who determines
to reform).

Pen is, at last, elected to Parliament upon his merits, and

coming into some unlooked-for wealth, he and Laura are able to settle down to a life of happiness and love.

SILAS MARNER

George Eliot

Mary Ann Evans, who used the pen name George Eliot, was born in Warwickshire, England, in 1819. The daughter of the manager of the farm and grounds of a large estate, she was largely self-educated, and undertook a translation of a scholarly German book as her first serious literary effort. At the age of twenty-two she became associated with many of the prominent intellectuals of the time, worked as a magazine editor, and adopted a rational, agnostic attitude in place of the strict evangelical religion in which she had been raised. At this time she became the common-law wife of George Henry Lewes, a philosopher, writer, and editor. Although recognized as one of the leaders of London literary and intellectual society, Mary Ann Evans was condemned by the public (Lewes had a wife whom he could not divorce), and therefore she published her fiction under the name of George Eliot. She became famous and acquired considerable wealth as a result of her writing, but she wrote always for serious readers and never compromised her genius.

Silas Marner, published in 1861, belongs to the author's early period. In a circumscribed setting, George Eliot writes of simple people who find new meaning in life through the power of love. Very much larger in scope and content are the later novels of George Eliot; Middlemarch, published in 1871, is one of these, and is considered the author's masterpiece. The first novel to be concerned with intellectuals, it is also the first consideration of characters in terms of complex psychological motivations. George Eliot stands, therefore, in contrast to those novelists of the Victorian period whose work is characterized by complacent morality and materialistic standards. George Eliot's union with Lewes lasted until his death in 1878; in 1880 she married an admirer whom she had known for some years. She died seven months later in London.

Silas Marner, having been unjustly implicated in a theft by his close friend William Dane, leaves his native town of Lantern Yard and settles in the distant village of Raveloe. There he sets up his weaving trade, and, shunning all human society, he devotes his next fifteen years to amassing a fortune in gold, which he hides in his cottage, a miserable dwelling by the swampy Stonepit at the edge of the valley.

If Silas's cottage is the shabbiest house in Raveloe, then surely the Red House is the grandest. There lives Squire Cass with his two sons: the elder, Godfrey, a splendid young man, reputedly in love with the town beauty, Nancy Lammeter; and the younger, Dunstan, a gambler, a spender, an idler—as common as his brother is fine.

Dunstan holds great power over Godfrey, however, for he alone knows Godfrey's dark secret—that Godfrey is married to a low creature, by whom he has fathered a child. Dunsey uses this knowledge to blackmail his brother; and when Godfrey asks for money he has collected in rents and rashly lent to Dunstan, Dunsey refuses to repay it, urging his brother to let him raise the sum by allowing him to sell Godfrey's prize horse, Wildfire. Furious though he is, Godfrey has no choice but to yield to Dunstan's presumptuous proposition.

The horse sale is never transacted, however, because through Dunsey's carelessness the horse is killed. Wondering how he is now to raise the sum of money he owes Godfrey, Dunstan thinks of Marner's hidden treasure. Making his way to the cottage at the edge of the Stonepits, he finds it empty. Quickly the theft is accomplished, and Dunsey strides off into the night.

For several days the robbing of old Silas Marner is the talk of the village—but soon it gives way to another mystery. The dead Wildfire has been found, and there is much speculation among the citizenry as to how he came to be killed. In the Red House, though, the speculation is more on the topic of Dunstan's disappearance, for he has not been seen since leaving with Wildfire for the hunt. But to connect Dunsey's disappearance with the robbery occurring on the same day occurs to none—not even to Godfrey, who has better reason than anyone else to know of what his brother is capable.

The robbery does provide the townspeople with an excuse to make Silas's acquaintance; and one of his comforters, the cheerful widow Dolly Winthrop, is to prove of great service in the years to come.

The following New Year's Eve, a ball is held at the Red House. Godfrey dances attendance on Nancy Lammeter, but she is put off by his reluctance (a long-standing one) to commit himself to marriage, never guessing his reason.

On the same night, Mollie Farren—the very woman who prevents young Godfrey from declaring himself to Nancy—

takes her daughter and, determined on vengeance, makes her way through the snow to Raveloe. She never arrives, however, for she is stricken in the snow, and dies. The child, a beautiful blond little girl, crawls to the nearest source of light for warmth. And when Silas returns to his cottage, he finds the little one asleep on the floor.

In his muddled excitement, he gathers the child up in his arms and goes to the Red House, where he bursts in on the assembled guests. His story is difficult for the gentry to comprehend, but eventually it becomes clear that the child is the daughter of the unknown dead woman in the snow; and, further, that Silas believes the little girl has been sent to him in place of his stolen treasure, and that he is therefore determined to keep her and raise her as his own.

Ultimately it is decided that Silas shall have his way—though Godfrey insists on contributing to the child's support. And, with the burial of Mollie Farren in an unmarked pauper's grave, all that exists of the child's past is banished forever—for all except Godfrey.

Dolly Winthrop immediately sets to and helps old Silas in his new role of father. She brings baby clothes outgrown by her own son, Aaron; she advises on the proper methods of caring for and feeding the baby; and, in general, makes herself invaluable, though Silas remains adamant that the child is *his*, and that she not be allowed to grow too fond of anyone but himself.

As Eppie grows—the child is christened Hepzibah in memory of Silas's mother—she fills the humble cottage at the Stonepit with warmth and joy such as Silas has never known.

Not long after the coming of Eppie, Godfrey—at last set free by the death of his first wife—marries Nancy Lammeter, and together they look forward to the day when their hearth will be gladdened further by children of their own. As for Eppie, Godfrey resolves in his heart that he will neither forget her, nor neglect to provide for her. For that, he tells himself, is a father's duty.

And so time passes. At the end of sixteen years, Eppie has become a beautiful and fond daughter to Silas; and such a change has come over Silas that none can even remember him as the dour young man who had first come to Raveloe so many years before.

One day Eppie unwittingly brings sadness to him. She tells

him that she has fallen in love with Aaron Winthrop, and
that they wish to be married. Knowing that her happiness
depends on it, Silas agrees that the marriage may take place
—though his heart aches at the thought that another man has
found a place in his Eppie's heart.

The very afternoon on which Silas learns of Eppie's plans,
Nancy Cass is anxiously awaiting her husband's return from
the Stonepit, where he has gone to supervise the draining
operations that have been in progress for some time. The
passing years have dealt kindly with Godfrey and Nancy, but
there is one void in their life: they have never had children.
Godfrey had at one time proposed their adopting Eppie—but
Nancy had not agreed, and so the matter was dropped.

Godfrey is later than usual in returning on this particular
afternoon, and when he does arrive at the Red House, Nancy
sees at once from his face that something is amiss. Godfrey
tells her that the Stonepit draining has been completed, and
that at the bottom the body of Dunstan has been found. To
add to the horror, beside the corpse are the sacks of gold
stolen so many years ago from old Marner.

Godfrey observes that with the passing of time *all* hard
truths must come out into the light; and, breaking down, he
confesses to Nancy the story of his first marriage, his relationship to Eppie, and the reason he wanted to adopt her when
she was still a child. Nancy tries to understand her husband;
forgive him, she does easily. They resolve that the wrong
done to both Marner and Eppie must be undone—that the
gold stolen by Dunstan must be returned to Silas, and that
Eppie must now be brought to the Red House to live, and
raised to the station in life to which she was truly born.

It is late at night when Nancy and Godfrey arrive at the
Marner cottage, and Silas and Eppie are amazed to see them.
Godfrey, trying to state his reason for coming without confessing too much, merely invites Eppie to live in the Red
House to be the daughter that he and Nancy never had. To
this proposal Silas refuses to listen. So at last Godfrey tells
the entire story, and makes his claim to Eppie.

Eppie asks Silas's advice as to what she should do. But
heartbroken though he is at the disclosure that another man
has the right to take his Eppie from him, he refuses to offer
a word, insisting that the decision be Eppie's alone. She,
after thinking for a brief moment, thanks Godfrey sincerely,

but explains that Silas is the only father she has ever known, and that having reared her, tended her, and cared for her, he has the only claim upon her which she will recognize.

Sadly Godfrey and Nancy accept Eppie's decision; and wishing her and Silas well, they leave the little cottage and move off silently into the night, returning to the empty Red House.

With the money returned to him, Silas resolves to go back to Lantern Yard, in the hope that at some point during the past years his name may have been cleared. So he and Eppie and Dolly Winthrop set out on their journey. But when they reach Lantern Yard, they discover that the town is gone. All that remain of the past are a few isolated buildings; a new factory is standing on what was once the center of the town. Whether or not the truth of his innocence was ever made apparent to his old townsfolk he will now never know. Silas accepts this fact, for through his life with Eppie, he has learned to forgive much, and to trust much.

Eppie determines that on her marriage to Aaron, the young man must come to live with her in Silas's house, for she resolves never to leave her father. And when the sun rises on Eppie's wedding day, the weaver of Raveloe has no cause in the world for unhappiness. He feels in his heart of hearts more strongly than ever that in acting like a father to a lone, motherless child, he has brought a blessing on himself.

MIDDLEMARCH

George Eliot

In the provincial town of Middlemarch, individual destinies cannot be played out in silence or in secret. Everyone knows everyone else—and has for generations. What touches one life must eventually touch all lives in the town.

Dorothea Brooke and her younger sister, Celia, orphans, live with their uncle, a good-natured but dull man of means. Though Dorothea is courted by Sir James Chettam, she rejects him in favor of the scholarly Mr. Casaubon. Old enough to be Dorothea's father, Casaubon attracts her for what she takes to be his largeness of intellect, his breadth of idealistic vision. Within six months of her marriage, however, Dorothea faces the bitter truth about the man she has married: he is selfish, unimaginative, petty, and cold.

Though she is introduced to Will Ladislaw before she marries, it is not until Dorothea encounters him in Rome, where she and Casaubon are on their wedding journey, that the young man catches her interest. He is a distant cousin of Casaubon's—the son of a woman who had been cast out of the Casaubon family years before because of her marriage to a foreigner of no distinction, who was to be Ladislaw's father. Casaubon has given Ladislaw an annual stipend; but under Dorothea's influence, Ladislaw rejects his cousin's support and determines to make his own way in the world as a newspaperman. Casaubon conceives a dislike for his young relation, and when it is evident that Dorothea admires him, the old man becomes intensely jealous. When Casaubon dies, a scant eighteen months after his marriage to Dorothea, a humiliating codicil to his will stipulates that Dorothea shall lose her inheritance if she ever marry Ladislaw.

Meanwhile, Celia Brooke—who has always scorned her sister Dorothea's interest in "ideas and notions" and who prefers to live a more socially conventional life—has captured Dorothea's rejected suitor, Sir James, and the two lead a pleasant, if unimaginative, life together.

Dr. Tertius Lydgate—like Dorothea, a crusader and reformer at heart—comes to Middlemarch determined to succeed in spite of the competition of two established doctors who are hostile to him, Dr. Sprague and Dr. Minchin. Obtaining the backing of the richest and most powerful man in town, Mr. Bulstrode, Lydgate at first prospers. Although he has been determined never to marry, he is deflected from his bachelorhood by the beautiful, shallow, materialistic Rosamond Vincy, daughter of Middlemarch's mayor, and they are wed. As Lydgate himself has always been improvident, he is at first unaware of his wife's extravagances. However, his practice falls off, and the expense of furnishing and maintaining a house on the scale Rosy demands soon drives him to the realization that he is severely in debt. Rosamond's scheming behind his back and her defiant attempts to thwart his every move toward economy only drive him deeper into despair. He finally swallows his pride and asks Bulstrode to lend him a thousand pounds. But the rich man spurns him, merely condescending to give him a lecture on the virtue of thrift.

Bulstrode is himself nearly driven to despair by the periodic reappearances in Middlemarch of the drunken wastrel Raffles, who is the one man who knows Bulstrode's secret, and who has, through the years, tormented and blackmailed him. It seems that early in life Bulstrode had become the second husband of a woman who made her living as a receiver of stolen property. The woman's rightful heirs had been Ladislaw and his mother, but they had been presumed dead. Bulstrode, however, knew of their existence, and, keeping it quiet, received a fortune—their fortune—upon his wife's death. It was this money that made it possible for him to set up life as a millionaire in Middlemarch.

On one of his visits to Middlemarch, Raffles conveys this information to Ladislaw, and in a burst of guilty generosity, Bulstrode offers to restore the original fortune to Ladislaw. The young man, however, rejects the offer, being unwilling—as his mother had been before him—to share the benefits of such ill-gotten gains.

Ladislaw and Dorothea have finally come to a realization that they love each other. But the terms of Casaubon's will make marriage impossible, Ladislaw having no money of his own, and the young man returns to the Continent.

Meanwhile, another Middlemarch romance has been in progress. Fred Vincy, the idle and spendthrift brother of Rosamond, has been for years in love with poor, homely, spirited Mary Garth. Mary has been nurse to the old miser Featherstone, a relation of Fred's; and it is Fred's hope that Mary will wed him when Featherstone dies and leaves him a fortune. Featherstone does die, but Fred is cut off without an inheritance. Mary is determined not to marry him, though she loves him deeply, until Fred has made a man of himself. With the help of Mary's parents, the fine Caleb and Susan Garth, and of the good-natured clergyman Mr. Farebrother (who denies his own affection for Mary in the aiding of Fred's cause), Fred begins to make a start as an estate manager. (This horrifies the elder Vincys, who have dreams far above this for their spoiled son.)

Once again Raffles turns up in Middlemarch, this time in a state of broken health. He blurts out the story of Bulstrode to Caleb Garth, who determines to resign his position under

Bulstrode. (Earlier, Raffles had told the tale to a number of wasters in the local billiard parlor.) Fearful that Raffles will repeat his story yet again, Bulstrode sends for Lydgate. The doctor gives strict instructions for the care of Raffles, not having any idea who the man is or why Bulstrode is so concerned about him. Under no circumstances, says Lydgate, is Raffles to be given any alcohol, or he will surely die.

Claiming a change of heart, Bulstrode gives Lydgate a check for a thousand pounds as a loan to tide him over. Lydgate does not realize that it is Bulstrode's way of assuring himself of Lydgate's loyalty. That night, Bulstrode allows Raffles to be given brandy, and by the next morning the blackmailer is dead.

Lydgate's joy at having been rescued from debt by Bulstrode is short-lived, however, for the entire scandal of Bulstrode's past is soon made public at a town meeting by one of the men who has heard it from Raffles. Moreover, it is suggested that the thousand-pound check was a bribe to Lydgate, knowingly accepted, to hush up the real cause of Raffles' death.

Bulstrode is ruined in the town, and Lydgate nearly so. It is only the intervention of Dorothea that enables Lydgate to return Bulstrode's thousand pounds and set off for London with Rosamond, determined to start life anew. Dorothea also helps make Rosamond realize her share in Lydgate's downfall and her wifely responsibility in standing by him.

Bulstrode is anxious to do anything he can to improve his reputation among the people of Middlemarch, and Caleb Garth—whom he has always respected—suggests that he make young Fred Vincy manager of all of Bulstrode's estates. This is done, and Fred and Mary are at last able to marry.

Dorothea now recognizes the emptiness of her life, and against the advice of her uncle Mr. Brooke, her brother-in-law Sir James, her sister Celia, and the town's social arbiter Mrs. Cadwallader, Dorothea determines to give up her inheritance from Casaubon and marry Ladislaw.

Thus, though neither the idealistic Dorothea nor the idealistic Lydgate manages to fulfill the youthful dreams of helping humanity on a grand scale, both are freed at last to pursue a degree of worthwhile happiness.

THE WARDEN

Anthony Trollope

Anthony Trollope was born in London in 1815. His father had been an unsuccessful lawyer, and his mother, Frances Trollope, was an extremely prolific writer whose popular success, however, came too late to mitigate the poverty of his years as a day student at Winchester and Harrow. He was unable to study further, and in 1834 he took a position as a post-office clerk in London; he was transferred to Ireland in 1841 as a postal inspector with a considerable raise in salary, and he prospered financially from this time on. In Ireland he married and began to write novels, the first two of which were failures. The Warden, his first novel to be well received, marked the beginning of the "Barsetshire Chronicles," a series of six novels which constitutes his most memorable achievement. Trollope was a methodical worker, and the revelation in his posthumously published Autobiography that he invariably worked two-and-one-half hours each day at the rate of 250 words per fifteen minutes had a damaging effect on his literary reputation for many years. Twentieth-century readers, however, find in his works one of the most comprehensive depictions in literature of Victorian middle-class society attempting to preserve itself against the inevitable arrival of the modern era. Trollope's novels number over fifty, and following his resignation from the Postal Department in 1867 he devoted himself exclusively to his writing and to the enjoyment of his substantial income. He died in London in 1882.

When John Hiram died in 1434, he willed to the town of Barchester certain tracts of land, the income from which was to be used to build a retreat and provide the necessities of life for twelve old men of Barchester to sustain them in their declining years. The bishop was to administer this trust by appointing a warden (who might also be the precentor if the bishop approved), and by seeing that when one of the twelve aged inmates of "Hiram's Hospital" died, another was selected to replace him. Thus has the trust been administered until the time of our story.

The present warden of the hospital is the Reverend Septimus Harding, a widowed clergyman of middle age, who lives quietly and gently with his beautiful twenty-four-year-old daughter Eleanor. Harding's older daughter, Susan, is the wife of the Reverend Doctor Theophilus Grantly, the militant and aggressive son of Harding's old friend, the bishop.

That Harding was appointed precentor of Barchester Cathedral shortly after Susan's marriage to the bishop's son had given rise to some small amount of whispered scandal. But as "the Warden" (as Harding is known) is the best-loved man, perhaps, in all of Barchester, the whispers soon quiet themselves.

A few years later, a second scandal begins to be whispered in the town. This time, gossip has it that old Hiram's will is no longer being carried out accurately. The twelve pensioners continue to receive the same daily amount of money they have always received, though the value of Hiram's estate has greatly increased since it was first willed to Barchester. Since the living this increased income affords Harding is still far from munificent, and since the twelve pensioners are all more than adequately provided for in terms of their real needs (Harding himself has added to their dole twopence a day each from his own pocket), it would seem that these whispers too will quickly die. But such is not to be the case.

The rumors reach the ear of John Bold, son of Dr. Bold, a now-dead boyhood friend of the Warden's. John Bold is handsome, intelligent, honest; he is in love with Eleanor Harding (and she with him). But he has a major failing: an almost irrational passion for justice. And when the whispers about old Hiram's estate being mismanaged reach Bold's ears, he determines to investigate. He consults with his lawyer, the grasping Finney, about how best to proceed in his investigation, and Finney, scenting a large amount in legal fees if the matter can somehow be inflated, urges Bold on in his task.

Through the efforts of Finney, word soon reaches the twelve pensioners that something is amiss in the way they are being treated; and, as rumors often are, this one is distorted until the men believe that they are really entitled to a hundred pounds a year under the terms of Hiram's will, and that Harding, the Warden, has been stealing the money from them. Soon the inmates of Hiram's Hospital are divided into two camps—one pro-Warden, led by old Bunce, and one anti-Warden, led by Abel Handy.

Having learned from his lawyer that there is, indeed, ambiguity about the correct interpretation of Hiram's will, Bold determines, in the interests of justice, to pursue the matter further. (Bold, of course, has nothing personal to gain in this matter; and he is pained that his investigations may, in any way, result in hurt to the Warden. But justice is Bold's god, and he must pursue it come what may.) Off to London he goes to institute legal proceedings against the administrators of Hiram's estate.

While in London, Bold spends a good deal of time with his friend Tom Towers, who writes for the *Jupiter*, London's biggest and most influential newspaper. And soon after—perhaps it is a coincidence—the *Jupiter* prints its first attack on the "grasping clergy" who are mismanaging affairs in Barchester.

The Warden has been stung from the first by the rumors that he might, in any way, be occupying a position or receiving an income to which he is not entitled. But the *Jupiter* article cuts him to the quick, and he confers with his son-in-law, Grantly (of whom he is afraid), as to what the best course of action might be. The Warden is all for writing a letter of explanation to the *Jupiter*, but Grantly, sophisticated and wise in the ways of the world, convinces him that this would be folly. Grantly urges that the Warden do nothing, but wait until the actual suit is brought against him. Meanwhile, Grantly tells him, he will retain the services of Sir Abraham Hazard to represent him. (Hazard is the most important—and most expensive—clerical lawyer in London.) The Warden is unhappy that his name cannot be cleared at once, but he sees no way to argue with his son-in-law.

With the appearance of the *Jupiter* article, what has been a topic for idle conversation in the village springs into prominence as a major conflict. Abel Handy causes a petition against the Warden to be circulated through Hiram's Hospital, and by harping upon the "hundred pounds a year," he gets most of the men to sign it. Bunce, however, remains loyal to Harding, his position being that no matter what the outcome of the lawsuit, the pensioners themselves will gain nothing, while their friend Harding may lose a great deal.

Events move apace in London, and an opinion on the case is received from Sir Abraham Hazard. He points out to Grantly that the opposition will fail in its case on a technicality, and the validity of the administration of the bequest will not therefore come to issue. Grantly communicates this news to the Warden, and is dismayed that it does not comfort the good man. Harding's position is that what is at issue is whether he does or does not have the right to the income he receives; and merely knowing that he will win the case on a technicality of law does not relieve him, but only depresses him further.

Eleanor, who has been watching her father's spirits sink lower with each passing day, at last resolves to go directly to Bold, plead on bended knee for her father, and then part from him forever. She braces herself for the interview, and all goes as she has planned—at least until she has finished her plea and John has agreed to do all he can to stop the assault on the Warden. What happens next is something Eleanor could not have anticipated; John sweeps her into his arms and forces her to declare her love for him, even as he declares his for her.

True to his promise to Eleanor, Bold goes to Grantly to tell him that he will drop the suit. Grantly, however, sure that victory will lie in his own hands, rejects him, and tells Bold that the only reason Bold wishes to drop the suit is that Bold knows he will lose. Further, says bull-headed Grantly, the Barchester clergy refuses to have the suit dropped, but insists on being vindicated in the courts. Bold is infuriated by this maddening and stupid position of Grantly's and he leaves in a rage.

He is not so easily deflected from his promise to Eleanor, however, and the next day Bold goes to London to urge Tom Towers to use his influence at the *Jupiter* to see that no further attacks on the Warden are made in that paper. Towers, however, is as infuriating as Grantly had been; and he and two other writers, Mr. Popular Sentiment and Dr. Pessimist Anticant, declare loftily that the press is not to be tampered with or the truth interfered with. Needless to say, the *Jupiter* continues its senseless and sensationalist attacks on the Warden.

At this point the Warden—who is by now thoroughly crushed and disillusioned by all that has transpired—determines to take matters into his own hands. He travels to London, where, after great effort, he manages to secure an interview with Sir Abraham Hazard. Hazard assures him that his case is foolproof, but after much debate, the Warden succeeds in getting Hazard to admit that the case will win on technical merits. The correctness of how old Hiram's bequest is now being administered is, indeed, open to possible question.

With this information, Harding announces his intention of resigning the wardenship. Though his daughter Susan, his son-in-law Grantly, Grantly's father, the bishop, and even Sir Abraham strongly recommend against it, believing it the sheerest madness to allow a vague question of right to stand between Harding and eight hundred pounds a year, the Warden remains adamant.

After his resignation, Harding goes with his daughter Eleanor (who has all along supported her father) to live in a small cottage. Out of respect for Harding, the bishop refuses to appoint a new Warden as successor, and the post remains vacant. All the twelve pensioners get out of the change is a reduction in their daily stipend—since twopence apiece of their ration was the Warden's personal gift, and he is no longer in a position to make it. Young Grantly is left to pay the exorbitant fees of Sir Abraham.

Several months later, Eleanor marries Bold, whom Harding has liked all along, ever refusing to allow the matter of the fight about the wardenship to interfere with their friendship.

Harding himself is happy in his new and quiet life, and for a long time people meeting him continue to refer to him as the Warden. When they do, Harding meekly reminds them: "No, no, not Warden now. Only precentor."

THE EGOIST

George Meredith

George Meredith was born in Portsmouth, England, in 1828, the son of a naval outfitter. He was sent to school in Germany, and upon his return to London was apprenticed to a lawyer. He soon gave up the legal profession, and became associated with the radical literary set in London. His first poems were published in 1849. Like the novels which he began to write a few years later, they were appreciated by a select and small group of readers and critics. He earned his living as a journalist and, from 1867, as an editor for a prominent London publisher, in which capacity he dealt with many notable writers of his time and was himself recognized as one of the finest editors and literary advisors in London. He continued to publish his own novels and poetry. His reputation grew as his advanced ideas began to appeal to a public emerging from

Victorian orthodoxy into the freer modern atmosphere. Meredith's novels were fictional expositions of his philosophy of life, which held that critical intelligence coupled with the "comic spirit" would lead humanity to its highest destiny. The comic spirit, to Meredith, meant rational observation and perception of the follies of mankind. Meredith called The Egoist *a "comedy in narrative," and acknowledged it to be based on his own folly and experience, with himself as the model for Patterne, the egoist, his first wife Mary Ellen Nichols as the model for Clara, and Thomas Love Peacock, the novelist who was Meredith's first father-in-law, as Clara's father, Dr. Middleton. Meredith belongs to the very small group of writers who were not only ahead of their own time, but who continue to seem advanced even to succeeding generations of intellectuals. He was, in his old age, the leading literary intellectual in England; his ideas and radical opinions precluded his burial in Westminster Abbey, even though King Edward VII and his Prime Minister had requested this honor upon Meredith's death in 1909.*

Virtually from his birth, Willoughby Patterne seems destined for his role as Egoist. Wealthy, landed, aristocratic—handsome, witty, accomplished, he is the son of an adoring mother, the pet of two loving maiden aunts, and the acknowledged petty prince of his part of the country.

Willoughby grows up petted and pampered, his every whim catered to, his every illusion about himself supported and augmented. Hearing, for example, of a Lieutenant Patterne who has distinguished himself in the field, Willoughby plays at generosity by sending the man a munificent sum, and an invitation to the ancestral hall; but when the naval man shows up to claim the proffered hospitality of his distant and suddenly acknowledging kinsman, Willoughby is disappointed in the man's homeliness and ragged appearance, and has him turned away. He comforts himself with the knowledge that he could not have exposed his beloved mother to such a man, and by sending the old tar another handsome gift of money, Willoughby proves to himself again his own boundless munificence of spirit.

When the Egoist assumes his majority and the title of Lord, speculation runs high among the gentry as to whom he will choose to become Lady Patterne. There are some who favor Laetitia Dale, the sweet but dowerless daughter of one of Willoughby's tenants. And, indeed, the girl herself worships Sir Willoughby with a quiet but persistent passion. Instead of Laetitia, however, Willoughby chooses Constantia Durham—robust, spirited, and rich. Laetitia, feeling her own unworthiness, resigns herself to worshiping her hero from afar.

Before long, however, Willoughby begins pressing suit upon Laetitia. She learns that he has been thrown over by Constantia; and, overwhelmed by her good fortune, consents to Willoughby's wooing her. Willoughby's mother having become ill, Laetitia moves into Patterne Hall as her nurse, and she basks daily in her lover's radiant attractiveness.

But Laetitia's happiness is not to endure. On his mother's suggestion, Willoughby leaves England for a round-the-world tour; and when, three years later, he returns to Patterne, he greets Laetitia merely as an old and valued friend.

Exercising his famous generosity, Willoughby sends for the eldest son of the distant cousin, the sailor whom he had turned away. The lad, Crossjay Patterne, is of course too high-spirited and low-born to reside in Patterne Hall itself, and Willoughby prevails upon Laetitia and her father to keep the boy in their home. Crossjay is a delight to Laetitia, and a balm for her wounded heart.

Shortly thereafter, Willoughby makes clear that he is to become betrothed a second time. This choice is Clara Middleton, a beautiful and intelligent girl of eighteen. From the outset of their courtship, it seems clear to the girl that she and Willoughby are hopelessly at odds in certain basic respects. She feels a strong need to be herself, while he looks only for a woman who will subjugate herself completely to his own needs, desires, and whims. Reluctantly Clara agrees to the betrothal, and pledges her constancy to him.

Soon after, old Lady Patterne dies. Though marriage is thus ruled out for the time of mourning, Clara and her father, the scholarly Dr. Middleton, come to Patterne Hall for a prolonged visit. It is during this time that Clara gets to know Willoughby better and better—and with each passing day, her horror of him grows, for it soon becomes inalterably clear to her that he is incapable of a single thought or emotion that does not directly bear on his own comfort.

For a while, Willoughby maintains that her unhappiness will be solved by their marriage. How can she help but love him? And, it follows in his mind, if she loves him, then she must needs adapt herself to his image of her and of himself. It is precisely this image of himself, however, that continues to alienate Clara.

They differ, it seems to her, in their views of everything. One source of conflict between them is the method of raising Crossjay and preparing him for his future. The boy seems admirably equipped for a naval life, and Clara, who adores the youngster, agrees with the boy's tutor, Vernon Whitford, that that is the only future for him. Willoughby disagrees; it is his plan to raise the boy as a gentleman—thus keeping him dependent for life upon his, Willoughby's, good will. If the boy shows affection and obedience, he will be provided for; if not—the boy merely shows himself an ingrate and worthy of any catastrophe that may befall him as a result of being out of favor with the master of Patterne Hall.

This method of tying people to him is ever present in Willoughby. Vernon Whitford, Crossjay's tutor, is himself a case in point. He is an impoverished dependent cousin of Willoughby's; but whenever he shows signs of breaking away from Patterne Hall to make a life of his own as a writer, Willoughby circumvents him by threatening to abandon Crossjay, whom Vernon has come to love.

The contrast between the fine, intelligent Vernon and the selfish, petty Willoughby is all too clear to Clara. Willoughby's deficiencies are further illuminated by the arrival at Patterne of an old friend of Willoughby's, the high-spirited Irishman, Colonel DeCraye. Constantly exposed to these two fine examples of manhood, and frequently in the company of the noble, patient Laetitia, Clara's revulsion for her betrothed reaches a boiling point.

She begs Willoughby to release her from her pledge. This he petulantly refuses to do, believing Clara to be the victim of a childish whim. In this he is supported by Clara's father, old Dr. Middleton, who has been thoroughly seduced by Willoughby's superficial charm and by the graciousness of life at Patterne Hall. (He is particularly seduced by the cases of ninety-year-old port in Willoughby's cellar.)

Clara's detestation reaches its climax one rain-swept morning when she runs away from Patterne Hall, determined to escape the marriage that is so abhorrent to her by flight to London. She is followed by Vernon, who begs her to return to Willoughby, stand her ground, and fight for her freedom. She is too desperate with fear for that, however, and sends him away. But when she is overtaken by Colonel DeCraye and seen with him by the town gossip, she agrees to return to Patterne Hall with him, being unwilling that any should suspect her of running away with the gallant Irish officer.

The abortive escape attempt cannot be glossed over entirely, however, and matters between Willoughby and Clara become more and more the topic of conversation. Clara reveals her soul to Laetitia, who proves a steadfast friend; she has herself begun—albeit at the age of thirty—to doubt Willoughby's perfection, and Clara's accusations ring true.

Only when he is finally convinced that he can by no means hold or punish Clara (as he would like to do) does Willoughby hit on a stratagem which he hopes will somehow manage to preserve the legend of his perfection and provide him with a bride.

In a secret midnight interview with Laetitia, he proclaims that he has renounced Clara and set her free, and that it is Laetitia herself whom he loves and wishes to marry. To his incredulity, Laetitia firmly refuses him. Shaken to the marrow by this display of inconstancy toward one of his perfection, Willoughby pretends the next morning (having already sworn Laetitia to secrecy) that he has never once wavered from his determination to hold Clara to her pledge and make her his bride.

Unbeknown to both Willoughby and Laetitia, however, their midnight conversation has been overheard by young Crossjay, who had been sleeping under a coverlet on a sofa in the room where the meeting took place. Crossjay reveals enough of the tale for it to spread across the countryside by afternoon.

Fighting with his back to the wall, Willoughby is determined to keep up appearances and provide himself with a Lady Patterne at all costs. He promises Clara that he will release her—only provided that she marry his cousin, Vernon Whitford; by this means, he hopes to guarantee that both Clara and Vernon will be dependent upon him for life, and will never desert him. At the same time, Willoughby resolves to propose marriage to Laetitia once again, this time insuring the success of his suit by getting her aged father to support his cause.

Clara refuses to marry Vernon. But when she confides this

news to Laetitia, that lady—who has grown markedly in her ability to see the true state of people's hearts—makes Clara see that indeed she and Vernon love and are suited to each other. Thus, Clara and Vernon are able to accept Willoughby's offer for their own reasons; and when Dr. Middleton, made aware at last of the overbearing egoism of Willoughby, assures them that they will not need to be dependent upon the lord of Patterne Hall, their joy is complete.

As for Willoughby, he finally does succeed in getting Laetitia to accept him, but only after she has plainly and publicly exposed him to the entire household for the Egoist he is. She makes it clear to him that she does not love him, and there is little prospect that she will ever cater to his vanity in a single instance.

Crossjay is assured of a sensible and profitable future in line with the ideas Laetitia, Clara, and Vernon have shared over him. Clara and Vernon go to Italy with Dr. Middleton. The dashing Colonel DeCraye, already beginning to get over his infatuation with Clara, goes off with the town's social arbiter, Mrs. Mountstuart, for further entertainment. Willoughby is left alone at Patterne with his elderly maiden aunts, and with the aging, cool Laetitia.

JUDE THE OBSCURE

Thomas Hardy

Thomas Hardy was born in 1840 near Dorchester, in the region of England called Wessex in his novels. At the age of sixteen he was apprenticed to a church architect. Although the quality of his work indicated a promising career in this field, he soon turned to the writing of prose fiction. His first novel appeared in 1871 and with the publication of successive books his reputation as a novelist was securely established. Hardy's major novels, set against the austere Wessex landscape and dealing with man as a victim of fate in a harsh universe, are today considered relentlessly pessimistic, and in the novelist's own time they were branded as obscene and immoral. Ironically, the author claimed that the true theme of his writings was the search for a better world. Jude the Obscure, published in 1895, caused a great public outrage because of its frank treatment of illicit love. Discouraged, perhaps, by this reaction, Hardy wrote no more novels. He produced a vast poetic drama, The Dynasts, in 1908, and from that date until his death he wrote several outstanding volumes of lyric poetry. Called "the last of the great Victorians," he was, in his old age, the most venerated man of letters in England, and on his death in 1928 he was buried in Westminster Abbey.

Young Jude Fawley is distraught when his beloved schoolmaster, Mr. Phillotson, leaves the village of Marygreen for Christminster. It is the schoolmaster's hope somehow to be able to enroll at one of the colleges of Christminster, and thus make something of his life. When he is gone, little Jude resolves that he too will one day go to Christminster University.

To that end the lad secures ancient, dog-eared Latin and Greek grammars, and by the time he is nineteen he is very well self-educated. His plans, however, come to nothing for he is seduced by the sensual Arabella Donn, who, on the pretext of having become pregnant, gets Jude to marry her.

The marriage is a miserable one from the beginning, and not long after Jude discovers that Arabella had lied about her pregnancy, she deserts him and goes to Australia with her parents. Jude is now free to resume his dream of an education.

He goes to Christminster, with the intention of working at his trade (stonemasonry) until he has earned enough money to enroll at the college. In Christminster he meets a distant cousin, the beautiful Sue Bridehead, with whose photograph he has already fallen in love. He also finds Phillotson, who had never managed to enroll in the university; and Jude is able to get Sue the post of assistant to Phillotson at the small school Phillotson runs.

Sue is the direct opposite of Arabella—intellectual where Jude's wife is dull, refined where Jude's wife is coarse, ethereal where Jude's wife is sensual. At first, Jude and Sue pretend to themselves that the affection they feel for each other is cousinly; but soon neither can deny the truth of what they feel.

Sue has meanwhile enrolled at a female seminary, with the intention of becoming a certified teacher. She has also become engaged to Phillotson, with the understanding that they will marry upon her graduation, though this rashly made promise to a man old enough to be her father distresses her. A visit by Sue to Jude is misunderstood by the mistress of the seminary, however, and Sue is expelled. Shortly thereafter, Sue learns of the existence of Jude's wife, Arabella. Overwhelmed, not knowing which way to turn, she marries Phillotson.

Arabella turns up, and reveals that, having thought Jude dead, she has married an Australian. Jude promises to do nothing that could make public Arabella's bigamous state.

Jude and Sue continue to see each other after her marriage—a marriage which is hopelessly unhappy, as Sue has developed a complete revulsion for physical contact with Phillotson. At last she becomes desperate. She pleads with Phillotson to allow her to leave him and to go to Jude. Not wishing to hold her against her will, Phillotson agrees and Sue flees to her beloved.

Jude, having long since recognized the futility of his dream to enter the university, is now content to be a stonemason. He is thrilled when Sue comes to him, but he is taken aback when she reveals that she does not wish to consummate their relationship. He agrees to her proposal, and they live together but not as husband and wife.

Arabella's new "husband" comes to England, and Arabella asks Jude to divorce her so that she may remarry the Australian and legalize her position. To this Jude agrees. When Phillotson hears of Jude's divorce, he determines to divorce Sue. At last Jude and Sue are free to wed—but Sue hangs back. She prefers to live as they have lived, and fears that a legal marriage would destroy her happiness and Jude's.

Arabella has yet another surprise in store for Jude. She tells him that eight months after she left him, she bore his son—a child her new husband has no wish to support. Without asking permission, she sends the boy (whose nickname is Father Time, because of his desperately sad and aged expression) to Jude. Jude and Sue become father and mother to the poor lad, though they cannot seem to alleviate his sorrow. For his sake, they again plan to marry formally—but once more, Sue recoils at the last minute.

Sue now agrees to the consummation of her relationship with Jude, but soon afterward regrets it; and their physical relationship is not entirely satisfactory to either of them. But Jude is happy, for he now feels that he is truly the husband of the one woman he loves.

Society being what it is, however, life for Jude and Sue is not easy. Because of the irregularity of their relationship, they must continually move from one town to another. After several years, they return to Christminster. Sue has had two children of her own, and another is on the way.

They have difficulty in finding suitable lodgings in Christminster, because landlords are unwilling to take children. At last they find a room for one night, but Sue confides to "Time" (Jude's son by Arabella) that their lot is difficult, that the children make it harder, and that yet another child is on its way.

Time takes it into his unhappy head to remedy what he mistakenly believes to be the cause of his parents' problems; and the next day Jude and Sue find poor Time's body hanging from a hook, next to those of his half brother and half sister. He has killed them and committed suicide, leaving a note which says, simply: *Done because we are too menny.* In the shock that follows, Sue loses the child she is carrying.

Following the death of her children, a major change comes over Sue. She is struck by a new religiosity, and it seems to her that Time's awful deed was meant as a sign to her that she has sinned. She decides that she is in the eyes of Heaven Phillotson's wife and can belong to no other; and she tries to assure Jude that he truly belongs to Arabella.

To Jude this is madness. He believes that, in every true sense, Sue and he belong to each other. He is more truly her husband than Phillotson, who repelled her. But Sue insists. She leaves Jude, and asks Phillotson if he will have her back. Phillotson has suffered socially from his generosity in having let Sue go; and he now sees in her return the chance to recover his position. He agrees to marry her, but only on condition that she obey him in all things. To this Sue submits, and she and Phillotson remarry. They continue, however, to maintain separate bedchambers as before.

Jude is totally destroyed by Sue's leaving him. Broken in health and spirit, he easily falls victim to the now-widowed Arabella. She feels that it would be better to have Jude as a husband than no husband at all, and with little effort she tricks Jude into remarrying her.

Life with Arabella is agony for Jude. He can think of no one but Sue. At last, fearing that death is upon him, he makes a last journey to see her. In a wild moment of passion, she confesses her love for him and smothers him with kisses. But instantly her sense of moral purpose returns to her, and she sends Jude away forever. To punish herself for what she regards as an act of sin, Sue determines to return to her husband's bed, though Phillotson repels her more than ever. Thus, she martyrs herself to an intellectual idea.

In the rain on the way home from his final visit to Sue, Jude contracts a serious lung ailment. His dreams of an education, of doing good in the world, of loving, and of being loved all having been smashed, he resigns himself to death. Mercifully, he has not long to wait. Believing his entire life to have been a lie and a waste, he dies alone in a garret room, even as Arabella is flirting with the man she intends to be Jude's successor.

As they are preparing Jude's body for burial, old Mrs. Edlin (who has been a firm and loyal friend through the years to both Jude and Sue) tells Arabella that Sue has said she has found peace at last.

To which Arabella astutely observes: "She may swear that . . . till she's hoarse, but it won't be true. She's never found peace since she left his arms, and never will again till she's as he is now!"

ALICE IN WONDERLAND
and
THROUGH THE LOOKING GLASS

Lewis Carroll

Charles Lutwidge Dodgson, who used the pen name Lewis Carroll, was born in 1832 in a Cheshire village where his father was the vicar. He studied at Oxford, where he stayed on as a lecturer in mathematics until 1881. In the academic world, and as the author of many books on mathematics, he used the name of Dodgson; his remarkable books ostensibly for children, of which Alice's Adventures in Wonderland and Through the Looking Glass are the best known, appeared under the name of Lewis Carroll. Although it was widely realized that Dodgson had written these enormously popular stories, he asserted publicly on many occasions that he had no knowledge of any books "not published under his name." It is perhaps as futile to speculate upon the exact nature of the author's double life as it is to seek a conclusive interpretation of the Alice books. In the last century, adult readers were most responsive to the elements of social satire and political allegory in Carroll's works, whereas modern readers see Alice's fantasies about the world of grownups as a rich source of psychological symbolism. Literary and critical fashions, however, have in no way diminished the delightful and nonsensical qualities of Carroll's books, and with their famous illustrations by Sir John Tenniel, they have become classics. Carroll lived at Oxford until his death in 1898.

(Alice in Wonderland)

Alice, as charming and proper a little English girl as you can imagine, was sitting, bored, on a mossy bank one afternoon, when a White Rabbit, wearing a waistcoat and carrying a pocket watch, went running by, declaring, "Oh dear! I shall be too late!" and dashed down a rabbit hole.

Without thinking, off ran Alice after him and crawled into the rabbit hole. Down, down, down she sailed—as though falling ever so slowly down a well—until she landed in a bed of soft leaves.

She looked about. The rabbit was gone—but she spied a tiny doorway cut into a wall, beyond which was the most beautiful garden she had ever seen. The door was too small for her to get through; but when she saw a little cake marked "Eat Me," she began to nibble it. Sure enough, she grew smaller—and smaller—and smaller—until she could go right into the garden.

In the garden Alice met a Caterpillar who was sitting on a mushroom and smoking a hookah. She decided to ask his advice about which way to go—but when she spoke, she discovered that all her words were coming out in a strange sort of fashion. She tried repeating a poem that she knew quite well—it was "Old Father William"—but though it rhymed as she spoke it, the meaning was utter nonsense.

Although he was an interesting conversationalist, the Caterpillar proved to be of no help, so down the road went Alice. Before long she came to a little house, in front of which a Frog Footman and a Fish Footman were bowing low to each other, their powdered curls tangling each other up. As *they* offered no useful advice either, Alice just walked into the house without an invitation.

She found herself in a smoky kitchen, where a Duchess was bouncing her baby on her knee, while the Cook was filling the air with pepper, and the baby was filling the air with squeals.

"There's too much pepper in that soup!" declared Alice.

"There's not enough," answered the Duchess abruptly, "and that's a fact." With that, she thrust the poor baby into Alice's arms. Imagine Alice's consternation when the baby turned into a pig! Not that anyone noticed; the Cook and the Duchess paid no attention whatsoever, while their Cheshire Cat, who had been grinning all the while, simply began to disappear, a little at a time: first his tail, then his body, then his nose, then his ears—until all that was left of him was his grin.

"Curiouser and curioser!" thought Alice to herself, as she dashed down the road in pursuit of the little pig, which had jumped out of her arms.

She hadn't gone very far when she came upon a long tea table, set out under a tree. Huddled at one end were three truly curious creatures: a Mad March Hare, a Mad Hatter, and—between them, being used as a cushion—a sleepy Dormouse.

"No room! No room!" they cried as Alice approached.

"There's *plenty* of room," she replied, seating herself. But she wasn't too sure, a few minutes later, that she had done the right thing. For the three of them were so strange—so rude—so utterly mad. The conversation went on for a bit, about riddles that didn't have answers, and clocks that told what day of the month it was, and whether Time was a *him* or an *it*; but when the Hatter became insulting, Alice decided that she had better go. So off she ran, casting only one glance behind her (which was just enough for her to see the Hatter and the March Hare stuffing the Dormouse into the teapot).

Without realizing it, she found herself back in the wonderful little garden. Now, however, the place was abuzz with people. Pages who looked exactly like playing cards were rushing about, trying to paint the white roses red. When Alice asked them why, they explained that it was almost time for the Queen of Hearts' croquet game, and that if the flowers weren't the right color, the Queen would order everyone's head cut off.

Sure enough, just then Alice heard an imperious female voice screaming, "Off with his head!" and the Queen of Hearts came into view, looking exactly like her counterpart in a deck of cards.

In a twinkling the croquet game was begun; but what a strange game it was! For mallets, there were live flamingos;

for balls, there were hedgehogs; and for wickets—why, the royal pages just wandered around, bending over wherever it suited their fancy!

Alice was becoming very discouraged with her inability to play well, when her old friend the Duchess took her in tow, and brought her to the seaside, where she was introduced to the Gryphon, and to the Mock Turtle, a most lugubrious fellow who sobbed as he told his story.

"We went to school in the sea," explained the Mock Turtle. "Our master was a turtle—but we called him tortoise, because he taught us. We studied Reeling and Writhing and the different branches of Arithmetic: Ambition, Distraction, Uglification, and Derision."

On and on went the Mock Turtle; but Alice never did hear the end of his story—or of the Gryphon's song, for that matter —for the White Rabbit came rushing by, announcing that it was time for the trial.

"What trial?" asked Alice of the Duchess, as they ran along.

"The trial of the Knave of Hearts, my dear," explained her companion. "Tart stealing, you know."

The trial, like everything else she had experienced during this eventful day, struck Alice as quite mad. The King of Hearts, who was presiding, didn't seem to know the first thing about proper courtroom procedure. And the jurymen weren't much better; why, they had to write down their names on their slates for fear they would forget them!

Alice tried to be patient with the meaningless testimony of such witnesses as the Duchess' Cook and the Mad Hatter. But when the Queen demanded loudly, "Sentence first! Verdict afterward!" that was just too much!

"Stuff and nonsense!" exclaimed Alice at this foolishness.

"Hold your tongue!" said the Queen, turning purple.

"I won't!" said Alice.

"Off with her head!" the Queen shouted at the top of her voice. Nobody moved.

"Who cares for *you?*" said Alice (who had been growing back to normal size all this time). "You're nothing but a pack of cards!"

At this the whole pack rose up into the air, and came flying down upon her; she gave a little scream, and tried to beat them off . . . and found herself lying on the bank, with her head in the lap of her sister, who was gently brushing away some dead leaves that fluttered down from the trees upon her face.

"Wake up, Alice dear!" said her sister. "Why, what a long sleep you've had!"

"Oh, I've had such a curious dream!" said Alice. And she told her sister, as well as she could, all these strange adventures of hers that you have just been reading about.

(Through the Looking Glass)

Tired of playing with the chessmen by herself, Alice was holding a quite intelligent conversation with Dinah, her cat, when the subject of Looking-Glass House came up. Alice did *so* want to get into Looking-Glass House. She was sure it must be a most marvelous place. If only the glass would turn to mist, she could step right through.

As she thought these idle thoughts, Alice pressed her nose right up against the mirror over the mantel, trying to see as much as possible of what lay beyond—when suddenly the glass *did* turn to mist, and into Looking-Glass House she stepped.

All about her were the chessmen—but they had come to life. Hither and thither ran the pawns, the knights, and the castles. Before she had a chance to speak to them, though, she began to float through the house and out the door and down the steps. When she alighted, she found herself in a garden of live flowers. They had scarcely begun a most interesting conversation, however, when up bustled the Red Queen, as haughty an individual as Alice had ever met.

The Red Queen was most helpful. She showed Alice how the garden was laid out like a chess board. All Alice had to do was successfully cross eight squares, and then she too would be a queen—which is what Alice wanted most. (All of this information was given as the Red Queen and Alice were running as fast as they could. When they stopped, Alice was surprised to note that they were just where they had begun, and the Queen explained that in Looking-Glass House, one had to run as fast as possible just to stand still; to make progress, one had to run twice as fast.)

After much additional advice, the Red Queen disappeared, and Alice found herself in a railway carriage with a number of curious passengers: a Goat, a Man Dressed in White Paper, and many highly unusual insects. Though bizarre, the journey was well worth while, thought Alice, for at the end of the carriage ride, she had reached the fourth square, where lived Tweedledum and Tweedledee.

What strange fellows they were! Part of the time they were as rude to Alice as one can imagine; the rest of the time, no one could have been friendlier. (During a friendly spell, they recited "The Walrus and The Carpenter" for her.) By way of making conversation with them, Alice recited the rhyme about them which she knew. This proved not to have been a wise thing to do, however, for it reminded them of the battle they had promised to have. Not wishing to witness their fury, Alice waited only long enough to help them into their unusual battle regalia before hurrying off to the next square.

There she met the White Queen, who was so absent-minded and vague that Alice worried for her. But the White Queen proved to have her admirable qualities, too. She remembered things in advance—she shrieked, for example, a full five minutes before she stuck her finger with a pin. She also offered Alice a job as her lady's maid at the rate of two pence a week, and jam every other day. "The rule is," confided the Queen, "jam tomorrow and jam yesterday—but never jam *today*." As they spoke, the White Queen's voice became stranger and stranger—until Alice noticed that she had become a sheep.

Not wishing to spend much time talking with a sheep, off went Alice to the next square, in which sat Humpty Dumpty atop his wall. And what a philosopher he turned out to be! He had his own meanings for words, which he made up on the spur of the moment; he explained the desirability of un-birthday presents; he recited a charming poem for her—indeed, he was such an altogether interesting person that Alice regretted very much to note, as she left him, that he was slowly falling off his wall.

The next square brought Alice into the midst of a battle between the Lion and the Unicorn. But though she was glad to meet the White King and a curious fellow named Hatta, whom she felt she had met somewhere before, she was altogether pleased when she reached the next square and was able to leave the sounds of battle behind.

It was here that she met the White Knight, who had been toppled from his horse by the Red Knight. Such a kindly old gentleman was the White Knight—and such a brilliant inventor. Among his inventions were a trap to catch mice that might be running about on a horse's back; a set of anklets to protect his horse from shark bites; a clever way of getting over a wall on one's head—oh, so *many* valuable things. As he courteously accompanied Alice to the end of the square, he sang a song for her called—well, he wasn't quite sure *what* it was called.

When they reached the square's end, Alice waved him goodbye—and suddenly felt a weight upon her head. Reaching up she discovered that it was—it *was*—a golden crown. Now, she thought, she was finally Queen Alice.

But not *quite*, as it turned out. For there were her old friends, the Red Queen and the White Queen, to give her an examination. And oh, what a difficult examination it was: "What's the French for Fiddle-de-dee?" they wanted to know, and "How much is one and one and one and one and one and one and one and one and one and one?" Oh, the questions they asked!

At last, however, the Queens seemed satisfied with her, and so they ushered Alice into a banquet hall for her coronation feast. But not a mouthful of food did Alice taste—for the various victuals insisted on rising from their plates and being introduced to her, and it isn't etiquette to cut anyone once you've been introduced.

Suddenly all of the food, and the plates and cups and saucers, and the Red Queen and the White Queen, and all of the guests, too, became most rambunctious; they began to pinch and squeeze and push, until Alice could hardly keep her seat, much less her temper. Faster and faster everything began to move; and, indeed, Alice herself began to float into the air. Then the candles all grew up to the ceiling, and the bottles began to fly about with the saucers—until, in desperation, Alice grabbed hold of the White Queen and began to shake her.

She shook her—and shook her—and shook her—until the Queen started to make the strangest sounds. Mewing sounds, they were.

The more Alice shook her, the smaller and smaller she grew; and mewing all the time, she kept on growing shorter

—and fatter—and softer—and rounder—and—and it really *was* a kitten, after all—Alice's own kitten, Dinah.

Only then did Alice realize that the entire trip to Looking-Glass House had been a dream. But *whose* dream—her own, or the Red King's—well, that she was never able to decide.

TREASURE ISLAND

Robert Louis Stevenson

Robert Louis Stevenson was born in 1850 in Scotland, the son of an engineer. He contracted tuberculosis at an early age, and having to travel extensively for his health, received little formal schooling. He decided to become a writer, to the great dismay of his parents, and went to live in France. Here began his liaison with Mrs. Fanny Osbourne, a married American woman ten years his senior. They went to California together and, after Mrs. Osbourne's divorce, were married in 1880. The couple traveled widely, eventually settling in Samoa, where Stevenson lived in baronial fashion until his death in 1894.

Stevenson is considered one of the foremost writers of the "Romantic revival" of the late nineteenth century; besides his novels of adventure he wrote essays on the values of the life of excitement and romance, and the famous volume of poems, A Child's Garden of Verses. Treasure Island *remains his best-known work, a classic tale of adventure with which younger readers have identified since its publication more than three quarters of a century ago.*

To an out-of-the-way inn, the Admiral Benbow, comes an old seaman known only as "Billy Bones." With his scarred face, tarry pigtail, and raucous singing of an old sea song:

> *Fifteen men on the Dead Man's Chest—*
> *Yo-ho-ho, and a bottle of rum!*

he manages to frighten everyone about. To the son of the landlord, young Jim Hawkins, the old sea dog gives a monthly allowance of fourpence in exchange for Jim's keeping an eye open for a seafaring man with one leg, of whom Billy Bones seems to be frightened.

One day, a blind sailor comes to the inn. Billy Bones recognizes him as Old Pew, and receives from him the dreaded Black Spot—a sign that he has been doomed to death by his former mates for treachery against them. Before the sentence can be executed, however, Billy Bones dies of an apoplectic stroke. Jim's mother is determined to have the sum of money to which she is entitled for the old sailor's board and lodging, which he has never paid. She and Jim open the dead man's sea chest, but before Mrs. Hawkins can find enough coins to make up what the dead man owes her, she and Jim hear Pew returning with his murderous comrades. Jim grabs an oilskin pouch to make up the difference, and he and his mother flee the inn just in time to save themselves from the desperadoes.

In the oilskin pouch Jim discovers a treasure map. This he reveals to the somewhat foolish Squire Trelawney and the good Dr. Livesey. They recognize that the map will lead them to an island on which lies buried the fabled treasure of the long-dead Captain Flint, and they determine to go after it, taking Jim along as cabin boy.

Trelawney buys a ship named the *Hispaniola*, and hires a crew. When Jim goes to Bristol to join the ship, he is appalled to find that the sea cook Trelawney has hired is a one-legged seafaring man named Long John Silver. He wonders if it can be the same man of whom Billy Bones was so frightened; but Long John rapidly convinces Jim, Trelawney, and Dr. Livesey that he is the most amiable, capable, and honest man alive.

Captain Smollett, whom Trelawney has also hired, reveals to the Doctor and the Squire that he is very uneasy about the entire project. He mistrusts the crew, and he dislikes the fact that all aboard know the object of the journey. He prevails upon Trelawney for safety's sake to make some changes in the sleeping arrangements and in the disposition of arms and powder, and then agrees to take command of the ship.

The voyage aboard the *Hispaniola* is uneventful until one night, shortly after Treasure Island has been sighted, young Jim Hawkins decides to get an apple from the barrel on deck. The barrel is almost empty, and he has to crawl right down into it. Before he can crawl out, he hears Long John Silver and Israel Hands, one of the sailors, approach; and the conversation Jim overhears is enough to glue him to his hiding place in terror.

Jim hears that the entire crew, save for a handful of honest sailors, is a mutinous lot of desperadoes under the command of Long John Silver. It is their plan to wait until the treasure has been safely stowed on board; then, they intend to kill the Squire, the doctor, the captain, and Jim himself, and make the *Hispaniola* and the treasure she carries their own.

This Jim reveals to his friends as soon as possible; and it is agreed that on arriving at the island, Smollett is to give all men leave to go ashore. This plan is implemented, and most of the mutineers take advantage of it. Jim, too, slips ashore, unbeknown to his friends; and when Long John Silver discovers Jim's presence, he shouts to him—but Jim dashes off into the woods on the island.

During his exploration of the island Jim encounters a strange man who proves to be one Ben Gunn, a sailor who had been marooned there three years earlier. Gunn prevails upon Jim, when he has heard his story, to use influence with Squire Trelawney and Dr. Livesey to guarantee him safe return to England. In exchange, Gunn promises to be of great help to Jim. The bargain is struck, but immediately their conversation is ended by the sound of gunfire, and Gunn takes off into the woods.

The battle between the loyal forces of Captain Smollett and the mutineers under Silver has begun earlier than anticipated. Smollett, Livesey, and Trelawney, together with three loyal sailors, have taken refuge in a rough-hewn pirate stockade they have found; Silver's men are encamped in the woods, with another two or three of them aboard the *Hispaniola* anchored off shore, and in command of her cannon.

Jim returns to the stockade just in time. The fighting begins in earnest, and after the first assault, Smollett's party is victorious. But the battle is just beginning, and will continue for days.

After several skirmishes, Long John arrives at the stockade under a flag of truce, and tries to effect a bargain; but Smollett, perceiving that he has nothing to gain and much to lose, refuses Silver's terms. The rejection of Silver is followed by another attack—this one far worse than any that have preceded it; and when it is over, the twenty-six men who had at first sailed on the *Hispaniola* are reduced in number to thirteen—four within the stockade and nine in Silver's camp.

Taking advantage of a stillness in the battle, Jim slips out of the stockade unnoticed, and is off on a further adventure of his own. First, he finds the boat which Ben Gunn told him he had made and hidden. In it, Jim pushes out to sea toward the anchored *Hispaniola*, determined to cut it loose and let the tides carry it away, so that Silver will not be able to escape to it.

Jim finds the ship in the hands of the desperate and wounded ruffian Israel Hands. Pretending to trust Hands, Jim gets his cooperation in steering the *Hispaniola* into a sheltered bay on the other side of the island. Once the ship is moored, Hands turns on Jim, determined to kill him. The boy is too swift, however, and he flees to the top of the rigging. Slowly, laboriously, Hands climbs up after him; but though he throws his knife at Hawkins, and manages to wound him in the shoulder, he himself falls to the deck from the rigging and is killed. Happy with the prize he has brought his friends—Jim recognizes the value of the ship—the boy waits till night, and then returns to the stockade.

To his surprise and terror, the first sound he hears is the screaming voice of Silver's parrot calling out "Pieces of eight!" A flare is lighted, and Jim discovers too late that Silver and his men are now in possession of the stockade. Though the men wish to kill Jim on the spot, Silver determines to hold him hostage.

The next day, Dr. Livesey arrives at the stockade, and Jim learns that in his absence Livesey had turned over to the pirates the stockade and its provisions, as well as the treasure map itself. This Jim does not understand in the least; but later, when the pirates take him along to the treasure site, they find that the treasure has been dug up already.

As the infuriated pirates turn on their erstwhile captain, Silver, shots are again heard from the trees. In this final battle, Silver is taken prisoner, after which it is revealed that the treasure had been found by Ben Gunn, who is now of Dr. Livesey's party. Only three of Silver's pirates remain at large on the island; and these men, it is decided, will be marooned there. Accordingly, a few arms and provisions are left for the villains.

The next day, the treasure is loaded aboard the *Hispaniola*. Livesey has given his word that he will take Silver back to England and put in a good word for him before the courts. But before the *Hispaniola* reaches her final destination, Silver steals a generous sack of gold and effects his escape, never to be heard of again.

The balance of the treasure is divided equitably among

Dr. Livesey, Squire Trelawney, Captain Smollett, Ben Gunn, and Jim Hawkins. And so ends the adventurous voyage to Treasure Island. But for many nights thereafter, young Hawkins wakes up in the darkness to the sound of rolling surf pounding in his ears, and to the awful cries of Silver's parrot screaming, "Pieces of eight! Pieces of eight!"

THE HOUND OF THE BASKERVILLES

Sir Arthur Conan Doyle

Arthur Conan Doyle was born in Edinburgh in 1859, and received a medical degree from the Edinburgh Royal Infirmary in 1885. Doyle's first story of the detective Sherlock Holmes, A Study in Scarlet, *appeared in 1887; so enthusiastic was the reception of the fictional detective that Doyle gave up his medical practice in 1890 in order to devote himself entirely to writing. The Hound of the Baskervilles appeared in 1902. Although remembered primarily for detective fiction, Doyle was also a writer of historical novels, plays, and non-fiction works of political and military history. In his later years Doyle became interested in spiritualism, and spent most of his time as a writer and lecturer on this subject. He was knighted in 1902. He died in 1930.*

Doyle must be credited with creating, in Sherlock Holmes, the prototype of the fictional detective: aloof and somewhat odd, brilliant beyond human capability, he begins work where lesser intellects have left off, and arrives at a solution as astonishing to others as it is elementary to him. This formula has inspired what is probably the most widely read fictional genre of our times, the English detective mystery; it appears, furthermore, that those subsequent fictional detectives who most recall the qualities of Sherlock Holmes find the greatest public favor.

Shortly after the death of Sir Charles Baskerville, his friend and neighbor, Dr. James Mortimer, goes to the world-famous detective, Sherlock Holmes, to tell him some elements of the Baskerville tragedy which have not appeared publicly. Holmes and his good friend and confidant, Dr. Watson, listen attentively as Mortimer tells them first of the legend of the Hound of the Baskervilles—a huge, fiendish hound that has supposedly caused the death of Baskervilles for centuries—and, second, that the night Sir Charles supposedly died of a heart attack on a garden path he was not merely taking a stroll, as has been supposed, but was standing at the garden gate for a period of about ten minutes, as though he had been waiting for someone. (The absence of any footprints but Baskervilles's suggests that the person for whom he waited never arrived.)

Mortimer, suspecting danger to the new tenant of Baskerville Hall, Sir Charles's heir, seeks Holmes's help—help which Holmes is glad to give. The new tenant is Sir Charles's nephew Henry—now Sir Henry Baskerville. (Sir Charles had never married; his younger brother, Rodger, the black sheep of the family, had died years before in Central America; and his second brother, Henry's father, had also died.) Arriving in London from America to take up residence in Baskerville Hall, Sir Henry receives an anonymous message warning him to stay away from the moors of Dartmoor, the family seat. This note of mystery intrigues Holmes; and when two boots are stolen from Sir Henry's hotel room—first a brand-new tan one, then, when that has been returned, an old black one which is not returned—Holmes decides that a plot of grave proportions is indeed under way.

Holmes notes that Baskerville and Mortimer are followed everywhere in London by a man with a pale face and heavy black beard. When he learns that this description fits that of the Baskerville butler, Barrymore (who with his wife are the only servants at the old mansion), he urges Baskerville to go at once to his new home in Dartmoor, accompanied by Dr. Watson, who is under no circumstances to let Baskerville out of his sight.

Neither Watson nor Baskerville is impressed with the first view of the Baskerville country. Shrouded in mists and fog, neighboring the Grimpen Mire (a complex of quicksand pits on a craggy hillside), within sight of some crude stone huts deserted by primitives during the neolithic age—the setting is grim. No less grim is Baskerville Hall itself, a smoky, dark mansion of towers and twisting corridors. Watson is little disposed to feel reassured, and the lugubrious Barrymores do not cheer him to any degree.

Not knowing how long it will be before Holmes himself comes to Dartmoor to investigate, Watson settles down for a prolonged visit at the Hall, and soon gets to know the few neighbors of Sir Henry. Most interesting are the Stapletons—the fair-skinned Jack, an enthusiastic lepidopterist, and his dark sister, Beryl. Beryl attempts to communicate with Sir

Henry when her brother is not present, her message being that Sir Henry is in the gravest danger; but only Watson hears her words, and she hurriedly and confusedly begs him to forget them. It is evident that she is in some fear of her brother.

To add to the chill atmosphere, a convict named Selden, one of the most heinous murderers known, escapes from nearby Princetown Prison, and is spotted once or twice near the Grimpen Mire, and he remains at large.

Keeping his eye on Barrymore, the tight-lipped butler, Watson catches the man in an obvious lie: Barrymore says he heard no sobbing in the night (a sound Watson had heard distinctly), and he assures Watson it could not possibly have been Mrs. Barrymore. The lady appears shortly, however, and her eyes are clearly red-rimmed from weeping. It also seems to Watson that Barrymore is heard walking through the house in the dead of night, and he and Baskerville determine to catch him at it. This they succeed in doing, and to their surprise, they find him signaling with a candle from a second-story window. He refuses to explain his conduct, but Mrs. Barrymore breaks down and tells them that Selden, the convict, is her brother, and that though they know he is an evil man, her sisterly love has not died, and she arranges to leave food for him every second night. She pleads so effectively that Baskerville and Watson agree not to tell the police.

Another night sound which disturbs the atmosphere is a strange, horrible baying of a hound far away. Though Watson and Stapleton attempt to allay Baskerville's fears about it, it is clear that the family legend of the fiendish Hound of the Baskervilles and its curse of death are preying more and more upon the nobleman's mind.

One happy note is struck—for Watson, at least—when it becomes apparent that Sir Henry is falling in love with Beryl Stapleton. From a distance Watson sees the two of them holding a tryst. The two are also watched by Jack Stapleton, who suddenly descends upon them and stages a hideous scene in which he reviles both Sir Henry and his sister Beryl, forbidding them to see each other again. Sir Henry is confused and angered by Stapleton's conduct; but a few days later Stapleton apologizes. He explains that his sister is his one companion in life, and that the thought of her marriage had unduly upset him. He assures Sir Henry that if he will wait three months before pursuing his romance with Beryl, Stapleton will adjust himself to the idea and will not oppose the match. To this Baskerville agrees.

While on a walk one afternoon, Watson spies, at a distance, the convict who has been hiding on the moors, and determines to track him down. He climbs the craggy mountainside and goes to the spot where he has seen the man. It is one of the deserted stone huts, and Watson steps in, his pistol drawn. No one is present, but it is clear that someone has recently occupied the hut. Suddenly Watson hears a step behind him. Whirling around, he finds himself face to face with—Sherlock Holmes.

Holmes explains that he has been on the scene for some time, though it has served his purpose to let everyone think that he has been in London. Now, Holmes declares, the time has come for him to make his presence known, and accordingly he joins Watson as a house guest at Baskerville Hall.

Fearing that the convict on the moors endangers the lives of those in the community, Watson and Holmes determine to seek him out and kill him. They move in on the misty Grimpen Mire, where Holmes knows the man to be hiding, but he eludes them. In their search, however, they hear again the frightful baying of the Hound; this time the terrible sound is close and clear, and it is obviously the moan of a crazed beast. As they listen to the nerve-shattering sound, rooted to the spot, there is a sudden shout nearby. They turn just in time to see the convict being pursued by a ferocious black dog with mouth and eyes that shine with an eerie glow. By the time they are able to reach the spot where they have seen the two, the hound has disappeared into the mist. They find the man, however—dead, clawed to pieces by the dog.

Curiously, the convict is dressed in an old suit of Sir Henry's. Holmes realizes at once that the Hound is a real dog, trained to attack by scent. This explains why the new boot that was stolen was useless, and was therefore substituted for the old boot. The criminal needed an object of Sir Henry's clothing with which to train the dog; and now, going on scent alone, the dog has killed the wrong man.

The attack makes it clear that the net around Sir Henry is growing tighter, and that the time to act is fast approaching. The question remaining, however, is who could be training the dog—and for what reason. This question is answered by

Holmes shortly thereafter; strolling through Baskerville Hall, he notes the ancestral portraits on the wall. One of them depicts a man of exactly the same countenance as Jack Stapleton.

Quickly Holmes moves into action. He perceives that a trap is being set for Sir Henry, and he allows the nobleman to walk into it—all the while, he and Watson keeping close watch. Things move exactly as Holmes has predicted; and when the giant Hound is set to attack Sir Henry, the detective kills it. On close examination, he discovers that the animal had been starved to make it more bloodthirsty, and that its teeth had been painted with phosphorescent paint—which explains the unnatural glow reported by those who had spotted the Hound.

In the confusion Jack Stapleton, knowing that he has been found out, manages to escape into the Grimpen Mire; but as no trace of him is ever found, it is assumed that he has lost his life in one of the quicksand pits.

Beryl Stapleton confesses that she was not Jack's sister, but his wife and an unwilling accomplice in his crime. He was, in reality, the nephew of Sir Henry—son of the family black sheep Rodger; and knowing the family legend of the Hound, he had worked out his ingenious plot to secure for himself the entire Baskerville fortune.

Thus, having solved the mystery and saved Sir Henry's life, Sherlock Holmes, ever the suave and cool-headed man of the world, finds himself free to invite Dr. Watson to the opera to hear the singer De Reszke in *Les Huguenots*.

KIM

Rudyard Kipling

Rudyard Kipling was born in 1865 in Bombay, India. In 1871 his parents took him to England, where he entered school; he returned to India in 1882, where his father, now curator of the museum at Lahore, secured for him an editorship on the Lahore Civil and Military Gazette. His verse and short stories began to attract attention, and upon his return to England in 1889, he found himself to be a literary celebrity. He married a young lady from America in 1892 and they lived in Vermont for five years. Upon returning to England, he found himself the most famous English author of his time, and in 1907 he received the Nobel Prize for

*literature. He lived until 1936, but his popularity and reputation
declined after the outset of World War I, and his imperialist con-
servatism made him seem archaic to new generations of liberal
Englishmen.*

*As a panorama of Anglo-Indian society and as a story of ad-
venture, Kim is judged the finest and most durable of Kipling's
longer prose works. Here, the author's gifts as a storyteller and his
knowledge of India, always his strongest assets, combine in one
of the last great narrative accounts to be set against the background of England's colonial glory.*

His mother having died in childbirth, Kimball O'Hara (known
as Kim) is left an orphan upon the death of his father, a
hard-drinking member of an Irish regiment stationed in India.
His only inheritance being a drunken prophecy of his father's
that Kim will one day be saved by a red bull in a green field,
Kim becomes a street urchin and lives by his wits. Browned
deeply by the Indian sun, and never lapsing into English but
conversing only in various Indian dialects, young Kim is
taken for a native. His one fear is that someday the fact that
he is a "Sahib"—a white—will be discovered, and that he will
be forced to give up his vagabond life.

Kim attaches himself to an old Tibetan monk who is on a
search for the mythical Holy River, believing that he will be
released from the Wheel of Toil only after bathing in the holy
waters. Kim—much taken with the lama's childlike sanctity,
and fearful that the old man will be forever taken advantage
of by the Indian natives—offers to go with the monk in the role
of his *chela,* or disciple. As their destination is to the north,
Kim accepts a commission from the secretive native Mahbub
Ali to a white man of the English army, Colonel Creighton,
stationed in the north.

After many adventures in which he outwits the natives
on behalf of his beloved lama, Kim has managed to attach
the old man to the retinue of a chatty old woman from Kulu.
While out adventuring alone, Kim sees soldiers carrying a
flag showing a red bull on a green field. Struck by the image,
he forgets his wits—and shortly he is taken in tow by two
Englishmen who discover, from papers Kim carries about in
a scapular, the boy's real identity. They determine to send
Kim to school and refuse to let him escape; and when the
disaster is revealed to the lama, that worthy man promises

to pay the high annual tuition for Kim at St. Xavier's in Lucknow, the best school for white boys in India.

Kim's sorry lot is made somewhat easier by the fact that he keeps in sporadic touch with his lama by letter, and by the fact that Creighton has taken an interest in him. The one concession the English must make to Kim is to allow him to spend his holidays as he wishes; and whenever school breaks, Kim again dons the garb of a native, dyes his face and body brown, and lives his carefree vagabond existence. Much to his surprise, he periodically encounters his old friend, the mysterious Mahbub Ali, from time to time, in places widely separated from Mahbub's usual haunts.

When he has reached his early teens, however, he discovers the reason: Mahbub and Creighton are both members of the Secret Service. Creighton has long believed Kim to be particularly gifted for this special and dangerous calling, and Mahbub has been watching Kim's growth and reporting on it to Creighton. At last, the time is considered ripe for Kim to begin intensive training in the Secret Service. He is put in the charge of Sahib Lurgon, who is a strict taskmaster. However, when Lurgon finds how very admirably suited Kim is to the Great Game—as the Secret Service profession is called among its practitioners—he initiates Kim into the secret details of becoming an adept spy. Together with another player in the Game, the fat Hurree Babu, Lurgon teaches Kim all that can be taught of this most perilous profession.

At last Kim is withdrawn from school—ostensibly to accept a post as an engineer—and he is set free on one last six-month holiday before he is to enter his lifework, the Game, in earnest. Kim immediately takes advantage of this holiday to become a "native" again, and to rejoin his lama. As usual, the two set out once more on the lama's quest for the great river.

Kim's freedom from care is short-lived, however, for traveling on a train with the lama, he encounters a member of the Secret Service brotherhood, whom he recognizes by certain secret signs and passwords casually uttered. The man is desperately hurt, and he makes clear to Kim that he is being pursued by a well-organized band that will stop at nothing short of killing him. Only by thinking quickly and acting with swift decision and ingenuity is Kim able to save his new-found comrade, who is known to him only as E.23, and the man eludes his pursuers and slips away from the crowd. Kim, feeling the mixed emotions of joy at having so skillfully managed his first encounter in the Great Game and despair at feeling that his part in the venture will never be known, is cheered considerably by the appearance of Hurree Babu (in disguise), who assures Kim that credit will accrue to him for the escapade.

Hurree explains to Kim that he is on his way to perform a desperate mission, and Kim eagerly agrees to join him. Using the innocent, holy lama as a mask for his real purpose, Kim travels northward in Hurree Babu's path. At last they encounter their quarry—a Russian and a Frenchman, ostensibly innocent hunters but actually European spies. Taking advantage of a temperamental outburst by the Russian, Kim and Hurree are able to separate the men from their party, and Kim secures the crucial documents which the men have been carrying. This is a far greater success than he had ever hoped for, but his pleasure is dimmed by the fact that the dear lama is in a weakened condition.

Painfully, Kim leads the old man back to the home of the Kulu woman, an arduous journey of many, many miles. Kim himself is unwell, and he is sustained in the trip only by his love for the lama and his desire to return the old man to the comforts of the rich Kulu woman's house. When that is accomplished, Kim passes into a deep coma.

He awakes many days later, to find the Kulu woman at his bedside, a tender and gentle nurse. On asking for the lama, Kim learns that the old man has found a river behind the Kulu woman's house which he believes to be the object of his years-long search; he is now at peace with himself, and ready to die happily.

Kim has two visitors during his recuperation—Hurree Babu and Mahbub Ali—both of whom come in disguise. Kim surrenders to them the documents he has taken from the spies, and receiving their understated congratulations, prepares himself for what he knows is to be a life of dedication, danger, and adventure—the Great Game.

ESTHER WATERS

George Moore

George Moore was born in County Mayo, Ireland, in 1857, the son of a member of the Irish parliament. In 1870 he went to Paris to study art and lived there for fifteen years. He was strongly influenced by the current trends in French art and literature, particularly the writings of Zola and the naturalistic novelists. Upon his return from France he lived in England, spending only a few years in Ireland, and thus he is generally placed among English, rather than Irish, writers. Esther Waters, which appeared in 1894 and is his best-known novel, is considered the first naturalistic novel in English. Whereas realism is concerned with a faithful depiction of actuality, naturalism emphasizes the sordid and degrading aspects of life. The English public thought this novel brutal and disgusting, and many bookstores and libraries refused to handle it; critics, however, were very much impressed with Moore's prose style and the quality of his perceptions. Moore was in close contact with the leaders of the Irish literary movement, the Celtic Renaissance, and many of his later works deal with Irish themes; yet his style continued to be influenced by French authors. Although never widely popular, he lived to see himself acclaimed as one of the major literary stylists of his time. He died in England in 1933.

At the age of twenty, comely, religious Esther Waters enters service as a kitchenmaid at Woodview, the home of the wealthy Barfields. Her father having died and her mother having married the brutal, alcoholic Spaulding, Esther feels alone in the world.

Her early days at Woodview are lonely. She is shunned by her fellow servants, who consider her loutish and rustic, and, as she cannot read, she is unable to find pleasant ways of passing her time. Gradually, however, she begins to adjust to her new life, and to make friends. Her mistress, Mrs. Barfield, proves to be a worthy woman who sympathizes with Esther; and when the two discover their mutual religious views—they are both members of the strict sect, the Plymouth Brethren—"Angel" (for so Mrs. Barfield is called by the staff) takes a keen interest in the kitchenmaid, and soothes her when she is chaffed by her fellow servants for being so religious.

Mr. Barfield makes his money by raising and racing horses, and the entire household (with the exception of Esther, Mrs. Barfield, and the cook, Mrs. Latch) takes a keen interest in betting and all other aspects of the track. Esther, however, finds it all repugnant; and her scruples against the evil of betting are enhanced when she finds that Mr. Randal, the butler, whom everyone supposes to be rich from winnings at the track, is actually all but destitute and has driven his wife and children to the edge of abject poverty.

Esther finds romance in the person of the ambitious William Latch, the handsome son of the cook. She has a rival for his attentions, the housemaid Sarah Tucker; but William prefers Esther, and at last seduces her, promising to marry her. Her guilt over what has happened, however, causes Esther to shun him entirely, and in a few months he elopes with a lady, the master's cousin, Peggy Barfield.

Esther discovers that she is pregnant, and receiving the commiseration and help of Mrs. Barfield, she returns to her stepfather's house. He treats her and her beloved mother brutally, however, and, somewhat impoverished by "loans" to Spaulding, Esther leaves. Shortly thereafter Esther's son is born, and in the same week, her mother dies and her stepfather emigrates with his remaining children to Australia.

To support herself, Esther boards her son Jackie and hires herself out as a wet nurse to the wealthy but selfish Mrs. Rivers. She leaves her position abruptly, however, when Mrs. Rivers makes it clear that she cares nothing for Esther's maternal feelings toward her own child, and when Mrs. Spires, who is looking after little Jackie, offers to do away with the infant for the sum of five pounds. The horror of letting her own child sicken, and perhaps die, while selling her milk to a wealthy woman's child is too much for Esther, and she determines to go into service.

Boarding little Jackie with the amiable Mrs. Lewis, Esther becomes a maid-of-all-work, but she is unable to hold a situation for more than a year or two. In one house she is dismissed when it is discovered that she has an illegitimate child; in another, the foolish young master makes advances toward her which she repels—only to find herself again out of work. It becomes increasingly difficult to find a position paying enough to support her growing boy, and at times she is almost resigned to returning to the workhouse (where she had spent a few weeks shortly after Jackie was born).

At last, however, she finds an ideal position with the kind, sympathetic, good-natured Miss Rice, a spinster novelist. Here, for the first time in years, Esther is happy. She begins keeping company with the upright Fred Parsons, also a member of the Plymouth Brethren, and he proposes marriage. Esther, who though she has let up on the formal religious observances of her youth has never wavered in her awareness of right, tells Parsons of her illegitimate child. Much to her surprise, Parsons goes with her to see Jackie. Convinced that Esther has repented of her sin, Parsons says that he will marry her and be a father to Jackie. Though she does not love Parsons, Esther accepts him, knowing him to be a worthy and honorable man who will provide a good home for her.

Much to her chagrin, however, Esther's plans are ripped apart by the chance reappearance of William Latch. He has left his wife, and declares his love for Esther, assuring her that as soon as he is divorced, he will marry her. Upon discovering that he has fathered a child, William becomes all the more insistent, and at last Esther—knowing that Latch is now a wealthy man, and wishing to insure Jackie's future—goes to live with him in the public house he now keeps. And, when he is divorced, he is true to his word and marries her.

As Latch's wife, Esther discovers domestic bliss. She and her husband and their son form a happy family, and their income is good. Esther's only anxiety is the bookmaking from which her husband makes extra money. She is particularly disturbed by the illegal bets passed frequently across the bar in their public house—but Latch assures her that no harm will come of it.

Latch's good luck does not hold, however, and year by year they find their financial reserves dwindling. At the Derby one day, Esther encounters her former beau, Fred Parsons. Now in the Salvation Army, Parsons warns Esther of the evil of betting, and later he comes to the public house to warn her that the Salvation Army is making a crusade against illegal bookmaking, and that at the least suspicion against Latch, the law will be down upon them.

Thus warned, Latch becomes more discreet. However, he is brought to court when Sarah Tucker, former maid at Woodview, is arrested in his house. She has been reduced to a pathetic state by her love of a racetrack tout, and has stolen some silverplate for him. Esther's dislike of betting is only increased by the sight of how it has degraded Sarah. Later, when Latch himself is arrested for making illegal book, the Tucker case counts against him, and he is heavily fined.

For a while he resolves to conduct no more illegal betting; but his luck becoming ever worse, he begins again. This time his undoing is brought about by the suicide of a bettor who has been driven mad by his losses. At the inquest, Latch's inn is mentioned, and he now loses his license.

His health having broken, he is at the edge of ruin; and when Latch at last dies of consumption, Esther and Jackie are penniless. Esther is once again faced with the prospect of the workhouse, but by taking a job as laundress in a cheap lodging house, she manages to hold body and soul together. At last, however, even that situation does not provide enough income for her and young Jack, and she is forced to go again into service. Her old mistress, "Angel" Barfield—now living alone, her husband having been ruined by betting and having died thereafter—takes her back into service, and helps Esther support Jack until he is a grown young man serving in a fine regiment. Reunited with her first friend, and returned to the observances of her childhood religion, Esther at last finds a measure of peace.

CHANCE

Joseph Conrad

Joseph Conrad was born Jósef Teodor Konrad Korzeniowski in 1857 in Poland. He studied in Kraków until 1874, when he left for France to continue his education. He became involved in smuggling activities, and went to sea as a hand on French ships. He joined an English ship in 1878, becoming a master seaman and an English citizen in 1886. He retired from the sea for reasons of health, and began writing; his first novel appeared in 1895. Erroneously considered adventure stories, Conrad's novels are profound explorations of the soul and condition of man; the exotic settings and situations are based on Conrad's own experience and are not literary ends in themselves. Heart of Darkness and The Secret Sharer are rich in psychological symbolism and deal with man's sense of moral responsibility. Chance, which is derived less from his own experience than his other works, was Conrad's first popular success, although he was fifty-five when it was published. So masterful is

Conrad's prose style that many readers find it difficult to believe that Conrad knew no English until the age of twenty-one. The last dozen years of Conrad's life were rewarded with fame and financial success. He made a tour of the United States in 1923, and died one year later in England.

Chance brings together into the same dining hall one evening two old seamen who entertain a company of their fellows with tales and anecdotes. One of them—Powell—describes how he came to get his first job, as second mate under Captain Anthony of the *Ferndale*. The other—Marlow—tells of having known Anthony's brother-in-law, a chap by the name of Fyne. Linking Fyne and Anthony is a mysterious girl named Flora, whose life and destiny seem shaped purely by chance. It is her story that, between them, Powell and Marlow eventually piece together.

An only child, Flora deBarral lives with her mother in a village some distance from London. Parvenus, they are spurned by all but a neighbor, the straightforward and sincere Mrs. Fyne, daughter of the famous poet Carleon Anthony. Flora's happiest times are the widely separated visits of her adored father, who showers her with gifts as proof of his affection, though he is by nature a quiet and morose person.

Most of deBarral's time is spent in London, where he is a financier. He lives alone in modest rooms, and when his wife dies, he determines to hire a governess to raise Flora in the comparative quiet of Brighton.

The governess proves not to be a happy choice—but of this deBarral is oblivious, as he spends little time with his daughter. Little Flora herself is an unimaginative child, and she accepts her governess's authority and goodness without question. This only helps the governess to further her own scheme. She introduces into the household a young man named Charley, passing him off as her nephew. He is, in reality, her lover—and it is her intention that he shall marry young Flora and secure her fortune.

By chance, Mrs. deBarral's old friend Mrs. Fyne and her family take the house next to Flora's in Brighton. They see the girl grow into a young lady; and though they have little intercourse with her, they continue to take an interest in her.

Suddenly the world of deBarral's making goes to smash. One after another of his businesses goes bankrupt, and he is charged as a swindler and a thief. At the first sign of the trouble, the governess and her "nephew" desert Flora—but not before stealing whatever money of deBarral's they can get hold of, and telling Flora that she is wholly unlovable and unloved, and that she will always remain so.

The crushing effect of this information—which she accepts completely—is only increased for Flora by the fact that she is turned over to the care of a brutish distant cousin of her father's. When deBarral is finally convicted and sentenced to prison for seven years, Flora's desolation is complete. Life in her cousin's household is agony for her, and several times she runs away to seek comfort at the Fynes'. They at last agree to take care of her, and with their aid Flora, under the name of Smith (the name deBarral having been disgraced by the notoriety of her father's crime), becomes a governess.

What little liveliness and sense of hope she had entertained is gradually dulled, and except for the belief that her father has been greatly wronged and that some day she will be able to make up to him for it, she gives way to despair. Indeed, during a visit at the Fynes' country cottage, where she goes from time to time as a grown young woman, she resolves upon suicide, but she is by chance twice deflected from her goal.

The first deflection comes in the form of the Fynes' dog. The second comes in the form of Captain Anthony—Mrs. Fyne's bachelor brother, who is also visiting the cottage.

Like Flora, Captain Anthony is a lonely, sensitive, taciturn person. Within a few days he has proposed marriage to Flora, and when he leaves for London, she follows him. At this the Fynes become indignant. They are convinced that Flora does not love Anthony; that, indeed, she is merely an adventuress. (The girl was introduced to Anthony under the name Smith, and the Fynes believe that Flora has kept from him the knowledge that she is really the daughter of the convict deBarral.) Mrs. Fyne dispatches her husband to London to lay the whole truth before Captain Anthony, making him see the impossibility of his proposed marriage to Flora.

The complications resulting from Fyne's interview with his brother-in-law are deep. Anthony comes to believe that Flora has agreed to the marriage primarily to insure a safe haven to which her father may retire, free from the chains of the past. (DeBarral is scheduled to be released from prison within a fortnight.) However, because he loves Flora deeply, Anthony refuses to break his engagement to her; it is his belief that he cannot live apart from her. At this news Fyne is indignant, and he and his wife wash their hands of Captain Anthony and Flora forever.

For her part, Flora loves Captain Anthony deeply; but believing herself unworthy of and incapable of inspiring love, she mistakes his proposal that they marry but live in separate chambers aboard his boat for the honorable offer of a man who had thought himself in love but finds to his regret that it is not so. Desperate to provide her beloved father with solace, she agrees to Anthony's terms, though in her heart she feels that she is selling herself. And so the marriage is performed—but not consummated.

DeBarral is released from prison, and Flora meets him at the gate with a carriage ready to take him to her new husband's boat, the *Ferndale*, which is to sail the next day. Flora is prepared to find a loving father who will appreciate what she has done for him. Instead, she finds a bitter, selfish man who berates her for having married a fortune-hunter (deBarral has dreams of beginning a new financial empire, greater than ever) and for forcing him to exchange one prison for another, the *Ferndale* appearing to him as no better than a jail.

Against his will Flora brings her father aboard, introduces him to the crew by the name of Smith, and installs him in his cabin. From the first, deBarral loathes Captain Anthony, and makes his loathing clear. This does nothing to lessen the tension between Flora and her husband; both are constrained constantly by their unspoken love—each thinking that his love is unreturned.

With the arrival on board of deBarral and the new Mrs. Anthony, the once-happy sailors become embittered. They have little love for the pale, quiet woman who, they feel, has stolen their captain's affection; and they have less love for her father, "Mr. Smith," who seems to them evil. And most crushing of all to the crew is the change that has come over their beloved captain; his tension is obvious from the start, and it is not long before his men, seeing through the pretense of his marriage, understand the reason for that tension.

The only man on board who continues to have pleasant feelings toward all three of the figures in this strange triangle is the second mate, Powell, who has joined the *Ferndale* on its second voyage after the captain's marriage. Though he listens to the crew's bitter talk, he refuses to take sides, and the captain, Mrs. Anthony, and "Mr. Smith" all come to trust him.

The tension on board, however, continues to rise. Flora's faith in her father's love for her undergoes a severe trial; and as she is convinced that Anthony hates her, all her childhood feelings of unworthiness and frustration return. She is haunted by what she sees as Anthony's nobility; he is equally frustrated and maddened by his love for her which seems so hopeless.

One night as Powell strolls the deck, he inadvertently sees into the captain's private chamber, where Anthony sits reading over a glass of brandy-and-water. Suddenly a hand which Powell recognizes as that of Flora's father reaches in between a pair of curtains and drops something into the captain's glass, and withdraws. The brandy has been poisoned.

Much to Powell's relief, the captain, oblivious to what has happened, rises and leaves the room. Hastily the second mate rushes below and into the private chamber. He lifts the glass, but before he can destroy it, Captain Anthony surprises him by returning. Quickly Powell explains that the drink has been poisoned, and he stands the contaminated glass upon the table.

Before Anthony can comprehend it, deBarral himself enters, and begins to revile his son-in-law. Attracted by the noise, Flora, too, enters. Suddenly overcome by weariness and a sense of bitter frustration, Anthony, in the presence of Powell and deBarral, releases her from her pledge. He explains that though he cannot imagine how he will live without her, he can no longer hold her to a promise which is so plainly abhorrent to her.

At this Flora falls upon his breast, crying that she does not wish to be released. Forced to choose between her husband and her father, she chooses the one whom she loves most strongly, and who, she suddenly realizes, loves her. Anthony gently leads her back to her stateroom to rest from the ordeal.

As soon as they have left the room, deBarral turns on

Powell, and exclaiming madly that his daughter and her husband have conspired to drive him mad by imprisoning him on this ship when he could be out building financial empires, grabs up the poisoned drink and swallows it off. Within seconds, he is dead.

To protect Flora's dream of her father, Anthony determines that deBarral's death shall appear natural. He and Powell drag the old man's body back to his room and prop it up in bed, where it is found next morning by the steward.

At last, Flora and the captain are free to confess to each other their mutual love. But their happiness does not last long. The *Ferndale* is struck by a passing freighter one night, and all are saved but Captain Anthony, who by an unlucky chance is thought to have been rescued. His absence is not discovered until too late.

Powell continues to befriend the widow, who now lives ashore. She has had one chance at happiness, and to one of Flora's temperament, that one chance seems more than enough. But Marlow (who with Powell has narrated her story) reveals to Flora Anthony—and, separately, to the sailor Powell—what has been secret to them before, namely that they love each other.

It is clear that both will seize this chance. . . .

HEART OF DARKNESS

Joseph Conrad

The cruising yawl *Nellie* is becalmed. As there is nothing to do but wait for the tide, a small group of men aboard her, bound by their common interest in the sea, pass the time in telling tales of their adventures. Marlow, the only one of the four who still follows the sea, begins. . . .

From childhood on he has always been fascinated by the white spaces on maps—the uncharted, unexplored regions of the world. And when, as a young sailor, he finds himself out of work, he determines to sail up the great river into the core of Africa.

Getting such a job is not easy, and the men whom he contacts all try to discourage him from such beastly, unhealthful work. But women, he finds, are ignited by the idea of men going into the dark continent, uplifting savages, carving out empires, and bringing civilization to the far reaches of the world. So it happens that he enlists the help of his aunt who has connections with a trading company, and eventually he finds himself on the coast of Africa, in charge of a small steamer bound for the interior.

The steamer itself is in a serious state of disrepair, and Marlow must spend over a month waiting for adequate parts to arrive for fixing it. During this long, hot waiting period he gets his first taste of life in Africa. Though it challenges his spirit of adventure, it is not to his liking. It is hard for him to know what sickens him more: the blacks—humiliated and enslaved savages—or the whites—grasping, avaricious, scheming, petty men whose dignity and honor seem to have evaporated in the heat of the blinding sun.

Marlow at last is able to begin his journey into the uncharted interior. His steamer, inadequate and ancient, is manned by a crew of mute, cannibalistic slaves, and for passengers there are several representatives of the Company for which Marlow works. On the whole, he decides that he prefers the crew.

The journey up the river is slow, and as one long, sickening day follows another, Marlow becomes more and more depressed by the disease and despair he sees on every hand—all caused by the white man's invasion of the continent and his bringing of "civilization" to the natives. Even the occasional stops at way stations and the encounters with other steamers do little to ameliorate his growing sense of disenchantment.

There is, however, one flame of hope that burns in Marlow's imagination. This is to meet a man of whom he has heard some interesting talk: a Mr. Kurtz. This Kurtz, it seems, is a rare and unusual individual. Gifted, intelligent, articulate, he has gone into the heart of the continent as an agent of the Company, and become the best trader of all, sending back more ivory than all the other traders put together. Moreover, Kurtz is said to be a man of the greatest vision; and it is generally believed that if anyone can bring the benefits of civilization to the natives, that man is Kurtz. Altogether, Kurtz is depicted as a most remarkable man; and the fact that the other men of the Company whom Marlow knows obviously envy and fear Kurtz for his superiority adds to Marlow's determination to meet this one man who has remained uncorrupted by his long absence from home, friends, and family.

On . . . on . . . on drifts the steamer in its journey to the Company's Inner Station, where it is believed that Kurtz is now staying. Communication in this part of the world hardly exists, and rumors are often the only guide. That Kurtz is somewhere in the interior is certain, for his shipments of ivory continue to arrive; though how he is managing, no one knows, for his supply of beads and trinkets—the usual medium of barter with the natives—must be long ago exhausted. There are rumors that he is ill . . . even rumors that he may be dead. These Marlow refuses to believe, for meeting this remarkable Mr. Kurtz, and talking with him, has now become for Marlow the single, concentrated point of his existence. Why it should be so, he cannot understand. But he accepts this compulsion, and so pushes on.

About fifty miles below the Inner Station the steamboat comes upon a rude hut, clearly that of a white man. Upon investigation, Marlow finds a tattered book—an ancient, much-thumbed volume on seamanship, and a crudely lettered warning of danger ahead: "Hurry up. Approach cautiously." The signature is not clear—but it is not Kurtz's.

Prepared for any trouble, the party moves on. Eight miles from Kurtz's station they are ambushed by natives, who keep themselves well concealed in the foliage, but hurl their spears and arrows in a furious rain. The white men traveling with Marlow—fools, all—make blundering attempts to fire back at the natives, to little avail. But when Marlow blows the steam whistle of the boat, the natives flee in terror of its sound, and the Company men are able to begin the last leg of their journey.

Arriving at the Inner Station, the party is greeted by a young white man, who tells Marlow his story. He is a Russian, making his own way through the interior by trading in ivory. It was he who had left the warning note as well as the book, which he now receives from Marlow with deepest gratitude, having despaired of ever replacing this one scrap of civilization with which he has comforted himself for so many years. The Russian says that not only has he met Kurtz, he has become Kurtz's slave. Such a talker as Kurtz—such a philoso-pher—he has never met before in his life.

On being pressed by Marlow for more details about Kurtz, the young man reveals that Kurtz is now dying and in a de-lirium; that the attack by natives was not their attempt to prevent the steamer from reaching Kurtz, but rather to pre-vent the white men from taking Kurtz away; that, in short, Kurtz has become a god to the blacks of the area.

Marlow recoils from this news; but when he finally meets Kurtz, it is confirmed. The man is, indeed, dying—and the natives do, indeed, regard him as their god.

Kurtz confides his confidential papers to Marlow, and night after night Marlow pores over them by the dull, swing-ing ship's lantern. With growing fascination and horror, he pieces out the decay of Kurtz's mind, the slow disintegration of his personality. It becomes clearer and clearer to Marlow that the man who several years before had entered the in-terior of this dark continent as a fine, intelligent man of noble purpose has been seduced—by what?—into becoming a hol-low wreck of a human being.

Against the protests of the despairing natives, Kurtz is taken aboard the steamer, though it is clear he cannot last long. Marlow spends as much time as possible with him, try-ing to ferret out for himself the secret of what has happened to this strange man. But he learns little, and at last—in a voice no more than a whisper—Kurtz murmurs, "The horror! The horror!" and rolls over. Shortly afterward, a black brings the news to those on deck: "Mistah Kurtz—he dead."

The journey back to the continent's edge is a nightmare for Marlow. He cannot rid his mind of the mysterious, awful thing that has happened to Kurtz—or of those final words: "The horror! The horror!"

Months later, in London, Marlow goes to see the young woman who had been Kurtz's fiancée, to turn over to her the confidential papers he had received from the man. It is a painful interview. The woman—so full of love and trust and faith in the man she remembered—cannot know about the *real* Kurtz—the man whom Marlow had known. And so, when she pleads with Marlow to tell her Kurtz's last words, he says: "Your name."

"I knew it—I was sure," is her reply.

When Marlow finishes his tale, there is a silence. Nobody moves. One of the listeners, looking up, notes the water, which seems to lead into the heart of an immense darkness.

THE SECRET SHARER
Joseph Conrad

The captain of a cargo ship watches as dusk falls over a calm and still Gulf of Siam, only to find his sense of peace broken by the sight of the masts of another ship protruding from the midst of a nearby group of deserted islands—an unusual position. Mentioning it to his two officers over supper, he finds out that it is the coal carrier *Sephora,* out of Liverpool. One of the mates tries to explain away the mystery: she is probably waiting in that sheltered place for an especially high tide to carry her over the bar and thence up the great river which cuts into the coastline.

As the crew has worked extensively for the past two days with little sleep, the captain orders all hands to turn in, and he, restless in the strangeness of his first command, himself agrees to take the anchor watch. His mates and the crew regard the captain suspiciously—as the only newcomer on board, having joined the cargo ship but two weeks ago, none of them entirely trusts him—and this odd whim of his to take the anchor watch himself only compounds their mistrust. Still, he is the captain. . . .

Passing on his way aft that night during his watch, the captain notices that the rope side-ladder has not been hauled in. He assumes that it was neglected because of his own peremptory dismissal of the officers, and goes to pull it in himself. Much to his surprise, it will not yield, and after tugging at it for a few moments, he puts his head over the rail to see what holds it.

He is aghast to see, clinging to the ladder, a naked man, exhausted as if he had just survived a great ordeal. The man is not a member of the crew—he identifies himself as Leggatt —but before the captain pursues any extensive conversation with him, he hurries him aboard the ship and into his own cabin, where he gives the man a dry suit of clothes. Only then does he hear the man's story.

Leggatt is a refugee from the *Sephora*, on which he has until lately served as first mate. He tells the captain how the *Sephora* had survived a typhoon, with all hands saved only through his own impulsive giving of an order which the *Sephora*'s captain had been afraid to give. One of the crew had given Leggatt a show of insolence while Leggatt was executing the maneuver that saved the ship; and, in another burst of impetuosity, Leggatt had turned on this man—and, after a great wave that all but inundated the ship had cleared away, the man was found in Leggatt's grip, strangled to death.

Immediately thereafter, he explains, the captain had dismissed him from his place and had had him locked in his cabin. For six weeks Leggatt had stayed prisoner, but taking advantage of the inward lie of the *Sephora* and the unlocking of his cabin door, he had escaped this very night. It was his intention to swim until he could swim no more—and then, he says, he came to the overlooked rope ladder. It hung from the side of the ship, like a miracle, where it had no right to be—and he had grasped it.

As for the murder itself, Leggatt feels no guilt about it. The dead man was a mutinous scoundrel. Nor, he assures the captain, was he fleeing from legal punishment. What drove him to his suicidal adventure was his unwillingness to have to try to explain his actions to a court of men who never knew the sea. To them, it would be unexplainable.

Leggatt is the same size as the captain, and seeing him sitting in the captain's cabin in one of his own suits of clothes, the captain feels as though he might be looking at himself. He feels a strong impulse to save Leggatt, though how it is to be accomplished he is not sure. Even were his crew to have complete faith in him, the harboring of a confessed murderer—and a seaman, too—would be difficult; as it is, the crew does not trust him. The risks are great, but the captain cannot deny his impulse of—what is it? Charity? Brotherhood? He leaves Leggatt to sleep in his own bunk, pulls the curtains tight across it to hide the man, and falls asleep himself on the sofa. There, the steward, much to his amazement, finds the captain the next morning when he brings him his coffee.

All that morning the crew notices that the captain is in a mood which is stranger, more eccentric, than any they have noticed heretofore. He becomes peremptory with them, and spends more time than is usual confined to his own cabin.

That day, the captain of the *Sephora* comes aboard, and tells the story of the escaped man. How the listening captain manages not to reveal what he knows about the secret sharer of his own cabin he, himself, does not understand; but somehow he manages to convince the *Sephora's* captain that the escaped seaman must have drowned. The insipid captain of the *Sephora* leaves—but there is no sign of relief for the captain who has equivocated, for he recognizes the complete impossibility of Leggatt ever being discovered by his own crew, now that they have heard the story of the killing and the escape.

Once the ship weighs anchor and moves on in its voyage, the hiding of Leggatt is more easily managed. The only difficult moment of the day is when the steward comes to clean the captain's cabin. At such times, Leggatt hides in the small adjoining bathroom; when the steward leaves the captain's cabin, Leggatt returns, and the steward enters the bathroom through its second door opening onto the saloon.

One day there is a close call when the steward finds a coat which the captain had left out on deck to dry. Much to the captain's discomfiture, the steward insists upon taking it into the captain's cabin to hang up; and the captain is unable to protest without exciting suspicion. He hears the steward enter the cabin, and then, horrified, he hears the steward open the bathroom door. But Leggatt, managing to crouch down into the tub just in time, is saved from discovery by the steward's opening the door only just enough to reach in and hang the coat on a hook.

Night after night, Leggatt and the captain hold whispered conversations, and though they do not touch on the matter much in their talk, they reach an understanding that Leggatt must be allowed to slip off the boat in the dark some night when they are close to land.

The time is ripe as the ship nears a group of islands off the Orient coast. The captain, somewhat to the consternation of his mates, orders the ship to be directed landward. Leggatt is to be spirited below to the quarterdeck, where he is to hide in the sail locker until all hands are ordered above to reset the sails once the ship has come as close as possible to land; and at this point Leggatt is to slip silently out a porthole and make his way to shore. In their final whispered conference the captain presses upon Leggatt a small sum of money with which to start a new life in this strange place; and Leggatt gratefully ties the pouch of coins around his waist, against his skin. And at the last moment, before leaving Leggatt in the sail locker, on an impulse, the captain takes his own broad-rimmed hat and gives it to Leggatt to protect him from the sun.

The captain goes above to find the ship dangerously near-ing land. Nevertheless, to give Leggatt the best possible chance, he delays giving the order to come about until the last possible moment. The crew, restive almost to the point of mutiny, sighs, audibly relieved, when the order is given; while the captain, still unused to his new ship, is for a mo-ment unable to tell whether the ship has succeeded in chang-ing direction or whether it is hanging motionless and out of control in the almost windless night, a prey to currents that will carry it disastrously up on the land. Looking over the side for some floating object to gauge by, he sees, momentarily lit by a phosphorescent flash, his broad-brimmed hat, which Leggatt has evidently lost, bobbing on the water. From it, he sees that the ship is indeed under way, heading back into the smooth, open sea. . . .

ZULEIKA DOBSON
Max Beerbohm

Max Beerbohm was born in London in 1872, and was educated at Oxford. He contributed essays to The Yellow Book *while still at the university, and in 1898 he succeeded George Bernard Shaw as drama critic of* The Saturday Review. *His main popular fame was a result of a remarkable series of caricatures of prominent persons, several volumes of which were published between 1896 and 1925; but his essays, reviews, and fiction were also received as works of wit, intelligence, and sophistication. Beerbohm acquired, in his lifetime, a reputation as perhaps the most civilized, clever, elegant, and urbane man in the world of the arts, and these qualities are not merely evident in his works, but are the essence of his achievement.* Zuleika Dobson, *Beerbohm's only novel, is much more a part of the tradition of English satire than it is of the English novel; and it is as satire, pure and delicious, that this book has been so widely enjoyed. Beerbohm lived in Italy from 1910 until 1939, when he returned to England to be knighted. He died in Italy in 1956.*

Zuleika Dobson, the beautiful, single, young conjurer of the variety halls and the toast of two continents, finding herself between engagements, comes to Oxford to visit her grandfather, the Warden of Judas College. Though she is the darling of princes, premiers, and prime ministers, the delight of mayors, majors, and millionaires, Zuleika has never loved. She recognizes in her inmost heart that one of her exquisite beauty can respond only to the man who is so superior as to be indifferent to her. To date, she has met no such man.

From the first, the undergraduates of Oxford fall instantly in love with Zuleika. No exception is the young Duke of Dorset, himself the pinnacle of perfection. Wealthy, intelligent, gifted, and handsome, the Duke is as idolized in his way as Zuleika is in hers. His aristocratic breeding is so fine, however, that he gives no sign to Zuleika of the passion within his breast; and she mistakes his calm exterior for rocky indifference. Needless to say, she falls headlong in love with him.

The day after their meeting, however, the Duke reveals the truth. He is head over heels in love with Zuleika, and offers her his noble hand in marriage, assuring her that in spite of her low-born origins, she will be welcomed as duchess in a family so old and aristocratic that on the eve of the death of a Duke of Dorset two black owls come and perch on the battlements, remain all night hooting, and at dawn fly away, none knows whither. Zuleika is horrified that the Duke has fallen in love with her, and of course she will have none of him.

The Duke confides his misery to the ugly, ill-born Noaks, a student who lives in the same place. Noaks too has fallen in love with Zuleika, and both men, entranced by this goddess, remain impervious to the loving stares of Katie Batch, the pretty young housemaid who waits on them.

As Zuleika continues to spurn his advances, in spite of all the desperate entreaties he can make, the Duke resolves to commit suicide. Zuleika is enchanted at the idea of a man actually dying for her (it is the crowning achievement of her career as an international beauty), and she elicits the Duke's promise that as he dies, he will shout out her name so that none may doubt that he dies for her sake.

The fact that every student he meets is in love with Zuleika causes the Duke, in a rush of humanity, to tell them that she is a heartless wretch who is driving him to his grave. Instead of having the desired effect of cooling the undergraduates' ardors, the Duke is horrified to find that they all resolve to commit suicide in Zuleika's name also. Reluctantly the Duke is forced to admit to himself that even in death he is the college's arbiter of taste and setter of fashions.

The next night, Zuleika and the Duke have a horrid scene. Driven by his passion for her and his jealousy of the hold she has on the other undergraduates, the Duke declares that he is not, after all, going to die for her but, instead, going to live for her. At this Zuleika is infuriated. How dare he thus insult her by refusing to die? She dumps a pitcher of ice water on his head. The romantic Duke catches cold.

The next day, his love of Zuleika has turned to hatred. He determines not only not to commit suicide, but also further to punish her by sending her a note explaining that both his marriage proposal and his gesture of death were little jokes. Before he can finish his letter, however, he receives a telegram from his ancestral hall. The message is clear:

DEEPLY REGRET TO INFORM YOUR GRACE LAST NIGHT TWO BLACK OWLS CAME AND PERCHED ON BATTLEMENTS REMAINED THERE THROUGH NIGHT HOOTING AT DAWN FLEW AWAY NONE KNOWS WHITHER AWAITING INSTRUCTIONS.

The Duke sees that the gods will have their will, and orders his family burial vault prepared for his funeral.

The Duke has arranged to meet Zuleika at the boat races that afternoon. For the first time Judas College's team has bumped three crews; if they can bump a fourth this afternoon, they will set a new record. Zuleika well understands the Duke's unwillingness to commit suicide until after this important race. What she does not understand is his statement that though he die with her name on his lips, he dies not for her.

Now knowing that he has not long to live, for so the gods have ordained, the Duke notices young Katie for the first time. He discovers that she loves him, and he bestows upon her the pair of pearl earrings he had earlier received as a token from Zuleika. The girl is enraptured and believes that the Duke has proposed to her. But he corrects this erroneous impression, and, dressing up in his magnificent robes of the Order of the Garter (he is the only undergraduate in history to be honored with that distinctive membership), he makes for the river.

But even here his plans are thwarted, for just as the race starts, it commences to rain. Driven to desperation by the ugliness of the day, the Duke screams out the name "Zuleika!" and dives into the river. Immediately thereafter, the cry of "Zuleika!" is heard on every hand, and hundreds upon hundreds of undergraduates dive to their deaths. The sight of the Duke's face bobbing up and down among the billows so upsets the crew of the opposing college that the Judas Eight wins the race.

Old Dobson is unaware that the entire undergraduate body has committed suicide *en masse* over his beautiful granddaughter. He thinks that their absence from the victory dinner is merely a practical joke. But Zuleika knows the real cause; and she is torn between her pleasure that so many have died for her, and her knowledge that one has not.

Meanwhile, Katie has discovered that Noaks is the only undergraduate still alive. Believing the reason that he did not drown himself is that he, alone, was impervious to the charms of "the horrid Miss Dobson," Katie resolves to marry Noaks, and that ungainly youth is delirious with joy that at last he is loved by a beautiful woman.

However, when Zuleika learns that Noaks is yet alive, she goes to him. Here at last, she believes, is the one man who can resist her, and, therefore, the one man whom she can love. Noaks is beside himself with joy, and casts Katie aside for Zuleika. Katie, however, declares that Noaks avoided killing himself only because he was afraid, and not for any want of admiration for Zuleika. She spurns Noaks for preferring Zuleika; Zuleika spurns him for loving her. As a final indignity to both Noaks and Zuleika, Katie displays the earrings of Zuleika's that the Duke of Dorset had given her, and crows that the Duke died loving not Zuleika Dobson but herself, poor humble Katie Batch. This final indignity is too much for Noaks; he throws himself from his window and is killed.

Zuleika is in despair. None have remained aloof from her

charms; none have been indifferent to her beauty. Only the Duke of Dorset did not love her; and the publication of this news by Katie threatens to discredit the entire mass suicide on her behalf. Frantic, Zuleika determines to renounce the world and hide herself in a convent. She tells her grandfather of her resolve, and wearily goes to bed.

The next morning, however, the glorious Zuleika Dobson has second thoughts. She orders her French maid, Melisande, to pack her trunks, and to inquire about the quickest train to Cambridge. . . .

THE OLD WIVES' TALE

Arnold Bennett

Arnold Bennett was born in Staffordshire, England, in 1867, where he remained until leaving for London in 1888. He published some short stories and articles, and attained the editorship of a successful woman's magazine. His early novels, the first of which appeared in 1898, were received as the work of a man with considerable talent, but with the publication of The Old Wives' Tale *in 1908, the author was elevated by the critics and literate public to the rank of a master of modern fiction. Successive novels and plays sustained his reputation, and he lived the cosmopolitan existence of a widely admired author until his death in 1931.*

Influenced by the French school of naturalism, Bennett possessed an unerring eye for detail, and was able to write of ostensibly dull people and situations in such a way as to render them extraordinarily vivid and interesting.

In The Old Wives' Tale, *as in the best of his other novels, the acuteness of the author's perceptions works to draw from the drab lives of disillusioned people a significant analysis of human life.*

The upbringing of two daughters, Constance and Sophia, is almost entirely the responsibility of Mrs. Baines, her husband having been confined to his bed by a paralytic stroke when the children were four and three respectively. Mrs. Baines is a typical wife of the lower-middle class, and she is determined to raise her daughters properly.

It is Mrs. Baines's wish that both girls leave school and work in the family shop—a draper's—which adjoins their house in the village of Bursley. Constance, the more pliant, conventional, and dependent daughter, agrees. But Sophia is too spirited to be tied to a shop. She is determined to become a schoolteacher, and at last her will prevails.

One day, while at home, Sophia is entrusted with the watching of her ill father. She gets caught up in a conversation with a dashing traveling salesman, Gerald Scales; and in her absence from the sickroom, old Baines dies. Guilty over the death, Sophia agrees to give up teaching and return to the shop.

The shop is now run by Baines's former apprentice, Sam Povey. Mrs. Baines is distressed to note that Sam (whom she considers beneath her family's worth) and Constance are falling in love. She is even more distressed at the attachment which, it is evident, Sophia has begun to form with Gerald Scales. Mrs. Baines contrives to send Sophia to stay with her widowed sister, Sophia's Aunt Harriet. But this does not achieve the desired effect, for one day Mrs. Baines receives news that Sophia has run away with Scales, married him, and gone to live in Paris.

Mrs. Baines is no more able to manage the affairs of her other daughter, and at last she yields to Constance's marrying Povey. She turns house and business over to the newlyweds, and goes to live with her sister Harriet.

Life proceeds satisfactorily for Sam and Constance. They love each other in a quiet, habitual fashion. Year by year, business improves. After six years of marriage, their only child is born—a son, named Cyril—and he becomes the darling of their hearts.

The only friend Sam has is his distant cousin, Daniel Povey, who lives nearby. Dan has for years kept up a brave front about his home life; but one night he comes home to find his beloved son Dick lying on the stairs in agony with a broken ankle, calling for help. On searching for his wife, Dan finds her drunk in the living room, past hearing her son's pathetic cries. In his rage at this slattern to whom he has been tied for years, Dan kills her.

The trial of Dan for murder absorbs all of Sam Povey's interest. He himself engages the best lawyers he can find to get his cousin off, but it is of no use. Dan is found guilty and, in due course, executed. This failure wrecks Sam in spirit; and his health already having begun to fail, he soon dies.

Constance sells the business, but continues to live in the

same house, and (her mother having by this time died) devotes herself to the raising of Cyril. Cyril proves to be a somewhat talented boy of shallow intellect. He gives his mother little enough satisfaction, and when he wins an art scholarship and moves to London, Constance is grief-stricken. She must content herself with Cyril's weekly letters. And so, after more than twenty-five years, Constance finds herself alone.

Life, in the meantime, brings many unhappy adventures to Sophia. Gerald Scales proves an idle, egocentric fool. Thwarted in his original plan to seduce Sophia, he eventually marries her, but their life is misery from the beginning. Within a few years Gerald has completely gone through a fortune he had inherited—money that should have been enough to last them a lifetime. When it is gone, Gerald deserts his wife.

After he leaves, Sophia discovers that he has robbed his one good friend, the French journalist, Chirac. Fortunately she is able to repay the money. While in Chirac's company, however, Sophia—whose health and mind have been severely strained by her life with Gerald—collapses.

When she recovers consciousness, several weeks have elapsed. She finds herself in the house of one Mme. Foucault, a demimondaine turned landlady. This Mme. Foucault, a friend of Chirac's, has nursed Sophia back to health, and in return, Sophia buys the furniture in the flat for the woman, rather than let it go to creditors. When Mme. Foucault leaves abruptly for Brussels to follow a young lover, Sophia determines to set herself up in Mme. Foucault's place, with a single intention: to get rich.

With shrewdness and skill, Sophia attracts honorable gentlemen (including Chirac) as lodgers. By careful management, she is able to build up a small fortune, and during the siege of Paris and the commune, she becomes wealthy. Chirac declares his love for her, but Sophia spurns him; she has no interest in men, now, but wants only to be rich.

With the profits she has made, she is able to buy from an English couple a much larger, more respectable lodging house —the Pension Frensham. With her customary zeal and hard work, Sophia makes of the Frensham one of the best-paying and most popular resorts among Englishmen in Paris.

Quite by accident, a young friend of Cyril's, Mr. Peel-Swynnerton, comes across Sophia and recognizes in her the long-lost aunt of whom he has heard Cyril speak. Through his offices, Sophia and Constance re-establish contact with each other, and Sophia determines to visit Bursley again. She sells her pension for a handsome profit, and returns to England.

It is not long before she has moved in with Constance on a permanent basis; and though the two elderly sisters have their differences, essentially they are as sympathetic and affectionate as they were in girlhood.

Cyril spends little time now with his mother, though Sophia tries to make him see the cruelty this is to Constance. The only young people visiting the old house regularly are Dick Povey (Daniel's son) and his fiancée, a dear girl named Lily Holl.

Word comes that Gerald Scales, of whom nothing has been heard in almost forty years, is dying in a nearby city. Dick and Lily drive Sophia there in Dick's auto. Scales is dead by the time she reaches his bedside; but the sight of an old, old man (he had reached his mid-seventies when death overtook him) is a profound shock to her. She ruminates on the meaninglessness and fleetness of much of her own life. On the way home, Sophia contracts a chill, and within hours she is dead.

Her death is the final blow to Constance, who is now quite alone. An order comes evicting her from the house which is the only home she has ever known—it is wanted for the new draper who has bought the shop that had once been Baines's. Mercifully, before she is to move, Constance is delivered from this final indignity by death.

Cyril, who has been holidaying with his friends in Italy, is unable to reach Bursley in time for the funeral. The only genuine mourners are Mary, the last in a long line of domestic servants, and Sophia's ancient French poodle, Fossette.

OF HUMAN BONDAGE

W. Somerset Maugham

William Somerset Maugham was born in 1874 in Paris, where his father was with the British Embassy. He was orphaned at the age of ten and went to live with his uncle, a clergyman, in England. He studied in England and Germany, and took a medical degree in London. He never practiced medicine, however; having had his first novel, Liza of Lambeth, *published in 1897, he abandoned a medical career in order to be a writer. Maugham's first commercial success was as a dramatist; he wrote, between 1907 and 1927, some of the wittiest and most popular comedies of manners of the time. He traveled widely, finding in his journeys material for his novels and short stories, and retired to the French Riviera, where he spent most of his later years writing critical works and essays. He died in 1965.*

Of Human Bondage, *which was published in 1915, has become one of the most admired and widely known novels of the twentieth century. It contains many autobiographical elements, but is not to be read as autobiography; for example, Maugham's own physical defect, a severe stammer, becomes fictionalized in the novel as the clubfoot of the hero. Introspective and complex as this novel is, it is the work of an author who is above all a born storyteller; Maugham's superb narrative talents are the means by which the reader is led to the deeper problems of this book.*

At the age of nine, Philip Carey is left an orphan, and goes to live with his uncle, William Carey. The man, a vicar, is a self-indulgent, hypocritical gentleman of narrow views; and his wife, Louisa, though well intentioned, is too inept with children to give Philip the sensitive, thoughtful upbringing which the intelligent lad requires. He is unhappy in his new home, and after several years he is sent away to school.

School proves to be an even greater agony for Philip. He is intensely self-conscious about his clubfoot (a deformity he has had from birth), and the insensitive, meaningless cruelty of the rough boys at school leaves its mark on his nature. He becomes a solitary child, and though he forms one or two friendships, he seems doomed to remain isolated.

A brilliant scholar, Philip is destined for Oxford and the ministry. But life at school is one long hell for him, and at last he prevails upon his uncle and upon the school's headmaster to be allowed to leave the classroom and embark upon a plan of self-education abroad. His elders see in Philip's determination to quit school a want of self-discipline and a needless casting aside of Philip's talents and gifts. But at last his will prevails, and he goes to Germany.

At the end of his year abroad, Philip returns to his uncle's house more polished, more articulate, and more worldly; but he still has not found a sense of purpose in his life. He distracts himself with his first real amatory adventure—the conquest of the older, foolish governess, Miss Wilkinson; but he discovers that love in real life is far less amusing and romantic than love in stories. And he is only too glad to escape the governess's passion for him by going to London, where he is articled in an accounting office.

The London adventure brings Philip no more satisfaction than his year in Heidelberg. After a year in which he comes to loathe office work, Philip determines to go to Paris to study art (he has always been facile at sketching). Uncle William and Aunt Louisa disapprove, and the minister refuses to release to Philip the money from his inheritance necessary to make the journey. But Philip's aunt, who loves him deeply, gives him her savings so that he may go abroad and follow his new interest.

Life in Paris is full of adventure for Philip, and at last he believes that he has found his true vocation. He meets many fascinating young intellectuals among the British colony of painters and writers, and their talk of life, love, and art do much to supplement Philip's education. One of the most gifted young men Philip meets is the poet Cronshaw, with whom he has several imaginative, if enigmatic, discussions on the meaning of life.

A fellow art student who makes a profound impression on Philip is the pathetic, homely Fanny Price. Though everyone but she recognizes her total want of artistic talent, Fanny believes herself a genius. She pours out her philosophy to Philip—namely, that if one works at a dream hard enough, and wants it badly enough, it will be bound to come true. She is applying this philosophy to herself as an artist. At last, however, Philip receives a note from Fanny summoning him to her room; and he arrives to discover that, having reached the limits of destitution, she has hanged herself.

Fanny's death causes Philip to re-evaluate his own life. Determining that his own talent will never make him more than a mediocre artist, he chucks his paints, says goodbye to his Parisian friends, and returns to England.

By now, Philip's uncle is convinced that the boy will never amount to anything. As his aunt is dead, however, and as he has come into his majority and may manage his own finances, Philip is not concerned at his uncle's position. He now determines that he will become a physician (his father had been a doctor) and he again travels to London, this time to embark upon a course of medical studies.

Though he begins his studies with adequate success, Philip is haunted by loneliness. His self-consciousness over his minor deformity makes it difficult for him to make friends easily. In his despair, he encounters a common, vulgar tea-room waitress, Mildred Rogers. Irresistibly he is drawn to return to the tearoom day after day, and he conceives a pathetic but monumental passion for her. She spurns him at first, but gradually allows him to escort her out to dinner and the theater. Philip is dizzied by his success with her—though he continues to wonder how he can be attracted by so low a creature—but his hopes are dashed when Mildred tells him one night that she is going off to be married to a German named Miller.

Crushed by Mildred's duplicity, Philip contracts an illness through which he is nursed by his fellow student, the jolly (if amoral) Griffiths. Later, Philip finds relief from his passion for the waitress in a love affair with the sprightly, tender, intelligent Norah Nesbit. He reminds himself time and time again of his luck in escaping Mildred and in finding Norah; but when Mildred shows up again, revealing that Miller had never married her, and, on learning of her pregnancy, has deserted her, Philip finds himself as much enmeshed as ever. He casts Norah aside and makes a home for Mildred.

Many times Mildred proclaims her gratitude to Philip, and it is resolved that, after her confinement, the two shall go to Paris for a "honeymoon," and that Philip may there take his reward. When the appointed time comes, however, Mildred runs off with Philip's friend Griffiths, with whom she has fallen in love.

Philip returns to Norah, but discovering that she has decided to marry a kind, good man named Kingsley (in spite of the fact that she loves only Philip), he determines to part from her forever.

Philip learns that his old friend from Paris days, the poet Cronshaw, is back in England. He looks the man up and finds him impoverished and desperately ill. He takes him home to live with him, insisting that Cronshaw give up cigarettes and alcohol. But the man is too far gone, and refuses to reform. One night Philip returns to his flat to find Cronshaw dead.

It is a bitter blow to him to see one of whom he has thought so much come to such an end.

Griffiths, like Miller before him, tires of Mildred and deserts her. Desperate, the girl becomes a prostitute. When Philip learns of this, he insists upon taking her and her child home with him, but he is firm in his determination that their relationship shall never be other than that of friends. His deep love for her, which she has so often abused, prevents Philip from forgiving Mildred for her rejection of him. Not understanding Philip's sensitive nature and temperament, and feeling herself somehow demeaned by his refusal to sleep with her (though she admits that she cares nothing for him), Mildred is driven into a frenzy of hatred and spite, and hurls at him every obscene epithet she can think of—culminating in the word Philip most of all hates: "Cripple!" The next day, while Philip is at the hospital, Mildred destroys all his furniture and personal effects, and Philip returns to a smashed apartment. Mildred and the child are gone.

Soon afterward, Philip loses all of his money in unlucky stock market speculations, and he is forced to drop out of school. Driven at last to sleeping in the park, he is rescued by the highly original Thorpe Athelny, a former patient whom he had befriended while a medical student. Athelny introduces him into the bosom of his family, and finds work for Philip as a floorwalker in a major dress manufacturing house.

This period is the lowest of Philip's life, and he lives only for the day when his uncle will die, for though the inheritance he expects will be small, it will enable Philip to return to the hospital to complete his medical studies.

One day he again encounters Mildred; she has sent for him because she is ill, and hopes that his medical training will be sufficient for him to help her. He diagnoses her illness as advanced syphilis. In spite of his remonstrances, Mildred insists upon continuing as a prostitute. At least, thinks Philip, Mildred's child has died and is out of misery. Knowing that he can never be of any help to her, Philip says goodbye to Mildred for the last time.

Though his uncle lingers on and on—it seems to Philip willful torture on the old man's part—he does, at last, die; and Philip comes into several hundred pounds. He is enabled to complete his medical studies, and at last he becomes a doctor.

His first assignment is with a crusty old curmudgeon in practice in Dorsetshire. The two get on famously, and Dr. South invites Philip into partnership. Now approaching thirty, Philip rejects the offer. He is too eager to travel and see the world. For the first time in his life, he feels free.

To celebrate this freedom, he joins the Athelny family in the country, where they are on vacation. Here, for the first time, Philip notices that Sally, eldest daughter of the family, has blossomed from a child into a beautiful young woman. Without planning to do so, Philip seduces her; and though the next day he is filled with remorse, Sally shows no sign of unhappiness or guilt, but is the same delightful creature as always.

At last, Philip determines to marry her and accept the partnership offered by Dr. South. After a life of searching for a meaning and a purpose to his existence, he believes that happiness will be found only by following the simplest possible pattern.

A PORTRAIT OF THE ARTIST AS A YOUNG MAN

James Joyce

James Joyce was born in 1882 in a suburb of Dublin. The son of lower-middle-class parents, he was educated in Jesuit schools with the Roman Catholic priesthood as the eventual object of his training. His years at University College in Dublin were marked by increasing dissatisfaction with the standards and values of his childhood; in 1902, after receiving his degree, he professed a total rejection of his religion, family, and country, and went to Paris. He returned to Dublin a year later on the occasion of his mother's death, remained less than a year, married, and in 1904 left Dublin with his wife—never, except for a short visit some years later, to return to the city of his birth. The remainder of his life was spent on the continent of Europe, where he wrote continually, supporting his family by teaching. Joyce's eyesight, always poor, failed in his later years. There was much opposition to his books; those who considered Joyce's work obscene, unreadable, or preposterous were engaged in constant struggle with the author's champions, who saw in Joyce the most significant literary genius of the century. Joyce lived to witness the vindication of the latter group; and by the time of his death in 1941 he could delight in watching the most brilliant and eminent critics of the time grappling with the profound complexities of his later writings.

A Portrait of the Artist as a Young Man, *which was published in 1916, is certainly the most accessible of Joyce's novels. It is frankly autobiographical, and deals with events in Joyce's youth. The names of the leading characters have been fictionalized, but the celebrated figures referred to in the book are called by their actual names—notably the great Irish patriot Parnell, whose political career was ruined by the disclosure of his adulterous affair with Kitty O'Shea. Stephen Dedalus is, of course, Joyce, who had signed his first published stories, Dubliners, with this pseudonym. The name Stephen refers to the first martyr of the Christian religion; Dedalus, to Daedalus, the great artisan of Greek mythology who designed the labyrinth to contain the dreadful Minotaur, and who fashioned for himself and his son wings of wax so as to escape from the island of Crete. The hero of Portrait, when he invokes his namesake at the end of the book, intends to employ the processes of artistic creation to escape from the institutions which have thus far confined his spirit.*

Stephen Dedalus, the eldest child of a prospering Irish family, is sent to be educated by the Jesuits at Clongowes Wood College. He is a lonely little boy, thin and bespectacled, talented in his studies, and isolated from the others who excel in athletics and smutty talk.

One of them has elbowed him into a sewage ditch, and he contracts a fever. In his delirium he imagines the pomp and sadness of his own funeral, the beauty of the vestments and the ritual. And then he dreams of the dead hero Parnell, at the edge of a darkened ocean, and the Irish people in mourning.

Home for Christmas, Stephen is old enough for the first time to sit with the grownups at table. The talk soon turns to Parnell. Full of whiskey, his father and Mr. Casey splutter with a bawdy and bitter indictment of the Church in its betrayal of Parnell and Ireland. Stephen's Aunt Dante, once as avid an Irish partiot as she is still a Catholic, is revolted by the men's talk, having turned, along with the priests, against Parnell after his having been caught in adultery with Kitty O'Shea. Screaming "Blasphemer! Devil!" she leaves the table. Raising his head, Stephen sees his father's eyes full of tears for Ireland's lost leader.

Back at Clongowes, Stephen is again shoved aside by a bully, and this time his glasses are broken. Although he has written home for a new pair and his teacher has excused him, the sadistic prefect of studies sees him idling and canes

him. A bigger boy has also been caned for blotting his copybook, and the boys encourage Stephen to speak up for both
of them to the head of the school. Stephen overcomes his
shyness and the head of the school sees that justice is done.
The boys cheer Stephen and hoist him on their shoulders as
a hero.

Summering at Blackrock, Stephen follows his father and
Uncle Charles to the places where the men talk sports and
politics. But he also makes up romantic adventures with a
gang of boys, and at night he is absorbed in reading *The
Count of Monte Cristo.*

His father's fortunes fail, and the family is forced to move
to the slums of Dublin. No longer able to go to Clongowes,
Stephen roams the streets. At a party he meets a girl about
whom he dreams and writes poetry.

His father gets him into Belvedere to continue his education with the Jesuits. Again, Stephen distinguishes himself as
a scholar and model youth. He is given the chief part in the
school play, and the girl is to be in the audience. As he waits
to go on, two of the boys compliment him on his taste in
women. "You can't play the saint any more," says Heron,
striking him playfully. "You may as well admit."

"Admit!" Stephen remembers the day the master had discovered heresy in his theme. It was not a serious point, and
his great ability had excused him, but among his schoolmates
he detected a malignant joy. After class they baited him into
defending his favorite poet, Byron. Heron declared Byron a
heretic: "Admit that Byron was no good!" "No. No," Stephen
cried, as the boys beat him. . . . "Admit!"

The play over, Stephen rushes out, but the girl has not
waited for him. He runs off into the night and, alone, comes
to terms with his anger and baffled desire.

Stephen's father takes him to Cork, where the last of the
family property is being sold at auction. They visit the bars
and the university, while his father maudlinly recalls the
sports and politics, the singing, flirting, story-telling, and
drinking of his youth. Stephen finds himself embarrassed and
repelled by such a life.

He tries to erect his own breakwater of order and elegance
when, as a composition prize, he wins a large sum of money.
He buys dinners for the family, goes to plays, paints his room;
but when the money runs out, he finds that his breakwater

has been a fraud. In a turmoil, he roams the streets and finds himself among the brothels; giving way to his desire, he visits them again and again.

He lives with a sense of mortal sin, which reaches a climax during a sermon at the school retreat as he ponders the terrors of eternal damnation. He passes a terrible night, alone with the foulness of his soul, but at last grace descends upon him and he is able to weep for his lost innocence. The next evening he seeks out a chapel in a strange quarter of the city, is able to confess, and receives communion.

His life begins anew. He stores up grace by praying for the souls in Purgatory; he mortifies each of his five senses; each day he dedicates to its holy personage or mystery, each hour to prayer, every thought, word, and deed to God.

Yet imperceptibly his sense of grace begins to slip away. The petty imperfections of others irritate him; he remembers the suppressed fury in the faces of his schoolmasters. The flesh begins to call him again, and in resisting it, he feels pride. The sacraments no longer relieve his sense of desolation. . . .

The head of the school, remarking on his exemplary conduct and scholarship, asks him if he has ever wished to join the Order. Stephen has sometimes thought of it—of the secret knowledge of the confessional, of the mystery and splendor of performing the Mass. Yet as the priest talks, Stephen's mind wanders to the texture and perfume of women's clothing, to his masters at Clongowes and Belvedere, and to their judgments of literature which lately have seemed childish to him. And walking home, as Stephen considers the irrevocable act of taking vows, an instinct rises within him not to acquiesce.

He returns to the disorder, misrule, and confusion of his father's home, smiling ruefully to think that this life instead should win out in his soul. Around the littered table his brothers and sisters are singing; and in their voices he detects only the weariness and pain of all past generations.

He has refused the priesthood; he is to go to the university. His father has been in the pub for an hour finding out something about it. The university! Stephen can wait no longer; he sets out toward the sea. He meets his friends bathing, and they call to him—"Stephanos Daedalus!" "Bous Stephanoumenos!" He cannot answer; feeling the prophecy of his strange name, he sees Daedalus, the fabulous artificer, rising above the sea on man-made wings, and his soul is overcome with a vision of its destiny. And then he wades out into the swirling water where he sees a girl, as beautiful as a sea bird, and his heart cries out in profane joy. . . .

Stephen is late for his lecture. He leaves his squalid home, the fury of his father and the mutterings of his mother, and picks his way through the rubbish outside to the screaming of a mad nun in the nun's madhouse nearby. But his mind flies above the filth and noise; each scene on the way to the university evokes a different work of literature; and meaningless poems of his own making jingle in his head.

Too late for French, he waits for physics to begin. The dean of studies has come to light a fire in the empty room. In talking to him Stephen senses the torpidity of the Jesuit's soul, the routine and confinement of the calling which he has so narrowly missed. But now Stephen has the intellectual power to surpass his Jesuit masters, an aesthetic to replace theology, and he brilliantly expounds this subject which concerns him most.

Coming out of class with his schoolmates, Stephen refuses to sign his friend MacCann's petition for world peace. Before the other students, he tells MacCann: "You are right to go your way. Leave me to go mine." Neither can he accept the position of his Irish nationalist friend Davin. "Ireland has failed Parnell and every other would-be deliverer," he says; "Ireland is a sow that eats her young." To Lynch, Stephen further expounds his aesthetic, rooted in the Thomistic philosophy bequeathed to him by the Church. And at the end of his walk with Lynch, he glimpses the girl. . . .

Toward dawn he awakes and in his mind are verses. He has been jealous of the girl's flirtation with a young priest. Is he not himself a priest of eternal imagination? As his thoughts center about the mystery of sin and woman the verses irresistibly take shape, until he is left with a poem, perfect and whole.

On the way to the library, Stephen sees a flight of birds circling in the dusk. He wonders what they augur for him, feeling that like the swallows he is destined to wander. To leave forever Ireland, Church, home—will it be folly?

He meets his best friend, and as they come out of the library together the intelligent and skeptical Cranly scoffs at the other schoolmates they pass. And then, seeing the girl, who nods to Cranly, Stephen is overcome by reverie and he walks off from the group of students. Is it the girl or the poetry he remembers that gives him such joy? He thinks romantically of the Elizabethans, but without pleasure, for they are remote from the girl; he thinks of her own sweet odorous body passing homeward, and then a louse crawls over his collar. Disgusted with his vermin-breeding mind and body, he returns to the group.

Finally he is able to take Cranly aside to tell him of an argument he has just had with his mother. He has refused to take Easter communion. Cranly asks him why: if he disbelieves in the sacrament, then he need not fear receiving it falsely. Surely he could do it to make his mother happy. Stephen says he neither believes nor disbelieves; he may be going to eternal damnation. But he cannot kneel to a symbol of two thousand years of authority and veneration which no longer has meaning for him. Looking at the handsome Cranly, who would take communion for the love of his mother, Stephen feels that he has never loved his mother, or anyone; he has tried to love God and failed. He feels utterly alone, but it does not frighten him. Even his friendship with Cranly is coming to an end.

Stephen's diary that spring records his final breaking away. He will not serve that in which he can no longer believe, be it home, country, or Church; it is in loneliness and exile that he must seek the immediacy of experience and the freedom of expression that will enable him to forge a new conscience for his race. He breaks off with an invocation to his fabulous namesake.

THE CROCK OF GOLD

James Stephens

James Stephens was born in Dublin in 1882. Of a poor family, he was forced to hold menial clerkships while he attempted to have his writings published. His literary efforts came to the attention of the influential Irish nationalist writer, A.E. (George William Russell), who had Stephens's work printed. The public and critical reception of the poetry and prose of James Stephens was immediately favorable; and his literary reputation was internationally established when The Crock of Gold *was published in 1912. A charming fantasy which has delighted audiences in many countries,* The Crock of Gold *clearly demonstrates Stephens's close association with the Irish Literary Renaissance, a movement which drew upon the rich heritage of Celtic folk literature and native Irish fairy tales. Stephens spent the remainder of his life traveling and writing poetry and prose, and he died in London in 1950.*

In the heart of the dark pine wood called Coilla Doraca live two Philosophers who know more than anyone else in the world. They are married to two witches—the Grey Woman of Dun Gortin and the Thin Woman of Inis Magrath, each of whom bears a child at the same hour. As each woman hates her own child but loves the other, they switch children; but soon forgetting which is the child she hates and which she loves, each woman decides to love both Seamus and Brigid equally, in fear that inadvertently she might decide to hate the wrong child.

Claiming that he knows all there is to know, one of the Philosophers decides to do away with himself. He speaks a magic charm, whirls and whirls, and is dead. His wife, the Grey Woman, decides to follow him. She speaks a magic charm, whirls and whirls, and is dead. The remaining Philosopher and his wife, the Thin Woman, bury the two beneath the hearthstones.

One day, a local farmer, Meehawl MacMurrachu, comes to the Philosopher to seek help in locating his wife's stolen washboard. By a process of deduction, the Philosopher determines that it has been stolen by the leprechauns of Gort na Cloca Mora. He directs Meehawl to a hole in the ground belonging to the leprechauns. Instead of finding his washboard there, Meehawl finds the leprechauns' crock of gold, which he takes home and buries beneath a thornbush. As thornbushes are sacred to fairies, the despairing leprechauns can do nothing to unearth their stolen treasure.

In revenge against the Philosopher, the leprechauns gently kidnap the children, Seamus and Brigid. And despite the entreaties of the Thin Woman of Inis Magrath, they will not release them.

Meanwhile, Meehawl comes to the Philosopher with a second problem. His beautiful young daughter, Caitilin, has disappeared. The Philosopher determines that she has run off with the great god Pan, and his two children being released by the leprechauns soon after, the Philosopher sends them after Pan to find Caitilin. (Only children and innocent souls can come near Pan.)

It is indeed with Pan that Caitilin stays. He frees her spirit for love, and she thinks no more of home. And when Brigid and Seamus find her, Caitilin is kind to them and gives them supper, but she declines to leave Pan, for even at the thought of her absence he begins to pine.

When the Philosopher hears of the adventure, he determines to rescue the girl, and off he sets on a journey to find Pan. On the road he meets many interesting travelers, and to all he speaks his pessimistic and materialistic philosophy.

Pan and Caitilin have gone to the cave of another god, the great Angus Og. Angus is also a god of love—but love of a human kind, a sorrowing and troubled kind. For whereas Pan's love is love only of self, Angus' love is love of all suffering people. Forced to choose between the two, Caitilin chooses Angus, for he has greater need of her.

It is, at last, to Angus's cave that the Philosopher's journey takes him. He and the god have a secret interview, the import of which is never known. And then the Philosopher begins his homeward journey. On the road he meets many interesting travelers, and to all he speaks his optimistic and loving philosophy.

When he walks into his hut, he greets his bitter and dried-up wife with affectionate kisses and honey-sweet words. Not knowing how it happens, for the first time the Thin Woman of Inis Macgrath loves.

Their happiness is short-lived, however, for in meanness the leprechauns have told the police about the two bodies beneath the Philosopher's hearth. These bodies the police find, and, accusing the Philosopher of murder, they carry him off to the City and gaol where he is to be hanged.

Seamus and Brigid go off by themselves to discuss these awful things. They sit beneath Meehawl's thornbush, and reenact in pantomime what the policemen have done. When they come to the part of the digging up of the hearth, they find a crock of yellow powder. This, because it is so pretty, they give to their friends the leprechauns, who are now repentant that they have made such mischief for the Philosopher.

The Thin Woman determines to go after her husband, and taking the two children by the hand, she starts out on her journey. As they walk, she starts to tell Brigid all the things that a woman must know, and she starts to tell Seamus all the things that a man must know—but somehow she begins to be unsure of herself, and so they walk on in silence.

Many are the folk they meet, and many their adventures, and the Thin Woman reacts to each and speaks to all in the strange way that is her own, just as the Philosopher had acted and spoken in the strange way that is his own.

Among the personages encountered are the three gods of redemption: the Most Beautiful Man, the Strongest Man, and the Most Ugly Man. All three offer themselves to the Thin Woman, promising her eternal happiness; but each she rejects in turn, giving her solemn whys and wherefores, and she continues her journey.

Mysteriously the Thin Woman and the children find their way to the Cave of Angus Og. Angus, the god of human love, tells them that all roads lead to him if the searcher wishes to find him; without the desire to find him, no traveler can ever locate the right road.

Angus Og agrees to rescue the Philosopher. He summons all the fairies, leprechauns, gods, and shee of Ireland. It is a glorious and marvelous and wonderful parade that they make, and they go to the City and free the Philosopher and reunite him with his family, and all then dance in the moonlight to the wonderful fairy music.

MRS. DALLOWAY

Virginia Woolf

Virginia Woolf was born in London in 1882. Her father, Sir Leslie Stephen, was one of the most eminent and influential critics in England. He was a Darwinian agnostic whose home was a gathering place for the great intellects of the time, and whose private library, in which the young Virginia spent much of her time, was among the finest in the country. Living in London from 1904, she was one of the leaders of the celebrated "Bloomsbury Group" of prominent intellectuals; in this circle was the author Leonard

Woolf, who married her in 1912. The Woolfs founded the Hogarth Press, which printed the works of authors too avant-garde for conservative publishers. Virginia Woolf's own novels were experimental in form, and although never widely popular, they have been held in tremendous esteem by intellectuals, literary critics, and serious writers. She allowed the characters in her novels to reveal themselves by means of the stream-of-consciousness technique, and she discarded conventional plot structure in order to achieve a fleeting, but deeply felt and carefully observed, impression of time and reality. Mrs. Dalloway, published in 1925, explores the thoughts of one woman and to a lesser extent, the thoughts of a few people close to her. Truth, time, and space become subjective, and are felt as impressions rather than as objective, measurable reality. The author of this remarkable novel wrote, besides several other novels, penetrating and original works of literary and general criticism. Virginia Woolf suffered periods of severe depression during all of her adult life; in 1941, in the course of one of these emotional breakdowns, she drowned herself.

Clarissa Dalloway, fifty-two, is having a party this evening. Now, this morning, she is on her way to select flowers for the fete. Her mind drifts back to the days when she was a girl . . . Clarissa Parry . . . at her father's country home, Bourton. Those were the days when the bright and promising Peter Walsh was in love with her . . . when Sally Seton, unconventional and original, was her dearest friend . . . when the handsome and proper Hugh Whitbread was a constant visitor . . . when Richard Dalloway had come into her life, sweeping her away in romance and causing her to throw over the quarrelsome Peter. . . .

Mrs. Dalloway runs into Hugh Whitbread, still handsome at fifty-three. His wife Evelyn is again ill . . . how sad! . . . poor Evelyn! . . . Hugh is off to the Palace now (he is a minor official at Court), but he will not fail Clarissa's party. Mrs. Dalloway thinks again of Peter . . . and of her own daughter, Elizabeth . . . whatever does seventeen-year-old Elizabeth find of interest in that awful, middle-aged, ugly, religious spinster, Doris Kilman? The backfiring of an auto disturbs Clarissa's reverie.

The backfiring of an auto enters like a shot into the mind of Septimus Warren Smith, who with his small, childlike Italian wife, Lucrezia, is walking along the street. Doctor Holmes must be right about Septimus, thinks Rezia. He cannot be mad! But what to make of his talking aloud to no one—to the ghost of Evans, his dead comrade in the War? Surely, this Harley Street doctor they are going to see will tell her that nothing is wrong with Septimus. Or if something *is* wrong, cure it at once. Yet, what to make of Septimus' talk of killing himself? Her husband pays no attention to her. They stop in a park to rest, and Lucrezia tries to interest poor, mad Septimus in an airplane which is writing letters in the sky. . . .

An airplane which is writing letters in the sky catches Clarissa's attention as she returns to her house. There is a message: Lady Bruton wishes Mr. Dalloway to lunch with her today. Old Lady Bruton—will she come to the party, Clarissa wonders—and Richard. She thinks of Richard . . . her love for him . . . her love for Sally Seton. Sally had wanted her to marry Peter Walsh, gone these past five years to India.

Peter Walsh, gone these past five years to India, bursts in upon Clarissa as she sits mending the gown she will wear tonight at her party. Dear Peter—where has he come from? He is the same. He is in love with the wife of an Englishman stationed in India. He is to divorce his wife, she to divorce her husband. (How pained Clarissa had been to hear that Peter had finally married; how calm she is to hear now that he is in love.) How exactly the same Peter is—though older, of course, thinks Clarissa. How exactly the same Clarissa is, thinks Peter—though older, of course. Will he come to her party? How is Richard?

Richard is lunching with Lady Bruton. Hugh Whitbread is the other guest. Together they help the fatuous woman write a letter to the *Times*. Hugh is a pompous ass, thinks Richard: but what matter? Richard is in love with Clarissa . . . in love with Clarissa.

Can he be still in love with Clarissa, wonders Peter, sitting in the park. Yes, he feels it; Peter Walsh is still in love with Clarissa. But what of Daisy, the woman in India? Yes, he is in love with Daisy. Why should people suffer, he wonders? He looks at the poor little woman and the strange man on the bench across from him.

Why should I suffer, asks Lucrezia Smith of herself. It is almost time for Septimus to see Sir William Bradshaw, the great physician. Surely he will cure Septimus of this— melancholy. (No, no, it cannot be madness.) The visit proves to be a difficult one. Sir William calls Rezia aside. The case

is serious . . . Septimus has no doubt threatened to take his
own life . . . yes, yes, of course. He will arrange for Septimus
to be removed to a small home in the country for complete
rest. The attendants will come for him later this afternoon.
But Rezia will not be separated from him, will she? My dear,
sometimes the ones we love best are the worst for us when
we are not well. Yes, yes, thinks Rezia; but they will not
separate me from him. . . . They will not separate us, Septimus, she tells her husband as she brings him home. It is
half-past one.

At half-past one Hugh Whitbread is on his way to Bucking-
ham Palace. He thinks placidly of his life. People think him
a fool, he knows. Ever since that young girl Sally Seton had
laughed at him—they had been visiting at Bourton, and he
had kissed her in the library to punish her for laughing—he
has been aware that some people thought him a fool. But
they are the fools. Hugh has everything he wishes . . . influence . . . wealth (by marriage—why was Evelyn always
so ill?) . . . looks . . . manners. . . . He has heard that Peter
Walsh is back in town. Yes, Peter was the one of promise
when they had been young; and now Peter would come to
him to use his influence and get him a job. Well, he would
do what he could.

Hugh could be counted on to do what he could, thought
Peter, and so would Richard Dalloway. It wouldn't be easy
for a divorced man to find a position, but they would help
him. Still, he couldn't decide whether or not to go to Clarissa's
tonight. . . .

Clarissa is surprised when Richard brings her flowers in the
afternoon. He tells her of lunch with Lady Bruton. Hugh
was there (Clarissa had seen Hugh this morning); Peter
Walsh is supposedly back in town (yes, he had come to see
Clarissa this morning). Richard is off to a committee meeting.
Elizabeth is off to the Army and Navy stores with Miss
Kilman.

Miss Kilman is almost in love with Elizabeth. Elizabeth's
beauty is an affront to her. Elizabeth's wealth is an insult.
Elizabeth's lack of greed is appalling. How she loves Elizabeth! They finish their tea, and the girl is off at the first
possible excuse. Heartbroken, Miss Kilman goes to church.
Thank God for God.

Elizabeth rides the top of an omnibus, not caring where it

carries her. Just to be free—to drink in life. If only she could be in the country. How she hates London. But Clarissa is so social. Elizabeth Dalloway is content to ride the omnibus.

An omnibus throws curious patterns on the walls of Septimus Smith's room. Rezia is delighted with him; how natural he has been all afternoon. It is as though the past few weeks were a dream. Now there is no ghost of Evans . . . no muttered truths of God. There is only her own dear Septimus. There is a knock at the door. It is Dr. Holmes, the impossible Dr. Holmes. Rezia tries to bar him from entering, but he pushes her aside. He is just in time to see Septimus leap from the window to his death below. An ambulance screams through the streets.

An ambulance screaming through the streets—what a triumph of civilization, thinks Peter Walsh on his way to his hotel. He finds a note from Clarissa: "Heavenly to see you. I must say so!" Yes, he will go to Clarissa's party.

Clarissa's party is a success. Even the Prime Minister is there. Poor Peter Walsh seems a bit lost, thinks Clarissa. But not Hugh—why does Richard think Hugh an ass? And there is Lady Bruton . . . "How kind of you to come." Elizabeth is very grownup, in a pink frock; but her Oriental eyes seem dulled, thinks Peter.

The butler announces Lady Rosseter. Who on earth? wonders Clarissa. Good heavens! It is Sally Seton. She had heard . . . only in London for a visit . . . had to come, though uninvited. Sally Seton, her dearest friend, now married to a wealthy manufacturer and mother of five boys. Sally and Peter have much to say to each other. What a pity Clarissa is hostess. She cannot join them—not yet—there are still guests arriving.

Guests arriving . . . last come Sir William Bradshaw and his wife. They apologize for being so late. One of the doctor's patients has committed suicide . . . really most dreadful.

Dreadful of them to introduce the subject of death at a party, thinks Clarissa.

Yes, thinks Peter, I still love Clarissa. What else could account for this ecstasy? Yes, it is she. . . .

LADY CHATTERLEY'S LOVER

D. H. Lawrence

*David Herbert Lawrence was born in Nottinghamshire in 1885.
His father was a coal miner and his mother a schoolteacher. He
studied at Nottingham University College, becoming a teacher
there in 1908. There he met Frieda von Richtoven Weekley, a
German woman married to a professor at the College, and in 1912
Lawrence and Frieda eloped to Italy; there they waited for Frieda's
divorce, and were married in 1914. They spent the war years in
England, leaving that country in 1919 to travel; they lived for a
considerable time in the American Southwest and in Mexico. Lawrence's poetry was the first of his work to be published; it was his
novels, however, which brought him his great fame. He died of
tuberculosis, from which he had suffered since childhood, on the
French Riviera in 1930.*

Lady Chatterley's Lover, *published originally in 1928, has been
a cause célèbre, and one of the most famous/notorious books in the
history of literature, since that date. Banned until the 1960s in
Britain and America in its original form, it had been printed in
those countries in several "authorized" editions which could not
have been further from the author's original intentions; unexpur-
gated English editions were, however, never difficult to locate. The
novel is a celebration of the sexual aspects of love, a motif present
to some degree in nearly all of Lawrence's fiction but here dominant and explicit. The frank use of four-letter words, and the carefully recorded descriptions of lovemaking are never gratuitous, but
are central to the novel. Long before the original edition of* Lady
Chatterley's Lover *was declared fit for human consumption, the
influence of the novel as a treatment of forthright sexuality had
been widely observed in the work of other writers.*

When his elder brother is killed in the First World War,
Clifford Chatterley becomes heir to the baronetcy of his
father, Sir Geoffrey. It is Sir Geoffrey's wish that Clifford
marry and perpetuate the family line, and almost as much
out of filial duty as out of genuine desire, Clifford marries
Constance Reid, daughter of a Royal Academy painter.

The couple seems well matched: he is an intelligent if
somewhat withdrawn young man, she an intelligent and
hearty young woman. After a month's honeymoon, Clifford
returns to his regiment, and there is nothing to indicate that

his and Connie's marriage will be anything other than "typical."

War changes this, however, for Clifford returns from the front a shattered man. His recovery is slow and steady, but ultimately he remains paralyzed from the waist down. The knowledge that Clifford will now never father a new generation of Chatterleys sends old Sir Geoffrey into a decline, and he dies. Thus, it is as Lord and Lady Chatterley that Clifford and Connie return to the English Midlands to settle down at Wragby, the ancestral Chatterley home.

At Wragby they establish for themselves a way of life that is, at least at first, satisfying. Clifford becomes interested in writing, and before long his superficial, "modern" stories, to which he dedicates himself wholly, begin to be published in the so-called "little magazines" of note. The Chatterleys entertain frequently, and the house is often filled with Clifford's old London friends.

The complete denial of her physical self, however, begins to tell on Connie. Even her father notices it, and on a visit to the young couple he remarks (to each of them, separately) that she was never cut out for such a life. Recognizing the truth of this, Connie takes as a lover the playwright Michaelis, a house guest whom Clifford dislikes but cultivates because of his literary prominence and influence. The affair is easily managed, as Connie's apartments are at the top of the house, whereas Clifford's are on the ground floor, inasmuch as he is confined either to his wheel chair or to a motorized bath chair.

Connie suspects that Clifford will not mind her having an affair so long as he is not made to face the reality of it. And this suspicion is confirmed when he suggests to her one day that she consider having a child by another man, a child that could then be raised as a Chatterley. Although she knows that Clifford would never consider Michaelis a suitable father for such a child, she returns to the playwright that night— essentially because she believes herself in love with him, even though she finds him inadequate in the sexual relationship.

Much to her shock, however, Michaelis reveals to Connie that he finds notable deficiencies in her as a sexual partner. Connie had believed that the dissatisfaction was one-sided. Michaelis' revelation is enough to kill her "love" for him, and to put further thought of her having another affair out of her mind.

Shortly after this, a change is made in the arrangements at Wragby. Hilda, Connie's sister, insists that Connie's health is being endangered by her constantly being cooped up in the house. Much against Clifford's will, one of the local women, Mrs. Bolton, is hired to take on many of the chores attendant on Clifford's being an invalid, and Connie is left freer to entertain herself.

This she does by taking long walks through the family estate. On these jaunts, the only person she ever meets—and then, not always—is Mellors, the gamekeeper. Of him she knows a little history: that he is a local man, the son of a collier in the Midland mines; that he is married, but that his wife, a loose woman, has left him, taking their child; and that he is more cultured and educated than he cares to admit, affecting a broad, dialectal manner of speech which Connie finds hard to understand. She has difficulty in deciding whether she likes the man or not; and she decides that, on the whole, she does not.

Even less does she like Clifford, who is now a virtual baby in the capable hands of Mrs. Bolton. Steadily, indeed, she comes to hate her husband, to be stifled by Wragby, to be driven by a sense of desperation. She feels that everything in her life is closing in on her, and that she is headed for some sort of crisis.

When it comes, it comes naturally enough: she commences an affair with Mellors, the gamekeeper. Once committed to this strange, strong, sensitive man, she surrenders herself completely. He becomes the focal point of her existence. For the first time in her life, Connie finds genuine sexual satisfaction, for Mellors is a patient and knowing tutor, and he leads her along the labyrinthine roads of physical experience with a tenderness and a frankness that is the most marvelous thing Connie has ever known.

Meanwhile, Clifford, too, has taken a new hold on life. Encouraged by Mrs. Bolton's reverence for him, he takes a revitalized interest in the local people, in the colliery and its operation, and in his writing. But the rift between him and Connie has become too great to be bridged, though he is not aware of it. When, a second time, Clifford raises the delicate question of whether she would consider having a child sired by another man, Connie realizes fully how far apart in values and in basic responses to life she and Clifford have grown.

The deterioration of their relationship only heightens Connie's awareness of the growth of her love for Mellors. For the lady and the gamekeeper provide for each other the completeness that each has lacked in his own life. Their affair becomes ever more intense, and finally Connie becomes pregnant.

At first, Mellors is put off by this news, for he believes that this was all that Lady Chatterley has ever wanted of him. But soon he comes to realize that she does truly love him deeply, and that he loves her as deeply—a confession it is difficult for him to make to himself, for he had long ago given up faith in human relationships.

Connie's one goal now becomes marriage with Mellors. With Hilda's help, and the agreement of an old friend of Connie's, the supercilious Duncan Ross, it is planned that Mellors will seek a divorce from his wife, while Connie will ask Clifford to divorce her, naming Ross corespondent.

Clifford, however, is not so easily persuaded. He has become an arrogant, petty, and self-important man. He cares nothing for Connie's protestations that she loves Ross—nor even for her confession that she is pregnant by him. It does not suit Clifford to be divorced. Driven to distraction by his smug selfishness and disregard for her wishes, Connie at last tells him the truth: that it is Mellors, the gamekeeper, whom she loves and wishes to marry, and who is the father of her unborn child.

The confession, which Clifford recognizes intuitively as the truth, calls up in him all the ingrained prejudices of class. He reviles his wife for having fallen in love with such an animal as the servant, Mellors. In bitterness and petty meanness, Clifford resolves that he will not divorce her—indeed, that he will even allow Mellors' son to inherit his own estate.

But Connie's love for Mellors and his for her is too deep to be thwarted by Clifford. She determines to leave Clifford, to sacrifice her title and her aristocratic position, and to wait for the day when she will be free to join her life with the one man in the world who has wakened her to the meaning of life. And so she leaves Wragby forever, knowing only that she is soon to bear the child of her lover, and that her heart is filled with hope. . . .

HERSELF SURPRISED

Joyce Cary

Arthur Joyce Lunel Cary was born in 1888 in Ireland of English parents. Intending to be a painter, he studied art in Edinburgh and Paris after his graduation from Oxford. He went to Africa in 1913, serving as an officer in the Nigerian Regiment during World War I. He returned to England after the war and settled in Oxford, where he began to write; his novels, which had a large and enthusiastic audience, were written between 1932 and his death in 1957. Herself Surprised, published in 1941, is the first part of a trilogy; although it may certainly be read as a complete work, the two subsequent novels in the group are To Be a Pilgrim and The Horse's Mouth. The trilogy is graced with a controlled and lyrical prose style, but its greatest asset, quite in line with Cary's intentions, is a galaxy of extravagant characters, realized with compassion, intelligence, and humor. Unconventional and willful, these characters are alienated from the society with which they are in constant conflict. This is not an alienation grounded in hostility or revolt, but an alienation of strong people driven by strong urges: the urge of Gulley Jimson to create art, the urge of Sara to make her own way in the world and to fulfill herself as a woman. The influence of the stream-of-consciousness writers upon Cary is evident, but it is to the tradition of the great comic heroes, the tradition of Shakespeare's Falstaff and of Dickens's wonderfully exaggerated characters, that Cary most clearly belongs.

When Mr. Matt Monday, the middle-aged bachelor son of the house at Woodview, begins hanging about the back stairs and poking into the kitchen at odd moments, the new cook, nineteen-year-old Sara, makes no mistake about what he is after. High-spirited and jolly, the fat Sara feels sorry for shy, henpecked Mr. Matt. And it really doesn't surprise her—though it does startle her a bit—when she finds herself married to him and off on a wedding trip to Paris.

Once back in town, Sara undertakes to help Matt assert his long-dormant masculinity. And though Sara—and her best chum Rozzie Balmforth—are coarser than the women he has known, under their tutelage Matt does begin to come out of his shell.

Most instrumental in this transformation is the millionaire Hickson. Sara catches Hickson's eye at a local fair, and he is captivated by her fleshy beauty and jolly air. Soon he is coming to tea at the Mondays'; and, before long, the rest of the town follow his lead and accept the young Mrs. Monday who was a cook such a short time before.

Matt positively blooms under Hickson's new interest. Hickson throws business his way, thus improving the Mondays' financial situation; he gets Matt Monday appointed as a town councilor; and when his own mild amorous adventures with Sara Monday are curbed, Hickson introduces into the Monday household the artist, Gulley Jimson. (Hickson claims that it is because Jimson is a genius and needs to be helped; but the artist himself observes that since Hickson has invested heavily in his canvases, he can't be blamed for trying to boost Jimson's stock in the world.)

Rumor has reached Matt on several occasions that Sara has been too free with her favors to Hickson; and when he discovers Sara modeling for Jimson, he puts the artist and the artist's wife, the tired, religious Nina, out of the house. Sara continues to see the Jimsons surreptitiously, however, and this humiliates both her husband and her four daughters. The Jimsons finally go away—the mural Gulley has been working on for some time comes to nothing—and Matt is once more at peace.

Several years later, Matt Monday dies, and Sara decides to set up a hotel in collaboration with her friend Rozzie. On the day that her household goods are being sold (none of her daughters, now grown, wants any of the old-fashioned furniture which Sara herself has prized), Gulley turns up. He repeats a marriage proposal to Sara—he has made it several times in the past—but she rejects him, and he is content to go away with the loan of a few pounds (a loan Sara fears he will never repay).

The irrepressible, slovenly Gulley Jimson turns up again in Brighton, whither Sara and Rozzie have come to establish their hotel. Nina having long since died and Rozzie having changed her mind about going into business, Sara finally agrees to marry Gulley. He now surprises her with the news that he is not sure that his first wife has really died, and that Nina, his "second wife," had never been legally married to him; and Gulley prevails upon Sara to live with him without benefit of the registry office ceremony.

Life with Gulley is maddening for Sara. She is convinced he is a genius, though his work is too *avant-garde* for most collectors. He is a wonderful lover—but then, too, he beats her now and then. Her zest for life, however—and Gulley Jimson is nothing if not full of life—ties Sara to him, though she resents the fact that her small inheritance is dwindling and that Gulley feels free to strike her on occasion.

After one particularly violent fight, Sara returns to consciousness to discover that Gulley has left her. She is now penniless, and in desperation she writes several bad checks, hoping that she can escape town before the checks are presented for payment.

She is not lucky, however, and charges are lodged against her. Fortunately, as it is her first offense, she is freed with a fine and the obligation to repay the money owed when and as she can.

Her character spoiled by her session in the dock, Sara is not able to get the kind of domestic situation she would like, and she is forced to accept a position as cook in the rundown country home of a Mr. Wilcher. This Wilcher, a middle-aged bachelor, has an unsavory reputation for being free with the female help, but as Sara has no choice, she joins the staff.

Much to her surprise, she finds that she likes being a cook again, and she likes the life at Tolbrook. (Indeed, Gulley has turned up again and begged her to return to him, but she refuses, and only gives him some money.) She gets on famously at Tolbrook, taking as her particular friend Clarissa Hipper, sister of the wife of Wilcher's heir. Neither of the younger couple—Loftus Wilcher and his wife Blanche—strikes Sara's fancy, however.

The years pass in comparative quiet, but when it becomes clear that Mr. Wilcher really does pinch young ladies in the park, and, further, that he is entangled in a debasing relationship with a common woman, Sara feels it no more than an act of Christian charity to become Wilcher's mistress.

Now, in order to keep Gulley from hounding her, Sara makes him a regular weekly allowance. (To raise the necessary money, she has got into the habit of lifting an occasional item from Wilcher's house and pawning it.) And when Wilcher moves her to his London home, Sara is thrown into further contact with Gulley.

He has now taken another "wife"—Sara has lost track of whether it is his sixth or seventh—named Lizzie. A goodhearted soul who has already borne Gulley a child and has another on the way, Lizzie is totally incompetent as a house-keeper; so once a week Sara goes to the Jimsons' to do their cooking, cleaning, mending, and so on. She also takes care of nine-year-old Tom Jimson, the gifted son of Gulley and one of Lizzie's predecessors.

Wilcher is slowly losing what little mind he ever had, and the grasping Blanche fears that Sara will get him—and his fortune—into her control. Indeed, Wilcher does propose to Sara, and even takes a house into which he plans to move with her after the wedding. But two days before the cere-mony is scheduled to take place, Blanche strikes.

She brings a policeman to Sara's room, where they find several trinkets Sara has lifted and not yet pawned, as well as the stubs and records detailing Sara's other petty thieveries through the years.

Clarissa is infuriated. She believes that Sara has done no wrong, but rather that she has been the only true friend Wilcher ever had. She begs Sara to defend herself against the charges.

But Sara Monday (or Sara Jimson, as she also sometimes calls herself) has always tried to be honest with herself. She is a Christian woman, and she knows that the charges against her are true. Moreover, she feels that she was always too ready to have a good time, and devil take the hindmost, and this charge against her is a punishment for that sin as well as for the ones for which she is formally charged.

At the trial, Blanche paints Sara in blackest colors, and once again Sara's character is ruined. She is sentenced to eighteen months in prison. But, as Sara comforts herself, it's only her due. And after all, when she gets out, she can go and be a cook somewhere else. It only takes twelve months of domestic service to get a good character again. And she resolves to keep her fleshly tastes more under control, now that she knows them so much better.

POINT COUNTER POINT

Aldous Huxley

Aldous Leonard Huxley was born in 1894 in Surrey, England. A grandson of Darwin's associate T. H. Huxley, nephew of the poet Matthew Arnold, and brother of the eminent scientist Julian Hux-

ley, he was exposed from childhood to the significant intellectual currents of the times. After studying at Eton and Oxford, he traveled widely, coming to the United States in the late 1930s. In 1947 Huxley settled in the desert region of southern California, where he lived until his death in 1963. He first wrote poetry and criticism, but turned to the novel in 1921. His last novel appeared in 1955; Huxley's final years were devoted to the study of Eastern religion and philosophy, and experimentation with consciousness-expanding drugs. His novels are the works of a brilliant social critic who employed the form of the novel in order to express his ideas; it had not been Huxley's intention to produce masterpieces of the art of fiction.

Point Counter Point, published in 1928, is the most ambitious and complex of Huxley's novels. The title refers to the musical technique of counterpoint, in which several themes are presented, developed, and played simultaneously; in the novel, the main themes are love and death, the basic human instincts according to Freudian theory. The characters play viciously at life, loving and destroying each other until nothing more is possible but a regression to the innocent ignorance of childhood.

Brave New World, published in 1932, is a brilliant satire, aimed at utopianists and advocates of a planned society. Huxley took the ironical title from a passage in Shakespeare's The Tempest. The author indicates that mankind would best be served if less attention were paid to advancing society as a body, and more attention devoted to the development of the individual.

At a huge, formal musicale and supper party given by the sophisticated, witty, and merciless Lady Tantamount, we meet a large number of her guests—the cream of London society. We listen to their conversations—seemingly endless variations on the themes of love, sex, life, death, religion, politics, and art—and we come to know them well. Many of them we follow for a span of several months, during which we are witness to all of the incidents—the trivial and the dramatic—of their lives.

There is the great artist and rake, the aging John Bidlake. Thrice married and participant in innumerable love affairs and scandals, Bidlake presents the same sharp tongue, the same virile appearance as always. But secretly he has begun to have fears. His paintings are not accorded the same enthusiastic reception given those of earlier years. One of his sons is already dead, at fifty, of cancer—and nothing terrifies Bidlake so much as the idea of death, of decay, of ceasing to exist.

There is Walter Bidlake, the painter's son. Walter is a writer who has carried off Marjorie Carling from her husband. Together they live without benefit of clergy in a dreary flat, and now Marjorie is pregnant. The frigid, vulgar, dull Marjorie is desperate because it is clear that Walter no longer loves her; and in her desperation, she only drives him further and further away.

The new passion absorbing Walter is Lucy Tantamount, daughter of the hostess of the musicale. Lucy is a miniature of her mother: arrogantly beautiful and desirable, inherently cold, sophisticatedly cruel. Lucy lives only for herself; and though she has given herself to many men, she never loves. She delights in being loved, however, and uses her lovers' tenderness to torture them. Walter is, indeed, tortured by Lucy, but though he despises himself for it, he continues his pursuit of her.

Walter's sister, Elinor, parallels in her relationship with her husband, the brilliant, witty, but aloof Philip Quarles, the desperation and hunger for love which Marjorie Carling feels for Walter. But Elinor is as much superior to Marjorie as Philip is to Walter. She understands her husband, and loves him deeply, but though she toys with the idea of having an affair in the hope of shaking Philip into an emotional state, essentially she believes that she will remain true to him.

The man with whom Elinor contemplates an affair is Everard Webley, the dynamic, if slightly monomaniacal, leader of a group of British neo-Fascists called the Brotherhood of British Freemen. Dressed in uniforms of lettuce green, the Freemen hold mass meetings at which Everard, in the role of incipient dictator, makes passionate harangues about the coming revolution in British society which the Freemen are to bring about. Desiring Elinor Quarles, Everard is determined that she will become his mistress, and when he has taken over the country, that she will leave Quarles entirely for him. At one of Everard's public meetings, a heckler shouts a remark, slightly obscene in tone, at him; and, breaking ranks, several of the uniformed Freemen attack the interloper and beat him up.

The heckler is a neurotic young scientist named Illidge. Born into poverty and educated by chance, Illidge is the laboratory assistant of wealthy Sir Edward Tantamount. He is also a Communist, though there is a wide gulf separating his theories from his concept of his own life. Illidge talks out his hostility toward Everard Webley to the idle, sponging, unhappy young artist Spandrell. Though Spandrell poses as a deliberate waster and parasite, he is, in truth, deeply troubled by his inability to give meaning to his own life or to derive any satisfaction from it. He spends most of his time in idle conversation at various bars in the company of a large number of young intellectuals.

Among these are Mark and Mary Rampion, the healthy, well-adjusted parents of several small children. Mark is a gifted writer and painter, born in the lower classes; Mary is an intelligent daughter of the aristocracy. Each has supplied the other with the necessary stimulus and challenge for living the successful life, and their love for each other is solid and mature.

There is also the publisher Burlap, for whose magazine Walter Bidlake writes. Burlap is an insensitive and imperceptive man posing under a glib façade of intelligence. He is a master at self-deception: when, for example, his secretary, Ethel Cobbett, commits suicide over him, he is wholly unaware of his responsibility in the act.

All of these people are, in the world's eyes, successful. But as they live out their days in pettiness and egocentrism, disaster brews.

Elinor and Philip Quarles have increasing difficulty in communicating with each other, and Elinor at last determines to become Everard Webley's mistress. Choosing a day when Philip is away, she invites Webley to her home for dinner. Shortly before he arrives, however, a telegram comes from her parents' home telling Elinor that her young son, Philip, is very ill there, and Elinor takes advantage of the opportune arrival of young Spandrell to ask him to phone Webley, explaining that Elinor has been called away. Instead, the idly evil Spandrell calls Illidge, and together they plot Webley's murder. When Webley arrives at Elinor's, the murder is performed. Illidge goes to pieces, but Spandrell remains calm and indifferent, and coolly arranges for the disposal of the body several miles away. Then he and Illidge go their separate ways.

Philip, meanwhile, has responded to a call from his own family. His father, the aging and foolish husband to a quiet, understanding wife, has pursued his lechery a bit too far, and a vulgar London secretary named Gladys is now pregnant and threatening a major lawsuit. The elder Quarles takes to his bed at this unfortunate turn of events, and determines to die. Philip assumes the responsibility for working with a lawyer to reach an out-of-court settlement with the girl. He then goes to join Elinor at the home of her mother, John Bidlake's third wife.

There, two patients are in the house: young Phil, suffering from meningitis, and old John, the artist, who is a victim of cancer. After a lapse of hideous suffering, the little boy rallies, but it is only a glimmer of false hope, and soon he is dead. The old man lingers. . . .

Walter has finally succeeded in making Lucy Tantamount his mistress, but she makes his life a hell for him by her incessant willfulness and her unwillingness to yield her love to him. From Spain, Lucy writes an imperious letter demanding that Walter join her, and on an impulse he gives up his job, breaks with the unhappy Marjorie, and goes to the continent —only to discover, on arriving there, that Lucy's reference to a trip to Spain was merely a joke. Lucy casts him aside by beginning an affair with an Italian whom she picks up in the street.

For days the murder of Everard Webley goes unsolved, and it becomes something of a *cause célèbre*. Finally, desperate to give his life some significance, Spandrell writes an anonymous letter to the Brotherhood of British Freemen, telling them that if they will go to a given address at a specified time, they will find Webley's murderer. The address he gives is his own. He invites the Quarleses up for a drink; and leaving them to answer the door, he is confronted by several green-shirted Freemen, as he knew he would be, and is shot to death.

Only the desperate Burlap, and an equally desperate woman who has adored him in virgin frigidity, Beatrice Gilray, find happiness; but for them it consists of going back to childhood, and together they play at life like six-year-olds.

BRAVE NEW WORLD

Aldous Huxley

It is the year 632 A.F. (After Ford). The world has long, long ago become one vast government, following the infamous Nine Years' War, and now stability reigns supreme.

Religion, art, literature, and love have been banished. The only god now is the father-figure Ford, whose original ideas about history and the values of mass production have been rarefied into the present governing theory. Men are now artificially produced (the words "mother" and "birth" are obscenities in this brave new world); and from the moment of conception, each being is conditioned for the role that he will play in society. Society is stratified into five distinct castes, ranging from the Alphas, the intellectually superior beings who do the creative and responsible work, through the Betas, Gammas, Deltas, and Epsilons, the latter being half-moronic creatures who perform the vile and menial tasks. Because of constant conditioning, however, all individual creatures in this world are content with their lot; the Betas would not exchange places with the Deltas, nor the Gammas with the Alphas.

The society is so structured and controlled that none within it can experience ill health, pain, desire, or want without immediate gratification. Sex is free and indiscriminate; there are no outmoded ideas like "loyalty," "familial solidarity," or "morality" to obstruct the individual in his search for pleasure.

Occasionally an individual proves to be a slight misfit in this ideal world. When such a creature is brought to the attention of one of the directors (a hierarchy of directors, culminating in the ten World Controllers, runs the earth), he is sent to a government-run Reconditioning Center, so that the wrinkles in his personality can be more harmoniously adjusted to his society.

One such misfit—not yet brought to the directors' attention —is the Alpha named Bernard Marx. Whether his alienation is caused by his smallness in stature (it is rumored that when he was being formed in the embryo room, some alcohol was inadvertently placed in his blood-surrogate—a procedure used

to stunt Gammas) or his determination to experience, to *feel*
(he generally refuses to take any *soma*, the universally used
tranquilizer), he does not know; but Marx clearly feels himself set apart from the others.

This is made painfully clear to him when his request for
a date with the beautiful Lenina Crowne is accepted. She
discusses their planned sexual escapade in the presence of a
crowd of others—a perfectly normal practice—but this somehow sets Marx off into a fit of depression. The one person
with whom Marx feels comfortable is Helmholtz Watson.
Watson, too, senses his own alienation from his fellow Alphas;
it is suspected by his superiors that he is a little too brilliant.
What these two men share is their knowledge that they
are individuals.

As a special treat, Marx decides to take Lenina to the New
Mexico reservation. This is an inaccessible part of the world
maintained by the Directors in its original state. Few Alphas
have ever been there to see the savages, and Lenina is
thrilled to be going with Bernard.

Bernard Marx goes to the Director to have their pass-
ports to the savage outstation stamped; and the Director in-
judiciously mentions that he has visited the New Mexico reservation—and had a horrible experience there. His date
for the weekend had been a blond Beta—he doesn't remember her name—and somehow she disappeared. The Director
had to return to London without her, and he admits he still
has bad dreams about the experience. As soon as Marx has
left his office, however, the Director regrets having let this
tale slip; and as Marx's behavior has been erratic of late, the
Director resolves to punish him on his return from New Mexico by banishing him to Iceland.

Once in New Mexico, Marx and Lenina are both fascinated
and repelled by the sickening sights. They see Indians performing ritual dances to gods; they see disease and filth; most
repugnant of all, they see a mother (obscene creature!) actually nursing at her own breast a child she has literally
borne. This is too much for Lenina, and she takes a heavy
dose of *soma*.

Later in their visit, they encounter the very Beta whom
the Director had mentioned. She is now a repulsive, fat,
middle-aged woman, with a beautiful, fair-skinned, blond son.
Both mother (who is called Linda) and son (John) have

been unhappy living among the Indians, who have continually rejected them for being white. The mother is a ridiculous, contemptible woman; but John is an original, intelligent, sensitive young man, with whom Bernard feels an affinity. Bernard is able to arrange to bring the two back to London, and they eagerly join him and Lenina on the return trip.

Back in London, the Director announces his intention of exiling Bernard. The announcement is made before a factory full of Alphas, as Bernard is to be made an example of. However, he turns the tables on the Director by producing Linda and John. The idea of the Director's having actually fathered a being is so repulsive and ridiculous to the Alphas that he is forced to retire from his post.

Linda is of little interest, and as she is in poor physical health and can perform no valuable function to the society, she is sent to a hospital where she subsists entirely on *soma*, which shortly causes her death.

John however is called the Savage, and becomes something of a celebrity, for he is the first person that most of the others have seen who is of woman born. At first the Savage enjoys this attention, but it quickly palls. Most sickening to him is Lenina's willingness to give herself to him physically; John, whose ideas have been shaped largely by his extensive reading of Shakespeare, is repulsed by the total amorality and soullessness he observes everywhere.

When he hears that Linda is dying, he goes to her bedside and breaks down in tears. This makes trouble, however, as a troop of little children are being brought through the hospital for death-conditioning, and the Directors wish them to associate death with pleasure and happiness, not with this disconcerting grief of John's. Not knowing how to cope with the Savage, they send for Marx and Helmholtz. When these men arrive, they are caught up in the Savage's vision of the horror of society, and the three cause a near-riot. They are eventually subdued, however, by tranquilizers, and brought to trial.

The trial is merely an informal conversation with Mustapha Mond, Resident Controller of Western Europe. Helmholtz and Marx he banishes to islands where they will find others of their ilk—"individuals" who cannot adjust to the needs of society and who cannot wholly integrate their personalities with those of their fellows. John asks to be returned to New Mexico, but this the Resident Controller refuses.

Recognizing in the Savage a man of rare intellectual accomplishment and insight, Mustapha Mond, in an attempt to convert him, discusses with him at great length the reasons and values that underlie this new society. But the conversion fails. At last, John goes away to an isolated spot, taking with him only a few tools with which he can build for himself a life completely independent of the rest of the society.

He is soon followed to his retreat by a news cameraman from the feelies (three dimensional movies in which sensations portrayed on the screen are experienced by each member of the audience). The cameraman records John's purifying ritual of self-flagellation, and within hours John becomes the laughingstock of society. Helicopter loads of tourists arrive hourly to watch this hilariously funny ritual of the Savage whipping himself. At last John realizes that even his soul is no longer his own in this strange new world; and the last group of Alpha tourists to arrive find the funny Savage Man hanged by his own knotted rope. Slowly, very slowly, his body revolves in space.

LOST HORIZON

James Hilton

James Hilton was born in Lancashire, England, in 1900, the son of a schoolmaster. He studied at Cambridge, and received his degree with academic honors. He began writing articles while still at college, and had his first novel published in 1919. After Cambridge he supported himself as a teacher, columnist, freelance writer and book reviewer. On the basis of his first successful novel he was asked by an editor to write a long short story which became the fabulously successful Goodbye, Mr. Chips, and on the basis of Goodbye, Mr. Chips, readers now turned to Lost Horizon, which had actually been published a year earlier. Lost Horizon soon became a runaway best seller, and from it a notable movie was made. It was also adapted as a play and a television drama. Shangri-La has become a household word meaning earthly paradise; it was the name given by Franklin D. Roosevelt to his wartime hideaway. It was also for many years the unofficial name of the most fashionable area of one of the most fashionable supper clubs in the world. Hilton moved to California in 1935, where he enjoyed the life of a successful author, writing books and articles, delivering lectures and broadcasts, and writing scenarios. He died in California in 1954.

Meeting by chance in Berlin in the early 1930s, three old school fellows spend the evening reminiscing at a restaurant. They are joined by a young man named Sanders, who, during the course of conversation, lets slip a curious episode which the government had wished to keep quiet: at the government airfield in Baskul, in eastern Asia, some native has managed to steal a plane and make off with it—and its passengers —undetected. Further inquiry reveals that one of the four passengers was "Glory" Conway, whom the three companions had known at school.

Leaving the restaurant together, two of the three companions continue their conversation about Conway, who was a most extraordinary man. Rutherford, the elder of the two, admits that he has seen Conway recently; that the man is not dead, as is generally believed; and that he had a most fantastic story to tell. This story Rutherford has written into manuscript form, and he gives it to his young companion to read—with the warning that he will find it all but impossible to believe.

The situation in Baskul having deteriorated, the white residents are being evacuated by the British Air Force. On one small plane are Hugh Conway of the Consul Service; Miss Roberta Brinklow of the Eastern Mission; Henry D. Barnard, an American; and young Captain Charles Mallinson, Vice-Consul.

During the trip out of Baskul, the four realize that a strange pilot is in command of the airplane, and, later, that they are flying quite a bit off course. It dawns on them that they are being kidnaped, but before they have a chance to deliberate action, the plane makes a crash landing. The pilot has suffered some sort of stroke, and is dying.

The passengers do their best to make the man comfortable, but he continues to weaken, muttering occasionally, and then he dies.

Realizing that they are stranded in some out-of-the-way corner of Tibet about which they know nothing, the passengers hold a conference to decide upon a course of action.

Seeing a beautiful white mountain, cone-shaped and glistening, in the distance, they decide to head for it; for Conway thinks it is there that they will find the place about which the pilot has been muttering—some strange land called Shangri-La.

Before they have proceeded very far, however, they are met by a train of Tibetans led by a blue-robed monk named Chang. Speaking flawless English and displaying a cordial, if reserved, manner, Chang insists on accompanying them up the face of the mountain Karakal and to the lamasery of Shangri-La, where they are ushered into splendid apartments and made to feel most welcome.

Mallinson begins at once to make high-handed and hasty demands that preparations be made for the travelers to be escorted back to what he calls "civilization." Chang remains evasive, however, and the best that he can suggest is that the travelers prepare to stay at the lamasery, where they will be treated as honored guests, until the next arrival from the outside world of certain supplies that have been ordered, and that those who bring the supplies might then be prevailed upon to take the lost travelers back with them. That such outside couriers are not expected for several months does nothing to calm Mallinson's state of mind.

Conway, on the other hand, finds himself fascinated with Shangri-La—its fantastic beauty (he concludes that the mountain is well named, Karakal meaning "Blue Moon"), its air of remote tranquility, its combining of the best features of Oriental and Occidental civilization. Further, he concludes that their arrival at Shangri-La was not accidental—that somehow Chang had expected him and his companions—though how and why Conway is unable to guess.

This conviction of Conway's becomes a certainty when he overhears two Tibetans refer to the dead pilot as one of their own people. He does not share this knowledge with his companions, however. They, albeit with less grace than he, have accepted the knowledge that they must stay for some time as guests at Shangri-La.

The lamasery is a source of endless amazement to Conway. It houses a magnificent library, and a collection of Oriental art that would be the envy of many a museum. He is most impressed of all with the fact that there is a harpsichord on which the finest Western music is played—Mozart, Corelli,

Rameau—and that it is played by a beautiful young Chinese girl named Lo-Tsen.

As the days slip by, the travelers find much to admire in the still, silent lamasery where time seems not to exist; and with the exception of Mallinson, who remains as high-strung as ever, the travelers become more relaxed and accepting of their fate. Even the discovery that Barnard is not the man he has pretended to be, but is in fact Bryant, a criminal wanted by the police of a dozen countries, does little to shake their calm.

At the end of two weeks, an unexpected—and to Chang, highly significant—event takes place: the High Lama sends for Conway.

Interviewed alone, Conway hears from the tiny old man the entire history of Shangri-La, from its founding by a French missionary named Father Perrault in 1719 until the present day. But it is not until much later in the interview that Conway suspects the amazing truth that the High Lama with whom he speaks is the same Father Perrault, and that time does, indeed, stand still at Shangri-La.

Conway learns, further, that there is one provision attendant upon the hospitality of the lamasery: none who come to Shangri-La may ever leave. The interview continues, and Conway learns much that will cause him to think deeply in the days to come. When at last the interview ends, it strikes Conway that for the first time he sees the valley of the Blue Moon and this mysterious, mystic lamasery in all its true loveliness.

As the days pass into weeks, Conway falls ever more deeply under the spell of Shangri-La. It reaches even Barnard and Miss Brinklow, who determine that they will not leave. Conway's interviews with the High Lama continue—though Chang assures Conway that this is most extraordinary. From the High Lama, Conway learns more about Lo-Tsen, with whom he has fallen silently in love. She has been in the lamasery since 1884, when she was eighteen.

After many important meetings, in which more and more of the philosophy of this strange community is revealed to him, Conway hears from the High Lama a staggering piece of news: the old man is at last dying, and believing that holocaust is soon to befall the world, from which only Shangri-La will be saved, he wishes to appoint a successor to the lamasery throne—one who will preserve Shangri-La as a repository of all that is fine in the world. And the man he has chosen to become the new High Lama is Conway himself.

The Englishman is staggered with disbelief, but before he can question further, the High Lama is dead. Conway walks about in a daze.

He is awakened from his reverie by young Mallinson, who tells him excitedly that the long-promised couriers have at last arrived, and that the time has come for Conway to prepare to leave. Knowing this to be impossible, yet wishing to spare Mallinson inevitable heartbreak, Conway gently tells him the entire history of Shangri-La.

Mallinson, of course, believes that Conway is mad—and climaxes his argument by telling Conway that Lo-Tsen has agreed to join them in flight, and that even now she is making arrangements with the porters. Seeing that he cannot possibly convince Mallinson, Conway resigns himself to letting the young man make whatever attempt at escape he likes.

Mallinson is not so easily put off as that, however, for he has determined that Conway, whom he has long idolized, shall come too. He badgers, argues, and reasons—and at last, convinces Conway that there is no danger, and that the whole myth of Shangri-La is nothing more than imaginative raving. Finally Conway agrees to the journey.

Together they prepare for their departure as quickly as possible. And when, a short time later, they reach the valley of the Blue Moon where the porters are resting, there is Lo-Tsen, waiting to leave with them, her beautiful young face alive with joy. . . .

When the young Englishman finishes the story about Conway which Rutherford has set down, he doesn't know what to make of it. But it is not until several years later, when he again encounters Rutherford, that he is able to ask the many questions that haunt his mind.

At their second meeting, Rutherford tells how he happened to meet Conway in a Chinese hospital, suffering from amnesia; and how Conway gradually recovered, told him his story, and then—disappeared.

After hearing Conway's tale, of course, Rutherford admits that he was disinclined to believe it. But he began checking, and more and more details were verified, all corresponding to Conway's account.

Most interesting of all, perhaps, is Rutherford's story of how Conway had first been brought to the Chinese hospital. He inquired, of course, and was told that Conway had been brought in by a woman—an Oriental woman, according to the admitting doctor. The oldest woman the doctor had ever seen. . . .

NINETEEN EIGHTY-FOUR

George Orwell

George Orwell, whose real name was Eric Hugh Blair, was born in India in 1903, the son of English colonial administrators. He attended Eton, then served with the Indian Imperial Police in Burma. From 1927 to 1936 he lived in Paris and London in extreme poverty. He fought with the Loyalists in the Spanish Civil War, and spent his last years in England, where he died in 1950. Orwell's writings consisted primarily of journals; fiction for him was a means of expressing his primary concern, the fate of human freedom. Nineteen Eighty-Four, one of Orwell's few novels, was published in 1949 shortly before his death. A prophetic novel of the ultimate totalitarian society, its impact is difficult to overestimate. Words and phrases from the novel, such as "Big Brother," "doublethink," and "Newspeak" (Oceania's official language, the principles of which are contained in an appendix to the book), have become part of the language. The mere mention of the year 1984, in any context, has an immediately ominous connotation; promises of bridges to be built or neighborhoods renovated "by 1984" sound ironic, and talk of "the 1984 elections" may well be, because of Orwell's novel, a delicate concern for politicians. Orwell had been attracted to and subsequently repelled by Communism and for Fascism he never felt anything but contempt; therefore it is not the dominance of one ideology, but the dominance of any, which he feels will result in the eventual enslavement and dehumanization of mankind.

WAR IS PEACE

FREEDOM IS SLAVERY

IGNORANCE IS STRENGTH

These are the mottos of Oceania, one of three totalitarian empires into which the world is divided. It is in the city of London in the nation Oceania that Winston Smith lives; it is under the ever-watchful eye of Big Brother that Smith fights a mental battle to hold on to his sanity.

For though he gives lip service to the ideals of the Party—indeed, how can he avoid it, when he is under the constant surveillance of the telescreen, the hidden microphones, and the Thought Police?—he is constantly tormented by memories of an earlier time, when his country was called England and when his thoughts, his heart, and his soul were his own.

Though Smith cannot resist petty infringements of the Party rules, he lives in constant terror of being found out and vaporized—a process by which people are made to disappear, leaving no trace that they ever existed. And when Syme, an intelligent Party member who works with Smith in the Ministry of Truth preparing a revised dictionary of the official language, Newspeak, is himself vaporized, Smith's anxiety becomes even greater.

Yet the doubts continue—and little wonder. Oceania is constantly at war with one of the two other world powers—sometimes with Eurasia, sometimes with Eastasia. And yet when Oceania is at war with one, no one is allowed to recognize —or even remember—that relations were anything but friendly with the other. When the enemies change, loyalties and hates—absolute, total—must change without thought. One day Eastasia is the enemy, the next day it is Eurasia; and no one is supposed to notice the difference. Indeed, it is Smith's job to "rectify" documents, so that the entire history of Oceania always conforms to the ideology of the moment. And though Smith has mastered the art of the rigid visage, in order not to betray his thoughts to the telescreen, he cannot help his anti-Party ideas.

He believes himself to be watched by two Party members in particular—a man named O'Brien, and a strange dark-haired young woman who wears the scarlet sash of the Anti-Sex League. When he discovers that the girl has followed him one night as he is taking an irregular walk through the prole quarter ("proles" comprise eighty-five percent of the population, and, being regarded as beneath consideration by the Party, they are the only free members of society), he is convinced that she plans to report him to the Thought Police. Only later, when she manages by extreme ingenuity to pass him a note, does he realize that he has found his first ally; for

in crude lettering the note contains just three crucial words:
I love you.

Overcoming nearly insurmountable obstacles to communication, Smith and the girl, whose name is Julia, begin an illicit love affair, meeting at first in open fields, and later in the prole quarter in a room over a junkshop supplied by a kindly prole, Mr. Charrington. Here, at last, they are safe from the privacy-invading telescreen.

During the course of the affair, O'Brien makes contact with Smith; and when Smith and Julia realize that he, though nominally a member of the select Inner Party, is actually a rebel, they arrange a rendezvous with him. O'Brien swears them to membership in The Brotherhood—the amorphous, unorganized underground movement against the Party—and gives Smith a copy of *the book,* the most treasonous document ever heard of, authored by Oceania's most hated enemy, Emmanuel Goldstein. O'Brien assures them that Goldstein still lives, and that someday The Brotherhood's message of truth and freedom shall prevail.

During their next tryst at the secret room Smith and Julia are hungrily reading *the book* when suddenly they hear a steely voice address them. A picture falls off the wall, revealing a hidden telescreen. Mr. Charrington enters, and they realize, too late, that he is a member of the Thought Police. Julia is beaten by Party Police, and taken to an unknown destination. Smith is taken prisoner separately.

He supposes that he is taken to the Ministry of Love, reputedly the torture chamber used by the Party for extracting confessions and "rehabilitating" political prisoners before they are shot. Though he experiences fear, it is a numb fear; and the one clear thought in his mind is that he will not betray Julia.

There is no recording of time in the prison; Smith cannot tell an hour from a week. Though he has sporadic encounters with other prisoners—among them, Parsons, a former neighbor whom Smith had thought to be a true believer, yet who has been arrested for *crimethink*—he waits in a suspension of anxiety for his punishment to begin.

Begin it does—merciless beatings, endless infliction of pain. At times Smith feels that he cannot endure more, and yet, somehow, as the pain is increased, he bears it.

Then he meets his Grand Inquisitor—who turns out to be O'Brien, the same O'Brien who had so skillfully pretended to be a member of The Brotherhood. Under O'Brien, the tortures become even more extreme, and Smith begs to be killed. But O'Brien explains that it is not Smith's death that the Party wishes, or his confession; it is his "reintegration." The Party wishes to reconstruct Smith's intellect and emotions, to "correct" his deviationist tendencies, to lead him to the light and truth of Ingsoc (the official ideology) and all it stands for.

Progress is made; Smith tries to conform, to please the Party. But he discovers that it is evidently not enough; for, when O'Brien asks him what his attitude is toward Big Brother, the all-seeing, all-powerful, but anonymous head of state, Smith says (he knows that it is pointless to lie), "I hate him."

Finally Smith is brought to Room 101, the most-feared chamber in all the Ministry of Love. O'Brien explains that here the prisoner's ultimate fear is exploited. This fear, of course, varies from individual to individual, but the Party has ways of discovering what it is that each man most dreads in the secret recesses of his soul. In Smith's case, it is rats.

O'Brien shows him a cage of starving rats, devised with an antechamber into which Smith's head is to be fitted. The rats can be released into the antechamber at any time. Smith's pleadings and attempts to escape the awful mechanism are pitiable indeed, but O'Brien is relentless, and Smith is strapped into place. In the absolute terror of the moment, however, he betrays Julia in a scream. And this is considered testimony to his complete reintegration. The rats are not released.

Smith is returned to the outside world, a physical wreck. He is allowed to spend his days at the Chestnut Tree Bar, where he drowns his misery in gin that bites like nitric acid. He even encounters Julia once again—at this point, the Party takes no interest in supervising them. In dull, emotionless tones, they confess to each other that, in the terrifying moments in Room 101, each has betrayed the other.

As Smith is sitting in the bar one day, he watches an appearance by Big Brother on the telescreen. For the first time, he notices something about B.B. which had escaped his attention all along—the man is smiling. Smith experiences a curious sensation: he discovers that he loves Big Brother after all.

A PASSAGE TO INDIA

E. M. Forster

Edward Morgan Forster was born in London in 1879, and was educated at Cambridge. He traveled extensively throughout the Middle and Far East, and returned to England after World War I. He was a leading member of the brilliant "Bloomsbury Group" of London intellectuals in the 1920s.

His first novel was published in 1905; his last, A Passage to India, in 1924. He is also the author of several important works of literary criticism. Forster is acknowledged as the century's great craftsman of the novel in its traditional form. His prose style is flawless, his plots are perfectly balanced and conceived with a thoroughness which leaves no loose ends, and his characters are believable and well motivated; and these varied elements are bound into a smoothly functioning unit by a calm intelligence and a pervasive wit. A Passage to India is considered Forster's masterpiece, and, like his other novels, it deals with the problem of communication between people, a theme summed up in the phrase from an earlier book: "Only connect." Forster here extends this phrase to include not only individuals, but entire cultures; the connection hoped for, however, is not to be realized, and the disparities which separate the English from the Indians are not to be bridged.

Forster uses symbols in his novels to represent the concepts of central concern; in A Passage to India, the Marabar Caves are the dominant symbol, for they represent in their darkness the mystery of India, and the disastrous events which occur in one of them indicate the confusion and helplessness of Western man in an alien civilization.

Colonial India is divided into two separate and seemingly irreconcilable societies. There are the rulers—the Anglo-Indians, representative of the Crown, preserving in their tropical outposts as much of British custom and civilization as they can; and there are the ruled—the Indians themselves of all faiths. Between the two lies a chasm, and on those few occasions when it is crossed, the results seem invariably to widen rather than close it.

To the small city of Chandrapore come the elderly Eng-

lishwoman, Mrs. Moore, and young, plain Adela Quested.
Mrs. Moore is the mother of the shallow, opinionated Ronny
Heaslop, a young government official; and Adela has come to
see Ronny in his Indian surroundings before reaching a final
decision as to whether to become engaged to him.

Visiting a mosque, Mrs. Moore encounters an Indian poet
and physician, Dr. Aziz, and the two strike up an immediate
liking and sympathy for each other. A few days later at a
party given by Mr. Turton, the Collector, Mrs. Moore and
Adela witness only too clearly the indifference and brutality
that Aziz has said is the prevailing British attitude toward
the Indians. The Anglo-Indians—Ronny, the Turtons, Lesleys,
Callendars, Burtons, and their like—are barely civil to their
native guests.

Mrs. Moore and Adela persevere in trying to see the Indians as they really are. Cyril Fielding, a schoolmaster, and
the one Englishman who seems genuinely to like Indians,
invites Mrs. Moore and Adela to a tea party at which Dr.
Aziz is present, along with several other distinguished Indian
guests. The ladies are charmed with Aziz, as is Fielding,
who rapidly establishes a warm friendship with him; and it
is arranged that Aziz will escort them all on a journey to the
famed Marabar Caves in the nearby hills. The tea is spoiled
only when Ronny arrives suddenly, and, treating the Indians
as though they are not present, insists on escorting his mother
and Adela to a polo match which he has arranged as entertainment for them. Neither woman wishes to go to the match,
but Ronny succeeds in dragging them away.

Ronny tries to explain to his mother and Adela the necessity of this disdainful attitude toward the natives, but the
women are unable to comprehend why Christian brotherhood
would not be more effective. Nonetheless, Adela consents
to become engaged to Ronny.

Aziz plans the trip to the Marabar Caves down to the last
detail, so as to make it an unqualified success; but from the
outset his plans go awry. Fielding misses the train, and only
succeeds in joining the group at the site of the caves through
the help of Miss Derek, a supercilious, condescending Anglo-
Indian spinster.

By mistake, Adela enters a cave different from the one
Aziz enters. On turning back to look for her, Aziz sees her
running down the hill to Miss Derek's car. The two then

leave, and Aziz assumes that Adela has had reason to join her friend in preference to returning by train with himself, Mrs. Moore, Fielding, and the rest of the party.

When the train pulls into Chandrapore, however, the full disastrousness of the trip is revealed to Aziz. He is arrested on Adela's testimony that he has assaulted her in the cave, and the poor man is carried away to prison.

The entire English colony is enraged at Aziz's wickedness, and banding together in petty and cruel snobbishness, they hurl charges, threats, and imprecations about until a major state of racial unrest is created, culminating in a riot.

Only Fielding and Mrs. Moore believe in Aziz's innocence. To save herself from having to testify at the trial, however, Mrs. Moore determines to leave Chandrapore at once, though the season is most unhealthy for traveling. Mrs. Moore dies on her homeward journey—and, aggravating the local trouble, a rumor is spread that an Englishman has caused his mother's death for trying to save an Indian's life.

Fielding, now humiliated and shunned by the other Anglo-Indians, perseveres in his belief that Aziz is innocent, and he communicates this information by letter to Adela. That young lady, now convinced that her mind has been playing her tricks, takes Fielding's message to heart. At the trial, things go badly for Aziz—all sorts of innocent facts are twisted by the British, who have never doubted for an instant the Indian's guilt; but taking the stand, Adela declares that she was mistaken—that Aziz did not follow her into the cave, nor did he make any advances toward her whatsoever. The charges against Aziz are dropped.

The Anglo-Indian community, however, cannot brook what they consider Adela's letting them down. They ostracize her, and she is forced to take refuge with Fielding until she can book passage back to England. A rumor is started to the effect that Adela and Fielding are intimate—but, fortunately, this is dropped when a scandal erupts concerning Miss Derek's being caught *flagrante delicto* with one of the married British officers.

None of the principals in the affair are allowed to resume their normal lives, for the British community demands vengeance. Ronny breaks his engagement with Adela, and soon he is transferred to a different province. Fielding, too, is transferred out of the district, and, for a while, he visits England before returning to his new post in India.

Even Aziz is persecuted, for though he has officially been cleared without a blot on his character, the British community believes he is guilty, and for the rest of his life he is kept under police surveillance.

Aziz, though he has trusted Fielding as he had never believed he could trust any white man, feels betrayed by Fielding's protection of Adela Quested after the trial, and the friendship between the two men is shattered.

Several years later, they meet. By this time, Fielding has married Mrs. Moore's daughter by her second marriage. Aziz greets him with hostility, and Fielding soon realizes that it is because Aziz mistakenly believes him married to Adela Quested. But even after that misunderstanding is cleared up, Aziz and Fielding cannot re-establish their former friendly intimacy. Everything around them seems to say that it is too soon for an Englishman and an Indian to be friends. Not yet . . . not yet. . . .

THE HEART OF THE MATTER

Graham Greene

Henry Graham Greene was born in Berkhamstead, England, in 1904, the son of a schoolteacher. He attended Oxford, and until 1940 held various newspaper editorships. While in his mid-twenties, he became a member of the Roman Catholic Church. His writings began to be published shortly before the outbreak of World War II; within a decade he became recognized as a major novelist, as well as a skillful author of detective and spy stories which he calls "entertainments." In his serious novels, which include The Heart of the Matter *(1948) and* The End of the Affair *(1951), Greene is intensely concerned with the spiritual condition of his characters from a religious, and, more specifically, Roman Catholic, point of view. Greene's characters suffer great emotional agony as a result of their sins; those who seek salvation recognize their sins and attempt to reconcile themselves with God, thereby ending their torment, whereas those who reject God are denied salvation and continue to suffer without hope. The themes of Greene's novels, in their preoccupation with sin and salvation, have been compared to those of Dostoevsky. It is difficult to find other contemporary English novelists who have been absorbed by the strivings of man to find his redemption in God, and certainly there are none besides Graham Greene who have written so powerfully on this subject.*

In a small, British-governed town on the west coast of Africa, only one man is universally admired, trusted, and liked by the whites. He is Henry Scobie, second-in-command to the Commissioner of Police. The others are subject to each others' gossip—gossip which seems as interminable as it is purposeless: who is sleeping with whose wife, who is ready to crack from nervous tension, which of the two local smugglers—Yusef and Tallit—is the more powerful or the less trustworthy. And then there is the War, which is the professional focus of the white colony: smuggling, submarines, spying. . . .

Henry Scobie is unhappily married to the pathetic Louise, a pale woman disliked by the whole community. She continually begs to leave Africa for a while, but Scobie—anxious as he is to see her go, so that he might have some peace—cannot afford to send her. Louise's one friend is the newcomer, Edward Wilson, who, it is rumored, has been sent by the government to spy on all the local officials and particularly on Scobie.

Scobie is indifferent to these rumors. Indeed, he is indifferent to the fact that Wilson obviously is falling in love with Louise. But when Scobie is passed over for the commissionership in favor of a younger man, Louise's demands to be sent away from Africa become so insistent that Scobie borrows money from the notorious Yusef, and arranges for Louise to book passage.

Louise's departure brings peace and quiet to Scobie. But Wilson, who hates Scobie for being "unworthy" of Louise, only increases his hatred when the woman is gone. He discovers the fact of Yusef's loan to Scobie, and reports the policeman to government officials. Fortunately, however, Scobie's reputation is untarnished, and nothing follows the brief questioning to which he is subjected.

One of Scobie's more unpleasant tasks is to superintend the arrival of several small boatloads of English who have escaped from the sinking of a British liner. One of these survivors is a pale girl of nineteen, the four-weeks' bride of a boy lost in the disaster.

Scobie is attracted to her from the first—there is something about Helen that reminds him, in a tenuous way, of his own daughter, Catherine, who died at nine—and Helen reciprocates his friendship. Before long, however, and in a moment of mutual discovery, their friendship turns to love, and Scobie and Helen become lovers.

Though Scobie exercises extreme caution in keeping the affair a secret—he is, after all, a policeman—it soon becomes fairly common knowledge. Scobie is so used to telling the truth that he cannot dissemble easily. His major apprehension, however, comes from his own conscience. Henry Scobie is a devout and believing Catholic, and the affair brings him many moments of despair. He is unable to give pain, and as Helen is obviously dependent on his love, Scobie can do nothing but continue their relationship and suffer silently.

Helen does not believe in Scobie's religious torment, and she accuses him of indifference to her. Abandoning caution, Scobie writes her a passionate love-letter, and slips it under her door. The note, however, disappears before Helen ever knows of its existence.

Determined that his official relationship with Yusef shall in no way be compromised by the loan he had received from the smuggler, and having thought he had made that point clear to Yusef, he is amazed one day when the smuggler begs him, as a favor, to sneak a certain package aboard a Portuguese ship arriving the next day. Scobie refuses, indignantly. But when Yusef produces the incriminating letter to Helen, Scobie capitulates, and delivers the package of diamonds to the ship's captain.

This act, feels Scobie, is the beginning of his destruction. If he has sunk so low, how much lower, he wonders, can he sink? To what ends will he go to spare the pains of others?

He is distressed to receive a telegram from Louise, telling him that she is returning to him. In conscience, he tries to break his relationship with Helen; but though she begins by reviling him, the upshot of their argument is that things will continue as they are. To add to his sense of loss, Scobie is now awarded the commissionership which, earlier, would have meant so much to him, and to Louise.

With Louise returned, Scobie's moral disintegration reaches its final point, and he commits, what is for him the unpardonable sin. Unable to make a true act of contrition concerning his adulterous relationship, Scobie accepts Holy

Communion at Louise's side without having received the necessary prior absolution in the confessional. From this point on, Scobie recognizes that he is irretrievably lost to God, and he works only at salvaging what happiness he can for the two women with whom he is involved.

Wilson has renewed his attentions to Louise, and when she rejects his advances, he blurts out the truth about Scobie and Helen. To this, Louise painfully but quietly replies that she has known about the affair. A letter had come to her from one of the women of the English community, and that was why she had returned to her husband.

Unable to give either Helen or Louise the love and satisfaction each woman requires, Scobie determines to commit suicide. He pretends to have the symptoms of *angina*, and manages to obtain twelve tablets of evipan, a pain-relieving drug. Hoarding these up, Scobie makes elaborate efforts to insure that his death shall appear natural. At last, he takes the tablets and dies.

His death is recorded as having been caused by *angina pectoris*, and no post-mortem is performed. But Wilson—ever the conscientious observer—points out to Louise all the little flaws in the elaborate disguise Scobie had rigged, and he forces her to the conclusion that Scobie has killed himself. Wilson presses his love upon Louise, and begs her to marry him, but she pushes him off, telling him that perhaps she will in the future.

Helen is ravaged by Scobie's death. Utterly desolate, she seeks, but does not find, consolation in drink. And when the ridiculous Bagster, a petty local official, tries to make love to her, Helen yields, utterly without feeling. There is no one she loves. . . . What difference does anything make?

Curious about the truth of what Wilson has revealed to her about Scobie's death, Louise goes to see the local priest, Father Rank. He concedes that suicide might have been possible for Scobie. At this, Louise is bitter and angry, and questions how Scobie could for eternity have given up God by his act of self-destruction. But Father Rank tries to tell her of his conviction that Scobie truly loved God, and that God can surely be counted upon to be merciful to him.

THE END OF THE AFFAIR

Graham Greene

One rainy night in 1946, Maurice Bendrix, a young novelist, encounters Henry Miles, whom he has not seen for several years. Henry seems to be wrestling with some problem, and Bendrix agrees to go to a pub with him to discuss it.

Unbeknown to Henry, Bendrix has had an affair with Henry's wife Sarah—an affair which ended two years before. Bendrix has never quite forgiven Sarah for the abrupt way in which she disappeared from his life.

It is about Sarah that Henry is now upset. He tells Bendrix that he suspects her of seeing another man. Mostly, Bendrix gathers, Henry is looking for assurance that this is impossible. But vindictively Bendrix says he believes it quite possible, and offers to have Sarah followed by a private detective. Henry refuses this gesture and apologizes for having been so absurd. But several days later, Bendrix decides to go to the detective agency on his own.

Parkis, the man assigned to the case, makes regular reports on Sarah to Bendrix. Using his own little son as a blind, Parkis has discovered that Sarah goes regularly to visit a certain Mr. Smythe.

Much to Bendrix's surprise, Sarah calls him and invites him to lunch, ostensibly to talk about Henry. Under the watchful eyes of Parkis and his son, the two meet. The flame of passion springs up again in Bendrix's bosom, but Sarah—suffering from a severe cough—seems remote. The meeting is a failure.

With the connivance of Parkis, Bendrix borrows his son and manages to gain entrance to Smythe's flat. Smythe, it appears, is an antireligious preacher. A handsome man, disfigured only by a large strawberry-colored birthmark across one side of his face, Smythe tries to convert Bendrix to atheism. Bendrix (who is an atheist) says he is not interested, but suggests that a friend of his—a Mrs. Miles—might like to meet Smythe. At the mention of Sarah's name, Smythe winces in obvious pain, and it is clear to Bendrix that she has now left Smythe, even as she had earlier left him.

Bendrix goes to Henry, and reveals that he himself has

been having Sarah followed. (He takes great delight in the pain that he causes Henry by this revelation.) He further says that Sarah is now seeing another man—for all he knows, a string of other men. He reveals the facts of his own affair with Sarah to Henry, and leaves poor Miles a crushed man.

Parkis, still involved in the case, delivers to Bendrix Sarah's diary, from which Bendrix at last learns the truth about the end of his affair.

Sarah had been passionately in love with him (as he had been with her). One night, as they lay together in his flat, there had been an air raid (the affair ended late in 1944). Bendrix had gone to investigate, and was pinned under the wreckage of the house's front door. Sarah had come upon him, and found him (she believed) dead. Although an atheist, she had prayed that if God would somehow restore Bendrix to life and give him another chance at happiness, she would renounce the thing most precious to her in the world —her love for Bendrix. Her prayer over, Sarah looked up—to find Bendrix alive and only slightly bruised.

Since that time, Sarah has been true to her vow. Her diary reveals in complete detail the spiritual struggle which she has endured—how she has passed from atheism to qualified belief, how she has altered from skepticism to faith and back to doubt. The diary also tells how she attempted to forget Bendrix with other men, and how that failed; sex and lust, she finds, have no meaning for her without love.

In an attempt to prove to herself that her vow to God was meaningless, and thus free herself to return to Bendrix, Sarah had gone to see the atheist Smythe. But though her visits to him each week gave her food for thought, they only intensified her belief in the existence of God. And when Smythe had fallen in love with her and proposed, she had had to desert him.

The most important thing about Sarah's diary to Bendrix is not the description of her approach to faith (he is a determined atheist) but the recurring evidence that Sarah loves him still. He determines that he will take her away from Henry forever. He phones Sarah, but she refuses to see him, pleading illness. He tells her that he cares nothing about her illness; he knows now that she still loves him and he is coming for her.

As Bendrix approaches Sarah's house in the pouring rain

that night, he finds her slipping out of the house. He follows her, and at last she goes into a Catholic church. There is a confrontation, and Sarah (her cough worse than ever) refuses to listen to Bendrix's plan. At last it is agreed that she will return to Henry until she is well, and that Bendrix will then come for her.

Before he sees her again, however, Sarah dies.

Henry, completely broken apart by Sarah's death, asks Bendrix to arrange her funeral. In spite of the remonstrances of a priest, who tells them that Sarah had been receiving instruction in the Catholic faith, Bendrix arranges for Sarah to be cremated. Though he, better than anyone else, knows fully of Sarah's spiritual transformation, he takes vindictive pleasure from denial of all suggestions that Sarah was anything but an atheist.

At the funeral, Bendrix meets Sarah's mother, and from the woman he learns that at the age of two, Sarah, though she was never told of it, had been baptized in the Catholic faith. He assumes that this news, revealed so shortly after he has learned definitely of Sarah's recent attempt to become a Catholic, merely presents an interesting coincidence.

Parkis's young son, who had become very attached to Sarah during the time that he and his father were "investigating" her, becomes dangerously ill. Henry sends the boy some children's books that had been Sarah's. One of these Parkis later returns, with a curious story: while the child was unconscious, at the crisis in his illness, he had dreamed that Sarah came to him and made him well. The next morning, the child is indeed better. And written in the book, in the six-year-old handwriting of Sarah as a child, is found the message: "When I was ill my mother gave me this book by Lang, If any well person steals it he will get a great bang, But if you are sick in bed, You can have it to read instead." The boy insists that Sarah had made him well. Bendrix chalks up another coincidence.

Shortly thereafter, Bendrix runs into Smythe again. The strawberry-colored birthmark is gone. The man, somewhat shamefacedly, tells Bendrix that when Sarah had deserted him, he began to question his own lack of faith. He refuses to specify how the birthmark has been got rid of, but suggests that it was not by medical science.

Bendrix has by now moved into Henry's home; they have

reconciled their differences since Sarah's death, and are some kind of solace to each other. Once again, Bendrix reads Sarah's journal. He at last recognizes the existence of God—but it is only to hate Him. (This was precisely what Sarah's first response to God had been.) Bendrix prays—a prayer that is almost identical to one Sarah had prayed during her first troubled months after leaving Bendrix: "O God, You've done enough, You've robbed me of enough. I'm too tired and old to learn to love. Leave me alone forever."

AMERICAN NOVELS

THE DEERSLAYER

James Fenimore Cooper

*James Fenimore Cooper was born in Burlington, New Jersey, in
1789, and one year later the family moved to Cooperstown, New
York, a settlement established by his grandfather and father. He
entered Yale at the age of thirteen, but left in his junior year and
went to sea, becoming a midshipman in the U. S. Navy in 1808. He
married the heiress of a landed New York family in 1811, and
lived on her estate in Westchester County before moving to New
York City in 1822, one year after the publication of his first successful work of fiction. In 1823 The Pioneers, the first published
book of* The Leatherstocking Tales *series, appeared; this book
earned for Cooper an international reputation as the first major
American novelist.* The Deerslayer *belongs to* The Leatherstocking
Tales, *and, although published in 1841, is first in the series in
order of narrative. Cooper, a literary celebrity, lived in Europe for
seven years, but returned to Cooperstown in 1833. In his later
years he assumed the role of a severe critic of America and of
Jacksonian democracy in particular; his criticisms were nowhere
appreciated, and in fact caused him to become extremely unpopu-
lar. He died in 1851.*

*Cooper's novels virtually created the romance of the frontier,
a fictional concept which is very much alive today as one of the
great sources of the American myth. Ironically the novels themselves are widely deprecated for their contrived plots, artificial dialogue, and excessive length; and they have been unfashionable for
generations. There is, nevertheless, much to be admired in Cooper's
writings. Readers of* The Deerslayer *cannot help but be impressed
by the author's sincere, and prophetic, concern for the future of a
nation which desecrates its own wilderness and places the acquisi-
tion of wealth above all moral considerations. If Cooper was overly
romantic about the Indian in his natural setting and overly pessimistic about the brutality of the white settlers, he has nonetheless
been vindicated in part, and much of what he believed has become a healthy thorn in the nation's conscience.*

On his way to the Huron country to keep a rendezvous with
his childhood friend, the Delaware Indian Chingachgook,
Natty Bumppo, called the Deerslayer, falls in with the gi-

gantic trapper Henry March, nicknamed Hurry Harry. Arriving at the isolated, beautiful lake Glimmerglass, the two make their way to the home of Tom Hutter.

Hutter's house is a most unusual one: called the Castle, it stands on pilings in the middle of the lake, so that Hutter can more easily protect himself and his daughters from Indians and unfriendly white hunters. In addition to the well-armed house and several canoes, Hutter has a sort of houseboat, called the Ark, in which he can comfortably navigate.

Hurry Harry is in love with Hutter's older daughter, Judith; but Natty Bumppo, though admitting that she is the most beautiful girl he has ever seen, finds her too self-centered and flirtatious for his taste. He is as pure a young man as ever crossed the countryside, and Judith's beauty is no snare for him. As for Hutter's second daughter, Esther (called Hetty), she is half-witted—though comely and a devout Christian.

A party of Huron Indians (also known as Mingos) is spotted on the shore, and the colonial governor having offered a bounty for Indian scalps, Hurry and Hutter determine to kill the Indian women and children. The Deerslayer, who believes strongly in refraining from shedding blood except in direst emergency, urges against the cruel expedition; but the coarser men have their way, and require that the Deerslayer accompany them to man the canoe.

The expedition ends in failure, however, for the first woman attacked screams so loudly that she attracts the attention of the men of the tribe, and Hurry and Hutter are taken prisoner. The Deerslayer alone escapes—but not before he sheds human blood for the first time, in an encounter with a treacherous Huron brave. In spite of the bounty, however, the Deerslayer refrains from taking the Huron's scalp, believing that scalping is right for a redman but not for a white.

The Deerslayer is now solely responsible for the protection of Judith and Hetty, but as he has the aid of Chingachgook, whom he now meets as appointed, he feels sure that no harm will come to them. (Chingachgook has come to this place to rescue his beloved, the beautiful Delaware maiden Wah-tal-wah, who has been held prisoner by the Hurons.)

Before Judith and the Deerslayer are able to implement a plan for the rescue of Hutter and Hurry, the half-witted girl, who is secretly in love with Hurry, makes for the Indian encampment by herself. Fortunately, as the Deerslayer assures Judith, the Indians will not harm Hetty because of her affliction, redmen holding that creatures of less than normal intelligence are the special love and care of the god Manitou.

During her sojourn with the Hurons, Hetty meets Wah-ta!-wah, and she brings back news that encourages Chingachgook. The Indian maiden has sent her beloved a message that she will sneak away at a given time and that he is to come to rescue her at a certain rock.

The Deerslayer at last succeeds in ransoming Hutter and Harry from the Hurons in exchange for some ivory chessmen that Judith finds in a locked chest of her father's. Far from being grateful, however, the two men blame the Deerslayer for their having been captured in the first place, and they are determined to get their revenge upon the Hurons.

At the time appointed by Wah-ta!-wah, Chingachgook and the Deerslayer slip away from the Castle in a canoe, not wishing to wake the sleeping Hutter and Hurry, who would only make trouble, and they head for the rock at which they are to meet the Delaware maiden. Much to their surprise, they discover that the Hurons have moved camp, and are now situated at the very place of their assignation with Wah-ta!-wah. After reconnoitering, the two men plan their attack, and it is successful—at least to the extent that Wah-ta!-wah is spirited away by Chingachgook and taken to the Castle. The Deerslayer, however, is taken prisoner.

The Hurons now declare war on the Castle, and though Chingachgook gives wise counsel, Hurry and Hutter are too stubborn to listen to him. Fortunately the Indian is able to protect the two women in the Ark, but he can do nothing to help the men, who are ambushed by Hurons. When the fight is over, Hurry has been severely beaten and humiliated, and Hutter has been left to die, after first having been scalped.

It is a sad occasion for Judith and Hetty when they must see to the burial of Hutter below the surface of the lake, at a spot where, two years earlier, their mother had been buried.

After the simple funeral, Hurry proposes marriage to Judith, and, much to his surprise, she refuses him. The girl has long ago recognized his lack of valor; moreover, she now loves the Deerslayer. (If the truth were known, Hurry is loved desperately by the half-witted Hetty, but as he has eyes only for Judith, he is destined never to know this.)

The Hurons propose to free the Deerslayer if he can get certain concessions from his friends: Chingachgook and Hurry are both to leave the Huron country; Wah-ta!-wah is to be returned to the Hurons; and Judith and Hetty are to take Huron husbands. These terms the Deerslayer knows will never be accepted, but giving his word that he will return freely the next day to the Hurons to face their tortures, he returns to the Castle to make the Indian demands known.

All reply to these demands as he expects, with the single exception of Hurry. Now that Judith has refused him, Hurry is determined to leave the Glimmerglass, and will stay neither to protect the women nor to help effect the rescue of the Deerslayer. He does agree, at least, to warn the colonials at the fort about the Huron uprising, and to send them to rescue his friends.

Though Judith begs him to break his word to the Indians and stay in safety, the Deerslayer cannot go back on his pledge. Accordingly he returns to the Huron camp.

For several days the Hurons use psychological torture upon the Deerslayer, convinced that he will break. But they underestimate the strength and courage of this white man raised by the Delaware Indians. At last it is agreed by the Huron chiefs that the Deerslayer must be tortured in earnest.

Before the torture has proceeded very far, it is interrupted by the intrusion into the Huron camp of Hetty, who tries to alter the Indians' intention by a pathetic reading from her Bible and a lecture on God's will. Recognizing her lack of wits, the Indians put her aside and proceed with the torture.

Again the horrible ceremony is interrupted—this time by Judith. She tries to deceive the Indians into thinking that she carries great influence with the colonial governor, and that she will punish their torture of the Deerslayer by bringing troops to suppress the Hurons. This ruse is exposed, however, when, by questioning the guileless Hetty, the Indians learn that Judith has no more influence than she.

Again the torture is begun—but this time it is interrupted by a far more serious threat to the Hurons: the troops of the colonial fort, alerted and led by Hurry Harry, are descending upon them.

A furious battle ensues, in which all of the Indians are

killed or routed. Sadly, a stray bullet has hit poor Hetty, who at least has the happiness of seeing Hurry Harry once more before she, too, goes to join the bodies of her mother and father at the bottom of the Glimmerglass.

Judith is now more convinced than ever that she loves the Deerslayer, and when she sees that he is not about to speak to her, she takes the initiative and asks if he will marry her. The Deerslayer makes clear to her that he has great respect for her, but that he does not love her. Trying to be brave, Judith leaves him and goes with the soldiers to the colonial fort. Hurry Harry strikes off on his own, and the Deerslayer follows his good friends, Wah-ta!-wah and Chingachgook, into the wilderness.

Some fifteen years later, the Deerslayer (now called Hawk-eye) returns to the Glimmerglass with Chingachgook and with the latter's son, Uncas, the last of the Mohicans. They find that all is just as they had left it so long ago, except that the Castle and the canoes are in a sad state of decay. With the passing of a few more winters, nothing will be left of them. They look for the graves at the lake bottom, but they cannot find them.

Later, Hawkeye visits the garrisons of the Mohawk, and tries to find out what has become of Judith. But none knows her there and he can find no trace of her.

BILLY BUDD

Herman Melville

Herman Melville was born in New York City in 1819. Forced because of family finances to end his schooling at the age of fifteen, he became a cabin boy on a transatlantic ship, and in 1841 joined the crew of a whaling ship destined for the South Pacific. He jumped ship in the Marquesas, however, and went to Tahiti, where he lived for some time before sailing for home in 1844. Upon his return, he wrote romances based on his adventures; these early works were extremely successful, and Melville enjoyed five or six years as a very popular author. In 1851 Moby Dick was published; it was poorly received, and Melville's reputation went into a steady decline. Although he continued to write he was no longer able to support himself on his literary earnings and so he took a position, which he held for close to twenty years, as a customs official in

*New York. When he died in 1891 his name was nearly unknown
and his artistic reputation nonexistent.*

Billy Budd, Foretopman, *written about 1889, went unpublished
until 1924, by which time a phenomenon which was extraordinary
but by no means unparalleled in the history of literature had occurred. An eminent critic, convinced that Melville had never been
properly understood in his own time, subjected Melville's writings
to new interpretations which left little doubt that the author, especially in* Moby Dick, *was concerned with subjects far more profound than whaling practices. Melville was reread, discussed, and
interpreted, and his reputation soon rose to its present gigantic
stature. Contemporary readers, attuned to literary and psychological symbolism and accustomed to a tragic and pessimistic view of
the condition of man, have little difficulty with the pervasive allegorical aspect of Melville's fiction. The characters in* Billy Budd
*are conceived not as realistic portraits but as symbols of human
qualities. Billy represents all the virtues of pure innocence; his
physical and spiritual beauty is unstained. Although it is his rôle to
destroy Evil, symbolized by Claggart, he cannot survive amid
the realities of this world; he is so far above being human, and
the world is so far below being divine, that his very presence is
a threat to the framework of a society based upon compromise.
Captain Vere is the Judge, the dispenser of order who acknowledges
the necessities of reality. The Christlike quality of Billy is affirmed
when he forgives his executioners, but the parallel cannot be continued further; in Melville's view of humanity, the establishment
of a kingdom of heaven on earth is not a possibility.*

It is the summer of 1797, and the impressment of sailors from
merchant ships is still the rule in His Majesty's Navy—notwithstanding the recent Nore mutiny. When Lieutenant
Ratcliff of H.M.S. *Indomitable* boards the merchant vessel
Rights-of-Man, he no sooner lays eyes on a young seaman,
Billy Budd, than he determines that this is the only man on
board that he will impress for service on his warship.

Captain Graveling of the *Rights* tells Lieutenant Ratcliff
that he has decided upon the one man Graveling is most
loath to lose. Before Budd had come aboard the *Rights,* says
Graveling, the men were a surly, uncooperative lot; but under Budd's influence, the crew is now happy and hardworking. All of the men adore Billy Budd—and Graveling fears a
return of their former sentiment should he be impressed. Ratcliff is determined to have the young sailor, however, and
without further ado Billy Budd is installed aboard the *Indomitable* as foretopman.

Twenty-one years old, Billy Budd—sometimes called "Baby" Budd, because of his beardless cheek—is a handsome, nay, beautiful young man. Tall, well built, fair, he reminds one of a Grecian statue cast in an Anglo-Saxon mold. Soft-spoken, hardworking, Billy is indeed the Handsome Sailor. He has but one blemish; in the fever of emotion, he stammers, and is unable to speak easily. (This affliction is not ordinarily evident.)

Billy takes hold in his new position at once—to the surprise of Captain the Honorable Edward Fairfax Vere, more commonly known as "Starry" Vere, who had expected some resistence, or at least some sullenness, from a man so newly impressed. However, as there is no trouble, Captain Vere pays little further attention to Billy Budd. The captain is a remote man, and though a martinet for maintaining order and discipline, he remains otherwise withdrawn from his officers and crew. He is something of a philosopher, and would rather read than spend his free time in social intercourse.

Another who has noted the arrival of Billy on board with particular curiosity is the Master-at-Arms, John Claggart. For no explainable reason, this man takes an immediate dislike to Billy, which he attempts to hide beneath a direct and almost jovial façade. But there is an innate wickedness in the breast of John Claggart, and something about Billy Budd stirs his hostilities. Whether it is the lad's physical beauty that Claggart resents, his willingness to work hard and uncomplainingly though impressed, or his clear-eyed and all-too-apparent innocence of evil, there is something about Billy that raises Claggart's hatred.

Shortly after joining the *Indomitable*, Billy witnesses a sight that fills him with horror. A young sailor, guilty of some minor breach of naval discipline, is publicly flogged on the deck. The brutality of the punishment, the cruelty of the flogger, and the look on the lad's face when he is at last set free, overwhelm Billy; and he determines to be punctilious in all things, lest a similar punishment be meted out to him.

Because he is so scrupulous in the execution of his duties, Billy is surprised to find that occasionally he is in minor trouble aboard the ship. It is always something petty—but always enough to bring down upon him a vague threat from one of the police of the underdeck. Disturbed by this, Billy asks for the advice of a veteran aboard, an old Dane whom he has come to love.

The Dansker has long since learned not to give advice; and when he hears Billy's story, he merely observes that "Jemmy Legs"—the crew's nickname for Claggart—is down on Billy. Billy finds this impossible to believe, but the Dansker repeats the charge.

The next day, Billy's suspicions are allayed when Claggart gives him a playful rap with his official rattan, saying, "Handsome is as handsome does." When he sees that his shipmates take this as a sign of joviality in Claggart, Billy is convinced that the Master-at-Arms cannot possibly bear him ill will. Unfortunately he does not see the sardonic smile or the hostile gleam in Claggart's eye as he walks away from Billy.

Claggart's passion against Billy is of a refined and subtle sort; and as Claggart has ready access to many of the ship's officers, and great influence over them, he is able to weave a tight but invisible web about the young sailor.

One night Billy is summoned surreptitiously to a secret meeting of those sailors who have been impressed. They tell him that they wish to mutiny, and ask if they can count on him to join them. In his horror at this proposal, Billy begins to stammer and finds it all but impossible to speak; but it is clear to the others that he wants no part of their scheme. But when Claggart arrives on the scene suddenly, Billy regains the use of his tongue, and loyal to his messmates, gives Claggart a plausible excuse for the men being there. Though the man who had summoned Billy to the assignation—a man who dines at Claggart's table—now smiles at him surreptitiously whenever he sees Billy, there is no further mention of the mutiny.

Now Claggart is ready to strike. He goes to Captain Vere and tells him that a mutiny is brewing. When Vere demands that Claggart speak plainly and name the ringleader, Claggart smoothly announces, "William Budd. A foretopman."

Vere can hardly believe the charge, having observed Billy many times, and having felt within himself a most positive warmth and admiration toward the young sailor. He has Billy summoned to his cabin and demands that Claggart repeat, to Billy's face, what he has charged behind his back.

Coolly, Claggart looks straight at Billy and repeats the

charge. Its monstrousness and injustice are seen at once in Billy's face, but he can only stammer. Vere asks him to defend himself, and noting the lad's affliction of speech, urges him to take time to calm himself before speaking. But Billy becomes more and more wrought up, and more and more unable to speak. The next moment, his right arm flies out, and Claggart falls to the deck.

"Fated boy!" gasps Captain Vere, "what have you done?" And, horrified, Vere goes to Claggart to find that he is dead.

Vere is terribly shaken by this. He is convinced that Billy is innocent of the charge, and that Claggart had been malicious in making it. But there is no doubt that Billy has killed Claggart, and must be tried according to naval law. So the innocent becomes the guilty, and the guilty innocent.

Billy is tried that very night by a court-martial, with Captain Vere presiding as well as serving as chief witness. The three judges feel precisely as Vere does. The provocation of Billy was such that it justified his action; the death of Claggart is justified by *his*. But the trial is to consider not what went before, but merely the event of Billy's striking an officer and killing him. There is no choice but to find Billy Budd guilty. Though the judges wish to mitigate his sentence, Vere himself points out how impractical that would be. The other men would wonder what accounted for the sudden leniency, and with mutiny in the air, leniency is the one feeling that must not be allowed to emanate from officers.

Billy is sentenced to be hanged from the yardarm the next morning.

He passes the night in irons, locked in a cell, where his only visitor is the chaplain. That good man recognizes the thorough innocence of Billy's soul in all respects, and when Billy does not respond to the comforts he would offer, he merely kisses the lad and goes away. Almost in a stupor, Billy sits thinking only of Captain Vere—of the captain's conviction that he, Billy, is innocent, and of his valiant attempt to make Billy see the necessity for his behaving as a captain must.

The next morning Billy stands on the deck, the noose about his neck. He is calm, almost serene. Asked if he has any last words, he merely shouts, "God bless Captain Vere!" And then his body flies straight upward and hangs motionless.

Many years later, when Captain Vere himself lies dying, he is heard to mutter in his unconsciousness a single name, over and over—"Billy Budd. Billy Budd." But the name has no meaning for his auditors.

Among sailors, however, the name does have meaning. Billy Budd has become something of a legend. There is a song they sing among them—none now knows how and where it originated—called "Billy in the Darbies," which tells his story. And even among those who are too young to have heard the true events aboard the *Indomitable*, pieces of the mast from which Billy was hanged are as revered as if they were relics of the true Cross.

THE MAN WITHOUT A COUNTRY

Edward Everett Hale

Edward Everett Hale was born in Boston in 1822. He was a member of a distinguished Boston family, and numbered among his forebears the great statesman Edward Everett and the patriot Nathan Hale. He attended Harvard, studied theology, and in 1842 became a Unitarian minister. Both as a preacher and as a prodigious writer of articles and books, he earned a reputation as one of the leading intellectual reformers of his day. He was particularly active in the antislavery movement, and in behalf of public education and improvement of the condition of the working classes. He was chaplain of the United States Senate from 1903 until his death in 1909.

The Man Without a Country, Hale's best-known work of fiction, was published in The Atlantic Monthly in 1863. If readers today are made slightly uncomfortable by the sentimental patriotism which is the theme of this novel, it must be remembered that it appeared in time of war, and did in fact have a rallying effect on the Union cause. The impact of the short novel was further increased by the fact that it was published anonymously and written in such a realistic style that many readers took it for a factual account. Regarded now as romantic rather than realistic, and ingenious rather than rousing, The Man Without a Country is today held in considerable affection as a piece of literary Americana.

In 1805 young Philip Nolan, lieutenant in the Western Division of the United States Army, meets Aaron Burr, and that glittering personality leaves a mark upon the young officer that is to bring him tragedy. For the next year, life seems very tame to Nolan in comparison to his experiences with the dynamic Burr, and he contents himself with writing letters to the great man—letters which go unanswered.

Later, however, rumors begin to circulate that Burr is raising an army to overthrow the government, and Nolan eagerly awaits developments. When at last he meets Burr again and is invited to join the scheme, he gladly throws in his lot with Burr.

The plot, of course, comes to nothing, and results in many courts-martial for those involved. The major figures in the scheme escape the law, but the lesser participants are not so lucky. Lieutenant Nolan is one of the unlucky ones, and he is tried for treason.

When Colonel Morgan, who is presiding at the trial, asks Nolan if he has any statement to make showing that he has always been faithful to the United States, Nolan spits out an impetuous oath: "Damn the United States! I wish I may never hear of the United States again!"

Nolan is found guilty, and his punishment is that he is to get his wish: he may never hear the name of the United States again. He is taken to a naval vessel which is just about to set off on a two-year cruise, and put aboard.

Thus begins the unhappy imprisonment of the Man without a Country—an imprisonment that is to last his entire life.

That the sentence may be properly executed, the following arrangements are made. Nolan is to move from one naval vessel to another, never coming closer than a hundred miles to the American shore. He is to be treated with as much courtesy as is due an officer of his rank. He is to be given the freedom of the ship and the company of her officers. But the name of his country, and news of his country are never to be mentioned before him. All reading matter given the prisoner is to be censored in advance. Though Nolan may wear the uniform of an officer, he may not wear the Army uniform's buttons, as they carry the insignia of the United States. (Thus, Nolan gets the nickname "Plain-Buttons.") Finally, no word of Nolan's unusual sentence, or of the man himself, is to be breathed outside the Naval Forces; no officer carrying Nolan on any cruise is even to mention him in official dispatches.

At first, Nolan treats his unusual fate as a lark. He swaggers, jokes, and laughs. But gradually, as the full implication of his fate dawns upon him, his spirits lower. Finally he has two bitter experiences which succeed in crushing him almost completely.

The first comes when he is reading Sir Walter Scott's *Lay of the Last Minstrel* aloud to some of the officers on deck. Neither Nolan nor any of the others has ever read the poem before. Thus the Man without a Country, reading on in his rich voice, is unprepared for the emotional shock of the lines:

> *Breathes there a man with soul so dead,*
> *Who never to himself hath said—*
> *This is my own, my native land!*
> *Whose heart hath ne'er within him burned,*
> *As home his footsteps he hath turned . . .*

Nolan's voice chokes up, and the officers listening squirm in painful embarrassment. But somehow the disgraced lieutenant forces himself on:

> *High though his titles, proud his name,*
> *Boundless his wealth as wish can claim,*
> *Despite these titles, power, and pelf,*
> *The wretch, concentered all in self—*

It is too much. Overpowered by emotion, Nolan heaves the book into the sea and retires to his stateroom.

His second crushing experience comes several years later. He is now confined to a naval ship which lies at anchor in the Mediterranean. The officers are staging a ball, to which a number of Americans from other ships, as well as those attached to the American embassy, are invited. Nolan stands at the sidelines and watches the festivities.

Suddenly noticing one of the women, however, he strides up to her and introduces himself. He had known her as Miss Rutledge back in Kentucky; she is now the famous Mrs. Graff.

Before the officer whose task it is to supervise conversation with Nolan can intervene, Nolan has asked Mrs. Graff to dance, and she has accepted him.

Nolan seizes the opportunity to ask her what is the news from home.

Coldly the woman turns on him. "Home! Mr. Nolan!" she says. "I thought you were the man who never wanted to hear of home again!" She turns on her heel and walks away from him.

Though his spirits have been crushed, Nolan has not lost his courage, as he is able to prove some time later. It is during the War of 1812, and the ship on which he stays is attacked by the British. Nolan leaps to the guns at once and takes command. He welds the men into a forceful fighting unit, and raises their spirits. When the attack is over and the British have fled, the commander of the vessel sends for Nolan and presents him with the commander's own sword. Further, the commander writes to the Secretary of War, describing the experience, and asking a full pardon for Nolan. The letter is never answered.

Nolan had cried when receiving the officer's sword. He cries again, but for a different reason, when a number of years later the ship he rides overtakes a schooner laden with slaves. The American party quickly frees the slaves, and Nolan is asked to serve as interpreter, as he speaks Portuguese.

Interpreting for the officer, Vaughan, Nolan tells the Africans that they are free, and that they will be taken to Cape Palmas. At this, the Negroes all protest: Cape Palmas is at the other end of the continent from their homes. They want to be taken to their wives, their children, their houses. In short, they want to be taken *home*.

The Negroes' passionate defense of the importance of going home is too much for Nolan. He weeps—and Vaughan, recognizing the privation to Nolan of *his* never being able to go home, agrees to take the Negroes to the northern part of Africa.

And so Nolan's life goes on—year after year, vessel after vessel, commanding officer after commanding officer.

At last, his health fails, and he feels that he is dying. (It is 1863—more than fifty years since he was first put aboard the *Nautilus* at New Orleans.) He sends for the captain of the *Danforth*, the vessel that is to be his last prison, and begs that, as he is dying, the punishment be ended and that the captain tell him of his own dear country.

Looking around Nolan's stateroom—it is the first time he has seen it—the captain notes that Nolan has made of it a patriotic shrine. A flag of the United States drapes a portrait of George Washington. A hand-carved American eagle hangs on the wall. There is even a pencil sketch of a map of the United States which Nolan has drawn from memory.

Realizing how greatly the Man without a Country has suffered, the captain relents and, in the half-hour that is left to Nolan, tries to compress all the history of the United States. How avidly, how eagerly Nolan drinks in every word.

Tiring, Nolan lies down to rest, but not before giving the captain an envelope to be opened after his death. The captain believes that Nolan's strength will come back, but he is wrong. In less than an hour, Nolan is dead.

Looking at the slip of paper left in his charge, the captain sees that it is a request from Nolan that he be buried at sea. Nolan asks further, though, that somewhere in America a monument be set up, so that he will not disappear altogether from memory. On the monument Nolan asks that these words be carved:

In memory of

PHILIP NOLAN

Lieutenant in the Army of the United States

"He loved his country as no other man has loved her;

but no man deserved less at her hands."

THE ADVENTURES OF TOM SAWYER

Samuel L. Clemens

Samuel Langhorne Clemens, who used the pseudonym Mark Twain, was born in Florida, Missouri, in 1835. His father's business failure forced him to discontinue his schooling in 1847, and he worked as an itinerant printer until 1856 when he became a riverboat pilot on the Mississippi. When the Civil War put a stop to traffic on the river, Clemens moved to Virginia City, Nevada, where he worked on a newspaper; here, in 1862, he adopted the pen name Mark Twain, a riverboat term which indicated a navigable depth of two fathoms of water. His humorous writings began to appear at this time, and he was soon famous; additional success came to him as a lecturer, and he traveled widely. He married a Connecticut socialite and settled in Hartford, where he invested in a publishing firm. His later years were darkened by the death of his wife and two daughters, and by the failure of his business. He eventually paid his creditors with the receipts of an exhausting world-wide lecture tour. Honored and beloved by the world, but

*increasingly bitter and melancholic toward the end, he died in
1910.*

*The first major American writer born west of the Mississippi,
Mark Twain both created and reflected a style, diction, and point
of view regarded as typically American. Brash, informal, humorous,
uneducated, self-sufficient, optimistic, innocent, democratic—these
were the qualities of the young country which the writings of Mark
Twain embodied. His two most famous novels,* The Adventures of
Tom Sawyer *and* The Adventures of Huckleberry Finn, *are based
to a large extent upon the author's boyhood experiences in Missouri, but the novels are quite different and not at all companion
pieces. Tom Sawyer's adventures are romantic in character. Tom
is wildly unrealistic, opposed to the logical world of adults; his
victories represent childhood dreams of glory. Huck Finn, on the
other hand, is realistic and anxious to learn about the world of men;
the novel of his adventures, furthermore, is much vaster in scope
than Tom Sawyer, and has been historically much the more important of the two. Huck's journey down the river symbolizes the
journey of life, in which the traveler undergoes the initiation
experiences that carry him to manhood. This is no idyllic voyage,
but a series of contacts with a society which is often brutal and
cruel. Huck's rebelliousness, originally boyish, is never mitigated;
finally Huck knows too much of the world to which he is expected
to conform, and he escapes from it again to seek those values which
he has come to appreciate. As the first novel to make full artistic
use of American English as a spoken language,* Huckleberry Finn
*has been called the most influential of American novels; Ernest
Hemingway was not greatly exaggerating when he remarked that
"All modern American literature comes from one book by Mark
Twain called* Huckleberry Finn."

Tom Sawyer, of St. Petersburg, Missouri, is typical of small-
town boys: he steals jam from the larder, picks fights with
every new boy in town, vacillates between scorn for all creatures of the female sex and desperate admiration of them.

He lives with his Aunt Polly, his parents being dead, and
the poor woman is often beside herself, trying to lead him
in the straight and narrow path without stifling his need to
be just plain boy. (Tom's lot isn't made any easier by the
fact that he has a half brother, Siddy, who is the very model
of perfection in youth. In comparison with Sid, Tom is indeed
a harum-scarum sort.)

Possessed of a vivid imagination, Tom manages to turn
even the most humdrum chore into a bully adventure. Set
to whitewashing Aunt Polly's fence one beautiful afternoon,

as a punishment, Tom pretends to the boys passing by that he actually enjoys the chore. His young friends, who had at first scorned him and teased him for having to waste time by working, soon are begging for a chance to do a little whitewashing. Tom is very reluctant to let them help; after all, Aunt Polly is very particular about this fence's appearance. When the boys plead and plead, however, and promise to be extra-careful, and when they begin to give Tom some of their treasures in exchange for the privilege of whitewashing Aunt Polly's fence, Tom kindheartedly relents and gives each boy a turn, supervising the operation himself while lying in the shade and munching an apple.

Tom's best girlfriend has been the dark-haired Amy Lawrence. But the fickleness of man is evident when a new girl moves into town, the beautiful Becky Thatcher. Tom is determined to win this new prize, and soon he devises a number of stratagems by which he is thrown into her company. His romance progresses brilliantly; indeed, Becky is on the point of becoming engaged to him. But at the crucial moment, Tom lets slip that he has already been engaged to Amy —and Becky deserts him in a huff.

Tom and his boon companion, Huckleberry Finn, the idle, dirty, shiftless, and altogether lovable son of the town drunkard, find a dead cat and plan to go to the graveyard one night at midnight to use it in trying out a wart cure they've heard of. Meeting at the assigned spot, they serve as secret witnesses to a horrible deed. Hoss Williams's grave is being robbed of its body by Muff Potter (a town ne'er-do-well), young Dr. Robinson, and Injun Joe, the last-named being the most feared and hated man in town. Doc Robinson refuses to give Injun Joe the money he wants, whereupon there is a fight. Injun Joe knocks Muff Potter unconscious, stabs the doctor with Muff's knife, and then, when Muff comes to, convinces the poor man that *he* is the murderer.

Huck and Tom, terrified, swear to each other that they will never reveal what they have seen. Some days later, Muff is arrested for the crime and put in jail to await trial. Huck and Tom, who have always liked Muff, smuggle small comforts to him, but are too frightened to speak up and own his innocence.

Afraid of Injun Joe, Tom decides to run away and become

a pirate. In this desperate adventure he is joined by his two best friends—Joe Harper and Huckleberry Finn.

The boys round up some provisions and, using an old raft, make for Jackson's Island. For several days life there is a lark, but eventually the lads begin to feel homesick. But Tom is able to persuade Joe and Huck to stay on the island, for he has returned home late one night and, unnoticed by Aunt Polly, overheard a conversation in which it is revealed that the townspeople, thinking the three boys drowned, are planning a funeral service. Tom convinces the boys to wait at Jackson's Island until the afternoon of the funeral. This they do, sneaking back to town just in time to hide, unnoticed, in the church gallery. At the appropriate moment, they appear in the middle of the congregation, to the confusion and joy of all.

At last, Muff Potter is scheduled to come to trial. Siddy overhears the conscience-stricken Tom muttering in his sleep, and goes to the sheriff. At the trial, therefore, Tom is called as a witness. Bewildered as to how it is known that he was a witness to the crime, Tom begins to testify; but before he can say what he had seen, Injun Joe bursts through a window and escapes. The men of the town search for him, but he is not found. Tom spends many nights of terror afterward, dreading his fate if Injun Joe should ever come after him.

Now Tom and Huckleberry determine to look for buried treasure. They go up by the old haunted house, and dig; but before they are able to find anything, they hear mysterious voices, and so they hide. Again the two boys are witness to a frightening scene. Two men talk about a great treasure they have found, and about getting revenge upon an unnamed person. The boys recognize one of the men as a deaf-and-dumb Spaniard who has been recently seen about town. Imagine their terror when they realize that he is none other than Injun Joe, disguised in a serape and false beard. They determine to track down the treasure themselves, overhearing the names of two hiding places mentioned by the men—"Number Two" and "the sign of the cross."

Huck discovers that Number Two refers to a deserted room in a tavern. He goes there, and sure enough finds Injun Joe—but no treasure. He determines to follow Injun Joe when he leaves the tavern late one night, carrying a strongbox. (Tom is off on a picnic with Becky and the other respectable youngsters of the town this particular night, and so misses the adventure.) Huck follows the villainous Indian, and though he doesn't find the treasure, he does overhear a plot against Widow Douglas, a kindly woman who lives alone. Acting quickly, Huck enlists the aid of a Welshman and his sons, who succeed in routing the villains before the widow can come to harm; but Huck is insistent that his name be left out of the story.

Meanwhile, Tom is having an adventure of his own. He and Becky (with whom he has now been reconciled) have been exploring some old caves with the other youngsters at the picnic, but somehow become separated from them, and get lost in the labyrinth. Their absence is not noted till late the following day, and a search party is sent out. For days the two youngsters wander about the cave without being discovered, and at last are given up for dead. At one point, Tom sees a light—and his heart stops when he recognizes Injun Joe holding a lantern. Fortunately, however, the villain disappears. At last Tom finds his way out of the cave by way of a partly closed entrance five miles from the one they originally used, and he and Becky return to town.

When he has thoroughly recovered from his days without food, Tom learns that Judge Thatcher, Becky's father, has ordered that the entrance to the cave be sealed, so that there can be no more episodes like the one Becky and Tom have endured. Horrified, Tom runs to the Judge and tells him that Injun Joe is in the cave. A party of men goes and opens the cave, and there they find the body of Injun Joe.

Tom realizes that the fortune Injun Joe had found must be secreted in the cave. (The other man involved in the crime has drowned—perhaps victim to another of Injun Joe's murders.) Tom and Huck go to the cave by way of the entrance Tom had found, and eventually they locate the treasure, buried at a spot beneath a cross marked on the cave wall. They are rich indeed!

On their way back to town with the treasure, they are stopped by the Welshman, who insists that they accompany him to Widow Douglas's house. There a party is in progress. Siddy has told everyone about Huck's part in the saving of Widow Douglas from Injun Joe, and she has now determined to adopt the boy so that he will not be penniless.

Tom explains that Huck doesn't need the widow's money —that he is rich. Tom and Huck display their treasure, and soon they are heroes in the town. Judge Thatcher invests each boy's share, and Tom and Huck soon have a regular income equal to that of the minister.

Widow Douglas insists that Huck live with her nonetheless; but after several weeks of being scrubbed, dressed in tight, clean clothes, and being forced to live a regular life, Huck finds it too much for him, and he decamps to his rags and dust-heap, where Tom finds him happy as can be.

Tom insists that Huck at least *try* the civilized life for a little longer, and at last Huckleberry agrees. But he makes it clear to Tom that it is to be nothing more than one last *attempt*.

How successful that attempt is, the author indicates, will be revealed in another book.

THE ADVENTURES OF HUCKLEBERRY FINN

Samuel L. Clemens

When Tom Sawyer and Huckleberry Finn come into twelve thousand dollars in gold and Huck is taken in by Widow Douglas to be civilized, the poor lad chafes pitifully against this new condition. On Tom's insistence, Huck tries to see the thing out, though clean sheets and new clothes and school don't agree with him.

The straw that breaks poor Huckleberry's back arrives one night in the form of his father. Old Pap Finn hasn't been seen for a year, but now the drunkard, determined to get his hands on Huck's fortune, comes to make life miserable for his son.

To further his own scheme, Old Finn kidnaps Huckleberry and secretes him in an isolated cabin in the woods. At first Huck is delighted to live once again the natural life. But finally the beatings of his brutal drunkard father get too much for him, and he waits until Pap goes off to town one day, and then effects his escape—not before making arrangements that will lead everyone to believe that he has been murdered.

In this adventure Huck proves himself Tom's equal for

imagination and detail, and as he drifts down the river to Jackson's Island, where he intends to hide, he hears the booming of cannon which indicates that the villagers have indeed assumed that he is dead and drowned.

Huck makes camp for several days on Jackson's Island, when much to his surprise he encounters Jim, the Negro slave of Aunt Sally Watson. Jim has run away, as he has heard Aunt Sally saying that she intends to sell him South. Huckleberry and Jim agree to help each other in their mutual escape.

It is flood time, and the two are easily able to secure a raft for themselves. When a deserted house comes floating down the river, they enter it to "borrow" such provisions as they can find. There is a dead man lying in the house—Jim discovers the body, which Huck refuses to look at—and that is enough to frighten the two away from their find. The house provides them with clothes and miscellaneous implements, which, added to the store that Huckleberry has taken from his Pap's cabin, see the boys well supplied for the long journey ahead.

Down the Mississippi float the two runaways on their raft, and many adventures befall them. On one occasion they come upon a group of men planning a murder. A different time, Huck disguises himself as a girl to reconnoiter, but is discovered to be a boy. Later they are overtaken by men looking for runaway Negro slaves. But each time, Huckleberry's fantastic imagination and quick-wagging tongue save the day.

Their first disaster occurs when the raft is hit by a passing steamboat. Just before it hits, Huck dives over one side and Jim dives over the other, and the two are separated. Huckleberry makes his way to the shore where he is taken in by the Grangerford family—an old, wealthy, and aristocratic clan that has been having a feud for two generations with the nearby Shepherdsons. Huckleberry enjoys this family—and particularly having his own bodyservant, a slave who is assigned exclusively to Huckleberry's care. It is from this old Negro that Huck learns of Jim's escape from the river. He is being hidden secretly in a clump of trees by the Grangerford slaves. Huck goes to visit him, and as Jim is as suited with arrangements as Huckleberry, they decide to leave things as they are. However, the Grangerford-Shepherdson feud breaks out in earnest, and when Huck and Jim see the wholesale slaughter that ensues, they decide to make their escape. Fortunately the raft has not been wrecked, and Jim has custody of it; so off down the river go the two runaways once more.

Several days later, Huck lands in order to gather wild berries and "borrow" any produce that he may find in a field or garden. Seeing two men run toward him, he bolts—but they soon catch up with him and beg him to save them. Never one to let an unfortunate fellow creature come to harm, Huck welcomes the two aboard the raft, and all hands quickly shove off.

It develops that the two men have not met formally, but that each was about to share a common fate, for both are confidence men who have been discovered, and the people of the town were after them with dogs.

Recognizing in Huck and Jim's comfortably furnished raft an easy, cheap, and pleasant mode of transportation, the two decide to stay. One passes himself off as the Duke of Bridgewater, and the other as the Dauphin, son of Louis the Sixteen and Marry Antonette. Huck doesn't believe this nonsense, but sees no harm in humoring the two. For simplicity's sake, he calls them "The King" and "Duke Bilgewater."

There isn't a trick known to man that these two don't practice: fake revival meetings, theatrical performances, phrenology readings, quack doctoring—the list is nearly endless. The raft stops at every town, so that the Duke and the King can ply their various trades—but, of course, with the law always one step behind them, they are forced to move pretty quickly down the river.

The most outrageous trick of all comes when the two charlatans learn about a bequest to two Englishmen who have not yet shown up to claim it. Pumping an innocent yokel for detailed information, they are soon in position to pass themselves off as the Englishmen, and they—and Huckleberry, who is forced to pose as their servant, Adolphus—are installed as guests of honor in the home of the late Peter Wilks, their supposed brother and benefactor.

Huck is all amazement and admiration for the ease with which these two operate in their attempt to steal the entire Wilks fortune from his three orphaned daughters. But when the three girls—Miss Mary Jane, Miss Joanna, and Miss Susan —are good to him, Huck determines to help them. Confiding in Mary Jane, he arranges for the exposure of the Duke and the King, and for the return of the property to its rightful heirs. Before the plan can be executed, however, along come two men who *also* claim to be the English brothers.

This turn of circumstance leads to a great commotion, with both pairs of men insisting on their rights to the inheritance. At last it is determined to dig up the body to check it for a tattoo mark; whoever accurately identifies the tattoo is to be considered legal heir. In the melee that follows, Huck determines to make his escape. He heads for the hidden raft and pushes off—but not without great heaviness of heart, for no sooner is he aboard when he discovers that the Duke and the King are also, their plans having been foiled. (Fortunately, however, they don't suspect Huckleberry.)

Further on in their journey, the King and Duke play the most dastardly trick of all. When Huckleberry is away from the raft, they sell poor Jim to a man named Phelps for forty dollars, telling Phelps that there is a reward of $800 posted for Jim which they themselves don't have time to collect, and which Phelps can collect instead.

This treachery on their part kills whatever spark of kindness Huck may have had left for the two scoundrels; and when they play their confidence games one time too often, and are ridden out of a town tarred and feathered on a rail, Huckleberry feels no compassion for them.

Huck now makes his way to the Phelps farm, determined to make up some story that will enable him to learn the fate of Jim. As he approaches, he is welcomed by old Mrs. Phelps as though he were expected; and discovering that the Phelpses *are* waiting for a boy named Tom and have mistaken Huck for him, Huck decides to play along. He is having a difficult time keeping undiscovered, however, as they keep asking him questions about "home" and "the folks" which he is at a loss to answer—until he discovers that the Tom they think him to be is none other than Tom Sawyer! From then on things go smoothly, since Huckleberry is as conversant with the Sawyer family history as if it were his own.

Intercepting the real Tom when he does arrive, Huck explains all that has happened; and Tom is content to pass himself off to his Aunt and Uncle Phelps as Sid Sawyer, his own younger half brother. Tom is as enthusiastic as Huck at the idea of rescuing Jim, who is kept locked up in a small shed behind the house.

Huck describes a plan for effecting the rescue which is simple and foolproof. But its very simplicity and lack of danger and guarantee of success are the things that turn Tom away from it. Tom Sawyer is too full of the books he has read about pirates and medieval prisoners and royal dungeons. He believes the escape must be done *right* if it is to be any good at all—and "right" means elaborate preparations of the most far-fetched sort, preparations which upset the entire Phelps household, which convince Jim that his last hour is at hand, and which postpone the actual rescue of the poor Negro for several weeks.

At last, all the arrangements suit Tom perfectly, and the escape is staged. In the ensuing confusion—Tom had written an anonymous letter *warning* the Phelpses that Jim is to be taken that night—Tom is shot in the calf of the leg.

Safely on the raft, Tom urges Huck and Jim to push off; but Jim refuses. He knows that were his position and Tom's reversed, Tom would not leave without getting a doctor. So Huckleberry fetches a doctor to care for Tom. Of course, the doctor spots Jim at once as the Phelps's runaway, and the poor Negro is taken back, this time chained in double irons.

Things seem to be going from bad to worse for the boys and Jim but all turns out happily. Tom's Aunt Polly arrives to see for herself why her sister talks about "Sid" in her letters, when Sid is still at home. She, of course, recognizes Huckleberry, and nearly faints as she thinks him to be a ghost.

Huckleberry tells all about his adventures. Tom reveals that Jim must be freed as he has been free all along, Aunt Sally having died and given the slave his freedom in her will. (Huck is disgusted that the escape plans were so elaborate since Tom knew Jim was already free and only needed to say so; but Tom is satisfied with the *adventure* of the thing.)

Huck does not want to return to St. Petersburg, as he still fears his father. But Jim quiets him on that point, telling him that the dead man in the house they had seen floating down the river was none other than old Pap Finn.

The Phelpses are so impressed with Huckleberry that they invite him to live with them and be "civilized." But Huck determines to escape. As he observes, "she's going to adopt me and sivilize me, and I can't stand it. I been there before."

WASHINGTON SQUARE

Henry James

Henry James was born in New York City in 1843 into a family whose members, thanks to the fortune amassed by James's grandfather, did not have to earn their own livings. James's father was a noted theologian; his older brother William was to become an eminent philosopher and psychologist. Henry James was educated by private tutors in the United States and Europe and he briefly attended Harvard Law School in 1862. He began to publish his stories in 1864 in The Atlantic Monthly. In 1876 he settled permanently in London, and became a British citizen in 1915, one year before his death.

Very much apart from the dominant American literary trends, realism and romanticism, James's writings were until some time after his death admired more in England than in America. A reappraisal by American critics in the 1930s has resulted in the virtual enshrinement of Henry James as America's greatest practitioner of the art of fiction; many distinguished critics, British and American, regard him as a stylist unequaled in the English language. James's fiction is the work of a highly sophisticated and intelligent observer of the subtleties of behavior among people who are themselves highly sophisticated and intelligent. A typical James novel contains little plot, less action, and no violence; James is not concerned with the active processes of living, but with the internal processes of experience. Referred to as "The Master" by his admirers, James has written, besides fiction, works of literary criticism which have the status of classics.

Washington Square (1881), from James's early period, has become one of the best known of his stories. Catherine Sloper, a prototype Jamesian heroine, must deal with men who either do not consider her, or who want to take advantage of her wealth; she eventually finds the moral strength which sustains her and provides her with a lonely, inner triumph.

The Turn of the Screw (1898), a product of James's middle period, is a chilling tale which has long fascinated readers and critics with its many unanswered questions. Is the governess reliable, or is she the victim of repressed fantasies which derange her faculties, and those of the children of whom she is in charge? Do the ghosts really exist? Are the children themselves possessed of evil? The arguments persist, and critics have found support in the story for widely opposing interpretations.

The Golden Bowl (1904) *was one of James's last major works. It is an example of the "international novel," or novel of Americans in Europe, a literary genre which James perfected. An extremely complex book, it deals with most of the themes which had concerned James in his earlier works; these themes are developed by presenting a series of factors which clash, interact, and eventually enrich each other: European versus American, life versus art, good versus evil, decadence versus vitality. These themes are woven by James into an elaborate tapestry, the very existence of which is its only meaning. In the art of Henry James, problems are raised, rather than solved.*

The scene is fashionable New York, in the early half of the nineteenth century.

Dr. Austin Sloper marries the wealthy Catherine Harrington; and, as he himself is a much sought-after physician, he is soon master of a large personal fortune. He suffers two grievous blows during the early years of his marriage: the first is the death of his three-year-old son; the second is the death, two years later, of his wife, who has just given birth to a daughter. Dr. Sloper never quite forgives this child for causing his wife's death and for being female, and little Catherine is raised in a remote and unloving atmosphere.

When Catherine is ten years old, Dr. Sloper introduces into his household in Washington Square his widowed sister, Lavinia Penniman, and puts her in charge of his daughter's upbringing. Childless and without money, Lavinia is an incurable romantic, and fancies that she will "make something" of Catherine.

Dr. Sloper has no such illusions. Completely objective about his daughter, he observes that Catherine is neither beautiful nor brilliant. He charges Lavinia with the responsibility, merely, of making her good.

During Catherine's sixteenth year, she goes to her first party. It is at the home of Dr. Sloper's second sister, Mrs. Almond, and is in honor of the engagement of young Marian Almond to Mr. Arthur Townsend. At the party, Catherine is introduced to Arthur's brother, the handsome and suave, if indolent, Morris Townsend. Lavinia is enraptured that the girl should have attracted the notice of such a dashing young man, and babbles on in romantic fantasy. Dr. Sloper, however, is unimpressed. Any man, he believes, who seeks plain, dull Catherine must be either a fool or a scoundrel. As for

Catherine, she maintains her usual façade of passivity; but the truth is that she has fallen in love with Morris Townsend.

The practical Mrs. Almond urges Dr. Sloper to encourage the romance. Even if Townsend should prove a fortune-hunter, she believes, it will be a good match for Catherine; for clearly the girl does have the requisite fortune, and Townsend is a more brilliant man than Catherine might otherwise hope for.

Dr. Sloper refuses to accept such a proposition. He believes Townsend to be after Catherine's money; and when the young man comes to him and tells him of his intention to woo Catherine, Sloper is only confirmed in his prejudices against Townsend.

Catherine and Morris continue their courtship nevertheless, encouraged by the romantic Mrs. Penniman. It is her belief that her brother will soon relent, seeing how fixed Catherine is on her choice, and will consent to the marriage. To Catherine, his yielding is imperative, as she is unwilling to do anything without her father's blessing. To Morris, Sloper's consent is equally urgent; for without it, he will lose the fortune on which he has set his sights.

Finally Catherine and Morris inform Dr. Sloper of their engagement, and Morris declares that he will never give up Catherine. The doctor, however, counts on inspiring terror in his daughter; and of course, he tells her that he will disinherit her if she marries without his consent. (She has, from her mother, inherited ten thousand a year—but this is not enough for Townsend, and he urges Catherine to win her father's consent.)

To substantiate his own impressions of Morris as a grasping rogue, Dr. Sloper pays a visit to Townsend's widowed sister, Mrs. Montgomery, with whom Townsend lives. The woman knows how important to her brother is the prospect of marrying the heiress of Washington Square, and she is reluctant to disclose anything to his discredit. But Sloper learns what he had set out to learn, and at the end of the interview, Mrs. Montgomery murmurs impetuously, "Don't let her marry him!"

Now the silent battle is on in earnest between the firm will of Dr. Sloper and the equally firm will of his daughter. Lavinia serves as emissary between the young lovers, and keeps Morris' hopes up about her brother's eventually relenting.

Indeed, she urges Morris to marry Catherine first, and get Sloper's approval later. But Morris is too shrewd for this advice; to marry the girl without her father's consent is to saddle himself with a dull wife and gamble on the future. Only by winning the doctor's consent—and fortune—first, is Morris willing to take on the burden of making Catherine his wife.

Dr. Sloper has, at least, come to appreciate Catherine's unaggressive obstinacy. He had not imagined that so dull a girl could remain so fixed in a single purpose. To force her to give up Morris, he pretends to believe that Catherine is merely waiting for his own death, so that she then may inherit his wealth and marry against his wishes. To this the girl replies simply that that is not her intention; if she does not marry Morris before her father's death, she says, she will not marry him afterward.

Seeing that his psychological attacks on Catherine are of no avail, the doctor now proposes that Catherine accompany him for a tour of Europe. She agrees. It is his hope that the six-month absence from New York will help put Morris out of Catherine's mind; it is her hope that, alone with her father viewing the scenic beauties of the Continent, she will find him in a more receptive frame of mind. And so the trip is made—but neither hope is realized. At the end of the six months' tour, Catherine is as steadfast as Dr. Sloper is intractable.

During the Slopers' absence, Lavinia has been in frequent contact with Morris, constantly encouraging him and urging him to marry Catherine, come what may. Morris cannot abide the meddlesome old woman, but sees that he must put up with her. When, however, on the Slopers' return to New York he sees that he is no closer to his goal than he had been six months earlier, he at last determines to give up Catherine—and tells Lavinia of his intention in no uncertain terms, opening her eyes for the first time to his lack of feeling for Catherine and to his real motive in wooing her.

Crushed by this disillusionment, and her heart breaking for her niece, Lavinia urges Morris to break with Catherine gently, and to this he agrees. In their final meeting, he proposes several unconvincing reasons for having to go away for a while, and assures Catherine that he will write and return to her soon. When the door closes behind him, however, Catherine sees that he is leaving her forever. For a day she is inconsolable and remains in her room; but the next day she emerges, seemingly as calm and passive as ever.

Sloper takes great delight in having, at last, been proved right in his estimate of Townsend, but Catherine is determined to give him as little satisfaction as possible. She tells her father that she has broken her engagement and sent Morris away. To this the cruel doctor, who insists on twisting the knife, replies that it was most unkind of her to have encouraged the young man for so long, only to disappoint him and break his heart.

The subject of Morris Townsend is not again referred to in the house in Washington Square for many years, and life goes on as if there had never been such a person. Catherine continues to be quiet, dutiful, and passive; and though Lavinia senses the deep wound that must burn in the girl's bosom, she is frustrated by Catherine's refusal to share it.

Then one day, believing that his death is not far off, Dr. Sloper raises the matter with Catherine once again. He asks her to promise that after his death she will not marry Townsend. This Catherine refuses to do. She says that she has already given her word on the subject once, and will not do so again.

Later, when Sloper dies, it is discovered that he has all but cut Catherine out of his will—using phraseology that makes public his suspicion that she will be prey to fortune-hunting blackguards. But even this seems to make no real impression on Catherine.

Shortly after Sloper's death, Lavinia again encounters Morris. She is impressed with the fact that he has aged, and is much more subdued in manner than before. Still single, Morris expresses interest in meeting Catherine again, but the girl declines, in spite of Lavinia's urging.

Unexpectedly, however, Morris arrives at the house at Washington Square, and is ushered in to Catherine. But the girl—as unemotional as ever—simply tells him that he should not have come. She has no wish to renew their acquaintance.

Sending him away for the last time, she hears the door close behind him, and quietly returns to the needlework that lies in her lap. The moment seems to prophesy the entirety of Catherine Sloper's future.

THE TURN OF THE SCREW

Henry James

It is during a house party at the Christmas holidays that
ghost stories are being told. A member of the party, Douglas,
indicates that he has a terrible tale to share with the others.
Rather than tell it, he sends to his home for a manuscript
written years before by the chief participant in the tale—a
governess. When the manuscript arrives, he reads it to the
assembled party. . . .

The governess has been hired by a London bachelor to
care for his orphaned niece and nephew, eight-year-old
Flora and, during his school holidays, ten-year-old Miles. The
governess finds oppressive the idea that she is to live in the
remote country house, Bly, with only the housekeeper, Mrs.
Grose, as a companion; and she finds odd the gentleman's
stricture that he is not to be communicated with concerning
the children. But she is young—just out of school—and so she
accepts the position.

Fortunately Bly, though an ancient home, is a comfortable
one; Mrs. Grose proves to be the best-hearted woman imaginable, and little Flora is an angel. The governess considers
herself fortunate.

The happy mood is dispelled, however, when a letter arrives from the boarding school at which Miles has been, saying that he is expelled. The governess imagines all sorts of
things—the letter does not specify a reason for Miles's ex-
pulsion—but when the boy himself arrives, the governess is
enchanted with him.

Miles and Flora are, without doubt, the most beautiful,
most intelligent, most sensitive children she has ever known.
Indeed, they are almost *too* good—but this thought does not
enter the governess's mind until she has a frightening experience. She sees, through a window, a strange man standing
on a hill, staring intently down at Bly. The man is handsome
and well dressed—but there is a coarseness about him, and
an air of evil, that frightens the young governess. However,
she decides that he must be a chance intruder, and when he

turns and walks away, she succeeds in putting him out of her mind.

Several days later, the governess is sitting over a book, when, looking up suddenly, she sees, pressed against the window glass, the face of the same man. She lets out a small shriek, and he again disappears.

Now the governess is truly frightened, and she confides in Mrs. Grose. Upon hearing the man described, Mrs. Grose explains that it can be none other than Peter Quint, who had been butler in the house several years before. When the governess asks where Quint works now, Mrs. Grose is forced to tell her that Quint is dead.

The governess determines to get Quint's entire story from Mrs. Grose. She learns that Quint was, indeed, a coarse and evil man who had achieved ascendancy at Bly, and had complete charge of the house. Moreover, he had carried on an affair with the former governess, the frail Miss Jessel—an affair about which Miles and Flora had known. Miss Jessel, too, is now dead.

When the governess sees the apparition of Miss Jessel in the garden a few days later, terror strikes to the very core of her existence. And after making a number of careful observations, the governess at last realizes what is happening: Quint and Miss Jessel have come back to Bly to claim the souls of Miles and Flora—to drag the innocent children into their world of evil and damnation.

Overcoming her initial feeling of helplessness, the governess determines that she must, at all costs, save the children's souls from the darkness that closes in upon them. She confides in Mrs. Grose, who agrees, in her simple way, to help in any way she can.

The task is not a simple one, however, because it soon becomes clear that Miles and Flora *know* what is happening—that they seek communication with Quint and Miss Jessel, and that they choose themselves to move closer and closer to the dark adventure which the spirits seem to promise.

The governess determines that she dare not speak of Quint to Miles until the boy has spoken first. She now recognizes that what she had imagined to be niceness in the children is, in fact, slyness and secretiveness. It is as though she and they have made a silent pact, under which all agree to say nothing at all about any subject that may prove unpleasant.

However, with the increasing reappearance of Quint and Miss Jessel, the governess finds it harder and harder to pretend with her little charges that she is unaware of what is going on. But when she does broach the subject in any way, no matter how obliquely, Miles's shrewd mind is too quick for her, as is Flora's. Both children give her glib, almost believable answers and explanations for their behavior. They remain the picture of sweetness and innocence, even when she knows they are dissembling.

Though the governess's skill at dealing with the crisis seems not to be increasing, her determination to deal with it does. At last she sees that she must take direct action.

Her opportunity comes on a Sunday afternoon when, despite her intense efforts to keep both children within her sight, they manage to separate. Miles is in the upstairs study, and Flora has left the house. The governess realizes that with the boy is Quint, and with the girl, Miss Jessel. Sensing that Flora is less involved with the spirits, being younger, she determines to leave Miles and go after his sister. Mrs. Grose accompanies her.

They come upon the child in an almost trance-like state, and know instantly that she has been with Miss Jessel. When Flora sees them, she begins walking toward them in silence, but with an expression of such evil knowingness upon her face that Mrs. Grose shudders.

Suddenly the governess sees Miss Jessel, and points her out to Mrs. Grose, as Flora looks terrified. But, alas! To Mrs. Grose the spirit is invisible—and when she says as much, Flora, too, denies seeing the dead woman and accuses the governess of being mad.

That night Flora sleeps in Mrs. Grose's room, and the old housekeeper hears and observes such things of the child that she can no longer avoid accepting the reality of what the governess has told her. Together, Mrs. Grose and the governess agree that Flora must be removed at once from Bly if she is to be saved from the danger that threatens her. Making sure that the child has no opportunity to communicate with Miles before leaving, Mrs. Grose takes her away to London early the next morning, leaving the governess to cope with Miles as best she can.

When Miles discovers that Flora is gone and that he is alone with the governess, the cultivated reserve behind which he has for so long masked his true feelings begins to crack. He struggles, it appears to the governess, to make a confession of some sort.

This is the moment she has waited for, and she presses her advantage. Bit by bit, fragments of emotion come from the boy. Clearly he is in great inner turmoil—torn between a desire to go on with the dark adventure, to learn more and more of the secrets Quint would share with him, and a desire to avail himself of the governess's love and protection, to find peace in her assurance that she will save him.

Suddenly, just as the governess believes that he is about to confess the entire experience, Miles's manner changes, and he says that he will tell her all later, but that he must go out of the house now.

Turning to the window, the governess sees the intense face of Quint, staring at the boy. She understands that to let Miles go now is to lose him to the powers of darkness forever.

Clasping her arms around the boy, she beseeches him to confess. Crying desperately, Miles tries—and at last he speaks Quint's name. The governess knows that she has triumphed, and that Miles is saved.

Holding his shaking body in her arms, she turns to the window in time to see Quint's look of pain and defeat. Slowly Quint turns and walks away, and the governess knows that he will never return.

Joyously she rocks Miles's body in her arms, knowing that he is saved. But her joy lasts only for a moment. Miles is dead.

THE GOLDEN BOWL

Henry James

Fanny Assingham is one of those London women who take a deep and sustained interest in the intimate lives of their friends. Perceptive, shrewd, witty, she is always on the alert for signs of change in the emotional climate. So when her good friend Amerigo, an Italian Prince, makes clear that he is looking for a wife—with a large fortune attached—Fanny thinks at once of dear Maggie Verver. Maggie, the only child of the American millionaire Adam Verver, is pretty, good-natured, and, above all, innocent of all evil; and as Fanny has the highest opinion of the Prince, she brings the two together. Maggie falls deeply in love with the Prince; and as she is equipped with the requisite millions, they become engaged.

The Prince is determined to earn his good fortune by being an exemplary husband and son-in-law. More than anything else, he wishes not to pain Maggie or Adam Verver. It is for this reason that several days before his marriage he is somewhat taken aback by the appearance in London of Charlotte Stant.

Several years before, he and Charlotte had been lovers. But she is as poor as the Prince; and as both recognized the Prince's need for money, they had agreed to part. Now, Charlotte insists on a final day with the Prince—ostensibly to shop with his help for a suitable wedding gift for Maggie. (Maggie and Charlotte have been friends from childhood, but Maggie has no idea that Charlotte even knows Amerigo, much less that she has been passionately in love with him.)

In an out-of-the-way curio shop Charlotte finds the perfect gift for Maggie: a small crystal bowl, gilded. The Prince demurs, however, as he has perceived that the bowl has a tiny crack, and that it, therefore, would be an ill omen as a wedding gift. He offers to buy it as a gift to Charlotte from himself; but she declines for the same reason. In their discussion of the bowl—they speak in Italian—their relationship of old is redefined. They are only slightly disconcerted to find that the curio shopkeeper has overheard and understood them. The day ends without their finding a gift for Maggie.

Her promised last hour with Amerigo over, Charlotte returns to America "to find a suitable match" for herself, and the Prince and Maggie are married.

A year goes by in complete bliss for Maggie. She has her handsome husband, whom she loves deeply; she has her beautiful baby, the Principino; and she has her adored father, Adam Verver. Life at Fawns, the English country home of the Ververs, is idyllic.

But two things bother Maggie. One is the comparative quiet of Fawns, and the idea that there is something wicked in the uselessness of the life that she leads. To remedy this, she proposes that Charlotte Stant—who is again in London—be invited to stay with them. Not only will Charlotte bring life to Fawns, Maggie thinks, but Maggie will be able to help her by relieving her poverty-stricken way of life, and by introducing her to people of social rank.

The other thing bothering Maggie is that her father remains single. The millionaire himself is disturbed by the fact that he is so often besieged by maiden ladies obviously intent on making him their prey. Maggie tells her father that for her sake—for her peace of mind—he should remarry; then Maggie will not feel as deeply as she does that her own happy marriage has taken her away from her father. Mr. Verver at last agrees for Maggie's sake to consider the idea of remarriage.

Charlotte arrives at Fawns, and the entire household is animated by her presence. Charlotte is a singular individual; poor and without relations, she nonetheless manages to live with a flair and verve that Maggie admires and almost envies.

Prince Amerigo has long been anxious to pay a visit to his native Italy, and with Charlotte installed at Fawns, Maggie finally feels that she can safely leave her father. So the Prince and Princess depart for the Continent, leaving Adam Verver and Charlotte behind. Before they return, a telegram arrives at Rome informing them of the change that has occurred in the relationship of the two left back at Fawns. Adam Verver, taking Maggie's instructions to heart, has found that he is entranced with Charlotte. And when the millionaire has proposed to her, Charlotte, hesitating only briefly, has accepted.

To Fanny Assingham, who has remained a confidante to Maggie, to Charlotte, and to the Prince, the news that Charlotte is to be introduced into the Prince's family is at first disquieting; and she is tempted to tell Adam Verver about Charlotte's past relationship with Amerigo. But at last she decides to hold her tongue. As she explains to her husband, Colonel Bob Assingham, she knows Charlotte and the Prince both to be the most scrupulous of individuals; if neither of them fears any complications from Charlotte's becoming Maggie's stepmother, what has she, Fanny, to fear?

The wedding performed, the Ververs take up residence in London's Eaton Square, and the Prince and Princess reside in nearby Portland Place. And the pleasant life that had been lived by the foursome at Fawns now continues in London.

Maggie and Adam Verver, however, find that they cannot do without each other's immediate presence as easily as they had supposed. Mr. Verver finds frequent excuses to drop in at Portland Place to visit his daughter and admire his grandson; and Maggie, in turn, often goes to Eaton Square to look in on her father. More and more, Charlotte and the Prince are thrown into each other's company alone. This unusual circumstance becomes public when Adam Verver refuses to go to a ball because he is sick, and Maggie insists that she, rather than Charlotte, stay behind and nurse him. At the ball, everyone is struck by Charlotte's beauty—and Fanny is not the only person to note that the Prince and Charlotte are together, unaccompanied by their *sposi*.

The relationship that has been so long dormant can no longer remain so under such pressures, and at last Charlotte and the Prince become lovers once again. They are the epitome of discretion, and both agree on the urgent importance of never hurting Maggie or Adam Verver. But those two, father and daughter, are so completely caught up in their relationship with one another that Amerigo and Charlotte, it would seem, can have their cake and eat it too.

They count on Maggie's innocence. They count on Maggie's goodness of heart. But what they fail to count on is the depth of Maggie's perception. That she does not always speak or act is no indication that she does not think. Soon the young Princess senses that something is amiss in her pretty family picture.

Fanny, who feels remotely responsible for what has come to pass, is determined to save Maggie from pain, even if she has to lie herself black in the face to do it. When Maggie broaches the topic of her suspicions, therefore, in confidence to Fanny, Fanny pooh-poohs them away, swearing that there can be nothing between Charlotte and Amerigo.

Fanny's deception is not to work, however. Shopping for a birthday present for her father, Maggie comes across the little golden bowl, rejected four years earlier by Charlotte and the Prince. Not suspecting the flaw in the bowl, she buys it, and at an exorbitant price. The curio dealer, however, is remorseful, and he goes to Maggie's house to tell her of the crack in the crystal. There, he sees on the mantlepiece pictures of the Prince and of Charlotte. They recall to him the scene of four years before, and innocently he repeats the details of it to Maggie.

When Maggie confronts Fanny with this evidence, Fanny perseveres in her attempt to convince Maggie that the girl is imagining much that is untrue. To symbolize an end to the matter, Fanny smashes the golden bowl. The sound of it brings the Prince into the room, and Maggie tells him all that she has learned. He neither denies nor defends himself, but asks merely whether Charlotte knows that Maggie knows about the liaison. "Find out for yourself," Maggie tells him.

Maggie is determined to win her husband back, but in such a way that her father, Adam Verver, may never be disillusioned about the fidelity of his own wife. This need for secrecy forces Maggie to think things through very carefully, and allows her to move and speak only very slowly and enigmatically.

The two families return to Fawns, and it is there that Maggie discovers, from sly hints that her father drops, that he, too, has suspected the relationship between Charlotte and Amerigo, and that he has refrained from speaking for fear that Maggie may not know of it and be pained. The two never discuss the subject openly, but each understands the other.

Maggie takes hope for herself from the observation that Amerigo has said nothing to Charlotte. And though Maggie has sympathy for Charlotte in the torments that she now must be enduring—Charlotte knows that something has caused the Prince to cool toward her, but cannot even guess at the reason—Maggie believes that Amerigo's silence is a sign that he will return to her.

To simplify matters, Adam Verver determines to go with Charlotte to America. He knows that he need not offer any explanations for returning to his native land, where he is in the process of building and endowing a great museum of fine arts; and he knows, too, that Charlotte cannot possibly protest the move.

It is Charlotte who breaks the news to Maggie, passing the decision off as her own. She tells Maggie that though she knows how deeply Maggie loves Adam Verver, he is, after all, Charlotte's husband, and Charlotte now wants him to herself. Maggie accepts Charlotte's version of the story without even hinting at what she knows to be the truth.

It is this nobility in Maggie that finally opens Amerigo's eyes to the true worth and value of his little American Princess. And before too long, he and Maggie are again to know the perfect happiness and purity represented by the little golden bowl—before it was cracked.

THE AGE OF INNOCENCE

Edith Wharton

Edith Wharton, born Edith Newbold Jones in New York City in 1862, was a member of a wealthy and distinguished family. She was educated in New York and Europe by private tutors, and married Edward Wharton in 1885. She settled permanently in France in 1907, where she maintained a brilliant salon of writers, critics, and artists. Her husband had a severe emotional breakdown in 1908, and the Whartons were divorced in 1913. For her efforts on behalf of France during the First World War, she was made an officer of the Legion of Honor. She lived in Paris until her death in 1937, returning to America once, in 1923, to receive an honorary degree from Yale University.

Edith Wharton was a great friend and admirer of Henry James, with whom she is often compared because of their similar backgrounds. Her fiction, however, is not imitative of James, and tends to be more pointed, sardonic, and tragic than his; both were elegant stylists, with Wharton the less cerebral and more direct of the two. Besides novels she wrote short stories, books of travel and criticism, and poetry.

The Age of Innocence, which was published in 1920, is a hard, penetrating look into New York society of the 1870s. This novel considers the social conventions which determine the feelings and actions of the characters, and finds these conventions unnatural and limiting, more likely to result in vulgarity than in any true refinement of spirit. Mrs. Wharton castigates not only her generation: young Dallas Archer, a man of the twentieth century, is no more liberated from the stifling values of his time than his parents were from the values of theirs.

The world of society in New York City in the 1870s comprises a very tightly knit group of wealthy families—*old* wealthy families. Mrs. Manson Mingott is related to Medora Manson; Newland Archer to van der Luyden Newland; Emerson Sillerton to Sillerton Jackson. Along with the Leffertses, the Dallases, and a few others, these are the families that dominate the *haut monde*. Their code is rigid, their way of life unassailable—at least from their own point of view.

Newland Archer, well-to-do young attorney, adores society, and all it stands for. As he sits in the Club box at the opera, continually gazing over at his beloved May Welland, who sits in Mrs. Manson Mingott's box, he feels how tremendously right he is to have picked her. Everything about May is perfect: her innocence, her charm, her fair beauty. Newland shares the surprise of the others in his set that Mrs. Mingott has seen fit to allow her other niece, Ellen Olenska, to attend the opera in May's company.

Ellen Olenska has suffered an impetuous, almost Bohemian, upbringing by her aunt, Medora Manson, with the result that the dark, beautiful girl has never been considered quite suitable by society. And, bringing scandal and shame to all her New York friends, the girl ran off when quite young, and married the European nobleman, Count Stanislas Olenski. The man proved to be a brute, and Ellen escaped him, but not without raising some rumors about the nature of her relationship with Olenski's secretary, the man who had been her protector during her marital crisis. Now Ellen has returned to America to begin life again, and only someone as defiant of authority—and as aware of her own wealth, rank, and power in society—as old Catherine Mingott would have dared present Ellen to society once more.

Catherine Mingott's show of bravado is, according to some, typical of the "deterioration" of good society. Each year, these pessimists observe, there is a lowering of standards. More and more "strangers" are admitted into the closed ranks. As one wag notes, it won't be long before they will be happy to marry their children to Julius Beaufort's bastards. (Beaufort is a parvenu, notorious for his relationship with the "fancy woman" Fanny Ring.)

Society is not so easily to be won over, however; and when Mrs. Mingott issues invitations to a dinner "to meet Ellen Olenska," most of the invitations are declined. Newland feels that it is his responsibility to intervene on Ellen's behalf, as May Welland, his fiancée, is Ellen's cousin. Accordingly Newland goes to the most influential society couple of all, the van der Luydens, and persuades them to "take up" Ellen. Thus, the rest of society is forced to accept the girl.

Newland's engagement to May is announced, and the pair

are enraptured with each other. The betrothal is to last about a year and a half; the marriage cannot possibly be hastened, in view of the elaborate preparations required: a house must be bought and furnished; May must secure her trosseau; linens, china, silver, plate must be purchased; and so forth.

May is particularly anxious that Newland be nice to "poor cousin Ellen." Accordingly, when the Wellands leave for their annual winter trip to St. Augustine, taking May with them, Newland resolves to perform little niceties for his dark, mysterious cousin-to-be.

Newland, who from time to time has had flashes of insight into the shallowness of the lives led by the people he knows best and admires most, has been able to suppress any chance thinking that life among the four hundred is not the only, or even the best, life available. But as he gets to know Ellen Olenska better, it becomes more and more apparent to him that to live life fully, one must live more as she does: impetuously, emotionally, freely.

Ellen has seen and suffered much, and her objective in returning to New York is to forget the pain of the past and begin life again. But she is unprepared for the many subtle demands that her family—for so half of society must be termed—finds necessary to make of her. For instance, one of the most vital men she has met in New York is Julius Beaufort, who is tolerated, if not accepted, by society for his having married society's own Regina Dallas. It is Newland's task to inform Ellen that it is not proper for her to be seen in Beaufort's company. Again, Ellen attends parties given by the *nouveau riche* Mrs. Lemuel Struthers, parties at which she can meet the artists, writers, and actors of the day; and society must inform her that this is quite improper of her, that Mrs. Struthers is not someone that Ellen may know.

The crisis in Ellen's readjustment to society comes when she asks her attorneys—the firm Newland works for—to secure her divorce. The families rise in horror at the scandal it would cause—Count Olenski has threatened to accuse Ellen of having been the mistress of his secretary, the man who helped her escape from the Count, if she insists on getting a divorce. Newland takes the responsibility for opening Ellen's eyes to the necessity of her remaining married to Olenski, and she bows to his superior judgment.

It is at this point that Newland makes a horrifying discovery: he is falling in love with Ellen. To save himself, he rushes off to St. Augustine, where he insists that May marry him immediately instead of waiting out their engagement. May, in the quaint and quiet way in which all society women manage to have things their own way without seeming in the least to have any opinions or preferences of their own, shows Newland that it is impossible. Newland returns to New York, believing himself free to declare himself to Ellen. She, in turn, avows that she loves Newland, too, but can only love him so long as he is true to May and makes no attempt to deepen the attachment which Ellen now sees growing between Newland and herself. Ellen manages to convince old Catherine Mingott that it is necessary that Newland and May be allowed to marry at once, and so May's parents consent. Newland and May are married at Grace Church in the wedding of the year.

During the honeymoon, Newland—whose values have begun to be reshaped by his acquaintance with the down-to-earth Ellen—has his eyes opened as to just what kind of woman he has married. May is, superficially, innocent and subservient; but in reality, she has all the prejudices and snobberies of her set, and in her own winsome way manages to have everything done as she likes. Newland finds her something of a bore. Indeed, the only interesting conversation he has during their Grand Tour is with a French tutor named Rivière, whom he meets in London. This Rivière gives Newland an increased appreciation of the fact that somewhere, somehow—outside the sphere in which Newland moves—a life of vitality, of action, of interest, and of energy can be lived.

It is several years before Newland sees Ellen Olenska again, but he is never able to hear her name without feeling in his bosom a strangling emotion. One summer, when "everyone" is staying in Newport, he learns that Ellen is staying not far away, in Portsmouth, with the unfashionable Blenchers. At first he resists meeting her, but when he becomes aware, from a slip May makes, that a plot is afoot among the families to force Ellen to return to her brutish husband—a plot of which he has been kept in ignorance, as it is known that he will be on Ellen's side in the matter—he determines to see Ellen. At the Blenchers', he learns that she has gone to Boston for two days, and, telling a few lies, Newland arranges to go there.

In Boston he meets Ellen—and the old passion rises. Ellen makes clear to him, however, that the instant he demands that she come to him to consummate their love, she will return to her husband. For the moment, she says, she will not go back to Europe; and her purpose in coming to Boston has been to give that message to an emissary from her husband. By chance, Newland meets the emissary. It is none other than M. Rivière, from whom Newland learns, once and for all, that Ellen's past has been entirely blameless. Newland and Ellen declare their love for one another, and then he returns to Newport and to May. Ellen shortly afterward moves to Washington, D. C., to escape the temptation that Newland presents.

Now there is a new scandal to concern the Mingotts, Mansons, van der Luydens, Wellands, Jacksons, and the rest. Julius Beaufort has been engaged in shady financial operations, and is ruined. His wife, the former Regina Dallas, commits the unpardonable sin of going to old Catherine Mingott and begging her to get the family to stand behind Beaufort until he is on his feet again. Such behavior cannot be countenanced, and Regina's proposal is enough to give Catherine Mingott a stroke.

During her convalescence, old Catherine sends for Ellen, and insists that the girl live with her. Ellen has always been her favorite in the family—she is the only one, thinks old Catherine, who shows the real Manson spunk. And when Ellen braves the scorn of all to go and visit poor Regina Beaufort, for whom she feels great sympathy, Catherine does nothing to stop her.

Now that he is confronted with Ellen's continual presence, Newland can no longer resist her, and he begs her to run off with him. This Ellen refuses to do. But after several clandestine conversations, she at last agrees to meet him several days later, with the understanding that they will become lovers. After this one meeting, however, Ellen assures him, she will return to Europe and her husband; but it is a threat that Newland does not believe.

On the morning of the assignation, however, Newland learns from May that Ellen has gone away—returned to Europe, though not to her husband. Newland is at a loss to explain to himself Ellen's strange behavior; but later he learns that May—clever, shrewd May—had suspected his deepening relationship with her cousin, and had prematurely "confided" in Ellen that Newland and she were to become parents. Again, May has managed, in all innocence and sweetness, to manipulate life so that her own desires are gratified.

Twenty-six years later, Newland has not forgotten Ellen, though he has no idea of her history since she left New York. May has been dead for two years. Newland's three children are all but grown. His eldest son, Dallas, is about to marry charming young Fanny Beaufort, bastard daughter of Julius Beaufort and Fanny Ring. Before his wedding, Dallas insists that his father join him for a tour of the Continent, a trip to which Newland agrees.

In Paris, Dallas tells Newland that he has a surprise for him. They are going to have tea with Aunt Ellen Olenska, of whom Dallas has heard much from his fiancée. Newland, however, refuses to go with his son to meet Ellen. It is the past that matters to him now.

SISTER CARRIE
Theodore Dreiser

Theodore Dreiser was born in 1871 in Terre Haute, Indiana, the twelfth child of German immigrant parents. He attended Indiana University for one year, and left to become a journalist. He worked for several Midwestern papers, eventually becoming a drama critic in St. Louis. He moved to New York in 1894, married, and began to write seriously. Sister Carrie, his first novel, appeared in 1900, and was followed by other novels, short stories, travel books, and autobiographies. Dreiser became interested in socialism in the late 1920s. A major, if continually controversial, novelist of his time, he died in 1945.

Sister Carrie proved to be too shocking and sordid for the American public, and was actually suppressed at the time of its appearance. It was felt that the immorality of the heroine would corrupt the young women of the nation; but, ironically, it was Dreiser's contention that the heroine had herself been corrupted by the society in which she lived. In this novel are contained many of the motifs which were to appear again and again in Dreiser's later novels, and which were, no doubt, inspired by the author's memory of his own youth: poverty, rejection by society, the power of money, and above all, the urgent need of the ambitious outcast to "make it big" at all costs. Sister Carrie was among the first novels to be concerned with the corruption of the American Dream, a theme which has become one of the dominant factors in American fiction of the century.

Eighteen-year-old Caroline Meeber—called from childhood "Sister Carrie" by her family—is on her way to Chicago, the great metropolis of the Midwest. She feels an indefinable yearning for a new and better way of life than she has known in the rural and provincial Columbia City in which she was raised.

On the train, she is pleased to note that she has caught the fancy of a traveling salesman; and though she knows that he is a "masher," she is happy to talk to him. He is the dapper, dashing Charles Drouet, and Carrie thinks him quite fine. When they arrive at the station, they exchange addresses, and Carrie says that he may call upon her.

Once installed in the flat of her married sister, Minnie Hanson, however, Carrie recognizes that she could never entertain Drouet in such a miserable place. Her sister and brother-in-law Sven lead a mean and narrow life. Carrie would rebel against it, but she does not know how she can do better, and so she accepts the confines of her existence.

Her first objective is to get a job, and in spite of her timidity she at last succeeds in finding work in a shoe factory. It is an awful experience for Carrie; the men and women with whom she works are crude and vulgar, the work is dull and tiring, the working conditions primitive, the pay only $4.50 a week. But she senses that she is trapped, and since she gives four dollars a week to Minnie for room and board, she cannot buy herself even a few nice clothes.

That winter she becomes sick, however, and when she recovers it is assumed that she has lost her job. Carrie goes out to find another. During her search, she encounters Charles Drouet, who recognizes her at once. He insists on taking her to dinner in a lovely restaurant, and this experience gives Carrie another glimpse of the fine world for which she longs. When Drouet presses twenty dollars on her, as a "loan," she reluctantly accepts it so that she can buy new clothes.

Such a purchase is not so easily managed under the watchful eyes of the Hansons, however. Carrie is torn between her conscience and her desires. At last she agrees to a proposal of Drouet's that she leave the Hansons and allow herself to be installed in a furnished room in another part of Chicago. And so, without a great moral struggle, Carrie simply becomes "Mrs. Drouet" without benefit of clergy.

Life with Charles is ever so much more to Carrie's taste. Now she has pretty clothes, small luxuries, ease. She feels that she has arrived at a truly satisfactory standard of living; and as Drouet promises to marry her soon, she is happy.

The only friend that Drouet ever brings to their home is G. W. Hurstwood, manager of the fine saloon, Fitzgerald & Moy's. Hurstwood is suave, sophisticated, handsome, mature—as much above Drouet as Drouet is above Sven Hanson. Carrie is impressed. The easygoing Drouet urges Hurstwood to visit Carrie while he, Drouet, is out of town on business. Carrie knows nothing about Hurstwood except that he is charming; he is, in fact, unhappily married to a grasping social climber, and he is more than delighted to find solace in Carrie's company. She is a pretty girl, innocent, sweet, and unspoiled. Soon, she and Hurstwood are in love with each other.

Drouet's lodge, the Elks, get up a benefit performance, and are in need of a young woman to play a leading role. Drouet urges Carrie to accept, and under the name "Carrie Madenda" (Drouet's lodge brothers know him to be single) she makes her debut. Hurstwood is in the audience, and Carrie's performance is so moving that both he and Drouet decide that they must marry her.

As a result of his being seen at the performance, Hurstwood is unable to continue lying to his wife about his activities, and Mrs. Hurstwood threatens to divorce him. He determines to run away with Carrie, and they make plans to do so. Unfortunately, however, Drouet finds out about Carrie's liaison with his friend, and reveals to her that Hurstwood is married. This shocks Carrie tremendously, and she writes to Hurstwood saying that she wishes never to see him again. At the same time, Drouet is too hurt by Carrie to go on with their relationship, and so the girl is now alone.

Hurstwood is desperate, driven mad both by Carrie's coldness and by his wife's insistent demands for money—demands that will lead to a scandalous divorce and his professional ruin. A chance accident at Fitzgerald & Moy's causes the safe to be left open one night, and in a rash moment of madness, Hurstwood steals ten thousand dollars.

The same night he rushes to Carrie's flat, and pretending that Drouet has been hurt in an accident and that he must take her to him at once, Hurstwood manages to get Carrie aboard a train for Canada. On the train he confesses his ruse, and tells Carrie that he cannot live without her. Will she go to Canada with him and marry him?

At first, Carrie is reluctant, as she feels that she has been betrayed. But at last she consents. The two register in a hotel in Montreal as "Mr. and Mrs. Wheeler," and the next day they go through a wedding ceremony, which Carrie, in her naïveté, believes to be legitimate.

Hurstwood—now "Wheeler"—has been tracked down by a detective, and at last he is forced to return most of the money to Fitzgerald & Moy's, in exchange for an assurance that they will not prosecute him.

Now, he and Carrie go to New York, where they take a flat on West Seventy-eighth Street. Hurstwood recognizes how far down he has come in the economic and social ladder, but he determines to make the best of it, and buys a third interest in a saloon.

Carrie gradually becomes more and more discontented with Hurstwood and with her life—it seems that they are continually watching their money—and when she meets and becomes friendly with the wealthy, showy Mrs. Vance, her own comparative poverty galls her.

Through Mrs. Vance she meets Bob Ames, Mrs. Vance's cousin. This handsome, assured young man opens Carrie's eyes to a world beyond that of money and fashion—a world of culture and taste. This new understanding only causes her to chafe more at the increasing narrowness and meanness of her own world.

Now, two years after making his impetuous investment in the saloon, Hurstwood is ruined. He and Carrie are forced to move to a shabbier apartment, and at last there is no money left. During one of their bitter arguments over Hurstwood's inability or unwillingness to get a job, Carrie learns that her marriage to Hurstwood is not a legal one. This is bitter news to her, but she feels duty-bound to stick by Hurstwood.

Now she determines to act upon one of her recurring

fantasies—that of becoming an actress. After making several attempts to find a position, she finally becomes a musical comedy chorus girl at a salary of twelve dollars a week. It is on this meager salary that she and Hurstwood now survive.

He does make one real effort to get a position. A strike has been called of trolley motormen in Brooklyn, and scab labor is being hired. Hurstwood gets such a position, but feelings in the community run so high that there are continual attacks on the scab workers, and after only several runs on the trolley line, Hurstwood bolts, grateful to escape with only minor bruises and wounds. This marks the end of his ambition, and Carrie recognizes that he will never again amount to anything. (She has long since ceased loving him, and has only stayed with him out of a sense of duty.)

A friend of Carrie's in the chorus line urges her to share a furnished room, and Carrie, recognizing that the only way out of her morass is to shed Hurstwood, agrees to go and live with the girl, Lola Osborne.

This move seems to mark a change in Carrie's career. She is raised to leader of the chorus, and then, catching the eye of the producer, is given a small featured role. When the ingenue of the company leaves, Carrie is given her role, and it is with great delight that she reads her name in the theatrical column for the first time, "Carrie Madenda." Meanwhile, her salary has been climbing steadily.

Following the shrewd advice of Lola Osborne, who knows the theatrical ropes, Carrie manages to get an even better role in a production opening that summer. By a curious chance, she becomes the hit of the show—although her role is a nonspeaking one, and all she does is stand about the stage in Quaker dress, frowning. Now her picture appears regularly in the newspapers, and Carrie Madenda is a celebrity. She signs a new contract for $150 a week.

Meanwhile, Hurstwood has deteriorated utterly. He begs for handouts, gets his lodging and food from missionary workers. Ultimately, aware that he is nothing more than a tramp, he spends his last ten cents on a poor furnished bedroom, turns on the gas, and dies. He is buried anonymously in potter's field.

Because of her celebrity, Carrie is now able to live in the fanciest hotels. (Managers give her a minimal rate, knowing that her name on their guest lists will attract customers.)

While staying at the Waldorf, Carrie encounters Charlie Drouet. As handsome and glib as ever, Charlie tries to re-establish his old relationship with Carrie. Having her back would be the biggest feather in his cap, now that she is a star. But Carrie is too experienced and too hardened for him now, and she dismisses him with only the remotest friendliness. From Charlie, she now learns for the first time about Hurst-wood's theft—but the news makes little impression on her. Unfazed, Charlie is soon setting up dates with other young women.

Now Carrie meets Bob Vance again, and he reminds her of the fine world in which she has never moved. He considers musical comedy superficial, and urges Carrie to become a serious actress in dramatic comedy. Lola is aghast at this advice, since Carrie is so successful as a soubrette.

But Carrie's heart is always set on higher goals and brighter worlds. Somewhere, she believes, is happiness. And she is determined to pursue it and track it down. She resolves to become a serious actress.

DEATH COMES FOR THE ARCHBISHOP

Willa Cather

Willa Sibert Cather was born in Winchester, Virginia, in 1876. Nine years later, her family settled in Nebraska on the prairie frontier. She attended the University of Nebraska, and graduated in 1895. After several years in Pittsburgh, she moved to New York, where she had her first collection of short stories published in 1906. She worked on the staff of McClure's Magazine, a journal devoted to exposing corruption in industry and politics. Leaving McClure's, she devoted the remainder of her life to writing; with the publication of her novels of the frontier, she was established as an important novelist. In her later years she wrote works of shorter fiction and critical essays. She died in 1947.

Death Comes for the Archbishop, which appeared in 1927, is one of her most popular books; the novel is set in historical New Mexico rather than on the Nebraska prairies which the author knew so well, and it is apparent that a good deal of research went into the background, an important part of the novel. Miss Cather was a fine craftsman who told her stories well, set them in an environment which she made complete and tangible, and populated them with believable, memorable characters. Her writing belonged not

*to any school of fiction, but to her own personal artistic standards,
which were high indeed.*

Into the harsh wilderness of New Mexico, still uncharted in
the middle of the nineteenth century, come two priests: the
newly appointed bishop of the diocese, Father Latour, and
his vicar, Father Vaillant.

The two men have been intimate friends from their days
as seminarians in France. They are as different from one
another as they can be, but the bond between them is an
unbreakable one. Jean Marie Latour, of patrician ancestry,
is handsome, sensitive, intelligent, and drawn by all that is
physically beautiful. Joseph Vaillant, sprung from sturdy
peasant stock, is physically ugly, with pale blue, watery eyes
and straw-colored hair, and cares nothing for material possessions. He is short of stature and somewhat frail, though
when he is driven by zeal he can accomplish great feats of
physical strength. Indeed, early in his life he had earned the
nickname *Trompe-la-Mort*, for his ability to outwit death.

When the two arrive in New Mexico, the priests there are
unwilling to acknowledge the supremacy of the bishop. There
has been virtually no contact with Rome for centuries, and
the local priests—petty tyrants, extremely lax in observances—
are reluctant to reform or to yield up their sways of influence. So Father Latour must make a trip to Mexico on mule-
back, through the wasted, rugged, unknown mountains, to secure documents from the bishop there that will prove his
right to the New Mexican bishopric. His journey lasts a year,
and when he returns to Santa Fe, he finds that Father Vaillant
has won over the local priests as well as the natives.

And so the two men begin to reclaim the souls in this
savage wilderness, and bring them back to the Mother
Church. Their life is hard, but both men are deeply committed to their work and to their love of God and the Blessed
Virgin. Each year sees some progress, and the bishop's chief
regret is that there is so much work to be done that he cannot
keep his beloved companion, Father Vaillant, in Santa Fe,
but must continually send him out to remote provinces and
settlements. Though Father Vaillant chafes at his constantly
needing to uproot himself just when he has made friends, and
go again among strangers, he is at heart a missionary, and
his gifts are the missionary's gifts.

In this bleak and blazing country—where all is austere but religion, which takes on an aura of theatricality—the two men meet many people, have many adventures, and make some close friends.

Once, when the two are traveling on their white mules, Contento and Angelica, through the remote Truchos mountains on their way to Mora, they lose their path, and stop at the isolated hut of a rude and evil-looking American. At first they accept his offer of a roof for the night, but when the man's terrified Mexican wife signals them of danger, they abruptly change their plans and leave, much to the consternation of their host.

When they arrive at Mora, they find that the Mexican woman has followed them, and they hear her terrible story. Her husband, Scales, makes his living by murdering such men as stop by his cabin. Also, he has killed each of the three babies she has borne him. A party is sent out to Scales's cabin, and the bodies of four men are unearthed at the spot the woman had indicated. Scales is tried for murder and hanged, and the woman, Magdalena, finds refuge in the home of the trustworthy Western scout, Kit Carson, and his wife. Later, when Father Latour has succeeded in bringing out to this part of the world five nuns who start a school, Magdalena goes to live with them, and for the rest of her life knows peace and contentment.

One of Father Latour's major responsibilities is to bring Catholic order to the many churches and parishes within his diocese. This is not always easy, since many of the priests are jealous of their privileges and of the private wealth they have been able to accumulate. Two of the most notorious of these are Antonio José Martinez, and his friend, Father Lucero. The former is a sensualist—he boasts to the bishop of the children he has sired; the latter is a miser. When they refuse to change their modes of life, Father Latour excommunicates them. Unfazed, they begin a schismatic church, and so great is the loyalty of the Mexicans and Indians that few are left in the old church. Not long after, the libertinous Father Martinez dies, and he is followed, shortly, by Father Lucero. Before Lucero dies, he sends for Father Latour, and confesses that Martinez had left a fortune to be spent on masses for the repose of his soul, and that he, too, has a fortune for the same purpose. On Lucero's deathbed, the old priest is received back into the Church by Father Latour.

Another major episode in Father Latour's life in the West concerns Don Antonio Olivares and his wife, Doña Isabella. Don Antonio is a fabulously wealthy man, and he and his wife are often charming hosts to Father Latour and Father Vaillant. They have one child, the spinster Inez, who lives in a convent in the East. When Don Antonio dies, he leaves his estate to Doña Isabella and her daughter Inez, but his brothers contest the will. Doña Isabella is a very vain woman, and has always passed herself off as much younger than she really is. If she is in her early forties, say the brothers, she could not possibly be the mother of Inez. Father Latour and Father Vaillant plead with the woman to admit her real age in court, thus saving Don Antonio's wealth for herself during her lifetime and for the Church afterward. At last, the priests prevail, and Doña Isabella asks what the youngest is she would have to admit to. They tell her she must admit to at least fifty-two, and in court she says that she is fifty-two. The admission seems almost to crush her. Later, however, at a celebratory party, she publicly takes the good priests to task "for the lie you made me tell about my age in court."

As the years pass, both Latour and Vaillant come to love their wild adopted homeland more and more. They begin to understand the natives, both Indian and Mexican, and learn to respect them. They take deep pleasure from the crude native arts, from the highly ritualistic elements of the native celebrations of Catholicism, from the legends they hear of Indians long dead, and early missionaries, and wicked priests of the past.

One of the most interesting of these tales is that of Fray Baltazar, a priest of the early seventeen hundreds. He made his home in a fantastic castle on a cliff, and lived as a petty tyrant. His only pleasure was his table, and he constantly sent Indians on errands to faraway places to fetch him rare foods and unusual seasonings; his only pride was his garden, for which he forced each Indian woman to give him a daily allotment of precious water. The Indians whom he subjugated hated him, but their fear of him was too great for them to act against this man who took, took, took—but never gave. One day Fray Baltazar could no longer bear the thought that only he knew of his beautiful garden, so he invited four neighboring priests to attend a dinner party. The four came, and were mightily impressed—even envious—of all their host, Fray Baltazar, showed them. At dinner, however, tragedy struck. An Indian serving boy accidentally spilled a tureen of hare *jardinière* as he carried it into the dining room. Instantly the host seized a pewter mug and flung it at the boy, killing him. Without waiting a moment, the four guest priests gathered up their skirts and departed, but Fray Baltazar did not move. That night the Indians revolted, and carried the priest to a high cliff, from which they flung him to his death.

The years move on . . . on . . . on. . . . When gold is discovered to the north, a priest is needed to go among the wild miners. So once again, Father Vaillant must uproot himself and leave. This time, he and Father Latour feel that it is their last parting. And though Father Vaillant does return to New Mexico from time to time—on several occasions to recuperate from illnesses or injuries—his final home becomes the Colorado country, where eventually he, too, is raised to bishop, and where he dies.

By now Father Latour has become an archbishop, and has seen the materialization of his greatest dream: the construction of a cathedral, in his beloved southern French Romanesque style, in the great Western plains.

At last Father Latour goes into semi-retirement, and a new bishop comes to take his place. But when his health begins to fail, he returns to the bishop's mansion in Santa Fe, wishing to die there.

In his last weeks, as his health inevitably slips away, he reviews all the events that he has shared with Father Vaillant since their boyhood. He writes, still, letters to Father Vaillant's sister Philomène, who is a Mother Superior in a convent in France. And when Father Latour closes his eyes for the last time, he is laid before the high altar in the church that he has built.

THE CALL OF THE WILD

Jack London

Jack London was born in San Francisco in 1876. Born out of wedlock, he took his name from a John London, one of his mother's husbands. He grew up in the teeming waterfront neighborhood, selling newspapers, hauling freight, and only occasionally going to school. He went to sea on a sealing ship in 1893, and on his return crossed the United States and Canada, largely on foot. In 1896 he went to the Klondike where gold had been discovered; this experience provided him with material for the Yukon stories which brought him fame when published in 1900. In the next fifteen years he wrote fifty-one books, covered the Russo-Japanese War for the Hearst papers, lectured, and traveled to Mexico and the South Seas. Suffering from severe depression and alcoholism, and on the verge of financial disaster, London committed suicide in 1916.

London's tales of adventure were commercially successful in many languages during his lifetime, and their fame continues. The Call of the Wild (1903) has been London's most popular work. Its appeal arises first from its qualities as an exciting tale of the northern wilderness, but more important is the chilling, elemental fascination in the story of a civilized animal becoming a killer in the course of its brutal struggle for survival.

Buck is the prize dog at the California showplace-home of Judge Miller. Half St. Bernard, half Scotch shepherd dog, he is a sturdy, rugged—but nonetheless pampered—animal.

It is his splendid stature that brings Buck to grief. The gold rush in the Klondike is on in earnest, and sturdy dogs are bringing fantastic prices. Manuel, a gardener on Judge Miller's estate, having run up gambling debts he is unable to pay, kidnaps Buck one night and sells him for fifty dollars to a brutal stranger.

The stranger puts a rope around Buck's neck, and the dog finds himself nearly strangled. After a horrible four-day ride confined in a crate in a freight car, during which he receives neither food nor drink nor exercise, Buck at last reaches his destination. He is taken in charge by a man wearing a red sweater and carrying a club; and it is from this man that Buck first learns the lesson of the wild, the law of fang and club. For the man beats Buck again and again with the club until the dog succumbs to the brute's superior weapons. Though cruelly beaten, however, Buck is not crushed in spirit.

Along with several other dogs, Buck is sold to a representative of the Canadian Government, one Perrault, and taken aboard a ship bound for Alaska. Reaching Alaska, Buck has his first experience with snow and ice—and it is a dreadful one for him. Such pain and misery he has never known . . . but he is soon to become used to this vast, white land.

Perrault and his partner François are couriers for the

Canadian Government, and Buck is to be one of their team of sled dogs. His initiation period is painful, but his spirit is as strong as ever, and soon he is as good a dog as any in the pack. (The other dogs are Curly, Billee, Joe, Dave, Sol-leks—and Spitz. Spitz is the lead dog, an animal of mean and vicious temperament; and Buck soon senses that this is the animal whom he must overthrow one day.)

Buck quickly adapts to the tasks demanded of him. His sinews stiffen, his muscles harden, and he accepts the primordial beast that is dominant within him. He becomes cunning, sly, shrewd—and, indeed, vicious. He and Spitz are forever challenging each other—but usually nothing comes of it, for Perrault and François are always ready to separate the two.

The first trip to Dawson that Buck makes in harness teaches him many things of value, not the least important being his pride in his ability to work. And though the dogs are pushed severely, all of them perform bravely and beautifully. On the return trip from Dawson, Buck at last has his chance to fight with Spitz to the death and prove his own supremacy. It is a bitter fight, with strength and viciousness on Spitz's side; but Buck has intelligence, and at last he succeeds in killing his rival. Buck is now lead dog, and with him at the head of the train, Perrault and François make their return journey in record time. Buck is a hero.

The Canadian Government has adopted a policy of selling any dogs that have been hard-pushed, rather than caring for them and allowing them to rest. Thus it happens that Buck and the other dogs in the team fail to get the period of rest and recuperation that their hard-pushed bodies need, but are sold instead for a paltry sum to two men, Hal and Charles, who are traveling with Mercedes, wife to one of them and sister to the other. This party is ignorant, helpless, and foolish. They overload their sled, overdrive and underfeed their animals, and bicker among themselves.

Although the task demanded of them is too great, the dogs nobly do their best until they are all nearing the breaking point. When the party reaches the camp of one John Thornton, he advises the men that they are abusing the dogs, and, further, that the snow bridges ahead are about to melt, so that it is folly for them to push farther.

To this Charles and Hal reply with disdain. Hadn't they

been warned that they wouldn't get this far? Yet here they are. Moreover, the dogs are merely lazy.

The men fall to and begin beating the dogs with whips to make them move. One by one, the exhausted dogs rise to make the effort. All, that is, but Buck. He will not budge another step, in spite of Hal's beating him nearly senseless with a club.

In a rage, Thornton interferes. He knocks Hal down, and cuts Buck out of harness. Driven by whips, the rest of the dogs move on with their three masters, and Thornton goes to comfort Buck. Suddenly a scream is heard from up ahead; a snow bridge has given way in the spring thaw, and the entire party is drowned.

For the first time in his life, Buck has a master for whom he can feel passion. John Thornton loves Buck and nurses him back to health. His kindness to the animal wins him a friend for life.

On three occasions, Buck is able to prove his love for Thornton. Once he saves Thornton from a raging flood near some torrential cataracts; without Buck, Thornton would certainly have been dead. Another time, Buck attacks a man who would strike Thornton, and tears the man's throat open. On a third occasion, Thornton has foolishly boasted that Buck could pull a frozen sled carrying a thousand pounds dead weight for one hundred yards. A bet is made, and the odds go shooting up to three to one. Thornton stands to lose all he has; but Buck seems to understand what is at stake, and for love of his master he accomplishes what all had considered an impossible task, and wins for Thornton a large sum of money.

Thornton now makes his camp with two partners, Hans and Pete. They have found a river of almost pure gold in the middle of untracked wilderness, and every day their panning earns them a fortune.

It is at this time that Buck reverts more and more to his true state. He begins to wander away from the campsite at night, drawn by an indefinable feeling. On one such foray he encounters a wolverine, and after some petty skirmishing, the two become friends. But still, Buck feels the pull of his love for Thornton, and he returns to the campsite regularly.

His forays into the wilderness become more and more regular, however, and he stays away for longer and longer periods of time. He has tasted blood once, when he killed one of his own kind—Spitz. Now he longs for greater prey.

His first success is in killing a black bear, which he slays and devours wolf-fashion. But the longing for blood becomes ever stronger. He manages to corner a bull moose, and for days torments the animal, allowing it neither to eat nor drink nor rejoin its friends. At last he kills it—an animal larger than himself.

Still, he returns to the camp periodically, to be fondled by Thornton. But the intervals between his visits become greater and greater.

Then one moonlit night, he encounters a pack of wolves. The leader of the pack attacks him—and Buck succeeds in killing him. Several wolves more attack this strange animal who is so much like them, and yet larger and smarter than they; but they, too, are killed. And then the wolves accept him as one of themselves.

But Buck deserts them for a final visit to the campsite. When he reaches it, he finds Thornton, Hans, Pete, and their dogs dead. They have been killed by marauding Yeehat Indians, who even now are dancing about the wreckage of the camp.

In a flash Buck attacks, and one by one the Yeehats fall, their throats ripped apart by the animal's teeth. Those that are not killed flee for their lives, never to return to this valley.

Now, for the last time, Buck leaves Thornton and goes to join the wolfpack as its leader. He has finally and irrevocably heard the call of the wild.

MAIN STREET

Sinclair Lewis

Sinclair Lewis, the son of a physician, was born in 1885 in Sauk Centre, Minnesota. He studied at Yale, graduated in 1907, and worked as a journalist, publishing articles, verse, and two novels which attracted little attention. The appearance of Main Street *in 1920 catapulted Lewis to fame, and the publication of* Babbitt *two years later confirmed his reputation as one of the most important and widely read American novelists of his time. In 1928 Lewis divorced his first wife and married Dorothy Thompson, the foremost woman reporter and foreign correspondent of her day; they were divorced in 1942. In 1930 Sinclair Lewis became the first American to win the Nobel Prize for literature. He died in 1951.*

Main Street *and* Babbitt *struck the American public with an enormous impact. The nation, since the end of World War I, had acquired a new sophistication and perspective, and was prepared to take stock of its shortcomings, even to laugh at itself. The eyes of the world were on America, and Americans were eager to show that they were well aware of the Main Streets and Babbitts (the latter soon became, and has remained, a generic term) in their midst. There are, to be sure, deficiencies in Lewis's art, but artistic shortcomings do not diminish his stature as the great satirist of the American bourgeoisie.*

Orphaned Carol Milford feels a strong need to "do something" with her life when she finishes at Blodgett College. Accordingly she rejects the marriage proposal of would-be lawyer Stewart Snyder. She doesn't quite see herself as merely a housewife in some sleepy little town. Instead, she goes to library school in Chicago, and after a year accepts a position with the public library in St. Paul.

Three years later she meets young Dr. Will Kennicott, of Gopher Prairie, Minnesota. She is impressed with this virile, handsome, straightforward man of the Midwest, and though she is slightly repelled by what she suspects is his too great devotion to making money, his forthrightness and honesty attract her. When Will tells her that she will find ample sphere for her talents and her humanitarian zeal in Gopher Prairie—according to him, the town and townsmen are just waiting for the influence of a cultured and good woman such as herself—pretty Carol agrees to become Will's wife.

Her first view of Gopher Prairie makes Carol wonder if she has chosen wisely. "G.P.," as its inhabitants are fond of calling it, is as ugly, flat, and uninteresting as thousands of other towns in the Midwest. Main Street here is indistinguishable from hundreds of other Main Streets. The local hotel—the Minniemashie House—is as monumentally repulsive as any building in the state.

Carol has no greater expectations or hopes for the people. The Sam Clarks, the Jack Elders, the Dave Dyers, the Jim Howlands—such men and women are, according to Will, the salt of the earth, good, wholesome folks that Carol will come to respect, admire, and love. But she sees in them only ignorance, pettiness, vulgarity, and self-righteousness.

Carol determines to like everyone, however, and to become liked by them. Fortunately, early in her residence she
finds several people who seem to offer some kindred viewpoint, some sense of reality, to comfort her. These include
the outspoken Miss Vida Sherwin, schoolteacher and spear-
head of all forward movements the town has witnessed in
the past decade (though Vida resists any relation with Carol
except one of distant and condescending sympathy); the
dreamy-eyed lawyer, Guy Pollack, who suffers from what he
calls "Village Virus"—a lassitude that makes it impossible
for him to leave Gopher Prairie, although he recognizes it
clearly for the cultural wasteland that it is; and Bea Sorenson, the fresh-scrubbed, naïve Scandinavian girl who is Carol's
maid-of-all-work. Only with Bea, however, is Carol able to
build a relationship of unquestioned security and mutual respect; and for this she is to know the scorn of the towns-
women, who do not approve of treating "Scandahoofian" servants as equals.

What depresses Carol most about her new life is its complete predictability, its relentless sameness. She determines
to liven things up, and, accordingly, her first party breaks
every Gopher Prairie social rule. Her guests, despite themselves, have a hilariously good time, and enjoy the exotic
Chinese food she has prepared instead of the traditional and
acceptable angel cake. But the next party that she attends
is so dull that she might never have given her own party,
and she recognizes that she will not change Gopher Prairie
in respect of its evening entertainments.

Carol now throws herself into the life of the community,
in a desperate effort to win recognition and acceptance for
herself and her ideas, as well as in an attempt to bring vitality
and culture to the people. But effort after effort fails. She is
equally unsuccessful at generating interest in building a new
civic hall, in enlarging the public school, in improving the
lot of the immigrant farmers, in bringing new life to the
library's collection of books. Typical of the reaction to all of
Carol's "new-fangled" proposals is that of the librarian, who,
when Carol asks if a librarian's chief job isn't to stimulate
people to read, replies, "No indeed! A *good* librarian's chief
job is to preserve the books!"

Undaunted, Carol makes repeated efforts to storm the
vacuous citadel. She joins the two "acceptable" ladies' social

groups—the Thanatopsis Club and the Jolly Seventeen. But she only succeeds in getting herself whispered and gossiped about. Everyone thinks Carol is pretty and well meaning—but all feel it their solemn obligation to set her right about the way things are done. (And, of course, in Gopher Prairie, the way things *are* done is the way they always *have been* done, and therefore the *only right* way they can be done.)

Even Will Kennicott is less enthusiastic over Carol's efforts to transform the town than he had been over her ideas when they were courting. He begins to accuse her of putting on airs, considering herself superior to everyone, and, as a result, of chasing away his friends. Virtually the only person from whom Carol derives wholehearted encouragement is Miles Bjornstam, a "socialist-anarchist" gadfly who is tolerated by the gentry of Gopher Prairie only because he is the best plumber and handyman available. But, of course, as Miles is a pariah in her circle, Carol cannot talk with him as frequently or as openly as she would like. For if she has learned nothing else, Carol has learned how effective, how malicious, and how destructive is the gossip of Gopher Prairie.

Now, at twenty-six, Carol recognizes that she must rethink her entire approach to life in the town if she is to find any happiness there. If her old values and ideals will not function, she must adopt new ones. She throws herself into a wholesale campaign of being the "adoring wife." She re-examines Will, and finds him to be a hero. Her admiration and love for him reach their highest point when she witnesses the calm, effective way her doctor husband performs a dangerous amputation in a country shack during a blizzard. To complete her marital happiness, however, one thing is lacking—a child. Will refuses to father children until he believes that they can "afford" them. Carol's infatuation with her husband does not last long.

Again, Carol begins her attempts to bring culture to Gopher Prairie. Again, she is unsuccessful. And she is slightly disappointed when Miles Bjornstam marries Bea Sorenson—partly because it means losing the honest companionship of Bea, and partly because Miles as a married man gives up much of the radicalism and forthrightness Carol had so enjoyed in him before. (Miles remains a rebel at heart; but he sees that unless he mends his speech, Bea will remain an outcast, socially, in the town. As it is, Carol is Bea's only regular visitor, and it is not until Miles has become fairly well-to-do as a dairyman that the gentry of the town begin to treat Bea decently.)

At last Carol does find an interest to lift her spirits and make her feel a real person again. She is pregnant. Wisely nodding, all of the matrons of the town tell her—and each other—that now that she is to have her own family she will give up all her high-falutin' nonsense and settle down.

For the first two years of little Hugh's life, their prophecy comes true. With her son, Carol is no longer lonely, and the shaping of the little boy's life is outlet enough for her creative instincts. Moreover, as Bea has had a son, Olaf, at about the same time, the two women renew their old intimacy, much to Carol's delight, and little Hugh and the even more beautiful little Olaf become playmates.

Now, Carol learns the secret of the distance between herself and Vida Sherwin. The poor spinster had, years ago, conceived an infatuation with Will Kennicott, and had believed that he reciprocated her feelings. She has never forgiven Carol for "stealing" Will from her. Vida, however, does manage to land a husband—the ineffectual, simpering manager of the shoe department at the Bon Ton, Raymie Wutherspoon. Everyone in town seems to accept this marriage at face value—everyone, that is, except Carol, who sees the real inadequacies that have led Vida and Raymie to each other.

She feels ever more stifled by a sense of creeping death. Ugliness and hypocrisy seem to her to shroud Gopher Prairie, and she fears that she will suffocate.

There is a brief respite for her in the amorous attentions of Percy Bresnahan, the local celebrity—a crude, vulgar, "hometown" boy who has become a millionaire in Boston. Everyone fawns over "Perce" except Carol; but she responds to his fumbling and tentative embraces, because they remind her that there are true flesh-and-blood people in the world. Though the affair comes to nothing, Carol recognizes that her marriage to Will is empty. They maintain separate bedrooms, and Will, in silent protest, drifts into an affair with Maud Dyer, the wife of his friend Dave.

Life goes on . . . and on . . . and on, in Gopher Prairie, and Carol feels more and more stifled. World War I breaks out—but it only makes the townspeople more smug and self-righteous. When Miles Bjornstam's wife Bea and son Olaf die of typhoid, Carol is horrified that none of the gentry attends the funeral. Indeed, remembering that on occasion he has questioned the sense and humanity of warfare, they talk of riding Miles out of town on a rail for being "unpatriotic."

Although again she has found several seemingly kindred spirits, each of them displays a deficiency to Carol. There is the aristocratic Mrs. Westlake, who takes refuge from the smallness of Gopher Prairie behind a wall of incessant reading. There is the eccentric Mrs. Flickerbaugh, who defies the town with her weird costumes and mannerisms—and who feels the pain of being rejected. There is the effeminate, artistic Erik Valborg—whom all in the town call "Elizabeth," and who leads a life of desperate loneliness. Carol falls in love with Erik—but the gossips of the town watch them closely and spread such malicious rumors about Erik that it is impossible for them to consummate their relationship, and he leaves Gopher Prairie in despair.

The crushing blow to Carol—the incident that illuminates for her all the evil in the way of life represented by Will Kennicott and his friends—is the scandal that befalls young Fern Mullins, a new schoolteacher. Cy Bogart, the most obnoxious, vulgar, and immoral youth in town, lies about Fern in order to save himself a tongue-lashing from his sanctimonious mother, and Widow Bogart succeeds in having the innocent girl fired and run out of town. As a result, Fern's professional and personal reputation are ruined—though everyone involved knows that there is probably no truth in the widow's accusations. But Widow Bogart is "of" the town, and Fern is not; so it is the girl whose reputation is sacrificed instead of the widow's vanity.

Carol at last works out an agreement with Will whereby she will leave Gopher Prairie, taking Hugh with her—not to return until such time (if ever) as she can do so freely.

She goes to Washington, where she gets a position with the Bureau of War Risk Insurance. (It is the last year of World War I.) Life is at first difficult, but gradually she makes some friends and begins to take advantage of the oasis of culture and intellect she has found.

Carol has always been scrupulously honest with herself, and as the months roll by, she sees much in Washington that she finds as oppressive as Gopher Prairie had been.

But she finds, too, freedom—a sense of her own individual integrity and worth as an individual—and she revels in this new awareness of her personality.

Much to her surprise, a year later when she runs into two people from Gopher Prairie, Harry and Juanita Haydock, whom she had always scorned, she greets them warmly and affectionately, and asks for all the news.

After Carol has been in Washington for thirteen months, Will comes to visit her. (She is secretly thrilled that he has come without her inviting him.) For several weeks she shows him Washington—and for the first time in their lives they come to see each other as whole people, flawed but worth while. Carol finds herself falling in love with him—truly in love with him—for the first time.

When he leaves Washington, Will humbly urges Carol to return to Gopher Prairie—but only if and when she can do so freely of her own desire and impulse.

The time for Carol's free return arrives after she has been away for two years. She takes Hugh back to Gopher Prairie with her, and she is carrying Will's second child.

She has no illusions about what waits for her in the blank Midwest. In less than a week she is aware again of all the ugliness, dullness, and meanness of life there. But she also recognizes her love and need for Will, and the fact that the worth of her own personality is not affected by her surroundings.

She accepts defeat—but she believes—she *knows*—that she has kept the faith.

BABBITT

Sinclair Lewis

George F. Babbitt, forty-six years old, is no different from most of the other middle-aged men in the city of Zenith. Like Vergil Gunch, Orville Jones, Chum Frink, Sidney Finkelstein, and all the rest of his friends, he is a member of the Elks, a member of the Boosters, a member of the Athletic Club, a member of the Chamber of Commerce, a member of the Presbyterian Church, a member of the Republican Party. Like them, George lives in a competent and glossy house, furnished in polite and impersonal taste. Like them, George drives—and worships—an automobile.

What distinguishes George F. Babbitt from the thousands of other men like himself are small details: he has a wife, Myra, and three children (twenty-two-year-old Verona, a graduate of Bryn Mawr; seventeen-year-old Ted, a high school junior; and ten-year-old Tinka, the darling of her daddy's heart). He is a member of the State Association of Real Estate Boards. And, perhaps most unique of all, he has a recurring fantasy in which he follows a beautiful, desirable, and loving female through wooded glades and sunlit dells. This female he comes to think of as his fairy child.

When George F. Babbitt was a student at State, he had dreams of becoming a lawyer, and vaguely of associating himself with liberal social causes. But that was long ago, and the only vestigial traces of his youthful dreams are his belief in the superiority of his skills as an orator and his friendship with Paul Riesling.

Paul had been George's roommate at State, and had shown great promise as a musician. But like George, Paul has allowed his dreams to slip away from him. Now he finds himself chained to the dull routine of a roofing business and the slavish demands of a nagging, hostile wife, Zilla. George has never lost his great admiration and affection for Paul, and though the two are now middle-aged men, George continues to see himself as a sort of older brother to Paul, a support and a comfort for the sensitive violinist.

George has moments of discontent, moments in which the pep and push of the Zenith Boosters seem inadequate answers to the problems of life. But he cannot seem to put his finger on his feeling of inadequacy, or find the solutions to the problems of which he is aware. He tries to communicate with his two older children, but Verona has the superciliousness of a recent college graduate, and Ted has the superiority of adolescence. George chafes at the dealings between his father-in-law and business partner, Henry Thompson, and the politician representing the transit company, Jake Offutt; but the fact that their shady operations have brought George his small fortune make it impossible for him to rebel against them. He sees in every pretty woman he meets a glimpse of what might have been—but his solitary attempt at flirtation, with his friend's wife, Louetta Swanson, ends in a sense of shame.

George notices this dissatisfaction—this sense of frustration —most vividly at a dinner party given by his wife. Fortunately, however, some bootleg liquor (it is 1920) manages to raise his spirits sufficiently so that he doesn't act on his impulse to shoo all the guests home.

There are bright spots in the life of George F. Babbitt. There is a trip to Maine which he and Paul manage to arrange for themselves alone, without their wives and children. There is a trip to Chicago with his son, Ted, during which he and the boy seem to draw closer together. There is the convention of the State Real Estate Board in the not-too-distant city of Monarch, during which all sorts of hijinks and hilarity occupy his time and energy. But from each of these little sorties George returns to Zenith only to find it as dull and predictable as ever.

A bitter blow comes to George—and to his wife, Myra— when they set their sights on enlarging their social circle to include the aristocratic McKelveys, whose parties are always written up in the papers. With persistence, the Babbitts finally manage to pin the McKelveys down to a specific night, and Myra goes all out in arranging the dinner party. The fete is a disaster, however, and the McKelveys make patent excuses and leave early. George and Myra hope for a while that the invitation will be returned—particularly when the local paper notes that the McKelveys are playing host to the British lord, Sir Gerald Doak. But the desired invitation never arrives, and George announces loudly that he hopes to goodness he and Myra *don't* get invited to one of the McKelveys' dull, stodgy old dinners. No get up and go to folks like them, he exclaims. The McKelveys are never mentioned in the Babbitt household again.

Some time later, however, George, on a business trip to Chicago, meets Sir Gerald Doak—and is delighted to find that the man is not a fusty aristocrat, but is a regular fellow. Indeed, he is the British counterpart of George Babbitt, and the two spend a delightful evening together talking business, Rotary, and conservative political opinion. George is pleased with this social success of his, and envisions returning to Zenith and being able to refer casually to "my friend, Lord Jerry."

This pleasant fantasy is driven from George's mind, however, when dining in the hotel he sees across the room Paul Riesling in close conversation with a woman who seems to George no better than she should be. George blusteringly goes up to their table, in spite of Paul's obvious pain and anger, and arranges to meet Paul later. Paul is furious with George for following him, and George is confused and unhappy over his friend's defiant protestations that women companions are his only solace from Zilla. In the end, George offers to cook up a story of having been in Akron (where Zilla thinks Paul is) and having run in to Paul. To that end, George does stop in Akron, en route to Zenith, and drops a postcard to Zilla. This subterfuge manages to allay Zilla's suspicions about Paul's latest wandering—though she knows quite well that he has had many casual affairs—but the episode introduces a coolness between George and Paul that had never been there before.

The ideas started in George's mind by Paul's amours are only increased by his chance meeting with the attractive widow Tanis Judique, and at last he determines to kick over the traces. He takes a pretty young manicurist to dinner—a girl named Ida Putiak; but it is only too painfully clear to him that she considers him a bore. George resolves to be moral.

Meanwhile, Paul has found Zilla unbearable, and in a fit of rage, shoots her. George is thunderstruck by this. Fortunately Zilla is not killed, and Paul goes to prison for three years. When George, some time later, approaches Zilla to ask her to appeal to the governor for a pardon for Paul, he finds that she has "got religion," and is determined to let Paul stay in prison as a "good example" to others.

The sense of desperation seems ever to be increasing with George, and a chance encounter with Tanis Judique starts a period of revolt for him. He falls in love with the attractive woman, and soon he becomes a regular member of the Bunch, an informal assortment of Tanis's friends who meet regularly to drink bootleg liquor, dance wildly, and discuss "Bohemian" subjects into the early hours. Though these people—so very different from the "right" element in Zenith—repel him at first, George learns to like them for Tanis's sake. Soon, he likes them for their own sake. They seem to have the spirit, the zing, the sense of liveliness that he lacks in his own life.

George's mild carryings-on are noted with much disapproval by the men in the Boosters Club, the Athletic Club, the Chamber of Commerce, the Y.M.C.A. (Myra is away visiting her sister, and George's men friends are willing to wink a little at his high living—but now he seems to be going too far.) This only adds to their anger at his defense of Beecher Ingram, a minister whom most decent Zenith-ites wish to run out of town. (George, as a result of a chance conversation with the radical Seneca Doane, finds himself becoming more and more liberal in his views.) At last the differences between George's opinion and the opinions of the other men are brought into the open. A Good Citizens' League is being formed, representing all the right-thinking element in Zenith—and George refuses to join. He laughingly passes the G.C.L. off as a fad.

He soon learns, however, that his rebellion from the accepted standards and virtues of middle-class Zenith will cost him dearly. He finds that his friends shun him. He is openly snubbed, deliberately excluded. Soon, his business begins to fall off, as the rumor is spread that George is some kind of crank.

The pressures that he is under in the community are not relieved by the demands now made on him by Tanis Judique and her friends; and with horror, George sees that Tanis, whom he had imagined to be a carefree, golden spirit, is in truth a grasping, ignorant middle-aged woman.

When Myra returns to Zenith, George resolves to be again a model husband. His resolve begins to crumble, however, in the face of Myra's complacency and stolidity. At last they begin bickering in earnest, and for the first time in more than twenty-five years of marriage, each reveals his true feelings of frustration, loneliness, and despair.

An emergency appendectomy performed on Myra is the crisis which brings the two together. During Myra's convalescence, George's old men friends note the change that has come over their friend Babbitt: he seems to be his good old regular self. Indeed, George has come to believe, again, in the sense and rightness of the middle-class Zenith values. Much to his delight, he is again invited to join the Good Citizens' League. Accepting the invitation reopens to him all the pleasures of life in Zenith. And when Myra twits him about the wicked, wicked woman who had, for a time, captivated her poor little George, he smiles at her indulgently.

Nonetheless, when young Ted elopes with silly little Eunice Littlefield and marries her, George interrupts the cries of righteous indignation set up by Myra, Verona, Eunice's parents, and Myra's father. He takes his son aside, and in an impassioned plea urges the boy to be true to himself. George tells Ted how much he admires him for knowing what he wanted and going out after it. The elder Babbitt pleads with his boy to go on in the same vein, never to allow himself to become another George F. Babbitt—afraid of his family, afraid of Zenith, afraid of himself.

THE LATE GEORGE APLEY

J. P. Marquand

John Phillips Marquand was born in Wilmington, Delaware, in 1893. He lived with his family in Rye, New York, and then in Newburyport, Massachusetts, until entering Harvard College on a scholarship in 1911. After graduation he was a reporter in Boston, served in France during the war, and then came to New York, where he worked as a journalist and an advertising copy writer. He devoted himself entirely to writing in 1922, and that year published his first novel, a detective thriller. A journey to the Far East inspired the creation of the detective Mr. Moto, and the Moto stories, appearing in magazines, were immensely popular. The Late George Apley (1937) established him as a novelist of prestige, and it was followed by further novels which satirized the executive suburbanites of the American Northeast. Marquand, married and divorced twice, died in 1960.

The Late George Apley, which won a Pulitzer Prize, was popular as a book, play, and movie. Not since the novels of Edith Wharton had the upper-class milieu of a particular American city been so mercilessly slashed in its most vulnerable area: the elaborate set of imposed values and restrictions by means of which it was able to maintain its inbred insularity.

The noted man of letters, Mr. Willing, undertakes to edit and publish in a limited edition, for circulation among the family only, the papers of George Apley (1866–1933). This undertaking is sponsored by the man's son, John Apley; and at

John's insistence that the late George Apley be presented, for once, as a real person, Willing reluctantly agrees to include documents which he, himself, believes would be better suppressed. In addition to quoting extensively from Apley letters, diaries, and journals, Willing supplies a tenuous narrative which both fills in gaps and justifies the actions and attitudes of his late friend, George Apley.

Born with a golden spoon in his mouth, George Apley learns early the importance of pride of family, place, and tradition. Virtually from the cradle, he is taught his responsibilities as a scion of one of Boston's oldest, most prominent, most influential, and wealthiest families.

He is sent to Hobson's School, where he forms his earliest friendships—friendships with such boys as "Wormy" Broughton, "Daisy" Partridge, and "Winty" Vassal. These boys, being like young George, are from the right families, and they will form his closest circle of friends throughout his lifetime.

George's boyhood is passed in conventional fashion, with winters divided between attendance at Hobson's and the dancing lessons at Papanti's class, and summers spent at the family estate in Milton. When George enters Harvard in 1884, he is typical of his class.

Once away from home and the moralistic influence of his parents, however, George blossoms. Much to his family's regret, he exhibits a strain of lightheartedness, and he drifts into easy camaraderie with boys who are not quite from the right circles. His father manages to impress upon him the idea that a man is known by the company he keeps; his mother reminds him continually of the importance of his family heritage. The older Apleys are gratified that at least George joins the right clubs and societies, and manages to do creditably well in his studies.

Toward the end of his senior year, however, there is a most distasteful episode for George's family. In spite of their conscientious attempts to lead their son in the right path, he falls in love with Mary Monahan, a young lady of no position. For a while his passion withstands parental assault, but at last, his health failing under the strain, he separates from Mary and agrees to go abroad in the company of his Uncle and Aunt Preston and their daughter Henrietta. (Henrietta, like George, is recovering from an attachment to a person of the wrong sort.) The Apleys sigh with relief when George embarks.

While in Europe, George receives continual letters from home, all of them reinforcing the concept of *noblesse oblige*. (All, that is, except those from his younger sister, Jane, who sympathizes with him in his great unhappiness. She, too, has been thwarted by the Apley standards. But Jane is an unstable girl, and her advice is not, of course, to be taken seriously. Indeed, eventually Jane suffers a nervous breakdown, and must spend the balance of her life in institutions.) George does his best to find the grand tour cheerful, but he is filled with a continual melancholy which he does not understand—a yearning to be free of his family and all it represents.

Nonetheless, he dutifully returns to Cambridge and enrolls in the Harvard Law School. Here again, his urge for frivolity breaks out. To sober him, he is sent to work during the summers in the cotton mills of his millionaire uncle, the bachelor William Apley. He is a failure there, however, and Uncle William advises against George's ever being allowed to go into business.

George now seems to lose his power to think for himself. Without quite knowing how it happens, in 1890 he finds himself engaged to plain but socially acceptable Catharine Bosworth. Soon they are married, but it does not take George long to discover how little he has in common with his wife. As he loathes friction, he decides that the easiest path is to allow her to make decisions in which he acquiesces.

It is after he has entered the law firm of Reid and Smith that George makes his first real mark in Boston society. At a meeting of the staid Browsers' Club, he reads a paper that he has written called "Jonas Good and Cow Corner." It takes him an hour and ten minutes to read it, and it details the careers of the one hundred and fifteen owners of a single piece of Boston real estate (Cow Corner) from its original owner (Jonas Good) to the present. The paper makes a great stir, and George finds himself invited to join a number of highly regarded clubs and to serve on many public-spirited committees. It is a great gratification to his parents—as well as to Catharine—that George seems now, at last, to be accepting his proper role in the highest sphere of Boston life.

He now begins to recognize the value of what his parents

have for so long been preaching; and after the birth of his own children—a boy, John, and a girl, Eleanor—he finds himself more and more in sympathy with the advice that his own father had given him.

Nevertheless, as the years move on, he feels a sense of frustration. Though he is constantly busy, he never seems to be getting anywhere. Catharine manages his life in such a way, however, that he cannot revolt; and in this she is abetted by George's older sister, Amelia. Married to Newcomb Swimmings, scion of a prominent family, Amelia has preserved intact the virtues drummed into her in childhood, and between Amelia and Catharine, George has little opportunity to move outside the prescribed track.

Suddenly George's father—whom he has come to regard as the fountainhead of all truth and virtue—dies. George is horrified to learn that his father has left, in New York City, a twelve-year-old bastard son. He manages to keep this quiet, however, by making the boy's mother a generous lump-sum payment.

Inch by inch, Catharine and Amelia succeed in remaking George Apley, and when, in 1905, Sargent paints his portrait, it is of an aristocratic, self-satisfied, slightly supercilious man. Now, for the first time, George begins to recognize that the world about him—the solid, secure world on which he has put so much reliance—is beginning to change. He senses that his caste is being threatened, and begins an energetic campaign to preserve the old values.

It is at this time, too, that for the first time (it happens at the Province Club, of which he is a leading member) George Apley is referred to openly as a snob. But he has too much respect for Apley responsibilities to be intimidated, and soon he is deeply immersed in the work of the Save Boston Association, a conservative group devoted to preserving the old values.

By now his son Johnny is twelve, and though George regrets that his relationship is not all he had hoped it would be with his son, he isn't quite sure how to improve it. He enrolls the lad at Groton, where the boy is miserable. But George sends him letters of encouragement, letters that spell out to Johnny the meaning of being an Apley, the great responsibility he bears. (In many respects, the letters that George writes are reminiscent of those his father had sent him when he was Johnny's age. But George is not aware of this.)

The greatest blow to George Apley during this period is the death of his beloved mother, who had always represented to him what was truest, best, and noblest—in Boston, and in all womankind.

Soon, it is John's turn to continue the family tradition of being educated at Harvard, and George writes his son a lengthy letter in which he outlines for the boy the pitfalls that lie before him. He even goes so far as to refer to the episode of Mary Monahan, and tells John how wise he had been to heed his father's advice. One is happy, he tells his son, only with people of his own class.

For a long time George Apley has been seemingly immersed in a torpor, but the rumblings in Europe that precede World War I serve to reawaken him, and he reasserts himself by writing letters to the newspapers, attending lectures, and subscribing to conservative causes. To John, George's stand seems to be one of pig-headed irrationality; but George recognizes how impossible it is for his son to understand the things he has come to learn in his maturity.

The fact that to George family is more important than the individual is clearly indicated at this time by the decision of a second cousin, John Apley, to divorce his wife in order to marry a woman with whom he has fallen in love. (Married, she too plans a divorce.) Fortunately George Apley controls the finances of his cousin, and he flatly refuses to give the man another penny if he proceeds with this scandalous action. The result is the lifetime condemnation of four unhappy people—and the preservation of the unspotted Apley reputation.

George has been becoming aware for some time that his children's values are different from his own, but now he recognizes that it is not merely a case of their sowing harmless wild oats. He is particularly dissatisfied with Eleanor's frankness and her freedom in choosing as men friends people of whom Apley has never heard; but even John is a disappointment to him in that he doesn't show the proper respect for the old values and associations.

Nonetheless he is unprepared for the shock of John's joining the National Guard to go and fight in Mexico. Bravely, however, he and Catharine rationalize their son's behavior in patriotic terms.

That the deterioration of family values is spreading seems to be indicated now on every hand. First there is the shocking experience of remote Aunt Henrietta's being buried in the part of the family plot George has always believed reserved for *his* branch; his insistence to his cousin that Aunt Henrietta's remains be exhumed and reburied elsewhere results in a feud that is never ended. Then perhaps most shocking of all, old Uncle William marries a practical nurse—a nobody—named Miss Prentiss. (George is somewhat soothed, however, when he learns that an ante-nuptial arrangement preserves Uncle William's millions for John and Eleanor.) And when Uncle William dies soon after, George sees (much to his regret) his two children become independently wealthy.

When World War I breaks out, young John goes right to the front, and George feels robbed of his son's companionship. Eleanor is more impossible than ever. To assuage his disappointment in his children, George throws himself into the war effort. Always on the reactionary side, he is against the League of Nations, believes that the Roman Catholic Church is building fortresses throughout America, and is convinced that the government in Washington is run by German sympathizers and spies. He is especially distressed at the influence now wielded by Catholics, Irish, Jews, and other such irresponsible minorities.

Relentlessly his desire for escape—a desire which he cannot understand—increases. This restlessness reaches a climax when he starts a lawsuit against a prominent and influential politician named O'Brien. But the wily O'Brien easily engineers the naïve George into a situation in which he is arrested in a hotel room with a prostitute. Only the intervention of his old flame, Mary Monahan (now Mary O'Brien), and the payment of a large sum gets the charges against George dismissed, and the case attracts no publicity.

When John returns from the war, he is unwilling to enter into the life that his parents have planned for him. Instead, he goes off to New York, which almost breaks his parents' hearts. Worse, they later learn that he has secretly married a divorcée, Louise McCullough. (Fortunately, however, she is one of the Connecticut Hogarths, which helps George and Catharine save face over the marriage.)

In 1929 the stock market collapses. George's fortune is not seriously affected, but the news finally shocks him into recognizing how completely out of step he has become with the times. He reappraises his entire life, but though he sees much that has been foolish, essentially he believes that it has followed the perfect pattern. He is grief-stricken that John will not return to Boston and take up his role as head of the important Apley family.

Finally John decides to bring his wife and son, John, Jr. (whom George has already had enrolled at Groton) to Boston. Two weeks after John returns, George Apley dies.

THE GREAT GATSBY

F. Scott Fitzgerald

Francis Scott Key Fitzgerald was born in St. Paul, Minnesota, in 1896. His family was in comfortable circumstances, and he entered Princeton University, where he wrote for the literary magazines and collaborated on the Triangle shows with his friend Edmund Wilson, who was to become his lifelong associate and editor of Fitzgerald's posthumously published writings. Fitzgerald left Princeton in 1917 to serve in the army, and while in training camp, he began a novel about Princeton. He first gained recognition through the magazine appearance of short stories, soon followed by the novel This Side of Paradise, published in 1920. Another novel and two collections of short stories later, he was the acknowledged spokesman and chronicler of his generation of flappers, bootleggers, and expatriates. He and his wife Zelda lived extravagantly in America and France, exhibiting the hedonism and abandon characteristic of the times, drinking to excess, dissipating talent and energy, unable and unwilling to slow down or to look behind or ahead. The market for his work declined when the era ended in 1929, and Fitzgerald went to Hollywood to work. He died in 1940, after years of desperate emotional decline.

The Great Gatsby, published in 1925, remains the most telling and powerful fictional account of the jazz era in all its amoral abandon. Tender Is the Night—appearing in 1934, at a time when Fitzgerald's reputation had declined and Americans were not interested in the emotional crises of the idle rich—was poorly received. It has since risen a great deal in critical esteem, and is appreciated as a sensitive, tragic story of love and dependence among people who appear more contemporary and believable now than they did when the book was originally published.

Nick Carraway, a young man who finds his native Midwest too confining and provincial after his return from World War I, and who is being pushed unwillingly into an engagement with a girl of whom he is only vaguely fond, decides to come East and "learn the bond business"—a popular field for young men during the 1920s. Renting a house in Long Island's West Egg, he settles down to his new way of life.

Across the bay in East Egg lives Nick's distant cousin, the former Daisy Fay, now married to handsome and wealthy Tom Buchanan. Nick looks the Buchanans up, and they greet him as a long-lost, best-beloved friend. Daisy is as beautiful as ever, Tom as athletic and successful—but Nick senses an emptiness in them and their way of life. Nevertheless he is charmed by them, and by Daisy's close friend, the hard but attractive young woman, Jordan Baker.

In telling the Buchanans and Jordan about the house he rents, Nick mentions the fabulous estate next door, which belongs to a Mr. Jay Gatsby. At the sound of the name Gatsby, Daisy seems to become tense. Later, when she and Tom are out of the room, Nick learns from Jordan that Tom is rumored to be having an affair with a married woman. This is thought to explain Daisy's nervousness and constraint.

Tom insists on bringing Nick to meet his mistress. She is the voluptuous Myrtle Wilson, wife of a local garage mechanic. Nick finds her vulgar and unattractive, and determines to have as little as possible to do with Tom's relationship with her.

The stories that he hears about his neighbor, Gatsby, stir Nick's curiosity; the man is the center of a great deal of gossip, but nobody seems to know very much about him. When at last Nick gets an invitation to one of Gatsby's lavish Saturday night parties, he attends with pleasure. At the party he again meets Jordan Baker, and from her learns that Daisy had at one time been very much in love with Gatsby. Indeed, they had become engaged, and though Daisy eventually threw him over, she has never fully gotten over her feelings for Gatsby. The two have not seen each other in many years.

Nick becomes a friend of Gatsby's, and finds him an enigmatic figure. Obviously proud of his wealth, Gatsby seems nonetheless very insecure. On the whole, Nick decides that he likes him, and when Gatsby asks Nick to arrange a tea party at Nick's place, inviting himself and Daisy (who is not to know in advance that Gatsby is coming), Nick agrees.

Though the expansive, sophisticated Gatsby almost bolts at the last moment, he is finally persuaded to meet Daisy, and she is obviously as delighted as he is to renew their acquaintance. Gatsby's whole career has been built single-mindedly with the objective of finding Daisy one day and re-claiming her; he is convinced—rightly, as it happens—that Daisy has married Tom for his greater wealth. For her part, Daisy remembers her deep love for Gatsby, and the strains present in her marriage make it all the easier for her to fan old sparks once again into flames. Soon she and Gatsby are more in love with each other than ever before.

Gatsby is not exactly the man Daisy believes him to be. Born James Gatz, the son of very poor Midwesterners, he had early in life determined to be wealthy, and seizing an unusual opportunity during his boyhood to attach himself to the fabulously rich financier Dan Cody, he had changed his name and became, in a few short years and as the result of various shady (if not illegal) business ventures, the man he had set out to be: the urbane, polished, well-known Jay Gatsby. It is this man—this attractive, sophisticated, rich man —whom Daisy loves.

Gatsby believes that by all rights Daisy Fay has belonged to him ever since they were engaged, and at a dinner party at the Buchanans, to which Jordan and Nick are also invited, he is determined to announce his intention of taking her away with him. The situation does not lend itself to the in-tended announcement, however—though Tom Buchanan be-comes aware of a degree of intimacy between his wife and Gatsby that he had never before imagined.

As the evening progresses, they all drink a great deal of champagne, and decide to drive into New York. Gatsby and Daisy go in Gatsby's car—a yellow roadster—while Nick, Jordan, and Tom follow in the Buchanan car. The latter group stops at Wilson's garage for gasoline, and when they leave, Nick notices the face of Myrtle Wilson at an upstairs window. She glares at Jordan, and Nick smiles to himself, thinking that Myrtle supposes Jordan to be Tom's wife, Daisy, of whom she is insanely jealous.

The five young people meet as arranged at the Plaza Hotel, and in a drunken scene, Gatsby declares to Tom that Daisy is *his*—that she has never loved Tom, and that he intends to take her away. Tom manages to wring from Daisy the confession that she did, at least, love him early in their marriage. This confession wounds Gatsby, but even worse is Tom's determination to take Daisy home and to reawaken in her her love for him.

The scene becomes an ugly one, and at last Daisy and Gatsby start back to East Egg, with Tom, Nick, and Jordan following. When the latter group reaches Wilson's garage, however, they are stopped by a tragic sight: the dead body of Myrtle Wilson lying in the road. From the men and women who are standing about, they learn that Myrtle had gone running into the road waving her arms, and that she had been struck by a speeding yellow car which had not even stopped. Wilson is murmuring incoherently, but the details are soon pieced together by Nick.

Wilson had discovered that his wife was having an affair with another man, and had locked her up in the apartment over the garage and beaten her. He had been determined to move out of town to take Myrtle out of the reach of her seducer. She had somehow escaped, and had run into the road trying to flag down the approaching car to ask for help —though Wilson is under the erroneous impression that she had approached the yellow car specifically because it was driven by her lover. He is now determined to find the owner of the yellow car, and get his revenge upon the driver.

When Nick gets home that night, Gatsby's house is ablaze with light. Nick learns from Gatsby what he has already suspected: that the reason Gatsby had not stopped the car when the accidental killing took place was that Daisy, not himself, was at the wheel. He is waiting now for a sign from Daisy—the flicking off and on of her bedroom light, visible across the bay—that will tell him that everything is all right, and that she loves him. He waits up nearly the whole night, but the sign never comes.

No one believes that Wilson will be able to find the owner of the yellow car, but Tom Buchanan had hinted to him that *he* could identify the driver. Nick warns Gatsby that he is in danger, but Gatsby does not listen. He is too consumed with his thoughts of the elusive Daisy Fay.

Several nights later, Gatsby's body is found floating face down in his own swimming pool, shot through the head. In a clump of bushes nearby lies Wilson's body, his gun clutched in his hand.

Nick tries to round up all of Gatsby's friends and business associates for Gatsby's funeral, but though they had all been proud to claim acquaintance with him during his lifetime, and had used and abused his hospitality, all of them find excuses not to attend. At the funeral Nick finds only one tired, owl-eyed man whom he had seen at a couple of Gatsby's parties, and Gatsby's old father, Mr. Henry Gatz.

He is most disturbed at Jordan's refusal to come; he has been half in love with her, but when she tries to put him off at this crucial time with flippant badinage, Nick hangs up on her. Several months later, when he runs into Jordan briefly, he finally recognizes her as the superficial, callous, egocentric girl she is.

A few weeks later, he meets Tom Buchanan, and gets from him the truth: it was he who told Wilson that Gatsby owned the yellow roadster. Tom tries to justify himself with the fact that he loved Myrtle, with the fact that Gatsby had been trying to lure Daisy away. . . . It is too much for Nick. Sadly he turns away, recognizing the colossal carelessness of people like Tom and Daisy . . . and at the same time believing that what happened was inevitable, and that it will happen again.

TENDER IS THE NIGHT

F. Scott Fitzgerald

When eighteen-year-old Rosemary Hoyt, the newly risen movie star, arrives with her mother, the twice-widowed but indomitable Mrs. Elsie Speers, at the Hôtel Gauss in the south of France, she decides at once that she doesn't like it, and determines to leave after three days. She changes her mind, however, when she finds herself accepted and drawn in by the one group at the hotel that seems to be the focus of everyone's attention—a group that is at once self-contained, self-effacing, and vastly superior to every other group. How much more sophisticated, more inviting they seem than the people she has known heretofore—people typified by Collis Clay, the Yale graduate who has been following her about Europe like a lost puppy.

At the hub of this group are handsome Dick Diver, a non-practicing psychologist, and his incredibly beautiful but remote wife, Nicole. Rosemary falls instantly in love with Dick, but she is enchanted, too, by the others—particularly Abe and Mary North and Tommy Barban. These people are intelligent, attractive, witty, and they live a life of such calculated self-amusement that Rosemary cannot resist them.

Before she knows it, Rosemary is caught up in the activities of her new friends—and in a clandestine (if unconsummated) love affair with Dick Diver. Both of them agree that Nicole must suspect nothing. Dick is tremendously attached to his wife, as Rosemary observes, and from a hint dropped by a guest at a party about a scene between Dick and Nicole which the guest had witnessed, Rosemary surmises that there is more to the Divers' relationship than she is aware of.

She at last gets a glimpse of the true nature of things one night when she and Dick come upon Nicole in a hotel bathroom, babbling hysterical and incoherent accusations. The next day, Rosemary is hurt but not surprised when Dick sends her away.

Nicole's madness is the secret grief of Dick Diver's life. He had first met her when, as a beautiful and very rich young girl of sixteen, she had been committed to a sanitarium in Switzerland run by one of Dick's friends and colleagues, Dr. Franz Gregorovious. Nicole had become schizophrenic as the result of having been seduced by her own father. When Nicole and Dick met, he was just going off to the front as a captain; and for two years, the mentally ill young girl and the handsome American doctor-soldier corresponded. At first the letters clearly revealed the depths of Nicole's disturbance. But the latter half of the correspondence indicated to Dick that she had, indeed, made a remarkable recovery.

When World War I was over, Dick returned to Switzerland. He and Nicole fell in love and determined to marry. Nicole's older sister, the well-intentioned but insensitive "Baby" Warren, believed that Dick was marrying Nicole for her money, and though this was not true, Dick saw no reason to disabuse "Baby" of her notion—particularly as she whole-heartedly approved of the match.

Life for Dick and Nicole was, at first, pleasant. Dick had always found his greatest joy in life in helping people; and with her husband to lean on, Nicole continued to improve. The Divers had two children—a boy, Lanier, and a girl, Topsy—and though Dick neglected his profession, they were leading an idyllic, pleasure-filled existence.

Now, however, Nicole has had a relapse. This seems to Dick the opportune moment to accept a long-proffered partnership with Franz; and the two doctors therefore buy a clinic in Switzerland, where they will try to cure wealthy Americans suffering from mental illness. (The clinic is financed by Nicole's money through "Baby" Warren, who manages Nicole's affairs; and it is understood that Nicole herself will be a quasi-patient at the clinic.)

At first things go well, but after some time Dick finds himself becoming more and more frustrated. He is drinking more than he should. At last he determines to take a leave of absence from the clinic; so, leaving Nicole behind, he goes to Paris.

It is in Paris that events seem to conspire against him. He gets a wire telling him of the death of his father, and he makes a quick trip to the United States for the funeral. He becomes highly introspective, thinking about the contrast between his father's life—he had been a minister—and his own.

Back in Paris, he learns that Abe North has been beaten to death in a speakeasy; and the parallel between his own career and that of the alcoholic Abe, a musical genius who never accomplished anything, is painful.

At his hotel in Paris, he meets Rosemary Hoyt—as beautiful as ever, still hounded by Collis Clay. In the four years that have passed since their last meeting she has become a woman and at last she and Dick consummate their affair. But now they realize that they do not love each other anymore, and they part.

After Rosemary is gone, Dick and Collis go out and tour the bars and bistros—a disastrous evening that ends with Dick being arrested for drunkenness and for assaulting a French policeman. "Baby" Warren finally manages to get Dick out of jail, and the story is kept out of the papers. But Dick recognizes that something serious is happening within himself.

Returning to Switzerland and Nicole, who is now again well, Dick tries to resume his life productively as a psychologist, but he cannot. He and Franz agree to separate; Franz—almost eagerly—agrees to buy out Dick's share in the clinic. The Divers return south.

The life of idleness, at which he had been such an expert just a few years before, now loses its fascination for Dick. There is a hollowness within him that he cannot stand, but which he does not know how to combat. He tries to be an attentive husband, a good father, but he knows that he is only partially successful.

When Mary North—now remarried to an Indian with the dubious title Conte de Minghetti—invites Dick and Nicole to visit her at her villa, they accept, primarily because they have nothing else to do. As they had suspected it would be, however, the visit is a disaster, and Dick accuses Mary of having become a bore. When she returns the compliment, he knows that hers is the more accurate judgment of the two.

Back at the Riviera, Dick watches Nicole drifting further and further away from him. Ironically, she is now almost completely well, and every day finds her stronger. When one afternoon she realizes that she has been maneuvering her own life successfully for some time, without referring to Dick, she understands that she is at last a whole woman.

Recognizing that the foundation of Dick's love for her is built on her weakness—on his ability to help her, to care for her—and that she can no longer offer him this weakness as she is no longer ill, Nicole decides to accept the advances of the long-patient Tommy Barban, who has always loved her. Soon they are engaged in a passionate affair, and Tommy determines to marry her.

Tommy goes to Dick and confronts him with the fact that Nicole now loves him (Tommy) instead of her husband, and that they wish to marry. Much to Tommy's surprise, Dick accepts the situation with complete equanimity, and makes no protests. (Nicole realizes that he had suspected what is between her and Tommy for some time; and his easy acceptance of the situation is yet additional proof to her that he no longer loves her.)

Dick and Nicole are divorced, and she marries Tommy.

From time to time they get news of Dick—but only of the sketchiest kind. He returns to America and becomes a small-town doctor in New York State. As the postmarks on the cards he sends change frequently, however, they gather that he has not yet settled down. The last one comes from Hornell, New York. . . .

SANCTUARY

William Faulkner

William Faulkner, born in 1897 in New Albany, Mississippi, moved with his family at an early age to Oxford, the site of the University of Mississippi. Faulkner did not finish high school, but joined the Canadian Air Force for a year, and returned in 1919 to Oxford, where he studied for two years at the university. He apparently decided to be a writer in 1924, when he went to New Orleans and became associated with a group of writers who had founded an experimental literary magazine. In New Orleans he wrote some poems and two novels of no great consequence. His first important long works appeared in 1929, and were followed by a steady stream of novels. Recognition of Faulkner's talent was belated but well within his lifetime. He received the Nobel Prize for literature in 1949, and was often referred to as the most significant living American author, a creative genius without equal among his countrymen in this century. From 1925 until his death in 1962 Faulkner lived in the same house in Oxford, Mississippi, relatively secluded for a literary celebrity of his stature.

The novels of William Faulkner are set in the Deep South, a region, as Faulkner describes it, of dissolute landed families and vulgar, newly rich merchants, of whites and Negroes, of isolated towns and lonely farms, of death, decay, violence, and hatred. In accepting his Nobel Prize, Faulkner spoke of the aim of his fiction —to describe "the human beast in conflict with itself." To achieve this end, while keeping the past always in mind, Faulkner created a new prose style; for conventional grammatical structure, he substituted long stream-of-consciousness sentences in which meaning is conveyed through the association of images which reach back in time to the sources of memory and experience. Sanctuary (1931) is a horrifying tale of criminality in a small town; its sequel, Requiem for a Nun, appeared in 1951. Both novels take place in the fictional Yoknapatawpha County, in which Faulkner set more than half of his novels and stories. Not in the Yoknapatawpha series, Light in August (1932) is a complex allegorical novel.

Horace Benbow, tormented to the breaking point by his nagging wife, Belle, determines to leave her. Deserting his law practice, he begins making his way to the home of his sister, Narcissa Sartoris. On his way he meets in a wood a small, tense man with a pistol, who leads him to a rundown plantation known as the Old Frenchman Place.

This plantation is the hideout of Lee Goodwin, bootleg liquor manufacturer. The tense man is called Popeye, and he is one of Goodwin's cohorts—though the exact relationship between the two is not clear. The others living on the plantation are equally disreputable: Ruby LaMar, a former prostitute who is the mother of Goodwin's infant son; the idiot Tommy; Tommy's father, an old blind-and-deaf man; and Van, Goodwin's tough and muscular truck driver. But Horace is trying to make his peace with the world, and he does not judge them.

Leaving the Old Frenchman Place the next day, Horace reaches his childhood home, now inhabited by Narcissa (widowed), her young son, Benbow Sartoris, and the old but sharp-tongued spinster Miss Jenny. Also in attendance is handsome Gowan Stevens, a suitor of Narcissa's, considerably younger than she.

Gowan senses that Narcissa is not responding to his passion, and so he decamps in order to meet a college girl with whom he has a date, the beautiful Temple Drake. By the time he meets Temple, however, the unstable Gowan is thoroughly drunk; and instead of taking her to the football game as he had promised, Gowan takes her to Lee Goodwin's place so that he can get more liquor. On the way, however, he manages to smash up his own car, and it is the sinister Popeye that leads Gowan and Temple to Goodwin.

At first Temple is not frightened by the strange people in this remote house. But as Gowan gets drunker and drunker, she becomes increasingly aware of the danger of her situation. Gowan is clearly in no condition to take her away; Popeye and Van are both openly eyeing her with lust; and the sullen Ruby blazes hatred at her. Suddenly the sophisticated veneer of eighteen-year-old Temple cracks, and the terrified child within bursts forth.

The hours that follow turn the experience into a nightmare. Van and Popeye become menacing, and only the interference of Lee Goodwin prevents their attacking Temple.

Gowan, drunk, is beaten up by Van, and Temple spends the night crouched in a miserable dark bedroom beside the snoring Gowan, terrified for her life.

The next morning Gowan recognizes that he cannot get Temple away from these strange people, and in his cowardice he slinks off the place and deserts her.

Now thoroughly unnerved, Temple begs to be taken off the place. But her only two allies are Ruby, who fears Temple's presence as a danger to herself, and the idiot Tommy; and neither of them can help her. In desperation, Temple runs to the barn and hides there in the dark.

Seeing her leave the house, Popeye announces loudly to the others that he is leaving the plantation for good. But, instead, he circles around and sneaks into the barn through a rear entrance, and hides himself in the loft.

Tommy has been sitting outside the locked front door of the barn, and Temple has felt him to be some protection. But suddenly she becomes aware of Popeye's breathing in the dark.

In the blackness and humidity, Temple is violently raped. She screams. . . .

Later, a shot rings out, and the kindly idiot boy, Tommy, lies dead. . . .

Several days later, Lee Goodwin is arrested for the murder of Tommy, and brought to the Yoknapatawpha Jail. He protests his innocence, but refuses to divulge any details of who was present at the Old Frenchman Place. Ruby LaMar, as much in love with Goodwin as ever, hires Horace Benbow to defend him, and in spite of the protestations of the self-righteous Narcissa, Horace takes the case. He believes that he has been for too long dominated by women, and that now, at last, he must take a stand for what he believes is just, in spite of the Southern prejudices and traditions by which he was raised.

Meanwhile, Popeye has taken Temple to Memphis, where he installs her in a locked bedroom in a whorehouse run by the genial Reba Rivers. (Hilariously, two other "nonprofessional" guests come to reside at Miss Reba's. They are the Yoknapatawpha hayseeds, Virgil Snopes and his friend Fonzo, who mistakenly believe Miss Reba to be running a lodginghouse for young transients.)

The gentry of Yoknapatawpha have prejudged Lee Goodwin, and found him guilty. They hound his poor mistress, Ruby LaMar, mercilessly; and she, aware of what Horace's handling the case will do to his reputation, urges him to give it up. But Horace is determined to see the thing through, and thus redeem his own manhood.

Horace learns from Ruby that Temple Drake and Popeye had been at the house at the time of Tommy's murder. In spite of Goodwin's protestations, Horace determines to track them down and pin the crime on Popeye.

From the venal Senator Clarence Snopes, who has learned the information as a result of a visit to Virgil and Fonzo in Memphis, Horace learns of Temple's whereabouts. (Of course he bribes Senator Snopes for the information.) Horace visits Temple, and learns the full horror of her situation. It appears that Popeye is impotent; he keeps Temple a prisoner in her room, and brings to her regularly a handsome young man named Red. It is Red who is Temple's lover, and their love must be enacted as a performance for the depraved Popeye. Temple agrees to testify in Goodwin's behalf.

Before the trial, Temple devises a scheme whereby she may have Popeye killed and then run off with Red, whom she loves. The scheme misfires however—the sinister, cruel Popeye has too many henchmen of his own—and it is Red who is murdered.

As Horace becomes more and more deeply involved in the lives of Lee Goodwin and Ruby LaMar, he finds himself growing increasingly stronger. For the first time he feels a glimmer of self-respect, and he determines to divorce Belle and begin living a life that will be true to his own needs and ideals.

His sister Narcissa, however, has far different ideas for him. Respectability is her watchword, and she is mortified that her brother should be engaged in defending people whom she considers degenerate murderers. Narcissa is also determined that Horace will not create a scandal by divorcing Belle, inasmuch as he had created one when he married her. (Belle was the divorced wife of a man named Mitchell.) To render Horace powerless and return him to his usual state of docile obedience, Narcissa recognizes the importance of Horace's losing the murder case.

She therefore goes to Horace's opponent, the prosecuting attorney Eustace Graham, and tells him what she knows about the information Horace received from Senator Snopes. Graham, a typical representative of Yoknapatawpha morality, has his men attack Senator Snopes at night, and wring from the beaten man the address of Temple Drake.

Although Goodwin steadfastly refuses to bring Popeye's name into the case—he knows that his own life would be snuffed out by Popeye's henchmen if Popeye were implicated—Horace is convinced that the jury will not convict Goodwin on the slim evidence available. And when Temple Drake arrives in court, Horace feels that his case is sewed up.

He does not know, of course, that Graham has been in collaborative conference with Popeye; and when Temple takes the stand, she tells the packed courtroom the hideous story of her rape. (Most gruesome of all the details she reveals is the fact that she was violated with a large corn cob, and a gynecologist corroborates this testimony.) But when asked what man perpetrated this crime upon her, Temple coldly and unemotionally points to Lee Goodwin. There is a clamor in the courtroom, and Temple is whisked away by a group of Popeye's strongmen, who surround her. Her eyes blazing with terror, she is unable to talk to anyone.

Goodwin is found guilty and sentenced to be hanged. But the self-righteous Yoknapatawphans determine to take justice into their own hands. They kidnap Goodwin from the jail, torture him, and roast him alive.

As the lynching is in progress, Horace recognizes that his fight for survival as a man is over, and that he is beaten. He tells Narcissa simply that he is going back to his wife, Belle. She replies, equally calmly, that she knew he would; indeed, she has already written to Belle to expect him.

Ironically, several months later, Popeye is arrested in Florida on a charge of murder—a murder he did not, in fact, commit—and he is found guilty. He awaits his death with great calmness. Indeed, Popeye's entire life has been one of surface calm, though a long history of bloodthirsty and unthinking violence would seem to indicate that there is constant turmoil within his mind.

As for Temple, her father, the wealthy and cultivated Judge Drake, takes her to Europe, where she may enjoy the

calm and beautiful scenery of the old world, and thus find
peace. Temple, however, views the splendor through cold,
unmoved eyes. . . .

LIGHT IN AUGUST

William Faulkner

Orphaned Lena Grove, living with her Uncle McKinley's family at Doane's Mill, Alabama, becomes the clandestine mistress of young Lucas Burch. When Lena discovers that she is
pregnant, Lucas tells her he must go away to find a better
job—but that he will send for her in due course and marry
her.

Lucas does not send for her, however—or, at least, thinks
Lena, he must have sent for her but his message has gotten
lost. As the time for her confinement comes closer, Lena decides to go in search of him. Setting off with thirty-five cents
and a satchel, she begins her long journey. Fortunately people are kind to her along the way, and give her lifts in their
wagons, or shelter for the night and food for the morning.

She hears a rumor that Lucas is now working in a planing
mill at Jefferson. When she finally gets to the mill, it is Saturday, and the only man there is named Bunch, not Burch.

Byron Bunch is immediately taken with Lena, and he tries
to comfort her. Reluctantly he tells her that there is no man
named Burch on the place. The two spot a building on fire
some distance away, and to take Lena's mind off her troubles,
Bunch tells her about the two men who live there: Joe Brown
and Joe Christmas. Bunch sees his mistake, however, when
the ferreting questions of Lena reveal that "Brown" is, indeed, the deserter Lucas Burch.

The fire that rages in the Negro cabin on the old Burden
place, where Christmas and Brown are staying, is the beginning of what will be the last chapter in Christmas's tortured
life.

His earliest memories revolve about the time when he was
three or four years old, living in an orphanage. Called Christmas, because it was on Christmas Eve that he was found
on the orphanage steps, he has no knowledge of his origins—

except that, as the children at the orphanage had teased him with the epithet "nigger," he is sure that he is part Negro, although he has never had any trouble passing for white.

He remembers a malevolent old man—the orphanage custodian—who had kidnaped him one night, and who had whispered strange oaths over him, calling down God's curse upon him.

He remembers more vividly the McEacherns, who adopted him. Old McEachern was a narrow-minded, puritanical farmer who had beaten young Joe regularly and had preached never-ending sermons on the evils of the world and the wickedness of the flesh.

When Joe was about eighteen, he had a chance encounter with a bleached blond waitress named Bobbie. Considerably older than Joe, Bobbie was touched by his innocence and strangeness, and soon she became his mistress, Joe sneaking out of the McEachern farmhouse window by a rope to go to her.

Joe's nocturnal adventures were discovered at last by McEachern, who followed the boy and the waitress to a country dance. There he denounced the girl as a harlot and his stepson as a lechering son of Satan. Pushed beyond the breaking point, Joe seized a chair and beat the old man over the head with it. He didn't even wait to find out if he had killed McEachern, but began running.

Fifteen years later, he was still running. Suffering from his own conflicts and hostilities, Joe Christmas, never accepted by either the white community or the Negro community, always felt an outsider.

When he reached Jefferson, he decided to stop running for a while, particularly as he found a sort of silent patroness in the old spinster Miss Burden, who gave him food and allowed him to live in one of the deserted cabins on her place.

Miss Burden had long been a sort of recluse on her own estate. The descendant of Northern abolitionists and herself a friend to Negroes, she was shunned by the townspeople, who after three generations continued to think of her as a stranger.

Her kindness to Joe Christmas, however, soon provoked his anger, and he felt a need to punish the strange woman who gave without asking anything in return. One night, he went to her darkened bedroom and raped her.

Strangely Miss Burden did not seem to be angry over the episode, which only frustrated and enraged Christmas the more. Eventually the two became lovers—but their relationship was a source of humiliation to Christmas, who could not bear that Miss Burden should maintain her own identity and strength of will. Christmas began to feel that Miss Burden had become the male in the relationship and himself the female.

At about this time Christmas had invited to live with him in the cabin a foolish young man named Joe Brown who, like himself, had drifted into town and who now worked at the planing mill. He believed that Brown's presence would force Miss Burden to leave him alone. But this proved not to be the case.

At last, in desperation, Christmas killed Miss Burden and set the cabin afire. Now he has begun running again.

Byron Bunch goes to his friend, the defrocked minister Hightower, to discuss the problem of Lena Grove. The ex-minister sees at once that Byron has fallen in love with the girl, and having devoted the past years of his own life to avoiding involvement with his fellow man, Hightower refuses to give Bunch counsel.

Joe Brown has been taken into custody by the sheriff as a possible accessory in the murder, though Brown insists on his own innocence and claims the thousand-dollar reward that has been posted for the murderer. He tells everyone that Christmas alone performed the deed. At first, of course, the townspeople do not believe him; but when he tells them that Christmas had confessed to being part Negro, they all believe in Christmas's guilt. A search party is sent out after the murderer, and Brown is kept in prison.

Byron Bunch determines to tell Lena nothing about the murder. Instead, he tells the girl that Brown (Burch) is away on business, but that as soon as he is free, Bunch will get him to come to her.

The manhunt for Christmas is on in earnest, and though the fugitive is desperate with the knowledge of what will happen to him if he is caught, he realizes that he cannot go on running for the rest of his life. Finally he all but asks to be arrested in nearby Mottstown, and is taken back to prison in Jefferson.

An old couple named Hines, living in Mottstown, hear of the arrest of the "white nigger" and become strangely agitated. The man, Old Doc Hines, begins trying to stir up a lynching party, but his wife manages to hustle him off to Jefferson. There they encounter Byron Bunch, to whom they reveal themselves as Christmas's grandparents. The murderer was the illegitimate son of their daughter, Millie, and a traveling circus man who claimed to be Mexican but was, according to Hines, part Negro. Hines has been convinced ever since that that child was specially marked for God's vengeance; indeed, he was the very man who arranged to be custodian at the orphanage just so that he could see what happened to his bastard grandchild.

Byron brings the old couple to Reverend Hightower, and tells the minister that if he will only say that Christmas was with him on the night of the murder, the man will not hang. But the minister fairly screams his refusal to become involved in the lives of others.

As the Hineses are not allowed to see Christmas in jail, Byron Bunch takes them to the cottage where Lena is installed. When Lena is delivered of her baby, Mrs. Hines's mind wanders, and she thinks it is her infant grandchild, Joe, that has been born.

With Christmas in jail, Brown is released, but he is not given the reward which he claims belongs to him. Byron gets the sheriff to force Brown to go to the cabin where Lena lies, though Brown is not told why he is being brought there. When he sees Lena, he pales, and glibly begins to promise the simple, devoted girl that they will be married soon, and that she will become Mrs. Lucas Burch.

But Byron, who loves Lena, recognizes that Brown is only looking for an avenue of escape. He follows Brown to an embankment on the outskirts of town where Brown has fled with the intention of waiting there until the sheriff sends the reward money. The two men fight, though Byron knows he is outmatched. At last Brown knocks Byron out, and, terrified that he has killed him, decides not to wait for the messenger to arrive with the money, but to hop on a passing train. Byron, lying on the ground in pain, is able to smile when he sees Brown depart, for he knows that Lena will never see the man again.

The sheriff is insistent that Christmas be given a fair trial; indeed, he even consents to an interview between Christmas and old Mrs. Hines.

A fanatic young man named Grimm, however, insists to the sheriff that there will be trouble with Christmas, and against the sheriff's orders, Grimm rounds up a band of gun-carrying men who surround the jail and town square, ostensibly to maintain order.

When Christmas is escorted out of the jail en route to the courthouse, he suddenly breaks away from the sheriff and disappears into the crowd. Immediately Grimm's posse is after him.

They at last track Christmas down in Hightower's house. (Why he should have gone there is a mystery, unless his grandmother had, in her wandering way, believed that Hightower stood ready to help Christmas and had told him this when she saw him in jail.)

Christmas knocks the ex-minister down and takes refuge in the man's study. When Grimm and his band burst into Hightower's house, the old man begins to shout loudly that Christmas had been with him the night of the murder, that it is all a mistake.

But it is too late for Hightower to do Christmas any good. Grimm corners him and shoots him; and while he lies crumpled on the floor, fatally wounded but conscious, Grimm whips out a knife and savagely mutilates Christmas. Shortly thereafter, Joe Christmas dies.

Occasionally, wagon drivers traveling through different states in the South encounter an odd band of travelers. They are a young woman, who wears no wedding band; an infant male, still suckling at her breast; and a middle-aged man. They are Lena, her child, and Byron Bunch. They are headed for nowhere in particular, but seem content simply to be wandering about together, having themselves a fine view of God's great world.

THE BRIDGE OF SAN LUIS REY

Thornton Wilder

Thornton Wilder was born in Madison, Wisconsin, in 1897. His father, the editor of The Wisconsin State Journal, *was appointed Consul General of Shanghai and Hong Kong in 1906; the boy's voyage to China with his family was the first of many extensive journeys which have occupied much of Wilder's later life. He entered Oberlin College in 1915, left after two years to serve in the World War, and resumed his studies at Yale, graduating in 1920. He taught in Rome, and returned to Princeton to take an M.A. degree, which he received in 1926, the year of the publication of his first novel,* The Cabala. *Not a prolific writer, Wilder has written only five novels and six plays. He has taught at Harvard and at Chicago, and has given lecture courses at European universities.*

Thornton Wilder has never been associated with a particular literary movement. He is a precise craftsman with a classical sense of form and style; his education, imagination, and superb taste are evident in all his writings, a few of which are derived from other literary sources. Entirely his own creation, The Bridge of San Luis Rey *brought the author international acclaim when it was published in 1927. It is a singularly beautiful parable in which the characters represent—perhaps—aspects of love: humility, sorrow, innocence, bitterness. The tragedy around which the book centers is poetically and dramatically timed in the lives of the victims, but it is, after all, an accident of fate for which no justification, other than the unknowable will of Providence, can be determined.*

It is five o'clock in the afternoon, July 20, 1714, when the bridge of San Luis Rey—that marvelous structure of vines built a hundred years before by the Incas, that bridge which all Peruvians consider indestructible—for no apparent reason breaks, plunging five people to their deaths in the gulf below.

The single witness to the breaking of the bridge is Brother Juniper, a good priest long devoted to discovering, to the extent of his abilities, God's true purposes and plans. Brother Juniper accordingly decides to investigate the lives of the five people killed in the accident, hoping to uncover in them a common theme by which he will discover why God determined that those five people should die. For years he searches for evidence. . . .

Doña María, Marquesa de Montemayor, is a well-known eccentric. Years ago the woman had borne a daughter, Clara, on whom she lavished all her love and affection. But Clara was a cold, arrogant girl, and loathed her mother. This is the one bitterness of Doña María's life. At the earliest opportunity, Clara had escaped her mother's clutching grasp through marriage to the Conde Vicente d'Abuirre, a petty nobleman of Spain. Now, the mother writes lengthy, detailed letters to her daughter in Spain—letters which are destined to become one of the pinnacles of South American literature —through which she hopes to regain the lost love of Clara. But the girl remains indifferent to her mother's grief as well as to her love.

As a companion, Doña María has living with her the twelve-year-old girl Pepita, taken from the local convent orphanage. This Pepita is the brightest of the girls in the orphanage, and the one whom the Mother Superior, Madre María del Pilar, has selected to train in convent administration. All of Pepita's affection is centered on Madre María, and she finds it difficult to feel anything warmer than a sense of duty toward the Marquesa, her mistress.

One day the Marquesa and Pepita are in a theater where the beautiful and beloved actress, La Périchole, is playing. La Périchole makes sarcastic jibes from the stage about the Marquesa; but the old woman does not understand that she is the butt of the comedienne's jokes. The Viceroy hears of the performance—La Périchole is his mistress—and, as he fears the influence of the Marquesa's son-in-law at the court of Spain, he insists that she apologize to the Marquesa.

The actress visits the old woman, and finds in her not an eccentric, laughable crone, but a cultivated, passionate, tragic figure. She goes away from the interview deeply moved.

The Marquesa's relationship with her daughter comes to a climax when Clara has a child. The Marquesa at last realizes that her affection for Clara has been exclusively selfish. She determines to go to the shrine of Cluxambuqua with Pepita to do penance. At the shrine she discovers a letter Pepita is writing to Madre María, in which the girl protests her love for the Mother Superior and her indifference toward her mistress. The Marquesa forgives the child.

Leaving the shrine, the two begin to cross the bridge of San Luis Rey.

Among the children raised in the orphanage at the Convent of Santa María Rosa de las Rosas were identical twins, left there in infancy. These two brothers, Esteban and Manuel, grow up to be singularly beautiful young men—but they are a mysterious pair. They speak little to others, and have established an intimacy of communication between themselves that is complete almost without language. They work together, eat together, live together. The only woman, it seems, who has any effect on them is the Mother Superior who raised them, Madre María del Pilar.

Because the boys have been educated in a convent, they are among the few men in the town who can write. Therefore, they become scribes, hiring themselves out to write letters for the illiterate. One day, Manuel is hired to write a love note for Camila, the beautiful actress called La Périchole, and he falls desperately in love with her.

It is this love for the distant beauty that causes the first rift between the twins. Although neither refers to what is happening, it becomes clear to Esteban that part of his brother's mind is focused elsewhere, and he soon discovers the cause. He offers to leave Manuel, and urges him to pursue his romance; but Manuel calls him a fool, and says that nothing can separate them. Indeed, Manuel goes so far as to send a message to the actress telling her, in harsh terms, that he will write no more letters for her.

Then one day, Manuel suffers a serious injury to his leg. Esteban nurses him as well as possible, but the wound festers and becomes worse. At last, a doctor is sent for. The doctor gives Esteban detailed instructions concerning the necessity of frequent applications of cold cloths to the wound. The pain that these treatments cause Manuel is intense, and in his agony he screams out curses upon Esteban. When the pain subsides, he apologizes to his brother, but the curses cut into Esteban's heart like knives, and he believes that he is the cause of all his brother's pain and grief.

Ultimately Manuel dies of the wound, and Esteban is inconsolable. He determines to kill himself, then changes his mind and signs onto a ship as a sailor. But before the vessel is to sail, he changes his mind once more. He is grief-stricken and will talk to no one. He feels that he is alone, alone, alone. . . .

At last the ship's captain convinces Esteban that he must

carry on with his life. The two set out for Lima, where the boat is to sail. Before they come in sight of the bridge of San Luis Rey, the captain finds that he has to stay behind to check some merchandise. Esteban goes ahead, and begins to cross the bridge behind an old woman and a little girl. . . .

There was a young man who, for years, lived by his wits. In different lands, in different segments of society, he changed his name and his position whenever he was bored, living always as an adventurer, one step ahead of the law. The illegitimate son of a Castilian nobleman, his only identity now is as "Uncle Pio."

The greatest event of Uncle Pio's life, without doubt, was his discovery of a singularly arresting young child, whom he determined to take and train as the greatest actress of her day. (Uncle Pio loves more than anything else the Spanish drama.) An actor himself, he works with the girl relentlessly, for he senses that she has great talent. Much to his surprise, he discovers when she matures that she has great beauty as well.

The girl, Camila, finds Uncle Pio a harsh and perfectionist taskmaster, and she longs for the approval from him that is never forthcoming. But though she rebels from time to time against his tutelage, she always returns, for Uncle Pio has kindled within her own breast the dream that they now share: she must become the greatest actress in the land.

At last Uncle Pio considers the girl ready, and as La Périchole she makes her debut. She is an instant success and becomes the darling of Peru. Soon she is mistress to the Viceroy himself.

Now the vain and impulsive Camila can have her revenge upon Pio, for he is old and the tables have turned. He is the one who needs her approval and recognition. This she withholds; indeed, she casts Uncle Pio out of her life. He tries many ruses to draw La Périchole into meetings and interviews with him, but she remains distant and will have nothing to do with him.

For a while La Périchole rides the crest: fame, fortune, and a perfect son, Jaime, child of the Viceroy, are hers. But then a tragedy strikes. Both La Périchole and her beloved beautiful child are stricken with the smallpox. When the disease is over, the great actress finds her face hideously scarred and her body old. Her son, still beautiful, is nonetheless sadly weakened by the ravages of the disease.

At this juncture Uncle Pio comes to La Périchole again. At first she rejects him, but finally she agrees to see him. To his proposal that she rejoin him she turns a deaf ear. But when he proposes to take her son—now penniless—and make a gentleman of him, she wavers. At last, understanding how successful Uncle Pio had been with her at this game, she agrees that he may take the boy, Jaime, though she understands that she will probably never see him again. At this her heart breaks, and she turns to the Madre María del Pilar for comfort.

The old man, Uncle Pio, and the young, sensitive lad, Jaime, set off together. The boy becomes tired, and the old man tells him they will rest when they have crossed the bridge of San Luis Rey. Ahead of them, he notices an old woman with a little girl, and a young man who seems to be a sailor. . . .

When Brother Juniper has learned all that he can about the lives and emotions of the five people killed in such a seemingly arbitrary fashion, he wrestles with the problem of finding a common thread running through his evidence.

At last he publishes a monumental work describing his findings. But the Inquisition does not approve of attempts to explain the methods of God, and the old priest is burned publicly, along with his great manuscript about the fall of the bridge of San Luis Rey.

FOR WHOM THE BELL TOLLS

Ernest Hemingway

Ernest Hemingway was born in 1899 in Oak Park, Illinois, where his father was a doctor. Hunting trips to northern Michigan made a profound impression on the young Hemingway, and inspired some of his first short stories. After high school he joined the editorial staff of the Kansas City Star, which he left in 1917 in order to join the army. He was rejected because of his poor eyesight, and joined instead an ambulance unit on the Italian front, where he was badly wounded. Returning to America, he grew bored and restless, and left for Paris where he was to become a leading member of the "Lost Generation" of American expatriates. Under the literary influence of Gertrude Stein, Ezra Pound, and Sherwood Anderson, Hemingway developed the distinctive, staccato prose style which has influenced countless modern writers. His first published work, Three Stories and Ten Poems, *appeared in 1923, and was followed by further story collections and his first novels; by 1929 he was realizing a substantial income from his writings. Hemingway became an international celebrity, and was often pictured in the press while boxing, mountain-climbing, at the bullfights, deep-sea fishing, hunting big game, covering a war-torn front. Not surprisingly, Hemingway drew from each of these activities a novel, story, or journalistic account.* For Whom the Bell Tolls, *published in 1937, was Hemingway's own favorite among his novels, and was based upon his own experiences as a reporter and Loyalist supporter in the Spanish Civil War. Hemingway was a reporter in Europe during World War II, after which he settled for a time in Cuba with his fourth wife. He wrote* The Old Man and the Sea *in 1952, and the publication of this simple tale did much to restore his declining literary reputation. In 1953 he won both the Nobel and Pulitzer prizes, well-deserved rewards for the man who instilled a new purity, vigor, and strength into the prose of his time. In 1961 he died of a self-inflicted shotgun wound.*

In May 1937, Robert Jordan, college instructor of Spanish from Missoula, Montana, finds himself behind enemy lines in the mountains of Spain, functioning as a "bridgeblower" for the Republicans in the Civil War. His current assignment is to reach a band of guerrilla warriors hidden in a cave, and with their aid to dynamite a specified bridge and destroy two Fascist-held guard posts. This demolition—to be precisely timed to coincide with a planned Republican offensive—will insure the successful campaign of the shrewd General Golz.

Guided by the rugged, white-haired Anselmo, Jordan succeeds in locating the guerrilla band in their mountain fastness; and setting down his sacks of dynamite, he surveys the men and women who will be his comrades-in-arms for the next four days.

It is a strange group. There is Pablo, nominal leader, but now stricken with fear, with craving for security, and with love of alcohol. There is his wife, Pilar; ugly, brave, eternally dedicated to the Republican cause, she is the real leader of the band. The others, Jordan finds, are not so easily assessed. Anselmo, who has been his guide, he trusts implicitly, though the old man himself seems to have fears of his own adequacy. The stolid, stubborn Fernando, with his punctilious

regard for etiquette and morality, is an unknown quantity—
as is Rafael, the twinkling-spirited, lackadaisical gypsy.
Rounding out the band are the quiet brothers, Agustin and
Andres, and the dark Eladio—and Maria.

Yes—there is Maria. Young, frightened, beautiful, she has
been a victim of the Fascists, whose shaving of her head and
physical abuses of her had left her nearly insane. Pilar, who
loves the girl passionately, has nursed Maria back to health.
Jordan instantly responds to the girl's strange, pathetic
beauty. Pilar notes this, and trusting Jordan implicitly, determines that Maria shall be his woman.

Pilar's trust in Jordan is not matched by the others, and
soon there is a debate in the cave as to the advisability of
joining in the expedition to blow up the bridge. Pablo is
against it; to dynamite would be to alert the enemy and
make it necessary for the band to escape to a remote region
in order to avoid capture. Here they are able to live in relative quiet and prosperity.

Pilar scorns Pablo for his cowardice, and she is joined by
the others, who believe that the bridge must be blown up if
the Republic demands it, regardless of the personal danger
and sacrifice involved. In the showdown that follows, Pilar
asserts her leadership, and Pablo sees that he is defeated.

Jordan does not trust Pablo, and wonders whether it would
not be wise to kill him. In this he is encouraged by Rafael,
but he determines to wait and see.

That night, as Jordan lies in his sleeping bag outside the
cave, the frail Maria comes to him, and at her own insistence
she becomes his woman. She has fallen in love with this
Inglés, "Roberto"—and he with her. For the first time in his
life, Jordan feels complete love and affection and tenderness.

A concentration of Fascist planes that fly over the next
morning indicates that real trouble is brewing. Pilar recommends leaving Pablo out of discussions of strategy; he is
smart, but his fear and disinclination to act make him, she
believes, more of a liability at the moment than an asset.
Therefore, Pablo does not join in the expedition to the nearby
stronghold of the guerrilla Santiago, called El Sordo, on whom
Jordan must rely for help.

As Jordan, Pilar, and Maria make their way to the camp
of El Sordo, Pilar tells of the early days of the revolution.
At that time Pablo was at his peak of action and dedication

to the Republican cause, and Jordan senses the strong emotion Pilar feels for the man Pablo once was. But Pilar makes clear, too, her revulsion for the atrocities committed in those early, savage days—tortures and killings by both Fascists and Republicans.

At the camp of El Sordo, Jordan finds the man to be a worthy ally. Aged and deaf, he is, nonetheless, a man whom he knows he can depend upon. Jordan details his plans for blowing up the bridge to the old man, who recognizes the difficulties involved in having to do the deed in daylight. But El Sordo accepts what must be, and maps out with Jordan the best strategy possible, as well as the best route to Gredos, the remote mountainous country to which the band must make its escape after the bridge is blown up.

On the way back to their own camp, Pilar leaves Maria and Jordan so that they may make love among the fragrant pines. The embraces of the young lovers are more ecstatic than anything either had ever dreamed possible.

That evening Pablo, drunk, predicts snow. This Jordan finds hard to believe, as it is the end of May; but sure enough, the flakes begin to fall, and soon a snowstorm is raging. All are confined to the cave, which serves as a storehouse for the band's ammunition as well as its home, and Pablo becomes steadily drunker.

He believes that the snow will cancel all of Jordan's plans for blowing up the bridge, but Jordan insists that the operation—now a day and a half away—must go forward as scheduled. The hostility between the two men builds and builds. (Jordan recognizes that Pablo is not as drunk as he pretends to be.) But the showdown that should occur never materializes, and Pablo, recognizing that he has won no allies to his position that the bridge-blowing is a mistake, leaves the cave.

Pilar is now for killing him. The rest of the band agrees, and Jordan consents to do the act. But when Pablo returns to the cave, he has changed his mind, and agrees to help blow up the bridge. Jordan is confused by this change of heart on Pablo's part, but the two establish an uneasy truce.

That night, as he lies in his sleeping bag outside the cave, Jordan's mind pursues many threads of the past . . . and of the future. He dreams of the day when Maria will be his wife, after the war. . . . He thinks of how he came to be here in this foreign land, fighting this foreign war. . . . He remembers Kashkin, the Russian dynamiter whom he had shot on the man's own insistence; Kashkin had been wounded, and was terrified of the Fascist tortures he would have to endure were he taken alive. . . . As he lies there, his mind wandering in many directions, Maria comes to him, and they make love under the stars.

The next morning a Fascist cavalry officer on horseback wanders into the camp unsuspectingly, and Jordan kills him. (How the man's arrival had gone undetected by the gypsy Anselmo, who was standing watch, remains unexplained until later the gypsy arrives with two fat rabbits which he has killed—confessing that he couldn't resist deserting his post for a few minutes at the prospect of so fine a dinner.)

Jordan knows that, missing their fellow, other Fascist cavalry will soon be upon them. Pablo is sent to lead the band's horses down the mountainside, and the rest set up fortifications from which they can cover themselves. The cavalry do arrive, but they are misled by the tracks of Pablo's horse; and though they get so close to the guerrilla band that Jordan can see their features through his gunsight, he wisely refrains from firing. When the cavalry disappear, the others see the wisdom in their not having notified the enemy, by shots, of their existence and whereabouts.

Now a great number of enemy planes go overhead, and by the direction of their flight and the sounds of their bombs falling, the band understands that El Sordo's stronghold has been attacked. Knowing that El Sordo's position is hopeless, Jordan refuses to allow any of his own band to go to the old man's rescue; and though El Sordo and his men make a valiant stand against the Fascists, their hilltop retreat is at last leveled. The enemy cut off the heads of El Sordo and his men to carry back to their city stronghold in triumph.

With El Sordo's men gone, Jordan determines that it would be wise to get Golz to change his plans. It will be all but impossible for Jordan to do what is needed with the few men he has. Therefore he dispatches a message with Andres, hoping that it will reach Golz in time for the planned offensive to be canceled.

The cavalry having departed, Pablo returns to the cave. Again he is drunk—and again he professes to agree with Jordan's plans. But that night Jordan is awakened by Pilar, who tells him that Pablo has disappeared, taking with him Jordan's supply of detonators, fuses, and caps.

It is soon morning, and the plans proceed for the attack on the bridge and the enemy posts. (Fortunately Jordan is able to improvise replacements for the material stolen by Pablo.) The atmosphere is filled with tension and fear. All know that the odds against their success are high.

Suddenly Pablo reappears, and listening to what he has to say, Jordan finds himself believing the old Spaniard for the first time. Pablo talks about the great loneliness he has felt all night. He has been jealous of Jordan, and resentful of Pilar's assuming leadership—but he cannot exist without companions dedicated to the Republican cause. Although he has destroyed the explosive material he took, he has brought with him a small band of shepherd tribesmen with horses to help in the assault.

Jordan not only accepts Pablo back, but allows Pablo to pose to the newcomers as the band's head. With these additional men, there is again hope that the assault may be successful.

As the time nears for blowing up the bridge, Jordan perceives that Andres has not managed to get his message through to Golz in time. Accordingly, plans move forward as arranged. Pablo is put in charge of the shepherds, and given the task of destroying one sentry post. Pilar and the other men are to destroy the second post. Anselmo and Jordan have the task of dynamiting the bridge.

There is fear, anxiety, nervous joking, praying . . . but all the while, preparations move steadily forward. At last the enemy is sighted, and the guerrillas spring into action. There are losses to the small band—but the enemy posts are taken, and the bridge is destroyed.

Now it is time for escape—though how it is to be managed with so few horses is not certain. Suddenly the band hears a burst of machine-gun fire coming from the direction of Pablo and his men. Then, the explanation of the shots is evident. Pablo has murdered the shepherds after they have done their work, so that he can take their horses. All are revolted at this wanton evil on the part of the conscienceless Pablo, but there is no time for moralizing or making choices. The group's escape must be carried out.

As they begin to cross a small bridge in single file, enemy

shots ring out. They have been sighted. Jordan moves quickly to arrange the safe passage of all over the bridge; but as he, himself, is dashing across, his horse is shot, and he is crushed beneath the animal.

Rafael and Pilar manage to pull him to cover by the side of the road, and there Jordan realizes that he has broken his leg badly, and cannot be moved. Knowing what he must do, he arranges that Pablo shall take Maria to safety, no matter what else may happen. Then, calling the frightened girl to him, he bids her goodbye, telling her that she will always be with him, that he will always be with her. The girl is reluctant to leave, but at last she does as her lover wishes.

Jordan is left alone by the side of the road, his machine gun set up beside him. He is in great pain, but he knows that though his own life will be sacrificed, he must fight for the Republic as long as he can. Carefully, in his agony, he lines up his sight on the end of the bridge. Thus he waits until the first enemy soldier shall begin to cross.

Soon, a young Fascist lieutenant strides onto the bridge. His heart beating, Jordan takes careful aim.

THE OLD MAN AND THE SEA

Ernest Hemingway

For eighty-four days the old fisherman Santiago has caught no fish. Some think his fishing days are over—that he is too old. Others believe that he has finally hit an unbreakable streak of bad luck. The only one who believes in Santiago is the boy Manolin. Manolin is learning to be a fisherman, and since he was five has gone out each day with Santiago. But now he sails with another fisherman, for his parents have refused to let him go with Santiago after the fortieth day of the old man's empty run.

In spite of being attached to another master fisherman, Manolin loves only Santiago. And when the old man comes back on the eighty-fourth day empty-handed, it is the boy who welcomes him, who cadges a meal for him, who discusses the day's baseball results with him.

And on the eighty-fifth day, it is the boy who supplies the fresh bait, and who helps the old fisherman down to his boat with the gear. But of course when the old man sets out on the water, he goes alone.

The old man considers the lucky possibilities of the number eight-five—and he resolves to get an early start and sail far out today, in an effort to break his luck. Accordingly he starts rowing long before the sky is light, and, as the current is with him, he finds himself in an excellent position when the sun rises. With professional dexterity he baits and lowers his four sets of hooks, each going down to a different depth, but all hanging straight from the side of the boat.

Some time goes by and all that the old man catches is a ten-pound albacore, which he hauls in to use for bait. As he sits waiting for his big catch, he talks aloud to himself, about the boy, whom he loves and understands . . . about their mutual hero, Joe DiMaggio . . . and about the sea.

The sea—the beautiful, mysterious sea. Some—notably the younger fishermen—call the sea *el mar,* and think of it as a masculine, malignant force. But to Santiago the sea is *la mar,* feminine and mysterious, but lovely like a woman and unpredictable like a woman.

At last he feels the tension in one of his lines that tells him a marlin has taken the bait. It is a huge fish, to judge by the pull, and the fight between the man and the fish begins in earnest. For hours the fish tows the boat with great force; but Santiago has expected a good fight—indeed, has hoped for a good fight—and he is prepared for it.

On . . . on . . . on moves the boat, pulled by the giant fish beneath the water. It is now night, and the old man begins to tire slightly. His left hand has cramped badly, and he cannot unfold the fingers; it is useless to him in this battle. "If only the boy were here," he thinks.

To maintain his strength, he waits till the sun is rising and then eats the raw tuna which he caught the day before, regretting only that he did not have the foresight to equip his boat with salt. Now the great fish surfaces, and Santiago sees that he has indeed caught himself a prize. It is at least two feet longer than the skiff itself, and must weigh well over a thousand pounds. Bigger than any fish Santiago has ever heard of!

But the fish is strong and a fighter, and Santiago grows tired. He says ten Hail Marys and ten Our Fathers, praying that the Virgin will help him to land this beautiful fish. He promises to visit the shrine of the Virgin of Cobre if he gets the fish.

To keep his mind clear during the struggle, and to give himself renewed strength, he thinks back to the time when he was much younger and had Indian-wrestled a mighty Negro in a tavern in Casablanca—and won. That fight lasted a day and night, and he had won, and everyone had called him The Champion. Surely he will win this fight too.

The pain in his back and hands is excruciating, and he reminds himself of the necessity for staying alert and strong in order to land this marvelous fish. He catches a dolphin, and forces himself to eat its sweet flesh, though it nauseates him. On the second night he sleeps for the first time.

"If only the boy were here!" he thinks when he wakes.

At last, on the third morning, the fish begins to circle, and Santiago is finally able to maneuver him into position where he can harpoon him. The harpoon blow is a sure one, and the fish is dead.

Because the fish is so large, Santiago cannot take it into the skiff, but must laboriously go through the details of lashing the fish to the side of the boat. This is at last accomplished, and the man starts to sail in.

An hour later, the old man encounters new trouble. A shark approaches and attacks the dead fish. The old man succeeds in killing the shark, but his harpoon goes down with the shark. Worst of all, the great marlin's blood is now streaming through the water, and the old man knows that this will attract many more sharks before he is safely ashore.

He lashes his knife to the butt of an oar, and when a school of sharks arrives, he succeeds in killing two of them with this improvised harpoon. But striking the third, he hears the knife snap. Now he resorts to clubbing the marauding sharks with a sawn-off oar, but eventually he loses the club, too.

Defenseless, he must accept the knowledge that the sharks are now devouring his fish.

After much effort, he manages to get to land and pull his skiff out of the water. Lashed to the side of the boat is the giant skeleton of his great prize—eighteen feet from nose to tail. Santiago staggers home and falls into his bed.

When he awakes, he finds Manolin sitting beside him. The boy has been crying. He tells Santiago that everyone has seen the giant skeleton. He tells him that the Coast Guard and planes have been out looking for him. He reads the scores of the baseball games. Then, pouring some coffee for his beloved old friend, he urges the fisherman to sleep.

Sitting beside the old man, the boy again weeps. But the old man is sleeping, and in his dreams, he smiles.

GONE WITH THE WIND

Margaret Mitchell

Margaret Mitchell was born in 1900 in Atlanta, Georgia, where her family had long been prominent. As a child, she developed an interest in the events of the Civil War; her father, president of the Atlanta Historical Society, provided her with ample accounts of the war that was so important in the history of that city. She attended Smith College for one year, then returned to Atlanta and took a job as a journalist. In 1926 a difficult ankle sprain caused her to leave her job, and, confined at home, she began work on her one novel, Gone With the Wind. Ten years later, in 1936, the historical novel was published and immediately it began to make its own history. The greatest commercial success of a single edition in the history of publishing, it sold a phenomenal two million copies in one year, was translated into twenty-two languages, and was made into the most successful motion picture of the century. The book owed its popularity to the great panorama it presented, to its always interesting narrative, and certainly not least to its hero and heroine; about the fate of Scarlett and Rhett after the novel ends, Margaret Mitchell received thousands of queries. In 1949 she died in Atlanta, after being struck down on the street by a car.

It is 1861, and sixteen-year-old Scarlett O'Hara, the belle of Clayton County, Georgia, feels that the world is in her palm. The eldest, best-loved daughter of Gerald O'Hara, owner of the plantation Tara, she is pretty, rich, and surrounded by beaux. Most important of these men to Scarlett is sensitively handsome Ashley Wilkes, of nearby Twelve Oaks.

When the handsome Tarleton twins bring word that Ashley is about to announce his engagement to his cousin, Melanie Hamilton, Scarlett refuses to believe them. The next day, however, at a barbecue at Twelve Oaks, Ashley and the meek, quiet Melanie make their announcement. In despair, Scarlett corners Ashley, and declares her passion for him, believing that this will be enough to make him desert Melanie and run away with her. But she has forgotten that Ashley is a true Southern gentleman, and he is horrified at her proposal. Scarlett's humiliation is increased when she finds that her interview with Ashley has been witnessed by the scandalous, sardonic Rhett Butler, a rich man of good birth, but one who is "not received" by nice people.

To revenge herself upon Ashley, Scarlett promptly accepts her least likely suitor—the weak-willed Charles Hamilton, Melanie's brother. And to climax this most eventful of days in Scarlett's life, news is brought to Twelve Oaks during the party that the long-anticipated war between the States has begun.

With men going off to the Confederate Army in great haste, the ordinary proprieties of a long engagement are not observed. The day before Ashley's wedding to Melanie, Scarlett becomes Charles Hamilton's wife. Two months later, she is his widow. And several months after that, she bears his child —a son, named Wade Hampton Hamilton.

With Charlie dead, it is considered only right that Scarlett go to live with his family, and so she and Wade move to Atlanta, where they live with Melanie and her flighty aunt, Miss Pittypat Hamilton. Melanie, as the wife of her own beloved Ashley, is a constant thorn in Scarlett's side. And Melanie's perpetual good-natured meekness grates on the spirited Scarlett's nerves. But life in Atlanta is so much more exciting than life at Tara, that Scarlett is satisfied.

It begins to become apparent to the Southerners that the war, which they had at first expected to win with only a battle or two, is going to drag on. And the longer it lasts, the more seriously everyone begins to take it. Scarlett soon becomes bored by the eternal talk of the war and the "Noble Cause"—and she is frustrated by the social rules that determine a life of seclusion and boredom for young widows.

The only kindred spirit she finds in Atlanta is the odious Rhett Butler, now a successful blockade-runner. Rhett has recognized Scarlett for what she is: a vain, scheming, conceited young woman. Because he is not taken in by her charming wiles, Scarlett loathes the dashing scoundrel, but she cannot deny a grudging admiration of him.

Now the war is on in earnest, and the Southern losses mount. Poverty begins to stalk the land, and the once-high hopes of the South begin to fade. Rhett Butler is the only one who seems to accept the fact that the South is doomed, and that worse days are to come; and for this he is regarded as an outcast.

After two years of the war, Ashley comes home on his first furlough. Scarlett is shocked at how changed he is—so gaunt, so spiritless. But she loves him as much as ever. When he returns to the fighting, and Melanie announces herself pregnant, Scarlett feels as though Ashley has been unfaithful to her. To add to her private griefs, Ashley is reported missing. Using his influence, Rhett finds that he has been taken prisoner.

By now the South is all but crumbling, and Atlanta is in a state of siege. Scarlett recognizes that they must escape, but the roads are blocked. Once again—as he has done so many times during the past awful months—Rhett Butler steps forward to rescue them. He manages to get a horse and carriage, and into it he puts Scarlett, Wade, Melanie and Beau, her new baby, and the ignorant slavegirl Prissy (who with Scarlett had brought Beau Wilkes into the world), and he drives them through the enemy lines. Behind them they can see the flames of burning Atlanta.

Once on the road to safety, Rhett leaves the party, having determined to join the Confederate Army, even now at the last gasp of the war. So Scarlett is left to bring the small band of refugees to Tara alone.

The situation at Tara is more grim than Scarlett has dreamed. Her beloved mother, the saintly Ellen, is dead. Both of Scarlett's sisters, Suellen and Carreen, lie ill with typhoid. Gerald O'Hara's mind is wandering. But at least there are the faithful slaves, Mammy, Pork, and Dilcey, and Scarlett determines to fight for the preservation and restoration of Tara.

The months that follow comprise one long, never-ending nightmare. Scarlett changes from a delicate, fragile lady to a coarse, tireless farm woman. Inch by inch she begins reclaiming the land; and though the family is broken, hungry, and weak, Scarlett drives them all mercilessly. She is determined to become rich, so that never will any of the family ever, ever be hungry again.

She finds that she is even able to commit murder, when she kills a Yankee marauder who invades Tara. She steals his wallet and the jewelry she finds in his knapsack, and takes joy in the act. Nothing, it seems to her, can hold her down; her lust for wealth, for land, for security knows no bounds. When a band of Yankees return to the nearly desolate plantation to pillage and plunder, Scarlett manages to outwit them and keep control of nearly all her small store of animals and food.

During these long, bitter months of relentless work and no reward, Scarlett comes to feel a grudging respect for Melanie. She senses a will of steel in her sister-in-law, and a never-ending fund of devotion and loyalty; but she still cannot forgive Melly for being Ashley's wife.

At last the war ends. The South is utterly destroyed.

But unlike most of her compatriots, Scarlett refuses to give in to grief, despair, or sentimentality. Come hell or high water, she will be rich again. Fortunately a young soldier who had rested at Tara while wounded decides to stay on and help manage the small farm; and with this Will Benteen to help her, Scarlett knows that Tara will rise again.

At last Ashley returns, and again he and Scarlett have a passionate confrontation. Ashley swears that he will never look at her again except as a sister—but at least Scarlett can hope, for she now knows that Ashley loves her.

If the war was awful, the Reconstruction that follows is worse. Between the carpetbaggers and the scallawags the Southerners are never left alone. It appears that Tara will be lost for failure to pay outrageous taxes. In desperation Scarlett goes to Rhett Butler—she knows that he wants her— and offers to become his mistress if he will give her money. He refuses her, but not before telling her a few more home truths about herself, as is his custom. Rhett tells her that she and he are both of a kind—rascals and opportunists. He assures her that she has not seen the last of him.

Scarlett is about to despair of raising the money she needs to save Tara when she encounters the beau of her sister Suellen—the middle-aged, weak Frank Kennedy. Frank has made money as an Atlanta merchant, and in his small fortune Scarlett sees her salvation. Shamelessly she lies to Frank, telling him that Suellen has discarded him. Though she has not had occasion to use her feminine wiles in years—it seems centuries—they have not deserted her. Within two weeks Scarlett becomes Mrs. Frank Kennedy. She must share her bed with a man for whom she feels contempt; she must live in Atlanta instead of on the plantation. But—Tara is saved.

Now, for the first time, Scarlett discovers that she has a shrewd head for business, and inch by inch she takes over her husband's store. With Rhett's financial backing, Scarlett also buys a lumber mill, and soon—having mastered the art of outsharping the sharpest practitioner—she is a success.

There are hard times for Scarlett. The horrors of Reconstruction are unbelievable. She is pregnant again—a state she cannot abide. The gentry have begun to cut her for her unconventional behavior. But she has money—and the encouragement of the realistic Rhett Butler—and that is enough for her.

Ashley has decided that his only hope for redeeming himself as a man in his own eyes is to leave Tara, where he lives on Scarlett's charity, and take a job in New York. Scarlett is desperate at this turn, and offers him a job running one of her sawmills. He turns her down, fearing to be too close to her; but Melanie—kindhearted, sweet Melanie, who can believe evil of no one—listens to Scarlett's plea, and in gratitude for all that Scarlett has done for her, agrees that she and Ashley will come to Atlanta. Having Ashley where she can see him daily brings joy to Scarlett once again.

Shortly after her daughter, Ella Lorena, is born, Scarlett learns that the men of her set have joined the forbidden Ku Klux Klan. One night law officers raid the Klan's secret meeting place. Only the quick thinking and glib lying of the town's two most disreputable characters—Rhett Butler and the madam of an Atlanta fancy house, Belle Watling—save the lives of Ashley and several others. But Frank Kennedy is killed.

On the very day of Frank's funeral, Rhett Butler—who has always claimed not to be a marrying man—proposes marriage to Scarlett. He has always wanted her, he says, but he sees that he must marry her to have her. Scarlett accepts. After their marriage several months later, Rhett indulges Scarlett's every fancy, whim, and desire. He makes but one rule: none of his money is, in any way, to go to Ashley Wilkes.

For a while Scarlett is happy with Rhett. In particular, he awakens a woman's passion in her. But he is too strong for her to twist and bend as she is accustomed to do with men, and there are frequent quarrels between them.

These are glossed over, for a while, by the birth of their daughter, nicknamed Bonnie Blue. Rhett adores the little girl, and Scarlett herself finds that she is fonder of this child than of her other two.

But soon she and Rhett are at loggerheads, for now Rhett has determined that he and Scarlett must, for Bonnie's sake, return to respectability. Rhett Butler, who for years has encouraged Scarlett to scorn "what people may say," recognizes that if Bonnie is not to be hurt when she reaches young womanhood, he and Scarlett must be accepted by the gentry, the people who count, the Old Guard—the very faction that long ago turned against both Rhett and Scarlett.

For a while Rhett manages to earn the respectability he suddenly desires, and, particularly through the good offices of Melanie, whom he considers the only truly great lady he has ever known, he and Scarlett begin to be received by the better families.

But then Scarlett induces a new scandal. She goes to the mill, where she knows Ashley is working alone, and confronts him. Ashley tries to maintain his gentlemanly honor, but he is no match for Scarlett. Unfortunately they are caught in their embrace by Ashley's bitter sister, India, and soon the news is all over town.

That very evening Rhett and Scarlett are due at a party at the Wilkeses'. Scarlett says she will not go; but Rhett, who has already heard the gossip, forces her to attend—and wearing her most shameless gown. Unbelievably, Melanie greets her at the door and kisses her; and it is clear to all present that Melanie has heard the story from India, and has refused to believe it. Thus, Melanie's loyalty and goodness save the guilty Scarlett's reputation.

The next day Rhett leaves the house and it is months before Scarlett hears from him. When he returns, their meeting is a bitter one. Scarlett lets slip the hateful news that she is again pregnant. Rhett sardonically remarks that she may hope for a miscarriage—whereupon Scarlett reaches out to strike him, slips on the stair, and falls.

She does indeed miscarry, and Rhett is grief-stricken. But in her pride, Scarlett refuses to send for him, and this once again hardens his heart against her.

The final tragedy of Rhett's life comes when his darling Bonnie, at the age of five, breaks her neck while taking her pony over a jump. It was Rhett who has allowed Bonnie to ride, over Scarlett's protests; and now Scarlett accuses him of killing his daughter. At this, Rhett seems to fall apart; he takes to drinking heavily, and moves into the fancy house of his old friend, Belle Watling.

Scarlett scarcely sees him again until, some time later, while on a trip to Macon she receives a telegram from him, telling her that Melanie is dying. She returns at once to Atlanta, and goes to the bedside of her sweet sister-in-law.

For the first time Scarlett seems to clarify her feelings toward the people with whom she has most intimately been connected. She sees that Ashley is a weak, idealistic child, and that what she has been in love with all these years was only a fancy of her own making. Melanie, she has come to recognize, is (with the possible exception of her own mother, Ellen) the only person she has ever known who could be called truly saintly. And as for Rhett—Scarlett recognizes that he is the only man in the world that she has ever loved.

When Melanie dies, Scarlett suddenly feels weak. The years of fighting, fighting, fighting have been too much for her. Now she wants somebody to lean on. Automatically, she turns to Rhett.

But it is too late. He tells her coldly that all the love he has had for her is gone. He is leaving her, for he cannot risk the pain that inevitably results from anyone's being so foolish as to love the imperious Scarlett O'Hara.

This final blow is too much for her. Almost numbly, Scarlett goes back to Tara, the one refuge she knows. But as she sets foot on the red clay soil of her beloved plantation, she is again able to raise her head. The old fighting spirit comes back to her. She is determined that somehow, some way, she will recapture Rhett and rekindle his love. After all, tomorrow is another day.

LOOK HOMEWARD, ANGEL

Thomas Wolfe

Thomas Wolfe was born in 1900 in Asheville, North Carolina, where his father was a stonecutter. After public school he attended the University of North Carolina, where he was a great success in his studies, as an actor, and as a writer of plays. He went to Harvard to study playwriting with George Pierce Baker, and there he received an M.A. degree. He began teaching at New York University in 1924; on a trip to England in that year he began work on his autobiographical novel, Look Homeward, Angel. *Five years later (after a heroic editing job by Maxwell Perkins at Scribner's), the book was published. It was well received, and was acclaimed by Sinclair Lewis in his speech of acceptance for the Nobel Prize. Wolfe's second novel,* Of Time and the River, *a sequel to the first, appeared in 1935. In 1937 he became involved in disputes with his editors, and withdrew from them the manuscripts of his third and fourth novels. The following spring, while in Seattle on a cross-country trip, Wolfe became seriously ill; he died in Baltimore several months later. His unpublished manuscripts were edited by Edward Aswell, and were published in 1939 and 1940, safely securing Wolfe's posthumous reputation as a major writer. All of Wolfe's novels are autobiographical; long, powerful, and written in a prose style which could be monumental, thumping, ringing, tedious, poetic, excessive, musical—but never insignificant—his books were vast and passionate expressions of the dreams of a young man.*

When stonecutter Oliver Gant's wife Cynthia dies, he leaves his home in Sydney and begins wandering through the South. At last he settles in the city of Altamont, and marries for a second time. His new wife is Eliza Pentland, twenty-four-year-old daughter of the eccentric Major Thomas Pentland. Of this marriage, ten children are born, of whom seven live: Steven, Daisy, Helen, twins Grover Cleveland and Benjamin Harrison, Luke, and—after a time—Eugene.

Gant is a hard-drinking, lusty, improvident man, while Eliza is a cold, sober, grasping woman. It becomes evident to them both, early in their marriage, that their wills and temperaments will be continually at loggerheads, but they work out a sort of truce. Though this truce is breached periodically by Gant's refusal to give up drinking and by Eliza's insistence on investing every spare penny in real estate, the family is, on the whole, a happy one—at least during the early years.

When Eugene is three years old, Eliza decides to take her young children to St. Louis, where the Fair is an established attraction. It is her intention to open a boardinghouse at which residents of Altamont visiting the Fair can stay; and for a while she is successful in this business, and happily sees her income grow. But typhoid strikes young Grover—the quiet, sensitive son—and the boy dies. Heartbroken, Eliza returns with her children to Altamont.

Now she determines to open a boardinghouse on one of the properties she has recently acquired in Altamont. Accordingly, the Dixieland is opened. (Eugene is now seven.) Gant continues to live in the family's former house on Woodson Street, with his daughter Helen serving as his housekeeper. Eugene, as the baby of the family, stays with Eliza. Eliza is too intent on making money to think of the possible effects this breaking up of the family may have upon the children. Certainly, living apart from her husband suits her own temperament. But the break is to wreak havoc with the emotions of the children, and soon the older ones are drawing up battle lines, some of them feeling their strongest loyalty to their father, others to their mother.

The one who remains aloof from all the bickering and backbiting is Ben. Quiet, roughly attractive, intelligent Ben has been an aloof boy ever since the death of his twin. He seems to feel equal bitterness toward both his parents. Indeed, the only member of the family toward whom he expresses any affection is young Eugene; and even with him Ben is as likely to be gruff in manner as he is kindly.

If life is made difficult for young Eugene by his mother's grasping protestations of poverty, it does offer challenges and interests and new sensations on every hand, and his young boyhood is passed in comparative happiness. When Eliza contracts Bright's disease, she begins making pilgrimages south in the hope of finding relief, and on each of these young Gene accompanies her, finding always new sights and sounds and smells to lure him and fascinate him. Each glimpse he has of the great world that lies beyond the narrow confines of the family excites him, and he feels within himself a longing, a yearning to reach out for new experiences. He is intrigued, too, by the curious assortment of "guests" residing at the Dixieland. (Eliza, too ready to think of profit, accepts as visitors people known to be disreputable, and closes her ears to the unsavory rumors she hears about them. Indeed, when the kindhearted Mrs. Pert, no better than she should be, is attracted to Ben, Eliza closes her eyes and continues to accept the woman's rent payments.)

The real beginning of Eugene's intellectual growth comes when he wins a five-dollar prize for a composition he has written in school, and he is invited to become a pupil at a private school for boys in Altamont. Reluctantly Eliza agrees to pay the tuition fee, and Eugene comes under the spell and influence of Margaret Leonard, the cultured and spiritual woman who heads the school. For the first time Eugene is exposed to great literature and great ideas, and his thirst—and capacity—for learning knows no bounds.

And so the early years of Gene's adolescence pass. He has the usual rough-and-tumble friendships, tentative broadening of horizons, and sexual fumblings of boys his age—and throughout these years he is aware of a bright and adventurous world lying just beyond the perimeter of his own life.

When Gene is fifteen, his beloved brother Ben tries to enlist in the Army—World War I has just started—but Dr. Coker tells him what he has begun to suspect: Ben is not a well man. Bitterly Ben listens to the doctor's verdict—and becomes more insistent than ever that Gene make something of himself and his life. The pain and torment of Ben's life show plainly in his face—but Gant and Eliza are too self-involved to notice what their son endures. Only with Mrs. Pert does Ben find solace.

It is at this time that Gant becomes seriously ill, and is operated upon. It is discovered that he has cancer. The news is kept from him—and Eliza, to whom Gant has become nothing but an inconvenience, refuses to accept the truth of the diagnosis. This drives Helen into an absolute frenzy. (Growing more and more like her mother with every passing year, Helen has become a replacement for Eliza in Gant's life.) Tired now of doing everything for her father without being appreciated for it, Helen marries the dull Hugh T. Barton. But her independence is not so easily won; she soon finds that she is tied too strongly, emotionally, to her father, and she and Hugh move in with Gant so that Helen can continue to care for him.

Gene has finished school, and Margaret Leonard believes that he should be sent to Harvard. Old Gant, however, as crusty as ever, refuses to allow Gene to go anywhere but to State University. And so, not quite sixteen years old, and already six feet three inches tall, slim, sensitively handsome Eugene Gant prepares for college.

The summer before he goes away to school, Eugene becomes closer than ever to Ben, and he begins to understand his brother's torment. Ben has felt cheated throughout his life by his parents' indifference to him; they have been too busy money-grubbing and fighting to give him his birthright. He is determined that Gene, at least, shall not suffer the same fate. He fights continually with Eliza and Gant to make them give Gene his due; and Gene is grateful.

Gene's college career begins unhappily. More than ever before he feels himself an alien, isolated from the main stream of life. He cannot quell the feelings that surge within him, telling him of the adventure and brilliance that lie in the great world . . . but he does not know how to act upon these feelings.

The summer after his freshman year at State, Gene meets the beautiful Laura James, who is staying at the Dixieland for the summer. She is five years older than he, but he falls desperately in love with her. (He is considerably more sophisticated about women than he had been a year before, having been initiated into the houses of ill fame in the back streets of the university town.) Laura is deeply touched by Gene, but she realizes the hopelessness of their relationship. When she leaves Altamont, she promises to wait for him—but several days later writes him a letter telling of her engagement to a doctor in Virginia. Eugene is inconsolable.

During the next few years, Gene comes to see more and more clearly the truth about himself and his family; and though he is still in search of his own identity, he comes to recognize that he is a combination of his mother's and his father's traits. And just as Eliza and Gant have warred with each other, so the Eliza within Eugene wars continually with the Gant within him.

He sees not only his parents' failings, but those of his sisters and brothers, too. And when the family is reunited dur-

ing the Christmas that Gene is seventeen, he is suddenly
stricken by the complete hypocrisy with which they have all
surrounded themselves. Getting riotously drunk for the first
time in his life, he speaks the truth aloud to the horrified
family. None of them can afford to admit the justice of
Gene's charges, however, and afterward he feels that he has
accomplished nothing by his outspoken stand.

Gene now determines not to return to school, but to go to
Virginia and try to find Laura James. For a while he merely
looks around this new environment, but when his money is
exhausted, he gets a job doing hard physical labor. For
months he works at backbreaking tasks, and though his body
weakens he is content, for he is able to lose himself completely and not think about the tormenting problems that
confront him. He does not find Laura.

Then one day he receives a telegram informing him that
Ben is very sick. Bitterly he thinks that the family cannot
even die without him—but he returns to Altamont.

Ben has pneumonia, and is dying—there is no doubt of it.
He lingers for several days, and during the course of his
death struggle, the various members of the family come to
realize how hollow and meaningless so much of their existence has become.

Most deeply wounded of all is Eliza, for Ben will not even
allow her to enter his sickroom. In bitterness, she turns upon
Mrs. Pert—the one friend Ben has had—and, calling her
"whore," throws the woman out of the Dixieland. But this
cannot erase the truth that the family is giving more care
to Ben dead than they had given to Ben living, and when
the boy finally dies, Eliza is all but destroyed.

Within days, however, she is as intent upon accumulating
more real estate as she ever was, and the aging, ailing Gant
is once again hurling curses at the world and at Eliza in
particular.

Gene returns to school for his last semester, and his parents come to his graduation. Eugene now recognizes that his
father is dying and that his mother is a stranger. He calmly
accepts what is, for him, the final disintegration of his family.

Eliza pleads with Eugene to come back to the Dixieland
to stay with her for a while, and to this he agrees. But soon
the bickering and the ugliness and the inhumanity begin
again, and Gene knows that he must make his final break

with Altamont. Accordingly he signs away his claims upon the estate of his parents (at the insistence of his brother Luke), announces his plans for going to Harvard, and, overcoming Eliza's objections, bids her farewell.

As he passes through the streets of Altamont, he stops by the stonecarving shop of his father, and there, standing beside a stone angel, he sees his brother Ben. He has a long, soul-racking conversation with this spirit of his dead brother, during which Ben urges upon Eugene the truth of his need to break free of the family and explore the world to find his own identity. As he bids Ben farewell and leaves Altamont for the last time, it seems to Eugene that the stone angel lifts its arm in salute.

OF MICE AND MEN

John Steinbeck

John Steinbeck was born in Salinas, California, in 1902, the son of a local politician and a schoolteacher. After six years at Stanford University, and no degree, Steinbeck went to New York in 1927, where he held a succession of jobs as laborer, editor, and chemist. His first books sold poorly, but the publication of Tortilla Flat in 1935 brought him attention; his reputation rose with Of Mice and Men in 1937; and in 1939, upon the appearance of The Grapes of Wrath, Steinbeck became a major literary figure. He continued to produce novels and short stories, many of them good or excellent, but no subsequent work has had the impact of The Grapes of Wrath. Steinbeck's work has been distinguished by a compassionate sense of social justice; it was this awareness that led critics to hail The Grapes of Wrath as the most important social document of its time, the Uncle Tom's Cabin (although Steinbeck was a far better novelist than Mrs. Stowe) of the twentieth century. For his literary achievement, John Steinbeck was awarded the Nobel Prize in 1962.

It is late afternoon when two rough itinerant workers settle themselves in a small wooded glade by the river. The small man is George Milton. The large man—with the strength of a giant and the mentality of a very young child—is Lennie Small.

George and Lennie—unlike most itinerant workers—travel everywhere as a team. Though they have little else, and will most likely spend the rest of their lives working other men's land, at least they have each other.

As they rest, George tries to pound a few instructions into Lennie's consciousness. When they get to the ranch to which they are headed, Lennie is to let George do all the talking. Lennie is not to get into any fights. If Lennie gets into any trouble at the ranch, he is to come back to this wooded spot and wait for George to come get him.

Lennie promises George that he will be good, promises that he will remember. But George knows it is pretty much hopeless. Lennie sits dumbly staring into the fire, stroking a dead mouse which he has carried in his pocket. George throws the mouse away, and Lennie is heartbroken. He loves to pet soft things—mice, velvet, fur. His vise-like hands, however, too quickly kill the tiny animals he finds. George promises that he will get a pup for Lennie as soon as possible; maybe Lennie won't kill a pup. As they get ready to eat their evening meal, Lennie begs George to "tell about the rabbits." Slowly George begins this recitation which he has delivered many, many times.

It is a fantasy that one day George and Lennie will get together enough of a stake to buy themselves a small farm, live off the fat of the land, and be beholden to no one. And especially for Lennie, there will be rabbits—soft, furry, many-colored rabbits. Not only does the endless retelling of the story quiet Lennie, but it mesmerizes George too, so that at times he too believes in the reality of the dream.

As soon as they reach the ranch the next day, George senses that there is going to be trouble, but he determines to keep a close watch on Lennie, and try to make the job turn out successfully. The threat of trouble is made tangible by the appearance of the boss's son, Curley. This Curley is a little fellow—and like many small men, he hates big men. Accordingly he takes an instant dislike to Lennie.

From Candy, an old hand, George learns that Curley is always looking for a fight. George fears the consequences of Curley's antagonizing Lennie—but at least he can take comfort from the knowledge of Lennie's overwhelming strength. But the threat of trouble is increased when Candy tells George about Curley's wife—a voluptuous, vulgar tart who is always trying to arouse the desire of the men around the ranch, much to Curley's enragement.

The other men on the ranch come in from their work, and meet George and Lennie. Most impressive is Slim, a tall, rugged jerkline skinner who is accorded deference by all the others. As the men sit around the bunkhouse, one of them, Carlson, begins badgering old Candy to shoot his dog. Candy's dog smells, says Carlson, and is old and decrepit. If Candy will let him shoot the dog, says Carlson, Slim will give him one from the new litter Slim's dog has just dropped. Candy is reluctant to give up the dog—he has had him since he was a pup—but the men all agree with Carlson that the old dog must go. Carlson finally gets Candy to agree, and he takes the old dog out and shoots him with his luger pistol. The next day, Slim gives Candy one of the pups—and George gets Slim to give one of the pups to Lennie.

Lennie is ecstatic with the pup, but it takes George's constant watchfulness to keep the child-minded Lennie from bringing the dog into the bunkhouse. As a result, Lennie spends most of his time in the stable with his new pet.

Candy overhears George and Lennie talking "about the rabbits," and George makes the dream of a farm of their own so vivid and warm that Candy begs to be taken into the scheme. He offers to put up $350—more than half of the money needed; and George excitedly realizes that for the first time the dream may become a reality. He and Lennie agree to Candy's becoming a partner in the farm.

Curley shows up at the bunkhouse shortly after this, looking for his wayward wife. The men have nothing but contempt for him, and Slim, particularly, makes clear to Curley how insignificant they all think him. As a face-saving gesture, Curley provokes a fight with Lennie. Under instructions from George not to fight, Lennie stubbornly refuses to defend himself. At last, however, George tells him to fight back, and Lennie seizes one of Curley's fists in his own great paw. Curley instantly screams in pain and goes limp, but Lennie—panicked—cannot let go. (Panic always causes Lennie to freeze and hold on tight.) Finally the men succeed in freeing Curley; every bone in his hand is broken. They persuade Curley to pretend that his hand was caught in a machine.

Over the weekend the men are free. On Saturday night, only Lennie, old Candy, and the hunchbacked Negro stable buck, Crooks, are left on the ranch, the other men having gone to the local bawdy house. Curley's wife comes around, and begins tantalizing the men; she is a wanton, vulgar, yet pathetic creature. At last they succeed in getting her to leave them alone.

The next day, however, when all the men are out playing horseshoes, Curley's wife—desperately lonely and longing for someone to talk to her—comes upon Lennie in the barn. He is holding his puppy in his lap, stroking it. The dog's neck is broken; Lennie knows he has been too rough with it, but hadn't meant any harm. He is fearful that now, because he has been bad, George won't let him tend the rabbits. (George's one threat against Lennie is that he won't let him tend the rabbits on their farm unless Lennie behaves himself.)

Curley's wife is too lonely to recognize Lennie's imbecility, and she begins pouring her heart out to him. She talks about how restless she is on this dump of a ranch—about how she could have been in the movies. To convince Lennie how beautiful she is, she urges him to feel the fine texture of her hair.

Lennie accepts the invitation, but he cannot stroke gently. His hands are too big and strong. The girl pulls away, but Lennie panics, and seizes her hair in a tight grip. The more the girl screams, the tighter Lennie holds her. At last, she drops to the ground, lifeless.

Lennie recognizes that, again, he has been bad. He has done to the girl what he had done to the mouse and the puppy. "George won't let me tend the rabbits," he says to himself.

Candy is the first to discover the girl's body, and he calls George. George recognizes at once what his dumb friend has done, but Lennie is nowhere in sight. Candy agrees to tell the other men, and to pretend that George knows nothing at all, so that when the news of the girl's death is publicized, George is able to act as though it is a surprise to him.

Slim suggests sending out a party to capture Lennie and bring him to prison—but the evil-tempered Curley, his hand still in a sling as a result of his fight with Lennie, is determined to lynch the imbecilic man. The discovery that Carlson's luger is missing, suggesting that Lennie is armed, only confirms his intention. The other men recognize that nothing will calm Curley short of killing Lennie, and reluctantly they agree to go out in search of him.

George is closely watched by Curley, but he manages to make his escape from the search party, having first established a set of misleading suggestions that he hopes will carry the others in the wrong direction.

Lennie is frightened that George will be angry with him, and worries about whether George will let him tend the rabbits. George tries to calm him down, assuring him that everything will be all right. He urges Lennie to look across the river while he, George, tells about the farm. That way, he says, Lennie will be able to picture it to himself.

Accordingly, Lennie looks away, and George begins telling "about the rabbits." All the while he speaks, he is aware that the search party is getting closer and closer. Finally, still talking about the rabbits, George shoots Lennie in the back of the head with Carlson's luger, which he had stolen for precisely this purpose.

When the searchers arrive, they find George sitting over Lennie's body. He had wrestled the gun away from Lennie, he tells them, and killed him.

Slim, however, instantly surmises what has really happened, and goes to George to comfort him.

Curley is jubilant at Lennie's death, and confused by the restraint in George and Slim. "What's eatin' those guys?" he wonders.

THE GRAPES OF WRATH

John Steinbeck

On his way home to his family's tenant farm in Sallisaw, Oklahoma, after having served four years of a seven-year sentence for homicide, Tom Joad meets the Reverend Jim Casy. The Reverend tells Tom that he has lost his faith and is no longer a preacher; he now devotes his life to wandering about, trying to figure out the meaning of life. Tom invites Casy to join him, and assures him of a welcome from the Joad family, who have always been glad to share whatever they have.

When Tom and Casy arrive at the Joad farmstead, however, they find it deserted. The explanation for this is supplied by Muley Graves, the lone neighbor they encounter in the entire area. Continual cotton planting has robbed the soil, explains Muley, and now, after several years of drought, the land has turned to dust. All of the tenant farmers are being pushed off their land by the corporations and banks that own the farms. Most of them, Muley tells the men, are selling off their belongings and heading west for California, in the hope that they will there find enough work to feed themselves and their families.

Tom finds his own family at the farm of his Uncle John. Sure enough, they are all on the point of departing for California in a rattletrap Hudson Super-Six sedan truck. They are frightened and confused—but their hopes are high that California will prove to be the Promised Land. Tom determines to break his parole and join the family in their westward trek. And when at last the truck begins its journey, it is loaded down with essential commodities to sustain the family, as well as a host of people: Ma and Pa Joad, Grampa and Granma, Uncle John, teen-age Rose of Sharon (called Rosasharn) and her husband Connie Rivers, Tom's older, silent brother Noah, sixteen-year-old Al, twelve-year-old Ruthie, ten-year-old Winfield, Tom himself, and Preacher Casy. (Grampa, at the last minute, stubbornly decides not to go on the journey, but Tom succeeds in drugging him with cough medicine and carrying him aboard the truck.)

Highway Sixty-six is the main route westward, and the Joad truck is not the only one making the pathetic journey. Migrants from the entire Midwestern section of the country, pushed off their lands by bank-financed bulldozers and tractors, are wheeling to the green promise of California in their ancient cars. They have seen the orange handbills promising work, and their starving children are the goads that keep them moving.

At their first stop, however, the Joads begin to hear disquieting rumors about the reception that awaits them in the West, and they see on the faces of others in their position the reflection of their own discouragement and despair.

The Joads meet a couple named Wilson, stranded by the roadside. Al and Tom are able to help Wilson fix his car, and the Wilsons and the Joads decide to travel together. Because the Wilsons can take several passengers, the load on the Hudson truck is lightened, and this doubling-up of their party is a help to all. The death of Grampa and the illness of Sairy Wilson, tragedies shared together, only serve to bind the two families into a more cohesive unit.

And so the flight across the Panhandle continues. When Wilson's car breaks a connecting rod, Tom suggests that the rest of the party move on, leaving him behind to fix the car and catch up with them later. But Ma is adamant. "All we got is the fam'ly unbroke," she says—and nothing can persuade her to leave a single member behind.

Now the Joads learn, in earnest, how far down in life their poverty has brought them. They camp in ugly, unsanitary places for fifty cents a night. They learn to build and tumble casual worlds of friendship every twenty-four hours. They hear the truth about the orange handbills promising work: they are a lure that bring so many workers West that wages are forced down and down and down. For every job, there are ten hungry men. They learn to humble themselves—to stifle their traditionally fierce pride—when sheriffs and deputies and policemen harass them. They learn to swallow the bitter insult of being called Okies.

Sairy Wilson's sickness continues, and at last she cannot move on. The Joads do not want to desert the Wilsons, but Wilson forces them to leave. With Rosasharn pregnant, and Granma senile, it becomes imperative that the Joads reach California, so that the men can work and earn money. And so the Wilsons are left behind. (Meanwhile, late one night, Noah has decided to leave the group; and though Tom argues with him, he cannot prevail against Noah's stubborn silence and determination. Noah disappears, and Ma recognizes how much she has changed when she can accept so stoically the fact of her firstborn's leaving.)

Finally, after much drudgery and pain and weariness and despair, the Joads cross the border into California one early morning just before sunrise. Everyone rushes out of the truck for a first view of the Promised Land—everyone except Granma, who has died in the night. The few dollars the Joads have left go toward burying Grannie, and so the family begins its stay in California at the very bottom.

They settle into a Hooverville camp—and, for the first time, the full horror of their situation is brought home to them. They are pushed around all the time by petty local officials. Worst of all, they now see for themselves that California offers no work. Tom and Casy learn from Floyd Knowles, a young worker who reached California before them, that the only hope for Okies is to band together and refuse to be pushed around. But when Floyd tries to speak his mind to a deputy, he is arrested, and a fight breaks out. In the melee that follows, Floyd is killed and Tom cracks the deputy over the head with a club. Knowing that if he is caught Tom will be sent to prison for many years, as he already has a record, Casy insists on giving himself up in Tom's place.

The Joads, desperate with fear, leave the campsite that night. The next morning, they learn that shortly after their departure the deputies had come and burned the camp to the ground.

Now, the Joad party is reduced again—this time by the desertion of the immature, weak Connie, Rosasharn's husband, who simply walks away without a word to anyone.

A brief respite comes for the Joads when they are able to find a place in a government camp at Weedpatch, where there are sanitary arrangements, a feeling of communal spirit, and a chance for the Okies to regain their dignity and pride. But in a whole month only Tom manages to find work—and that for only five days. Reluctantly the Joads decide to move again, this time hoping to find work up north.

On the road they are stopped by deputies who, learning that the Joads want work, commandeer them and force them to accept a pathetic wage on a ranch where peaches are being picked. The work is long and backbreaking, the living conditions primitive, and the prices of food so arranged that all wages must be spent at once in the company store. There is no freedom, no choice, no dignity. Ma learns that when she is in trouble she must look to poor people like herself; they're the only ones who understand, and who can be counted upon to help.

Taking a stroll late at night, Tom Joad wanders outside the camp where he encounters Casy. Casy is leading a group of striking workers in a picket line, and Tom learns that the reason the Joads were impressed into work by the deputies is that the local officials are trying to break the strike. Tom and Casy have not been in conversation long when, again, the Okies are attacked on the trumped-up charges of the police. Tom is a witness when Casy is killed; in rage, he himself clubs a man.

Now there is nobody to take Tom's place, and he is forced

to hide. The Joads escape from the peach ranch late at night and make their way to a cotton ranch where they make their home in one end of an unused boxcar. Tom hides out in the woods, and every night Ma brings food to a secret place and leaves it for him.

For a while, things begin to look up. There is a little money coming in, and though the work is exhausting, at least the family is eating meals regularly. But their good fortune is not to last.

Fighting with another girl over a box of Cracker Jacks, Ruthie lets slip that Tom is hiding nearby. Ma goes to Tom to warn him that the secret is out, and that men may be after him. Tom decides that he must go away, in order not to endanger the rest of the family. Ma protests; it seems to her that life has been nothing but one desertion after another. But Tom knows what he must do. He is too much of a man to live in hiding—or to accept the bullying of the police and the landholders. Casy, Tom now sees, was right in his philosophy that the poor must stick together and fight for their rights, and Tom is determined to go off and preach Casy's message. He knows that he will be killed sooner or later, but he prefers to die like a man doing an honest man's work. Ma, at last, yields; but she knows that she will never see this, her best-beloved, son again.

Now, it seems, there is nothing but one trouble following another. Winfield becomes sick, and the small allowance of milk that should go to Rosasharn for the unborn baby must be given to the little boy instead. Al talks continually of leaving the family to get married—though without him, there will be nobody to drive and care for the truck.

And then the rains come—day after day. There is no work in the fields. Money runs out. The supply of food is exhausted.

The boxcars in which the Joads live, along with other families, border on a small river; and the men watch in alarm as the river rises each day. Soon they will be flooded out; even now, several of the cars and trucks are flooded. Desperately the men try to build a dike that will prevent the river's rise from washing them out.

As the men work day and night, Rosasharn's time comes, and the women stay inside the boxcar, helping her through her delivery. Her baby is born dead.

In spite of the men's efforts, the river's rise is too rapid to be forestalled, and it becomes inevitable that the boxcars must be deserted.

Ma gets Pa to help her lead the weakened Rosasharn onto the road. Pa protests; they don't even know where they are going to, where they will find shelter. But the animal need for survival within Ma is indomitable. That they must move on is all she knows. And so the remnants of the Joad family, tired and spent, move on. . . .

ALL THE KING'S MEN

Robert Penn Warren

Robert Penn Warren was born in Guthrie, Kentucky, in 1905. He graduated with high honors from Vanderbilt University in 1925, where he was associated with several of the South's most eminent critics and poets. He continued his studies at the University of California, at Yale, and at Oxford. A noted critic and scholar, he has taught at several American universities, and has been at Yale since 1950. Although Warren achieved his first fame as a poet, his novels have constituted his most important and widely known achievement.

All the King's Men was published in 1946, and won the Pulitzer Prize the next year. Based unmistakably upon the political career of Governor Huey Long of Louisiana, the novel reveals the author's acute sense of history, and his understanding of the way in which men determine the larger events of their times; it is unusual and impressive for a poet and literary scholar to be so much at ease among the more violent political myths of America.

Willie Stark is a self-educated small-town Southern lawyer who determines to buck the entrenched politicians and expose their corruption. Encouraged by his good, patient, religious wife Lucy, he runs for the state legislature. Willie believes that he has the backing of Tiny Duffy, an influential manipulator in state politics. But he is disabused of this notion by the tough-talking, cynical Sadie Burke, who is a member of Tiny Duffy's entourage, and by Jack Burden, a young newspaper reporter who is trying to get through life without experiencing emotion. They tell Willie that he is merely the straw-man candidate chosen to split the rural vote in the coming election. At first, this news unsettles Willie; but then he becomes known throughout the state as the champion of the little people.

When Willie becomes governor, he hires Jack Burden as a confidant and general secretary, though with the understanding that Jack's conscience is to be his own. By now, Sadie too is in Stark's camp. With her shrewd political insight and long experience, she is determined to make Willie the biggest political figure the state has ever known. She is also in love with him, and though she rails against him for picking up women occasionally, she remains faithful to him. (Some time after Lucy and Willie have a son, Tom, Lucy leaves her husband—though they keep up some sort of appearances so that his political career will not be hurt.)

One of Willie's major tactics in getting things done is to pressure his opponents by finding out any scandal about them. It is frequently Jack's job to dig up the scandal. He is horrified, however, when Willie asks him to get any dirt available on Judge Montgomery Irwin, who is backing an opponent of Willie's. Irwin, a highly respected man in the state, is one of the few people Jack remembers from his own childhood with pleasure. Irwin had been like a father to Jack—his own father having deserted his mother during Jack's earliest years—and Jack has admired Judge Irwin more than anyone else, with the possible exception of former Governor Stanton (now dead), father of Jack's two closest childhood friends, Anne and Adam Stanton.

Jack is convinced that he will find nothing on Irwin, but Willie insists that he dig anyway. So Jack digs—and unearths the fact that many years before, Irwin had taken a bribe and, indirectly, caused the suicide of a man named Littlepaugh. Jack is so disturbed by this news that for the time being he tells no one about his discovery.

One of Willie's biggest dreams is to build a hospital for the state that will surpass any hospital in the country. Willie envisions it as the one landmark of his career to be absolutely untouched by corruption. As the best man to head the hospital is the patrician Adam Stanton, now a world-famous surgeon, Willie orders Jack to "get" Adam to head the hospital. Adam at first refuses, but finally his own inclination to do good (and he recognizes that the hospital will be a tool for doing good) coupled with the insistence of his sister Anne that he take the position cause Adam to accept Willie's offer.

This re-entry into his life of Anne and Adam Stanton makes Jack uneasy. He knows that they disapprove of Willie and everything he stands for. (At least, he is correct as far as Adam is concerned; later he learns that Anne has become Willie's mistress, and even plans to marry him some day.) Since walking out on his master's thesis—the life story of a complex Southerner of Civil War days, Cass Mastern—and on his wife, the former Lois Seagar, Jack is desperately trying not to become emotionally involved in life. But his long affection for Adam and his long love for Anne combine to make him most uncomfortable.

Both Anne and Adam feel guilty over their relations with Willie Stark, whom they regard as an evil man. To make them see Willie as he sees him—as a pragmatic but worthwhile achiever—Jack discloses to the Stanton sister and brother what he has learned about Judge Irwin. This news shakes them both desperately, because it reflects discredit upon their own father, who had shielded Irwin at the time. Jack realizes that he has accomplished nothing.

Tom Stark, now grown to young manhood, is the idol of Willie's life—but it is through him that disaster begins to strike. One of Willie's opponents, a politician named Mac-Murfee, charges that Tom has fathered the unborn child of a girl named Sybil, but that the girl will be paid off and the story kept quiet if Willie surrenders the hospital's new clinic contract to Gummy Larson, a corrupt building contractor. Willie knows that only pressure from Judge Irwin can call MacMurfee off—so he sends Jack to Irwin.

Jack at first simply asks Irwin to call MacMurfee off, and make him drop the pressure on Willie. When he refuses, Jack is forced to reveal the documents he has concerning Irwin's shame. Irwin agrees to think things over for twenty-four hours. But that night, Jack's mother comes screaming into Jack's bedroom, and Jack learns that Irwin has killed himself. Jack learns also that Irwin was his father, and the only man his mother ever loved. He now understands why Irwin had been so good to him for so many years.

With his trump card—Judge Irwin—gone, Willie is forced to capitulate, and he gives the contract for the hospital clinic to Gummy Larson. But it is only the beginning of the end. Willie's son, Tom, is a star athlete, but he has become a self-ish, headstrong youth. Refusing to keep to training rules, he gets out of condition, and in the big football game of the season he is critically hurt.

Adam Stanton does all he can in operating on the boy, but Tom comes out of the operation a hopeless invalid, almost completely paralyzed. This is a crushing blow to Willie, but because of it Lucy is able to make him see how far he has drifted from his original goals. He agrees to go back to her, and begin again.

Several days later Anne calls Jack, in a frantic state. She tells him that Adam has received an anonymous call in which the caller has told him about Willie's relationship with Anne. The caller said, further, that it was for this reason that Adam had been made director of the hospital; but that now that Adam has let Tom become paralyzed, Willie is going to have him fired. Anne urges Jack to find Adam, as she is sure that he is in a desperate frame of mind.

Jack looks all over town for Adam, knowing full well that what Adam has learned about Anne is enough to drive him mad. But before he can locate Adam, Jack is summoned to the Capitol for an emergency meeting with Willie. Standing with Willie in the Capitol, Jack finally sees Adam standing by a pillar. Jack and the governor move toward him, when suddenly Adam whips out a gun and shoots Willie down. Adam, in turn, is killed by a burst of fire from Willie's bodyguard, Sugar-Boy. Willie lingers in pain for several days, but at last he dies.

Jack determines to find out who had made the anonymous telephone call. At last he learns from Sadie Burke—who is now in a sanitarium—that Tiny Duffy was the caller. Sadie agrees to provide Jack with whatever evidence he needs to make the charge against Duffy stick. And Jack does go to Duffy, to tell him that he knows how Willie—"The Boss"— came to be killed. Tiny, who has succeeded Willie as governor, is terrified of what Jack will do, and tries to buy Jack, but without success.

Several months go by, during which Jack tries to sort out the entire series of episodes he has lived through. For the first time he is able to see his own mother as a real woman. He visits Lucy Stark, and finds a measure of meaning in the dignity with which she is pushing forward. (Tom has died, and Lucy has arranged to adopt the child born to Sybil; she has named the baby after Willie.)

At last Jack comes to realize that for years he has been trying to pinpoint guilt and responsibility in other people, without examining himself, to see his own responsibility in the affairs of the world. He discards his idea of having revenge upon Tiny Duffy, and instead determines to return to his master's thesis; he now believes that he can make an adequate interpretation of the confused and guilt-ridden life of Cass Mastern.

And he and Anne together begin to build a new relationship which will draw upon the strengths of the past, while discarding the old inadequacies and evasions.

THE CATCHER IN THE RYE

J. D. Salinger

Jerome David Salinger was born in New York City in 1919. After being sent to a military academy, he studied at Columbia College. He served in World War II, and began contributing short stories to The Saturday Evening Post *and* The New Yorker *shortly after the war ended. His one novel,* The Catcher in the Rye, *appeared in 1951. Since its publication, he has written a number of complex short stories about the fictional Glass family, some of which approach novella length. He lives in New England with his family, avoids publicity, and, although public interest in his career is enormous, he will not answer any questions on his published or planned writings.*

The Catcher in the Rye *has been one of the most widely read of contemporary American novels. It was quickly adopted as the book of the generation born during the late depression and World War II years, for the good reason that it was the only novel in recent times to deal honestly, intelligently, and appealingly with the problems of contemporary urban adolescents. Holden Caulfield's rebellion against the adult world was quite unlike any previous literary treatment of the subject of growing up, or, for that matter, any previous literary treatment of severe emotional distress. He does not experience alternate periods of lucidity and confusion, but is, as a result of his neurotic hypersensitivity, always lucid, always perceptive, always vulnerable. The final image that he recalls in his narrative is that of his little sister going around and around on a carrousel; this is the last of many symbolic representations of Holden's dominating, but unconscious, desire: to be himself a child again, never to grow up, never to go ahead, as a person on a carrousel never goes ahead. The reader never learns the real causes of the hero's disturbance, nor is there any indication of what is to become of him; but to a generation of readers who identify with him, Holden Caulfield is the most sympathetic and loved creation in contemporary fiction.*

Adolescent Holden Caulfield is recovering from an illness in a sanitarium. He tells the story of how he spent the weekend before Christmas vacation the year before.

He has been notified that he is being kicked out of the school he attends, Pencey Prep, for not applying himself. (He is flunking four of his five subjects.) But that doesn't really bother Holden; he's been flunked out of several schools. What bothers him most is that the news will shake up his parents when they learn of it. His mother has been somewhat nervous ever since Holden's younger brother, the brilliant Allie, died at the age of ten. (Holden has an older brother, D.B., a gifted writer, now in Hollywood, and a younger sister, the incomparably bright and genuine Phoebe.)

Holden is relieved to be leaving Pencey, in a way. He has no real friends there—unhappily for him, he sees people much too clearly, and is constantly torn between his loathing of their phoniness and his compassion for their inadequacies.

It is the weekend of the big game at Pencey, and Holden is one of the few boys not caught up in the excitement. (He has just returned to campus, as a matter of fact, in a state of mild disgrace. The fencing team, of which he is manager, was supposed to have a meet with a New York school, but Holden had left all of the foils on the subway, and the meet had to be called off.)

He pays a visit to his history teacher, the ill, aging Mr. Spencer. Holden senses Mr. Spencer's genuine concern for him, but the man makes him uncomfortable, so he leaves.

He returns to his dormitory, but fails to find the sense of companionship he seems to seek—either with the outcast boy next door, pimply Robert Ackley, or with his own roommate, the handsome and superficial Stradlater. Stradlater is having a date with a girl Holden had known several years before, Jane Gallagher. Holden remembers with pathetic pleasure how, when he had played checkers with her, Jane had always refused to move her kings. He tries to communicate to Stradlater the special feeling this gives him . . . but Stradlater is too concerned with the prospect of necking with the girl.

Stradlater's egocentric concentration on his own physical attractiveness and gratification sickens Holden more than anything else that day, and in a sudden burst of determination, he decides to leave Pencey early. (It is Saturday, and the Christmas vacation does not begin until Wednesday.)

He packs his bags, and late at night makes his way to the station, where he boards a train for New York. On the train he meets the mother of a boy whom he loathes at school— Ernest Morrow. Holden finds the woman touching—there is something warmly appealing about her—and he tells her a fantastic tale of what a great guy her son Ernest is . . . all the while wondering why he has such a strong need to tell lies. (In telling his own story, Holden is frank about the strength of his fantasy life. He is always telling people that he has a brain tumor, or imagining that he has been shot in the gut, or something.)

Once in New York, Holden decides to go to a hotel. (He can't go home until his parents have had time to assimilate the news of his flunking out of school; he figures that will be by about Tuesday.) In the taxicab, he asks the driver what happens to the ducks in the Central Park lagoon in winter, but the driver thinks he's a little bit crazy. (Holden is always wondering about such things as the ducks in winter; ideas like that "kill" him.)

He checks into a sleazy hotel, and then goes out and wanders about the city. He dances with three pathetic spinsters from Seattle in one nightclub, and then goes to another in Greenwich Village. Here he meets a girl named Lillian, who knows his brother D.B.; but she is such a phony that Holden gets away from her as fast as possible, and walks the forty-one blocks back to the hotel.

Sex is an almost constant preoccupation of Holden's, and when the elevator operator in the hotel offers to send a prostitute up to Holden's room, the boy accepts eagerly. While he waits for the woman to arrive, he stares out of the window, and sees several upsetting scenes of a sexual nature in adjoining hotel rooms. They depress him.

The prostitute finally arrives, but Holden, torn by conflicting feelings, is unable to make love to her. They fight about how much money he owes her, and when she fails to get as much as she wants, Sunny, the prostitute, brings Maurice, the elevator operator, to Holden's room. Maurice hurts Holden by twisting his arm, and the boy is finally forced to come up with the extra money.

The next morning Holden phones Sally Hayes, a pretentious social-climbing girl he has known for some time, and makes a date to take her to the theater. He then goes to breakfast, and encounters two nuns whose simplicity he finds moving. He insists on giving them ten dollars for their charitable work. But something about them saddens and depresses him.

While wandering around the city until it is time to meet Sally, Holden has several interesting conversations with children. Children move him, perhaps, more than anything else; he responds to their sincerity, their directness—their lack of phoniness. Later, when he hears a little boy singing "If a body catch a body coming through the rye," he can't get the song out of his head.

The date with Sally is a disaster. She says all the phony things about the play (*I Know My Love*, starring the Lunts) that Holden knew she would say. Finally, after they have been skating at Rockefeller Center, Holden gets fed up with her and insults her. He is now again alone.

He calls a boy named Carl Luce who had been his senior advisor when they had been at Whooton together, and they meet for a drink. Carl is now at Columbia, and now having no patience with Holden's adolescence, he takes a patronizing tone toward the boy. Holden spends several hours in the bar after Luce leaves, just getting drunk. (Holden is very tall, and has a good head of gray hair, so that he is served alcohol in some places—the darker ones.)

After nearly passing out, he douses his head with cold water and decides to pay a sneak visit to his sister Phoebe. He walks to the apartment house where his family lives, and lets himself in surreptitiously. (It happens that his parents are out, so he is able to operate a little less furtively after a while.) He wakes up Phoebe, and the two—who love each other deeply—have a long and touching visit with each other.

Phoebe, who is ten, knows instinctively that Holden has flunked out of school, and she is beside herself with grief. She lectures him, and protests that he doesn't even know what he wants to do with his life. He insists that he does, and when

Phoebe presses him, Holden tells her that his favorite idea is to be standing in a field of rye, where a lot of little children are playing. He is standing at the edge of a cliff, and it's his job to catch the little children before they fall over the edge. That's what he wants to be—the catcher in the rye.

Holden's parents return, so Holden sneaks out of the apartment and goes to visit a former teacher of his, Mr. Antolini. The man is most considerate of Holden, and treats the boy like a human being. He talks to him earnestly about Holden's future, but in such a way that gives Holden pleasure. The evening is ruined, however, when Holden wakes up—he is sleeping on a couch in the Antolini living room—to find the man patting him on the head. Holden is terrified that the man is a pervert, and making a flimsy excuse, he dresses in the dark and leaves. He spends the rest of the night sleeping in Grand Central Station.

Walking about the city the next morning, Holden suddenly believes that he will disappear every time he gets to a street crossing. So he asks his dead brother Allie to help him. Whenever he reaches a curb, he asks aloud for Allie not to make him invisible; and when he reaches the opposite curb, he thanks Allie.

Holden now determines to hitchhike west, and spend the rest of his life pretending to be a deaf-mute, so that he will never again be bothered by phonies. He can't leave without saying goodbye to Phoebe, however, so he goes to her school and leaves a note for her, telling her to meet him at the Museum of Natural History at lunchtime.

While he waits for her, Holden sees an obscenity written on a wall. It disgusts him—particularly when he thinks of all the little children who will see it. But he decides that if he spent his whole life going around rubbing out such signs, there still would be more of them. It is hopeless.

Phoebe is late, and she arrives carrying a suitcase. She has determined to go with Holden rather than be left behind. He realizes that it is impossible, and is curt with her, which wounds her so that she won't speak to him. Finally, as a peace offering, Holden takes Phoebe to the zoo, and by the end of the afternoon, as he sits watching her ride around and around on the carrousel, he realizes that he will not go west, but will go home with her.

Now, observes Holden, he is getting ready to go to a new school in September. But what bothers him is the way the psychiatrists keep asking him if he's ready to *apply* himself. But how is he to know, he wonders, until he tries? It's all so phony. . . .

FRENCH NOVELS

THE PRINCESS OF CLEVES

Mme. de La Fayette

Marie-Madeleine Pioche de la Vergne, who became the Comtesse de La Fayette, was born in Paris in 1634, where she was educated privately. She became a member of the great intellectual circles of Paris, and was acquainted with the eminent literary figures of her day; among her closest friends were Mme. de Sévigné and the Duc de la Rochefoucauld. She married the Comte de La Fayette in 1656; they were apparently separated after the birth of her second child, when she left the Comte's country estate and settled in Paris for the remainder of her life. Mme. de La Fayette wrote four novels, and, as was proper, publicly denied any knowledge of them. Testimony of literary associates, however, has established her authorship. Furthermore, as the most educated and brilliant woman in the court circles of the time, she appears to be the only one of her contemporaries who could have written these astonishingly clever, sophisticated books. La Princesse de Clèves was published in 1678. Considered the first great French novel, this book is remarkable for its psychological insight, intelligence, simplicity, and familiarity with the manners and intrigues of the French aristocracy. The Comtesse de La Fayette died in Paris in 1693.

During the last years of the reign of Henri II, the glittering French court is the scene of petty intrigues and grand schemes, ambition and flirtation, passion and despair. There are two political factions warring with each other: one headed by the queen's uncles, the Messieurs de Guise, the other by the king's governor, the Connétable de Montmorency. And there are three social factions, each headed by a royal lady: Catherine de Médicis, the king's wife; Marguerite de France, the king's sister; and Diane de Poitiers, Duchesse de Valentinois, the king's mistress.

In these circles, a constant topic of interest, speculation, and intrigue is *l'amour*—and recognized outstanding in the lists of love is the Adonis-like Duc de Nemours. Even by his enemies Nemours is acknowledged to be handsome, charming, witty, gallant, *distingué*. And if his gifts are not enough to make this bachelor interesting to all, the fact that he has many mistresses but is thought never to have loved makes him the focus of constant speculation.

So splendid and far-reaching is the reputation of the Duc de Nemours that word reaches Henri's court that Elizabeth, the newly crowned virgin Queen of England, seeks Nemours for a consort. Encouraged by the king, Nemours agrees to allow emissaries to be sent to England on his behalf, and he himself goes to Brussels to await developments that promise to bring him to the throne as Elizabeth's consort.

Nemours would be grieved to know that shortly after his departure from court a beautiful young woman, innocent and unpromised, appears. She is Mlle. de Chartres, wealthy heiress of a distinguished family. Under the protective wing of her shrewd mother, Mme. de Chartres, the girl makes an instant sensation among the bachelors near the court.

Two rivals for the girl's hand are the Prince of Cleves, who has fallen in love with her at first sight, even before knowing her name, and the Duc de Guise. Over these, however, Mme. de Chartres prefers the Duc de Montpensier, and under her maneuverings it appears that the connection between her daughter and the duke will take place.

A shift in power among the cliques at court, however, makes this impossible. Indeed, not only Montpensier but Guise as well must withdraw their suits because of political developments. Thus, virtually by default, Cleves wins the hand of the beautiful Mlle. de Chartres.

The one unhappiness Cleves feels at his betrothal stems from his awareness that his fiancée does not love him; that, indeed, she is all but indifferent to him. However, he loves her desperately, and in the hope that she will learn to love him, he makes her his bride. Thus Mlle. de Chartres becomes the Princess of Cleves.

Shortly after the marriage, Nemours returns to court to report to the king on the progress of his suit to Elizabeth. At a ball, Nemours and Mme. de Cleves dance together even before they are introduced. The reputation of each is so brilliant that they suspect each other's identities; and when formal introductions are made, both appear calm. Secretly, however, each feels a mysterious transport of delight.

Innocent and unsuspecting, the Princess does not attempt to interpret her feelings, but she notes that her pleasure in-

creases at every encounter with Nemours. Unaware, she is
falling in love with him. Her secret—which even she herself
only dimly suspects—is known to two other people who have
perceived the changes in the Princess's emotions. One is the
gallant Guise, who must love her from a distance and in
silence. The other is the Princess's mother, Mme. de Chartres.

At first, Mme. de Chartres intends not to speak to her
daughter about the dangers that attend her growing affection
for Nemours, as she hopes that the girl herself will recognize
the pitfalls of such a relationship. But falling ill, Mme. de
Chartres is no longer able to supervise her daughter's conduct, and her fears increase. At last, knowing that she is on
her deathbed, she determines to speak to the Princess.

She warns her daughter of the hardships that lie before a
woman of the court who lets scandal touch her name. She
cites instances of women who, indulging their folly when
friends are in power, are made to pay with shame and disgrace when different factions achieve prominence.

The Princess of Cleves is horrified at the picture her mother
paints for her, and she recognizes the importance of ceasing
all contact with Nemours immediately, before he has a
chance to guess her feelings. Accordingly, when her mother
dies, she uses the period of mourning as an excuse to escape
from the court—and from Nemours.

The Prince, her husband, cannot understand her extended
absence from the court, and at last he prevails upon her to
return. Sure that her feelings for the handsome bachelor are
dead, she accedes to her husband's wishes. When, however,
she hears from the gossiping Mme. la Dauphine that Nemours is rumored to be so deeply in love that he has forsaken
his suit to Queen Elizabeth, the Princess of Cleves trembles.
When the innocent gossipmonger adds that it is apparent
that the woman Nemours loves does not return his passion
and is not his mistress, the Princess becomes almost certain
that she herself is the object of his love.

At her first re-encounter with Nemours, the Princess is convinced of it. He loves her! She is thrilled at the thought—
but more determined than ever that he shall not know the
true state of her own feelings for him. Accordingly, she
avoids him as much as possible. Nonetheless, she is deeply
gratified when she observes him, during one of his visits to
her husband, stealing a miniature portrait of herself. The

Prince of Cleves merely assumes that the miniature has been lost through carelessness.

At a tennis match held during a court festivity, a letter is dropped by one of the contestants, and word is whispered that it is from Nemours' unknown beloved. The letter is given into the Princess's custody—the donor never dreaming her particular interest in it—and it causes the poor girl great grief. In an unknown woman's hand, the letter contains accusations of perfidy and deceit against the unnamed recipient. What horror! Not only does Nemours love elsewhere, he has been deceiving his beloved with yet another woman! The Princess rereads the letter several times, and on each occasion her agony and jealousy increase.

In truth, however, the letter was written to the Vidame de Chartres. Learning that it is supposed to belong to Nemours, the Vidame begs Nemours, who is his good friend, to accept ownership, for if the truth of the Vidame's two mistresses were known at court, he would be ruined. Nemours agrees, only to be horrified himself at learning that the letter is in the possession of his beloved Princess. He goes to her, bringing with him proof in the Vidame's hand that the letter is *his* and not Nemours'. Consoled at last, the Princess is restored to happiness, and her interview with Nemours makes it clearer to both the feeling that they have for each other.

Now the Princess recognizes that she is truly endangered by her love for Nemours, for he loves her in return. To escape temptation, she gets her husband to allow her to go to their country home, Coulommiers.

Unbeknown to the Princess, however, Nemours is visiting near Coulommiers. Finding himself at the edge of her estate, he enters the gardens, intent on calling upon her. (His friendship with the Prince of Cleves is adequate justification for his visit.) Before he can make his presence known, however, he eavesdrops on a heated conversation between the Prince and Princess.

Believing that her only salvation lies in the full confidence of her adoring husband, the Princess confesses that her repugnance to life at court stems from her unwillingness to expose herself to the attentions of a man there whom she loves. Heartbroken at finding the love he has been unable to win bestowed on another, the Prince of Cleves nonetheless nobly understands his wife's predicament, and agrees to help her in her pure resolve. His only bitterness arises from the fact that the Princess will not reveal the name of the man in question.

Nemours, in his hiding place, is convinced that he himself is the man. So enraptured is he by this turn of events—by this amazing frankness on the Princess's part, and by her virtuous and pure behavior—that he repeats the story to his friend the Vidame, pretending that it happened to "a good friend." The Vidame, however, perceives Nemours' true emotions, and passes along the tidbit about Nemours' unknown beloved. Soon the story is repeated by an unsuspecting gossip to the Princess of Cleves herself.

In rage she accuses the Prince of having betrayed her. He, in turn, knowing his own innocence, protests that she must have been the one to tell about the confession in the garden. Both are convinced that neither would have any sane motive for telling the story; yet neither can understand how else the story can have been circulated. In her confusion and grief, the Princess focuses her hostility on Nemours, and believes that she hates him.

At a court tournament, however, at which her presence is required, the appearance of Nemours, who wears colors that she alone understands are meant to be hers, changes her hatred to joy. Unfortunately the king is seriously wounded in the tournament, and the wound leads to his death. Without being able to speak with her, Nemours is called away to Rheims for the coronation of the new king.

At Rheims, Nemours cannot conceal his anxiety to slip away to visit Coulommiers; and he offers the excuse that he must visit his sister, who lives nearby. The Prince, now convinced that Nemours is his rival for the Princess's love, sends a spy to follow Nemours and report upon his behavior.

The spy sees Nemours go to the garden wall at Coulommiers, and drop out of sight. He does not reappear until morning. The next night, the spy watches as, again, Nemours climbs into the Princess's garden. On the third day, the spy sees Nemours arrive at Coulommiers in a carriage with his sister. Convinced he has the evidence wanted by his master, the spy returns to the Prince of Cleves and tells what he has witnessed.

What the spy could not know was that the Princess, walking in her garden the first night, had seen Nemours climb the wall, and had instantly gone into the house, locking the doors against him. On the second night, fearing his reappearance, she had stayed behind her locked doors, and so both nights Nemours had wandered in the gardens, alone.

Stricken by what he takes to be proof of his wife's perfidy, the Prince of Cleves falls ill of a fever, and takes to his bed. Within days, the doctors despair of his life. The Princess, who had flown to his bedside, is at first at a loss to understand his accusations against her. But at last, perceiving how mistaken he is, she tells him fearlessly the truth about Nemours' visits to Coulommiers. The news of his wife's innocence makes the Prince happy, but it comes too late to save him, and he dies.

Now the Princess gives way to genuine grief. For the first time, it seems to her, she appreciates the true value of the man she has lost, for the Prince loved her steadfastly and without reproaches, knowing that his love was not returned, and indeed was placed elsewhere. The Princess determines never to see Nemours again, and through the Vidame she sends him word of this total rejection.

For months the Princess buries herself in solitary mourning. At last she reaches a point where thought of Nemours does not bring a guilty flush to her cheek, although she fully acknowledges to herself that it was her love for Nemours that caused the death of her noble husband.

After a long period of mourning, the Princess learns, by chance, that Nemours is still hopeful of pressing his suit, and that he has been watching her, unnoticed, from a distance. She remains adamant about seeing him. Indeed, on one occasion she notices him, and though her heart struggles in her bosom, she is grateful that he turns away before recognizing her, and she does not call to him.

Nemours is now more desperately in love with the Princess than ever, and he is convinced that if he can but once achieve an interview with her, he will win her for his wife. His friend, the Vidame de Chartres, who is the Princess's uncle, intercedes, and invites the Princess for a visit, not telling her that Nemours is to be present too.

And so the fateful interview is arranged. Nemours presses his suit, but before his emotions reach their height of expression, the Princess silences him. She confesses to him that she does love him, and that she has always loved him. But, she says, she is determined never to see him again—both because of her sense of duty to her late husband, and because she believes that her love for Nemours and his for her will wither upon fulfillment. It is only the obstacles between them that have made such steadfast love possible; indeed, she suspects that the reason the Prince's love for her endured was because he knew it was not returned.

Determined to fulfill her pledge never to see him again, the Princess goes on a long journey to the Pyrenees, where she falls ill. Thither Nemours follows her, but she will not receive him.

It is many years later before he, at last, forgets her; for her part, she decides to live out the balance of her life in a convent, where no one will inquire into the history of the beautiful Princess of Cleves.

MANON LESCAUT
Abbé Prévost

Antoine François Prévost d'Exiles, later called the Abbé Prévost, was born in Flanders in 1697, and educated at Jesuit schools in his village and in Paris. He served a novitiate, but for unknown reasons left school to join the army, from which he eventually deserted. Shortly before 1720 he became involved with a girl who is said to have been the inspiration for the character of Manon Lescaut, but the affair ended tragically and Prévost entered the Benedictine abbey of Saint-Maur, becoming ordained soon afterward. Later he went to the abbey of St. Germain-des-Prés, in Paris, where he remained until 1728 when he quit the order and sailed to England. There he began to write long tales of romance and adventure. He spent several years in Holland, then rejoined his religious order; he secured for himself, however, a position which did not require him to remain in a monastery. In 1754 he became Abbé of St. Georges de Gesnes. He died in 1763.

Prévost is an important figure in the history of French romantic literature. Of his several romances, Manon Lescaut, published in 1731, has become the most famous. Two noted operas are based on it: Massenet's Manon and Puccini's Manon Lescaut. He was also the author of biographies, and translated the poems of Dryden and novels of Richardson into French.

At seventeen, the Chevalier des Grieux, accompanied by his closest friend, Tiberge, aged twenty, is on his way back to the Academy at Amiens, his holidays being at an end. Stopping at an inn, the young man cannot help but notice a girl —the most beautiful he has ever seen—who appears to be led against her will by an older man.

Striking up a conversation with her, he learns that she is Manon Lescaut, sixteen. Having offended her father, she is now being taken by an old family servant to a convent, where she is to spend the rest of her days.

Des Grieux has fallen instantly in love with Mlle. Lescaut, and the thought of her being hidden forever from the world is too much for him. He proposes to help her escape. Manon sees only unhappiness lying ahead if she should be so rash as to accept des Grieux's offer—but how else is she to escape the cloistered life which she dreads?

It is an easy matter for des Grieux to elude the old Lescaut servant, and soon he and the bewitching Manon have made plans to travel to Paris, where they will be wed. They have between them the sum of one hundred and fifty crowns, which, in their innocence, they suppose will last them forever. Tiberge, a sober young man destined for the priesthood, does all he can to dissuade des Grieux from his folly, but the chevalier is determined to bind himself to the beautiful creature whom he has found. At last, des Grieux realizes that he must even escape from Tiberge, who disapproves so heartily of his plan. Accordingly he invents a plausible tale— and when Tiberge wakes the next morning, he finds des Grieux and Manon gone.

At Saint Denis, en route to Paris, Manon and des Grieux must spend the night at an inn, and there, without benefit of clergy, they become man and wife. Des Grieux, who until this hour has been innocent of women, knows ecstasy such as he has never dared dream of, for Manon, though barely out of her childhood, is a skilled and charming mistress.

The romantic couple establish residence in Paris, and though they cannot marry—des Grieux would need his father's permission—they are idyllically happy. The one blot on his serenity is des Grieux's growing realization that his bewitching Manon loves luxury and extravagance—and that his purse is dwindling. Broaching the subject to her, he offers to write a letter to his father, begging for funds. Much to his surprise, Manon begs him not to do so rash a thing, as she fears des Grieux *père* would take her beloved away from her. Instead, she says, she will call upon resources of her own.

Thinking that she means to write to friends, des Grieux is calmed; and sure enough, there is soon abundant evidence that Manon has received the money they need. Then one day, having noticed several odd occasions of behavior on Manon's part, and, having heard some indiscreet whispers among the servants, des Grieux begins to suspect that Manon's money has come from a new lover, a certain M. de B____. Before he can confirm his horrible suspicions, however, he is kidnaped (it appears to him that his abductors have Manon's connivance) and returned to his father's house.

Overcome at this treachery which has carried him so far from his beloved Manon, des Grieux learns from his father the awful truth: Manon has indeed become the mistress of the wealthy M. de B____, who, to rid himself of the annoyance of a rival, has written the elder des Grieux of the young chevalier's whereabouts. Accordingly, the elder des Grieux has had his son "rescued" from his folly.

For six months young des Grieux is kept a virtual prisoner in his father's house, and he gives way to the greatest griefs and lamentations. Gradually, however, he begins to convince himself that he has gotten over his passion for the traitorous Manon, and when Tiberge sets off for the Seminary of Saint Sulpice, it is agreed that young des Grieux will accompany him, and study for holy orders. Thus the Chevalier des Grieux becomes Abbé des Grieux.

A year later, it is time for the young seminarian to present his public disputation at the Sorbonne. As luck would have it, he sees in the congregation Manon—now eighteen, and more beautiful than ever. As the two young people look into each other's eyes, the flame of passion bursts into new life. In a clandestine interview, the lovely Manon swears her repentance for her conduct of the past and, vowing eternal fidelity to des Grieux, agrees to go with him. Deserting her present protector, B____, and taking with her as much money and as many jeweled trinkets as she can lay hands on, Manon goes with des Grieux to the suburb of Chaillot, where they rent a house.

Giving not even a second thought to the sacred calling which he renounces, young des Grieux is swept away by delight and rapture with his entrancing mistress. Soon, however, Manon's taste for luxury reappears, and the two resolve to go again to Paris, where life is gay and lively.

In Paris, des Grieux meets for the first time the brother of Manon, a rude, surly Guardsman. Lescaut makes no objection to des Grieux's relations with his sister; indeed, he seems heartily to approve, and goes so far as to move in with the young couple. Not daring to say anything to Lescaut for fear of wounding Manon, des Grieux puts up with his brother-in-law as best he can. But soon it is apparent that they are on the brink of ruin.

Lescaut's advice as to how to get out of this predicament reveals his full baseness to des Grieux: he suggests that Manon should sell her favors, and keep the three of them on the proceeds. Des Grieux would rather die than submit Manon to such horrible indignity. He summons his old friend Tiberge, and begs him for money. Tiberge, steadfast and loyal, gives des Grieux all that he has, and preaches a short sermon to his friend on the immorality of the life he is leading. Manon, impatient with Tiberge's sermonizing, sends him packing.

When Tiberge's money is gone, des Grieux is again desperate, and he agrees to become, under Lescaut's skilled tutoring, a professional card cheat. But soon, having fallen victim to a theft, des Grieux is again at the edge of ruin.

Now Lescaut comes forward with a cunning scheme. The wealthy elderly Monsieur de G. M____ is attracted by Manon. By pretending that she will become his mistress, Manon can get him to give her money, with which she can then decamp without having sullied her virtue. To add verisimilitude to the tale, des Grieux must pose as Manon's brother. The scheme works perfectly. De G. M____ is gulled, and Lescaut, des Grieux, and Manon escape with a tidy sum.

Unfortunately, however, de G. M____ has them followed and arrested, and they are sent to prison. In his cell at Saint-Lazare, des Grieux feigns repentance, hoping to secure an early release. But when this fails, he smuggles a message out of the prison to Lescaut, who had escaped imprisonment, begging him to help him escape. The two use the innocent Tiberge as a courier, and at last a daring plan is worked out. Fantastic as it is, it works, and des Grieux escapes, but not without having to kill a guard.

Now des Grieux's energies are bent on rescuing Manon. He finds that the warden of the prison in which Manon is lodged has a handsome young son. Sure that the lad will be sympathetic to the lovers' plight, des Grieux speaks with this M. de T——— and, sure enough, finds him a most willing listener and collaborator. With M. de T———'s connivance, Manon is smuggled out of the prison in the garb of a man, and together the lovers fly to Chaillot, taking their now-intimate friend, M. de T———, with them. (Unfortunately, during the escape Lescaut is assassinated by a fellow Guardsman whom he had cheated at the gaming table.)

Soon, of course, owing to Manon's passion for luxury, the daring young couple is again enmeshed in debts. This time, des Grieux resolves to write to his father, begging for money. (He does not scruple, however, to accept more money from the ever-constant Tiberge, as well as from M. de T———.)

Now Manon becomes the object of the attentions of another rich gentleman—none other than the son of de G. M———, the elderly man already gulled. At M. de T———'s suggestion, it is agreed to play the same ruse upon the son as was played upon the father—but de G. M——— *fils* is cleverer than they had suspected, and Manon finds herself a prisoner in his house. With great ingenuity, however, des Grieux has de G. M——— abducted, and he and Manon determine to spend the night eating de G. M———'s food and lying together in his bed.

A servant who had witnessed the abduction, however, sets up an alarm, and just as they are preparing for bed, des Grieux and Manon are surprised by the intrusion of the elder de G. M——— with armed guards. The lovers are quickly subdued, and again transported to prison—this time to the Petit-Chatelet.

The next day, des Grieux receives a visit in his cell from his father, who has come to Paris in response to his son's earlier letter, and who has just learned of his imprisonment. In tears, des Grieux makes a passionate plea for forgiveness and help—and the old man relents, but only part way. He agrees to arrange for his son's release, but he insists that Manon must be imprisoned for life, or, at the very least, transported to the Americas. (The elder des Grieux has had an interview with the elder Monsieur de G. M———, and the two fathers have agreed that this Manon is clearly a menace to all rich young men.)

Since his father's mind cannot be changed, des Grieux contents himself with his own release, confident that he will be able to arrange an escape for Manon. But he is in despair when he learns that she is to be taken the very next day, along with a number of common prostitutes, to Le Havre, and from there sent to America where she will become the wife of some bachelor pioneer.

Des Grieux sees as his only hope the kidnaping of Manon as she is being taken from Paris to Le Havre. To that end he hires a band of ruffians to help him in his attack; but at the crucial moment, the hirelings take fright of the men who guard the prisoners, and desert. Alone, des Grieux is powerless, and he must content himself with bribing the guards generously to allow him to talk with Manon.

She tells him that he must leave her, as she has brought him nothing but grief; but, as much in love with Manon as ever, des Grieux swears that he will follow her to the ends of the earth. Accordingly he books passage on the vessel that transports the women to the New World.

During the two-month voyage, the captain of the ship is most taken by the open and deep affection between Manon and des Grieux, and when the prisoners reach New Orleans, the captain tells the American governor that the pair are husband and wife. Thus Manon is not sold into marriage as are the other prisoners. And, because of the captain's good report, the governor himself hires des Grieux as petty clerk at the fort, which provides the couple enough to live on.

During the early months of their new life, Manon and des Grieux find themselves undergoing a reformation. They no longer pine for luxury and gaiety, but are content with their simple lot. Now the only thing they lack for complete happiness is to be joined as true man and wife in the sight of God.

Believing that the governor's permission is necessary to all marriages, des Grieux goes to him and tells him the truth of his relationship with Manon, and begs permission for a priest to marry them. The governor is enraged at this duplicity; and finding that Manon is, in truth, a single woman, vows that she shall be wed to his own nephew, a bachelor called Synnelet.

Manon is as grief-stricken as des Grieux by this new development, and des Grieux sees no way out of the difficulty but to have a duel to the death with Synnelet. Therefore the two men fight, and soon the Chevalier des Grieux—a superb swordsman—sees his enemy fall senseless to the ground before him.

Having murdered the governor's nephew, des Grieux recognizes that he must escape for his life. Manon begs to be taken with him, and at last he yields to his mistress, although he knows that their road will be a hard one. And so the two make their escape from the colony.

Manon, however, is not used to walking endless miles on country roads, and by nightfall she feels that she is at her last moment. Passionately she takes des Grieux in her arms and clasps him to her. A few moments later, she is dead.

The next day the governor's men find des Grieux lying on the rude grave that he has dug for Manon, prostrate with grief. They use the unexplained death of Manon as an excuse for arresting him.

It turns out that Synnelet had not been killed, and that he had begged his uncle for mercy toward Manon and des Grieux. At last the governor had yielded, and had given his consent to the marriage of the lovers. This consent, of course, comes too late—but at least the governor's intercession produces a full pardon for des Grieux, and he is freed.

Since Manon's death, however, des Grieux has lain in a high fever, and it is a long time before he regains his strength. During his convalescence, he returns again to the pious thoughts of his youth, and when Tiberge arrives in the New World to bring him back to France, he returns with his friend in the conviction that he will devote the remainder of his life to the service of God.

THE CHARTERHOUSE OF PARMA

Stendhal

Marie Henri Beyle, who used the pen name Stendhal, was born in Grenoble, France, in 1783. He joined Napoleon's army in 1800, resigned in 1802, and after several years rejoined the army and served until the fall of the Emperor in 1814. He lived in Milan for seven years, and then in Paris. In 1831 he attained a position, which he held for the rest of his life, as a French consular officer in Trieste and later in Civitavecchia. He died in Paris in 1842.

Stendhal's first writings consisted of critical articles, which were printed largely in British journals. His first novel, Armance, appeared in 1827, and attracted little attention; but even his two great novels, The Red and the Black (1831) and The Charterhouse of Parma (1839), were poorly received by his contemporaries, and it was not until the end of the nineteenth century that Stendhal's reputation as one of France's greatest novelists was established.

The Charterhouse of Parma is based upon Stendhal's intimate knowledge of northern Italy. It is at once a detailed and carefully observed picture of the entire life of a community, and a romantic tale of love and adventure. Critics used to argue endlessly about classifying Stendhal as a romantic or a realistic writer, until it was realized that his great distinction was that he had successfully combined the two literary traditions as no writer before or after had been able to do.

Fabrizio del Dongo, a high-spirited, starry-eyed youth of seventeen, is determined to live a life of heroism and grandeur, and he announces his decision to run off and join the armies of the great Napoleon. This news lacerates the hearts of the two women who love him best in the world: his mother, the Marchesa del Dongo, and his aunt, the Contessa Pietranera (who was, before her marriage, Gina del Dongo).

The women, however, have no male ally to stop Fabrizio in his rash plan, for the lad's father, the Marchese, a greedy and stupid man, all but ignores Fabrizio, preferring his elder son, Ascanio, who is so much more like himself. (Indeed, there is even the possibility that Fabrizio is not del Dongo's son at all, but was sired by a handsome lieutenant of Napoleon's army who had been billeted in the del Dongo home in Milan in 1796.) So Fabrizio is off to war.

So naïve is he in the ways of the world, however, and so unconvincing is his presentation of the forged passport that allows him to cross the border, that he is immediately clapped into prison for thirty-three days as a spy. When at last he is freed, he makes his way to Waterloo, and there, in a brief skirmish, he kills his first—and only—Prussian, almost by mistake. The rest of his adventures at war are similarly comic as the result of his naïveté, and he is quickly urged to make his escape from the army. Wounded lightly, and using a succession of horses—it is fortunate that Fabrizio is rich, for he has a singular knack for letting his horses be stolen from him—he at last makes his way home.

Back in Milan, however, the political situation is chaotic, with various factions vying for power. A petty official of the ruling faction is determined to arrest Fabrizio for having fought with Napoleon, and it is only the audacious flirting of Fabrizio's beautiful aunt, the Contessa, with the powerful but unscrupulous Canon Border that saves Fabrizio. (Having devoted much of her life to serving as a second mother to this handsome nephew of hers, the now-widowed Contessa finds herself willing to go to great lengths to save his neck.) In spite of the Contessa's intervention on his behalf, however, Fabrizio must go into hiding.

In Milan the Contessa, reputedly the most beautiful woman in the city, meets a visiting celebrity, the middle-aged Minister of Parma, Conte Mosca. Mosca, though married, falls in love with the Contessa, and is amazed to find himself acting like a moonstruck schoolboy. Though she is quite candid about her not loving Mosca in return, the Contessa recognizes the superior qualities of the man, and at last she agrees to a daring, but foolproof, plan Mosca presents to her.

He proposes that he arrange a marriage for her with the elderly Duca Sanseverina-Taxis of Parma, who is desperate to earn an honor from the Court of Parma, an honor which Mosca is in a position to grant. Following the marriage, the Duca Sanseverina will agree to leave Parma forever, after installing the Contessa in his house as Duchessa. There, as a respectable married woman of the nobility, the Contessa will be free to receive Mosca, and she may then, without fear of scandal, become his mistress.

The Contessa yields, attracted as much by the livelier atmosphere in Parma as by Mosca himself and the fortune that she will guarantee herself by this marriage. So, the Contessa becomes the Duchessa.

Her success at the court is triumphant; she is easily the most beautiful woman in Parma—though there is a young girl newly presented, Clelia Conti, daughter of the unscrupulous General Fabio Conti, who threatens some day to outshine the Duchessa. Particularly impressed with the new Duchessa is the Prince himself, Ranuccio-Ernesto IV, the absolute monarch of Parma, in whose good graces Mosca, as Minister, stands high.

The Duchessa's only unhappiness stems from her uncertainty over the future of her charming nephew, Fabrizio. How can she insure his present safety and future brilliance? Mosca is delighted to supply an answer—not only because he wishes to give in to every caprice of his bewitching mistress, but because he is slightly jealous (baselessly, he admits to himself) of this handsome youth, Fabrizio del Dongo, who seems to be so important to the Duchessa. Therefore it is decided that Fabrizio must be sent to Naples where he will be trained for the priesthood. Eventually, and if Mosca's influence at court remains steady, Fabrizio will be called to Parma, and someday raised to the archbishopric.

Time passes quickly for Fabrizio in Naples. He is an ideal student, and he enjoys both his studies and the passing affairs he has with a parade of mistresses. His one regret is that he cannot seem to form a lasting affection for any of these beauties, and he fears that he will never know real love and deep-seated passion.

At the end of four years Fabrizio is a Monseigneur, and is called to Parma. At first, the Prince is interested in the young priest, but soon he becomes jealous of the all-too-obvious affection held by the Duchessa for her nephew. He vows that given the opportunity, he will punish Fabrizio severely.

Encouraged in flirtation by Mosca, who is also jealous of the Duchessa's evident affection for her handsome nephew, Fabrizio starts a petty and innocent *amour* with the vivacious and attractive actress Marietta, who is under the protection of a hideous actor called Giletti. Mosca is delighted at the progress of the romance as reported to him by his spies; but the Duchessa so fears for Fabrizio's safety—Giletti is reputedly a violent and jealous man—that Mosca arranges for the acting troupe to leave Parma and for Fabrizio to be called home to his mother's estate in Milan.

Fabrizio is bored in Milan, and after three days he is ready to return to Parma. He pays a visit to the tutor of his youth, the eccentric priest Father Blanes, who prophesies for Fabrizio a dark future: imprisonment for a crime that is not a crime, and the ending of life on a rude bench, garbed in white. Fabrizio is amused.

Back in Parma, Mosca's influence brings great success to

Fabrizio. The lad is named Coadjutor to Archbishop Landriani, and his right of eventual succession is proclaimed. All of Fabrizio's hopes are dashed, however, when he has a chance encounter with Marietta and Giletti. The two hot-headed young men are soon at swords' points, and in the melee that follows, Fabrizio kills Giletti in self-defense, and is forced to flee across the border. Once again, the youth finds himself traveling on a forged passport; and, again, as at Waterloo, it is the simple peasants of the countryside who protect him from his own innocence and save his neck for him. Fabrizio is delighted to be living such a life of high adventure!

Ordinarily, the killing by a noble of the house of del Dongo of a wandering, baseborn actor the likes of Giletti would cause no stir; but Mosca's enemies at court—particularly the fiendish Minister of Justice, Rassi, and the wild-eyed radical, the Marchesa Raversi—see in the murder an opportunity to destroy Mosca's influence over the Prince. Accordingly, they secure a warrant for Fabrizio's arrest and imprisonment.

Innocent of all these machinations against him, Fabrizio, as carefree as ever, resides in Bologna under the assumed name of Giuseppe Bossi. In Bologna he not only renews his relationship with the minx Marietta, but also carries on an extensive—and expensive—flirtation with the famed opera singer Fausta. His adventures in connection with his pursuit of Fausta, with the necessary attendant humiliation of Fausta's rich protector, keep Fabrizio hopping. But though he enjoys all the hubbub and commotion of carrying on a public and scandalous flirtation, he still regrets that he is incapable of feeling true passion and abiding love.

Upon hearing of the warrant for Fabrizio's imprisonment, the Duchessa, who now begins to suspect herself of loving her nephew more than is quite appropriate for one of her age and familial relation to the boy, determines to make the Prince sign a pardon for him. In the most daring ploy of her active career as a court beauty, the Duchessa succeeds in raising the Prince's passions, rescuing Fabrizio from the sentence he is under, and having her enemy, the scheming Marchesa Raversi, banished from court.

But when he realizes that the Duchessa has raised hopes which she has no intention of fulfilling, the Prince determines to save his vanity and extricate himself from her grasp by reneging on his promise. He changes Fabrizio's sentence merely from one of death to one of long imprisonment. Learning of this, the Marchesa Raversi—more bitter than ever—stirs a plot or two of her own; and before anything can be done to warn Mosca and the Duchessa, Fabrizio is lured back to Parma, arrested, clapped in irons, and taken to the infamous prison, the Citadel.

As he stands in the office of the Citadel's chief general, Fabio Conti, Fabrizio, who regards his current plight as something of a lark, sees for the first time in many years the beautiful, modest young daughter of the general, Clelia Conti. The two fall instantly in love—and Fabrizio now knows, for the first time, the bliss of passion.

Though Fabrizio's imprisonment causes great anguish to all his friends—particularly to the Duchessa, who finds herself more passionately attracted to her nephew at every encounter—he himself is delighted to be in the Citadel, for through the lone window of his cell he can see Clelia Conti at a distant window.

Soon the prisoner and the beautiful warden's daughter are signaling each other daily messages in an elaborate code they have devised, and though they are unhappy at their enforced separation, each knows that love—great, romantic love —hovers in the air between them.

The Duchessa recognizes that any future efforts on her part to free Fabrizio will reflect discredit upon Mosca, and she therefore gives the good man his *congé*. As the months go on, Fabrizio's continued imprisonment brings despair to his three best friends: to the Duchessa, whose love for him knows no bounds; to Mosca, who understands that he cannot have access to his erstwhile mistress, the Duchessa, so long as Fabrizio is imprisoned; and to Clelia, who is now under orders from her father to marry the richest man in Parma, one Crescenzi.

An elaborate plan is worked out whereby Fabrizio's escape from the Citadel may be effected. At first he protests that he doesn't *want* to escape—he loves Clelia too much!—but at last the girl herself and the Duchessa combine their efforts and convince him. In the most daring escape ever attempted at the Citadel, Fabrizio makes off, and is taken into hiding by the Duchessa.

Now the Duchessa's rage against the Prince and against

Rassi, the Minister of Justice, knows no bounds. Availing herself of the services of a mad Liberal poet named Ferrante Palla, who is desperately in love with her, the Duchessa orders the poisoning of Prince Ranuccio-Ernesto IV. And when his son, who loves the Duchessa as much, if not more, than his father had, ascends the throne of Parma as Ranuccio-Ernesto V, the Duchessa is returned to Court in triumph. At last she is in a position to ruin Rassi—and this she does. Conti is also at her mercy, and because Fabrizio is so desperately in love with Clelia, before she exacts her price from Conti also, the jealous Duchessa forces him to guarantee the marriage of Clelia to Crescenzi.

After Clelia's marriage, Fabrizio seems to lose all interest in life about him, and he throws himself deeply into his work as a priest. The Duchessa is in despair; she had hoped that in freeing her nephew she would restore him to a position by her side from which, together, they could rule the most brilliant and lively society of Parma. But Fabrizio is simply not interested any longer in the gay life of society.

Now the new Prince becomes insistent, even as his father had been before him, that the Duchessa grant the ultimate favor—even going so far as to offer her the Prime Ministership of Parma in exchange for her affections. The Duchessa protests, even though she had promised that on granting a full pardon to Fabrizio the Prince could claim his reward. The Prince determines to hold her to her promise, however, and the Duchessa has no choice but to yield.

A single half hour of love is all that the Prince gains for his efforts, however, and he is in despair when he learns that no sooner had he left the Duchessa's house when she herself left Parma, determined never to return. In Perugia she joins Mosca, who by now has accumulated a handsome fortune of his own and whose wife—from whom he had long been separated—is now dead. And so at last Mosca and the Duchessa (who has, for many years, been a widow) are married, and both are deeply satisfied by the match they have made.

Fabrizio's reputation as a preacher soon grows, and eventually a foolish rumor—involving a rich young woman named Annetta Marini, who has fallen in love with his preaching—reaches the ears of Clelia, now Marchesa Crescenzi. Clelia has not seen Fabrizio for several years—indeed, she has taken an oath to the Madonna never to look upon his face again—

but she cannot resist going to church to hear his sermon. When he sees her in the congregation, Fabrizio's passion bursts into flame; and Clelia experiences a similar emotion at hearing Fabrizio's beloved voice.

It is not long before the two cannot resist a meeting, and they hold a tryst one dark night in the Crescenzi gardens. Clelia, who had vowed only not to *see* Fabrizio, feels free to meet him in the dark, and soon she becomes his mistress, insisting only upon their never meeting by daylight, so that she is not forced to break her vow to the Madonna.

Several years later, Fabrizio, as much in love with Clelia as ever, finds himself unsatisfied by these midnight trysts. To give pleasure to his life, he wants to have with him one of Clelia's children—the little boy, Sandrino, who is, in truth, Fabrizio's son.

Since Crescenzi would never relinquish "his" son to Fabrizio, an elaborate scheme is concocted whereby the boy may be abducted while Crescenzi is away from Parma; and, to avoid a search being made for the child, it is further planned to have a mock burial, and to report the child as having died.

Unfortunately the excitement and derring-do of the plot prove too much for the frail child's health, and Sandrino does, indeed, die. It is not long before the unhappy Clelia has followed the boy to the grave.

Mosca now lives once more in Parma, where Rassi, Conti, the Marchesa Raversi, and other old enemies have gradually made their returns to power, too. The Duchessa, who has steadfastly refused to return to the court of Ernesto V, maintains a villa and a glittering salon at Vignano. But Fabrizio can no longer be attracted by the charms of either of their worlds. He feels that he must atone for the death of Clelia. Therefore he resigns his archbishopric and retires to a nearby monastery, the Charterhouse of Parma, where he lives out his remaining years on a rude bench, garbed in white.

SALAMMBÔ

Gustave Flaubert

Gustave Flaubert was born in Rouen, France, in 1821, the son of an eminent doctor. He was educated locally, and in 1840 went to

Paris, where he studied law for three years. He had already been involved in several amorous adventures, and had exhibited attitudes typical of the romantic youth of his generation—boredom, dreaminess, dissatisfaction, depression. While at law school, he suffered a nervous breakdown, and spent a year in recovery, during which time he decided to abandon law in order to write. A patrimony came to him in 1846, and he was able to write without having to earn a living. He had also, by this time, become less romantic and was developing cynical ideas about humanity. In 1851 he began working on Madame Bovary; five painstaking years later it was completed, and the author was rewarded with the admiration of the critics and educated public. The next five years were occupied totally with the preparation and writing of Salammbô, which appeared in 1862. Although the novel had a poor critical reception when it was published, it is today held in some esteem. Far from a typical historical novel, it is a cynical study of cruelty, inhumanity, treason, and the betrayal of innocence, and is written with the superb craftsmanship which distinguishes all of Flaubert's writing. In his later years Flaubert, though he had never solicited fame, was considered the foremost literary artist in France. His scorn for humanity, but not his rigorous, self-imposed standards, had somewhat softened by the end of his life. He died in 1880.

Disgusted with his people for their failure to give him the support he had asked for during the First Punic War, the Carthaginian general Hamilcar Barca, after achieving an honorable peace with the Romans, has absented himself from Carthage. The Carthaginians still hate Hamilcar—some, because he did not win a greater victory, others because they fear that he will want to seize power in Carthage.

The Carthaginians are no more reasonable in their dealings with General Gisco, who has remained in Carthage. He has advised that the many mercenaries who fought for Carthage as one great army of Barbarians be speedily paid and dispersed. But the Carthaginians hope that by temporizing they will be able to avoid paying the Barbarians. To appease these unruly soldiers, they hold a huge feast for them —in the gardens of the absent Hamilcar's house, knowing full well that Hamilcar will have to bear the expense of the entertainment.

The feast soon becomes an orgy, and the Barbarians—drunken and satiated—commit havoc among Hamilcar's precious possessions and slaves. One of the mercenaries, Mathô, a Libyan general, cuts the bonds of Spendius, a middle-aged slave of Hamilcar's; and the shrewd, ambitious Spendius, once a rich man himself, swears lifelong devotion to the man who has freed him from slavery.

At the height of the chaotic feast, a woman appears on a distant terrace. It is Salammbô, Hamilcar's beautiful and mysterious daughter, who has devoted her life to worship of the moon goddess, Tanit. The eyes of all the Barbarian men are upon her, but only two dare approach her: Mathô, the Libyan, and Narr' Havas, prince of Numidia. Before Mathô can reach the girl, Narr' Havas pinions Mathô's arm with a spear. When both men turn again to the palace, Salammbô and her slave-nurse, Taanach, have disappeared. Of this encounter is born a hate between Mathô and Narr' Havas, and their love for Salammbô.

The Barbarians, believing that they will shortly be paid, camp outside the gates of Carthage. But the Carthaginians, thinking themselves now rid of the mercenaries, have no intentions of treating honorably with them. They send to the Barbarian camp as their spokesman the obese, leprous Suffet Hanno; and Hanno tries to appease them. As none of the Barbarians understands the Carthaginian tongue, however, an interpreter is needed, and Spendius steps forward to claim the role.

Deliberately the newly freed slave, who is consumed with hatred for Carthage, misinterprets Hanno's speech, and tells the Barbarians that they have been vilely insulted by Carthage. The Barbarians turn upon Hanno, who barely escapes with his life. Capitalizing on this ferment of unrest—and upon Mathô's determination to capture and subdue the beautiful Salammbô—Spendius soon works the Barbarians up to the point where they are ready to make war on Carthage.

Spendius determines that for complete success, the Barbarians must somehow steal from Carthage the veil of Tanit —a sacred cloth, called the Zaimph, which the Carthaginians worship. He recognizes that without the Zaimph, the Carthaginians will be utterly dismayed, and feel themselves deserted by their gods; with it, the Barbarian soldiers will believe themselves invincible.

To this end, Spendius conceives a daring plan. Telling Mathô that he will take him to Salammbô, he leads the general to a cistern outside the city walls. They climb into it, and soon find themselves propelled along by a great current of water. They are inside the conduit that brings water to Carthage—and after a difficult and painful trip, they manage to emerge within the city's walls.

It is not long before they have made their way into the innermost room of the sacred temple, and after murdering a priest, they steal the iridescent Zaimph. Spendius is all for leaving Carthage with the prize at once, but Mathô is determined to confront Salammbô, convinced that the girl, who worships Tanit and the Zaimph, will be unable to resist him when she sees that he has the sacred veil.

When he does find Salammbô and confronts her, however, the girl's reaction is one of rage at the sacrilege he has committed. To his own surprise, Mathô finds himself unable to seize the beautiful maiden; instead, he is content to let her eyes burn into his consciousness, and without a word, he allows Spendius to lead him away to safety outside the city walls.

The theft of the Zaimph has the precise effect predicted by Spendius, both within and without the Carthaginian walls. The Carthaginians are terror-stricken, the Barbarians sure of victory. Now to the Barbarian camps comes Narr' Havas, with an army of his own. Recognizing that victory will lie with the Barbarians, he pledges his allegiance to them, and his enmity with Mathô is ended in a bond of friendship.

The war begins auspiciously. Carthage's great generals have all been slain except for Gisco, who is a Barbarian prisoner, and Hamilcar, who is still absent from the city. Hanno, who now commands the Carthaginian army, is a fool, and his pretentiousness and self-importance cause the thwarting of any sound military strategy that is proposed. With every day, the Carthaginians suffer greater and greater blows, and it seems that it will be no time before the Barbarian victory is complete.

Now Hamilcar returns to Carthage. At first, he is deaf to the pleas of his fellow citizens to lead their armies. He remembers too well how the patricians had failed him at the battle of Eryx. But when Hamilcar sees the destruction and havoc that the Barbarians have wreaked upon his own possessions, and when he learns that Mathô, after stealing the Zaimph, is known to have gone to Salammbô's chamber, he changes his mind, and accepts command of the Carthaginians.

At the very first battle after Hamilcar resumes command of the troops, the Carthaginians win a major victory, and Hamilcar seizes for his city two thousand captives. But now, again, the patricians, led by the jealous Hanno, go back on their word, and refuse to send the reinforcements that Hamilcar requests. Seething with rage, Hamilcar has no choice but to fight as best he can.

The people of Carthage are convinced that without the Zaimph they are lost. It is on this pretext that the high priest of Tanit, Schahabarim, tells Salammbô that she must go, alone, to the Barbarian camp and retrieve the treasure. His real reason is that he loves Salammbô, and this order is an expression of his perverse jealousy over not being able to possess the beautiful daughter of Hamilcar himself.

In her innocence, Salammbô does not question what will happen to her, but makes herself as beautiful as she can, following Schahabarim's instructions, and goes to the enemy camp with a guide provided by the high priest.

Through the guide's skill and cunning, Salammbô at last finds herself alone in the tent of Mathô, face to face with the Barbarian general. He is more overwhelmed than ever with Salammbô's beauty, and he draws her to him in a passionate embrace. The girl is at a loss to understand the strange feelings that now capture her.

Early the next morning, as Mathô lies asleep, Salammbô gathers up the sacred Zaimph. She draws a dagger from its sheath, and is about to plunge it into Mathô's bosom, when something—she knows not what—arrests her. She is content merely to steal from the camp with the veil of Tanit, carrying it with her to the nearby encampment of her father's army.

Narr' Havas, ever the opportunist, has recognized that with Hamilcar leading them, the Carthaginians will win the war. Therefore, he has gone over to his erstwhile enemy, and pledged to Hamilcar his fidelity, and a large army which he will raise among his own people. Hamilcar, however, is not as naïve as Narr' Havas thinks. To guarantee the Numidian's loyalty, he determines to betroth him to Salammbô. In this way he can also get Salammbô—who, he realizes, must have traded her virginity for the return of the Zaimph, and whom therefore he would not give to a man he respected—conven-

iently married off. Accordingly, Salammbô and Narr' Havas
are betrothed.

Because the Carthaginians have steadfastly refused to send
reinforcements, Hamilcar's army suffers greater and greater
blows. Unable to wait until Narr' Havas shall return with
reinforcements of his own, Hamilcar at last manages a retreat to Carthage, where he and his fellow citizens must stay
locked up; for no sooner have the gates of Carthage closed
behind Hamilcar's forces than the Barbarians lay siege to the
city.

At first the Carthaginians are hopeful of eventual victory,
but when Spendius executes a particularly daring maneuver,
they believe, at last, that hope is gone. What Spendius does
is to find loose brickwork in the Carthaginian aqueduct outside the city walls; destroying the aqueduct, he cuts off all
water supply to Carthage.

Now, in their desperation, the people determine that blood
sacrifices must be made to the god Moloch. (As Tanit is the
supreme female goddess to the Carthaginians, so Moloch is
the supreme male god; and there has long been a controversy
over which is more powerful.) Accordingly, hundreds of innocent children are rounded up to be fed into the flames
within the great idol. Only through a most daring ploy is
Hamilcar able to substitute a slave child for his own bastard
son, little Hannibal, the treasure of Hamilcar's life.

The sacrifice seems to be effective, for the skies open, and
the long season of heat and drought is ended with the coming
of rains. The people take heart—and even Schahabarim, high
priest of Tanit, acknowledges the superiority of Moloch.

Now, Narr' Havas arrives with six thousand Numidian
troops. The Carthaginians, convinced at last that Hamilcar's
advice is sounder than Hanno's, depose Hanno and replace
him with Hamilcar as Suffet. With Hamilcar's complete leadership, the course of the war is changed.

Now it is the Barbarians who suffer greater and greater
losses. Though the tide of battle sees some shifts—during a
period of three years it is inevitable that no side should always
maintain supremacy—and the Barbarians even manage to
break through the walls of Carthage, victory seems surely
on the side of Hamilcar.

And, at last, the Barbarians—or what is left of them, for
those taken prisoner have been brutally tortured and killed,

and those in the field have been driven to near-madness by their starvation—surrender. All who survive are put to the sword—all, that is, but Mathô. (Spendius, who earlier had come to Hamilcar's camp to sue for peace, has been crucified, and only Mathô is left of the Barbarian generals.)

With peace restored to their city, the Carthaginians spend days of revelry and rejoicing. The only serious conversation seems to be on the topic of finding a suitable torture for Mathô, for he has come to personify all of the Barbarians, and the Carthaginians are determined that he shall suffer in recompense for the Carthaginians tortured and killed during the three years of the war. At last it is decided that Mathô will run the gauntlet.

On the day chosen by the priests as being most propitious, the Carthaginians turn out in great numbers. Not only are they to witness the death of Mathô, but the marriage of Salammbô to Narr' Havas as well.

A great stage has been erected before the idol, Moloch, and there sits the beautiful Salammbô, now recognized for her retrieval of the Zaïmph as the savior of Carthage. On one side of her sits her bridegroom, Narr' Havas; on the other, her victorious father, Hamilcar Barca.

At a signal from the priests, Mathô is released from his prison at the far end of the city, and begins to run through the streets of Carthage. The streets are lined with citizens, and at every step he is struck with whips, pelted with stones, sprayed with vinegar. Soon his body is a mass of hanging flesh and flowing blood—but the whips of his guards will not allow him to falter a step. On . . . on . . . on he must run, beaten, stoned, ripped to pieces.

At last, a murmur goes up in the great square before Salammbô's throne, and the gruesome figure of the all-but-dead Barbarian general appears. He staggers forward to the dais, and Salammbô half rises from her seat. For an instant, Mathô looks into the eyes of the beautiful girl of whom he has so long dreamed—and then collapses at her feet, dead.

Salammbô, as she looks at this man whom she has loved so deeply and hated so intensely, is overcome by a feeling that she has never before experienced. She sways, and Narr' Havas reaches out his strong arm to support her.

But Salammbô is dead.

AROUND THE WORLD IN EIGHTY DAYS

Jules Verne

Jules Verne was born in Nantes, France, in 1828. He studied at local schools, and went to Paris to study law. He paid little attention to legal studies once in Paris, and began to write operetta librettos and short plays. His first published fiction, Five Weeks in a Balloon, appeared in 1863, and was a great success. He wrote more stories and novels dealing with scientific innovation and fantasy against a background of scientific and geographical fact, and each work was more popular than the last. Verne had caught the imagination of a world intrigued with the possibilities of the new technology, and he became one of the most widely read authors of his time. Around the World in Eighty Days was published in 1873, and retains its interest as a delightful and imaginative tale of adventure. Verne's scientific prophecies, considered extravagant when they were published, were soon realized; and the author must be given credit for his remarkable foresight, even if modern technology causes Verne's details to appear quaint today. Greatly honored in his lifetime, Verne died in France in 1905.

One morning in the fall of 1872, the efficient Londoner Phileas Fogg hires as manservant a jolly young Frenchman named Jean Passepartout after the shortest and most peremptory interview Passepartout has ever had. No sooner is the Frenchman hired than Fogg is off to the Reform Club.

Passepartout looks about the Fogg household in Savile Row and notes the extreme efficiency with which it is run. There are schedules everywhere, and Fogg has made clear that he expects the utmost precision from his new servant. As Passepartout has had a hectic and varied career—he has been everything from circus acrobat to municipal fireman—he decides he will enjoy the change of working for a machine of a man who likes life orderly, routine, and simple.

At the Reform Club, to which Fogg goes each day (nobody knows anything about him, though it seems certain that he is a man of independent wealth), the members are all chatting about the daring daylight robbery of the Bank of England. A man described as "a gentleman" has made off with fifty-five thousand pounds; a reward has been posted of two thousand pounds plus five percent of whatever amount is recovered.

Fogg's whist partners—Stuart, Sullivan, Fallentin, Flanagan, and Ralph—debate whether the thief is likely to make good his getaway. One of them mentions that it is certain; according to a chart in the newspaper, one can now make a complete circuit of the world in eighty days.

The other players pooh-pooh this idea; eighty days, they say, is the ideal time, and does not take into consideration inevitable accidents and delays. At this point Fogg takes up the argument, stating categorically that the trip around the world *can* be made in eighty days.

Before long the debate on the topic is quite heated, and at last Fogg determines to prove the feasibility of his thesis. He bets twenty thousand pounds that he, himself, can go around the world in eighty days. Flabbergasted, his friends agree to the wager—and then, calmly, Fogg picks up his cards, as though nothing has happened. "Diamonds are trump, I believe," he says.

Passepartout is staggered at his master's announcement that they must leave on a trip around the world—but there is no time to waste on protestations. While he packs a few items of clothing for his master and himself into a suitcase, Fogg fills a carpet bag with an enormous quantity of money —and then, the two are off on the first leg of their journey. As they settle into their seats on a railway car, Passepartout suddenly remembers that he has forgotten to turn off the gas in his room.

Fogg is imperturbable. "It will burn, then," he says, "—at your expense."

The early stages of the journey go smoothly and uneventfully—at least so far as Fogg knows. What he is unaware of is that a detective named Fix, reading of Fogg's bet in the newspaper, has put two and two together and come up with the (incorrect) conclusion that Fogg is none other than the bank robber. Determined to capture Fogg for the reward, Fix follows in his trail.

Unfortunately for Fix, however, the telegram granting him a warrant to arrest Fogg when he lands in Suez does not arrive in time. As he can only arrest Fogg on English soil, he determines to dispatch to London for a warrant to be sent to Bombay—and follow Fogg there.

The *Mongolia*, on which Fix, Fogg, and Passepartout sail for Bombay, makes excellent time, and they arrive at their destination two days early. This gain of time is a source of joy to Fogg—and a source of consternation to Fix, for the warrant has not arrived. He has no choice but to wire for another warrant to be sent to Calcutta.

Next on Fogg's itinerary is a train journey to Allahabad. Imagine his surprise when, fifty miles before reaching his destination, the train is stopped and all passengers must alight. Asking the meaning of this, Fogg is startled to learn that the newspapers were premature in announcing the completion of the railway line; the tracks have not been laid beyond the hamlet of Kholby.

Passepartout is in despair, but Fogg remains as calm as ever. He finds a peasant with an elephant, and though he must pay an extravagant price for the animal, he succeeds in purchasing it. He then hires a Parsee to be driver of Kiouni, as the elephant is called. And so Fogg and Passepartout, along with Sir Francis Cromarty, a fellow passenger in need of transportation to Allahabad, begin their journey on elephant back.

Fogg is convinced that he will be able to make up the lost time once he reaches Calcutta—but he does not count on the adventure that awaits him during this journey. The elephant driver hears some strange noises in the forest, and stops to investigate. It is discovered that in a clearing nearby, a beautiful young woman (the Parsee identifies her as the widow of the newly dead Rajah of Bundelcund) is held prisoner by a band of Brahmins, who intend to burn her alive with the corpse of her husband.

Passepartout is enraged; the Englishmen are aghast; but there seems to be nothing they can do to help the miserable young woman. Though they remain unobserved, they can see clearly that the Brahmin band outnumbers them, and is well armed. Fogg, though he feels helpless, is determined to watch through the night in the hope that some chance will present itself to rescue the maiden.

In the early hours of dawn, Fogg and Cromarty are amazed to hear shrieks from the Brahmin camp. They look— and are flabbergasted to see that the corpse of the dead man has risen from his bier and has picked up the beautiful widow. Too stunned to move, Fogg watches as the corpse carries the girl directly toward himself and his elephant— and then, suddenly, Fogg recognizes that the "corpse" is none other than Passepartout. By a clever ruse, the Frenchman has abducted the girl and insured her rescue.

Immediately she is taken into the howdah, and the strange band of travelers is on its way. The girl, when she recovers her senses, reveals herself to be Princess Aouda, as beautiful a young woman as any of the men has ever seen. English-educated, she is a charming person—and Fogg willingly offers to take her to Bombay, where she can live with a Parsee relation of hers.

Reaching Benares, Sir Francis takes his departure, and Fogg plans to move on. But again his nemesis, Fix, has a plot. He has discovered that Passepartout, quite unwittingly, has committed a minor offense against a local Indian religious sect; accordingly, Fix arranges for charges to be brought against him and Fogg, hoping thus to delay Fogg long enough for the arrest warrant to arrive.

But Fogg will not let a minor fine and jail sentence delay him. He posts extravagant bail for himself and his man-servant, and is on his way. Even Fix is overwhelmed by the coolness with which Fogg relinquishes so much money, for it is to Fix's advantage (he thinks) that Fogg spend as little as possible. (After all, part of the reward Fix anticipates is a percentage of the recovered money.)

Fix's last hope lies in getting a proper arrest warrant in Hong Kong, the last British ground that Fogg will touch. But again luck fails him, and the warrant is not there when they arrive.

Fogg's schedule is now very tight, for he has lost precious time all along the way. He must make connections with the *Carnatic*—and is dismayed to find himself arriving in Hong Kong after its scheduled sailing. But, fortunately, the *Carnatic* has been delayed by boiler trouble, and now is not sched-uled to sail until the next day. Accordingly, he decides to spend some time looking about the city, and also bringing Princess Aouda to her relative's house. Therefore he sends Passepartout to the steamer office to book passage on the *Carnatic*.

Passepartout is joined in this trip by Fix, who by now has become quite friendly with the jolly Frenchman, without revealing his true motive. At the steamer office, they learn that the *Carnatic* is to leave earlier than expected, and they get their tickets. Desperate that Fogg will slip away from him, Fix decides that the man must not learn of the *Carnatic's* earlier sailing, and must miss the boat. Therefore, in all friendliness, he offers to show Passepartout the sights. The naïve Frenchman agrees—and before too many hours have passed, Fix has succeeded in having him drugged, and he leaves him unconscious in an opium den.

Fogg and Aouda have discovered that her relative no longer lives in Hong Kong. The girl is frightened at the prospect of what may become of her. Fogg insists that she allow him to escort her to England, where surely she will find friends. With a trembling heart, the girl accepts the offer of the handsome Phileas Fogg; as imperturbable as ever, he does not seem to notice her emotion.

The next morning, Fogg cannot understand why Passepartout has not shown up. Then, when he learns that the *Carnatic* has sailed during the night, he surmises that the Frenchman had learned of the earlier sailing, had assumed that Fogg himself knew of it, and had got to the boat on time.

It seems that this accident to his planning will altogether upset his chances of winning the wager, but Fogg is not one to give up easily. He hires a pilot boat, the *Tankadere,* and gets her captain, John Bunsby, to agree to try to get the vessel to Shanghai, where he expects to connect with the *Carnatic.* Fix now finds himself in the humiliating position of having to ask Fogg to take him along, and Fogg, having no idea who Fix may be, courteously agrees to having Fix as his guest.

Now adventures pile up thick and fast, and one disaster after another seems to present itself. Never losing his calm, however, Fogg handles each as it comes—and though he seems to be losing time on his schedule, he still believes that he can complete his journey in the required eighty days.

At Yokohama there is joy for both Fogg and Fix. Much to Fogg's delight, he discovers Passepartout working in a traveling circus with an act called the Long Noses, and master and servant are reunited. For Fix the pleasant surprise is the arrival—finally!—of a warrant for Fogg's arrest. It can do no good except on English ground, of course—but as this mad bank robber, Fogg, seems serious about returning to England, Fix decides to follow him, warrant in hand.

Passepartout, thrilled to be reunited with his friends, notes with evident satisfaction the emotion with which Aouda regards Fogg. But the Frenchman thinks his master an arrant fool for being so cold toward the girl; a Frenchman would certainly not behave as Fogg behaves with such a beauty.

From Yokohama the band sails for California—and from the moment they touch land, it seems, they are faced with problems more severe than any experienced in Asia. There is a major political riot in which they become embroiled. (Fogg, assuming that at least the election of a president must be at stake, is flabbergasted that all this turmoil is over a lowly justice of the peace. Curious breed, these Americans!) There is the railroad bridge at Medicine Bow, which the engineer dares not take the train over; at Fogg's suggestion, all the passengers walk across the bridge one by one, and the engineer races the train across at full throttle. It is no sooner across when the bridge breaks behind it, and plummets into the bottomless ravine below.

Next Fogg is challenged to a pistol duel while the train is in motion—but before the duel can take place, the train is attacked by gun-bearing Sioux Indians. In the ensuing fight, Passepartout is taken prisoner, and Fogg—with Fix close behind him—throws his schedule to the winds and spends days in the rescue of his loyal servant.

Fix, of course, is as eager as Fogg himself for the strange Englishman to return to British soil, and now it is Fix who comes to the party's rescue, by contriving a sledge with sails to carry them across the frozen Midwest until they can connect with their train.

When at last they reach New York, they are three quarters of an hour too late, and have missed the sailing of the *China*, bound for Liverpool. Still undaunted, Fogg hires a trading vessel, the *Henrietta*. Ordinarily the *Henrietta* would never sustain an ocean voyage—much less make the kind of time Fogg believes necessary. So Fogg ties up the reluctant captain, Andrew Speedy, and captains the crew himself. When fuel runs out, he orders the boat itself to be burned. By the time the weary band of voyagers reaches England, all that is left of the *Henrietta* is her engine and her iron hull.

At last, within hours of succeeding at his fantastic wager, Phileas Fogg is in England. Fix asks him: "Are you truly Phileas Fogg?" Assured that he is, Fix then slips out his warrant and arrests Fogg for the robbery of the Bank of England.

In prison, Fogg puts his watch on a table before him, and sees the minutes ticking away into hours. As the time passes, so does Fogg's dream of winning the bet. When at last Fix's error is revealed, it is too late. Fogg has lost!

When Fix comes to the cell door to announce Fogg's release and to apologize, Fogg looks at him stonily for a moment—and then hits him, knocking him out cold.

Back in his rooms at No. 7, Savile Row, Fogg believes himself now free, at last, to declare his love for Princess Aouda. The girl is overwhelmed; she had not imagined that her own love for him had been returned. Fogg tells her that, having lost the wager, he is penniless, but the girl accepts his proposal nonetheless, and the two are lost in rapture.

Suddenly Passepartout bursts into the room. "You have won the wager, Monsieur Fogg!" he exclaims.

Aouda and Fogg are flabbergasted—and then Passepartout explains. By traveling always east in their journey around the globe, the travelers had gained a full day's time. It is not Sunday, as Fogg imagines, but the day before. He has yet twenty-five minutes to win his wager.

Hastily Fogg dashes off to the Reform Club. Stuart, Sullivan, Fallentin, Franklin, and Ralph are gathered there as agreed, but they doubt that their mad friend Fogg will appear. Just as the clock begins to strike the appointed hour, the door flies open. The members of the Reform rise as a body, and gasp.

It is Phileas Fogg! He has returned! He has won the twenty thousand pounds! He has gone around the world in eighty days!

THAÏS

Anatole France

Jacques Anatole François Thibault, whose pen name was Anatole France, was born in Paris in 1844. His father owned a bookstall on the Seine, and sent his son to a religious school where the boy received a disciplined education in religion and the classics. He began writing novels in his twenties, and achieved his first success in 1881 with The Crime of Sylvestre Bonnard. *He acquired a wealthy and cultured patroness who introduced him to Paris literary society and encouraged him to champion in his writings the liberal causes which were having a profound impact on the French nation at the end of the nineteenth century. In each of his works his style became progressively more mature, his sentiments more ironic, his satire more powerful and controlled. Anatole France was deeply involved in the Dreyfus case, and many of his works were violent attacks on the Church and the Army as institutions. He became allied with the political Left, but his inherent skepticism obviated intense involvement with any cause, and he eventually aimed his satire at the socialists and anarchists, much as he had done, and continued to do, with the institutions of the Right. Anatole France is most admired for his style, for his rationalism, and for his penetrating exposure of foolishness and pretension. He was a widely honored man at the time of his death in 1924: he had received the 1921 Nobel Prize for literature, and had been often acclaimed as belonging to the great French rational tradition of Voltaire. Thaïs, published in 1890, was one of Anatole France's bitterest attacks on Christianity, revealing as it does the author's sympathetic treatment of the pagan courtesan and his undisguised contempt for the hermit Paphnutius.*

The scene is Egypt in the fourth century A.D. Of all the ascetic monks who live on the banks of the Nile, none is as zealous, as holy as Paphnutius, priest of Antinoë. (This does not include the famous Anthony, the most religious of all the Egyptian ascetics, who lives away from the river, on a mountain.)

As a young man, Paphnutius had lived in Alexandria, son of well-to-do parents. There he studied philosophy—indeed, he was an atheist for a long period—and followed the usual rounds of pleasure as practiced by young Alexandrians. He drank freely, sported merrily, attended the theater frequently, visited houses of ill-fame regularly. But, at the age of twenty, under the tutelage of the priest Macrinus, he experienced a sudden conversion to Christianity and, as a penance, went to live in the desert.

For the past ten years, then, Paphnutius has lived in a small hut, surrounded by his twenty-four disciples in their huts. He wears a rough hair shirt, whips himself mornings and evenings, and often lies prostrate upon the sand for days at a time in total abstinence from food and drink.

One day, as Paphnutius meditates upon his holy books, he sees as in a vision the voluptuous face and form of an actress he had once seen in Alexandria—the renowned courtesan, most beautiful of women, Thaïs. Try as he will, the priest cannot rid his mind of the image of this sinful woman, and at last he perceives that the vision of Thaïs is a sign from God. He, Paphnutius, must rescue this woman from her life of lust, carnality, and wickedness, and restore her to God. Trembling, Paphnutius decides to go to the evil city, Alexandria, to meet with Thaïs.

He consults a simple holy man named Palemon, who also lives in the desert, about the wisdom of his plan. Palemon advises Paphnutius that to go to Alexandria will swerve him from his holy course; mixing with men can only lead to the soul's downfall. Leaving Palemon, Paphnutius is disheartened by the advice; but he comes upon a pair of plovers which appear to him as messengers from God. The female plover is entrapped in a net, and the male pulls at the net with his beak, carefully ripping it thread by thread, in order to free the female. Thus does Paphnutius recognize that God intends for him to rescue Thaïs from the net of her own iniquity. (He is alarmed a little to notice that in the process of freeing the female plover from the net, the male has got his claws completely entangled in it. But Paphnutius remains undeterred.)

Accordingly he sets out on his journey, first leaving one of his disciples, Flavian, in charge of the others, and urging him to be particularly watchful of the idiot disciple called Paul the Simple.

During the course of his journey, Paphnutius encounters an old mystic—ascetic, like himself—and the two talk. But to Paphnutius the mystic seems a fool, having rejected both the glories of this world and those of the next to find what he calls contentment. Paphnutius believes it pointless to talk to a man so benighted that he does not dedicate his life to God, and he moves on.

Reaching Alexandria, he goes to the house of the rich man Nicias, who had been a schoolmate of his ten years before. Nicias greets Paphnutius warmly, and when the priest asks for a bath, rich clothes, and sack of money with which he can go to Thaïs, Nicias says he is glad that his old boyhood friend has at last renounced his religious foolishness and is returning to the world of pleasure. Enraged, Paphnutius declares that he is on a holy mission, and is destined to save the soul of the harlot Thaïs. Nicias, who seeks no quarrel with any man, wishes the priest well, mentioning that Thaïs had once been his own mistress and that she is, still, the most beautiful woman in Alexandria. At the idea of Nicias' having lain with Thaïs, Paphnutius is filled with a rage that he is at a loss to explain, and he hurries away.

Thaïs is performing this evening in a theater, and Paphnutius goes to see her. From the conversations he hears around him, he gathers that all have come to the theater with the same purpose—to see Alexandria's darling, Thaïs, in the role of Polyxena. The courtesan-actress is, indeed, every bit as breathtakingly lovely as Paphnutius had remembered her, and he watches her performance transfixed. At the end of the play, he rises in his seat and shouts aloud that Thaïs must be sacrificed as a willing victim to God.

He rushes out into the streets of men, learns the house in which Thaïs lives, and sends a frightened servant to announce his arrival.

Her performance over, Thaïs is resting at home in the Grotto of the Nymphs—perhaps the most voluptuous room of all in a house built by Thaïs of nothing but beautiful and voluptuous rooms. She lies on a gilded tortoise-shell couch, a looking glass in her hand, and she wonders how long her fabled beauty will last.

Thaïs' life has been a strange one. The daughter of a bestial father and a miserly mother, the only pleasure she knew in childhood was her friendship for the house slave, Ahmes. This Negro delighted in the little daughter of his master, and told her stories, played games with her, and kept her warm with his own blanket at night. Ahmes was one of the few slaves in those days with the courage to remain true to Christianity, for the Saved were persecuted on every hand. He told Thaïs the story of his religion, and of how he had been baptized and given the name Theodore. To the little girl, his stories were magical—she was a highly superstitious child, and was never to lose her superstition—and when Ahmes proposed that she be secretly baptized, she assented.

Shortly after being received into the Church in a secret midnight ceremony held in a cave, Thaïs forgot all about her new religion; she could not separate in her mind the Christian stories from the myths of the other gods. But when Ahmes was charged wrongfully of a theft—merely to conceal the fact that his master hated him because Ahmes was a Christian—and was tortured to death by three days of crucifixion, little Thaïs was deeply moved, and resolved to run away from home.

Soon she fell into the clutches of a wicked old crone, who beat her mercilessly in order to teach her to dance gracefully. The crone's effeminate son, as wicked as his mother, taught Thaïs to act. There was no doubt that the girl would grow up to be a beauty, and these two hoped to make something out of her by fitting her for the stage. But Thaïs again ran away, and fell innocently and easily into the role of courtesan. At last she became renowned—winning fame and riches as much for her abilities on the stage as her abilities in the rites of love.

Now she is at her peak of perfection—the darling of Alexandria, wealthy beyond reckoning (countless men have squandered entire fortunes on her). But Thaïs is still superstitious. She knows that her beauty cannot remain unparalleled forever, and what will become of her when her loveliness fades? She is desperately afraid of death.

When Paphnutius is shown into the Grotto of the Nymphs where Thaïs lies, he is stunned by her beauty. The blood suffuses his face, and then rushes away from his head. Clearly this is a sign from God that he must save Thaïs from her own wickedness.

The woman is frightened, at first, by the strange holy man, and when she hears his name, she becomes terrified that he may bring her death. (Paphnutius' fame is wide, and many erroneous legends about his powers have been spread abroad.) But soon the priest's warnings about the wickedness of a life of pleasure put her at her ease; that pleasure is wicked is such a foolish notion to Thaïs that she thinks Paphnutius is joking with her. It is only when he talks about death and life after death that she becomes frightened. Thaïs does not know quite what to make of this strange man.

As Thaïs has promised to go to a banquet this night, Paphnutius urges her to go and witness the folly and emptiness of the life she leads; but he vows that he will go with her. At the banquet, Paphnutius is the only Christian, and the other guests—Cotta, Hermodorus, Dorian, Nicias, Zenothemis, Callicrates, the heretic Marcus, and others—discuss their ideas of religion. Paphnutius says nothing.

At the end of the banquet, however, something happens which upsets Thaïs deeply; young Eucritus plunges his dagger into his own bosom. Thaïs is terrified of death—and this episode reminds her of an incident that has occurred recently. She had seen a number of Christians doing homage to a tomb, and had learned that it housed the great martyr, Theodore the Nubian, who had been none other than her own childhood friend, Ahmes. These events—coupled with the fact that the abbess of the nunnery into which Paphnutius resolves to place Thaïs is a daughter of Alexandria's famed proconsul, and therefore a woman of great esteem—cause Thaïs to agree to what Paphnutius proposes. She follows him into the night.

Before Thaïs' redemption can truly begin, Paphnutius believes it necessary for her to destroy utterly every trace of the life she has led, and at his instigation she submits to having a hug bonfire built, in which all of her possessions are destroyed. (At first Paphnutius had considered making Thaïs donate her riches to a church or monastery—but in a flash he sees the wickedness inherent in this plan. How can the work of God be furthered by wealth earned from wickedness and carnality? No, all of Thaïs' past life must be destroyed, utterly and completely.) When her wealth is gone, Thaïs dons the meanest robe of one of her slaves, and follows Paphnutius into the night.

Thaïs, still not quite aware of what is happening to her, but conscious that she is being saved from death, is entrusted to the Abbess Albina, and Paphnutius returns to his own rude hut in the desert, conscious that his mission has been accomplished and that the vilest woman in the world has been redeemed and brought to God's love.

But Paphnutius finds that he cannot exorcise his thoughts of the beautiful Thaïs. Night after night, day after day, his mind has room only for visions and fantasies of the actress-courtesan. The harder he tries to meditate upon holy matters, the more he is overcome by thoughts of Thaïs. At last he has a dream in which a giant pillar appears; there is a voice urging him to go and live atop the pillar. So once more he leaves his twenty-four disciples and goes off by himself. Finding a ruined temple, he mounts to the top of a column, determined to stay there until his soul be cleansed.

Even atop the column, however, the dreams, fantasies, and visions of Thaïs persist. Days, weeks, and months go by —and the legend of the monk who lives atop a column in the desert spreads. Soon pilgrims begin coming for Paphnutius' blessings, and the word of his miraculous cures spreads far and wide. Eventually, an entire city grows up around the base of Paphnutius' column, and he is considered the greatest holy man in the land. But the visions of Thaïs in all her voluptuousness persist, and Paphnutius comes to recognize that even greater submission is needed before God will cleanse his soul.

He therefore crawls down from his pillar in the still of night, and goes off into the wilderness. (Later, his disciples swear to having seen him carried off his column by archangels.) He takes up his residence in a deserted tomb, in which he hopes utterly to hide from the world. But even in the tomb, the fantasies from the Devil—for so Paphnutius has come to identify them—continue, and his desires grow stronger than ever. The crowning horror of this stage of his penance is that he finds he is, at heart, a heretic and an unbeliever.

Shrieking in despair at this revelation, Paphnutius falls in a dead faint. When he revives, he finds himself in the company of some monks led by the famous Zozimos. These monks are on their way to a final meeting with the saintly Anthony, whose hour of death is at hand.

When all the monks are assembled at the appointed place, Anthony comes among them to give his final blessing. The dying man singles out one monk of the crowd—Paul the Simple—and asks him what visions he sees.

In a trance Paul tells of seeing Thaïs on her deathbed. She has been redeemed, and is the greatest nun of her order. Through her acting and her singing and her flute playing, she has brought all of her sisters-in-Christ closer to God.

Paphnutius, in great anguish, believes that as it was he who brought Thaïs to redemption, now he too will at last be saved. But Paul the Simple sees a different vision of Paphnutius; for him, says Paul, there are the words "Pride, Luxury, and Doubt."

Thunderstruck at this betrayal, Paphnutius can think only one thought: "Thaïs is dying! Thaïs is dying!" At last he recognizes that he should have acknowledged his own love and desire for her long ago. To have enjoyed one carnal hour with Thaïs would have enabled Paphnutius to laugh at hell.

Determined that Thaïs shall know the truth before dying,

Paphnutius rushes to the convent where she lies, as beautiful as ever, at the edge of death. He proclaims her name, and throws himself upon her—but it is too late. Thaïs sighs a final prayer for forgiveness of her life of wickedness, entreating God to take her to His throne. Then she is dead.

Paphnutius feels his heart breaking within his bosom. Suddenly the nuns shriek and draw away from him. "Vampire! Vampire!" they scream—and Paphnutius, passing his hand across his face, feels how hideous he has grown.

THE IMMORALIST

André Gide

André Gide was born in Paris in 1869. His family were pious French Protestants who provided him with a thorough education and enough financial support to begin writing at an early age. Gide became a center of controversy because of his writings. He made, however, no attempt to court the attendant publicity nor, on the other hand, did he ever try to bring his ideas into line with conventional tastes and standards. Although he married in 1895, he did not disguise his own sexual inclination; The Immoralist (1902) is a fictionalized account of his own marriage, and the sufferings of the hero and his wife closely parallel Gide's own tormented domestic situation. The Counterfeiters (1926) is also autobiographical, and treats the struggles which the writer endured in the course of choosing to obey his own emotional and artistic impulses. Gide traveled widely and wrote—besides several novels—plays, poems, critical studies, travel sketches, and journals. He was attracted to the ideal of a communist society, but came away from Russia in 1936 disillusioned and cynical; his report on the failure of the 1917 revolution, in terms of the ideological changes he had hoped for, greatly antagonized the powerful left-wing intellectuals of France.

Gide was guided at all times by his expressed aim: to be true to one's self and to what one feels and believes, whatever the cost. He was rewarded with the 1947 Nobel Prize for literature; this was in effect recognition that an artist's achievement can be rewarded without necessarily sanctioning his beliefs. Gide died in Paris in 1951.

To console his dying father, twenty-four-year-old Michel takes as his wife the friend of his childhood, twenty-year-old Marcelline. He knows very little about her, and does not love her, though he likes her a good deal; and he imagines that her feelings for him are about the same.

After his father's death, Michel takes his bride to Tunis. A scholar of renown in spite of his comparative youth, Michel intends to resume his research and writing activities. He is prevented from this, however, by an illness which he contracts at the time of his marriage. It begins with only an annoying cough, but it becomes steadily worse, and soon he begins spitting up blood.

Michel tries, at first, to keep Marcelline from knowing how seriously ill he is, for he has come to recognize that she loves him deeply. But at last her knowing cannot be prevented, and Michel sinks back, content to let her minister to his needs. Marcelline consults a doctor, whose verdict is cruel. Michel has tuberculosis, and can be saved only by removing him immediately to Biskra, in Algeria.

Between the arduous journey and the death sentence under which he is placed, Michel despairs of life, and he is in the greatest anguish. But his health does begin to return, and soon he is well enough to sit up in bed, and even to take short walks in the afternoon, leaning on his wife's arm.

One day Marcelline brings a beautiful young Arab boy to Michel's room, hoping that the lad will amuse him. Michel finds himself strongly attracted by the boy's animal grace, and especially by the boy's robust health. The boy is brought every day, and soon Marcelline has found other boys to come and amuse her husband.

Now, when Michel has a hemorrhage, he is profoundly disturbed, whereas he had been comparatively calm over the first hemorrhages, which were so much more serious. But Michel wants to get well. He begins to read everything he can lay hands on which deals with his disease, and suddenly he realizes that he has been treating himself unwisely. It is necessary to rebuild his body, and to that end he begins gorging on food, whereas in the past he had been indifferent to meals.

Now Michel becomes obsessed with his body. He begins to throw the windows wide open at night, though in the past he has always slept in a closed room. He forces himself to go for walks, each day walking a little farther. He is particularly fond of walking to a distant orange grove where, in the afternoons, one of his favorites among the Arab boys, Bachir, can be found playing a flute. He envies the beautiful Bachir his dark, glossy skin, and one day determines that he must tan himself. Accordingly he begins visiting an isolated spot that he knows and, each day, strips himself and gives his body to the heat of the sun. One day he even goes so far as to plunge impetuously into a clear mountain stream nearby, but the chill shocks him. Soon, the whiteness of his body, which he had so much loathed, turns to bronze.

One day in January, Michel has a curious experience. He is alone in a room with Moktir, one of the beautiful Arab lads, but his back is turned. Moktir, not realizing that Michel is watching him in the looking glass, steals a pair of scissors from the table. What is amazing to Michel is that he himself says nothing; rather, he seems obscurely pleased by the boy's theft. After this event, Moktir becomes Michel's favorite.

His health considerably restored, Michel and Marcelline decide to travel on, so that Michel may begin his work. But now Michel is amazed to discover that he cares nothing for the abstruse subjects that interested him in the past. It seems to him that he has been suffering from the veneer of civilization, and he determines now to strip away all artificiality, all pretense, from his own character, and find out who Michel really, in essence, is. It seems to him he is going to discover a new self. To that end, he even shaves off his beard and begins to let his hair grow, thus altering his external appearance and making it more natural. At the same time, he is aware of a growing love for Marcelline.

One day Michel decides to set out early for a nearby village on foot, and Marcelline agrees to follow him in a carriage, joining him for lunch. After several hours of walking—hours which are sheer joy to him—Michel suddenly hears a strange sound. He turns back and sees Marcelline's carriage approaching at breakneck speed, the driver standing up, shouting loudly. As they approach, Michel sees that Marcelline is petrified, and that the driver is drunk. The carriage passes too swiftly for Michel to stop it, but up ahead, the horse falls, and Marcelline escapes. Instantly Michel is down upon the driver, and pummels the brute soundly. He succeeds in tying up the man, and dumping him into the carriage. That night Michel possesses Marcelline for the first time, and it is an experience of unutterable ecstasy.

In picking up his studies again, Michel discovers that he

has completely lost his taste for the dead works he had before concerned himself with. He decides, instead, to investigate the life of young King Athalaric, the fifteen-year-old who worked with the Goths to overthrow his own mother. It is his intent to use this material to illustrate his thesis that culture and civilization lead to the death of man. Accepting a chair at the Collège de France for the following year, Michel decides to spend the summer at an estate he has inherited at La Morinière.

Once installed in their summer home, Michel divides his time, at first, between necessary visits to the bailiff, Bocage, to settle the administering of the tenant farms, and pleasurable visits with Marcelline, who is now expecting a child.

His devotion to these two, however, gives way at the arrival of Bocage's younger son Charles, seventeen. Michel is immediately attracted by the lad's vitality, health, and graceful beauty, and soon he is spending more and more time in the boy's company. Charles, who has been studying agriculture, opens Michel's eyes to the abuses being perpetrated on the farm, and Michel is grateful to have so charming and informed a friend.

In the fall Michel and Marcelline move back to Paris, and install themselves in a large apartment, where they will live until the following summer. Michel's first lecture on his new thesis is poorly received; for the most part, his auditors do not seem to understand him. The one exception is Menalque.

Menalque, currently in disrepute owing to a scandal which received wide publicity in the newspapers, is a man whom Michel has known for many years. Now, for the first time, he finds himself in sympathy with the mysterious Menalque, whereas before he had always found him slightly distasteful. Menalque begs Michel to visit him several weeks hence, just before Menalque is scheduled to leave the country, and Michel agrees.

At the time of the appointed visit, Michel debates the advisability of keeping the appointment, for Marcelline has been lying ill with a fever. At last, however, he decides to go, for Menalque seems the only person in the city who is alive. Even Marcelline seems to have changed and to have taken on the superficial values which he, Michel, has been trying to cut away.

The visit with Menalque proves to be a disturbing one,

but it is nonetheless stimulating. Menalque tells of having heard about Michel's sojourn in Biskra, and even produces the scissors which the Arab boy, Moktir, had stolen. To Michel's amazement, Menalque tells him that Moktir had seen Michel looking at him in the mirror at the time of the theft, and had wondered why the man had not spoken. Thus, explains Menalque, while Michel thought that he was fooling the boy, it was really the boy who was fooling him.

Menalque also describes to Michel his own way of life. He is totally without possessions, so that he may always be free. Possessions, he warns, tie one down—and Michel is clearly too fond of possessions. Michel turns this idea over in his mind for some time. . . .

When he returns to his apartment, he finds a doctor there. Marcelline has taken a turn for the worse, and has lost the baby she has been carrying. At this news Michel feels as though he is falling headlong into a bottomless hole.

With the doctor's consent, Michel takes Marcelline to La Morinière, hoping that the climate there will be beneficial to her. As for himself, he is content to be at the country place, though he at first misses the companionship of Charles, who is back at school.

Becoming more and more obsessed with finding the reality of life, Michel begins to spend increasing amounts of time with the peasants who work the tenant farms. At first, these men are wary of him, but gradually they begin to trust him. One, in particular, a coarse fellow named Bute, fills him in on all the gossip of the local families, and Michel sees that the façade presented by these people to the world masks essential passions and depravities. Michel finds the truth more interesting than the pretended piety and virtue.

Bute also shows him the snares set by a poacher who is none other than Bocage's elder son, Alcide. With Bute's help, Michel catches Alcide in the act of poaching—but to his own surprise, he ends by giving the boy money in exchange for showing him how to set snares. Michel is a little chagrined, later, when Bute asks for money to buy more copper wire for new snares; Bocage, he explains, has found the old ones. Michel pays—and then must pay Bocage a promised bounty on the snares he has found. This goes on for some time until Bocage mentions that it is Alcide who should get the bounty, for he is the one who finds the illegal snares. Thus, for the second time, Michel finds himself duped in a situation in which he has believed himself to be duping.

Charles now returns to La Morinière, and Michel is disgusted that the beautiful boy has turned into a priggish, homely, would-be man. Charles repeats to Michel a lesson which he himself had taught the boy a year before: if one has possessions, one must devote care and energy to their preservation. Michel determines to sell the estate, and travel with Marcelline, whose health continues to be poor.

Now it is discovered that Marcelline has tuberculosis, and Michel resolves to be to her during this illness what she had been to him during his. But he is too consumed by his searching for his own identity to become the self-effacing nurse which the virtuous Marcelline had been at Biskra. Nonetheless, he determines to pretend.

Trips to various climates and cities and cure centers proving of no avail, Michel decides to ignore the doctor's advice and take Marcelline back to Biskra, in the hope that she will find there the cure that he himself had found. Patiently the sick woman endures the journey, but she has little hope for her recovery.

In Biskra, Michel is sorrowed to find that all of the beautiful Arab boys have grown up and become ugly—all, that is, but one: Moktir. Newly out of prison, Moktir is as ravishingly beautiful as ever, and Michel invites him to live with him and Marcelline. Happily the Arab boy accepts.

Michel finds in the boy the perfect companion, for Moktir knows all the dark corners of the native quarter, and Michel, more intensely interested than ever before in finding the essential qualities of existence, believes that he will experience them under Moktir's tutelage. All day Michel stays by Marcelline's bedside, but when night falls, he steals out of the house and with Moktir goes to Moorish cafes and bordellos.

Marcelline accuses Michel, one day, of liking what is inhuman—but he notices how her eyes hunger for the sensations and experiences which she is too weak to endure.

One night, after Michel has spent several hours lying with a Moorish woman who is also Moktir's mistress, he returns to find Marcelline hemorrhaging. He tries to reassure her that everything will be all right, and he picks up her rosary beads from the floor where they have fallen, and tries to put them back into her hands. But deliberately she lets them fall again. Toward morning, Marcelline dies. . . .

Michel stays on at Biskra, living on next to nothing. An innkeeper provides him with food, and he has a young servant boy, Ali, to take care of him. This lad is very fond of Michel, but when he finds the man making love to a prostitute who is his own sister, he goes away for several days. Michel finds this jealousy of the lad's foolish, since the boy knows how his sister earns her money. But to please little Ali, he sends the girl away.

She is not offended, but whenever she meets Michel she laughs, and tells him that he is falling in love with her beautiful little brother. Michel admits that perhaps she is right. . . .

THE COUNTERFEITERS

André Gide

When adolescent Bernard Profitendieu discovers a packet of his mother's old love letters, he learns that he alone, of her four children, was not fathered by her husband. This knowledge that he is a bastard relieves Bernard of the guilt he he has felt over being unable to love his "father," and he determines to run away from home, never again to be dependent upon Profitendieu money.

Leaving behind a melodramatic letter for his "father," he goes to spend the night with his closest friend, Olivier Molinier. Olivier is the beautiful son of Profitendieu's partner. From Olivier and his younger brother, George, who shares the bedroom, Bernard learns that their elder brother, Vincent, has been keeping a mistress. Bernard tells Olivier of his plans for making his own way in the world, and Olivier is amazed at his young friend's bravado; but when Bernard asks him to spend the next day with him, Olivier must refuse. He has secret plans of his own; he intends to go to the train station to surprise his Uncle Edouard, who is en route to Paris. Olivier had spent some time with Edouard, who is a minor novelist, several years before, and had fallen in love with him; but he is sure that his uncle finds him boring. Nonetheless, he de-

termines to see him. Therefore, the next morning Bernard
must go away alone.

Vincent Molinier, Olivier's older brother, is in desperate
circumstances. His mistress, Laura Douviers, is pregnant.
(They had become lovers at a tuberculosis sanitarium at Pau,
where both had believed they were dying.) Vincent at first
intended to give Laura the money he had saved for his next
year's education; but under the suave tutelage of the decadent, homosexual Comte Robert de Passavant, author of the
bestselling novel *The Horizontal Bar*, Vincent used the
money to gamble, in the hopes of making more. Now he has
lost everything, and has deserted Laura. Passavant introduces
Vincent to the idle and superficial Englishwoman, Lady Griffiths. Soon this cold and aloof creature has Vincent enmeshed;
she makes him her lover, and convinces him that he has done
well to abandon Laura.

In her unhappy, desperate plight, Laura has written to the
one friend whom she believes she can count on to help her:
Edouard. It is ostensibly to give her money that Edouard
now travels to Paris; but in reality it is in the hopes of seeing
again his beautiful nephew Olivier, with whom he is in love
(though, unhappily, Edouard recognizes that in all likelihood
he bores the poor lad).

Reaching the train station, Edouard is overcome with excitement when Olivier greets him; but the interview between
them is stilted and artificial, and both are made unhappy by
it. In his nervousness, Edouard drops the claim check to his
luggage, which he intends to get later.

The check is found by Bernard, who has jealously followed Olivier to the train. Retrieving the suitcase of
Edouard's, Bernard finds himself the possessor of a sizable
amount of money; a suit of decent clothes, only a little too
large for himself; Edouard's notebooks and diaries; and a
letter from a girl named Laura.

From the notebooks and diaries, Bernard learns of
Edouard's passion for Olivier. He learns, too, that Edouard
is planning to write a major novel called *The Counterfeiters*,
and Bernard reads the notes about this novel with keen interest, as he and Olivier both have hopes of becoming writers
themselves.

Though no names are mentioned, from the details of the
letter, Bernard realizes that this Laura is the woman

abandoned by Vincent Molinier. He takes some of Edouard's money and goes to the hotel where she is staying, determined to rescue her. (He recognizes that he is the only one, besides Laura herself, who knows who her lover is.) Laura is overcome with horror when Bernard confronts her; but they are interrupted by Edouard, who understands at once that Bernard has his lost luggage. The upshot of this strange interview is that both Bernard and Edouard agree to help the miserable Laura, and Bernard is hired as Edouard's secretary. Thus, when Vincent sends a packet of money to her, money he has won gambling with Passavant, Laura is able to return it marked simply "Too late."

Passavant has had his own reasons for befriending Vincent. He is infatuated with Vincent's beautiful young brother, Olivier, and urges Vincent to introduce him. Olivier is overwhelmed at meeting the smooth, famous author—and particularly flattered that the wealthy Passavant wants him to be editor of a new literary review which he plans to publish. He is a little taken aback, though, when Passavant suggests that he accompany him on his travels during the coming summer. But the older man is sure that he can get Vincent to overcome his younger brother's reluctance.

While in Paris, Edouard pays a visit to the ancient music teacher, La Pérouse, a close friend of Laura's grandfather. From La Pérouse Edouard hears something about the agonies of growing old. La Pérouse has but one joy in life—his love for his thirteen-year-old bastard grandson, Boris—a child whom he has never seen (the boy is being raised in Poland), but whom he loves with a single-minded passion. La Pérouse is determined to see the child once, and then commit suicide.

Edouard, convinced that if La Pérouse but once sees the boy he will give up all thoughts of death, promises to bring Boris to the old man. He learns that the child is now at Saas-Fee in Switzerland, with a woman doctor who is trying to cure him of his nervousness. Therefore Edouard, Laura, and Bernard go to the Alps.

In his naïve joy at his good fortune, Bernard writes a long letter to his friend Olivier, describing all of his adventures with Edouard and Laura. Enraged with jealousy over Bernard's having "stolen" his beloved Uncle Edouard, Olivier deliberately goes to Passavant and accepts his offer.

At Saas-Fee, Edouard finds young Boris. The boy is in treatment with the mystic psychotherapist, Mme. Sophroniska; and his one friend—whom he obviously adores—is the doctor's young daughter, Bronja.

Laura now realizes that Edouard is the one whom she has loved all along, and is driven to despair by his seeming aloofness. She does not, of course, understand that his passions are centered on Olivier. When Bernard falls in love with her, it is too maddening. She writes to her husband, Felix, in England, telling him all. In reply, he sends her protestations of his love and forgiveness, and begs her to return to him, promising to love Vincent's son as his own. And so she returns to her husband.

Now Edouard brings young Boris back to Paris, and enrolls him in the school of Laura's puritanical grandfather, Azais-Vedel. Because La Pérouse himself is to be a teacher there, because while remaining in Edouard's employ Bernard has agreed to tutor at the school part-time to keep his eye on Boris, and because among the new pupils there are some, particularly George Molinier, whom Edouard believes will be a good influence on Boris, Edouard is satisfied that all will turn out well, and he is able to pick up work once more on his complex novel, *The Counterfeiters*.

Unbeknown to Edouard, however, young George is not at all a fit companion for Boris. He has fallen in with a group of idle lads like himself, who are being taught such minor vices as petty thievery and deceit by older lads who, in turn, get their orders from one Victor Strouvilhou. This Strouvilhou, a friend of Passavant's, is determined to use the young boys to further his own schemes of blackmail and passing counterfeit ten-franc pieces.

Edouard and Bernard both find a measure of satisfaction in their lives in Paris—Edouard from his writing, Bernard from his love affair with one of Laura's sisters, the independent Sarah. (Laura's brother Armand assures Bernard, however, that only his sister Rachel is worth anything.) Both Edouard and Bernard are distressed, however, at the change that has come over their beloved Olivier as the result of his connection with the loathsome Passavant.

Olivier is annoyed, at first, by the coldness of his friends. Then he becomes more and more distressed. At last he realizes the superficiality and artificiality of his own life, and desperate for the affection and admiration of Edouard and Bernard, Olivier deserts Passavant, and attempts to kill himself. Fortunately he is saved by Edouard, who nurses him back to health.

Edouard now receives a visit from his half sister Pauline, the mother of Olivier. From her he learns for the first time of the hell it can be for the mother of three such handsome and intelligent sons as George, Olivier, and Vincent. Pauline realizes that she has lost both of the older boys, but begs Edouard to use his influence on George before it is too late. She is convinced that the boy has stolen a hundred-franc note, a theft which he denies; and she suspects that he has also stolen a packet of letters written to her husband by his current mistress.

Edouard does speak to George, but he finds his youngest nephew brazenly indifferent to his entreaties.

Bernard, who now lives with Edouard (having been asked to leave the school of Azaïs-Vedel by Rachel, who has learned of his affair with her sister Sarah), goes to take his examinations for the baccalaureate degree. While he is away, Edouard is visited by Bernard's "father," the prosecuting attorney Profitendieu. He tells Edouard that an investigation is under way into a ring of counterfeiters who are using young boys to pass their false coins. So far, he explains, he has been able to hold the investigation in check, because he knows that George, the son of his partner Molinier, is implicated. (Molinier, in turn, believes that the investigation is being held back by Profitendieu to protect his bastard "son," Bernard.) He begs Edouard to use his influence on George while there is still time for the boy to extricate and protect himself, and to this Edouard agrees.

Soon the conversation turns to Bernard, and old Profitendieu breaks down in tears, explaining that he has loved Bernard better than he has loved his own three children. Edouard, however, cannot bring himself to promise that he will get Bernard to return to the Profitendieu home.

Bernard passes his examinations, and shortly thereafter he has a mystical experience, in which he is led about by an angel. As the result of this encounter, which lasts for many hours, Bernard determines to dedicate himself to work that is truly significant for an artist.

Edouard now has another interview with his nephew

George. At first the boy is as indifferent as he had been earlier, but when Edouard tells him of the police's interest in the counterfeiters, the boy pales, and Edouard knows that he has succeeded in frightening the boy out of his illicit practices. George returns to school and warns his two closest friends—Philippe Adamanti and Léon Ghéridanisol—of the impending danger. Quickly they get rid of all the counterfeit coins in their possession. Now, however, they must find some new way of titillating their jaded juvenile palates. How can they amuse themselves, now that passing counterfeit coins has been ruled out?

The answer is provided by Boris. The lad has never been happy at the school—the other boys have always been offended by his pale good looks, his musical voice, his graceful body—and this exclusion has been agony for him. And recently Mme. Sophroniska has come to tell him that his beloved Bronja is dead. The boy is miserable.

For their own amusement, George, Ghéri, and Phiphi hatch a plot to torment Boris. They pretend to have formed a secret society to which they will not admit him, because they believe that he is a coward. Desperate to be included, Boris is willing to go to any lengths to prove his courage—precisely what the fiendish youths had expected him to do. As an initiation, they tell him that the four of them must draw lots; whoever draws the marked lot must shoot himself. By pre-arrangement, Boris is selected. He is given a pistol stolen from old La Pérouse—the very pistol with which the old man had tried, and failed, to commit suicide when he found that Boris did not return his love. George and Phiphi believe that the terror of handling a pistol which he believes to be loaded will be too much for Boris, and they await his ordeal with eager delight; but Ghéri is even more eager than his friends, for unbeknown to them, he has loaded the pistol. At the appointed time, Boris raises the gun to his temple and fires, killing himself.

This puts an end to Azaïs-Vedel's school, which has been in tottering financial shape for years. Sarah, furious that Rachel has driven Bernard away, runs off to England where she will be free, leaving Rachel alone to patch up the pieces of the school, although Sarah knows that her virtuous sister is going blind.

Even Armand, the girl's handsome, gifted brother, who

had also worked at the school, decamps, choosing to immolate his brilliance and wit in a superficial world of cold cruelty and sophistication. He has accepted the post deserted by Olivier; he will become Passavant's new protégé and editor of the review.

Visiting the recuperating Olivier to tell him this news, Armand, disdainful and pretending indifference to life as always, shows Olivier an "amusing" letter he has received from his older brother, Alexandre, who has for years been living in Africa. The letter describes a mad Frenchman of about thirty whom Alexandre has taken into protective custody. It seems this madman had recently murdered a British woman. . . . Olivier is too weak and too tired to be amused by the letter, and he does not finish reading it. Nor does he suspect the truth of it—that the letter describes his brother Vincent, who has murdered Lady Griffiths.

Bernard, at last able to accept responsibility for himself and his actions, has become a whole person. He is able to return to the home of Profitendieu, and to take the old man's genuine love, and find comfort in it.

And Edouard, too, is happy. Pauline has charged him with looking after his beloved Olivier. Now he will return to work on *The Counterfeiters*.

THE WANDERER

Alain-Fournier

Henri Alban Fournier, who used the pen name Alain-Fournier, was born in 1886 in a village in France near the city of Bourges. His father was a schoolmaster, and young Henri was sent to a fine lycée near Paris in order to prepare for the distinguished École Normale Supérieure. He failed the entrance exam twice, and in 1905 went to England where he worked as a French secretary. He served in the military from 1907 to 1909, and after that supported himself by tutoring while he worked on his novel. Appearing in 1913, Alain-Fournier's one novel was titled in French Le Grand Meaulnes; the English translation, titled The Wanderer, was published in 1928. The novel was a moderate success when it first appeared; critical appreciation has grown steadily since that date, and the book now enjoys the status of a small masterpiece. A beautiful allegory, The Wanderer has defied precise classification, although at one time or another it has been claimed by the sym bolists, the impressionists, the surrealists, and the existentialists as an example of their respective schools of writing. Alain-Fournier was working on a second novel when he was called into the army at the outset of the First World War; he was killed in the trenches in September 1914.

When, on a November day in the 1890s, seventeen-year-old Augustin Meaulnes is enrolled by his widowed mother as a boarding student at Sainte-Agathe's School, one of the students in particular senses that a new life is beginning. This student is François Seurel, son of the schoolmaster. At the age of fifteen, François feels somewhat alienated from his schoolfellows because of his limp. He senses that this affliction will not be an impediment to friendship with Meaulnes, and his spirits brighten.

As Meaulnes shares a garret room with him, François soon gets to know him well—as well, that is, as one can get to know him, for Meaulnes is a silent boy, with a faraway look in his eye. Because Meaulnes immediately becomes unofficial leader of the boys in the form, he is given the nickname Admiral; but none of the other boys—Moucheboeuf, Dutremblay, Fromentin, Delouche, Coffin, and the rest—is able to establish with him the rapport that exists between him and François.

Shortly before the Christmas holidays, M. Seurel announces that his parents-in-law, the delightful Charpentiers, are to arrive, and he asks for a volunteer to go with François to the station to meet them. Meaulnes hopes for this privilege, but is too proud to ask for it. Therefore M. Seurel chooses the foolish Moucheboeuf.

Meaulnes, regretting that he has been passed over, frames in his mind a harmless little plot by which he can both serve as escort for the Charpentiers and play a practical joke as well. François and Moucheboeuf are to pick the old folks up in a mule cart at the local station at two minutes past four; Meaulnes, therefore, will get the jump on them by borrowing the mare and cart of a neighboring farmer, Fromentin, and, with this swifter conveyance, meet the Charpentier train at the stop ahead, Vierzon, at three o'clock.

François surmises what his idol is up to, but on the chance that Meaulnes may lose his way, as he is unfamiliar with the local roads, François decides to go to the train station with

Moucheboeuf as planned, "just in case." As it happens, he does meet his grandparents, as scheduled, at two minutes past four. No, they tell him, they had not seen a young man fitting Meaulnes's description at the Vierzon station.

As the evening grows late, the whole Seurel family begins to wonder and worry about the "escape" of Meaulnes, but silence on the subject prevails, for fear of upsetting Grandfather Charpentier. Much later, however, things begin to look serious, for a stranger knocks at the door to deliver Fromentin's mare and cart, which he has found abandoned some distance away.

Meaulnes remains absent all that night, and in the morning—convinced that all will end well—M. Seurel announces that Meaulnes has gone to visit his mother. No one questions this—but François, who knows the truth, is in an agony of worry and speculation.

It is three days before Meaulnes returns, his clothes torn and dirty, his face weary. He offers no explanations, and none are asked for.

That night, as he lies in bed watching his friend undress, François notices that Meaulnes is wearing an elegant and expensive embroidered waistcoat instead of his own plain one. He asks Meaulnes about it, whereupon the older boy, saying nothing, immediately puts on his shirt again, covering the waistcoat, and lies down on the bed fully dressed.

Now a subtle change occurs in the relationships among the boys at school. All of those who had followed Meaulnes so unquestioningly in the past draw away from him, sensing that his recent adventure has somehow set him apart from them. Only François remains loyal. Meaulnes doesn't even seem to notice that now it is the brutish Jasmin Delouche who is leader of the school. He is abstracted and distant in manner, and spends much of his time working on the drawing of a map, which he allows nobody to see.

Several times François wakes up at night to see Meaulnes, fully dressed, standing by the door of their garret room. He seems on the verge of leaving—but always, at the last moment, shrinks back. One night, at this scene, François impetuously begs Meaulnes not to leave him behind. The older boy comes to François' bed and promises him that when he does leave for a second journey to his "Lost Land," he will surely take François with him. Always excluded before from journeys because of his limp, François is more grateful than he can say. From that night, Meaulnes and François are like brothers.

Now François learns what had transpired during Meaulnes's adventure.

Planning only to go to the station at Vierzon, Meaulnes had somehow lost his way. Convinced that he could not be too far from his destination, he had continued driving in the direction that he thought was right, but by nightfall he recognized that he was truly lost in a strange area. He left the mare and cart to go ask for directions at a peasant hut; but when he left the hut later, he could not find his horse and cart. So he plunged on afoot. Eventually he came to a château in ruins. Seeing nobody about, he decided to spend the night there. In the distance, he noticed several children in strange garb, and overheard their conversation, but he could make nothing of it.

Entering the château, he found it to be not in ruins, but merely deserted. He found a bedroom, and pushing a jumble of antique toys and musical instruments off the bed, he lay down and was soon asleep. He was awakened by voices. Looking up, he saw two strange men in carnival costumes stringing lanterns about. One of them—tall and thin, with a strange voice—told him that he was welcome to the fête, but that he must come in costume.

Rising, Meaulnes discovered trunks of clothes that had obviously belonged to a wealthy young man of another age. He threw a cloak about himself and descended to the salon.

The château was now alive with merrymakers, all of them in masks and carnival dress. Meaulnes learned that this was a fête celebrating the betrothal of the young master of the house, Frantz de Galais, who was soon expected to arrive with his bride. Gayer and gayer became the entertainment, and Meaulnes found himself caught up in it; but as the time for the bridegroom's arrival drew near, people began to get nervous.

One of the merrymakers who particularly caught Meaulnes's eye was a beautiful young woman. He had several elusive encounters with her, and in her eyes he saw that she was as moved as he, but she always drew away, as if afraid of him. At last he did succeed in learning her name and in telling her his. She was Yvonne de Galais, sister of the expected bridegroom.

When it became clear that the bridegroom would not appear, the party began to break up. Back in "his" chamber Meaulnes was changing into ordinary dress when he saw a young man at the window.

The young man—as pale and handsome as Yvonne—was the unhappy Frantz. In a few words, he told Meaulnes his tragic tale, singling him out, he said, because he was a stranger. His fiancée had deserted him; there was to be no wedding.

Meaulnes said nothing to the departing guests about his interview with Frantz. As some of the travelers were destined for the area of Sainte-Agathe's School, they invited Meaulnes to ride with them. As they moved along, Meaulnes heard a shot and saw a flash of smoke. (The other travelers were too busy talking to notice.) Looking out the coach window, he saw the tall, thin man with the strange voice running through the woods, carrying a pale white man in his arms.

Once back at the school, Meaulnes cannot rid his mind of this strange adventure—and particularly he thinks of the beautiful Yvonne. He is determined to find the Lost Land again and return. François persuades him to wait until he has finished the map, so that once on their way they will have no trouble finding the château. Meaulnes agrees.

By now the other schoolboys have come to hate Meaulnes and François for their secret air of mystery. One night they ambush the two in the town. Though all are masked and muffled, François recognizes each of his schoolmates, but notes that the leader of the band is a stranger. It is this stranger, who seems older than the others, who wrests the treasured map from Meaulnes. Then Meaulnes and François are released.

The next day there is a new student, a young man attached to a gypsy wagon seen about town. (The only other person known to be attached to the wagon is a thin old man called Booby.) François suspects the gypsy lad of being the leader of the previous night's ambush. This is confirmed when, finding himself alone with François and Meaulnes, the gypsy returns Meaulnes's map. "You will note," he says, "that I have added what information I can to what you already had on the map."

Shortly thereafter, Booby and the gypsy lad, whose face is always masked by the bandage he wears tied about his head, give a circus for the townspeople. Booby, dressed as Pierrot, proves to be the thin man from the château.

At the circus, Jasmin Delouche heckles the performers mercilessly, confident that he will get away with it, as he alone knows that the police are on their way to arrest the two performers for having stolen some chickens. Before the end of the performance, however, the performers surmise what is afoot, and make their escape—but not before the young man has pulled off his bandage before Meaulnes, revealing himself as Frantz, and given Meaulnes a slip of paper with Yvonne's address in Paris. Then, Frantz and Booby are gone. The townspeople are disappointed.

For some time after this, Meaulnes is downcast. It does not surprise François, therefore, that suddenly he announces one day his intention to go to Paris to look for the girl from the Lost Land. Meaulnes and François swear eternal friendship, and the older boy goes away. François eventually receives three letters from him.

The first is written two days after Meaulnes's arrival in Paris. He says that he has spent all day sitting on a bench outside the specified house, watching, but without success. He wonders if he is mad—and then observes that a young girl has sat on the same bench all day too. If he is mad, there are others in Paris mad also, he notes. In June a second letter arrives from Meaulnes. All hope is gone. He has just learned that Yvonne, who has never appeared, is married.

At the end of November comes a third letter. Meaulnes cannot escape the thought of Yvonne. He is going now to his mother's house in the country, but eventually he will take up his search again.

François is convinced that poor Meaulnes will now never find again his Lost Land—or his lost lady. He tries to put his dear friend out of his mind, convinced that he will never see him again.

Then, the following August, the stupid Jasmin Delouche innocently tells him a story about a fête at a château near his parents' home. Three days of revelry had been followed by the desertion of a young woman, the fiancée of the master of the château, leaving the merrymakers to break up their party, their reason for celebrating—the master's betrothal—no longer applying. Idly Jasmin wonders if this was the secret fête that that fellow Meaulnes may have been to the time he disappeared.

Excitedly François realizes that he is in a position to bring his dear friend back to the Lost Land. Getting the particulars of the château's location from Jasmin, François finds that it is in a province where he has relatives. Accordingly he goes off to visit his Uncle Florentin, from whom he hopes to know more.

Sure enough, Florentin not only knows the château, but he is friendly with old Monsieur de Galais, father of the unhappy Frantz, who has disappeared, and of the beautiful Mlle. Yvonne. The story of the girl's trip to Paris and marriage proves to have been false. An interview between Mlle. de Galais and François is arranged. She is the most beautiful woman he has ever seen, and they get along well.

Uncle Florentin suggests arranging an outdoor party for François, old man Galais, and his daughter. "Perhaps," he says innocently, "that friend of yours that you mentioned might like to come—you know, that fellow Augustin Meaulnes." At the name, Yvonne pales, and François sees that she, too, is deeply in love with the stranger whom she met at the party so long ago.

On his way to the home of Meaulnes, François stops to visit another of his relatives in the area, his Aunt Moinel. From this woman he hears a strange tale. She too was at the fête—but afterward, on her way home, she had met a poor girl on the road who begged to be taken into the carriage. The girl was Valentine Blondeau, the fiancée of Frantz, who deserted him at the last minute, fearing that he was in love with a dream vision of her and not with herself. The girl is now in Paris, Aunt Moinel continues—but then cuts her story short. "Why on earth should you be interested in the tales of an old woman like me?" she says humorously to François.

At last François reaches the home of Meaulnes's mother. There he is reunited with his dear friend, and tells him the good news of his having found Yvonne and located the château. Meaulnes, who is on the point of leaving on a journey, seems abstracted, but agrees to go with François to the outing planned by Uncle Florentin.

The outing is not a great success, and the meeting of Yvonne and Meaulnes seems to bring sadness to them both.

But before the day is ended Meaulnes and Yvonne are betrothed, and after five months, they are married. They go to live in the château, now all but destroyed.

The day after the wedding, François hears a strange sound near the château. He recognizes it as the secret call of Frantz, whom he discovers. The handsome, sensitive Frantz is in despair. He must find his beloved Valentine, he says, and François and Meaulnes must help him to find her. François, not wishing to rob Meaulnes of his new-found happiness, promises Frantz that he will track down Valentine alone. Frantz must return to this spot in a year. Taking him at his word, Frantz, in despair, announces his intent to leave immediately for a tour of Germany with Booby. Then he is gone.

Inside the château, Meaulnes and Yvonne have heard Frantz's signal, too. At first they try to ignore its message for them, but at last Meaulnes realizes that he must go to Frantz. He has a secret reason, he says. Reluctantly Yvonne releases him—but François must tell him it is too late. Frantz has already left for Germany.

Meaulnes, a desperate look in his eye, seizes his cloak. He will not return, he says, until he has found Frantz.

Yvonne is desolated by Meaulnes's departure, but she is used to indulging men. All her life she and her beloved father have pampered handsome Frantz, who has remained a child at heart. Her only friends at the Sand-Pit, as the château is called, are now her old father and François. From them she derives the strength needed to carry her through the months without a husband—for she is expecting a child.

At last the child is born—a daughter—but it has been a difficult delivery, and Yvonne lies in a fever. Within a week she is dead—without ever having had a word from Meaulnes. Several months afterward, her father, Monsieur de Galais, follows her to the grave.

François teaches school. He lives on at the Sand-Pit, to oversee the care of the little girl, and to await the return of Meaulnes. In his rambles through the château, François discovers a copybook that had belonged to Meaulnes, and from it he learns the secret of his friend's recent air of sadness, and the reason for his abrupt departure in pursuit of Frantz.

The girl who had watched with him in front of the de Galais house in Paris was a seamstress named Valentine

Blondeau. Eventually, drawn by similar sorrows, Valentine and Meaulnes had fallen in love, and were to be married. Before the wedding, however, Valentine, desiring to be honest, had given Meaulnes the love letters she had received from her fiancé of the past—and from them Meaulnes had learned, for the first time, that she is the girl who cast Frantz aside.

Convinced that Frantz had been the means of helping him in his fruitless search for Yvonne, Meaulnes now thought Valentine, who had rejected Frantz, a horrible creature. Therefore, he cast her aside, turning a deaf ear to her protestations that she would end up in the streets.

A final entry in Meaulnes's journal, written following his marriage to Yvonne, tells of his hearing Frantz's cry, and of Meaulnes's determination to find Valentine and restore her to Frantz before ever again looking at his own beloved, Frantz's sister.

Time goes on. Meaulnes's child is now a pretty little girl a year old, and François loves her devotedly. He is saddened to note, however, that the child seems indifferent to him.

Then one day François sees a bearded man approach the château. It is Meaulnes. The two men fly to each other. Meaulnes is in joyous spirits: he has found Valentine and Frantz, and reunited them. Now he is free to love his beautiful Yvonne.

François tells him the sad news of Yvonne's death, and Meaulnes gives way to tears of bitter despair. Then, François introduces him to the child of whom Meaulnes knows nothing—his daughter.

Instantly, on being placed in Meaulnes's arms, the little girl's face lights up with delight. The spark returns to Meaulnes's eyes.

Sadly François recognizes that he has lost the little girl—that she responds at once to Meaulnes, a stranger, as she had never responded to him whom she knows so well.

François envisions the day when Meaulnes will sweep the little girl up in his cloak, and take her off on one of his wandering adventures. . . .

THE LITTLE PRINCE

Antoine de Saint-Exupéry

Antoine de Saint-Exupéry was born in Lyon, France, in 1900. He joined the French Army Air Force in 1921, and in 1926 became a commercial pilot, flying between France, West Africa, and South America. His first two novels appeared in 1928 and 1931, and were about flying; supposedly André Gide suggested to Saint-Exupéry that he abandon the form of the novel in favor of personal autobiographical essays. In the mid-1930s Saint-Exupéry worked as a correspondent, covering the Spanish Civil War, and it is probable that this experience, which affected his political and religious thinking profoundly, plus Gide's advice, led to Wind, Sand, and Stars, *which was published in 1939. After the fall of France in 1940, Saint-Exupéry came to the United States, where he gained a wide and admiring audience as a spokesman of the French Resistance.* The Little Prince, *published in 1943, is, on the surface, a delightful and imaginative children's tale; readers of the time, however, did not miss the allegorical implications, dealing with the alarming growth of Fascism, which are fundamental to the story. Greatly admired in his lifetime, Saint-Exupéry disappeared in 1944 on a reconnaissance flight over occupied southern France. Although presumably he was shot down, no traces of the man or his aircraft were ever found.*

An aeronaut, forced down alone with his plane by mechanical trouble in the midst of the Sahara, is surprised to meet a small person who demands that the pilot draw him a picture of a sheep. The mysterious person—a boy with yellow hair, innocent expression, and magnificent military costume—will answer no questions until the pilot has drawn a satisfactory picture. But after the picture is finished (it is a picture of a box, and the sheep is inside the box) the boy and the pilot talk; and gradually the pilot pieces together fragments of conversation which tell him the story of this beautiful, strange boy.

The boy is the Little Prince, sole human inhabitant of a tiny distant planet (which the pilot surmises to be Asteroid B-612). On this planet are three volcanoes (two of them active); many small, pretty bushes; the seeds of the dreadful baobab trees, which the Little Prince is careful to pull up each morning, lest they spread and grow and choke out the lovely bushes; and—perhaps most important of all—a unique red flower, so beautiful and so delicate that the Little Prince has fallen in love with her.

Indeed, it was this rare flower that brought about the Little Prince's sadness, for she is a vain and silly creature, the flower, and had used imperious and conceited phrases to the Little Prince. He, in his innocence, had misunderstood her, and felt himself rejected. He had therefore decided to leave his beautiful little planet. Too late, the flower, who truly loved the Little Prince, realized her folly; but in her pride she had been unable to declare her love. And so the Little Prince left on his journey.

He visited, first, a series of neighboring planets, on each of which he met a curious person. The first was a King, who hailed the Little Prince as his first subject. But the Little Prince did not see the point in being a subject; nor did he understand why the King wanted to be a King, so he traveled on.

Next, he met a conceited man, who hailed him as an admirer. The Little Prince found him as hard to understand as the King, and so he went to the next planet.

There he met a tippler—a man who said he drank all the time to forget his shame. When the Little Prince asked him what his shame was, the tippler said that his shame was drinking. The Little Prince left the tippler in a state of deep dejection.

On the fourth planet, the only inhabitant was a businessman, who claimed to own all the stars, and who devoted all his time to counting them. But the Little Prince was confused by the man's need for senseless ownership, and so he moved on.

On the next planet—the smallest of all—the Little Prince met a lamplighter, whose orders were to light the lamp at sunset and to extinguish it at sunrise. Unfortunately the planet had been revolving faster and faster ever since the lamplighter had received his orders, and now he was forced to light and extinguish the lamp every thirty seconds. The Little Prince was satisfied that *this* grown man, at least, was capable of thinking of something besides himself—but he was saddened by the lamplighter's inability to extricate himself from the bondage of a foolish and outdated order; so he left him.

On the sixth planet, the Little Prince met a geographer, who warned him against concerning himself with anything ephemeral. But when the Little Prince realized that the things the geographer considered worth while were things he himself considered dull, whereas the geographer considered his beloved flower "ephemeral" and therefore insignificant, the Little Prince decided not to stay. He asked the geographer's advice as to which planet he should visit next, and the geographer told him: "Earth."

The first creature that the Little Prince met on Earth was a deadly golden snake. At first the snake was going to strike —but when he realized the complete innocence and sadness of the Little Prince, he became compassionate, and talked with him instead. When the snake saw that the Little Prince was weak, he promised that whenever the Little Prince should ask him, he would help him to return to his own star.

The Little Prince traveled on, in the hopes of meeting some grown men whose ways he would understand. As he wandered, he came across a garden—and was surprised to find it full of hundreds of flowers, all just like the flower he had loved on his own planet. He was deeply saddened by this evidence of his beloved's perfidy in telling him that she was unique when she was only a common rose. But the more he thought about his rose, and his volcanoes, and his shrubs and baobabs, the sadder he became, though he could not understand why he should miss such simple things so intensely.

The next creature he encountered was a wild fox, who begged the Little Prince to tame him. Asking what "tame" meant, the Little Prince learned an important lesson: "tame" means to create ties between beings, to cause each to need the other and to recognize the other's essential uniqueness. The Little Prince tried to explain to the fox that he didn't have enough time to tame him; that because he would be going away soon, it would not be fair to the fox to tame him. But the fox insisted, and so the Little Prince tamed him. Sure enough, when it was time for the Little Prince to go away, the fox cried, because now he was tame and he loved the Little Prince. But the Little Prince recognized his responsibility to his beloved flower, and so he left the fox, sadly.

The Little Prince met several other creatures on earth—all of them grown men—but he did not understand any of them, and so he continued to wander through the desert, until he encountered the disabled airplane and his new friend, the pilot.

It has taken eight days of conversation before the pilot has learned the Little Prince's history—and now, as the tale ends, he discovers that he has no more water. The Little Prince, too, is thirsty, but unlike the pilot, he does not despair, for the fox has given him an important secret: what is essential cannot be seen with the eye, but only with the heart.

The Little Prince is convinced that he and the pilot will find water, and together they begin to wander through the desert in search of a well. The Little Prince becomes tired, and the pilot, who is skeptical of being successful in the search, tenderly carries his small friend in his arms. Gradually, as they travel through the night, the pilot begins to understand the truth of the fox's secret. And, just at daybreak, he finds a magnificent well, and their lives are saved. Without saying it in so many words, the Little Prince now makes clear that he must soon return to his own planet. He asks the pilot to draw him a muzzle for the sheep, so that the sheep will not eat the beautiful flower. Unhappy, the pilot complies with this request, though he hopes that the Little Prince, whom he has come to love, will not find a way of returning to his planet, but will stay on earth.

The next evening, when the pilot returns to their usual meeting place after working on the plane, he sees the Little Prince, at a distance, in conversation with a deadly golden snake. The pilot is about to shoot it with his revolver when the snake slithers away and becomes invisible.

The Little Prince comes up to the pilot visibly frightened but trying to be calm. And then the full meaning of the interview with the snake becomes clear to the pilot.

Horrified, the man tells the Little Prince that he must not keep his appointment with the snake, but the Little Prince only smiles his sad smile. The pilot's plane is now fixed, the Little Prince explains, and it is now a year since he himself came to Earth. It is time for him to return to his star. He confesses that he is afraid, but he knows what he must do.

The pilot wants to accompany the Little Prince to his final interview with the snake, but the boy thinks it unwise. The pilot will see his body lie still on the ground, he explains, and will think that he has died; but that will not really be the case. His body is merely too heavy to make the journey to the star, and the Little Prince must go without it.

Before going to the meeting place, however, the Little Prince gives the pilot a gift: the power to hear stars singing. Then, he goes off into the night to keep his appointment with the snake.

The pilot follows him. He thinks that his heart will break, and he begs the Little Prince not to go ahead with his plan. But the Little Prince explains in his quiet, sad way, that he must: he is responsible for his flower.

There is a flash of gold, and in an instant, the Little Prince falls motionless to the ground. There is no sound.

Only later does the pilot realize that he had neglected to draw a strap on the muzzle he had given the Little Prince, and he wonders whether the sheep will eat the Little Prince's beloved flower. Sometimes he thinks that everything will be all right, that the Little Prince will find a way to protect the flower; but at other times he feels certain that the sheep has eaten the flower, and then his heart is filled with anguish.

And when he looks up at the sky, the pilot can hear the stars singing. It is a beautiful sound, but it only seems to make him long for the Little Prince all the more.

WIND, SAND, AND STARS

Antoine de Saint-Exupéry

In 1926 Saint-Exupéry, a young man, begins a romance that is to endure his whole life long. He enrolls as a student airplane-pilot with a company operating flights between southwestern France and French West Africa. His romance is with flying, with space, with planes, with wind, sand, stars. . . .

He remembers so clearly the rainy night before his first flight. He had spent it with the great pilot Guillaumet, who, by the light of a lamp, taught him the reality of maps. To a pilot, Guillaumet explained, the things that are left off a map are often more significant than the things that are depicted. A stream, for instance—so tiny, so temporary that it is ignored by the cartographers—the pilot must know of its existence, and the direction in which it runs. For if it does not appear on the map, how is the pilot to avoid it in making a forced landing?

As he rides the omnibus the next morning, bound for the hangar and his first flight, Saint-Exupéry looks at his muffled fellow passengers—complacent bourgeois clerks, caught up in their attempts to salvage a few last, reluctant moments of sleep. He is a little surprised that they do not see, do not notice his own intense excitement. But pilots are a special breed of men, a race apart. The petty clerks cannot understand the special and rare camaraderie that binds together this new breed, the pilots. . . .

He thinks of the pilots he has known: Bury . . . Bourgat . . . Riguelle. . . . He thinks particularly of two: Mermoz and Guillaumet.

Mermoz had been a true explorer, a pioneer of flight. It was he who had first surveyed the flight lines across the great Sahara. Once he had been taken prisoner by the Moors, who had never seen a pilot. They kept him prisoner for a while, and eventually he was ransomed. Then, when the South American line was opened, it was his task to find the best flight routes over the treacherous Andes. So perilous was this mission that he was forced down with his mechanic—but he persevered, and triumphed. And when flying the Andes had been perfected, he turned his attention to night flying, and when he had mastered that, to transoceanic flight. So Mermoz pioneered—the desert, the mountain, the night, the sea. . . . He was lost in the Atlantic.

Guillaumet too was a superior specimen of a special breed. His was the integrity of a fine craftsman, the dedication of a master artist. Lost in the Andes in winter, he had outlasted even the most optimistic hopes. In spite of hunger and lack of sleep and frostbite, he had gone on. "What I went through," he said later, "no animal would have gone through." But, though he had thought many times during his ordeal of simply giving up, he remembered that his comrades still hoped that he would survive. And so he survived.

Saint-Exupéry remembers his own battles against the elements—and, in particular, the first time he had flown through a cyclone. He cannot explain—for there is no word that can describe horror, but only many words and still more words that circle about the sensation, yet in the end fail to communicate it. But he remembers that the cyclone was for him a spiritual experience rather than a physical one.

He spent much time in the Sahara, where the pilots' only companions were the few French soldiers stationed at their lonely outposts. And the Moors—strange men of strange ideas. He comes, at last, to understand a little of their way of thinking, feeling, living. But only a little. He no more understands the Moors than they understand the French general Bounafous, their most hated enemy. (When Bounafous leaves the desert and returns to France, the Moors feel that they have lost a best-beloved friend. So does Saint-Exupéry feel about much of what he experiences: hate that is love, love that is hate.)

Saint-Exupéry and his fellow pilots in the Sahara meet a slave called Bark. Unlike most Sahara slaves, Bark does not accept slavery, and he does not relinquish his erstwhile identity. He begs to be taken to his home, Marrakesh, where he may again be with his family and enjoy his rightful name, Mohammed ben Lhaoussin. The pilots at last buy Bark, and restore him to freedom. And they learn from him that man is free only when he is loved and needed.

One day, forced down in a stretch of uncharted Saharan waste never before known to man, Saint-Exupéry finds a meteorite. It seems to him that this contact with a long-dead shooting star puts him at one with eternity, and insures the survival of his own spirit.

In 1935 the pilot is flying the Paris-Saigon mail route in his plane, the *Simoon*. His only companion is his mechanic, Prévot. As they begin their flight, all is serene. The pilot rediscovers the majesty of nightfall in mid-air.

But eventually the two men recognize that they are lost. They are flying over uncharted sands, and are loath to put down so far from civilization, so they fly on. But their fuel cannot last, and they crash. They pull themselves free just as the *Simoon* bursts into flames.

They do not know where they are. There is no sign of life anywhere—no, not so much as a blade of grass. There is only a pint of liquid and a few pieces of fruit for the two of them. Saint-Exupéry rapidly calculates how long they can hope to last without finding water. Not long, not long at all . . . At best they can hope to be found in a week, and that will be too late.

Each day they tramp the wastes of the desert, hoping to be seen, hoping to find water, some sign of life. They leave a huge bonfire behind them each time they leave the wreck—both to guide their own return, and to serve as a signal to any plane. But there are no planes. . . .

The thirst becomes unbearable. They must make do with the little moisture that condenses in the cool of the morning on the plane. The heat becomes intense—and with it come the mirages.

One day, his eyes affected by the glare, Saint-Exupéry returns from a solitary expedition. As he approaches the plane, he is overjoyed to see Prévot in conversation with two Arabs. He shouts to them, but they do not hear. Stumbling painfully, he runs toward them. When he reaches the wreck, he finds Prévot alone. There are no Arabs. . . .

How simple is life! How simple is death! Three days are an eternity. . . .

Now Saint-Exupéry sees another mirage: camel prints in the sand. But no, Prévot sees them too! It is no mirage. The two men are saved by wandering Bedouins.

They drink and drink and drink of the Bedouins' water, and then they are fed, and put to sleep. Returned at last to civilization, they are happy all the time. Bread makes them happy. Honey makes them happy. But a telegram expressing joy that he has been found safe and alive brings tears to Saint-Exupéry's eyes, and shatters him. . . .

Life is simple. Death is simple. Why do men choose to die? Saint-Exupéry does not understand. He goes to Barcelona during the Spanish Civil War, hoping to find an answer. But there is no answer. The Republicans, the Loyalists, the Fascists—he cannot tell the difference among them. They are men, simple men, and they choose to die, though they have never lived. It is so in Madrid; it is so in Barcelona; it is so in Guadalajara. Saint-Exupéry does not understand. It fills him with horror, with terror, with loathing.

He thinks of a train ride he had once taken. He had seen

two ugly peasants, man and woman, their mouths hanging open, lying asleep in their seats. Between them slept a beautiful child—their son. He remembers the child's face—it had seemed to him the face of the child Mozart. With a shudder, he realizes that these vacuous sleeping peasants were once like the beautiful child, and that one day the beautiful child will become a sleeping peasant.

That is the source of his anguish! He grieves at the sight of so many murdered Mozarts. . . .

The pilot thinks again of the smug, complacent clerks who rode the omnibus on that first night, that night when he was to make his very first flight. Those musty civil servants—they were the same as the pilots, but with a difference: they never knew that their spirits were hungry.

THE STRANGER

Albert Camus

Albert Camus was born in 1913 in Algeria of a Spanish mother and an Alsatian father. Albert had to work his way through school and received, in 1936, a degree in philosophy from the University of Algiers. After graduation he began a career in journalism, and was involved with theatrical companies as an actor and manager. He spent a short time working on a newspaper in France, and returned to Algeria in 1940, where he wrote The Stranger, *his first novel. In 1942, the year* The Stranger *was published, he went back to France as a member of the Resistance. He edited the important underground journal,* Combat, *and began to attract critical attention for his fiction and his powerful wartime editorials. Camus became associated with Jean-Paul Sartre and the existentialists, but broke with Sartre because of political differences. Camus' own philosophy deals with what he calls the "absurd." Defined in the essay,* The Myth of Sisyphus, *Camus' philosophy holds that man exists in a meaningless universe, and must be aware of the absurdity of his position in order to gain any value from his experience. In* The Stranger *and* The Plague *(1947), Camus presents powerful accounts of the existential dilemma of modern man in his futile search for the meaning of life. Camus has been very influential, both as a stylist and as a literary philosopher. He received the Nobel Prize for literature in 1957. He showed promise of becoming increasingly important; but his life came to a tragic end in an automobile accident in France in 1960.*

When he learns that his mother has died at the Old People's Home in Marengo, the insignificant clerk Meursault requests a two-day leave so that he may attend the funeral. He travels the fifty miles from Algiers by bus, and as he rides along he cannot help but resent his mother a bit for making it impossible for him to enjoy this glorious day.

Mme. Meursault and her son had never been close, and when the old gatekeeper of the Home chats with the young man he is a bit surprised at how calm he is. Meursault not only offers the gatekeeper a cigarette in the presence of the coffin, but declines to have the lid of the coffin removed to give him "a last look."

All through the night Meursault keeps vigil by his mother's coffin, along with ten or twelve silent old people resident in the Home. The next day—in intense heat—the pathetic cortège makes its way to the red clay cemetery. Meursault thinks mostly of how uncomfortable he is under the broiling sun. Indeed, the only demonstration of grief at the funeral comes from Thomas Perez, an ancient inmate of the Home who had been particularly fond of Mme. Meursault. When the funeral is over, Meursault takes a bus back to Algiers.

When he awakes the next day, Saturday, he feels at loose ends and decides to go swimming. At the beach he runs into Marie Cardona, a pretty girl with whom he had had an innocent flirtation some months before, when she worked in his office. Now he and Marie go for a swim, and she allows him a few liberties. They agree to go to the movies together that evening—a Fernandel film which Marie is very anxious to see is playing locally. After the film, Marie goes back to Meursault's apartment with him.

As Marie must leave early Sunday morning, Meursault feels at a loss for something to do. He looks out of the window at the passers-by. He thinks about cooking himself his dinner—easier than making the effort to go out and dine at Celeste's restaurant. He listens to the commotion caused in the hall by his neighbor, Salamano, who is trying to get his mangy pet dog to behave. Most of the tenants of the building find Salamano's behavior toward the animal disgusting, but Meursault is indifferent to it.

There is a knock at the door, and Meursault opens it to find Raymond Santes, the young man who lives across the hall. Though they have occasionally exchanged a word on the stairs, there has been little contact between them. Most of the tenants agree that Raymond is a pimp, and they avoid him; but Meursault has no antipathy toward the young man, and when Raymond invites him to dine in his room, he accepts.

Before he can prepare the meal Raymond must bandage his hand, which is bloody. As he prepares the meal, he tells Meursault how he came to be hurt. He had been keeping a girl—an Arab girl, he explains—paying the rent on her flat, giving her enough for food, buying her an occasional present. Though she wanted more money from him than he thought she was worth, Raymond considered it acceptable to continue the arrangement between them. Then he discovered strong evidence that she had started deceiving him with other men. He had beaten her up—and the man who attacked him just now in the street was the Arab girl's brother. (Raymond assures Meursault that the Arab gave less than he was given in the scuffle.)

Now Raymond wants to punish the girl even more. He asks Meursault to write a scabrous letter of accusation to her, one that will incense her. To this proposal Meursault makes no objection, and he writes the letter. Raymond is delighted, and asks if Meursault will be his regular pal. The clerk sees no reason not to become Raymond's pal; he accepts.

Meursault's liaison with Marie Cardona continues each weekend. Before long, she asks if he loves her. He says that it is a foolish question; and when she presses him for an answer he replies, "Probably not." When she asks if he will marry her, however, he tells her he will if she wishes him to. Confused, Marie asks why. "Why not?" answers the clerk.

One day Raymond invites Meursault to go with him to the seaside to visit friends of his who have a cottage there, the Massons, and to bring Marie along. It sounds like an agreeable idea, so the outing is arranged.

Marie and Mme. Masson hit it off together beautifully, and the men are quite comfortable at leaving them alone together while they go for a stroll on the beach. On the way out to the seaside Raymond had pointed out to Meursault a small group of Arabs lounging near the bus stop with their eyes on him, and had indicated which of the group was the brother of his ex-girlfriend. Now, as Meursault, Raymond, and Masson stroll along the sand in the morning sun, they encounter two Arabs strolling toward them. One of them is the same man Meursault had pointed out earlier.

Raymond goes up to him and says something which Meursault cannot hear. Suddenly there is a fight, and Masson pounces on one Arab while Raymond tackles his special antagonist. Meursault sees the man whip out a knife, but his warning comes too late, and Raymond is slashed. The two Arabs take to their heels, and, cursing bitterly, Raymond allows himself to be led back to Masson's cottage where a doctor can treat his cuts.

After lunch Raymond determines to have revenge and, taking his pistol, starts out toward the beach. Meursault, hoping to dissuade him, follows. The sun is now high in the sky and the sand is red hot. Indeed, the atmosphere seems to Meursault like a furnace.

At the end of the beach they see the Arabs again. Raymond asks Meursault what he should do, hoping that Meursault will urge attack. Instead, Meursault wisely invents a plan by which Raymond surrenders his pistol to him. While the two stand in debate, the Arabs slip away. Raymond and Meursault walk back to the cottage, and Raymond goes inside to lie down.

Meursault, however, is plagued by the intense heat. He is restless, fidgety. At last he decides to walk upon the beach. The brine sprays his face, the sun beats upon his head, but he walks on. Suddenly he comes upon the figure of one Arab— the brother—lying on the sand. Meursault fiddles with the pistol, still in his pocket. Then, without thinking, he takes it out, and fires a shot at the Arab, killing him instantly. He waits a moment, and then fires four shots more into the corpse.

Although he is arrested and put in prison to await trial, Meursault does not really believe what is happening to him. Not that he is incredulous; he is merely indifferent. The police who question him also seem indifferent; the matter has little importance to any of them. Even when some emotion is finally shown—the examining magistrate becomes disturbed at Meursault's calm refusal to acknowledge God and the redemption of suffering—Meursault finds it more curious than interesting. The magistrate appoints a lawyer to handle Meursault's case.

At first Meursault finds life in prison unreal, and he sorely feels the deprivation of not having access to women and tobacco. But he recalls something his mother had often said to him when he was little: "You can get used to anything." He finds that it is true, and soon he has so ordered his time and thoughts so that life in his cell is quite bearable.

A single visit from Marie makes the fact that he is in prison real to him again; but knowing that she will not be allowed to visit him again, as she is not his wife, Meursault finds that he can get used to her not visiting. Soon he virtually ceases to think of her.

He takes little interest in his interviews with the lawyer who is to defend him. At last, in despair of getting Meursault to cooperate, the lawyer simply assures him that everything will turn out well, and begs him not to volunteer any information of his own during the trial.

Toward the end of the eleven months he spends in prison, Meursault discovers that for some time now he has been talking to himself. He accepts the knowledge without alarm.

On the day of the trial's beginning, Meursault finds himself looking forward to the event with great curiosity. He has never been to a trial. He is surprised to find the courtroom so full; but his lawyer explains that many observers and journalists have come down to Algiers from Paris not for this trial but for the one scheduled immediately afterward, a sensational case of parricide.

Meursault is also surprised at the witnesses who have been brought to testify. There is the gatekeeper from the Old People's Home in Marengo, for instance, and his mother's ancient mourner, Perez. Meursault does not see what they have to do with the case.

But as the prosecuting attorney begins, Meursault understands. The prosecution's tack is to establish in the jury's mind the idea that Meursault's crime was premeditated, and that he has always had a criminal disposition. To this end, much of the case is devoted to establishing the events of the weekend of the funeral: Meursault's coldness, his indifference to his mother's death, his willingness to smoke by the coffin, his not wanting to have the coffin lid unscrewed for him to take a last look at his mother's body. From the funeral itself, the prosecutor moves to the events of the next day, and dwells on the fact that Meursault was so "inhuman" as to go to the beach, to attend a comic motion picture, and to begin his carnal liaison with Marie, with his mother not yet cold in the grave.

To all of this, of course, the defense attorney makes objection, but Meursault sees that the jury is impressed by the lurid—if irrelevant—details raised by the prosecution. The witnesses for the defense, who try to speak in Meursault's behalf —Raymond, Salamano, even the restauranteur Celeste—pale in comparison. Indeed, Meursault recognizes that they cannot make him seem an angel, for he has always been a lackluster, indifferent sort of person. He himself is more impressed with the prosecuting attorney than with his own lawyer.

The prosecution discusses the letter Meursault had written for Raymond to the sister of the now-dead man, and presents this as proof of premeditation. Further, it is declared that Raymond is a known procurer, and Meursault's friendship with him betrays his criminality. Finally, the prosecuting attorney manages in his summation to connect Meursault in the jury's mind with the parricide who is to be tried later.

When the jury retires to consider its verdict, Meursault's lawyer assures him that he will get off with a light sentence. He is not surprised, however, to hear himself declared guilty of premeditated homicide, and sentenced to decapitation.

Now that he is under sentence of death, prison is no longer tolerable to Meursault. The scrap of sky he sees from his cell window torments him. He can find no consolation in religion, and refuses steadfastly to allow the prison chaplain to visit him. Instead, he rests his hope in the appeal which his lawyer has instituted.

He knows that he can have no real expectation of success in this appeal, but the chance—be it one in 999,999—excites him. And when he knows the appeal has failed, he begins to wrack his brains trying to find a loophole through which he can escape from his dilemma. He curses himself that he did not read books on criminal law when he was free. He is bitter that he never attended a public execution, for much of his thought now focuses on the guillotine that awaits him.

For the first time in his life, Meursault appreciates the fact that he is alive, and he is beside himself that this knowledge should come so late. All night he lies awake, dreading the dawn, listening for the footsteps approaching that will tell him it is his last day. At each sunrise, when no footsteps have come, he is grateful for life, and he can fall asleep.

One day the prison chaplain enters Meursault's cell unannounced. At first, Meursault is merely annoyed at this pretentious man with his chatter about God, redemption, conscience, suffering. But then he can stomach the man's cant no longer and, grabbing the priest by his collar, forces him to the wall and begins to lecture him.

Passionately he declares his love for earthly things, and his refusal to hope for any existence after life. He has little time left to him, and he refuses to waste any of those precious hours on God. Reality—the only reality man can ever know—is sacred. All of the priest's thoughts and ideals together are not worth, to Meursault, a single real hair of a woman's head. The terrible thing about death is to disappear, for every man's life, no matter how petty and insignificant, is privileged because it is real.

By now he is yelling at the top of his voice, and two guards are needed to release Meursault's hold on the priest.

When the chaplain is gone, and he is again alone, Meursault feels himself purged. He recognizes that he was happy, and that he is now, again, happy. He has the certainty, the reality of his death to look forward to. The only thing that can add to his pleasure is the prospect of a large, screaming mob to turn out for his execution.

THE PLAGUE
Albert Camus

In the dull, sleepy town of Oran, a French port on the Algerian coast, Dr. Bernard Rieux sees, for the first time, a dead rat outside his door. He pays no attention to it; his mind is occupied with his wife, who is going to a sanitarium several hundred miles away, in the hope that she will find a cure for her racking illness. It is April 16.

Within three days, however, Rieux has reason to remember the first dead rat that he had seen, for now there is a full-scale epidemic of some sort, and peaceful Oran is shaken to the core. Rats are seen lying in the gutters everywhere, each with a blot of blood on its stiff muzzle. By the hundreds, and then by the thousands, rats come up from wharves, cellars, and sewers to die. Special efforts are made by officials to have the streets cleaned each morning; but by noon, there are more dead rats.

Dr. Rieux has several cases at this time which interest him. One is that of the strange M. Cottard, a would-be suicide who has been saved at the last moment by his neighbor, the elderly Municipal Office clerk Joseph Grand. Obviously Cottard is very tense and nervous, but when Rieux tells him that the police must be informed of the attempted hanging, Cottard becomes almost paranoid in his reaction.

The other interesting cases are of a grimmer nature. Rieux is at a loss to identify the disease from which both patients suffer, but the dreadful symptoms are the same: raging thirst, high fever, vomiting, swollen ganglia, torturously painful buboes—and then death. Comparing notes with other doctors, Rieux learns that each of them has had three or four cases of the same kind.

No official action is taken until it becomes clear that the mysterious disease is reaching epidemic proportions. A meeting of doctors is called, and it is there that the liberal and outspoken Dr. Castel uses, for the first time, the word that everyone dreads. He is convinced that the disease is bubonic plague. The rats have been the carriers, and the fleas from the infected vermin have spread the disease to the people.

Several of the doctors are reluctant to take Castel's verdict seriously, and they argue that to put stringent measures of sanitation into effect without first being positive about the nature of the disease may have a bad effect on the attitude of the population. But several days later, as the daily death toll climbs from ten to twelve to fourteen, the Prefect declares a state of plague, and the town is closed.

Though at first the population of Oran can hardly take the news seriously—or, at best, believes that the closing of the gates is a temporary measure only—it is soon clear that Oran has been closed in earnest, and its people are prisoners and exiles. As day moves after day, the people are stunned to find that mail is prohibited, that commerce dies. They feel themselves outcasts, deserted by the rest of the world, and despair sets in.

To counter the mood of depression—the death tally spirals upward each day—a Week of Prayer is organized by the Catholic priest, Paneloux. In his sermon the priest warns the people that God is punishing them for their wickedness and for their indifference to His love. But the sermon does not have the desired effect; the people remain as aloof from religion as always. Ironically it is from the Week of Prayer that Rieux dates the feeling of panic and hopelessness that settles over the town.

For some, there are merciful ways of forgetting about the plague that rages. Raymond Rambert, for example, who had been a visitor to Oran when the gates were closed, now finds himself desperately anxious to escape and return to his wife; and his endless visits to bureaucrats begging for special consideration occupy his mind, so that he has no time to think about the disease. There is the clerk, Grand, who is determined to write a great novel that will be perfect in every word; for years he has been rewriting and rewriting its opening sentence, and now he immerses himself in this project of polishing his prose. There is Tarrou, a man of no certain occupation, who keeps extensive journals, sardonic but highly perceptive, in which he records the events around him.

For Rieux, there is no such mental respite; as a doctor, he is immersed in the plague for eighteen to twenty hours each day. It is a relief to him when he notes that his usual sense of pity for sufferers has died.

As the summer heat blazes on, the death toll continues to mount. It reaches seven hundred deaths a week; on the ninety-fourth day of the plague alone, one hundred and twenty-four victims die. Now, a new variety of the disease, even more contagious than the first, breaks out—and the batches of plague serum currently arriving from Paris seem less effective than the first batches.

Though the petty officials of the town have tried to provide effective sanitation methods, they are woefully inadequate. Tarrou approaches Rieux with a scheme for organizing ordinary citizens into voluntary sanitary groups as a means of effectively dealing with the plague, and Rieux is enthusiastic. Attracted by a feeling that they must *do* something during this crisis, many join Tarrou, and the squadrons are soon operating efficiently and effectively.

Two who do not join in the effort are Cottard and Rambert. Rambert is still obsessed with the idea of escaping from Oran, though desertion from the epidemic-stricken community is stopped, when possible, with bullets. As for Cottard, he has suddenly become an expansive individual, highly active in the black market activities made inevitable by the plague. (Cottard had been in hiding from the police, and had lived in daily panic of being apprehended for a crime he had committed; but now that the plague has sealed off the town, he feels safe.) Cottard assures Rambert that he can help him escape, and the two begin a long series of clandestine meetings with men in the criminal world of Oran. Garcia . . . Raoul . . . Gonzales . . . Louis . . . Marcel. . . . Their faces merge, but Rambert is hopeful that one of them will enable him to quit Oran, and he is tortured by the slowness with which they move, and with the inevitable delays.

By mid-August there is not a soul left in Oran who is not in some respect a servant of the plague. There is no hope, no rest—and no preoccupation with anything but the plague. With the summer winds, the town falls victim to flying sheets of dust—but the atmosphere is no heavier than the morale. Martial law is instituted.

September . . . October. . . . Exhaustion wears everyone down. Food is scarce, and only obtainable on the black market at exorbitant prices. The poor of Oran create a rallying slogan: "Bread or Fresh Air." But there is nothing that can be done for them.

Only Cottard seems to be satisfied. The longer the plague lasts, the more relentless it becomes, the more sure he is of his own safety. He becomes loquacious, and more and more encouraging about Rambert's plans for flight. But Rambert has changed his mind: he has come to recognize that the plague is every man's responsibility. When he gets word that the details for his escape have been worked out, he sends a note to the bribed sentry telling him he has changed his plans. He then goes to Rieux and volunteers his services.

His meeting with Rieux is held at the dispensary where a new serum, devised by Oran's Dr. Castel, is being tried for the first time on a victim whose case is considered hopeless. It is the son of the Prefect, and gathered around the suffering boy's bedside are Rieux, Tarrou, Grand, Castel, and Paneloux, each watching intensely. The child's agony continues, almost unabated, for hours, and the men find it excruciating to watch the tortures that he suffers. Suddenly the boy dies.

Shaken to the core by the sight of the innocent child's

suffering, Rieux challenges Paneloux over the existence of a God. The result of their conversation is that the two men hold irreconcilably opposed opinions—but are firmer friends than ever, for each is committed body and soul to the extermination of suffering. Because of the child's death, Paneloux himself re-examines some of his beliefs, and the sermon he preaches later shows that he has accepted a much blinder, firmer view of Christianity than he has ever held before. He believes so intensely in the need to accept God's will unquestioningly, in fact, that when he himself falls ill, he refuses to summon a doctor. When Father Paneloux dies, Rieux feels he has lost a close friend.

Several weeks later, two cases in which Castel's serum has been used result in cures. Whether it is as a result of the treatment, no one can say, but it seems clear that bubonic plague is beginning, slowly, to decline. The pneumonic variety increases, however, so that the weekly death toll is at first unaffected.

But the decrease continues, and when the November rains arrive, there is, for the first time, a feeling of mild relief.

One night, after having put in a particularly wearisome day at the hospital, Rieux and Tarrou climb to a rooftop terrace and determine to indulge themselves in a respite from the plague by talking simply as friends. Tarrou tells Rieux his life story, and the doctor is deeply moved as he recognizes in Tarrou, who early determined to devote all his energies to the elimination of suffering in mankind, the closest thing to sainthood he has ever encountered. Later, the two men use their special passes to win for themselves a chance to go swimming alone under the stars. Rieux is deeply gratified by this experience, both because for the first time since the plague struck he has had a chance to relax, and because he has become so close to the soul of Tarrou. But both men understand that the next morning they must once again come to grips with the exhausting demands of the plague.

Christmas approaches, and it is the dreariest Christmas Rieux has ever known. But then something startling happens: poor Joseph Grand, who is stricken with plague and given up as hopeless, makes a miraculous and complete recovery for no apparent reason. This is the first in what proves to be a series of miraculous recoveries, and, at the same time, the number of new cases of plague reported daily sharply declines. It seems too much to hope for, but it is true: the plague is on the wane.

On January 25 the epidemic is regarded as officially stemmed. It is almost with hysterical joy that someone, for the first time since the previous April, reports seeing a live rat. The sense of shock that had greeted the first announcement of the plague's remission gives way to hopefulness—and then to relieved joy. Oran is to be free! Only Cottard reacts adversely; for him the end of the plague means the end of freedom, and he becomes again the morose, paranoid personality whom Rieux had met so long ago.

The one blight, for Rieux, on this wave of hope is that Tarrou, who has been living with him, is suddenly stricken with plague. For the first time, Rieux ignores the requirement that all new victims be sent immediately to the hospital. The doctor and his mother nurse Tarrou through his agony in their own home, heedless of the risk of infection. When at last Tarrou succumbs, Rieux is more grief-stricken that if he had lost a brother.

The next day, when a telegram arrives telling Rieux that his wife has died in the distant sanitarium to which she went a few days before the plague began, Rieux feels almost nothing.

In February the gates to Oran are opened. There is rejoicing in the town, as loved ones are reunited, and as all can feel free of the disease for the first time in months.

Walking through the riotously gay streets, Rieux comes upon a cordon of police surrounding the house in which Grand and Cottard live. Grand finds the doctor, and tells him that Cottard has gone mad. He has barricaded himself within his room, and is shooting it out with the police. Finally the police overcome Cottard, and drag him into the streets where they beat him, and then take him away.

Rieux climbs to the rooftop terrace and looks down at Oran. He recognizes the joy experienced by the townspeople, and he notes that it is tempered by a seriousness, by a special sense of dignity as the result of what they have all endured. But he is forced to recognize, too, that though they have won against the plague, the germs of the disease lie dormant somewhere. Someday, he thinks, it may rise again, and send its rats forth to die in a happy city.

THE DEATH OF A NOBODY

Jules Romains

Jules Romains, whose real name is Louis Farigoule, was born at St. Julien-le-Chapteuil in France in 1885. He studied at the prestigious École Normale Supérieure, and received a degree in philosophy in 1909. He is closely associated with the unanimist school of writers, who, having been influenced by contemporary sociological theory, consider that the groups to which men belong—family, religious, national—are to be studied in order to determine their effect upon the individual; and the individual is to be studied in order to determine his effect upon the group.

Romains has been a prolific writer in the fields of poetry, drama, and the novel. His principles are set forth in an early book of verse, La Vie Unanime. The Death of a Nobody, *which appeared in 1911, is based upon unanimist doctrine, exploring as it does the memory of a dead man in terms of the society in which he lived. Jules Romains has lived in France all his life, except for the years 1940 to 1946, when he was in the United States. His major achievement has been the cycle of novels,* Men of Good Will, *a twenty-seven-volume work published in France between 1932 and 1947. Set in Paris and spanning a quarter of a century, the series shows the author's erudition, intelligence, and knowledge of the broad area of social psychology.*

On an afternoon in spring Jacques Godard decides on an impulse to go to the top of the Panthéon to enjoy the view that has attracted so many tourists. As he surveys all of Paris from this new perspective, he realizes that, were he to die, nobody in that great city would grieve for a moment. Except for a few members of a club, the Enfants de Velay, to which he belongs (though he seldom attends meetings) and a few railroad men who still work on the line for which he worked until his retirement five years ago, nobody in all this city, in which he has lived for thirty-five years, may be said even to know him.

If Godard has any real existence at all, it is in the minds, hearts, and memories of his aged parents. Now past eighty, both Old Man Godard and his wife live still in their remote provincial village which they have never left, and between them, hovering like a spirit, is the presence of their long-absent beloved son, "young Jacques."

Two days after his visit to the Panthéon, Godard feels a pain in his back. At first the middle-aged widower refuses to acknowledge it, but each day it grows in intensity. Except for a few attentions from the porter in his building, Godard is aware of nothing but his ailment.

On the eighth day he wakes to feel two successive sensations. The first is a complete absence of pain. The second is the sensation of death.

Thus, alone and friendless, Jacques Godard, a "nobody," dies in his tenement room. For several hours it is as though he had never been. But when that evening the porter decides to look in upon the ailing man and finds his corpse, Jacques Godard begins what may be called a second life. For though he is dead, the very fact of his death causes experiences, events, emotions. It is as though there is yet power emanating from the dead man, power that controls the lives and actions of a number of people.

For a while the porter tells no one of his discovery. Rather, he savors the knowledge which he has, and feels that he possesses some special power, some significance, knowing what nobody else in the world knows: that Jacques Godard is dead. But the porter senses that his power will diminish if he does not share his news, so he notifies the Medical Examiner, sends a telegram to Old Godard, and begins to pass the word along among the tenants in the building.

The residents of the building, as if by common consent, have always avoided one another. Beyond an occasional nod in the hall, one tenant has never acknowledged the existence of the others. Indeed, they have all been members of a tacit conspiracy to pretend that the others do not exist. But now, this death in their building provides a bond for them. A small group of neighbors go into Godard's room and stand about, looking at his corpse. They try to think sad thoughts; they try to remember Godard. And as they stand together in silence, they feel that they are welded into a unit by some invisible force, some mutual calamity. One of the tenants— later, nobody is quite sure which one—has the idea that all should chip in and buy a funeral wreath for Godard. Two little girls of the house, holding between them a fresh white paper for subscribers' signatures, go from door to door, taking up the collection. At the florist's, three of the women of the house—women who have never before spoken to each other

—discuss, like sisters, the proper wording to be put on the wreath. On their return to the tenement, they stand in the hall, with nothing to say, yet unwilling to break the spell of commonality that binds them.

As Godard's parents live some distance from the village post office, their son's death is known, talked about, and forgotten before they themselves get the news. When the telegram does reach them, they are devastated with grief. Old Godard decides to go to Paris, beginning his journey that very night, for the funeral. Mother Godard is too aged to make such a long and tiring journey.

The old man walks to the village, where he will take the coach to the train station. As he walks, he thinks continually of his dear son, now dead. He tries to remember his face, but the features come back to him only dimly. He never does succeed in remembering what his son's eyes looked like. Periodically he breaks down, weeping.

Sitting in the coach with six other passengers, Old Godard debates with himself whether he should tell them of his son's death, or whether he should wait to be asked. It would be presumptuous to volunteer the information, he feels, but on the other hand, no one may happen to inquire of him where he is bound, and his moment of certain celebrity, the moment in which his loss will make him the center of attention among the travelers, might never transpire. At last, by staring relentlessly at a man in the corner, he forces him to open a conversation, and immediately he is given a chance to tell his sad news. All of his companions are sympathetic, and though Old Godard takes pleasure in the attention, it does not seem to him to be quite as satisfying as it should be. Well, at least he will be able to tell Mother Godard the kind things the travelers have said. Periodically he must remind himself not to think of the passing scenery, but rather to concentrate his thoughts upon poor dead young Jacques.

In the fourth-floor flat in Paris, the body of Jacques Godard is beginning to decay. But the "second life" of Jacques Godard goes on. On the second floor, a little girl dreams, as she clutches her blanket, of carrying an enormous sheet of paper round to the tenants. On the fourth floor, a woman falls asleep with frightening thoughts of Godard's body whirling in her mind, and dreams that she sits by a coffin at which Godard appears, draped in gray, and maliciously blows out the candles. The butcher, whose shop is on the ground floor, dreams of passing the time of day with Godard, when suddenly, quite casually, Godard says to him, "I am dead." On the fifth floor, a woman who never dreams passes the night in what seems to be the mist of a cemetery. In the next room, two lovers, lying apart after an embrace of passion, depleted and exhausted, think of the dead man, and reach their hands out to touch the warmth of each other's bodies. And in Godard's fourth-floor flat, the man is decaying, crumbling into bits that filter into other men's lives.

The next morning, the porter recognizes the old man at once as Godard's father, and invites him to take a drink with him. But as they drink, the porter begins to feel bitter. Godard's death is no longer his property, and besides, the other tenants have excluded him from their purchase of the wreath—have excluded *him*, who was the very first to *tell* them of Godard's death. But when the few guests gather for the cortège—some of the tenants, three members of Godard's club—the porter feels more reconciled.

The cortège is a small one, but the marchers are all aware of the cluster of people who stand in front of the house to see the funeral go by. The tenants of Godard's house recognize their superiority at this moment, and the bystanders are aware of a slight feeling of envy. None of them knows the dead man.

When the cortège moves out of the street, however, the feeling of superiority slips away and is replaced by boredom, then tiredness, and then irritation. After a long walk in the hot morning, the leaders of the small procession see trouble up ahead. It is a street fight between strikers and scab workers at a factory. There is a flurry of confusion among the walkers in the little procession; should they turn back, or should they march on? Suddenly the fighters notice the cortège; the fighting stops, the mob breaks apart to provide a path for the procession, and the bloody fighters and the policemen take off their hats to pay their respects. The mourners are deeply touched.

What might be called the high point in the "second life" of Jacques Godard comes in the little church, where an anonymous priest conducts the funeral service, and where Godard's body finally comes to rest in an ancient cemetery. Then begins the gradual decline of Godard's influence.

Several tenants, that evening, talk about the events of the day with their families. During the next few weeks, there is an occasional reference—a passing reference only—by one or another of the members of the Enfants de Velay. Then Godard is forgotten in Paris.

His fame survives somewhat longer in his native village. It takes many days for Old Godard to relate all the details of the funeral to Mother Godard.

The last time anyone thinks of Godard in Paris is when the porter rents Godard's old flat to a young couple. For an instant Godard's face floats before the porter's eyes. Then it is gone.

One night, old Mother Godard begins to cough. Though her husband tries to make her more comfortable, both of the elderly folks realize that she will not recover. One day in winter she dies. And not many weeks go by before Old Godard himself realizes that his end is near, and he too dies.

The following March, a young man is walking the boulevards of Paris. He is intensely aware of his own zest for living, of the vitality of his own life. His thoughts wax philosophical: Time . . . Life . . . Death . . . Eternity. He thinks about a man whose funeral he had attended just a year ago. What was the man's name? Bonnard . . . Bollard . . . ? Anyway, it was a friend of his father's. The more he thinks about that man, whose funeral cortège was so pathetically small—wait a minute, it wasn't *quite* a year ago, come to think of it—the more aware he becomes of his own mortality, and of his own insignificance. Reluctantly he admits to himself the fact that someday he, himself, will die—and in all probability, what will it signify? It will be the death of a nobody. . . .

MAN'S FATE

André Malraux

André Malraux was born in Paris in 1901, of comfortably situated parents. He studied at a lycée, then transferred to the School of Oriental Languages, where he learned Chinese and Sanskrit, and studied Far Eastern art. He went to Indo-China with his father in 1923, and there, after some archaeological work, became allied

*with nationalist political youth movements in Cambodia and China.
His first two novels tell of rebellion in Hong Kong and Indo-China.
Man's Fate, Malraux's third novel, was published in 1933, and
brought him international fame. A sprawling novel of Sun Yat-sen's
Chinese Revolution, the book is populated with a diversity of characters, and is set against a China which has rarely been so well
depicted by a Western author. After the failure of the Chinese
Revolution, Malraux conducted archaeological explorations in
Persia, Afghanistan, and Arabia, where he claimed that he had
found the buried capital city of the Queen of Sheba. Malraux was
active in the Loyalist cause in the Spanish Civil War (the subject of his novel Man's Hope, 1938). Captured by the Germans in
World War II, he escaped and was a guerrilla in the French Resistance, served the British command, and supported de Gaulle and
the Free French. He has written no novels since 1937, having
turned to art criticism and aesthetic theory, the profundity and
scope of which have been extremely significant. In recent years he
has held the post of Minister of Cultural Affairs.*

At twelve-thirty one night in March 1927, not long after the
abortive February Uprising in China, a Communist terrorist
named Ch'en Ta Erh kills a man for the first time. It is Tang
Yen Ta, and Ch'en murders him to secure a document which
will enable the Communist to take possession of a shipload of
armaments arriving the next day.

The experience of committing murder is an overwhelming
one for Ch'en, but by the time he reaches the phonograph
shop at which a secret meeting of fellow Communists is taking place, Ch'en has succeeded in masking his own terror and
horror.

Present at the clandestine meeting are Hemmelrich, an ex-
patriate German married to a sickly Chinese woman; his
partner, Lu Yu Hsuan; Katov, a Russian, one of the most
important organizers of the proposed insurrection; and Kyoshi Gisors, called Kyo, the half-Japanese, half-French intellectual who, with Katov, is an organizer of the insurrection
planned for the next few days in Shanghai.

Plans call for the insurrection to begin when the trainload
of revolutionary soldiers reaches the last railroad station before Shanghai. The Communists, fighting with the forces of
Chiang Kai-shek's Kuomintang, will take the city. But
whereas Chiang's men are well armed, the Communists are
not. Therefore it is essential for Kyo and Katov to get their

hands on the arms shipment destined for the governmental forces.

Kyo makes contact with Baron de Clappique, a bizarre Frenchman who traffics in all manner of goods—legal and illegal—to make a living. Without telling Clappique much, he arranges for the Frenchman's services in connection with the arms shipment arriving on the *Shantung*. Clappique is successful in executing the mission Kyo has generously paid him for, and early the next morning Kyo manages to board the *Shantung* with a band of his own men; binding the officers, the Communists quickly despoil the vessel of her precious cargo of arms, and make off with them.

Kyo lives with his father, Old Gisors, formerly Professor of Sociology at the University of Peking, who had been dismissed for making a particularly Communistic speech. Old Gisors and his son have a great love for each other, though they do not talk about the work of the Party with which Kyo is so much engaged. Also living with Old Gisors is Kyo's wife, May—an emancipated woman, a physician, dedicated to the Communist cause, whose passionate love for her husband does not prevent her from having a casual affair with a doctor at the hospital. Kyo is driven to despair when he realizes that he is capable of profound jealousy over this meaningless liaison of May's.

Another young man dedicated to Old Gisors is Ch'en, who had found in Kyo's father a source of stability and wisdom. The night of the murder, Ch'en goes to Gisors in the hope that he will be able to find relief from his own terror in the words of the old man; but Gisors is unable to say anything that offers promise or peace to Ch'en.

Deeply affected by the political unrest in Shanghai is the President of the Franco-Asiatic Consortium, a shrewd, ruthless, and polished financier named Ferral. If Shanghai should fall to the Communists, Ferral would be ruined—both in China and in France—for the extensive financial empire which he has built in Asia with French funds would crumble. He is gratified by rumors that Chiang Kai-shek, who is clearly destined to rule China, intends to make short shrift of the Communists as soon as he has no further need of them.

At last the signal for the outbreak of the insurrection is heard, and the fighting begins in earnest. Ch'en is in charge of a small brigade whose task it is to take the police station and appropriate its arms. In the grueling battle that follows, Ch'en finds a sense of fulfillment in his task as murderer, and with fanatic devotion he throws himself savagely into the fight. When the police station is won, Ch'en is no longer a novice, but an old, experienced soldier, with no horror of blood, and no terror of death.

During the course of the insurrection, Ferral nervously keeps track of each skirmish, and with every phone call, every messenger, he becomes surer and surer that ultimate success will go to the Kuomintang, and that Chiang will expel the Reds from power as soon as the city is taken. He is satisfied that his empire will stand—Chiang will need French support. It is with reduced anxiety, therefore, that he meets his mistress, the sardonic, infuriating Valerie, who insists that she is a person in her own right and who refuses to let herself be used. Ferral, however, is not accustomed to being thwarted, and he imposes his will on Valerie, and forces her to surrender to him.

The next day the Communists all but succeed in taking Shanghai; when the Kuomintang army arrives in a few hours, victory will be certain. But though they are gratified by their military success, the Communists have serious worries.

A courier arrives from the Kuomintang, with news that the Communists are being effectively reduced in power in Chiang's Central Committee—and further that Chiang has ordered that the Communists surrender their arms to his Blue Army, which has greater need of them. It is now clear to Ch'en and Kyo that Chiang has merely been using the Communists to gain his own ends, and that he has no intention of helping the proletariat, but rather of bolstering his own support among the bourgeoisie.

Kyo believes that the Communists' only hope is to get the support of the Communist officials at Hankow, the one Chinese province in which Communism has really taken hold. But Ch'en is a Communist of the terrorist tradition, and to him the only hope lies in the assassination of Chiang Kaishek.

Kyo and Katov both agree to make the difficult and dangerous journey to Hankow, and for several days they are out of touch with developments in Shanghai. Reaching Hankow, they secure interviews with the two most important Communist officials—Vologin and Possoz. From them they learn the disheartening news that Communism is not the success in Hankow that it is reputed to be; that hunger and unemployment are as great, that discontent among the poor is as rampant as at Shanghai. To Kyo's chagrin, the two Hankow Communists recommend a policy of accommodation with Chiang. They advise that the Communists go along with the demands of the Kuomintang for a while, and wait until the moment is right; then, they assure Kyo and Katov, Chiang will welcome the Communists back into power. Disheartened, Kyo and Katov have no choice but to make their way back to Shanghai.

Two weeks later, the Baron de Clappique meets, by appointment, Count Shpilevski, a member of Chiang's police force. Clappique had once done Shpilevski a great favor, which Shpilevski now intends to return. He advises Clappique that his part in the raiding of the *Shantung* is known, and that he has only two days in which to get out of China alive. Clappique protests that he did not know that it was a Communist plot, but he sees that Shpilevski is not impressed. Shpilevski does give him gratuitously the information that Kyo Gisors is also implicated, and Clappique rushes away to warn his young friend.

A half-hour late, Ch'en is awaiting anxiously the execution of a plan he has carefully worked out. Chiang Kai-shek is expected to be driven through a certain street within the hour; and Ch'en, along with two other terrorists, Pei and Suan, have plotted to throw bombs into his car. The plot, however, miscarries, and the three are unable to do anything but watch helplessly as Chiang's car rolls by.

They seek a hiding place in Hemmelrich's shop, but the old German—who loves his wife and his frail son desperately—is too fearful for his family to hide the terrorists, and so they move on. Now Ch'en realizes that the only way to accomplish his mission is to fling himself under Chiang's car with a bomb clutched in his arms. He proposes that Pei and Suan resolve to do likewise, to insure success, but the men are too fearful. Still resolved, Ch'en goes off by himself. Never in his life has he felt so alone.

Clappique, meanwhile, has been waiting at Old Gisors' house for Kyo to come so that he can warn him. At last Kyo arrives, and Clappique tells him of the reprisals Chiang is planning against the Communists for the *Shantung* affair.

Kyo sees the danger, but he cannot run away. He is needed at the Central Committee.

Kyo's wife, May, begs him to take her with him to the Committee, knowing the danger he is in. Kyo has still not recovered from his pain at May's infidelity, but after a passionate confrontation which is agony for them both, May and Kyo are reconciled.

Katov arrives looking for Ch'en. Word of Ch'en's intention to assassinate Chiang has leaked out, and the police are looking for him. But the Gisors have not seen the young terrorist, so Katov decides to look for him at Hemmelrich's, while May and Kyo go to the Committee.

Ferral, who has been watching developments daily with a practiced *sang-froid*, is assured by Chiang's emissaries that there will be no mercy shown toward the Communists. Calmly he goes to keep his assignation with Valerie. On arriving at her hotel, however, he finds himself the victim of a small practical joke played by the woman to demonstrate her independence and her refusal to submit her will to his. In fury he contrives an elaborate joke to punish her, and drives off into the night. His rage and his lust combine to form sadistic fantasies in his mind; and even with a prostitute, he is unable to forget the insult of his independent mistress.

At half-past ten that night, Ch'en stands alone at a spot where he is certain to see Chiang's car approaching. It is with ecstatic joy that he throws himself under the vehicle, the bomb clutched in his hands. A few seconds later, he is aware of a great, all-consuming pain. Somehow he manages to whip out his revolver and point it into his own mouth. A guard, giving him a violent kick, causes Ch'en's muscles to contract in a spasm, and the trigger is pulled.

Clappique has been desperately trying to raise money enough to make his escape from China, but he has not been successful. On his way to an assignation with Kyo, made when Kyo promised to bring him as much money as possible, Clappique stops at a gambling casino in the hope of increasing his small hoard of money. He is determined to play only a short time, for he has heard that Chiang's police intend to raid the Committee meeting, and begin their reprisals against the Communists. He wants to warn Kyo to avoid going to the Committee. But as he loses play after play at the gaming tables, Clappique becomes strangely mesmerized, and deliberately he lets the hour of his appointment with Kyo slip by.

Kyo and May wait for Clappique at the appointed place until it is apparent that the droll Frenchman will not show up. This confirms for Kyo his suspicions that the rumored reaction of the Kuomintang will not take place so soon—that Clappique is alarmed for nothing, and that no danger will follow immediately from the *Shantung* raid. At last he and May decide to go on to their meeting. As they walk through the dark streets, they are attacked by Chiang's police from behind. May is left unconscious in the road. Kyo is whisked away in a prison-bound car.

When Hemmelrich hears that Chiang's car has been attacked, he runs to find out the details. Learning that Ch'en's gesture had been futile—Chiang's car was empty when it was attacked—he returns to his shop in bitterness. He feels, more than ever, guilt and remorse at having turned Ch'en away earlier. Entering his shop, Hemmelrich stops with shock and horror. The Kuomintang have been there; the reprisals have started. He finds his wife and son lying dead, their bodies mutilated. Hemmelrich realizes that he is now free to act— free for the first time in his life. He runs to the Post where he knows the militant Communists are hiding.

Only minutes after his arrival, the Kuomintang begins firing on the building in which the Communists are hidden, and a pitched battle is waged under the generalship of Katov. But this time the Communists have little hope of success, and soon, of the small band that has tried to hold the building, only Hemmelrich is left neither dead nor unconscious. Determined that he will make one valiant stroke in the Party's cause, he lies in wait for a Kuomintang officer. When the man approaches (convinced that the building holds no more live soldiers), Hemmelrich kills him brutally. He strips the man of his uniform, and in the disguise of a Blue officer, he is able to make his escape.

Old Gisors, learning of Kyo's capture, seeks out Clappique, whom he knows to have friends and influence in many circles, and begs the Frenchman to do whatever he can to secure Kyo's release. Clappique feels guilty for having stood Kyo up—perhaps having caused his capture—and he therefore agrees to go to see König, General of Chiang's police.

König admits Clappique, but when the Frenchman reminds him that he, König, owes Clappique a favor, König says that it is already repaid; it was he who ordered Shpilevski to warn Clappique of the danger he was in. König thus considers the slate wiped clean. There will be no saving Kyoshi Gisors.

Clappique now raises himself from the passive torpor in which he has wandered since losing his money at the gaming tables. Suddenly the urge to live reasserts itself, and he is determined that somehow he will escape from China. He is delighted to find that his wits have not deserted him; now all his experience at making his way in the world through nerve and brilliance alone comes to his rescue. Within a few hours Clappique is safely on board a vessel bound for France, disguised as a common sailor. Once on board and realizing that his life is secure, he becomes, again, a droll braggart and expansive conversationalist.

Kyo finds himself segregated in prison from most of the other prisoners, and he learns that he is one of a select group that is to be put to the torture. Also in this small band is Katov, who has been wounded but not killed during the Kuomintang attack on the Communist Post. Both men wear a belt with false buckle, in which is secreted a single cyanide tablet. As they wait for death, Kyo is able to swallow his, and he dies in suffocating convulsions. Katov, however, believes that his tablet is large enough for two, and he determines to share it with his fellow prisoner, Suan. In breaking the tablet surreptitiously, though, the pain-racked Katov drops both pieces. Suan manages to find one, but the second is found by another prisoner. Both die quickly, and Katov realizes that he will be one of those left to be roasted alive.

It is several months later that Ferral, in Paris, finally comes to a realization that his financial empire is ruined. At a meeting with the banking interests of France and the Minister of Finance, he learns that there will be no hope of their saving the intricate, bankrupt Consortium to which he has devoted years of his life.

And in Japan, May goes to visit her father-in-law, Old Gisors, who has found refuge with the painter Kama. She begs the old man to accompany her to Russia, where he has received an appointment as professor at the Sun Yat-sen Institute.

But the old man refuses. Having lost the two young men

he loved best in the world—his son, Kyo, and the strange, fanatic, Ch'en—he has given up his dreams of the new, glorious world to be built by Communism. He wants only to be left alone to die. But May, thinking of the sacrifices made by the Katovs and the Kyos of the Revolution, is determined to vindicate them by throwing her own life completely into the struggle.

RUSSIAN NOVELS

DEAD SOULS

Nikolai Gogol

Nikolai Gogol was born in 1809 in the Russian Ukraine, the son of a Cossack landowner. He studied at regional schools, then went to St. Petersburg, where he acquired a government post and began to write. His writings, particularly his stories of Cossacks, were well received by the critics and public. He planned to become a historian, and received a university post, but this he resigned in 1835; having abandoned his researches, he proved a poor and unprepared teacher. When his satirical play The Inspector General *was hailed by the intellectuals in 1836, Gogol was encouraged to devote himself entirely to writing. He traveled in western Europe from 1836 to 1848, sending everything he wrote back to Russia to be published. His work was lavishly praised, and Gogol came to consider himself the most important living Russian writer. Dead Souls appeared in 1842, and is considered his finest work; as a satire of the Russian bureaucracy, it was praised, perhaps beyond its merits, by intellectuals and reformers. Gogol had planned to write a second part of* Dead Souls *(which was to include the story of Chichikov's redemption and turn to virtue), but his mind began to fail in the late 1840s. Feeling that he had been a bad Christian, he made a trip to the Holy Land, returning unredeemed. Thereupon he began to destroy his manuscripts, including the sketches for part two of* Dead Souls. *He died in Moscow in 1852.*

One bright day a carriage drives into an innyard in the provincial city of N., and a young man alights. His two serfs unload his baggage, the man rents a room, and then goes to have dinner. From his detailed inquiries about all the local landowners and petty officials, the waiter deduces that the man has come for an indefinite stay.

Thus does Pavel Ivanovitch Chichikov launch his adventurous visit. As N. is a comparatively quiet city, with little of interest occurring from one month to the next, it is not long before word of Chichikov's arrival spreads. Losing no time, Chichikov himself sees to it that he makes the acquaintance of all the city's important people; and as he has a smooth tongue and a flair for flattery, he readily makes himself the most sought-after guest at all the local dinners, suppers, card parties, and balls.

Having entrenched himself in everyone's opinion as the best of good fellows, Chichikov begins to pay a series of calls upon the local gentry.

The first estate he visits is that of the genial Mamilov, who is delighted to see him and who entertains him royally. After a time Chichikov hints that he has a business proposition to discuss, and the two men settle down to serious talk.

Chichikov's proposal to Mamilov is a strange one. He says he wishes to buy all of Mamilov's dead souls. (Serfs were, in those days, called souls by the men who owned them.) Mamilov is sure that he has not understood Chichikov correctly, but Chichikov goes on in greater detail, leaving no doubt of his meaning. Since landowners must pay taxes for every soul they own, and since a soul stays on the government roll books as taxable from one census to another, even though some of the souls may have died since the last census, Chichikov wishes to relieve Mamilov of the burden of paying taxes upon his dead souls, and wishes to buy them from him. Mamilov is delighted to be thus relieved of a tax burden by the good Chichikov, and he readily agrees to drawing up a bill of sale transferring to the stranger all of his souls who have died since the last census.

His business thus concluded most pleasantly, Chichikov (along with his own two serfs, Selifan the driver and Petrushka the valet) leaves Mamilov's and heads for the next estate on his list, that of one Sobakevitch.

Selifan, however, is somewhat partial to vodka and somewhat indifferent to directions. The result is that they get hopelessly lost, finding themselves miles from anywhere—and night is falling fast. Spying a large, isolated mansion with a few lights blazing, Chichikov directs Selifan to drive thither.

It is now the middle of the night, and Chichikov has some difficulty in making the house serfs understand that he is not a thief, rogue, and murderer come to do away with them and their mistress, but only an honest gentleman who has lost his way and is in need of a bed for the night. At last he is brought face to face with the mistress of the tumble-down farm. She proves to be an ancient and eccentric lady named Nastasya Petrovna Korobochka; but she has a good heart, and she makes Chichikov comfortable and allows him to spend the night on an old sofa.

The next morning Chichikov interviews the woman, and discovers that on her estate, too, many souls have died since the last census. He offers to buy them, but the old woman stubbornly refuses to sell, presenting first one excuse and then another. Chichikov is about to leave the house in a rage of impotent fury when he tries one last ploy. Lying, he says that he is a government contractor, and that if the woman will sell him her dead souls now, he will surely return in a few months with government contracts to buy up all her pigs, chickens, oats, lard, feathers—in short, whatever she wishes to sell.

At this, old Korobochka begins to sing a different tune, and delightedly she makes out a bill of sale to Chichikov transferring to him all of her dead souls. It is therefore with a light heart that Chichikov sets off again, this time determined to get directions to Sobakevitch's house.

Stopping at an inn for that purpose, Chichikov encounters the notorious Nozdryov, a liar, braggart, and gambler whom he has already met at various parties at N. Nozdryov greets him like a long-lost relation—the man is sick and tired of his present companion, his brother-in-law Mizhuyev—and insists that Chichikov must come home with him. Knowing Nozdryov to be a wealthy landowner, Chichikov decides that he might as well go with him, as it is likely that Nozdryov can be as easily persuaded to sell his dead souls as Sobakevitch. So off goes Chichikov with his loud-mouthed acquaintance.

Nozdryov's estate is in run-down condition, and Chichikov is determined not to stay as a guest there any longer than he needs to. The dinner that he is served is most disgusting, and Chichikov is outraged at the great quantity of liquor that is served—and consumed—at table.

After dinner Chichikov broaches the subject of the dead souls to Nozdryov. Instead of giving a straight answer, however, Nozdryov—the gambling instinct ever to the fore—begins to offer Chichikov various deals. He will sell the souls if Chichikov will also buy his horse; he will sell Chichikov his second-best carriage and throw in the souls gratis; he will sell. . . . But whatever outlandish proposal Nozdryov offers, Chichikov turns him down; he wants the souls, only the souls, and nothing but the souls. The two men arrive at a stalemate and the matter is dropped.

Chichikov is now interested in getting away, his errand having failed. But Nozdryov, who is quite drunk, insists that first they must play draughts together. Reluctantly Chichikov agrees—but it soon becomes apparent that Nozdryov is cheating enormously, and Chichikov refuses to play. Outraged at this accusation of dishonesty, Nozdryov calls out for his body servants to come and beat Chichikov to a pulp in payment for this insult. Two burly serfs bound into the room with rods in their fists, and Chichikov is convinced that his last moment has come. Just as the serfs are about to beat him, however, Chichikov is saved by the arrival of the police, who have come to arrest Nozdryov on a charge of assault and battery. In the confusion that follows, Chichikov makes good his escape, but it is not until long after Nozdryov's house has disappeared in the distance that Chichikov's teeth stop chattering.

Chichikov again sets out to call upon Sobakevitch. On the way, Selifan gets Chichikov's carriage entangled with the coach of another party, but Chichikov is not disconcerted, for one of the occupants of the coach is a beautiful blond girl—about sixteen years of age—whom Chichikov cannot cease gazing upon.

The relaxed and pleasant mood engendered by the encounter with the pretty Miss is soon destroyed, however. Sobakevitch leads Chichikov a merry dance in this matter of purchasing dead souls. He begins by demanding the outrageous price of a hundred rubles for each serf; at last, Chichikov is able to beat him down to two-and-a-half rubles per serf—but even at this price Chichikov feels he is not doing too well.

Next Chichikov goes to see the man who is regarded as the worst miser in all of Russia, one Plyushkin. At first, Plyushkin treats Chichikov rudely—assures Chichikov that he himself has already eaten, so that Chichikov need not hope for dinner; tells him that he has just run out of wine, and that he never drinks tea; and so forth. But when he learns that Chichikov has actually come to relieve him of the burden of paying taxes on his dead souls, Plyushkin sings an altogether different tune. He even orders the housemaid to unlock the cupboard and take from it the rusk of a cake he has had since last Easter. After the mold is scraped from the bit of dead pastry, Plyushkin offers this tidbit to his benefactor Chichikov—but Chichikov declines the delicacy, and returns that very night to the city of N.

By now Chichikov has acquired a total of almost four hundred dead souls. The next day, he brings his collection of documents to the local registry office, and after being given the run-around by bureaucrats all on the lookout for a bribe, he succeeds in having the sales registered and notarized in legal form.

Word of Chichikov's enormous purchase of serfs soon spreads about the city, and it is rumored that the man must be a millionaire. At that magic word, Chichikov—who had always been regarded as an indifferent sort of man—is suddenly considered a paragon of manly good looks and virtue. Half a score of women fall instantly in love with him—and one (anonymously) even sends him a passionate and hysterical billet-doux. Chichikov looks forward to the governor's ball that night, hoping that he will discover there the writer of this amorous epistle.

The ball, at first, is a personal success for Chichikov. All the ladies outdo themselves in paying attentions to him—as do all the men with businesses requiring capital, with marriageable daughters, or with both. But in an instant, tragedy overtakes Chichikov—and he doesn't even realize it.

The governor and his family arrive, and the governor's daughter proves to be the beautiful blond sixteen-year-old whom Chichikov had seen at the time of the carriage accident. Instantly Chichikov ceases paying attention to the other ladies, and has eyes only for this young beauty; and in the same instant, all of the ladies, seeing how the ground lies, withdraw their affections and loyalties from Chichikov, and begin to make up the most vicious scandals about him, which pass from one to another in a burst of feverish whispering.

To add to Chichikov's problems, Nozdryov is present at the ball. Quite drunk, and still angry at Chichikov for having escaped a thrashing, Nozdryov spills the fact that all the souls Chichikov has been buying and on which his reputation as a millionaire is based are *dead* souls. This fact is confirmed to the scandalized community by the old lady Korobochka, who has come to town to verify a suspicion that she has been cheated in her dealings with Chichikov—that dead souls may be worth a good deal more money than he paid for hers.

Buzz-buzz-buzz. The next days see one rumor after another circulated against poor Chichikov. Doors are closed to him. No one is at home to him. A series of secret meetings is held to determine who this strange scoundrel Chichikov may be, and what it is that he is up to. The ladies of the town agree that he has come to abduct the governor's daughter, and that purchasing dead souls is merely a blind. As for the men, they cannot settle the matter so easily, and are divided between those who think Chichikov is a brigand outlaw wanted for forging counterfeit rubles and those who think he is Napoleon in disguise, escaped from Elba. To fan the flames, Nozdryov goes from one house to another, telling ever greater lies about Chichikov's roguery.

When Chichikov at last discovers that he is in disgrace, he doesn't know what to think, for he finds himself blameless of all wrongdoing. At this point, Nozdryov comes to him and, protesting the deepest affection and eternal friendship for Chichikov, tells him of all the unbelievable stories circulating about the town. (Nozdryov protests that he himself has done nothing but defend Chichikov's behavior, but that everyone else is convinced that Chichikov is a blackguard.)

Seeing that his reputation is forever ruined in the city of N., Chichikov determines to set off for a new city in his quest for dead souls. Accordingly Petrushka packs up his things, Selifan mounts the box of the carriage, and the three turn their backs on N. for ever and ever, leaving the townspeople to wonder about who Chichikov really is and what he really wanted.

What none of them could imagine was the truth of the matter: that Chichikov is a bright young man determined to be rich; that he has gone through several fortunes already, each one made by some illicit handiwork and each one unmade by legal discovery; and that he is now embarked on his greatest get-rich-quick scheme of all: namely, to buy up as many dead souls as he can; to present the roll lists to the government showing so many hundred souls as his own possessions; and then to mortgage these mythical souls to the government for a tidy fortune.

Chichikov sits back in his carriage and muses. He gives little thought to N. and its foolish gentry; instead, he thinks about the next city he will visit, and he makes some mental computations about his chances of success in purchasing more dead souls. . . .

VIRGIN SOIL

Ivan Turgenev

Ivan Sergeyevich Turgenev was born at Orel, Russia, in 1818. He was the son of a cruel, very rich woman and a handsome colonel who had married for money. Turgenev traveled to western Europe with his family at an early age. He was educated at the universities of Moscow and St. Petersburg, graduating from the latter in 1837. He studied in Berlin, and returned to Russia in 1841, where he had his first literary sketches published. He traveled in Europe from 1847 to 1850, returning home upon the death of his mother, who left him a considerable inheritance. He was jailed briefly for anti-Czarist sentiments in 1852, and upon his release that year, he found that his books were being acclaimed not only in Russia, but throughout Europe; he was the first Russian author to achieve international fame and popularity. After 1863 he lived for the most part in Germany, France, and England, and was acquainted with the foremost European authors of the time. Some of his novels were extremely controversial, dealing as they did with political themes in a manner which pleased no existing political faction; these novels, the last of which was Virgin Soil (1877), were in fact quite prophetic about the future of Russia, where they were poorly received. In France, England, and America, however, Turgenev was acclaimed for his liberalism, as well as for the qualities of his fictional art. He was a master of description, able to create moods and to penetrate motivations on a personal or social scale. His influence was vast; some say he brought Russia to the world and the world to Russia. It is not too much of an overstatement. Turgenev died in Paris in 1883.

In the small St. Petersburg apartment of Alexei Dmitritch Nejdanov, four young revolutionary spirits are gathered, each dedicated in a greater or lesser way to the Cause—the great movement in which the intelligentsia (or a small portion of the intelligentsia) is allying with the peasants, to teach them, to inspire them, and to foster small village revolutions against the landholding classes.

These four are: Pemien Ostrodumov, undying in his dedication to the Cause; Sila Samsonitch Paklin, a limping, inadequate clown of a fellow; Fiekla Mashurina, a homely girl whose devotion to the peasants of Russia is matched only by her secret passion for her handsome young leader, Nejdanov; and Nejdanov himself, the intelligent, sensitive bastard son of an aristocratic general.

Word has been received from Moscow that Mashurina and Ostrodumov are needed there, and they have come to Nejdanov's to get money for the trip. Paklin begs to be allowed to contribute some funds to the Cause, and reluctantly Nejdanov accepts. None of the inner circle really trusts Paklin, but the young people are so fiery and impassioned that they cannot help letting slip secret information in his presence, and so they decide to regard him as a trustworthy ally.

Nejdanov has been running an advertisement in the newspaper in order to seek a position, and he accepts a well-paying post in the country home of the liberal aristocrat Boris Andreyevitch Sipiagin as tutor to the man's son, little Kolya. Nejdanov is favorably impressed with the delightful Sipiagin and with his beautiful country estate; but he is less impressed with the people he finds in Sipiagin's house: the man's plain, intense niece, Mariana, who is reduced to living on his charity; Anna Zaharovna, Sipiagin's ancient spinster aunt; and Simion Petrovitch Kollomietzev, a dandified, Frenchified aristocrat (although something of a parvenu) who scorns all nihilists, reformers, revolutionists, and intellectuals-in-general.

The one person who makes a favorable impression upon Nejdanov is Sipiagin's wife, Valentina Mihailovna, an attractive and accomplished hostess. Without realizing it, however, Nejdanov incurs the lady's wrath by proving immune to her flirtatious blandishments.

After living in the house for a while, Nejdanov re-evaluates Mariana, and feels a bond of sympathy with her. When he overhears her in intense conversation with Sergei Mihailovitch Markelov, the swarthy and outspoken older brother of Valentina Mihailovna, he thinks nothing about it. Later, however, Mariana confides in him that Markelov has proposed to her but that she has refused him. In spite of her dislike for the superficial people with whom she is surrounded and of the humility of having to live on Sipiagin's charity when it is clear that her aunt, Valentina, hates her, Mariana is too noble to marry a man whom she does not love, even if such a marriage should provide an escape for her. (She is most of all loath to marry the man her aunt has in mind for her—none other than the slick and artificial Kollomietzev.) As a result of their getting to know each other's past histories and inner secrets, Nejdanov and Mariana find that they are both passionately devoted to the Cause—and madly in love with one another.

Even in this remote rural community Nejdanov remains in touch with the movement. Markelov reveals himself as a member of the revolutionary brotherhood, and introduces him to Solomin, a young man who manages a nearby factory, who is also one of the group. Nejdanov finds Solomin a strange creature; in spite of his obvious success at working with and being accepted by the peasants (something the others have tried to accomplish but at which they have failed), in spite of his intelligence, in spite of his dedication to the peasants of Mother Russia, Solomin warns continually against any strong action in behalf of the Cause. While the rest are calling "The time is ripe for revolution!", Solomin urges a policy of watchful waiting. In spite of this passivity in the man, however, Nejdanov decides that he likes him enormously.

One day, while meeting with Solomin and Markelov, Nejdanov encounters Paklin, and introduces him to his fellow conspirators. The three repair to the home of the crude, sycophantic merchant Golushkin, who is so desperate to be liked by these bright young men that he flings his money about as though it were valueless to him. All get quite drunk at Golushkin's house—with the exception of Solomin—and make proud and fiery speeches on behalf of the Cause.

On leaving Golushkin's, Nejdanov notices that Markelov is in a dark mood, and presses for an explanation. At last Markelov reveals that he has received a letter from his sister, Valentina, in which the spiteful woman has told her miserable brother about the growing passion between Nejdanov and Mariana. Markelov's unhappiness at losing his beloved Mariana makes Nejdanov realize what a precious pearl he has found in the young woman, and he and Markelov part in sincere friendship, with Nejdanov promising to be worthy of Mariana and to make her happy.

Sipiagin has been tolerant of Nejdanov so long as the young man conformed to the pleasant, innocuous image of an employee. But now that Valentina has opened his eyes concerning the romance blooming between his niece and the tutor, he becomes a different person toward Nejdanov. The tutor, however, is indifferent to his benefactor's ill will. Sipiagin is even more enraged by the refusal of Solomin to leave his present employer and come to work for Sipiagin. This is too much! Sipiagin decides that perhaps Kollomietzev has been right about young reformers and nihilists after all.

The night that Solomin turns down Sipiagin's offer, he has a secret interview with Nejdanov and Mariana. The young couple pour out to him their dreams and ambitions. They are determined to run away together and go among the peasants, doing good and preparing themselves to die in the coming revolution. Solomin tries to point out to them the folly of their romanticism, urging that they reconsider this disastrous step, but the young couple is adamant. At last he agrees to supply them with a hiding place where they will be safe from Sipiagin's wrath.

Accordingly, a few days later, Nejdanov (who has been ordered off the premises by the enraged Sipiagin) meets Mariana in a deserted lane, and the two—each carrying his meager bundle of possessions—go to Solomin, who takes them in and hides them in a small attic apartment in the factory. In spite of—or perhaps because of—the romanticism of their escape and situation, Nejdanov tells Mariana that he will not ask her to live as his wife until he can feel noble enough to be worthy of her. The young man and woman live, therefore, as brother and sister.

At first, everything goes smoothly for the young lovers. They dress in peasant garb, and talk about how they will go out among the people, disseminating propaganda and helping to bring about a revolution. Soon, however, the situation begins to seem to them a farce, their peasant clothes merely theatrical costumes. They want danger, they want to be doing great things—but Solomin tells them that they will be far more useful to the peasants by helping them with menial tasks—carting a barrow of manure, combing the lice out of a child's hair. Indeed, Nejdanov, in a frenzy of urgency, does go out among the peasants to distribute revolutionary pamphlets, but he is met with ridicule and rejection by them, and begins to realize that there is more to becoming one with the peasants than he had imagined.

Even more bitter to him is the fact that Mariana seems to

love him less than she once did. She remains determined to abide by her vow to stay with him forever—and to marry him if he should ask her to—but Nejdanov sees that she does this only from a sense of honor; in her heart it is Solomin whom she adores. And Nejdanov is sure that Solomin returns the girl's feeling, and that he declines to speak only out of loyalty to Nejdanov.

Nejdanov thinks that he will go mad from this farcical existence, when suddenly word comes that Markelov has succeeded in igniting one of the long-hoped-for peasant uprisings in the next town. Nejdanov and Mariana are impatient to be off to join their comrades in this great and violent battle for freedom—but again, Solomin warns that their excitement is premature. In spite of Solomin's warnings, Nejdanov is determined at least to go to the scene of the riot and report on its success, and Mariana agrees to wait for him. (Solomin sends his trusted assistant, the peasant Pavel, after Nejdanov to look after the fiery, romantic youth and see that he comes to no harm.)

Alone, Mariana is in a fever of excitement and confusion. She cannot sort out her emotions. Is it Nejdanov she loves? Or Solomin? Or the Cause? Suddenly a strange woman comes to her room looking for Nejdanov. It is Mashurina, the homely girl of burning revolutionary zeal. Hearing that Nejdanov has gone, she leaves word that he is in great danger, and must find a new and better hiding place. Although the two women talk together only briefly, Mariana can see how desperately Mashurina loves Nejdanov, and how nobly she gives him up so that he may be happy. She is humbled by this knowledge.

Shortly after Mashurina leaves, Pavel brings Nejdanov home, bruised and drunken. It seems the young man had been proclaiming his revolutionary sentiments aloud and the peasants had not made the appropriate response. Rather, they had punished him by forcing him to drink great quantities of bad vodka and, just for sport, by giving him a drubbing.

Now Paklin arrives with the news that the revolution in the next town has been a major disaster. Instead of winning the support of the peasants, Markelov only stirred them up against him, and they turned him over to the police. An informer also turned in Golushkin, who even now is begging to be let go and promising that he will build a huge orphan asylum for the town if only the police will be lenient with him this once.

Paklin is, in truth, afraid that he himself will be betrayed, but he pretends to Solomin that his concern is for Nejdanov and Mariana. He offers to go to Sipiagin and tell him of his brother-in-law's arrest. Paklin is sure that Sipiagin—who is very influential—will help not only his wife's brother Markelov, but also his own niece, Mariana, and Nejdanov as well. Solomin agrees to the plan.

At Sipiagin's house, however, Paklin—in his desperation to present himself in the best possible light—manages to betray the young lovers and reveal their hiding place. Sipiagin determines to have his revenge upon them.

Fortunately, word of this reaches Solomin in advance, and he urges immediate and hurried preparations for flight. Nejdanov, though he behaves strangely, agrees to be ready in an hour, and he, Solomin, and Mariana go their separate ways to make their preparations to go into hiding.

Meeting at the appointed time, Solomin and Mariana find Nejdanov's body. He has shot himself in the head, and left a letter for them in which he tells them that they deserve each other. His last wish is that Mariana and Solomin be married.

Carefully disguised, Solomin and Mariana make good their escape, and eventually Sipiagin gives up his search for the niece who, he believes, has brought shame and scandal to the family name. A year later, Solomin and Mariana are married, and live happily with one another.

As for the Cause, Solomin is tried on charges, but they are of an insubstantial nature and the penalty is not stiff. Markelov, determined to be true to his ideals and play the martyr's role to the hilt, is found guilty and heavily sentenced. Golushkin buys himself out of his ticklish role as a conspirator. Ostrodumov is killed by a shopkeeper whom he is trying to propagandize.

Several years later, in a quiet back street of Moscow, the aging Paklin meets Mashurina, who is now traveling for the Cause in the guise of an Italian contessa. Paklin begs her to tell him the name of her superior—the man from whom she, and all of the workers in the Cause, receive orders—but Mashurina will not divulge the information. "Perhaps, then, he is anonymous?" jokes Paklin as Mashurina leaves his apartment.

Then, to the closed door, Paklin observes, "Yes, anonymous. Mother Russia."

THE IDIOT

Fyodor Dostoyevsky

Fyodor Mikhailovich Dostoyevsky was born in Moscow in 1821. His father, a physician, an impoverished aristocrat, and a strict disciplinarian, was murdered by his serfs in 1839; Dostoyevsky's mother had died some years before. He was forced to study military engineering, but in 1844 turned to writing. After years of misfortune, his first novel, Poor Folk, was published in 1846, and was successful. In 1849, however, Dostoyevsky, a member of a group of political radicals, was arrested, and sentenced to be shot. At the point of the execution the sentence was commuted to four years of slave labor in Siberia, and another four years in the army in Siberia. In 1858 he returned to St. Petersburg, having undergone a religious conversion. His first wife died after seven years of marriage, and in 1867 Dostoyevsky married again. With his new wife he spent four years in western Europe, during which time his reputation grew both in Russia and abroad. He produced his greatest works toward the end of his life, and died in St. Petersburg in 1881.

Dostoyevsky is now recognized as one of the very greatest novelists of all time. His concern with the agony of man, his profound psychological penetration into the meaning of love and hate, his comprehension of moral and metaphysical philosophy, and his concern with evil and suffering mark him as less a product of the nineteenth century than a herald of the twentieth. Modern psychology and philosophy acknowledge their debt to Dostoyevsky, and there are few important contemporary writers whose work has not been influenced directly or indirectly by him. The Idiot, which appeared in 1868, is an allegory with parallels to the story of Christ; Dostoyevsky here is examining the existence of evil and good as separate entities, and the possibility of reconciling humanity with the spirit of the divine.

Returning from a sanatorium in Switzerland, where he has been a patient for epilepsy, idiocy, and nervous disorders for four years, twenty-seven-year-old Prince Lyov Nikolayevitch Myshkin strikes up a conversation with two of his fellow travelers. Completely open and ingenuous, Prince Myshkin tells them his life story, and they, in turn, become confidential with him.

One of the men is Parfyon Rogozhin, also twenty-seven. Rogozhin is hopelessly infatuated with the infamous beauty, Nastasya Filippovna Barashkov, a young woman who had been seduced and debauched some years before by one Afanasy Ivanovitch Totsky, and who now lives an impetuous and luxury-filled existence in Petersburg. Rogozhin explains that he has just come into a fortune—that he is, indeed, a millionaire—and that he is now, therefore, in a position to offer himself in marriage to the captivating Nastasya Filippovna.

On hearing that Prince Myshkin is completely impoverished, the expansive Rogozhin, impressed by Myshkin's complete openness and naïve simplicity, invites him to live with him for as long as he likes. The third traveler in the compartment—the middle-aged, sycophantic Lukyan Timofeyevitch Lebedev—accepts Rogozhin's offer of hospitality at once; but Prince Myshkin is noncommittal, though polite.

On arriving at Petersburg, Prince Myshkin goes to call upon the only family with whom he has any connections whatsoever: the Yepanchins. Ivan Fyodorovitch Yepanchin's wife, Lizaveta, is the last Princess Myshkin, representing a distant branch of the Prince's own family. At first the Yepanchins are suspicious of the goodhearted Prince, and are sure that he has come to beg some favor of them. But soon they become convinced that he is both honest and good-natured, and they welcome him as a visitor.

Strangely enough, on his first visit to the Yepanchins' house Prince Myshkin again hears the name of Nastasya Filippovna. It seems that Yepanchin's secretary, young Gavrila Ardalionovitch Ivolgin (called Ganya), has been offered a small fortune by Nastasya's seducer if he will marry the woman. Money-mad, Ganya has made up his mind to agree to the bargain, provided that Nastasya Filippovna accepts him— this, in spite of the fact that he is in love with the Yepanchins' third and prettiest daughter, Aglaia; that he knows that Nastasya Filippovna scorns him for his avarice; and that marriage with such a notorious creature will shock and shame his own family.

Yepanchin himself is anxious that Ganya shall succeed in marrying Nastasya Filippovna, for after Ganya becomes rich by the marriage, Yepanchin hopes with Ganya's connivance to make Nastasya Filippovna his mistress. The two men anxiously await the birthday fête at which the haughty woman has announced she will make known her decision about Ganya's proposal. A further note of anxiety is introduced into their speculation about whether she will accept Ganya when it is learned that Rogozhin, now a millionaire, is intending to do his best to marry Nastasya Filippovna himself.

All of this Prince Myshkin observes with interest. (Because of his piety and openness, Myshkin is accepted by all who meet him as a rare and good person—though frequently his observations are so impractical and idealistic that his friends regard him as an idiot.)

The birthday fête at Nastasya Filippovna's proves to be a crucial occasion for several people. Prince Myshkin, who has seen Nastasya Filippovna by this time, is struck both by the woman's beauty and by the extreme suffering mirrored in her eyes, notwithstanding her flippant and arbitrary manner, and he is in love with her. He watches in horror as she haughtily castigates Ganya for his meanness in offering to marry her for money, and when, promising to abide by his decision, she asks Myshkin if she should accept Ganya, Myshkin tells her, "No."

Instead, Myshkin produces a letter which makes clear that he himself has inherited a fortune. Myshkin offers this money to Nastasya Filippovna, and asks her to marry him. The woman looks at the simple-minded, frail young Prince with a penetrating, strange gaze, but she says nothing.

Rogozhin, meanwhile, has arrived with a band of drunken friends to make his offer. He presents Nastasya Filippovna with a package containing a million rubles. On an impulse, she tells Ganya that she will hurl Rogozhin's bundle of notes into the fire; if he is sufficiently greedy to snatch the burning money out of the fire with his bare hands, he may keep it. All are horrified at this cruel proposal, but the woman proceeds to throw the money into the flames. When the packet catches fire, Ganya faints. Nastasya Filippovna seizes the singed packet with fire tongs, and tells the company that the money is to be given to Ganya when he recovers. She then goes off into the night with the jubilant Rogozhin.

Upon Yepanchin's recommendation, Prince Myshkin has taken rooms with Ganya's family, and there he comes to know both the Yepanchin and the Ivolgin families quite well. Ganya himself has undergone a marked change since the evening at Nastasya Filippovna's, and he even tries to give the burned banknotes to Prince Myshkin. Myshkin is deeply touched by the fact that Ganya thus gives evidence of having reformed—but Aglaia Yepanchin is as indifferent to him as ever.

Not long afterward, Prince Myshkin himself leaves the city without saying goodbye, and it is soon rumored that Nastasya Filippovna has left Rogozhin and is living with the Prince.

Several months go by before Myshkin returns to Petersburg. When he does come back, it is during the summer, a time when the Ivolgins and Yepanchins—along with many other families—are living in the country at Pavlovsk. Therefore Prince Myshkin lodges with the venal Lebedev, with whom he agrees he will go, later, to Pavlovsk.

One of Myshkin's first calls on returning to the city is made upon Rogozhin. More in love with Nastasya Filippovna than ever, the rejected Rogozhin is going mad with desire. He cannot long keep up his pose of hatred toward Prince Myshkin, however; the man is too saintly and too open for Rogozhin to hold out against him, in spite of his belief that Myshkin has robbed him of Nastasya Filippovna. The two men end their interview by exchanging crosses—Prince Myshkin taking a gold one from Rogozhin and giving Rogozhin the one of tin which he has been wearing—and swearing eternal brotherhood.

Returning to his rooms later that day, however, Prince Myshkin feels that he is being followed and watched. As he mounts the stairs, he is suddenly confronted by a man wielding a dagger. It is Rogozhin, his eyes blazing with murderous hate. In the instant that he is about to plunge his dagger into Myshkin's breast, the Prince goes into an epileptic seizure. This sufficiently frightens Rogozhin into making his escape, and thus Myshkin's life is saved.

Lebedev and Myshkin soon move to Pavlovsk, and there Prince Myshkin is again caught up in the lives of his Petersburg friends. The eccentric Lizaveta Yepanchin continues to blow both hot and cold toward him—particularly as she has begun to suspect that her youngest daughter, Aglaia, is in love with this mad Prince.

Myshkin, himself, has recognized a growing feeling of love

for Aglaia, but he cannot believe that this feeling is reciprocated. He fails to appreciate the peculiar nature of the girl's character; Aglaia does, indeed, love Prince Myshkin, but she cannot refrain from tormenting him and teasing him over his naïveté, even going so far as telling him that he is, indeed, what everyone has called him: an idiot.

One evening, there is a large gathering at Lebedev's. Among those present are the Yepanchins, with their three daughters, Alexandra, Adelaida, and Aglaia; Yevgeny Pavlovich Radomsky, a young man paying court to Adelaida; Lebedev and his daughter, Vera; Ganya Ivolgin and his drunken father, General Ivolgin; Ganya's sister, Varvara, and her husband; and Ganya's younger brother, Kolya, who worships Prince Myshkin. And, as luck would have it, it is in the midst of this great assembly that two scandals erupt.

The first occurs when four nihilistic young men burst onto the veranda demanding to see Prince Myshkin. They are Antip Burdovsky, a wild-eyed youth who seems to be the central figure in the group; a former hanger-on of Rogozhin's named Keller; an imperious young man named Vladimir Doktorenko (nephew of the scurrilous Lebedev); and Ippolit Terentyev, an impassioned friend of Kolya's who is dying of consumption. These men produce a fantastic story of illegitimacy, immorality, and skullduggery, the upshot of which is their contention that Myshkin is enjoying a fortune which, by right, belongs to Burdovsky. It is a long time before Prince Myshkin can speak, and he must listen to a series of shameless lies and scandals about himself; but ultimately he is able to prove, with Ganya's help, that the whole plot is nonsense. The four ruffians are at last somewhat mollified; indeed, Ippolit agrees to stay on in Pavlovsk as Prince Myshkin's guest, so that he may spend his last weeks of life in the serene countryside.

This commotion naturally cuts the evening short, and the guests begin to make their departures. Suddenly a carriage drives by the house and a woman—identified readily as Nastasya Filippovna—yells a series of suggestive and compromising remarks to Adelaida's suitor, Radomsky. He protests to the gathered assembly that he has never even met this awful woman, but Nastasya Filippovna's accusations against him are so specific that none believe poor Radomsky.

During the weeks that follow, Nastasya Filippovna becomes ever more open and outrageous in her assaults upon Radomsky's character. She even goes so far as to strike him in the face with a riding whip in the park. Needless to say, Yepanchin and his wife feel that they must send Radomsky packing, and bar him from further suit for Adelaida's hand.

Myshkin believes that Nastasya Filippovna has gone mad. He is further convinced of this when Aglaia tells him that Nastasya Filippovna has been in regular correspondence with her. The tenor of the letters is that Nastasya Filippovna is convinced that Myshkin loves Aglaia, and that Aglaia must marry him and make him happy. Nastasya writes that her own marriage to Rogozhin will follow within a few days of Myshkin's marriage to Aglaia. (In fact, the reason for Nastasya's attacks on the innocent Radomsky is that she believes him to be Aglaia's suitor, and she wants to "save" Aglaia for Myshkin.)

At last Myshkin believes that Aglaia does, indeed, love him, and he declares himself a suitor for her hand. And in spite of the fact that he totally disgraces himself by his awkwardness and naïve gaucherie at a betrothal party the Yepanchins have arranged for him and Aglaia, the Yepanchins resign themselves to the idea the Myshkin and Aglaia will marry.

The fiery Aglaia, however, wishes to settle relations between Myshkin and Nastasya Filippovna, and she begs Myshkin to accompany her one night to the house where the woman is staying with Rogozhin. Aglaia is convinced that Myshkin will, once and for all, declare that he wants nothing to do with Nastasya Filippovna. She does not reckon, however, on the older woman's superior skill at handling men. Insulted by Aglaia's tone and manner, Nastasya Filippovna decides to show the girl how much control she has over the innocent Myshkin, and she forces him to choose between them. Poor Myshkin loves Aglaia deeply and feels only pity for Nastasya Filippovna, but he is powerless to resist her claim that she will kill herself if he deserts her. He therefore chooses to stay with Nastasya Filippovna, and Aglaia, horrified and heartbroken, leaves, swearing never to see him again.

The entire community of Pavlovsk is scandalized at this turn of events, but plans for Myshkin's marriage to Nastasya proceed on a grand scale and with great bravado. As the marriage date approaches, however, Nastasya herself begins to have grave doubts. She believes herself a vile and wicked woman, and recognizes that Myshkin is marrying her only out of pity. She wavers constantly, but at last determines to go through with the wedding.

Myshkin is already waiting at the church when a carriage is sent for Nastasya Filippovna. A roar of approval goes up from the crowd gathered at her door when she appears, radiantly beautiful in her wedding finery. Suddenly from the crowd one man steps forward. It is Rogozhin. Nastasya Filippovna recognizes that this is her last chance to escape and to avoid doing Myshkin irreparable harm, and she accepts Rogozhin's arm. Before anyone can stop them, the two are off in a carriage.

When word of Nastasya's last-minute decampment reaches Myshkin, he determines to follow her. It takes several days, but at last he locates Rogozhin. The man greets him simply and tells him that he will take him to Nastasya Filippovna. They go into Rogozhin's darkened apartment, and there Myshkin finds Nastasya's body. Rogozhin has murdered her. With no word of reproach, Myshkin agrees to stay with Rogozhin, and he spends the night rocking the poor crazed murderer in his arms. When the police break into the apartment, they are amazed to find the saintly Myshkin gently nursing the deranged Rogozhin.

Friends of Myshkin's arrange to have him returned to the sanatorium in Switzerland where he can be cared for to the end of his days. There can be no doubt that the man is, indeed, an idiot, and cannot be trusted to look after himself. There, the Yepanchins come to visit him. Aglaia has run off with a Polish emigré who has proved to be nothing more than a soldier of fortune; worst of all, she has deserted the Orthodox Church and become a Roman Catholic. But looking at dear Myshkin, Lizaveta Yepanchin cannot bear to be gloomy. So she cheers up and talks of pleasant things.

WAR AND PEACE

Leo Tolstoy

Count Leo Tolstoy was born in Russia in 1828, the son of an aristocratic landowner. He studied at the University of Kazan, but did not take a degree. He joined the army in the Caucasus in 1851, and while stationed there wrote his first major work, a series of autobiographical sketches entitled Childhood. *Tolstoy served in the Crimean campaign, then left the army in order to travel abroad. Returning unimpressed with what he had seen of western Europe, he settled on his estate and attempted to improve the condition of the local peasantry. In 1864 he began writing* War and Peace, *finishing this monumental work five years later. Although he wrote fiction all his life, a good deal of Tolstoy's time and energy was spent on disseminating his personal moral philosophy, which had as its ultimate goal the replacement of all social, religious, and political institutions with a simplified Christianity based upon the Sermon on the Mount. His teachings were widely admired; and, in the last twenty years of his life, Tolstoy was the most venerated moral philosopher in the world. His attempt to divest himself of all his personal property brought him into severe conflict with his wife; he left his home in 1910, but caught pneumonia on the way and died in a railway station.*

War and Peace, often called the greatest of all novels, is an account of two noble Russian families during the Napoleonic Wars. The families, which are based upon Tolstoy's own maternal and paternal ancestors, contain a memorable galaxy of fictional characters. Tolstoy's own view of history, explicated at length in the course of the novel, is illustrated by the events of War and Peace; *Tolstoy saw history as an inevitable force, a flow of events not determined by humanity but carrying humanity along with it to an unforeseen destiny.*

The Kreutzer Sonata, published in 1889, is a criticism of the false social and moral premises upon which the institution of marriage is based. The narrator sees himself and his unfortunate wife as victims of the hypocritical attitudes that they had been taught—attitudes which do not take into account the actual sexual and social needs of men and women.

The rise of Napoleon and his years of conquest have their effect on virtually every life in Europe. In Russia, in 1805, there is a tenuous peace, and the nobility seem all but unaffected by the thirteen years of turmoil that have already racked the continent. All too soon, however, they are to be affected by the Corsican whom they now refer to contemptuously as "Bonaparte."

Young, handsome Prince Andrei Bolkonsky finds himself chafing irritably against the strains of marriage. His wife, Lisa, is attractive enough, but her foolish interests and petty concerns drive Andrei into morose fits of silence, in which he longs for freedom. He warns his closest friend, Pierre, against ever marrying.

Pierre is the illegitimate son of the multimillionaire Count Bezukhov. Dissipated, carefree, Pierre pays scant attention to his father, and he is indifferent to the fact that he is not received by whole segments of the Russian nobility.

One who has a special reason for detesting Pierre is Prince Vasili Kuragin, who—unless Bezukhov, who is dying, should legitimatize Pierre at the last minute—stands to inherit all of Bezukhov's millions. As Prince Kuragin is himself an avaricious man, and as his three children—two reckless and debauched sons, Ippolit and Anatol, and a beautiful, vain, and selfish daughter, Elena—have accumulated mountainous debts, he is particularly anxious that Bezukhov and Pierre should not be reconciled.

Pierre finds an ally, however, in Princess Anna Mikhailovna Drubetskoy. Impoverished, Anna Mikhailovna is unable to provide all the expensive luxuries for her son, Boris, that she feels he deserves. Therefore, her mind ever alert to an opportunity for shrewd dealing, she allies herself with Pierre and, by preventing old Bezukhov's will, in which he recognizes Pierre, from falling into Kuragin's hands, helps him assure his inheritance from the Count. As a result, when the Count dies, Pierre becomes the new Count Bezukhov and inherits all of his father's millions; in gratitude to the fawning Anna Mikhailovna, he gives her a generous sum with which she plans to finance her son Boris's future.

Boris himself, a lad of sixteen, is a frequent visitor at the home of Count Rostov, a wealthy nobleman. (His shrewd mother encourages Boris's intimacy with the Rostovs in the hope that he will one day marry Natasha Rostov, and thus gain himself a fortune.) Indeed, young Natasha loves the handsome Boris, and the two youngsters swear eternal fidelity to one another. There is also another pair of adolescent lovers in the household: Nikolai Rostov, Natasha's handsome brother, and Sonya, an orphaned, impoverished second cousin who lives in the house as though she were Rostov's daughter.

War is declared between Napoleon's France and Russia, and young nobles begin to join their regiments. Andrei, delighted to be liberated from the ties of marriage, deposits his pregnant wife, Lisa, at the country estate of his father, the eccentric elder Prince Bolkonsky; and knowing that she will be cared for by his sweet and devoted sister, Princess Maria, Andrei is easy in his mind. Nikolai and Boris, too, go off to the war, and Sonya and Natasha draw together in their girlish admiration of their young, beloved "heroes."

Prince Kuragin, having lost the Bezukhov fortune for himself, determines to secure it for Elena. To that end, he continually arranges for Pierre and Elena to be thrown together, and soon the rich young man is under the spell of the bewitchingly beautiful young woman. Pierre recognizes that he does not love Elena Kuragin—that, indeed, she is a vain and selfish creature. But he cannot resist her physical charms, and he consents to be married to her.

Having settled Elena's fortunes, Kuragin now turns his attention to the future of his son, the amoral spendthrift, Anatol. He takes him to the Bolkonsky country estate, intending to arrange a match between Anatol and Princess Maria. The girl, plain, devout, naïve, falls in love with Anatol, and is about to accept him. But old Prince Bolkonsky, who cannot bear the idea that his daughter will leave him, cruelly makes Maria aware of Anatol's flirtations with Mlle. Bourienne, a French governess in the house; and heartbroken, Maria gives Anatol a refusal.

Meanwhile, Andrei finds on the battlefield a sense of freedom and vitality such as he has long dreamed of. He fights valiantly and recklessly, but at the Battle of Austerlitz, he is grievously wounded, and no word of him reaches the Bolkonsky family for a long time.

In 1806, though the war is still officially in progress, there is, in effect, an armed truce. Nikolai comes home on leave, and though he is delighted to be once again in the bosom of his loving family, he begins to question his feelings for Sonya—particularly since she, poor girl, gives every sign of loving him as steadfastly as ever.

Pierre, his delights in the physical side of his marriage to Elena having long since departed, is made increasingly aware of his wife's infidelities. He sees that she married him only for his money, and that now she scorns him for his hulking physique, his indifference to "society," and his contemplative nature. When Pierre learns that Elena has been carrying on an affair with the rake Dolokhov, Pierre challenges the scoundrel to a duel, and succeeds in wounding him. He then demands that he and Elena live apart, maintaining their marriage in name only.

The delight which prevails in the Rostov household is not shared on the Bolkonsky estate. Lisa's time of confinement has come, and old Prince Bolkonsky and Princess Maria, who are convinced that Andrei has been killed, do not tell Lisa for fear that it will make her delivery more difficult. Even as Lisa lies in childbed, a man suddenly bursts into the house. It is Andrei. His return, however, though it brings joy to his sister and father, has no effect on his wife. She is too immersed in her physical agony even to notice his presence. Within a few hours, Andrei's son, Nikolusha, has been born and Lisa is dead, her frail body crushed by the ordeal of giving birth.

After his duel with Pierre, Dolokhov begins a flirtation with Sonya, but she makes clear that her heart belongs to Nikolai. The immoral Dolokhov then revenges himself by entrapping Nikolai in a card game in which the stakes escalate rapidly. At the end of the game, Nikolai has lost a small fortune to Dolokhov, who insists on being paid immediately. Nikolai must confess his loss to his father, who assures his son that in spite of the family's feeling some financial pinches at the moment, the debt will be paid. Thus it is in deep humiliation that Nikolai returns to his regiment.

When fighting erupts again, the embittered Pierre begins to question the meaning of life. He encounters an aged Mason, Ossip Alekseyevitch Bazdeyev, who initiates him into the rites and philosophies of the Masonic Order. Pierre feels that he is now on the road to finding a satisfying answer to his questions about existence.

Meanwhile Elena, from whom he is estranged, begins a flirtation with Boris. And that young man, having learned as the result of his experiences in the army that success in the world depends upon such things as what society one moves in and which women one flirts with, is overwhelmed with delight at the attention paid him by Elena, for the Countess Bezukhov's salon is considered the brightest in the city.

By 1808 the Czar has made peace with Napoleon, and Russia sides with France in her battles with other nations. This tenuous peace is to last only until 1810—but while it endures, a new sense of serenity settles over Russia.

Because of his belief in the Masonic rules, Pierre believes it incumbent upon him to return to his wife, and he allows himself to be swayed by the cajoling arguments of Prince Kuragin, who urges him to return to Elena. The reunion is not a happy one, however, for Pierre sees readily the relations between Elena and Boris, and he is consumed with jealousy.

With the death of his wife, Andrei finds that a numbness has overcome him. He takes no delight in his child, no pleasure in the affection of his devoted sister; he senses only that he is half-dead. One day, however, he catches a glimpse of a young girl, and this laughing, dark-eyed slip of a thing entrances him. He feels that only one such as she can bring him back to life.

The girl is Natasha Rostov, who has grown from an angular creature into a beautiful, ripening young woman. Indeed, Natasha has already received more than one marriage proposal. Boris, however, has not been among her suitors. He now seeks richer fields in which to graze than those offered by the Rostovs, and his "engagement" to Natasha is broken off.

The sight of Prince Andrei has had upon Natasha a strange effect, and she thinks of him as frequently as he does of her. At the first ball she ever attends, she and Andrei are brought together by their mutual friend, Pierre, and as they dance both realize that they are falling in love. Soon, Andrei is calling upon the Rostovs every day, and at last he makes his proposal. It is agreed that Natasha and he will marry if, after a year's waiting period, neither's mind has changed. In rapture, Andrei goes away for a sojourn in a warmer climate, where it is hoped he will regain his strength. (He has been severely weakened by the ordeal following his being wounded at Austerlitz.)

In 1810, Nikolai once more comes home on leave. Now it is apparent that the Rostov fortunes are seriously diminished, and that soon the family will be in desperate financial straits. Nikolai's mother, Countess Rostov, pleads with him to propose marriage to the beautiful heiress, Julie Kuragin, telling him that it is only through his rich marriage that the family can be saved. Nikolai is not sure of his love for Sonya, but his repugnance at marrying for money coupled with the infectious example of Natasha's romantic pining for the absent Prince Andrei combine to light sparks of love in his heart. To the Countess' dismay, Nikolai declares his love for Sonya, and the cousins are betrothed.

In 1811, frictions between France and Russia become ever greater, and it is apparent that the two nations will soon again be at war with one another.

Pierre, his faith in Freemasonry gone, is, in his inability to find the meaning of life, again driven to a sense of bitter emptiness, and he finds consolation in drink. As for Elena, she too begins to feel unhappiness, and she throws herself into an ever-widening circle of frivolity and recklessness.

Anna Mikhailovna now sees an opportunity to settle her beloved son Boris's future once and for all. She tells him that Anatol is suing for the hand of Julie Kuragin; thus goaded by the thought that so much money shall fall into the hands of a scoundrel, Boris decides to throw Elena over and propose to Julie himself. He is accepted, and finds himself the possessor of a fortune far greater than any he might have dreamed of during those childhood years when he played and flirted with Natasha Rostov.

Natasha, who is visiting in Moscow at the home of the old, eccentric Marya Dmitrievna Akhrisomova, is indifferent to Boris and his new fortune. She has been captivated by the handsome brother of Elena Bezukhov—Anatol Kuragin. And what starts as a harmless flirtation between the two soon grows into a serious situation. The naïve Natasha is sure that because she finds the gay and handsome Anatol attractive she must be in love with him. As for the unprincipled Anatol, he is determined to seduce the beautiful young girl. He makes all sorts of wild promises and proposals, and at last arranges to elope with Natasha and marry her. The girl believes his every word; she has no way of knowing that Anatol is merely toying with her. Indeed, he has been secretly married to a Polish girl whom he had seduced, and the mock marriage ceremony he plans to go through with Natasha has been arranged by a venal defrocked priest.

It is only through the determined intervention of the loyal and high-principled Sonya that the elopement is thwarted. Sonya and Marya Dmitrievna send for Pierre, whom they know they can trust, and he handles the situation masterfully, silencing the gossiping tongues of Moscow, arranging for Anatol to leave the city at once, and convincing Natasha that Anatol is no more than a scoundrel.

Natasha, overwhelmed at what she has done, writes to Andrei breaking off her engagement, and swallows arsenic.

Fortunately she is saved—again by Sonya and Marya Dmitrievna; but it is only in Pierre that Natasha feels she has a friend. As for Pierre, he is both horrified and thrilled to find that he is falling in love with Natasha.

In June 1812, Napoleon invades Russia. Andrei, in despair over his loss of Natasha, goes back to war, hoping to lose himself in the excitement of battle. His only emotion now is hatred for Anatol Kuragin, and he determines to track down the scoundrel who has robbed him of his happiness, even if he must go to the ends of the earth. Anatol, however, suspects Andrei's plans, and manages continually to elude him.

Nikolai, like Andrei, finds war a thrilling and exciting experience. He writes with pleasure to Sonya of all his daring exploits. (He is now a captain of cavalry.) War, however, becomes ever more intense, and Napoleon makes greater and greater gains, leveling all before him and burning all behind him.

Word soon reaches the Bolkonsky country estate that Napoleon's troops are only a day's march away, and that all must flee to safety. Princess Maria is grateful that her beloved father, Prince Bolkonsky, dies on the eve of the French army's arrival, so that he never knows how grievously his country is suffering. The death delays her departure, however, and it is only through the miraculous appearance of a handsome young Russian officer that she is able to make good her escape with Andrei's young son. The officer is Nikolai Rostov. By the time Nikolai and Maria arrive at their destination, they are in love.

At the battle of Semenovskoye, Andrei is again wounded, and he is taken into a makeshift operating tent. There is no anesthetic, and Andrei faints from the pain of the operation. When he comes to, he hears from the next operating table the agonized screams of a man whose leg has just been amputated. He looks over and sees that the victim is none other than Anatol Kuragin. Andrei is amazed to find no hatred in his own heart, but only forgiveness for the mutilated soldier.

Napoleon's advances are steady, and Russia's plight continually worsens. After defeating the Russians disastrously at Borodino, just outside of Moscow, Napoleon marches upon the city itself, and the Russians believe that the end has come.

Elena, in Petersburg, has impetuously converted to Roman Catholicism, and is determined to marry someone other than

Pierre. Her only problem is deciding which of two suitors to accept. She writes a fatuous letter to Pierre, demanding a divorce, and waits anxiously for an answer.

This letter does not reach Pierre, however, for he is no longer at his home, but is roaming about the streets of Moscow, one thought burning in his brain: that he himself must assassinate Napoleon and thus save Russia.

In their flight from Moscow, the Rostovs take into their wagon as many wounded Russian soldiers as they can, for these men would otherwise be left to the advancing enemy. It is only after several days of travel that Natasha discovers that one of the men in their party is the grievously injured Prince Andrei. Courageously, quietly, she goes to him, and in silence she reads forgiveness and love in his eyes. From that day forward, she becomes his devoted nurse.

Pierre, in a half-crazed state, wanders about the streets of Moscow, watching the looting, pillaging, and incendiarism. But he does not ever succeed in seeing Napoleon, whom he wishes to kill; and, instead, he is taken prisoner by the French.

When winter sets in, Napoleon's army is forced by food shortage and low morale to begin its march from Moscow, and the severity of the Russian snows begins to reverse the French Emperor's fortunes.

In Petersburg, Elena, driven to desperation by the persistent silence of Pierre about her proposed divorce, takes an overdose of drugs and dies.

Nikolai, at Voronezh, again meets Princess Maria Bolkonsky, and finds that he loves her as much as ever. But his family is now impoverished, and Maria is wealthy, and he fears that she will think that he loves her for her money. Moreover, he feels himself bound by his pledge to Sonya, and so he does not propose to her.

Like a miracle, a letter arrives from Sonya just as Nikolai is about to leave Voronezh. In it, she releases him from his pledge to her, and gives him the happy news that Andrei is safe and recovering. Thus, Nikolai and Maria are both made happy, and they pledge their love to one another before Nikolai rejoins his men at the front.

What Nikolai does not understand is that Sonya has released him from his promise only at the importuning of Countess Rostov, who is more anxious than ever that Nikolai make a rich marriage. Moreover, Sonya believes that because it now seems clear that Andrei and Natasha will soon marry, and because there is a law banning double interfamilial alliances, it will prove impossible for Nikolai and Maria to marry, anyway.

After receiving Sonya's letter, Princess Maria goes to the Rostovs', to be with her wounded brother. She and Natasha are united through their mutual love of Andrei, and the two women plan to nurse him back to health.

Pierre is kept prisoner by the French for four long, bitter weeks. But during this period a light breaks in his soul, and he at last finds peace. With the arrival of winter and Napoleon's imminent defeat, it seems certain that Pierre will be shot. Miraculously, however, he is saved, and is forced to march in the ranks of prisoners as the French army leaves Moscow.

The French troops, however, find that marching out of Moscow is not as easy as marching in. Weakened and demoralized, they are continually assaulted by Russian troops, and in one battle after another, the French ranks are decimated. In one battle, the Russians liberate all of their countrymen whom the French have held prisoners, and Pierre finds himself free. The same battle, however, sees the death of Petya Rostov, Natasha's little brother, the pride of the family who had gone to war against his parents' will.

News of Petya's death drives Countess Rostov mad, and is the final divisive influence in the family, which has long been crumbling under the strain of war. For only one person is the Countess's madness a blessing, and that is Natasha. Andrei, in spite of the loving ministrations of Maria and Natasha, has died, and since his death Natasha has been little better than dead herself. Now Natasha is revived by her mother's need of her attention and loving care, and she is able once again to face the business of living. In work Natasha finds her salvation.

Returning to Moscow, the Rostovs begin to rebuild their old fortunes. Fortunately the Bolkonsky mansion has been spared by the departing French, and Maria is able to help the Rostovs make their new beginning. It is at Maria's Moscow home that Pierre once more meets Natasha. And before long, Princess Maria has read both their hearts, and urges Pierre to hope. Natasha, she says, has not forgotten Andrei; but she will forget one day. And even now, says Maria, without knowing it, Natasha loves Pierre.

By 1813, Moscow is rebuilt, and life proceeds there almost as though there had never been a Corsican named Bonaparte. In time, Natasha marries Pierre, and the two find true happiness in one another—albeit in a quiet and settled spirit far different from the high-pitched passions and romantic fancies of their earlier years. With the coming of children, their lives assume a placid glow of contentment and mutual fulfillment.

Following the death of old Count Rostov, Nikolai assumes his father's debts, and with hard work he soon manages to improve the family's lot. At last, he marries Maria, and welcomes Andrei's son, Nikolusha, into his home as his own son.

But it is Pierre that Nikolusha loves best, and it is Pierre whom he asks endless questions about his idol, a man he never knew: his father, Prince Andrei Bolkonsky.

THE KREUTZER SONATA

Leo Tolstoy

In a carriage on a provincial Russian train, several passengers have been in each other's company for more than twenty-four hours; and, as is frequently the case in such circumstances, a general conversation springs up among them.

The topic turns to love, and one of the passengers—a cigarette-smoking lady—declares that mutual love is the only valid basis for marriage. If a man and woman do not love each other, why should they remain shackled to each other? The other passengers agree and, thus encouraged, the woman waxes enthusiastic on her subject.

Suddenly she is rudely interrupted by a passenger who has heretofore remained silent. Love, he says, is nonsense; what people imagine to be love is merely lust disguised—and, besides, it never lasts more than an hour, a week, a few months at most.

The woman begins remonstrating with the stranger, but he will not be put off. Indeed, he becomes quite voluble—but suddenly he shuts himself off by saying that the company has probably guessed his identity and wishes no more to listen to him. No, the others protest, they do not know who he is. The man introduces himself as Pozdnyshev, an acquitted wife-killer. At this announcement, silence descends on the carriage. At the next stop, the cigarette-smoking lady and her companion get off the train. . . .

As the train starts up, one of the passengers, a young man, sits down across from Pozdnyshev, and agrees to listen to his story.

From childhood, Pozdnyshev says, his life has been warped by the hypocrisy and viciousness of the polite society in which he was raised. Men are but beasts—and to disguise their lasciviousness and baseness from themselves, they concoct elaborate theories and rationalizations to justify their vicious conduct. Sexual gratification is healthy for young men, yes, even necessary, they say. And the doctors—for their own gain—repudiate truth and tell this same lie which society wishes to hear. It is normal for every young man to gratify his lusts—it is even encouraged. The governments sponsor bawdy houses.

It was in one of these houses that at the age of fifteen Pozdnyshev had debased himself for the first time.

Not that he had then realized the wickedness of what he was about. No, that was long before he had reasoned out this whole matter of sexuality and its evil influence, its all-embracing grasp on man's life. No, at that time he considered what he was doing most normal—even worth while, if you will.

Oh, the cant of a society that encourages young men to pursue such experiences, and then pretends—when the young men waltz in drawing rooms and whisper to innocent virgins —that the men are so pure!

Thus Pozdnyshev lived until he was thirty. At that age, he began to look for a wife. He was not amazed, he says, at the idiotic discrepancies of his behavior: he, a libertine, ever on the lookout for the woman who should arouse his passions yet be a model of unsullied innocence! Not that there can be such creatures, he now understands. God knows women are not pure; even the virgins are little better than prostitutes —only less open, more subtle and hypocritical.

He found the girl—a beauty!—and fell madly, rhapsodically

in love with her. They were betrothed. Such purity, such innocence, such beauty, such loftiness! But they had nothing to say to each other when they had finished discussing arrangements for their home-to-be. (And the indecency of *that!* Society thinks it quite proper that a girl should speak by the hour about sheets and pillowcases, mattresses and blankets!) And because he and the girl ate too much rich food and spent their time in idleness, what could one expect but that their passion for each other should grow?

They were married. The honeymoon—what an ironic misnomer that is!—was a disaster. Vile, shameful, pitiable, and, worst of all, unspeakably boring. The only moments of communication between young Pozdnyshev and his bride were when they were behaving like animals. The honeymoon—ha!—is nothing but official and approved sanction for the practice of uncontrolled lewdness.

As early as the fourth day of the honeymoon, his young bride picked a quarrel with him on the most stupid of grounds. At first, Pozdnyshev was at a loss to understand. Did she not love him? Was not marriage rapture? But at last he, too, saw the truth: marriage was farce, not rapture.

Soon he was enmeshed in a pattern of behavior that was to become permanent. There would be a petty quarrel with his wife—sometimes provoked by her, sometimes by himself. It would be resolved eventually by their physical embraces. But then, when the passion was over, the quarrel—or another —would break out afresh. And, truly, it was through his passion for his wife, says Pozdnyshev, that he killed her, for he used her at his will, never leaving her alone, regardless of her pregnancies, the nursing of her children. And this demand that a woman forever yield to her husband's desires—which he now recognizes to have been insane, and contrary to natural law—is promulgated and approved by society. Yes, and by the doctors! And because he was not committing adultery with other women, the young husband Pozdnyshev thought he was a model and virtuous husband. In reality, he sees now, he was a pig.

Ironically enough, through the whole of his married life, though he hated his wife more and more with every passing year, Pozdnyshev suffered from an insane jealousy. At first he was jealous of other men; then he was jealous of his own children, of the attention that their mother lavished upon them. His children! What a laugh, what a lie it is to say that children are a gift from God, as everyone says in society. Children are a curse, they are brought into the world to satisfy their parents' vanity and lust!

By the end of the fourth year of their marriage, Pozdnyshev and his wife had agreed tacitly that they hated each other, and their quarrels grew more intense. Their hatred would be temporarily overlaid with passion, but then it would blaze again; and the more violent their love-making, the more intense the hatred that followed.

For the children's sake, she claimed—but in reality for her own sake—his wife insisted that they move to the city. For a while the mechanics of hiring a house, of furnishing, of decorating occupied their attention and effected a truce between them. But the hatred and the boredom and the passion and the hatred and the boredom began again. It was like a trap to young Pozdnyshev, a trap!

During their second winter in the city, Pozdnyshev's wife became ill, and the doctors advised her to have no more children. To that end, they showed her how she could continue to indulge her husband's senses and her own without the danger or difficulty of becoming pregnant. Yes, screams Pozdnyshev to his traveling companion, it was the doctors—those eminent men of science and truth and nature—who helped him and his wife to practice their vileness in spite of God.

Her childbearing days over, the woman began to regain her looks. Though now no longer young, she still was pretty, plump, and rosy. It was at this time that men began again to notice her.

One in particular—a society violinist, vile, dandified, Frenchified—seemed to take particular notice. And Pozdnyshev, who knew only two emotions toward his wife—hatred and jealousy—for some perverse reason found himself fanning their acquaintance. He encouraged the man to come to his house to play—Pozdnyshev's wife was fond of playing the piano, and he took a fiendish delight in the maddening duets these two played behind the door of the music room. But hatred and jealousy grew in Pozdnyshev's bosom, for there was no doubt of the meaning of the glances that flew between the pair. They were already committing adultery by looks!

Once Pozdnyshev burst out at his wife in jealous rage over the violinist—and for the first time in months she smiled at her husband, and assured him that he was imagining things. They made up their quarrel in embraces . . . but soon Pozdnyshev's doubts raised themselves again. Again there were scenes, hysterics, recriminations. His wife tried to commit suicide more than once. Oh, it was madness!

One day, Pozdnyshev had to leave the city on business. On taking his leave from the violinist, the dandy intimated that he, too, would be away from the city at the same time. Pozdnyshev was able to leave in a calm frame of mind.

After only one night away, however, he suspected great treachery, and changed all his plans so that he could return home. He arrived unexpected and on opening the front door of his house, saw the violinist's fine cloak hanging upon the coatrack. So, he would catch the guilty couple unsuspecting!

He heard their voices in the dining room, and tiptoed thither. Suddenly he was terrified and frightened. If only it were a dream! But by some mad impulse he was propelled forward, and suddenly he flung open the dining-room door. The guilty couple started up. Their faces bore an expression of complete horror.

Instantly the couple tried to pretend that nothing was wrong. "We were not expecting you. . . ." "We were having some music. . . ."

Dashing for his wife, Pozdnyshev seized her by the throat and whipped out a dagger. The violinist tried to stop him, but realized he could do nothing and fled. Violently Pozdnyshev stabbed his wife, again and again, until she slumped to the floor.

The next morning, the police came for him, and brought him to the bedside of his dying wife. Thinking that she wished to confess her wickedness, he went to her; but she, with her last breaths, merely fired at him a volley of hatred and abuse.

At the trial, he was acquitted of murder, on the grounds that his wife was an adulteress and that in killing her he had merely defended his own honor. His wife's sister, however, has taken his children from him to raise as her own. And now, they, too, are to grow up in a world of sin, of shame, of hypocrisy, cant, viciousness, evil. . . .

Pozdnyshev sighs. "If I had known as a young man what I know now about life, about truth, I would not have married her, I would. . . ." But he realizes that he has talked a long time, and the young man is probably bored. "Excuse me, excuse me," he mutters. The young man shakes his hand, as the train pulls into the station.

"Excuse me. . . ."

NOVELS OF VARIOUS COUNTRIES

THE GOLDEN ASS

Apuleius

Lucius Apuleius was born in Numidia (now part of Algeria) about
A.D. *125. Virtually all that is known of him is based on his own*
Apologia, in which he claimed to have been educated in Carthage
and Athens, to have traveled the ancient world studying its reli-
gions, and to have married the widowed mother of his best friend.
He wrote in Latin. He probably spent most of his life in Carthage,
where The Golden Ass, *or* Metamorphoses, *as the author titled it,*
was written. Drawn from well-known sources, The Golden Ass *is*
one of the most delightful prose romances of ancient times, and it
has been over the centuries an inspiration for subsequent authors.
Its qualities of humor and satire, ordinarily extremely perishable
literary features, have survived quite intact to this day. Of Apuleius'
other writings, some philosophical fragments remain; no trace can
be found of the many poems he claimed to have written. Apuleius
probably died in Carthage about 175.

On his way to Thessaly, young Lucius Apuleius falls in with
two strangers who are debating tales of witchcraft. One of
the young men scoffs, but the second swears that he himself
has been victim of several witches' pranks. Lucius agrees
that witches abound in this world—women capable of wreak-
ing all sorts of havoc, from turning a man into an insect to
moving an entire city to a distant mountaintop. Although he
has a certain dread of such women, Lucius is nonetheless
anxious to reach Thessaly, long considered the home of
witches, and to see one of them perform her tricks.

Reaching the city of Hypata, Lucius goes to the house of
Milos to deliver to him letters from his friend Demeas of
Corinth. Milos invites Lucius to accept the hospitality of his
house during his sojourn in Hypata, and Lucius accepts—
though he soon regrets his acceptance, for Milos proves to be
as stingy a miser as Lucius has ever known, and the young
man sees that Milos sets a very meager table. He takes heart,
however, from the fact that Milos' wife Pamphile is a warm
and beautiful woman, and further, from the presence of

Milos' most winsome serving girl, Fotis. Perhaps, he thinks, his stay at Milos' house will not prove so unpleasant after all.

Encountering his foster aunt Byrrhaena in the streets of Hypata one day, Lucius goes to her house to dine, and there he is entertained by many tales of witches. His aunt tells him that one of the most feared witches of all in Hypata is none other than Pamphile, and she warns Lucius against falling in love with the woman. Lucius agrees that he must not do such a thing, but he fails to confess to his aunt that he has already made the beautiful maid Fotis his mistress, and that she is so perfect a lover that he wishes to seek no other. Byrrhaena reminds Lucius that the following day is to be devoted to celebrations in honor of the god Laughter, and she sends the youth on his way.

Approaching Milos' house in the dark, Lucius sees three brigands about to break down Milos' door, and so Lucius draws his sword and kills them. The next day he is arrested for the murder, and dragged in fear and humiliation to the public theater to be tried. After a terrifying ordeal, Lucius is at last made aware that the men were only pretending to be brigands, and the corpses were only stuffed clothes—indeed, the whole plot has been an elaborate hoax contrived in honor of the god Laughter. And so the youth is freed to return to Milos' house.

Lucius has long pestered Fotis to let him watch Pamphile when she is about her witchcraft, and at last Fotis agrees, swearing him first to secrecy. That night Fotis leads Lucius to a corridor near the top of the house. Through a chink in the door, Lucius watches as Pamphile undresses herself, rubs her body with salve taken from a small casket, and turns into an owl who flies away. His excitement at this witchcraft is so great that nothing will do but that he too must turn into an owl. Reluctantly Fotis fetches a casket of salve. Doing as he has seen Pamphile do, Lucius undresses himself, rubs his body with salve taken from the casket—and feels a horrible sensation. Fotis has made a mistake and brought the wrong salve. Instead of turning into a bird, Lucius finds himself turning into an ass.

Recovering from her first fright, Fotis tells Lucius that he can be turned back into his manly shape by eating fresh roses. She promises to gather some for him the very first thing next morning, and unhappily Lucius allows himself to be led into the stable for the night.

As luck would have it, however, that very night a band of thieves arrives to rob Milos' house. They steal, loot, and plunder—and Milos being so wealthy a miser, they gather more booty than they can carry away by themselves. Therefore the thieves steal Lucius—along with another ass and Lucius' own horse which are with him in the stable—and load the animals with their treasures. Thus, Lucius gets his first taste of what life is like for an ass—and it is not a pleasant one.

At last the thieves reach their hideaway, and Lucius is turned out to pasture. His first thought is to go and eat some roses in a nearby garden—but the gardener surprises him and beats him mercilessly. Lucius then decides that it would be better to wait until he gets away from the thieves before eating roses and transforming himself back into human shape; for surely the thieves would kill him instantly if he were to appear in manly form.

When the thieves go off on their next expedition, they leave Lucius behind. On their return, he sees that this trip was not one of looting but one of kidnaping, for they bring back to their den a beautiful maiden whom they intend to hold for ransom. The maiden weeps piteously, for she has been stolen on the very day of her wedding. To comfort her a little, the old woman who keeps house for the brigands tells the girl the pitiful and beautiful ancient tale of Cupid and Psyche. But the girl remains in misery and will not leave off her weeping.

Lucius takes great pity on this maiden in distress, and when an opportune moment comes, he breaks free of his rope and goes to her. The girl is on his back in an instant, and the two go galloping down the road, both eager to escape the wicked robbers. These men, however, overtake the girl and the ass upon the road and take them once more into custody. In punishment they determine to kill both the maiden and Lucius, and they devote a great deal of time to a debate about the most suitably horrible death they can devise. Poor Lucius shakes in his hoofs.

Before the death sentence can be executed, however, a handsome, robust young man enters the brigands' camp and says that he wants to join their band. He introduces himself as the renowned thief Haemus the Thracian, and he is speedily welcomed into the band. When a scout arrives from Hypata with the news that the robbery of Milos' house has been blamed on a house guest of Milos', one Lucius Apuleius, who had disappeared with his horse the very night of the robbery, the brigands, delighted that no one is on their trail, plan a celebration. Soon the camp is filled with merriment, and Lucius is disgusted to notice that even the captive maiden's spirits are lifted. She has smiles and even a few kisses for the handsome thief Haemus the Thracian.

When Haemus serves around the flasks of wine, however, Lucius notices that he himself does not drink, and suddenly he realizes that this Haemus is none other than the bridegroom of the captive maiden. Sure enough, all of the brigands soon drop off into drugged slumber, and Haemus makes off with his bride. He returns shortly with a band of police, and all of the brigands are killed. As for Lucius, he is taken as a special prize for the girl, for she has told her husband about how the ass had nobly tried to help her escape.

Now Lucius expects to live a life of ease, because the girl's parents have supplied money so that the good ass who helped their daughter may be put out to pasture for the rest of his days. Such bliss is not to be, however, for the man who takes Lucius in charge turns him over to a cruel woodcutter's boy, and Lucius is treated miserably by the lad—scourged, overloaded, and worst of all (for though an ass, Lucius retains his human sensibilities) accused of lechery. The boy, however, gets his just deserts when he is rent limb from limb by a vicious bear.

Lucius hopes now that his good friends Tlepolemis and Charite (for those are the real names of Haemus the Thracian and the young damsel kidnaped by the robbers) will come to his aid; but a messenger brings word that they are both dead as the result of their friendship with the perfidious seducer Thrassylus.

Now Lucius' ill-fortune overtakes him in earnest, for he passes from owner to owner, each more cruel and inhuman than the next. He is often faint with hunger and abuse, overworked to the point of death, and in agony from the beatings he sustains. His one source of comfort in life is the chance that is afforded him, in ass's guise, to become familiar with all natures of men and conditions of life; and Lucius is continually surprised by the evidence of lechery, deceit, and hypocrisy practiced on every hand. Most degrading of all is his service at the hands of a group of so-called priests, who use the statue of a Syrian goddess as a cover for the most loathsome abominations and thefts and deceptions of which Lucius believes man to be capable.

These priests, however, are finally revealed for the vile sinners that they are, and are put to death by an irate populace. Lucius is then sold to two brothers, the first kindly masters he has known since becoming an ass. One is a baker, the other a cook—and in their house Lucius is at last able to eat the delicacies for which he has not lost his human taste, instead of the rye and hay which he so much loathes.

The improved diet brings renewed luster to Lucius' coat and increased jauntiness to his step, and soon he is as handsome an ass as ever lived. Word spreads of his amazing taste for the food of human tables, and a wealthy captain summons Lucius to be brought into his presence.

The captain is so delighted with Lucius' beauty and human appetite that he buys him and makes a special pet of him. Soon, Lucius has been trained to do a host of wonderful tricks that amaze all witnesses, and he attracts a wide following. (The tricks, of course, are not so amazing when one considers the ass's human intelligence and spirit.)

Of all who see him, the most impressed with Lucius is a beautiful matron, who falls deeply in love with the ass. She bribes Lucius' keeper to bring the animal to her house one night, and there, after being wined and dined on all manner of dainties, the woman makes herself Lucius' mistress. The nights of love are repeated frequently, and Lucius finds life at last blissful.

Word soon spreads, however, of the amazing ass's new talent, and it is planned that Lucius shall give a public exhibition of his amatory prowess with a human woman at the theater. Engaged as his partner for the exhibition is a vile harlot who is under sentence of death.

Lucius' sensibilities are profoundly shocked at the contemplation of the show he is expected to give, and every fiber within him resists the idea. Therefore, just before he is to be brought out into the theater, Lucius makes a dash for freedom. As all eyes are focused on the stage, where a magnificent tableau is in progress, Lucius makes good his escape.

He does not stop running until night falls and he is many miles from the city.

Lying down in an empty field, Lucius prays to the queen of all goddesses in all her aspects and under all her names, begging her to restore him to human form. He realizes that his life as an ass has taught him much of value about the world, and he is now prepared to live a holy life. In a vision, the goddess appears to Lucius and responds to his prayers. She promises that the next day Lucius will witness a grand procession in which will march a priest bearing a garland of fresh roses. These Lucius must eat, and he will then be restored to human form.

The next day, all transpires as the goddess had prophesied. On tasting the proffered roses, Lucius feels a profound physical change taking place within himself, and in a few moments he is standing before the priest in his own shape, a man restored.

After notifying his family that he is indeed alive and safe, Lucius becomes a priest in the service of the great queen goddess, and devotes the rest of his life to holiness and prayer, always remembering and benefiting from the lessons he learned during his life as an ass.

THE TALE OF GENJI

Lady Murasaki

Murasaki Shikibu was born in Japan, about A.D. 978. Her father belonged to a lesser branch of a powerful feudal family. She sat in on the Chinese lessons which her father gave her brother, and thus learned the Chinese language, an extraordinary accomplishment for a girl at that time. Murasaki married at some time between 994 and 998, bore two daughters, and was widowed in 1001. At the age of twenty-six, she was placed in the service of the Empress Akiko, a girl of sixteen. From a diary which Murasaki kept until the year 1010, we learn that she felt rather stifled at the court of the Empress, and would have preferred to serve one of the livelier great ladies of Japan. The date of Murasaki's death is not known; she was alive in 1025, but it is believed that by 1031 she had died.

The Tale of Genji was probably begun in 1001, and completed while Lady Murasaki was at the Court of the Empress. It consists of six parts which bear the collective title The Tale of Genji; this is also the title of the first part, which is here summarized. The

*English translations of the work were published between 1925 and
1933. Murasaki's contemporaries knew the book, and it was discussed and read at the Imperial Court. It is considered one of the
very greatest works in the literature of Japan, and has been compared, as examination of a decadent nobility from a psychological
and temporal viewpoint, with Marcel Proust's* Remembrance of
Things Past.

When Kiritsubo, beloved young concubine of the Emperor,
gives birth to a son, the child proves to be the most beautiful
ever seen in Japan. From infancy the boy makes such a deep
impression on the Emperor, and stirs such love in his heart,
that he wishes to appoint the child Heir Apparent. This he
is unable to do, however, because the Empress, Kokiden, is
adamant that her own child shall someday become Emperor.

Kokiden's wrath against the newborn child extends to the
baby's mother, Kiritsubo, of whom she has always been jealous. Soon young Kiritsubo's life is made an agony by the
petty meannesses and tricks perpetrated upon her by Kokiden
and Kokiden's ladies, and before long she goes into a decline.
When her son is only three years old, Kiritsubo dies, and the
Emperor is prostrate with grief.

Several years later, the Emperor takes as his concubine
the Princess Fujitsubo, because she reminds him so much of
the dead Kiritsubo. She becomes the special friend of little
Genji, as Kiritsubo's son is called, and her beauty, as well as
her resemblance to his mother, makes an indelible impression on the little prince's mind.

Upon reaching the age of twelve, Genji goes through the
ceremony of initiation and leaves childhood for manhood.
His sponsor for the ceremony is the Emperor's trusted advisor, the Minister of the Left. Husband to the Emperor's
sister, the Minister of the Left has an only daughter, the
beautiful and noble Aoi. Though the girl is four years older
than Genji, it is agreed that they shall be betrothed. After
the marriage ceremony, however, Genji returns to the palace;
for the Emperor, who loves this son best of all his sons, cannot do without Genji's presence. Aoi, feeling herself rejected,
and indignant that her husband is a mere child, remains in
her father's house. And Genji, though he is relieved not to
have to live with Aoi, whom he finds cold, is not happy at
the palace. As a man, he may no longer have the free access

to the women's quarters which he was allowed as a child, and therefore he now seldom sees Fujitsubo.

When Genji is seventeen, people note that his visits to Aoi are few and far between. From this they conclude that he is not interested in women. But this is not so. It is Genji's lot that he should be attracted only to ladies who would be unsuitable for a Prince of the Blood Royal to take as mistresses, so he must conduct his amours most privately and circumspectly. It is at this time of his life that he forms a liaison with the Princess Rokujo, a lady considerably his senior. She is the widow of the Emperor's brother, Prince Zembo, and she is to play an important part in Genji's life.

Genji and his close friends, young men of the court, frequently talk far into the night about the different kinds of women in the world, and about which make the most suitable concubines and mistresses. Genji has little to contribute to such discussions, but he listens eagerly—particularly to the tales of his closest friend, To no Chugo, brother of Aoi. To no Chugo is considered an accomplished lover, and Genji learns much about women from him. Especially interesting is the story of a beautiful girl whom To no Chugo had made his mistress, but whom he had later discarded; the girl is reputed to have borne a child by this liaison, but To no Chugo has never been able to find a trace of either mother or child. . . .

One night, because of the inauspicious position of the stars, Genji is forced to stay in the house of one of his noble gentlemen-in-waiting, Ki no Kami. There he sees Utsusemi, second wife of Ki no Kami's father, and he falls desperately in love with her. The lady, though she seems flattered, will not yield to him.

Hoping to further his own cause, Genji persuades Ki no Kami to arrange for Utsusemi's little brother to become his page boy. And the lad does serve as a useful intermediary, carrying letters, poems, and gifts back and forth between his master Genji and his sister Utsusemi. Utsusemi remains adamant, however, in not yielding to Genji's supplications.

One night the page boy sneaks Genji into the house of his sister, and there Genji observes his beloved Utsusemi playing a game of go with another lady, one who seems coarser but more spirited than his beloved. That night he slips into Utsusemi's bedroom, but she has heard him coming and has disappeared. When he lies down beside the woman he finds there, she proves to be Utsusemi's guest, Nokiba no Ogi. Genji makes her his mistress. The next day he pretends to Nokiba no Ogi great love for her, and promises to write to her when he can do so without being discovered. And, indeed, he remembers the night and the woman with great pleasure. But it is the filmy scarf of the unyielding Utsusemi that he takes away with him in the morning as a token.

One night, returning from a visit to Princess Rokujo, Genji stops to visit the home of his old childhood nurse. In the house next door, there lives a mysterious lady, reputed to be a great beauty, and Genji determines to make her his mistress. With his nurse's son, Koremitsu, as intermediary, Genji soon gains entrance to the house. The girl there is indeed a beauty, and Genji falls in love with her, visiting her often in the dark of night to possess her. Her manner is aloof, however, and he resents his mistress's behavior; she has guessed that he is Prince Genji, and she is perturbed that he should continue to come to her only in darkness and with his face veiled. She therefore refuses to tell Genji her name.

At last Genji determines to take the woman to a deserted palace that he owns in the country, there to reveal himself and to spend a full day freely with her. The girl agrees, and with her maid Ukon and Koremitsu, she goes with Genji to the isolated palace. Their hours are at first blissful, but suddenly Genji is wakened from sleep to find a phantom woman bending over his mistress, who stares in terror. Instantly the phantom disappears, but the girl goes into a fit and it is clear that she is bewitched. Ukon and Koremitsu try to summon help, but it is too late. The beautiful girl who has never revealed her name to Genji dies. Koremitsu hurriedly makes secret arrangements for the girl's burial. Genji is desolate with grief, as is Ukon. From the weeping maid he learns that the dead girl was Yugao, the same girl loved and then rejected by To no Chugo. Genji resolves to make Ukon a lady-in-waiting at court, and to find Yugao's daughter in order to raise her in wealth and comfort at the palace of the Emperor.

One day Genji falls seriously ill with a fever, and at last it is decided that he must be spirited away to a distant province, where lives an old holy man reputed to be able to work wondrous cures. The holy man's medicinal herbs take effect, and Genji feels that he is getting better. During his period of recuperation, Genji encounters a middle-aged nun sitting with a little girl of about ten. The child makes a profound impression upon Genji, so beautiful is she. She reminds him of Fujitsubo—and indeed, the little girl proves to be Fujitsubo's niece, illegitimate daughter of the former Emperor's son, Prince Hyobukyo. Genji begs to be allowed to adopt the child, but the nun—grandmother to the girl—fears that Genji wishes to make the little one his concubine, and therefore she refuses.

Soon after, the girl's grandmother dies, and Genji, who has not been able to forget the child, goes to the girl's nurse, Shonagon, and presses his request for the child. Shonagon is too fearful to surrender the child, but she allows Genji to visit often. One night, however, Genji learns that Prince Hyobukyo has decided to claim his little girl, and rather than let the child go to another, Genji takes her away. Shonagon has no choice but to go along with Genji, and be installed in his palace. Hyobukyo, upon hearing from the house servants only that Shonagon has gone away with the child, thinks that the nurse fears the treatment the child would receive from his own wife, and he is not too dispirited, though he hopes someday to find his child.

Genji calls the little girl Murasaki, and he takes great delight in her. Never has he seen such perfection, such delicacy, such childish sweetness. He and Murasaki are like playmates, and spend hours together painting pictures, building dollhouses, and playing games. To Shonagon, however, Genji confides that someday he will make Murasaki his mistress, and that he will always love her.

Despite the pleasant hours spent with the little girl, Genji is still despondent over the death of Yugao, and he feels utterly desolate. Utsusemi continues to reject his advances, Fujitsubo is all but inaccessible, Aoi is cold and distant—is there none to love him, none that he can love? It is at this point that he hears of a mysterious princess whom none has seen. She is Suyetsumuhana—and though Myobu, the court lady from whom Genji first hears of the princess, urges him not to attempt a conquest, Genji resolves that he will love Suyetsumuhana. At first the lady resists all overtures, but Genji persists; finally she agrees to meet him, but only on condition that they talk through a closed door. All of the lady's shy and eccentric demands only increase Genji's pas-

sion, and he becomes more insistent than ever. When he finally succeeds in meeting the princess, however, he realizes
his folly, for she is graceless, dull, old-fashioned, and—worst
of all—ugly. Genji is particularly revolted by her long red
nose. It takes all of his ingenuity to withdraw from a relationship which he had pursued so relentlessly, and he is
ashamed of himself. Two other mistresses with whom he becomes briefly involved are an aging, foolish flirt of a serving
woman, and Princess Oborojukiyo, youngest sister of Kokiden,
the Empress. But neither *amour* brings him any satisfaction. . . .

Through a fortuitous set of circumstances, Genji is at last
able to consummate the great love of his life when he spends
a night with his father's concubine, the beautiful Fujitsubo.
Soon, however, the blissful memory of love turns to ashes for
them both, for Fujitsubo discovers that as a result of their
love, she is with child. Fortunately things are arranged so
that it appears that the child is the Emperor's, and no one
questions this. But when Fujitsubo and Genji look at the
child, both see his striking resemblance to Genji.

The Emperor, for the first time since Genji's birth, finds
himself interested in one of his newborn children; this baby
is a paragon! When he decides to surrender the throne to
Kokiden's son, it is this child of Genji's and Fujitsubo's that
is named the new Heir Apparent. Kokiden lives on at the
great palace as Empress Mother, her son now having
ascended the throne, and the Emperor and Fujitsubo retire
to their country palace.

Genji has, at last, begun to reconcile himself to Aoi, his
wife, and the hours they spend together are less bitter than
they have been. And when Aoi discovers that she is pregnant,
her coldness melts further, and Genji begins to hope that he
will at last have a loving wife.

The news of Aoi's pregnancy, however, brings unhappiness
to Princess Rokujo, for though Genji has long been a faithful lover, she fears that his new relationship with Aoi will
alienate him from her. Moreover, as her own daughter is to
become Vestal Virgin at Ise, as part of the ceremonies attendant upon the ascendancy of a new Emperor, Princess
Rokujo is to be absent from the Imperial City for a long
time. She is deeply saddened by these changes in her life.

At a street procession, to which crowds have come from all

over the province to see Genji the Shining One pass by in splendor, the servants of Aoi and the servants of Princess Rokujo have an altercation, and Rokujo's carriage is damaged. She does not believe, however, that Genji's wife was in any way responsible for the trouble.

As for Aoi, she is taken suddenly ill after this episode, and the doctors despair of her life. Genji rushes to Aoi's bedside, and even Princess Rokujo offers up prayers for the lady's recovery. The doctors are convinced that Aoi is bewitched, that the spirit of one who hates her has entered her body, and that there is no hope.

Miraculously, however, Aoi's child is born easily and quickly, even earlier than had been predicted, and Aoi takes a turn for the better after the birth of her son. She and Genji are finally reconciled with each other, and Genji looks forward impatiently to her recovery. But it is not to be.

Seemingly calm and contented, Aoi calls for Genji to come to her side one evening. When he approaches, however, he sees with horror that Aoi is indeed possessed. Her expression and her voice are those of another. Terrified, Genji recognizes in his wife the demon of Princess Rokujo. Before he can even scream for help, Aoi is dead.

Princess Rokujo, hearing of Aoi's death, racks her brain for any evil thought she might have had against the woman, and can find none. But she fears that unconsciously she may have been the cause of Aoi's death. Resolving never to see Genji again, she departs from the Imperial City and goes with her daughter to the distant province of Ise.

For a long time Genji is disconsolate and in despair at having lost his wife at precisely the moment he had learned to value her. His only pleasure is in his young son—and in the child, Murasaki, who is now old enough to become his second wife.

DREAM OF THE RED CHAMBER

Tsao Hsueh-chin

Little is known about Tsao Hsueh-chin, author of the Dream of the Red Chamber. *He was born after 1712, and died in 1764. He was a grandson by posthumous adoption of a wealthy patron, but for some reason he had been reduced to poverty by 1742. Although he knew little of the family that adopted him, it has been proven that Dream of the Red Chamber is indeed about that family. Some eighty chapters of the novel were left by the author at the time of his death, and in spite of the claim of one eighteenth-century editor that he had discovered forty more chapters, which he added to the original eighty, modern scholars believe that the eighty original chapters are the only authentic work of the author. The novel had not been intended for publication, and is therefore only more or less edited by the original author. Nevertheless, Dream of the Red Chamber is generally regarded as the greatest Chinese novel. Even for those readers unable to judge its relative worth, it is a rich and complex account of Chinese civilization in the eighteenth century, a civilization which becomes less alien as one's familiarity with the book increases.*

A single stone of the 36,501 gathered by the goddess Nugua to repair the Dome of Heaven remains unused in the labor. The goddess' touch, however, endows the stone with life, and the stone conceives a longing to go into the world and learn how men live. A Buddhist monk and a Taoist priest decide to grant the stone's wish, and for convenience's sake, they transform it into a piece of engraved jade.

When Pao-yu is born with a piece of engraved jade in his mouth, it is recognized by the entire Chia family—the wealthy and influential house into which he has been born—that this child has been singled out by the gods for some special role. Pao-yu is the youngest member of a household numbering some three hundred persons, and his life is so closely intertwined with the lives of the other members of the family and the servants that to tell his story is to tell the story of them all.

The family and servants all live on a great estate in the Capital, which estate comprises the two great Chia mansions, the Ningkuofu and the Yungkuofu. At the head of the family is Pao-yu's grandmother, Mme. Shih, called the Matriarch, for she is the oldest surviving member of the Chia family. All of the Matriarch's hopes for the family reside in her favorite grandson, Pao-yu.

When Pao-yu is still a boy, there comes to live in the Yungkuofu the orphaned granddaughter of the Matriarch, Black Jade, a beautiful but fragile girl. The girl is overwhelmed by the great family—particularly by Phoenix, the shrewd, power-loving wife of Chia Lien, nephew of the Matriarch. (Phoenix is also the niece of Mme. Wang, Pao-yu's mother.) Though the Matriarch has formal authority, it is Phoenix who in reality runs the family's business and financial affairs. Black Jade finds Phoenix formidable, particularly when she learns that one of Phoenix's nicknames is "Black Pepper"—but when the Matriarch assures her that Phoenix is a good person, she is able to relax a bit. Soon she meets Pao-yu, and the meeting is a strange one for both youngsters and has a profound effect upon them; for both Pao-yu and Black Jade believe that they have met before—perhaps in an earlier incarnation. A bond of sympathy springs up between them.

Pao-yu is no less attracted by another of his young female cousins, Precious Virtue. She returns his admiration, and, as she has a golden locket with an inscription which matches that on Pao-yu's powerful jade, it is assumed by the family that the two are destined some day to wed.

Pao-yu's best friend is Chin Chung, the poor brother of Chin-shih, who has committed suicide over her adulterous relations with Pao-yu's uncle, Chia Gen. Chin Chung is accepted into the Chia household to attend the family school, and he is soon a favorite of all. The young man falls in love with a nun at the Water Moon Convent. When his father discovers the liaison, however, he is so incensed that he beats Chin Chung severely. Soon after, the lad dies. Pao-yu is most unhappy at the death of his beloved friend. Indeed, because of his sadness, he is the only one in the family who does not rejoice that Cardinal Spring, his older sister, has been chosen by the Emperor for the signal honor of becoming Imperial Concubine.

Though Pao-yu is a bright boy, he is indolent, and pays no attention to his studies. He is able to get away with this because his father, Chia Cheng, is often away from home on long trips of business and cannot supervise him properly, and because his grandmother, the Matriarch, dotes on him and excuses his lapses of behavior. Thus it happens that Pao-yu spends most of his time in the compound of his girl cousins, Black Jade and Precious Virtue, and in the company of the many pretty serving maids of the Chia household: Purple Cuckoo, Snow Duck, Pervading Fragrance, Bright Design, Musk Moon, Lotus, and Oriole. Black Jade, who is highly sensitive, frequently resents the affectionate attentions lavished upon these girls by Pao-yu—and her resentment is not always without cause, for Pao-yu is a pleasure-loving lad.

Pao-yu is not adored by everyone in the Chia household. One woman, in particular, hates him: Chao Yi, his father's concubine. Because Pao-yu is the son of his father's wife, she thinks, he gets preference over her own son, Chia Huan. (She fails to realize that because her son Chia Huan is a loutish, stupid brute, even were he the son of a wife rather than of a concubine it is doubtful that he would be the preferred one.) Chao Yi also hates Phoenix, because the woman has openly slighted her son. To revenge herself upon these two, Chao Yi bewitches them, and Phoenix and Pao-yu fall ill. It is only through the efficacy of Pao-yu's precious piece of engraved jade that the two recover.

Pao-yu is now a young man. His father, Chia Cheng, returns to the Yungkuofu after a long absence, and is distressed over his son's waywardness. He discovers that because of a flirtation with one of the maids, Golden Bracelet, Pao-yu has inadvertently caused the girl's suicide. (Unfortunately, Chia Cheng hears the story from the treacherous Chia Huan, who grossly exaggerates the details, so that it appears that Pao-yu, who is in fact innocent of any real wrongdoing, had raped the girl and caused her to be beaten.) Added to this is the humiliating revelation by an emissary from the Imperial Palace that Pao-yu has been helping to hide the beautiful actor, Chi-kuan, from the Prince, who would use the young man ill. Enraged, Chia Cheng orders Pao-yu to be bound, and though both his mother, Mme. Wang, and his grandmother, the Matriarch, beg for mercy, Chia Cheng beats his disobedient and errant son mercilessly with a stout bamboo rod. Only the tears of the Matriarch prevent the chastisement from causing the death of her beloved grandson, and Pao-yu is put to bed in great agony. During his convalescence, Pao-yu finds himself more than ever attracted to Black Jade, and the two no longer hide their feelings for each other.

It is at this time that Phoenix learns that she cannot control everything that happens within the Chia family. She is humiliated to find that her weak-willed husband, Chia Lien, has been having an adulterous relationship with the wife of one of the servants. Though he is forced to apologize to his shrewish wife, Chia Lien is still determined to find a pleasurable female companion.

Chia Huan and Chia Lien are not the only men in the family to engage in scandalous conduct. Precious Virtue's brother, Hsueh Pan, is perhaps the most vicious and libertinous of the lot. Therefore he falls under suspicion (by those who do not know of Chia Huan's treachery) for being responsible for the beating administered to Pao-yu. Further, at an entertainment, he sees a beautiful young man who is part of the acting company, and desires to possess him. This young man, Liu Hsiang-lien, is deeply offended at this insult, but pretends to go along with Hsueh Pan's invitation. They meet, by appointment, in a deserted field, and Liu Hsiang-lien beats Hsueh Pan mercilessly, and forces him to abase himself most humiliatingly. As a result, Liu Hsiang-lien is forced to go into hiding.

Now, the good luck and prosperity which have belonged to the house of Chia seem to depart, and one calamity after another befalls the family. Phoenix's husband Chia Lien secretly takes as a concubine a young woman called Er-chieh. Because it is illegal to take a concubine without the consent of one's wife, he hides her in a house outside the Chia estate. Er-chieh has a sister, San-chieh, who has set her heart on marriage to the actor Liu Hsiang-lien. To make her happy, Chia Lien arranges a marriage for the two. When Liu Hsiang-lien discovers the irregularity of Chia Lien's relations with Er-chieh, he breaks his engagement to Er-chieh's sister. At this rejection, San-chieh commits suicide. Her death makes Liu Hsiang-lien recognize what a pearl he has lost, and in remorse he abjures forever the ways of the world.

Phoenix now learns of Chia Lien's relationship with Er-chieh, and insists that the girl be brought to live in the Ning-kuofu. She pretends affection and devotion for her husband's concubine, but in reality she hates the girl and concocts many plots against her. As a result, the girl goes into a decline and soon dies.

As if the shame of these proceedings is not enough for the family, there are new griefs. Hsueh Pan takes to wife a virago who makes life unbearable for all who come near; and Welcome Spring, one of the Matriarch's favorite granddaughters, marries a man from a distant province and goes away from her home forever. Further, Pao-yu's father Chia Cheng has been dismissed from the Imperial Service for incompetence, and Pao-yu's uncle Chia Gen, also of the Imperial Service, is found guilty of graft and corruption. And Cardinal Spring, loved as deeply as ever by her family in spite of her living away from them, falls ill, and her life is despaired of.

Black Jade, who has always been fragile, now goes into a serious decline. It is decided that all must pretend before her that she is to marry Pao-yu, since her affection for the boy is well known. Thus the poor girl takes hope at the precise moment when all hope for her happiness is lost—for Phoenix has decided that Pao-yu must marry none other than Precious Virtue.

Now mysterious omens appear: a begonia tree blossoms during the wrong season, and Pao-yu's jade is lost. It is clear that disaster must soon follow—and, indeed, without his precious jade, Pao-yu loses his mind and lies for weeks in a coma. It is decided that the same ruse that has been practiced upon Black Jade must be used with Pao-yu. Accordingly he is told that he will marry his beloved Black Jade. At the wedding ceremony, however, a veiled Precious Virtue takes Black Jade's place as bride, and she and Pao-yu are married. During the same hour, Black Jade, who has learned of this treachery, dies.

Soon after this, the Matriarch and Phoenix are both called to their eternal rewards after lengthy lives of service to the family.

Pao-yu's jade is mysteriously returned to him by a Buddhist monk and a Taoist priest, and he recovers his health and wits. Though he grieves for his dear Black Jade, he is aware of the vicissitudes that have beset the House of Chia, and he determines to apply himself to his studies. Everyone is delighted at the new Pao-yu who emerges, and hope begins to spring up that the ill-fortunes of the house will now take a turn for the better.

Indeed, the hopes seem justified, for in the Imperial Examinations, Pao-yu scores seventh highest of all the scholars in China, and Chia Lan, his cousin, scores one hundred and thirteenth. Because of these successes from the House of Chia, the Emperor decrees a pardon for Pao-yu's father and uncle, who were dismissed in disgrace from the Imperial Service.

The jubilation at the Ningkuofu and Yungkuofu is cut short, however, when it is discovered that Pao-yu is missing. For on his way home, Pao-yu has met an old Buddhist monk and an old Taoist priest. They tell him that his earthly mission is over, and while Pao-yu's father, Chia Cheng, who has come out to meet his son, looks on in horror, the three figures disappear. They are never seen again.

The fortunes of the House of Chia, however, do improve. The Emperor takes a personal interest in the family—his grief is ever-fresh over the death of the Imperial Concubine, Cardinal Spring, and he feels a bond with this family—and, in due course, a child is born to Pao-yu's wife, Precious Virtue. The child is a son.

THE SORROWS OF YOUNG WERTHER

Johann Wolfgang von Goethe

Johann Wolfgang von Goethe was born in Frankfurt-am-Main, Germany, in 1749. His father was a prominent lawyer, and his mother was a charming, cultured woman who instilled her love of learning in her son, who bore the signs of genius at an early age. He gave up the study of law in order to write verse and plays, and in 1770 undertook the study of medicine in Strasbourg. Here Goethe came under the influence of Herder, who taught that the true spirit of a nation was evident in its folk poetry, that it was wrong for one country to imitate the literary styles of another, and that honesty, feeling, and the expression of emotion are the proper subjects of literature. Goethe fashioned his own early writings on these precepts of Herder, and inaugurated with The Sorrows of Young Werther the Sturm und Drang (storm and stress) movement, which dominated German literature for years.

In Werther Goethe attempted to emphasize the power of sentiment and emotion and to disregard classical form and restraint. The character of Werther—sensitive, passionate, depressed, suicidal—became the model for romantic youth all over Europe. It is perhaps unnecessary to add that this book, which divided the generations as had nothing in memory, was sensationally controversial. Although The Sorrows of Young Werther strikes today's readers as mawkish, it retains some of its power and is fascinating as the first, and still the best, work of its sort. After 1775 the author spent most of his life at the court of Weimar, where he studied mathematics, optics, geology, and biology, and wrote poetry, drama, philosophy, autobiography, and his great masterpiece, the poetic drama Faust, which in its complete form was published in 1831, one year before the author's death. Goethe had long since abandoned the unrestrained romanticism of Werther, and had imposed classic disciplines on his later and more mature work; elsewhere, however, the impact of Werther *continued to be strongly felt in the writings of the Romantic authors throughout the Western world.*

In May 1771 the young man Werther leaves home and goes to a province to settle for his mother the tangled matters that surround an inheritance of hers. While in the country he writes letters to William, his friend at home, describing his impressions.

A would-be painter, Werther is enchanted with the countryside, and spends hours wandering over fields, meadows, hills, and the banks of streams. His favorite place is Wahlheim, a hilltop community a little distance from where he is staying, and it is to Wahlheim and its unspoiled scenic beauties that Werther escapes whenever he can.

The young man is as delighted with the rustic people he encounters as he is with their homeland. Tired of the pretensions and artificiality of city dwellers, Werther is refreshed by the simple, straightforward folk of the province, who care nothing for rank or wealth, but are willing to make friends with him for his own sake. One of the local people whom Werther finds particularly appealing is a young serving man who has fallen desperately in love with his employer, a widow considerably his senior. The lad's devotion to the woman, and his idolization of her charms and beauty, are touching to Werther, and stir profound feelings within him.

Werther forms no close attachments during the early part of his sojourn, and though he is not unhappy, he does philosophize on the dreamlike quality of the world and of life itself. Nonetheless he is willing to mingle with people, and when a ball is given he willingly accepts an invitation.

It is at the ball that he meets for the first time the beautiful Charlotte S., daughter of a magistrate. He is instantly taken with Lotte's warmth, natural charm, and divine beauty. Glad that the young man to whom she is reportedly engaged —one Albert—is away on an extended business trip, Werther passes the entire evening in transports of delight, dancing with Lotte whenever he can, keeping his eyes on her constantly.

The next day Werther goes to the home of Magistrate S. to pay a call. There he finds Lotte taking care of her eight younger brothers and sisters (her mother is dead), and the simple, unaffected grace of this wholesome beauty fills Werther with rapture. He has found the woman of his dreams in Lotte, and he loves.

The next few weeks make Wahlheim seem like heaven to young Werther. He spends as much time as possible with the girl, and it seems to him that with every one of his thoughts, with every one of his ideals, she is in complete accord. Their views on life, on literature, on art, on nature—all, all coincide. Werther is the happiest of mortals. By mid-July he is convinced that Lotte loves him in return . . . but whenever she mentions her absent betrothed, a shadow of doubt passes across his mind.

Werther's correspondent, William, taken aback by his friend's passionate letters, urges the young man to accept an offered post traveling with the Ambassador. But young Werther refuses. Is not love a more profitable business to devote oneself to than politics—or even art?

In August, Lotte's betrothed, Albert, returns—and Werther finds him to be a worthy, respectable young man. The two strike up a friendship, and young Werther continues to be as welcome in the S. household as before Albert's return.

The first time that Werther is in disagreement with Albert occurs when, playing idly with a pair of Albert's pistols, Werther puts one of them to his temple. This leads to a discussion of suicide, which Albert finds wholly indefensible. Werther is unable to make his friend see his reasons for defending suicide as an action of manliness and courage; it is the painter's conviction that a man is no more to be censured for dying from suicide than for dying from disease. But Albert cannot accept this proposition. Werther recognizes how difficult it is for men to understand one another.

With Albert's return to Wahlheim, however, things cannot go along unchanged, and Werther feels how completely—and how hopelessly—he is the slave of his love for Lotte. He is reduced to a state of restless indolence. He cannot paint. Even the kindness of Lotte and Albert oppresses him, for Werther does not enjoy the role of trusted friend. At last, frustrated beyond endurance, Werther decides to accept the post with the Ambassador and go away. Lotte and Albert bid him a fond goodbye, confident that they will see Werther again in the next world if not in this. With a passionate "Farewell!" Werther leaves them, his heart pounding violently in his bosom.

In October, Werther joins the Ambassador's entourage in a city distant from Wahlheim, and throws himself into courtly life. But he and the Ambassador do not get along together at all. Werther finds life at court petty, foolish, and unsatisfying. Even the friendship of Count von C. and a flirtation with Fraulein von B. cannot keep the unhappy young man from thinking of the good people of Wahlheim, of the beautiful, fresh country scenery and atmosphere, and—of Lotte. He forces himself to continue in his post, but by March he cannot endure life away from Lotte any longer. When a foolish mistake leads to Werther's being branded as a social climber, he resigns his post and returns to Wahlheim.

When he goes to visit Lotte he finds that she has married Albert in January. He can now no longer regard Albert as a friend—Albert, whom God has seen fit to place by Lotte's side in a role that Werther alone was born to fulfill! At times Werther is at a loss to understand how Lotte can love her husband; at other time he thinks that she is divinely right for preferring her bourgeois, solid husband to himself, so unstable and emotional.

At this point Werther encounters again the young man who had so impressed him when he first came to the province. The adoring serving lad tells Werther that he has been turned out of his mistress' house by the woman's jealous brother; nonetheless, says the young man, he will love the woman forever, even if he never sees her again. The young servant's passion finds an echoing response in Werther's breast.

When in September Albert is again called away on business, Werther begins to pay calls upon Lotte with increasing regularity. Though the girl cannot help but be aware of the love she inspires, she is always careful to treat Werther as a good friend—nothing less, but nothing more. And with every look of friendship from Lotte, with every word of warmth, Werther's passion for her blazes more brightly.

Though he is happy when in Lotte's company, Werther is miserable when away from her. He becomes a man obsessed, and his mind is constantly revolving around his unhappiness. He is in despair that he, who was born to give so much love, should be prevented from giving it by the unhappy accident of his beloved's having been already promised to another man. In his unhappiness Werther takes to rambling in the countryside at night, and he finds in the turbulent skies a sympathy with his own mood of depression.

One day, while out on one of his rambles, Werther meets a harmless young madman, who rants about days of past happiness and glory. From the man's mother Werther learns that the happy days the man longs for were those when he was completely mad, and locked up in an asylum. Werther thinks deeply on the fact that this man is happy only in insanity. The next day Werther makes the alarming discovery that the young man had once been secretary to Magistrate S., and his passionate love for the magistrate's daughter—Lotte—is what has driven him to madness.

Now it seems to Werther that he cannot endure his misery any longer. He is continually haunted and tortured by visions of Lotte. As for the girl herself, she can no longer avoid knowing what is obvious about Werther's feelings for her—and this knowledge frightens her. Lotte and Albert agree that they must become less intimate with young Werther.

One day, word comes that the young serving man whom Werther had befriended has been arrested for murder. He has killed the new servant of the employer whom he has so passionately loved. When Lotte, Albert, and Lotte's father excoriate the lad, Werther sees how completely out of sympathy he is with them. He is a man apart from the mainstream of life.

At last, determined to save herself from the embarrassment of Werther's violent passion, Lotte tells him that he must not come to visit her until Christmas. Werther, destroyed by this order, takes leave of his beloved.

Now, a plan which has been floating half-formed through Werther's mind takes definite shape, and Werther determines to kill himself. He writes a long and passionate letter of farewell to Lotte, intending that it should be delivered to her after his death. Then, he goes to take his leave of her in person.

It is the night before Christmas, and Lotte is startled at Werther's visit—particularly since Albert is away from the house. Werther is strangely calm, however, and soon Lotte agrees to let him read aloud to her passages from Ossian which he has translated into German expressly as a gift for her.

As he reads, Lotte is aware of her own emotions, and she

recognizes that, in her heart, she has never wanted Werther to go away. Rather, she has wanted to keep his love and his passion for herself.

Listening to Werther's low, steady voice, Lotte becomes caught up in the passages he is reading—passages of love and death. Suddenly the two young people are overcome with emotion. Werther falls to his knees and seizing Lotte's hand, covers it with kisses. The girl sobs, pushes the young man away, and flees from the room. But Werther has recognized the truth: she loves him!

In a strange state of elation, young Werther returns to his hotel and gives orders that he is not to be disturbed until morning. The next day Werther sends a servant with a note to Albert, begging the loan of Albert's pistols for a trip Werther plans to take.

When she hears the request that has been made to her husband, Lotte turns pale—but silently she obeys Albert and fetches the pistols to deliver to the servant. Trembling, silent, terrified, Lotte returns to her needlework.

The next morning at six, the servant finds Werther lying on the blood-soaked rug. He sends for a doctor, but it is too late. By noon Werther is dead.

A simple funeral is held, and Werther is buried between two favorite linden trees. Albert finds himself incapable of attending the service, and of course Lotte is not present. Workmen carry the body. There is no priest in attendance.

THE THREE-CORNERED HAT

Pedro Antonio de Alarcón

Pedro Antonio de Alarcón was born of a poor family in Guadix (near Granada), Spain, in 1833. He was intrigued at an early age with the writings of the Romantic novelists, but by 1855, when he published his first work, Romanticism had been superseded by French realism, and Alarcón's early book was scorned. Alarcón served in the war in Africa in 1859, wrote several travel books, and returned to Spain in 1872. His writings from this date were well received by the critics and public. The Three-Cornered Hat, which was written in 1874, has been acclaimed as one of the finest humorous works in literature. It was based partly on a current ballad, and partly on the author's childhood memories. Alarcón was elected to the Spanish Academy in 1875; he nevertheless was

*subject to continuous hostile criticism and wrote no fiction after
1881. He died in Madrid in 1891.*

All of Europe may have been in a social and political uproar
in 1805, but in the sleepy province of Andalusia—that is where
this tale takes place—life proceeds as it has for hundreds of
years, without taking so much as a by-your-leave of the rest
of the world.

The most goodhearted fellow in Andalusia is one Tío Lucas, the miller. Tío Lucas may be ugly as sin—but then, he
has a wife who makes up for it. For none is as pretty, none
as appetizing, none as plump and ripe and juicy-sweet as
Seña Frasquita. And how Frasquita and Lucas love one
another—well, it is something to behold.

Every Sunday the dignitaries of the town make their way
to Tío Lucas' mill. They like to listen to the birds singing and
the water rippling. They like to taste the sweet grapes and
luscious honey which Tío Lucas always serves. And at least
one of them—the Mayor (Don Eugenio de Zúñiga y Ponce
de León)—likes to admire the miller's beautiful wife.

Now the Mayor is very vain. No one is more impressed
than he himself with the power and authority symbolized by
his huge three-cornered hat of mayoralty. And so he reasons
that Seña Frasquita must infinitely prefer him to that ugly
Tío Lucas of a husband. And therefore the Mayor begins a
flirtation.

Seña Frasquita sees at once what he is up to, and she
makes Tío Lucas hide himself in the branches of the grape
arbor to eavesdrop on the Mayor's love songs. Frasquita coyly
leads the Mayor on, and he is aflame with carnal longings at
the prospect of promised delights when Tío Lucas jumps
down from the arbor. At first the Mayor is suspicious, but
he gathers that the fool of a husband has overheard nothing
(Tío Lucas and Seña Frasquita are accomplished dissem-
blers), and he goes away quite pleased with himself, convinced that the citadel will not need to be stormed but that a
drawbridge will be let down instead.

For several days the Mayor schemes about ways to insure
his conquest. At last, egged on by his constable, the rascally
Garduña, he hatches a plan and, on a propitious night, puts
it into effect.

On the appointed night, there is a knock at the mill door.

It is a rustic constable from a nearby village, who has a warrant for Tío Lucas' arrest. Since there's no help but to follow when the law beckons, Tío Lucas saddles up his donkey, shuts his wife up in the mill, and rides off behind the constable.

He does not ride far, however, when he spies the Mayor's tricorn etched against the sky. The Mayor is riding toward the mill. Seeing what is what, Tío Lucas resolves to get home as fast as possible.

This is not too difficult to arrange. Juan López, mayor of the neighboring village to which Tío Lucas is taken, is a congenial sort of fellow, and though he is party to the plot against the virtue of Seña Frasquita and intends to lock up her husband till morning, he is quite obliging to Tío Lucas. Taking advantage of his host's cordiality, Tío Lucas easily makes his escape, and is soon galloping back toward his mill. And when he gets there—damnation! The mill door stands open!

A million questions buzzing in his brain, Tío Lucas enters the kitchen—and there, on a chair by the fire, he sees the Mayor's clothes. Seizing his blunderbuss, he goes to the bedroom he has shared in so much happiness with his dear perfidious wife. At the door, his suspicions are confirmed. From inside the room he hears a sneeze—and there is no doubt that it is the sneeze of the Mayor. So Frasquita has succumbed!

Tío Lucas returns to the kitchen to think things out. Suddenly he concocts a fiendish plot of revenge—one that will pay out both the scurvy Mayor and his own treacherous wife. He strips quickly, puts on the Mayor's clothes, and rides off into the night, his mind full of visions of the charms of the Mayor's wife.

Meanwhile, here is what has really happened. Shortly after Tío Lucas left the mill, Frasquita heard cries for help coming from the mill-race. She opened the door to find the Mayor, dripping wet and shivering from head to toe. In his attempt to scale the walls of the mill, he had fallen into the stream.

At first Frasquita tried to throw the Mayor out, proclaiming that her husband was not home and that her virtue would not allow her to have a strange man in the house. But at last her human sympathies got the better of her and, fearing for the Mayor's health, she allowed him to hang his wet clothes by the fire and crawl into the bed until they were dried out.

The Mayor, however, was not shivering too hard to make amorous advances—and he even produced a document giving Frasquita's nephew a long-sought-for appointment. This appointment, he said, would go through—*if.* . . .

Frasquita, however, seized up her husband's blunderbuss and aimed it at the Mayor. Threatening to blow his brains out, she succeeded in intimidating him to the point where he gave her the document with no strings attached.

Now the Mayor was shivering in earnest. Frasquita was afraid that he really would catch his death. Unwilling to stay in the house with him, however, she saddled the family's second donkey, and rode off. Left alone, the Mayor buried himself under the bedclothes and tried to get warm while waiting for his clothes to dry. This was the real state of affairs at the mill when Tío Lucas jumped to his hasty conclusion.

Now Garduña appears at the bedside, and tells the Mayor that he has just seen Frasquita riding off—to fetch a doctor, no doubt. But the Mayor realizes that it is more likely she has gone to tell his wife where he is and what he is up to. The Mayor announces that he must leave the house at once. Unable to find his own suit of clothes, he is forced to dress in some old rags of Tío Lucas'.

In actuality Frasquita has gone to neither the Mayoress nor the Doctor. She has gone to the neighboring village to see Tío Lucas. Juan López sends a jailer to fetch Tío Lucas to see his wife—and it is discovered that he has escaped. Instantly Frasquita tells them what is going on, and, realizing that Lucas must have set off for the mill to kill the Mayor, she leads a band of village officers back to the mill in haste.

They arrive at the mill just as the Mayor is dressing in Tío Lucas' clothes. Juan López tries to arrest the supposed Tío Lucas, and the Mayor resists, whereupon a free-for-all erupts, in which several noses are bloodied and many eyes are blacked. At last, however, the truth dawns on everyone: that Tío Lucas supposes Frasquita to be a fallen woman, that he has gone off dressed as the Mayor, and that he is—perhaps—even now in the Mayor's own bedroom. Shocked, frightened, and angry, the band sets off for the city.

It is half-past midnight when they arrive in the city and begin pounding on the locked door of the Mayor's house. At last a servant appears and tells them that they cannot disturb anyone; the "Mayor," who had come home not long before, left strict orders that nobody is to be allowed into the house until morning, and then went straight to bed.

At this news the real Mayor begins sputtering and fluttering and muttering as though a lightning storm were going on in his chest. He begins to scream at the servants that *he* is the Mayor and that the man in the Mayoress's bedroom is an impostor, but they are not convinced and remain adamant about throwing him out of the house.

Suddenly all falls silent as a woman enters the room. It is the Mayoress. She gazes stonily about, and then, her eyes resting on her husband, she says calmly and clearly, "What can I do for you, Tío Lucas?"

This is too much for the Mayor, and the pandemonium breaks out again. But in spite of all his entreaties and protestations and threats and curses, the woman remains adamant in stating that her husband, the Mayor, is in bed; she has just left him there.

Then, who should enter the room but Tío Lucas himself, dressed in the Mayor's clothes. Now Frasquita bursts into a furious tongue-lashing, such as the Mayor had already given to his wife. But Tío Lucas, still convinced that he has been wronged, refuses to talk to her.

At last the noble Mayoress sends her husband out of the room, acknowledging him to be the real Mayor, and urging him to change into more civilized clothes. In his absence she silences the recriminations between Tío Lucas and Frasquita, convincing both that neither of them has been wronged. And peace is restored between the miller and his wife.

Now the Mayor comes into the room once more, dressed in his official regalia. Everyone, he says, has had a satisfactory explanation but himself. He demands to know the truth about what has gone on between the Mayoress and Tío Lucas.

But the Mayoress—who is, in truth, as innocent of sin as a babe unborn—has been bitterly hurt by such public broadcasting of her husband's infidelities. To punish him, therefore, she tells him that so long as he lives, he will never know what happened in her bedroom on this night.

Tío Lucas insists that Frasquita give all of the mattresses and linen from their bed to the poor, for he is unwilling to touch the stuff on which had lain the naked, shivering Mayor. That minor change accomplished, he and Frasquita go on loving each other, taking pleasure in the good things of life, and living to a ripe old age.

THE WORLD'S ILLUSION

Jakob Wassermann

Jakob Wassermann was born near Nürnberg, Germany, in 1873, the son of a Jewish merchant. His family was not sympathetic to his literary aspirations and attempted twice to establish him in business with relatives. Wassermann joined the army rather than stay in business, then took a government post. He subsequently wandered across Bavaria and Switzerland, writing and taking odd jobs. In 1895 he secured a good position as secretary to a writer, and shortly thereafter joined the editorial board of a new literary magazine, in which several of his poems and stories were published. His first novel appeared in 1897 and was well received; thereafter he wrote several important novels, short stories, biographies, and autobiographical works. It was from 1915 on, after he married and was living comfortably in Vienna, that his most famous novels were written. Wassermann died in 1934.

The World's Illusion was published in 1919, the title in the original being Christian Wahnschaffe. It is Wassermann's masterpiece, and has been translated into many languages, appearing in English in 1920. In its search into the depths of its characters, The World's Illusion reveals the profound, and at the time relatively recent, influence of Freud and psychoanalysis; and it is perhaps the first great novel in which Freudian interpretation is fully absorbed into the powerful development of the narrative. Important also in the story is the rapid change of scene from one part of Europe to another, creating strikingly a sense of essential unity in the diverse European countries and cultures.

Bernard Gervasius Crammon von Weissenfels—handsome, independently wealthy, sophisticated—leads a glossy, sybaritic life in the pleasure spots of Europe. The noted, the accomplished, the titled are his friends; the capitals and resorts of the Old World are his playgrounds. Vienna—Nice—Paris—Edinburgh . . . a mad adventure with a countess, a love affair with a ballerina, a confidential friendship with an actor: this is his life.

Indicative of the world's regard for Crammon as an exemplar of manhood is the fact that when the wealthy, middle-aged von Febronius realizes that he will never father a child to whom he can leave his riches, it is Crammon whom he selects to become his wife's lover for a night in order to sire a Febronius heir. Indicative of his personality and view of the world, Crammon regards the adventure lightly, never afterward making inquiry concerning the child he has fathered.

During his fortieth year, Crammon discovers a dancer named Eva Sorel—the most beautiful, the most entrancing creature he has ever known. He determines that he must possess her, but Eva is not so easily won. With a mind of steel and a driving sense of perfection, Eva rejects Crammon, though she is delighted to have his friendship.

Of all the attractive men and women he meets, none affects Crammon as profoundly as wealthy, blond, virile Christian Wahnschaffe, a young man who reflects, in his notable good looks and his ready acceptance of all the world's treasures as though they were his birthright, the young man Crammon himself once was. Crammon determines to make Christian his protégé, and Christian accepts the older man's friendship as he accepts all the world's glories: easily, naturally, and indifferently.

While staying as a house guest at one of the many Wahn-schaffe estates, Crammon meets for the first time the girl whom he now knows to be his own child: Laetitia von Febronius. He is delighted with the girl's beauty, disappointed in her innocence, and determined—when it becomes evident that Laetitia is in love with Christian—that she shall not have him. Christian is too great a treasure to be wasted on unsophisticated Laetitia; Christian must be saved for perfection—indeed, he must be saved for Eva Sorel.

Hamburg . . . the Riviera . . . Silesia . . . Geneva. . . . Christian and Crammon live an epicurean existence, tasting delight here, sampling pleasure there, indulging their minds and senses everywhere, being touched nowhere. Much to Crammon's surprise, Christian even seems impervious to the charms of Eva Sorel.

But this is because Crammon cannot see into Christian's

heart. Eva does have an effect on Christian, who finds himself strangely drawn to her, as she is to him. But their feeling for each other—their sensation of having, for the first time, encountered a worthy mate—remains unspoken. Christian is uneasy with some of Eva's coterie—notably with Ivan Machailovitch Becker, a mysterious Russian said to be at the heart of a revolutionary movement that is determined to overthrow the Czar. Eva, for her part, is distressed by Christian's calm, cool air of self-sufficiency.

Berlin . . . Majorca . . . Naples . . . Moscow. . . . Eva is a brilliant success wherever she dances, and her star rises steadily. Christian, however, remains unmoved—untouched—by all that transpires before him. He watches as a mistress whom he has rejected, the circus lion-tamer Adda Castillo, is clawed to death before his eyes—and he feels nothing. Paris . . . Bayreuth . . . Rouen . . . Ghent. . . .

A house party at the Wahnschaffe castle is upset, temporarily, when a worker in one of the Wahnschaffe factories—a man named Kroll—attempts to kill Christian's father. Though the elder Wahnschaffe escapes virtually uninjured, Christian, for the first time in his life, feels a deep and nameless stirring within him. Nor is he consoled by Crammon, who uses the episode as an example of the need for more repressive measures against the poorer classes. Wondering at himself for his folly, Christian allows himself to be led into the night by Ivan Becker, who takes the handsome young millionaire to the hovel in which live the wife and children of the imprisoned Kroll. Strangely moved, Christian first gives the woman all the gold he has about him—a small fortune, as it happens; then, he kneels at her feet. Becker whispers to him that this gesture holds the promise of his eventual salvation.

Laetitia, despairing of ever winning Christian, who has merely toyed with her affections, consents, under urgings from Crammon, to be betrothed to a sadistic Argentinian, Stephen Gunderman. Influenced by Laetitia's decision, Christian's sister Judith accepts the ambitious young businessman Felix Imhof.

On the night before her wedding, Laetitia arranges a secret meeting with Christian, at which she offers herself to him. Still moved by strange indecision, Christian rejects her. (Neither Laetitia's marriage nor Judith's, both impulsively made, brings happiness to the women involved. Laetitia leaves her husband after the birth of twin daughters, only to find that the man whom she has chosen to take his place is, indeed, one she does not—cannot—love; while Judith, finding Imhof too ambitious and self-contained to need her, divorces him and marries the ineffectual but brilliant actor Edgar Lorm, whom she proceeds to nag at unmercifully, making herself miserable in the process.)

Crammon senses that somehow Christian has changed; the young man is now moody, silent, unpredictable. As a change of pace, he suggests another grand tour, to which Christian agrees. Switzerland . . . France . . . Austria . . . Yugoslavia. . . . But Christian's torment will not cease, and at last he begs Crammon to leave him. Christian is determined to find an answer to the unspecified question that troubles him.

Losing interest in people—who all seem superficial and base to him now—Christian lavishes increasing attention on things. His purchase of Ignifer—the most famous diamond in the world—makes headlines throughout Europe. When he learns that Eva Sorel has also coveted the fabulous gem, he bestows it upon her.

Christian now encounters a man who is to have a profound influence upon him. This is Amadeus Voss, misanthropic son of a forester. Voss has trained for the priesthood, but his bitterness against all mankind for the suffering inflicted upon him throughout his poverty-stricken life prevents him from taking his vows. Nonetheless, he strives desperately to live a pure existence, though he is tormented excruciatingly by carnal desires.

Voss seems to offer Christian the answers to the suffering he feels within himself, and he calls the fanatic, ugly young man "brother." Christian—because of his good looks, wealth, and charm—seems to offer Voss a solution to his misery, too. The two have long and deep conversations together, and soon they are inseparable.

Eva Sorel has attracted the eye of Count Maidanoff, who pursues her relentlessly. She withholds herself from him, but realizes the futility of her action; for Maidanoff is the assumed name of the Russian Grand Duke, the most hated, most feared, most evil, most powerful man in the Czar's court. Tempted by the power which she will be able to wield as mistress to this man, she agrees at last to become his—but only on condition that she may first spend a month with Christian.

At the beginning of these days together, their passion for each other burns brightly, and their affair is sublime. But gradually Christian realizes that he cannot surrender the core of his being to this most beautiful of women, and he makes this clear to her. In an agony of torment and self-doubt, Christian sends Eva away; and he does not know whether he is pleased or fearful at the idea that he will probably never see her again.

Now living permanently in Berlin, sharing his comfortable quarters with Amadeus Voss, Christian is determined to pursue peace of mind at whatever cost. He gradually senses that he must simplify his mode of life, and so he takes humble lodgings. These, however, he judges not to be sufficiently austere, and so he moves into cheaper lodgings. Again and again he moves, each time to a place meaner, barer than the one before. Voss, however, who has become used to the income that Christian has made available to him, at last refuses to move, and so Christian begins living alone.

Two friends from his past come to see him in Berlin. One is Crammon, who is repelled by what he regards as Christian's folly. At last, Crammon throws up his hands in despair, vowing never again to interfere with Christian, though this decision to cast off the most marvelous, the most enchanting person he has ever known costs Crammon great pain. The other friend is Johanna Schöntag, the homely, acid-tongued, but sympathetic girl whom Christian had known during his affair with Eva Sorel. Johanna seems to be understanding of his pain and his dilemma—but eventually he decides that he must dispense with her friendship as well, in his fight to find peace of mind. Johanna, who loves Christian, forces herself to maintain a friendly relationship with Voss, whom she detests, but who is the only person in regular touch with Christian. Her constant exposure to Voss, however, and his endless importunate pleading finally bring her to become his mistress. She loathes Voss—but she has always bitterly assumed that her life would be nothing but pain and degradation; therefore succumbing to him somehow seems to her to be fulfilling her destiny.

By now Christian's friends and family have all but despaired of his sanity. He has rescued from the streets a common prostitute named Karen Engelschall, and installed her in his apartment. He has ordered all of his estates and possessions sold. (These his family buy back secretly.) He has turned over to a prison chaplain all of his wealth save the small amount he needs to subsist from day to day.

Though with each new gesture of self-denial Christian feels that he comes closer to the answer he seeks, he still feels mute apprehension about whether he will ever achieve his final goal of feeling at one with humanity and the purposes of life.

The single ray of pure joy in his life at this point comes in the person of sixteen-year-old Ruth Hofmann. The young Jewish girl is saintlike, devoting her life to the easing of other lives, though she herself is little richer than a pauper. Ruth is drawn mystically to Christian, and in her simple, uneducated way, she finds words that bring him deep comfort. Christian is now able to endure loathesome experiences which, before, would have made him ill merely to contemplate, simply because it is Ruth who leads him to them.

Unbeknown to Christian, Ruth has attracted the attention of Niels Heinrich Engelschall, the conscienceless criminal brother of the prostitute Karen, and of Niels's simple-minded companion Joachim Heinzen. So convinced is Christian of Ruth's sanctity that he cannot imagine anyone wishing the girl harm. Therefore, when for several days she is absent from the rude room which is her home, Christian suspects no trouble.

One night, as Christian sits nursing the dying Karen, he receives word that Ruth has been killed; her tortured body has been found. This horror and its shattering of Christian's hopes is so staggering that Johanna, present with him at the time, feels that she has seen the heavens themselves open and spew out smoke. It is only because Karen needs his help during her last illness that Christian somehow continues functioning.

The police quickly arrest the simple-minded Joachim Heinzen for Ruth's murder.

Shortly after Karen's death, Christian receives a visit from her insolent brother, Niels Heinrich. Christian talks to the young criminal about Ruth's murder; and gradually Niels's cocky air of assurance gives way to nervousness. Christian makes no accusations, but he begins dogging Niels's footsteps. Finally Niels becomes almost hysterical with fear. At last Niels confesses to Christian that he had terrorized, raped, and murdered Ruth, and then fastened the blame on Heinzen. Christian in his complete collapse makes the mad gesture of begging Niels for forgiveness—an act so overpowering that Niels nearly goes to pieces.

Christian's name has, by now, been mentioned in the papers; his friendship for Ruth and Niels's confession to him are reported in accounts of the murder and in the succeeding trial. This is the last blow to his family. The elder Wahnschaffe determines to have one final interview with his son, in which he will beg Christian for a rational explanation of his behavior—something that Christian has never been able to supply. If that fails, the old man determines to have Christian declared incompetent and have him locked in an institution.

The interview is a painful one, as Christian tries to make his father understand that he cannot give reasons for his way of life. He only knows that the life of his father—the life he himself was raised to live and believe in—is nothing but a sham, an illusion. Shaken to the core, the elder Wahnschaffe grasps something of what his son is trying to tell him.

Christian resolves to spare his family any further annoyance; he will change his name and leave Berlin. He promises that none who know him will ever hear from him again. His father asks him where he will go, what he will do. Christian can only answer that he does not know, but that he must continue his search.

THE MAGIC MOUNTAIN

Thomas Mann

Thomas Mann was born in 1875 in Lübeck, Germany, where his father was a rich merchant. Thomas was sent to military school where he was extremely unhappy; upon the death of his father and subsequent loss of the business in 1890, the family moved to Munich, where Mann sat in on lectures at the university. His first story was published in 1894, and he left Munich a year later to join his older brother, a writer, in Rome. Here he began work on his first novel, Buddenbrooks, which he finished after returning to Munich two years later. It was published in 1901, and although not an instant success, it began after a year or so to attract attention; the publication of additional stories at this time enhanced his reputation, and by the time of his marriage in 1905 Thomas

Mann was a famous author. His writings continued and his reputation grew; he won the Nobel Prize for literature in 1929, and is considered the greatest German novelist of the twentieth century. Mann was in Switzerland in 1933 when his family warned him not to come back to Germany. His books were burned by the Nazis in 1936, and two years later Mann moved to the United States. He became an American citizen in 1944, but returned to Switzerland to spend his last years. He died in Zurich in 1955.

The Magic Mountain (1924), Mann's most famous novel, is concerned with the themes and ideas which dominate most of his work. Disease and death, the position of the artist in society, the fate of man, the decay of civilization, the relation of the individual to time and space—these vast problems are all considered in The Magic Mountain, *in which the mountain sanatorium becomes the symbol of the Western world, with its content of dying humanity.*

Young Hans Castorp is somewhat anemic and run-down at the completion of his education, so it is decided that, before embarking upon his apprenticeship as a maritime engineer, he should go for a three-week rest to a tuberculosis sanatorium, high on a mountain near Davos, Switzerland. The reason for choosing this particular sanatorium is that Hans Castorp's cousin Joachim Ziemssen is a patient there. Hans, who is phlegmatic by nature (perhaps as a result of his having a comfortable inheritance left to him by his parents, both of whom died when he was quite young), agrees readily to the proposal. He likes the idea of spending three weeks doing nothing but resting, eating, smoking, and otherwise enjoying himself; and he considers his cousin Joachim his best friend in the world, one whom he will truly enjoy visiting.

Hans's first impressions of the mountaintop sanatorium, however, are negative. The patients there—an international group—strike him as somewhat boorish and uncultivated. Joachim, too, seems different: Hans remembers him as having been an alert, vital young man, eager to join his regiment (Joachim is a soldier), but finds him now remote and vague. Most distressing of all is the very atmosphere: Hans has difficulty breathing, finds himself tiring easily, and even falls victim to dizzy spells. When the head doctor of the staff, Herr Behrens, suggests that the young man would do well, during his three-week visit, to follow the regimen of the regular patients, Hans Castorp agrees.

This regimen follows a set pattern: breakfast, an hour of

rest cure, second breakfast, a walk, lunch, rest cure, tea, a walk, dinner, social hour, sleep. (For the regular patients there is, in addition, the taking of temperatures five times a day.) At first Hans chafes at this program—he finds the endless rest cures singularly monotonous, and the atmosphere continually depressing (the patients spend all of the rest cures and most of the nights out-of-doors on their balconies). However, as each day makes him feel weaker and more out of sorts, he begins to look forward to the rest that is thus imposed upon him.

Hans continues to find the patients at the sanatorium—admittedly an odd lot—annoying. He meets only a few of them personally—language barriers and social distinctions limit each patient to a fairly small circle within the large clientele—but with none of them is he warmly impressed. Among those making strong impressions on him are Ludovico Settembrini, an impoverished but highly verbal philosopher of the humanist school; Frau Stohr, a vulgar woman prone to coining the most outrageous malapropisms; and Hermine Kleefeld, a young woman who disconcerts Hans Castorp by whistling at him in a most strange manner. (He later learns that this is a knack that she has acquired as the result of having a pneumothorax; she belongs to a group of patients who have given themselves the macabre name, the Half-Lung Club.)

Nor does Hans limit his disapproval to those whom he knows personally. He feels vaguely ill-at-ease with the two doctors—Herr Behrens and his assistant, Dr. Krokowski, who practices psychoanalysis in addition to his other duties. And Hans Castorp is even sensitive to the personalities of patients who remain virtual strangers to him; one in particular, a young Russian woman, Frau Chauchat, makes herself particularly disagreeable to him by slamming the door every time she enters the dining room.

At last, Castorp finds that life in the sanatorium is getting too much on his nerves, which accounts, no doubt, for his feeling physically unwell. He determines to take a long solitary walk in the mountains one morning, to clear his head and take a new hold on himself. For a while his walk is effortless and pleasant, but soon he is overcome with dizziness. He sits down on a bench, then lies down, and has a strange dream—or, rather, vision. He finds himself again in the presence of a boy—the fair-haired, gray-eyed Pribislav Hippe—

whom he had worshiped from afar when they were both lads at school. Only once had Hans summoned the courage to speak with him, and that was to borrow a pencil. When Hans is finally able to get to his feet again, the vision over, he finds that he has coughed up some blood.

Toward the end of his three weeks, Hans is persuaded to take his temperature—and finds that he is running a fever. He insists that he suffers only from a catarrhal cough, but Behrens prevails upon him to let himself be X-rayed. The results of the examination are clear: Hans Castorp has tuberculosis.

Much to his own surprise, Hans accepts the doctor's verdict with equanimity, and he and Joachim make the necessary purchases for what will now be Hans's indefinite stay at the mountaintop sanatorium.

Breakfast, rest cure, second breakfast, a walk, lunch, rest cure, tea, a walk, dinner, social hour, sleep. . . .

Breakfast, rest cure, second breakfast, a walk, lunch, rest cure, tea, a walk, dinner, social hour, sleep. . . .

Hans finds himself slipping easily into the timeless world of the sanatorium. He is as interested in charting his own temperature curve as the other patients are in charting theirs. He carries about with him the small X-ray plate showing his diseased lungs as though it were a talisman. And he begins altering his attitude toward his fellow invalids.

Settembrini, the loquacious Italian, becomes a boon companion for Hans and his cousin Joachim. The taciturn Joachim —his mind ever fixed on the distant day when he will be well enough to rejoin his regiment—adds little to the conversations; but Castorp and Settembrini talk endlessly about life, death, time, humanity. Hans finds his mind is stretching under the influence of the older man. For the first time in his life, philosophical questions fill his mind and keep him occupied for hours.

One aspect of life at House Berghof (as the sanatorium is called) to which Hans refuses to adjust is the practice of keeping all word about the bedridden and hopeless patients from the ears of the ambulatory clientele. It is as though a conspiracy were afoot to create two separate worlds within the sanatorium—the world of the dining room and social hall, and the world of serious illness and death. Though the management has done this to spare the sensitivities of the less-sick patients, Hans determines to bridge these two worlds, and accordingly he begins, on Joachim's behalf as well as his own, to send small bouquets of flowers to the terminal patients. Soon the two cousins are regular visitors in the previously forbidden sickrooms of the dying. Hans delights in the warmth and gratitude of these patients and their families for the attentions he pays them; and he finds a distinct pleasure in the close contact with death which these visits afford him.

During this period the most subtle change of all in Hans's feelings is reflected in his new attitude toward the boisterous Clavdia Chauchat. Although he has not succeeded in meeting the beautiful Russian woman—indeed, he shuns all opportunity to do so—he finds himself strangely attracted to her. It is not long before he identifies his feelings for her as love; and soon his love has become a grand passion. The girl reminds him, in some way which he cannot identify, of his long-ago idol, Pribislav Hippe—though why it should be so he cannot understand.

Breakfast, rest cure, second breakfast, a walk, lunch, rest cure, tea, a walk, dinner, social hour, sleep. . . .

It is many months that Castorp has been a patient at House Berghof. The season is carnival, and a masquerade ball is planned. At the height of the festivities Herr Behrens introduces a new game to the patients: each is to try to draw a pig while blindfolded. Instantly all are eager to try to match the doctor's skill at this childish sport. Hans makes one pathetic effort but is determined to make another. Before he can essay the task again, however, his pencil is snatched from his hand by a fellow patient. For some demonic reason, Hans is obsessed with making another attempt immediately, and he rushes out of the salon in search of a pencil. He encounters Clavdia Chauchat, and immediately asks her if he may borrow a pencil from her. She answers in precisely the words that Pribislav Hippe had used so many years ago in the schoolyard.

This first encounter of Hans Castorp and his long-adored Clavdia leads to a lengthy conversation between the two, a conversation conducted mainly in French, as the young woman's German is inadequate and Castorp speaks no Russian. Hans declares his passion for Clavdia, who is amazed. She tells him that she is leaving House Berghof the next day, a piece of news which staggers him. But she assures him that she will one day return. The invalids exchange strange tokens—their X-ray plates—and when their lengthy and revealing interview ends, Hans is a victim of strange and highly ambivalent emotions.

Clavdia's departure from the sanatorium seems to set off a series of departures—both authorized and "wild." One of the "wild" departures is that of Joachim Ziemssen, who cannot bear to postpone rejoining his regiment in the "flat land" below any longer. Herr Behrens warns against Joachim's leaving, but the intense young man can no longer be put off; he feels that Behrens will never willingly announce him cured, and he warns his cousin Hans not to stay at the sanatorium much longer, or he too will fall into Behrens' clutches and will be given a "life sentence." Although he himself is far less sick than Joachim, Hans cannot bring himself to entertain the notion of leaving the sanatorium without Behrens' verdict of "cured."

Settembrini, too, leaves the sanatorium, having decided that his case is hopeless. He takes up residence in a nearby village, so that he may at least reap the benefits of the mountain air, and thither Hans Castorp goes frequently to visit him.

Also resident in the building in which Settembrini has taken rooms is the Jesuit priest Naphta, like Settembrini a tubercular. Naphta is as verbal as Settembrini, but the two represent opposite poles of philosophy. Each warns Hans against the ideologies of the other, but Hans enjoys debating with both of them, taking what each has to say with a grain of salt. He is concerned, however, at the apparent hostility between these two intellectual antagonists, who, in spite of their irreconcilably opposed points of view, need each other for intellectual stimulation.

Breakfast, rest cure, second breakfast, a walk, lunch, rest cure. . . .

Joachim's flight from House Berghof proves to have been premature indeed. He is brought back to the sanatorium after only a brief stay with his regiment in the land below. This time he knows it is a life sentence for him and, before long, Joachim dies.

Breakfast, rest cure, second breakfast, a walk, lunch. . . .

When the long-awaited day of Clavdia Chauchat's return to the sanatorium arrives, Hans Castorp is unable to feel the delight and unalloyed joy he has for so long anticipated, because his adored comes in company with a wealthy and dynamic Dutch colonial, one Herr Peeperkorn. There can be no doubt about the relations between Clavdia and Peeperkorn; they share adjoining rooms at House Berghof, and their luggage arrives in common. Hans feels his love for the girl as much as ever, and is distressed both at her new relationship and at her seeming forgetfulness of what passed between himself and her on that fateful night when he asked if he could borrow a pencil.

In spite of himself Hans finds himself attracted by the dynamic, insistent personality of the wealthy and flamboyant Peeperkorn, and as a result he is frequently thrown into Clavdia's company. Eventually Peeperkorn suspects a past relationship between his mistress and this Hans Castorp, and he presses the young man for an explanation. Hans tells him the truth, and Peeperkorn swears eternal brotherhood with him, begging Castorp to forgive him for having been the cause of what must be a painful situation.

After this interview Clavdia notes a change in Hans, and she feels able to talk with him freely. She confesses that though she loves Peeperkorn deeply, she is also tormented by the strain of so dynamic a man, and that she has brought him with her to House Berghof precisely in the knowledge that Hans would help her bear the burden of her relationship.

Shortly after his interview with Hans, Peeperkorn—a desperately sick man in any case—commits suicide. Following the funeral, Clavdia leaves the sanatorium, never to return.

Breakfast, rest cure, second breakfast, a walk. . . .

A nineteen-year-old Danish girl named Elly Brand comes to House Berghof as a patient. It is discovered that she has supernatural gifts, and under the direction of Doctor Krokowski, a series of experiments and seances is held. At one, Hans is invited to be present. It is determined to ask Elly's familiar —a long-dead poet named Holger—to produce the spirit of one who has died. Hans calls for an apparition of Joachim Ziemssen to be made palpable. Sure enough, he sees—as do the others present—the ghost of his dead cousin. He gasps— murmurs the words "Forgive me!" to Joachim—and then abruptly leaves the room. He has nothing further to do with the spiritualists.

Breakfast, rest cure, second breakfast. . . .

An emotional chaos seems to overtake House Berghof for no apparent reason. There is a fist fight between two patients, one an avowed anti-Semite, the other a Jew. A petty incident among several of the Polish invalids spreads and grows until it becomes a minor *cause célèbre* in international circles. The violent atmosphere seems even to have penetrated to the village below. One day, on an outing, Settembrini and Naphta become abusive about each other's philosophies, and before Hans Castorp knows how it has come about, the Jesuit and the Italian humanist have determined to duel to the death.

Hans cannot believe that the affair will actually take place; it is too stupid for men to fight over intellectual affront. But it is soon clear to him that the duel is on in earnest, and he is powerless to stop it.

At the appointed time, Settembrini confides to Hans that he could never kill another human being, and he fires his pistol into the air.

"Coward!" shouts the enraged Naphta, who has come to duel in earnest. Naphta raises his pistol and shoots himself in the head. He dies instantly.

Breakfast, rest cure, second breakfast. . . .

It is seven years that Hans Castorp has been resident at House Berghof. He has long ago given up any contact with the "flat land" down below, and is pleasantly reconciled to living out his life within the enclosed world of the mountaintop sanatorium.

It is 1914, and at Sarajevo the Austrian archduke is assassinated. With the start of the world conflict that follows, suddenly there is an extensive stream of departures from House Berghof—both authorized and "wild"—as patients hasten to join their families and friends in war-torn Europe down below.

Hans Castorp finds himself propelled into instant action. He leaves the sanatorium, knowing that his life of inactivity and passivity is at an end. He has found something to live for.

When we see him last, it is through the smoke of a battlefield. He is in the thick of the fight, and looks somewhat strange in his German soldier uniform. He is aglow, and a folk song comes lustily from his lips.

STEPPENWOLF

Hermann Hesse

Hermann Hesse was born in 1877 in a small German town in the Black Forest. His father was a religious writer and a missionary, and Hermann was sent to a theological school to study. His earliest writings were recollections of childhood and youth, set in the small towns of southern Germany. His mature novels, which can be dated from the outset of the First World War, are psychologically oriented. Steppenwolf, published in 1924, is concerned with the nature of man, and the division in the human personality between the rational and the brutal. Hesse's later works are increasingly complex, and deal with the social and political values of Western society. He lived in Switzerland from 1919, received the Nobel Prize for literature in 1946, and died in 1962.

When middle-aged Harry Haller takes lodgings in the house of a bourgeois German woman, the woman's nephew takes an instant dislike to him. During the following weeks, however, the young man becomes more and more curious about Haller, and eventually finds that he actually likes the strange, aloof, older man. Haller refers to himself always as "the Steppenwolf"—wild wolf of the steppes—and the young man finds this an appropriate name for the strange, withdrawn man who is so obviously solitary by choice and yet deeply saddened by his own homelessness.

After ten months Haller leaves the house suddenly and unnoticed. All that remains of him is a manuscript which he has written. The young man reads the journal, and does not believe that it is a literal description of Haller's experiences, but merely symbolic. The young man is convinced that Haller has not gone away to commit suicide, but that somewhere, still, he lives on, trying to work out the problems of his unhappy existence.

Reading the manuscript, the young man plumbs the depths of Haller's soul. . . .

Haller believes that within his single body live two separate beings—the man of civilization, to whom art, literature, and music (particularly the music of Mozart) have noble and inspirational value, and the steppenwolf, who is aggressive, uncivilized, wholly natural and impulsive. Haller's entire life has been tormented by the inner struggle between these two aspects of his nature, each of them trying to gain ascendancy for possession of his soul and destiny.

One night, walking about the city in a state of despair and pessimism, Haller sees a beautiful little Gothic gateway cut into a wall in which no gate has ever been before. The sign over the gateway warns him that admittance is not for everyone; only madmen may pass through the gate. When he tries to gain entrance, he finds the gateway locked against him.

Later he encounters a mysterious peddler, from whom he purchases a cheaply bound pamphlet. On the cover of it he reads that the book is not for everyone—that it is intended only for madmen. Taking it back to his room, he is surprised to find that it is a treatise on the steppenwolf. He reads it avidly and carefully.

Much to his surprise, the little book perfectly anatomizes the case of the man with the steppenwolf in his breast. The book so closely parallels his own feelings that even the exemplary case cited has his own name—Harry. From the book he learns that such creatures as himself do not comprise only two opposed souls within a single body, as he had supposed, but thousands and thousands of souls. For several days he wanders about Berlin, brooding upon the unhappiness of his condition, the ambivalencies between nature and spirit which he is unable to reconcile.

One day he joins a passing funeral procession, but the artificiality and pretense of the Christian rites make him unhappier than before. He thinks of his own isolation from society; not even Erica, from whom he is divorced, would miss him were he to die, nor would he grieve over the death of any single being known to him.

After the funeral he encounters a professor with whom he had been friendly many years before. The man is delighted to see him, and invites him to dinner. Haller accepts, and then immediately regrets having done so. The evening, indeed, proves to be worse than he had anticipated. The conventionally minded professor launches a tirade against the writer of a protesting letter appearing in a jingoist newspaper, and though Haller himself is the author of the pacifistic letter, he says nothing. Later, however, Haller himself becomes rude over a prized portrait of Goethe in the professor's living room, and the evening ends in harsh words and Haller's sudden departure.

As he wanders about the city, Haller's thoughts turn more and more to suicide. Death, it seems to him, offers the only solution to the unbearable dilemma of his life. At the same time, however, he fears killing himself. To gain time, he goes into a small café and dance hall.

As he enters, his eye lights upon a prostitute seated at a table. Something about her appearance calls to him and he approaches her. She, in turn, has been attracted by something about him, and she invites him to join her. Though he cannot explain the sensation to himself, Haller feels that he is under this girl's spell.

Immediately the girl begins ordering Haller about. She makes him eat, tells him how to behave, insists that he take an interest in what is going on about him. Without protest, Haller submits to her demands.

The girl continues to surprise Haller, for in spite of her apparent coarseness and ignorance, she is able to see to the depths of his soul. With incredible perception she tells Haller all about himself, and lets him see that she is a kindred spirit. She too is torn by conflict between nature and spirit. She ends the evening by telling Haller that she is going to revive his interest in the world—the first step in the process will be her teaching him to dance; that then he will fall in love with her; and that finally he will perform her ultimate command, and that will be to kill her. Haller is not surprised by this, and goes home eagerly, already anticipating his next meeting with the girl.

At their next meeting the intimacy between them becomes even greater. Hermine—that is the girl's name—seems to anticipate Haller's every thought, every need. She introduces him to jazz music, café dances, people of an insubstantial sort—and he accepts all that she shows him.

Two of Hermine's friends, in particular, have a profound effect upon him. One is the Latin saxophone player Pablo, an incredibly handsome youth who seems to live in another world, but who perceives that Haller is deeply unhappy. The other is the prostitute Marie, whom Hermine sends to Haller's room to become his mistress. Amazed at Hermine's thoroughness in renewing his interest in the world, Haller throws himself into a liaison with Marie with a recklessness and joy he has never before known. She proves to be an incomparable mistress, and even knowing that she dispenses her favors to Hermine and to Pablo as well as to a host of men picked up casually does not diminish Haller's passion for her.

After several weeks of dancing lessons and mad, reckless activity, Hermine declares that Haller is ready to attend a forthcoming masked ball. As the evening approaches, Haller suddenly begins to doubt the purpose and value of his relationship with Hermine, but nonetheless he attends the masquerade.

The first part of the evening is a failure for Haller. He cannot find Hermine anywhere; Marie is occupied in the arms of other wooers; and the remote Pablo is too busy playing in one of the orchestras to pay much attention to him. Haller, who has not put on fancy dress, suddenly feels that he is an old and desperately unhappy man, and he decides to leave the ball.

At the checkroom, he pulls out the check which will claim his hat—only to find on it an invitation to attend a Magic Theater which is for madmen only. The price of admittance marked on the card: "Your Mind." Haller determines to stay at the masquerade after all, and suddenly the entire color of the evening changes for him. Furiously, with passionate abandon, he enters into the dancing, constantly changing partners, stealing passionate kisses from the beautiful women who surround him. Still, he cannot find Hermine.

Sitting down at a bar to take refreshment, he finds himself beside a youth who is the image of his childhood companion Herman. Haller turns—and finds that Herman is none other than Hermine disguised. Now, at last, Haller recognizes that he is desperately in love with Hermine.

On and on and on whirls the party, and Haller keeps up the pace as frantically as anyone. At last the dawn arrives, and Haller finds himself alone with Hermine (now dressed as a black and white Columbine) and Pablo. It is Pablo who invites them to attend the Magic Theater.

First, the three indulge in rare and exotic cigarettes to put them into the appropriate mood. And then, Haller finds that they are in the theater. The theater is curiously arranged, comprising a seemingly endless corridor with an infinite number of doors, each labeled. Pablo tells Haller that here he will find answers to all his questions about himself; Haller has only to open whichever door he chooses.

Thus begins a night of strange discovery.

The first door is labeled "Jolly Hunting." Haller enters, and finds himself on a vast battlefield in which everyone rides in automobiles. Joyfully, recklessly, he begins to shoot at all who approach in autos, and in a steady, never-ending stream the victims fall before him.

In another room, there is a mysterious chessboard, on which all the pieces are slivers of different parts of himself, seized out of a miraculous looking-glass which has shown him thousands of instant images of his own past and present. The Oriental with whom he plays the strange chess game is able to rearrange these few selected pieces of Harry's past into an infinite variety of patterns—each of which bears a common relationship to the others, but each of which is unique and different. There is, seemingly, no end to the different ways that pieces of Haller's past can be arranged and organized to form a coherent whole.

A third room shows him a man and wolf, each torturing the other in turn. The man first forces the wolf to behave like a man; then the roles are reversed, and the wolf seizes the whip and forces the man to behave like a wolf. But the man cannot behave like a man, nor the wolf like a wolf; each must continually deny his own proper role in order to gain ascendancy over the other.

In a room labeled "All Girls Are Yours," Haller relives his entire growing-up period. Every woman he had ever noticed now comes back; but in this reliving, Haller is not the fumbling, foolish, awkward, and embarrassed creature he had been in reality. Instead, he now sees the sexual content and passionate opportunities in each encounter; now, he is able to take from each woman what was uniquely hers to give, and to give to each what he had uniquely to offer. Never in his life has Haller known such pure, simple, physical completeness and joy as he knows in this chamber of the Magic Theater.

The last room carries the legend "How One Kills for Love." It terrifies Haller, and he runs back to the magic looking-glass. This time, however, his reflection shows him only a slavering wolf of the steppes. Transfixed by this image, he listens as music from *Don Giovanni* swells in the background, and in an instant he finds himself standing beside Mozart. The two engage in a long conversation, and Haller learns from Mozart that peace and forgetfulness will only come in eternity. As Mozart tunes in a wireless set to listen to the music of Handel, Haller seems to lose consciousness.

When he comes to himself, his image in the glass is no longer that of a wolf, but rather of his own external self. He plunges into the last room of the Magic Theater.

There, lying on the floor, are Hermine and Pablo, asleep. They are nude, and have clearly finished a bout of love. Haller pulls a knife from his pocket and stabs Hermine to death.

Now Pablo wakes. Seemingly unconcerned, he tells Haller that it is time for the execution—that death which Haller has so long wanted. With great relief, sensing that at last his torment is to be ended, Haller allows Pablo to lead him to a public square, where a group of black-robed judges stand before a giant guillotine.

At the word of command, Harry kneels before the guillotine and rests his head beneath the blade. Suddenly, however, the judges and all the spectators burst into hysterical laughter.

When Haller comes to himself, Mozart is again beside him. The musician tells him that Haller's sentence is to live and be laughed at. It is too easy to prefer the grand and dramatic gesture. Haller may be ready for moments of great passion— he is clearly even ready to murder a beautiful girl—but what he must learn is to accept the horrible gallows humor of life. Haller is willing to die; his sentence is that he must live.

Suddenly Mozart is transformed into the person of Pablo, who tells him that it is time to leave the Magic Theater. Haller realizes that all the pieces of himself that had been used in the strange chess game are still in his pocket. He determines to start the game once again. One day, he hopes, he will be better ready to join Pablo/Mozart for eternity.

KRISTIN LAVRANSDATTER

Sigrid Undset

Sigrid Undset was born in Denmark in 1882, the daughter of an eminent Norwegian archaeologist, in whose work Sigrid took an early interest. She had been educated at a girls' academy, and wanted to study art, but her father's death made it necessary for her to go to business school and to take up clerical work. She lived in Norway from 1899. While holding her job, she began to write after hours, and had three novels published by the time she left office work to devote herself in 1912 to her new career as a housewife. Her first successful novel appeared in 1911, but the most fruitful period of her career began with the publication, in 1920, 1921, and 1922, of the three novels which were to form the great trilogy Kristin Lavransdatter. This trilogy of medieval Norway was extremely popular in many countries, and led to Sigrid Undset's being awarded the Nobel Prize for literature in 1928. In the late 1920s she wrote a tetralogy about medieval Norway called The Master of Hestviken; and she later wrote fiction set in other times, and a notable collection of essays. She became a Roman Catholic in 1924, and was outspoken in advocating religious tolerance; she fled Norway upon the Nazi occupation of her country in 1940, and spent the years until the end of the war in the United States. She returned to Norway in 1945 and, widely honored, lived her last years in an old Viking house, where she died in 1949.

Against the darkly glowing tapestry of fourteenth-century Norway unfolds the epic story of a woman whose life is one long struggle to reconcile her passionate nature with her sense of honor.

The lord of the feudal estate at Jorundgaard, Lavrans Bjorgulfson, and his wife, Ragnfrid Ivarsdatter, are left after the death of two infant sons with but two daughters, Kristin and Ulvhild. (A third daughter is born later.) Lavrans, the most respected and one of the wealthiest men in the community, adores his two girls, particularly Kristin, for after Ulvhild is badly injured in an accident, Lavrans regards Kristin as the only unspoiled thing in the countryside. As a result, the girl grows up petted, pampered, and adored.

At the age of fifteen Kristin is betrothed to an upright, stolid, but somewhat passive young man named Simon Darre, son of Adres Gudmundson of Dyfrin. Kristin's sisters—the crippled Ulvhild and the very little Ramborg—take to Simon at once, but Kristin herself is not attracted to him, though she readily accepts her father's choice. Her own affection lies in another direction—with young Arne Gyrdson, handsome son of peasant stock, of a class that precludes anything developing between them. When Arne is about to go away on a journey, Kristin meets him at night to bid him farewell.

This innocent interview is witnessed by the scurrilous Bentein Priesten, who thinks that Kristin has given her favors to Arne and that therefore she will be free with *him*. Kristin's screams drive Bentein off, but he harbors a deep grudge, and not long after, he murders Arne Gyrdson.

The death of Arne starts rumors about Kristin's not having behaved as a daughter of a noble house should, and Lavrans and Simon agree that it would be well for Kristin to go to the convent at Nonneseter for a while before her marriage, to give the rumors a chance to die out and also to give Kristin an opportunity to mature and to master the finer domestic arts.

The decision has an unlooked-for result, however—one that is to affect the rest of Kristin's life. For during her sojourn at Nonneseter, the girl encounters the dark and handsome Erlend Nikulausson, who comes to her rescue one day when she is set upon by a group of scoundrels. Unaware that the man has a considerable reputation as a rogue with a light way with women, and that he is the nephew of Lady Aashild of Haugen, who, in Kristin's home province, has achieved notoriety for living in open adultery with Sir Bjorn, Kristin thinks only of Erlend's dashing good looks. When she meets him by chance on a second occasion, the girl is delighted. Soon the pair meet regularly—no longer by chance—and Kristin finds herself hopelessly in love. She and Erlend pledge eternal devotion to one another, and unabashed by the fact that he has fathered two bastards, a son Orm and a daughter Margret, Kristin becomes Erlend's mistress.

When Simon goes to the convent to visit Kristin, she asks him to release her from her betrothal pledge, inasmuch as she has fallen in love with someone else. Simon is hurt by the girl's behavior, and is especially dismayed when he learns that she loves the disreputable Erlend Nikulausson—but he is too much of a gentleman to hold her to her word, and he has too great respect for her father, Lavrans, to humiliate him by taking Kristin against her will. So it comes about that Kristin returns to her family's home, shamed for having thrown over so fine a man as Simon Darre.

Lavrans is unwilling that Kristin should marry against her will; but he is equally unwilling that she should marry the rogue Erlend. (Lavrans is, of course, unaware that Kristin has already surrendered her virtue to the man.) Kristin is in despair, and her problem worsens when she discovers that she is with child. At last, her father having refused Erlend's offer for her, she agrees to elope with Erlend, and therefore she goes to the home of his aunt, Lady Aashild, where she is to meet her beloved.

Before they can make good their elopement, however, a visitor arrives. It is Eline Ormsdatter, Erlend's mistress of ten years' standing and the mother of his two children. The woman is mad with rage and jealousy—Erlend has long ago grown tired of her—and she is unwilling to give him up, wishing now to hold him to a promise he made in his youth that he would wed her when her husband died. In the confrontation between Eline and Kristin, the older woman tries to poison the girl—but she and Erlend are too quick for the madwoman, and Erlend, his knife at Eline's throat, compels her to swallow the poisoned drink. This sudden change in matters makes it necessary for Erlend to carry away Eline's body, and Kristin must therefore return to her father's house.

Shortly thereafter, Kristin's crippled sister Ulvhild dies. After this, Kristin notes a softening on her father's part toward her; and when Erlend's kinsmen, the nobly born Sir Baard and Sir Munan, make suit on his behalf, Lavrans agrees to Kristin's marrying Erlend. (Simon, meanwhile, has married a widow, Lady Halfrid.)

At the wedding, it is clear to all that Kristin is pregnant. In their shame, Lavrans and his cold, remote wife Ragnfrid are led to confide more fully in each other than ever before. Ragnfrid confesses that she had not been a maid at her marriage; indeed, the first son she bore might not have been Lavrans'. As for the husband, he feels great pain that he has never understood these two women who are most precious to him—his wife, Ragnfrid, and his daughter Kristin.

Kristin now goes to Erlend's estate at Husaby, over which she is to be mistress. She is appalled that things are so carelessly run; the whole estate is in disrepair, and waste and profligacy are on every hand. It is a marked contrast to the orderly life she had known in her father's house. With a will, she sets to work changing things so that Husaby may one day become again a fine and thriving estate. In this work she has the help and support of two loyal men—Ulf Haldorsson, a bastard kinsman of Erlend's who serves as steward, and Orm, Erlend's son by Eline Ormsdatter. (Kristin is surprised to find that she genuinely likes Orm—though she and Erlend's daughter, Margret, are unable to be anything but hostile toward each other.) Another source of moral support to Kristin at this period of her life is Erlend's younger brother Gunnulf, who is a priest.

Kristin is dismayed to find that Erlend seems so often remote from her. He has no interest in farming or in managing his estate, and spends most of his time discussing the political troubles of the day, matters which he does not share with her. When, however, after an excruciatingly painful delivery, their first son, Naakve, is born, Erlend draws closer to Kristin for a while.

And so time passes, with Kristin dividing her days between care and management of Husaby and the raising of her growing family. A second son, Bjorgulf, comes a year after the first, and then a third, Gaute, is born. Her fourth child Kristin miscarries as a result of a scarlet fever epidemic; and in the same epidemic, Orm falls ill and dies.

With the passing years Kristin finds Erlend more and more remote from her. He chafes at being confined to the farms—his whole life has been one of fighting and adventure —and he is indignant that Kristin should constantly be pregnant or nursing. More and more, Erlend absents himself from home, going on long journeys of mysterious political import. When her fourth and fifth sons are born, the twins Ivar and Skule, Kristin feels again the bitterness of knowing that Erlend does not care much for his children.

Simon's wife having died childless, he now marries Kristin's youngest sister, Ramborg. As Kristin goes home for the wedding for the first time in eight years, it seems impossible to her that so much time can have gone by. She is distressed to see how aged her parents have become, and she is overcome with guilt and remorse for all the grief she has caused them.

After the wedding, Kristin stays on at her father's estate, both because Lavrans is dying and because she is so near to the time for delivering another child. Indeed, shortly after her sixth son is born, her father expires, and the infant—who has remained unnamed until his grandfather should die— is christened Lavrans. (By custom, children are not named after living persons.) Two years later, in 1332, the strange, remote Ragnfrid follows her husband to the grave, and Kristin is saddened that she and her mother had never been able to communicate with one another effectively.

Now, it seems to Kristin, life at Husaby consists of nothing but trouble. Erlend is contentious with his brother Gunnulf over the latter's handling of certain estates which they share in common. Added to her distress at seeing this bitterness divide these two who were once so close is the problem of Erlend's anger over her being pregnant again, and their disagreement about the proper upbringing of their sons. Worst of all is the illicit relationship that Erlend's bastard daughter Margret forms with a married man, Haakon of Gismar. Erlend, discovering the man in his daughter's chamber one night, attacks him and wounds him severely, even to the cutting off of his hand. As a result of this scandal, Margret must be married off far below the station Erlend had hoped for her; and when she weds Gerlak Tiedkensson, son of a humble goldsmith, Erlend vents his anger on Kristin, and blames her for all of Margret's misfortunes. Kristin can only suffer in silence.

The estrangement between her and Erlend grows ever greater. Soon after the birth of their seventh son, Muhan, Kristin and Erlend have a series of bitter quarrels. The impetuous Erlend feels justified in breaking his fidelity to Kristin, and he begins an affair with the flighty but jealous Lady Sunniva Olavsdatter. Guilt very quickly overtakes him, and he casts her off.

Lady Sunniva, however, is not to be so lightly dealt with. One night as Erlend had slept at her side, Lady Sunniva had read some confidential letters that he was carrying. When Erlend deserts her, she reports the contents of these letters to the authorities, and the result is that Erlend is arrested on charges of treason.

After long imprisonment, Erlend is found guilty, and his life and goods are forfeit to the crown. Execution is postponed for a year, however, as the king wishes to have Erlend tortured (which is against the law) to find out the names of his co-conspirators. It is only because at this juncture Simon comes to Erlend's defense that he is saved. Backed up by the powerful intercession of Sir Erling Vidkunsson, Simon manages at last to have Erlend's life spared and the man himself released. All of Erlend's goods and lands, however, are forfeit. Therefore, he and all his sons must remove to Kristin's estate, Jorundgaard, which she has inherited from Lavrans.

Life at Jorundgaard is even worse for Erlend than life at Husaby. In addition to his loathing of farming and management, he suffers the indignity of knowing that he is living on his wife's wealth, and he has lost everything he might have left to his sons, who will now go unprovided for. There is also the unpleasantness of being constantly in company with Simon and Ramborg. This last problem, however, is ended when Simon confesses to Erlend that he has never once left off loving Kristin, and that he has decided never to see them again.

With the break between Simon and Erlend, Kristin becomes more argumentative than ever. She does not know about Simon's feelings for her, and only feels a great debt of gratitude toward him for having come to Erlend's rescue; accordingly she blames Erlend's habitual selfishness and thoughtlessness for alienating Simon. At last Erlend can stand being at cross-purposes with Kristin no longer, and he deserts her to live on the tiny farm at Haugen, a run-down estate which he has inherited since the seizure of his property from his late aunt, Lady Aashild.

Not long after, Simon falls sick, and Ramborg being too ill to attend him, having recently been brought to childbed, Kristin—known as an excellent leechwoman—is asked to come to Simon's estate, Formo, to nurse him through what is to prove his last illness. During this time the two become very close, but though Kristin tells Simon that she loves him as a brother, he never breaks his silence to confess his deep and long-lasting passion for her.

Kristin now goes to Erlend's retreat at Haugen to beg him to return to Jorundgaard. Adamantly he refuses. After five days of bliss with Erlend—he is again the young man she had first seen at Nonneseter, without the cares of children and farming and families—she returns, disheartened, to Jorundgaard alone. Several months later, when she learns that she is again pregnant, she sends one of her sons to Erlend with the news, and the request that he return. Erlend, however, is steadfastly stubborn, and again refuses.

When Kristin is delivered of another son, she bravely carries it to church and has it christened Erlend, thus violating custom and tradition. The scandal this causes is matched in viciousness only by the rumor that the child is by her husband's steward and bastard kinsman, Ulf Haldorsson. (None of the townspeople know, of course, about Kristin's sojourn with Erlend at Haugen. They know only that he has been gone from Jorundgaard for more than a year.) When little Erlend dies before he is three months old, Kristin thinks that surely her husband will return to her; but he does not come.

Now the rumors about Kristin's adultery with Ulf are brought into the open when Ulf's wife sues the bishop to grant her a divorce on the grounds that Ulf had fathered Kristin's child. The whole town turns against Kristin, and she has only her sons to defend her. Hearing at last of this vicious charge against Kristin, Erlend returns to Jorundgaard in haste to clear her. He is met by a mob of villagers and, in his usual hasty manner, begins a fight without thinking. During the melee, in which he kills several men, Erlend is severely wounded in the groin; and several days later, with all his sons gathered about his bedside, Erlend Nikulaussen dies.

For several years Kristin lives on at Jorundgaard. Except for Munan, who dies in an epidemic the spring after Erlend, all her sons live on. Lavrans has taken service with Jammaelt Halvardsson, Ramborg's second husband, who promises to make the lad's fortune. Ivar marries a rich widow. Skule enters the service of a nobleman, with whom he can travel and experience high adventure in the world. Naakve and Bjorgulf —the latter now nearly blind—have become monks.

Only Gaute lives on at home, and he is now the master at Jorundgaard. Kristin is appalled to learn that Gaute has fathered a bastard daughter by a serving wench—and when the little girl dies, she does not know whether she feels sadness or relief.

Now Gaute determines to marry, and Kristin watches as the drama of her son's life reminds her painfully of her own youth. Gaute has fallen in love with the beautiful Joffrid Helgesdatter, whose father, a wealthy nobleman, would never consent to her marrying the son of Erlend Nikulaussen. Accordingly the girl runs off with Gaute, and comes to live at Jorundgaard. When she bears a son, Erlend Gautesson, her father relents, as she knew he would; and Joffrid and Gaute are married. Later, a daughter is born to them.

Kristin, now in late middle age, is not happy in her daughter-in-law's house, and, as with the passing years she has turned ever increasingly to a love of God, at last she determines to become a nun. She joins a convent as a lay sister, and when the black plague breaks out, she proves her courage and her faith by undertaking tasks that no other dares. On one such errand she finds herself face to face with Ulf Haldorsson, and over the body of a woman newly dead, the two remember the man that they both loved and devoted their lives to—Erlend Nikulausson.

Word arrives that the plague has overwhelmed a nearby priory, and that both Naakve and Bjorgulf are dead. But Kristin Lavransdatter has little time to grieve, for it is only a matter of hours before she too is stricken. Thus dies Kristin Lavransdatter.

THE CONFESSIONS OF ZENO

Italo Svevo

Italo Svevo was born Ettore Schmitz in 1861 in Trieste, of a well-to-do Austrian father and an Italian mother. Due to the failure of his father's business, he was forced to give up his studies at the age of seventeen, and to take a job in a bank. His first novel, Una Vita, published in 1893, attracted little attention, and Svevo remained in the financial field. In 1902, while making frequent trips to England to oversee a branch of his now-prospering business, he engaged as his private English tutor one James Joyce. He showed Joyce his writings; Joyce was ecstatic, and encouraged Svevo to go on with his literary work. In 1923 Svevo, now retired from business, wrote The Confessions of Zeno, and had it published, as with his first two novels, at his own expense. He sent a copy to Joyce, who by this time had already become extremely influential as an author and critic, and Joyce recommended it to leading French and Italian critics. At once Svevo was discovered, and hailed as a great modern master of Italian literature. He was writing a sequel to The Confessions of Zeno when he was killed in an automobile accident in 1928.

The Confessions of Zeno was published in English in 1930. A masterpiece of irony, wit, and intelligence, it is rich in its perception of the intricacies and contradictions of human nature. Even though everything in the book is described as seen by the lazy, indecisive, and grotesquely pathetic Zeno, the observations are ultimately those of a man with compassion, humor, and a great deal of wisdom.

From earliest childhood, when he first became addicted to smoking, Zeno Cosini has been a most methodical person. Therefore when, as a young man, he decides to give up smoking, he selects a date that will be most propitious for discarding the habit. After all, one can't just select any time at random for one's last cigarette; there must be a certain neatness to one's choice of time, so that the gesture of renouncing nicotine will be of some significance. So Zeno sets the date—marks on the flyleaf of a book "Last Cigarette"—and stops smoking.

His last cigarette, however, leads to another. He therefore selects another propitious date, again makes the journal entry "Last Cigarette," and stops smoking. He has no better success this time. Thus begins a series of "last" cigarettes that is to endure his whole life long; each of his attempts, it must be noted, is accompanied by a sense of high purpose, firm resolve, and a notation on a book's flyleaf (or next to a dictionary listing) of the date and the words "Last Cigarette." Before long, this is abbreviated to the date and "L.C."

(At one point—this is some time later in the story, after he has been married—he even has himself incarcerated in a private sanitarium run by a Dr. Muli, where cigarettes are to be withheld from him by his nurse, a pathetic middle-aged widow. However, Zeno manages to get around this problem by suggesting to the nurse that cigarettes have a profound effect on his amatory powers; after he has smoked ten cigarettes, he tells her, women must be locked up if their safety and virtue are to be preserved. A few minutes later the nurse surreptitiously provides Zeno with the specified number of cigarettes. When he hears her go eagerly to her room, he calmly and successfully makes good his escape from the sanitarium.)

In April 1890, while Zeno is still a young man, his father lies dying. Zeno's mother had died when he was fifteen, and he had never in the past been close to his father. During his father's last illness, however, Zeno has long conversations with him about the meaning of life and death and the hereafter—but Zeno's flippant pronouncements are too much for the old man, who has long been half convinced of his son's madness. (When Zeno had been at the university, his constant changing of fields of study had led the old man to accuse his son of being mad. As a joke, Zeno went to Dr.

Canestrini and got a certificate proving his sanity. The old man did not think this funny, however; to him it only *proved* that Zeno was mad.)

Zeno's flippant attitude toward his father turns to remorse during the final stages of the man's illness, and he attends his father constantly. At the moment of death the old man raises his arm and strikes his son. Zeno cannot believe that this was what his father had *meant* to do; surely he was merely reaching for something and lost his balance. His father's death moves Zeno (briefly) to return to religion. He is grateful, now that the old man is gone, that he has had such a fine filial relationship with him. Zeno marks on the flyleaf of Ostwald's *Positive Philosophy*, which he is reading at the time, the words "4:30 A.M. My father died. L.C."

Zeno's father leaves his estate in the care of an old broker, Olivi, who is to manage the money for Zeno. Therefore the young man has nothing with which to occupy himself all day long. He resolves to marry. He has a friend, much older than himself, named Giovanni Malfenti, a crude, boorish business-man. This Malfenti has four daughters, all of whose names begin with A, and Zeno resolves to meet them.

Finally he is invited to Malfenti's house. The daughters, however, do not live up to his expectations. Augusta is homely; Alberta is a feminist; Anna is only ten years old. Ada, alone, is a beauty, and Zeno instantly falls in love with her. It appears, however, that she does not return his emotion.

Nonetheless Zeno persists in visiting the house night after night, in the hopes that Ada will relent. Since Zeno believes himself to be amusing to Augusta and Alberta, he hopes that they will put in a good word for him with Ada. (As for Anna, she openly accuses Zeno of being mad.)

With every day that passes, Zeno's love for Ada grows stronger and stronger. Imagine his surprise, then, when one day, on coming to the house, he is greeted by Signora Malfenti, who chastises him for toying with Augusta's affections in such a manner. If he does not mean to make the girl an offer, after having made her fall in love with him, says Signora Malfenti, Zeno had better stay away from the house for a while. Zeno is flabbergasted at this turn of events—and he stays away from the Malfentis.

Eventually, however, he finds that he cannot keep himself away from the jolly evenings at the Malfenti house, or from the prospect of seeing Ada. Accordingly he accepts an invitation from them to attend a party. A few days before the party, he meets Ada walking in the street with a handsome young man who is introduced as Guido Speier. That Ada prefers this popinjay is clear, and Zeno is in a rage of jealousy. His emotion is every bit as intense on the night of the party itself, for he finds Guido among the guests—and the center of attention. Zeno gets fairly tipsy, and makes a fool of himself, but he doesn't mind since this seems to offend the hated Guido.

When the party is about to break up, Zeno feels he must tie himself to the delightful Malfenti family at all costs. Accordingly he abruptly proposes to Ada, who turns him down. He then seeks out Alberta, proposes to her, and is rejected. Next, he goes to Augusta. He tells her that both of her sisters have just turned him down, and then he proposes to her. Humbly grateful to him for having her, ugly as she is, Augusta accepts. Soon afterward, Zeno and Augusta are married.

Betrothed only a short time after Zeno's own betrothal are Guido and Ada. Zeno resolves that all is over between him and Ada, and he cheerfully wishes her luck. He is delighted to find that he regards Guido now as a bosom friend—for after all, Guido really is a remarkable fellow.

After the two marriages, Guido decides to go into business, and he invites Zeno to help him. The two make endless arrangements and preparations—Zeno's methodical tendencies come in handy here—and soon they have bought furniture, hired a suite of offices, and engaged a pretty (if incompetent) stenographer named Carmen. The only problem is that neither Guido nor Zeno knows much about business. Zeno offers to ask old Olivi, who has proved an excellent manager, for advice; but Guido violently objects. He is sure that he and Zeno, without outside help, will be able to figure out how to run a successful business. Indeed, Guido seems to spend most of his time, now, at the office; but Zeno surmises that it is because he is having an affair with Carmen.

Zeno himself spends less and less time at the office, for he too is now having an affair. His mistress is the beautiful young singing student Carla Gerco, who had been the beneficiary of a private subscription fund to which Zeno had contributed. Zeno has great anxiety and guilt over his deception of Augusta, who really is the most admirable of women. Indeed, he finds that he dearly loves Augusta and never thinks of Ada anymore. Still, Carla is so pretty, so delightful. Zeno is especially pleased by her innocence; he must *force* her to accept money from him. (This money he hoards assiduously in a little envelope, so that he will always have some to bring Carla.)

The girl eventually begins importuning Zeno to tell him all about the misery of his marriage (he has, of course, told her he is unhappily married to a woman who does not understand him). Zeno is reluctant to talk about Augusta, but at last he agrees to point his wife out in the street to his young mistress. For some perverse reason which he himself doesn't understand, Zeno indicates to Carla as his wife none other than his sister-in-law Ada. Carla is so touched by the beauty of Zeno's "wife" and by her unhappy expression—Ada has by now learned of Guido's relations with his pretty secretary, Carmen—that she determines to give Zeno up. Accordingly Carla accepts the marriage proposal of her poor (but young and handsome) singing teacher. Zeno is touched by the girl's altruism, but bitter over her rejection of him. He cajoles and begs Carla to take him back, but she remains adamant in her decision that all is over between them, and Zeno goes back to Augusta. Later, he is able to congratulate himself on his virtue in having ended this tawdry alliance; Augusta is a jewel, a prize; he must love her and her only.

Because of his two-year-long affair with Carla, Zeno has paid little attention to Guido's business, of which he is the accountant. When he returns to the office, he is horrified to find that Guido's losses are staggering. He warns his friend at once that he must declare legal bankruptcy or face the consequences, which may be nasty.

Guido becomes hysterical at this advice; clearly Zeno does not trust him, and thinks he is an incompetent businessman. Guido's tirade brings on an attack of Zeno's mysterious limp —he has long suffered from a host of nervous and physical disorders of the most bizarre kind. Guido resolves that Ada must sign over to him half of her own fortune (Malfenti having died and left each of his daughters fairly well off). Zeno points out that this will accomplish nothing, and advises Ada (through Augusta) not to consent. Faced with Ada's refusal to give him her money, Guido stages a mock suicide attempt, and tearfully Ada (who loves her handsome husband) capitulates.

But it is as Zeno had predicted; and soon Guido's business affairs are in a worse mess than ever. Zeno warns Guido that he will go to prison if he doesn't straighten out the business, and Guido promises that he will "do" something. The first thing he does is to go off on a hunting party with Carmen to "clear his head for action"; his next step is to begin gambling on the Bourse, buying stocks on margin, selling short, and so forth. This leads Guido from one catastrophe to another. Again, he determines that Ada shall come to his rescue, and again he stages a suicide attempt. This time, however, Guido is not so lucky, and he dies.

Zeno becomes the man of the family by arranging everything so that Guido's losses are reduced and some of Ada's money is preserved. Everyone adores him—except Ada. She cannot forgive him for missing Guido's funeral (by mistake, Zeno had got into the wrong funeral procession and had found himself at the Greek Orthodox ceremony). When Ada goes away to South America to live with her children at the home of Guido's father, she castigates Zeno for his hatred of Guido. Zeno is flabbergasted at this wild accusation of Ada's, but she persists in taking the position that Zeno has always hated Guido, and brought about his downfall.

Some years later, Zeno goes into psychoanalysis. (Indeed, all of these, his confessions, are written at the suggestion of Dr. S., his analyst, who believes that they will help Zeno get to the root of his problems.) But the analysis is not a success —Zeno hasn't even been able to give up smoking, and certainly all his nervous ailments are no better than they were— so he gives up his venture in psychiatry. It was particularly grating that the doctor—the fool!—had insisted that Zeno had had an Oedipus complex and that he had hated not only his father (his dear father!) but also Malfenti and Guido Speier. Really, it was too taxing on Zeno's imagination to keep coming up with make-believe dreams to tell the doctor to substantiate this Oedipal theory.

The First World War has broken out, and though the fighting has not yet got near them, Zeno moves his family to their country home at Lucinico, where he believes that Augusta, their son Alfio, and their daughter Antonia will be safer. One day he goes out for a stroll in the countryside (and has a harmless flirtation with a farmer's daughter, who laughs at him and calls him an old man). On his way back to his estate, he is stopped by German soldiers who have encamped nearby and who will not let him through. So the war has come to Lucinico!

There is nothing for it but to begin the long trudge on foot to Trieste to get the necessary papers that will allow him to join his family. In Trieste he cannot get documents to allow him to return to Lucinico, but learning that his family is safe, he settles down in the city. Soon he is actively engaged in the world of high finance—and making a great success of it. He finds for the first time in his life a sense of satisfaction and contentment in a life of activity and purpose. He anticipates with great glee the fortune that he will make from his humming business deals.

THE TRIAL

Franz Kafka

Franz Kafka was born in Prague in 1883, the son of a Jewish businessman in comfortable circumstances. He received a law degree at the German University in Prague, and later held a minor government post in Austria. He suffered from poor health, and spent many years of his life in sanatoriums. He died of tuberculosis in Austria in 1924.

Some of his short stories had been published during his lifetime, but his three novels remained at his death in the form of unedited manuscripts. Kafka had, in fact, ordered a friend to destroy his unpublished manuscripts, but the author's friend, Max Brod, disobeyed this final request, and prepared the manuscripts for publication. The three novels—The Trial, The Castle, and Amerika—are closely related in content and style; Kafka's heroes are lonely men, confronted by a universe which oppresses them as they seek to discover its meaning, and their own place in its scheme. The Trial, which appeared in 1925, has the surrealistic quality of a nightmare; the central character is never apprised of the charges against him, nor is the identity of his prosecutors ever ascertained. He is guilty of existing, and because he exists, he must suffer in solitary anguish, unable to learn the direction, if any, of his salvation.

Joseph K., aged thirty and a bachelor, is awakened one day by a knock on his bedroom door. This in itself is unusual, as he is ordinarily awakened by Frau Gruber, the landlady of

the rooming house in which he lives, who brings him breakfast. K.'s surprise is heightened when he finds that the person
knocking is a stranger.

This man politely but firmly tells K. that he is under arrest, and asks him to step into the sitting room for a hearing.
K. dresses hastily and presents himself, only half believing
in the reality of the situation. He surmises that this is somebody's idea of a practical joke.

He revises his opinion, however, when he finds several
persons standing about the sitting room. All are strangers except two—Franz and Willem—who are clerks of low position
in the bank at which K. himself is chief clerk, a man of some
importance.

K. is now ushered into the bedroom of another tenant,
Fräulein Bürstner—a girl he has only noticed casually in the
past—and here he is informed briefly that he is under arrest,
though the strangers cannot tell him the charges against him,
as that is not allowed. Oddly, K. finds that what annoys him
most about this mysterious affair is that Franz and Willem
freely handle some photographs belonging to Fräulein Bürstner. The officials (none of them uniformed) then tell K. that
he will receive instructions about presenting himself for interrogation, and that in the meantime he may consider himself free to go about his business.

Put out of sorts by these strange goings-on, K. has a conversation with the landlady, but when Frau Gruber drops an
unpleasant reference to Fräulein Bürstner, K. is highly offended. He determines that he must make amends to the
young woman personally, and that night, when Fräulein
Bürstner returns home from work, K. approaches her. He
fumblingly begins apologizing to her for the Court of Inquiry's having used her premises for its hearing, but she does
not seem too upset by this. Before he knows how it has come
about, K. finds himself kissing and caressing the young
woman; and to this also she makes no objection. After their
innocent love-play is interrupted, however, by the arrival in
the next room of Frau Gruber's nephew, a captain, the young
woman's attitude suddenly changes, and she sends K. away
indignantly.

For the next few days K. goes about his business uncon-
cernedly; indeed, he devotes more time to thinking about
Fräulein Bürstner than he does to the unspecified charges

against him. The following Sunday, however, he receives a telephone call notifying him to present himself at a given address for interrogation.

The address is in a slum neighborhood, and K. has great difficulty in locating the specific apartment in which the first interrogation is to take place. At last he finds the room—a dirty, foul-smelling, overcrowded attic, jammed with strange, chattering men who seem to be of two factions. There is little order to the proceedings, so K. takes the situation in hand by making an impassioned speech to the court in which he declares his innocence and his absolute refusal to take any further part in this trial nonsense. At the end of K.'s declamation, he is told by the presiding judge that in making this plea he could not have done anything that would have a worse effect on the outcome of his case. K. is sent away and is told that he will be informed of proceedings in due time.

All week long, K. waits for a summons by the court, but receives none. Accordingly the following Sunday he goes back to the tenement courtroom of his first interrogation, only to find it empty. A slatternly woman—wife of the court's usher —engages him in conversation about the curious courts and the strange cases always being heard, but she is unable to give him any specific information about these extralegal goings-on. She begins to flirt with K., and he is on the point of seducing her when an arrogant and unpleasant student of the courts arrives and carries the woman bodily off to the Examining Magistrate who, like the student himself, has made the woman his mistress.

The court usher arrives just in time to see his wife carried off, and he makes bitter complaint to K. of the abuse he continually suffers as a menial of the court. He offers to show K. about the premises, knowing that as K. is himself under charge of the court, he will find a tour fascinating. They mount to an attic gallery, and K. sees in a sort of waiting room the most dejected band of men and women imaginable. The usher tells him that these are the accused whose cases are pending. K. thanks his lucky stars that he is not as abject and impotent as these poor creatures seem to be.

It is not long, however, before K. feels his own strength and vitality leaving him in these fetid premises. And though he has a conversation with an attractive young woman who apparently is connected with the court, and a dapper man who proves to be the Clerk of Inquiries, both of whom seem genuinely concerned about making him more comfortable, he finds himself growing weaker and weaker. Finally he prevails upon them to help him through the labyrinthine passages that lead to the street. It is only when K. finds himself again in the cool, fresh air that his spirits revive and he feels himself again.

During the next few days Fräulein Bürstner avoids K. assiduously, and he is more determined than ever to renew a pleasant relationship with her. At last, however, it is apparent that this cannot be, for Fräulein Bürstner has invited an unattractive girl to share her room, and this girl gives K. a brief interview in which she tells him he must leave Fräulein Bürstner entirely alone. K. cannot resist taking one last look around Fräulein Bürstner's room, but he senses that the strange, ugly girl and the captain are both aware of what he is up to, and this disconcerts him.

Now K. thinks more and more about his disturbing situation; and elements of it keep returning to haunt him. One day, in the bank where he works, he hears a sigh emanating from an unused storeroom. He opens the door to find Franz and Willem, both stripped, about to be flogged. They tell him that they are being punished because K. had complained about them during his first interrogation. K. is horrified, and implores the whipper not to carry out his orders on the two clerks, but the man is adamant. At the first shriek from the victims, K. closes the door and goes his way.

One afternoon K.'s elderly uncle arrives from the country and visits K. at the bank. The old man is beside himself with grief and despair over the fact that the charges, about which he has heard, have been made against K. He prevails upon K. to accompany him to the home of the famous lawyer Dr. Huld, who will, Uncle Albert believes, solve everything.

Dr. Huld proves to be desperately sick, but K. and his uncle are admitted to his bedroom by a voluptuous serving maid, Leni. The more Dr. Huld babbles about the strange extralegal courts and his experiences with them, the more convinced K. is that the lawyer is a fool and cannot help him. At the first opportunity K. slips away and finds Leni, to whom he makes love. At the end of the evening, Uncle Albert is disgusted and infuriated with K. for taking so little interest in his own case.

It is only after the interview with the lawyer, however, that K. seems fully to realize his own predicament. He becomes so obsessed with his case, with the unspecified charges against him, and with the futility of trying to prove his own innocence, that he pays less and less attention to his work at the bank. The thought that this laxness will give his rival, the Assistant Manager, a chance to rise to new heights only adds to K.'s gloom.

One day a manufacturer, who is a client of the bank, notices K.'s abstracted and preoccupied air. The manufacturer says that he has heard something of K.'s case, and recommends that K. go and visit Titorelli, a painter who is in some way attached to the court, and who may be of some service to K. Eagerly K. accepts the manufacturer's letter of introduction to the painter.

Titorelli lives in a tenement on the opposite side of town from the slums where the court has its offices, and K. is pleased to find him a congenial sort of fellow. Titorelli explains that as official court painter, he has access to much information as well as having friendships among many of the justices. He explains to K. that if K. is innocent—K. assures him that he is—there are three verdicts one can hope for. The first and best, definite acquittal, is unheard of, except in legends, and should be discarded as unattainable. The other two possibilities are ostensible acquittal and indefinite postponement. In ostensible acquittal, the prisoner goes free, but the case is not officially closed, and may be reopened at any time; indeed, sometimes a prisoner, having just heard a verdict of ostensible acquittal, goes home in jubilation only to find officers already there with a warrant for his arrest. Indefinite postponement, on the other hand, requires endless work and attention, since it is based upon never allowing the case to reach trial in the first place. Titorelli says that he stands ready to help K. in either alternative. After buying three paintings—all of them identical scenes of a heath—K. says he will think the matter over.

By now, months have dragged by, and K. can think of nothing but his case. He believes more in Titorelli, who claims that he can bribe the judges, as an ally than in Dr. Huld, who has in effect demonstrated to K. that lawyers are worse than useless. (Indeed, K.'s only reason for having called on Dr. Huld from time to time was the opportunity

such calls gave him to make love to Leni.) K. now decides
that he must dismiss Dr. Huld as his lawyer.

Accordingly he goes to the lawyer's house, this time to be
admitted not by Leni but by a strange, unhappy-looking man
who proves to be a tradesman named Block. This Block tells
K. his story; he has been under charge of the court for five
years, and Dr. Huld is only one of six lawyers he retains to
handle his case. His business has gone to ruin in the process;
indeed, his whole life revolves around his case. This man
interests K. greatly—he seems to have a good deal of inside
information about the strange workings of the courts—but
when K. notes that Leni seems fond of Block, his manner
cools, and he asks to be announced to Dr. Huld.

Ushered into the lawyer's bedroom, K. declares his intentions of dismissing the old man from the case. Dr. Huld, however, tells him to watch something before making up his
mind finally on the matter. Summoning Block to the bedroom, Dr. Huld lets K. see how totally subservient and dependent upon him is this accused man, Block. Indeed, Block
even goes so far as to crawl on his hands and knees and kiss
the old man's hand just to get the lawyer to reveal one crumb
of information about how his case is progressing. K. is sickened at this display, and further angered when Dr. Huld
tells him that Leni finds irresistible all men who are accused,
and that she is as free with her favors toward Block as she is
toward K. himself. K. leaves the lawyer's house in dark indecision.

K.'s superior at the bank seems not to notice how absorbed the young Chief Clerk is in extraprofessional matters,
and one day he asks K. to meet an important Italian client
and show the man the beauties of the city. K. sets up an
appointment to meet the visiting client in the city's cathedral. At the appointed time, however, the Italian does not
show up, and K. begins to wander about the cathedral by
himself. He notices, for the first time, a curious pulpit, seemingly designed so as to torture whoever might stand in it.
Then K. sees a priest actually going up into this pulpit to
preach a sermon, although the cathedral is empty.

Suddenly the priest calls him by name—"Joseph K."—and
K. stands riveted to the spot, to hear what the priest has to
tell him. First, the priest says that the case is going very
badly—that it is certain that K. will be condemned, and that

the verdict will come soon. Then he tells K. a lengthy parable about an ancient man who guards the gates of justice, and a petitioner to whom he bars admittance. Ultimately the petitioner, after having waited at the gate his entire life, dies, and the guard locks the door. The priest and K. have a long conversation, in which all of the various interpretations of the story are investigated, and ultimately K. finds he does not know how to interpret the tale accurately.

When the time comes to leave the cathedral, K. begs the priest to tell him if he wants him for anything more. But the priest replies that he is a prison chaplain. Therefore he is attached to the court, and has no more need of K. than the court has. The court is merely there to receive K. when he comes and dismiss him when he goes.

Not long afterward—on the evening of K.'s thirty-first birthday—two top-hatted men arrive at his house. K. immediately feels that a verdict has been announced in his case, and that these men are his executioners. The two men grip K.'s arms like two vises, and lead him through the streets, and ultimately out of the city.

At the edge of a stream, they strip K. of his coat and shirt, and stretch him on the ground. The two men begin passing a long knife from one to the other across his body. K. realizes that they expect him to seize the knife and kill himself, but he is determined not to do this. K. believes that help must be at hand, and he stretches out his arms, spreading all his fingers toward the sky. But the hands of one of the men are already around his throat, and the other plunges the knife into K.'s chest. In his final moment, K. senses that even his death will be a shame that will outlive him.

DARKNESS AT NOON

Arthur Koestler

Arthur Koestler was born in Budapest, Hungary, in 1905. His father was an inventor whose business was ruined by the outbreak of World War I. The family moved to Vienna, where Arthur attended the university. In 1926 he went to Palestine for a short time in order to work for the Zionist movement. He then edited a German newspaper in Cairo, and later became a correspondent for a newspaper chain. Koestler joined the Communist Party in 1931, and was a member until 1938. He visited Russia, and, while in Spain in 1937, was captured by the Fascists and sentenced to be executed. His release was secured by the London newspaper for which he had worked, and he was subsequently imprisoned in France and in England, presumably because of his Communist affiliations. After his release from prison in England, he was appointed to the Ministry of Information for the duration of the Second World War. He has lived in England since then.

Most of Koestler's writings deal in one way or another with his experiences as a Communist. Darkness at Noon, which was written in English, appeared in 1940 shortly after Koestler's final break with the Party. One of the most effective antitotalitarian fictional works of our time, it is the product of an intellectual who had come to realize that the Communist movement could not permit its adherents to think independently. Having witnessed the enslavement of a nation as a means to an end which now seemed far less attractive to him and others than it once had seemed, Koestler was convinced that it was not worth the sacrifices that the leaders of the movement demanded.

Awakened from a deep sleep by a pounding on his door, the middle-aged Rubashov thinks, at first, that he has had a recurrence of his old nightmare of being arrested by the secret police. But this time it is no nightmare. He is indeed being arrested, and he is numbed by the reality of being whisked away in the night.

It is only when the door of his solitary cell swings closed behind him that he begins truly to comprehend that what he has long regarded as inevitable has indeed occurred. One of the few survivors of the Old Guard of the Communist Party, he has found himself increasingly out of sympathy with the tactics and objectives of the Party's leader, Number 1. And though he has moved and spoken cautiously, he has had no doubt that sooner or later he would be regarded as an inconvenience.

He manages to sleep a few hours—he is quite calm in accepting the idea that he is to be shot—and the next morning, when Gletkin, the hard young warder, interviews him briefly in his cell, Rubashov is able to act indifferent with him, even supercilious. He reminds Gletkin of his own high rank and importance in the Party's history.

After Gletkin leaves, Rubashov begins the methodical pacing and turning in his cell—a habit he developed during earlier periods of imprisonment. Suddenly his step is arrested by the sound of ticking. He locates the sound as coming from the next cell—Number 402—and he realizes that the prisoner there is using the quadratic alphabet code, tapping each letter out slowly and methodically.

The two men communicate by means of this tapped code, and Rubashov learns that the man in the next cell is a long-imprisoned counterrevolutionary. He had not believed that there were any such men left. To think that counterrevolutionaries still exist—that they are not just bogeymen dragged out by Number 1 to frighten the people, or to be used as scapegoats in any emergency! The prisoner in 402 begs Rubashov to describe the last time he slept with a woman. Resignedly, almost humorously, he obliges. . . .

Later Rubashov thinks of the first time he had betrayed one of his comrades for the good of the Party. It had been Richard—that stuttering young man whom he had been assigned to meet in an art gallery, and whom he had been forced to destroy. Strange, he had not thought of him in a long time. Fortunately none of the Party workers made close ties with their comrades. They seldom even knew their last names. It was better that way, for sometimes—as in the case of Richard—one would be hampered by sentiment, by conscience. The end justified the means, and the end was the glory of the Party and the liberation and elevation of the Motherland. Richard, of course, had been correct in asserting that the Party was fooling nobody by calling defeat "strategic retreat," by refusing to face the demoralization of the people. But the Party line was not to be questioned, for to do so would mean questioning the wisdom of Number 1, indeed of the entire Party. There had been no choice but to betray Richard.

From the prisoner in 402 Rubashov learns that the harelipped prisoner in 400—a "political" like Rubashov—has been tortured. Rubashov wonders if he too will be tortured. And when prisoner 402 sends the message "Harelip sends you greetings," Rubashov is confused.

Later he thinks of his early days in the Party. There had been the time when he was imprisoned and tortured and had admitted nothing. Two weeks after his release from prison and a hero's welcome by the Party, Rubashov had gone to Belgium and begun the Party's work again. In Belgium, too, he had been forced to betray a comrade—Little

Loewy. What a fool that man had been to protest the Party's orders. The end justifies the means.

At last Rubashov is summoned for his first hearing. Ushered into a prison office, he is surprised to find that his inquisitor is none other than his old comrade, Ivanov. Their reunion is, at first, stiff, but soon Rubashov finds himself relaxing in the presence of his old friend.

Ivanov tells him of the charges against him—outrageous charges to the effect that at the instigation of foreign governments Rubashov has headed a plot against the life of Number 1. Nor is Rubashov impressed by the accumulated data Ivanov presents to substantiate these charges; he himself knows only too well how innocent conversations can be twisted and the meaning of actions subverted in order to substantiate any position at all.

From the specific charges against Rubashov the conversation moves into a more general discussion of the Party's purposes and methods, and Rubashov finds himself becoming quite heatedly articulate.

But Ivanov remains calm. He is even affectionate toward Rubashov, pointing out that he has not even brought a stenographer to this first hearing. He tries to reason with Rubashov, and tells him that he will do well to sign a confession and make a public recantation. The sentence, he promises, would be about twenty years—but this would be reduced to three or four, and then Rubashov would be free again to pursue his life's work—the work of the Party. Rubashov curtly tells him that it is useless, that he will not sign the confession, but Ivanov urges him to take two weeks to think about it.

After Rubashov is gone, Ivanov has a disagreement with Gletkin over the handling of the case. Gletkin believes that the only way to deal with Rubashov is to torture him; but Ivanov, who is Gletkin's superior, assures him that with a man of Rubashov's intellect, reason and logic will prove far more effective than torture.

After his first hearing, Rubashov finds that his life is made more pleasant. He now is supplied with tobacco, and he is allowed to take his exercise publicly in the prison yard.

During the two weeks that follow, Rubashov thinks more and more about his commitment to the Party, his divergences from the position of Number 1. He does not bother himself about the absurd charge of the plot against Number 1; the charge, Rubashov well knows, could be proved against him if the Party wished. Anything could be proved against him. . . .

The longer he thinks, the more he begins to see the reasonableness of Ivanov's offer. He remembers Arlova, his mistress as well as his secretary at the Foreign Trade Commission. He had allowed her to be shot by the Party, rather than come to her defense; for he had known that to defend her (which would have been just) would have weakened his own power for effective action in the Party. And he had been the more useful to the Party of the two. So Arlova had been sacrificed. Is he now to sacrifice himself, rather than save himself for maximum usefulness? With every day, he finds himself moving closer to the conviction that he will accept Ivanov's offer.

The night before the second week expires, a message is passed from cell to cell that a political prisoner is to be executed. It is Bogrov—and this comes as a shock to Rubashov, for Bogrov had been, like himself, along with the man who is now Number 1, one of the founders of the Party.

As the time of execution approaches, Bogrov is dragged whimpering alongside Rubashov's cell. Through the judas-hole in his cell door, Rubashov sees his fallen comrade, and is sickened at the wreck he has become, obviously the victim of torture. Even worse, he hears Bogrov give a strangled cry —and the cry is his own name: "Rubashov."

Those few seconds of agony serve to reverse Rubashov's stand. He will not give in to Ivanov. What a fool the man must be to arrange this spectacle—as clearly it has been arranged—to make him waver and capitulate.

That night, when Ivanov comes to his cell, Rubashov tells him how disgusted he is with him. But Ivanov protests that it was Gletkin's idea to frighten Rubashov with the sight of Bogrov—that, indeed, he himself had protested this folly.

Gradually Rubashov realizes that Ivanov is telling the truth, and the two, again, have a prolonged discussion on the advisability of Rubashov's signing the confession. At last Rubashov agrees to make his decision the next day.

All night he lies awake, and at last he concludes that he will sign, as Ivanov has recommended. Indeed, he recognizes that the decision had been foreordained all along; he cannot sacrifice any chance of being useful to the Party. He sends word to Ivanov that he has capitulated.

Strangely, it is several days before he is sent for. He thinks, surely, that Ivanov will not want to waste time now that he knows that Rubashov will confess. On the third day after sending the message, Rubashov learns the reason for the delay. He is summoned once more to the prison office, and this time it is Gletkin who is his inquisitor. Gletkin tells him that Ivanov had been charged with negligence and favoritism in the handling of Rubashov's case, and had, the night before, been shot.

Instantly Rubashov recognizes that Gletkin himself is the one who had reported Ivanov, with whom he had been in disagreement. And Rubashov perceives that Gletkin intends to make of his treatment of Rubashov a spectacular success, so that his own effectiveness and loyalty to the Party will not be questioned. Rubashov braces himself for the ordeal that he knows is to come.

Gletkin's tactics are not Ivanov's. An intense, burning spotlight is kept on Rubashov's face during the entire inquisition. The inquisition itself is dragged on day after day, with only the shortest periods of rest between questioning sessions. Where he had been ready to do all that Ivanov had asked, Rubashov now steels himself against Gletkin. He knows that he cannot hope to win, but he takes a perverse pride in making Gletkin work as hard as possible to wring from him each necessary admission, the signing of each of the seven charges against him.

The battle between the two men is a subtle one, and though Rubashov knows that he is foredoomed, he is determined to endure it as long as possible. Indeed, he is amazed when he does win one minor victory; he refuses to sign one of the seven confessions and, instead of pressing the point, Gletkin dismisses the charge for "insufficient evidence."

But Rubashov cannot win all the victories. He is confronted with the harelipped prisoner from cell 400, and sees that the man has been so brutally tortured that he will say anything. It is on this man's testimony that Rubashov is convicted of having plotted to poison Number 1. At last, after many days, the relentless inquisition is over, and Rubashov is allowed to sleep. Gletkin is convinced that Rubashov has succumbed not to Ivanov's "logic" but to his own more direct methods of exhausting the prisoner.

The public trial that follows is summary. Rubashov knows that he is being made a scapegoat, that his guilt is necessary to the Party for some obscure but nonetheless real reason. He plays his part to perfection, and is reviled by the judges and spectators alike. The press coverage of the trial makes clear that all the years that Rubashov had been regarded as a hero of the Party, the villain was actually in the service of foreign governments. Stolidly Rubashov accepts the sentence of death.

During his last days Rubashov reviews his life—a life in which he has given forty years of love, work, pain, devotion, and hope to the Party, and in which the Party has given him nothing. His faith in the ends justifying the means—a faith that had already begun to desert him—is now quite gone. He asks himself again and again what he is dying for. But he has no answer. All he can look forward to now is a great darkness.

Even as he is led to the cellar execution chamber, his mind continues to turn over these questions. Why is he dying? How has the Party failed? Where is the Promised Land?

The first shot fired into his skull takes him unawares. He feels himself rocking over the seas, floating in the mists upon the waters. The second shot sends him to the fringe of eternity.

CRY, THE BELOVED COUNTRY

Alan Paton

Alan Paton was born in Natal, South Africa, in 1903. Originally a science teacher in a school for African children, he later became the principal of a reform school for delinquent African boys. He and his wife have worked extensively on improving the condition of the African natives and are members of the white minority in Africa that favors equal citizenship for natives. Paton is one of South Africa's outstanding experts on prison reform, and has written non-fiction books about the governmental and sociological problems of that troubled country.

Cry, the Beloved Country was published in 1948, and has had an enormous success. Few of the problems described in this novel have been mitigated since its publication, and, as the uneasy situa-

*tion between European settlers and African natives grows more
tense, it is very possible that Paton's writings will prove to be
prophetic, and that the beloved country will be torn one day by
violent racial strife.*

When the Reverend Stephen Kumalo, the Zulu parson of the
hill-country village of Ndostheni, receives a letter telling him
that his younger sister Gertrude is sick, he and his wife decide that he must take the little stock of money that they
have long hoarded and go with it to the great city of Johannesburg in order to help her. Stephen is frightened by
this journey, partly because he is an elderly man who has
never left the hill country, and partly because of the stories
one has heard about the wickedness of Johannesburg. But he
goes, because his sister needs him, and because he may find
news of his other relatives who have disappeared into the
great city and from whom no word has come for several
years: his brother, John Kumalo, and his own beloved son,
Absalom.

Johannesburg proves indeed a terrifying place to Stephen,
and no sooner has he arrived in the great metropolis than he
is robbed of a pound by a young man. Fortunately, however,
he meets a fellow priest who guides him to the house of the
man who wrote the letter: Theophilus Msimangu. Msimangu
proves to be a middle-aged priest of great dignity and inner
strength, and Stephen knows that he has found a friend.

Stephen is installed as a roomer in the house of the
pious Mrs. Lithebe, a good woman, and between her and
Msimangu he feels that he will be safe. On the first night in
Johannesburg, Stephen learns of the great troubles between
the whites and the blacks. As he listens to his fellow priests,
both black and white, he hears of many deeds of wickedness
that trouble his soul.

The next day Msimangu takes Stephen to the house of
Stephen's sister Gertrude. Stephen is appalled to find that his
sister has become a prostitute and brewer of illegal alcohol.
She lives in a wretched condition with her young son. She
begs Stephen to take her and the boy back with him to
Ndostheni, and when she promises to mend her ways—she
believes it will be a simple thing once she is removed from
the great temptations of Johannesburg—he agrees. He takes
Gertrude and the child back to Mrs. Lithebe's house. The

good woman is skeptical of Gertrude—she recognizes at once what manner of woman this is—but she agrees to take Gertrude and the boy in for Stephen's sake; for Mrs. Lithebe feels deep respect for the good priest Stephen Kumalo.

The next day, the search for Stephen's son, Absalom, begins. No one seems to know just where Absalom is, and Stephen and Msimangu must track down every lead. It is not easy to do this, and their task is not simplified by the boycott of the bus lines by the blacks, which inconveniences them greatly but which they must respect, for are not they blacks too, and is not the cause of the blacks just? There is further the tension created by a recent series of murders of whites by natives—the latest is the murder of Arthur Jarvis, a white man who has devoted his life to the cause of the blacks. Johannesburg is a terrible place, thinks Stephen.

The search for Absalom continues for several days, and each clue gathered about the boy is more distressing than the last: bad companions, petty crimes, licentiousness—these are the things Stephen hears his boy accused of. The trail leads at last to the reformatory, from which Absalom has just been released. The young white man in charge of the reformatory gives Stephen an excellent report on Absalom; he tells him how the boy had been discharged early because a girl was pregnant by him and the pair seemed deeply in love and wished to be married. Stephen takes the girl's address.

Stephen's reunion with his brother John is as dispiriting as his search for Absalom. John, a golden-tongued orator, has become a wealthy carpenter, and has his own shop. He has turned away from God, however, and pretends to himself that he is a petty demagogue. He lectures to the blacks in the streets, under the close eye of the police; but because he is a coward, John Kumalo goes so far and no further in his speaking, so the police leave him alone. Msimangu warns Stephen that John will be in serious trouble one day.

It is a Tuesday when Stephen locates the girl who has been made pregnant by Absalom, and she has not heard from him since Saturday. The girl proves to be little more than a child herself, and Stephen sees in her the whole story of the native who goes to Johannesburg. It is a story of shame, misery, and evil.

The search for Absalom having reached a dead end, Stephen feels himself consumed with fear. And then disaster overtakes him: Msimangu brings the terrible news that Absalom, along with two other young men—Matthew Kumalo, son of John, and a youth named Pafuri—have been arrested for the murder of Arthur Jarvis. And Absalom has confessed.

How Stephen could have survived the days that follow without Msimangu he does not know, but the strange, quiet priest seems to put his entire life at Stephen's disposal, and the words of this city priest bring comfort to the troubled heart of the parson from Ndostheni. Together, they go to the prison to see Absalom. The boy tells his father that he and his companions intended to rob the house, and when they were surprised by the white man, he fired at him out of fear. He is deeply repentant, and Stephen believes him, but his heart is heavy. Absalom agrees that he would like to marry the girl who carries his child, and Msimangu promises to make whatever arrangements are necessary. Msimangu also arranges to get the services of the great white lawyer Mr. Carmichael, who will take Absalom's case without charge. (Carmichael will not, however, represent Matthew Kumalo or Pafuri; John Kumalo has a lawyer of his own who will plead that the two were not with Absalom, who alone has confessed.)

The next day Stephen goes again to see the young girl who carries his unborn grandchild. After a long conversation Stephen asks if the girl would like to return with him to Ndostheni. He is impressed with the earnestness and simplicity of her joy at this proposal. He takes her with him to the house of Mrs. Lithebe, and the good woman welcomes the child, for she sees that this girl is of a different sort than Gertrude. And Gertrude is happy, for now there will be a young person to talk to, and the girl is happy, for now she will be cared for and safe.

James Jarvis is a white planter of the hill country of Ndostheni, and when word comes that his only son, his beloved Arthur, has been murdered, Jarvis and his wife go to Johannesburg for the funeral. They stay with the parents of their daughter-in-law, and this couple discusses with them the black problem. Jarvis finds himself in agreement with them about the danger of the blacks and the need to suppress them, and he wonders how his son and his son's wife could have taken up the cause of the blacks. In his grief

Jarvis wanders around his son's house, looking through books and papers. He finds several of his son's manuscripts concerning the problems of South Africa, the problems of the whites, and the problems of the blacks. He reads them with deep interest.

The trial for murder begins, and Absalom tells his story in court just as he had told it to his father, and he swears that it is the truth—that Matthew and Pafuri were with him; that Pafuri planned the crime; that he, Absalom, out of panic and fear fired the shot that killed Arthur Jarvis; and that he is repentant. It appears that the trial will last several days.

To take his mind off the trial, Stephen decides to perform an errand which he has promised to do for a man at Ndostheni. This man has a daughter who went off to work for a white couple named Smith, who live in Springs, a section of Johannesburg, and the man has not heard from her. He has asked Stephen to find news of the girl.

During the course of the trial James Jarvis and his wife go to Springs to visit a niece who has married a man named Smith. Thus it happens that Jarvis is the man Stephen sees when he reaches the house at Springs. He recognizes the white man instantly—for he has seen this man, Jarvis, at Ndostheni—yes, even as he had often seen the white man's handsome young son, Arthur. Stephen is overcome with fear and trembling at this chance encounter, and when Jarvis finally calms him, Stephen reveals himself as the father of the man who has killed Jarvis's son. At this news Jarvis is shaken —but he is also touched at the look of fear, unhappiness, and gentleness in the black priest's eyes. He gives the information that Stephen has come for, and then bids him, "Go well, umfundisi."

"Stay well, umnumzana," replies Stephen.

The trial is over, and there is no reason to stay longer in Johannesburg. Absalom has been found guilty of murder, and is sentenced to be hanged. Pafuri and Matthew, who have steadfastly claimed that Absalom was merely trying to bring them trouble, are found not guilty, for there are no other witnesses besides Absalom. John Kumalo has used a good lawyer.

The final meeting with Absalom is heartbreaking for Stephen, for the boy is a good boy, and he is terrified of the hanging. Msimangu has arranged with the good white priest,

Father Vincent, for the marriage to take place, and the shy little girl so great with child thus becomes Stephen Kumalo's daughter.

Stephen goes to bid farewell to his brother, John. So bitter is he toward John over the lies John's son has told in court that he feels a great need to hurt his brother. He tells John that he has heard that the government has sent a spy to John's shop—a man who poses as John's friend—to take down the secret conversations held there against the government. Stephen takes delight in the unmistakable signs of fear which this produces in John. But the city brother tries to pretend that he is not frightened. "What kind of friend is that," he asks, "who would lead me into such trouble?"

Stephen looks at him coldly. "My son had two such friends," he says, and leaves.

Msimangu promises to write Stephen of the outcome of the plea for mercy that has gone forward on Absalom's behalf, and then the two men bid each other goodbye. Msimangu has announced his intention of going into a monastery—the first black man in South Africa to do such a thing. He gives Stephen his savings, as the bishop has said he might, and this money is like manna to Stephen, for he has spent all of his own money in Johannesburg. Stephen, the two women, and the child are to rise early the next morning to set out on their journey. When the time comes, however, it is discovered that Gertrude has slipped away in the night, leaving no message. Johannesburg has proved too great a temptation for her. Sadly Stephen takes Gertrude's little boy and his pregnant daughter-in-law, and bidding thanks and farewell to the good Mrs. Lithebe, he sets out for Ndostheni.

Stephen returns to his native village to find the yearly drought at its height. Poverty is everywhere; children are dying from lack of milk. Though the love of his wife, the goodness of his daughter-in-law, and the childish laughter and beauty of Gertrude's son do much to raise his spirits, Stephen finds himself in despair. After what he has seen in Johannesburg, he has no hope for the lot of the black man. Where will help come from? How will they be saved?

One day a little white boy rides by Stephen's house on a pony and stops to chat with the old parson. He is the grandson of Jarvis—a bright, eager lad. The boy is trying to learn the Zulu language, and Stephen is delighted with him. They talk. When the boy asks for a glass of milk, Stephen tells him that the natives have no milk, that children are dying from lack of milk. The next day a wagon arrives bearing cans of milk. They are from Jarvis, with instructions that the milk is to be used only for the children and the sick; and there is the promise that milk will be sent every day until the drought ends.

Stephen prays steadily for the restoration of Ndostheni—for how will the families keep their young people from leaving for the wickedness of Johannesburg if they cannot find food or work at home? He confers with the tribal chief, but there is nothing that the man can do. Then one day Stephen sees Jarvis walking about the fields of Ndostheni with a group of men; they are putting sticks into the ground. Several days later, a young, educated native arrives. He has been hired by Jarvis to teach the natives how to plant wisely, how to irrigate, how to graze their cattle. This agricultural engineer will bring life to Ndostheni.

Stephen cannot understand the actions of Jarvis, but he begins to understand a little when he and Jarvis take shelter together from a sudden storm. As they stand in the dark, dilapidated native church, Jarvis asks him: "Is there mercy?"

A letter comes from Msimangu telling that mercy has been denied to Absalom, and that the boy is to be hanged on October fifteenth. The night before the hanging, Stephen goes to a hilltop to keep a prayerful vigil. All night long he thinks of the things that he has seen and the people whom he has known. He thinks of the evil that has fallen on his race—of the sadness of such people as Gertrude and Absalom. He thinks, too, of the good he has seen: from blacks, like Mrs. Lithebe and Msimangu, and from whites, like Father Vincent and Mr. Carmichael and the young man at the reformatory—and James Jarvis.

On the night of the vigil, he again meets Jarvis. The man has remembered what is to happen to Absalom the next day; and he too has griefs to share with the sky, for Mrs. Jarvis has died, and the little boy must go away to school. Jarvis tells Stephen that he is going away from Ndostheni, and for an instant Stephen worries about what will happen to the natives. For the progress that has been made has been made only through the goodness of Mr. Jarvis. But Jarvis promises to rebuild the native church, and to send money to Ndostheni.

When the dawn comes the next morning, Stephen has hope for the future of his people and for the future of Africa. But when the dawn will come to emancipate the natives, that he does not know, for it is a secret.

EHRENGARD

Isak Dinesen

Baroness Karen Blixen, who used the pen name Isak Dinesen, was born in Denmark in 1885, the daughter of a naval officer who had spent some time exploring wilderness areas in the north-central United States. She studied painting in Copenhagen, Paris, and Rome, and in 1914 married her cousin, Baron Blixen. The went to British East Africa, now Kenya, where they managed a coffee plantation which had been purchased for them by the family. The Baron and Baroness were divorced in 1921, but she remained on the plantation, where she began to write; she was equally fluent in Danish and English. She reluctantly gave up the plantation in 1931 because of a fall in the coffee market, and returned to Denmark. Her Seven Gothic Tales, which was written in English, appeared in 1934 and brought her considerable fame in England and America. The same mood and the same exquisite perfection of style is found in Winter's Tales (1943). She lived on her estate near the coast north of Copenhagen, and died there in 1962.

Isak Dinesen's tales are generally supernatural or dreamlike, set against a background which is timeless and vaguely medieval. Ehrengard, published posthumously in 1963, was written in English, and was her last completed story. It is characterized by a comic, pastoral quality which is elegant, contrived, and, typically, rather bizarre. Isak Dinesen employs the plot of the story to investigate the oddities of human nature—particularly the grotesque sensibilities of Cazotte—and above all to describe and create a fascinating aesthetic experience.

The great grief of the Grand Duke and Grand Duchess of Babenhausen is that they have no child to perpetuate their name and authority in the small German principality over which they are sovereign. After fifteen years, however, joy prevails: the Grand Duchess gives birth to a son and heir, Prince Lothar.

As the prince grows up, he proves to be a paragon of intelligence and manly beauty. But—alas!—he has no interest in the fair sex. The Grand Duchess grieves. Has the dying

out of her husband's family merely been postponed for a
generation?

The Grand Duchess confides her fears to the masterly
court painter and roué, Herr Cazotte—a man in his middle
forties, as noted for his amorous conquests as for the divine
portraits and nudes that materialize under his brush. Cazotte
determines to take young Prince Lothar, now seventeen, on
an artistic tour of Europe. To this proposal the intellectual
youth agrees—though he is ignorant of Cazotte's plan to make
long sojourns at the courts of princes with beautiful and
eligible daughters.

The ruse has the effect anticipated by Cazotte: Lothar
falls desperately in love, and is betrothed to Princess Ludmilla, daughter of the worthy Prince of Leuchtenstein.

Shortly after the marriage ceremony, however, a new grief
strikes the Grand Duchess. Prince Lothar confides to his
mother that the first child of the generation-to-be—the infant
who shall insure the continuation of the Fugger-Babenhausen
line—will make his (or her) appearance a full two months before propriety allows.

Fearing that such a scandal would cause the overthrow of
the legitimate branch of the family and bring a lateral branch
of doubtful legitimacy to power, the Grand Duchess is distraught; and again she turns to Herr Cazotte with her troubles. At first Cazotte recommends that the royal family
merely put a good face on it and ride out the scandal; but
the Duchess finds this proposal unthinkable. Accordingly
Cazotte comes up with a second plan.

Word is to be given out that an heir is expected—but the
date is to be announced as mid-July rather than early May.
Further, it is to be announced that the Princess has been ordered into total seclusion by her doctors until her child shall
be born. This, says Cazotte, will explain Lothar and Ludmilla's remaining in hiding—which they shall do at the charming, isolated Schloss Rosenbad. There at the castle, accompanied by only a small band of courtiers and servants whose
loyalty cannot be questioned, the child will be born and kept
secret for two months. In mid-July, the cannons will announce a new heir—and soon thereafter the child can be dis-
played to the amazement and delight of all as the halest,
biggest baby ever born to the Fugger-Babenhausen dynasty.

The Grand Duchess is ecstatic with the plan, and orders

Cazotte to make all the necessary arrangements. These are soon completed with the exception of the hiring of a wet nurse for the infant-to-be, which is necessarily postponed, and the deciding upon the right noblewoman to serve as Ludmilla's maid-of-honor.

Cazotte himself selects the lady for the latter position: Ehrengard von Schreckenstein, daughter of a general, highborn, beautiful, and of unquestioned loyalty. Ludmilla is delighted with the choice, and soon the royal party is installed happily and secretly at Schloss Rosenbad.

The Grand Duchess is kept informed of the delightful life at Schloss Rosenbad by an endless flow of letters from Cazotte. One of the things he writes about in detail is his determination to seduce Ehrengard von Schreckenstein—not physically, but spiritually. It is Cazotte's ambition to create a situation in which the virginal, rigid Ehrengard will suddenly realize that Cazotte has utterly mastered her soul, that he possesses her more fully than if he had been her paramour. With fiendish glee Cazotte delights in the anticipated sensation of sending Ehrengard to her marriage (she is betrothed to one of the royal guards, Kurt von Blittersdorff) spiritually ravished. He even details to the Grand Duchess the slow, burning blush that will overcome Ehrengard at the moment she realizes that she has been seduced. The Grand Duchess, eternally grateful to Cazotte for his help in her hours of crisis, cannot but smile indulgently over his little scheme.

Life at Schloss Rosenbad is an idyl of bliss and joy, and each day passes in a rosy haze. At first, Cazotte does not know precisely how he is to accomplish his conquest of Ehrengard, but then one day a lucky accident shows him the way. He comes upon the girl bathing in a stream *au naturel*, observed (she believes) only by her maid. From the women's conversation Cazotte surmises that Ehrengard is in the habit of thus bathing nude each day, and in a flash he realizes how he is to accomplish his ambition: he must watch her, himself unobserved, and commit the picture of her to canvas. He will paint her with her face turned away, so that at the moment when he unveils his painting to the court, she alone will know of whom it is a picture. Already he can imagine the slow, burning blush that will suffuse Ehrengard's body at that moment—how she will gaze at him with both horror and passion when she realizes how he has possessed her. . . . He sets to work with a will.

On the eighth of May, Princess Ludmilla gives birth to a son as beautiful and perfect as Prince Lothar had been. A nurse, a loyal peasant woman named Lispeth, is engaged—and Ehrengard is left freer than ever for her afternoon bathing.

Each day Cazotte goes to the appointed spot, and works on his picture—and each day his dream of overwhelming this cold, austere beauty grows more intense. Then one day a sudden movement of Ehrengard's maid tells Cazotte that he is discovered at his watching post. What will be the effect of this premature revelation upon Ehrengard, he wonders?

He is not to wonder long. She approaches him shortly thereafter and says, in her measured, emotionless way, that she understands that he wishes to paint her picture. She invites him to meet her each morning so that she may pose for him.

Cazotte is shattered.

His plan for the seduction of Ehrengard is not the only one to go awry. The great secrecy surrounding the seclusion of Lothar and Ludmilla at Schloss Rosenbad cannot help but give rise to conjecture among the branch of the royal family that has illegitimate designs on the throne. And, since they cannot guess the real reason for the secrecy they conclude that it must be that Lothar is impotent, and that the entire story of Ludmilla's being *enceinte* is a myth. It is intended that a base-born infant shall be smuggled into Schloss Rosenbad and passed off as the royal child, thus preventing the sinister branch of the family from claiming the throne.

Duke Marbod—the head of the pretending branch—is convinced of the truth of this conjecture, and he determines to unmask the Babenhausens. Two of his partisans accordingly take up residence in a tavern called the Blue Boar, not far from the secret castle, in the hope of hearing scandalous rumors that will aid their cause.

As luck would have it, they encounter the husband of the woman hired as wet nurse to the secret prince. Lispeth's husband is drunk, and readily pours out his tale of woe to the eager ears of Marbod's henchmen. The drunkard—Matthias by name—feels himself ill-used by his wife's absence

from home, and by her refusal to tell him why she must
needs stay at Schloss Rosenbad. He has concluded, he avers,
that there is no baby there, and that a plot is afoot to rob
him of his wife, Lispeth.

Egged on by Marbod's henchmen, Matthias insists upon an
interview with Lispeth; and she, merely to satisfy her husband's curiosity, agrees to meet him at the castle gate with
the infant in her arms, to prove that she really is nursing a
child. When she keeps the appointed rendezvous, however,
she finds herself pulled quickly into Matthias' cart—for the
peasant has been told that he must kidnap his wife if he
wishes to save her from the "plot" of Schloss Rosenbad.

Lispeth sets up a scream of protest, but there is none to
hear her, and her fool of a husband drives the cart along at
breakneck speed. All the poor nursemaid can do is clutch
tightly to the infant prince.

Marbod's partisans had hoped to meet Matthias and his
victims at the Blue Boar, but they had not counted upon a
company of royal guards taking up residence there. Fearing
that they will be recognized as enemy agents, they decide to
lie low until they can safely meet with Matthias.

As for Matthias himself, he soon begins to have second
thoughts about what he has done. When he reaches the Blue
Boar, therefore, he merely takes Lispeth and the child to a
small attic room and glares at them in silence.

Meanwhile, the kidnaping has been discovered at Schloss
Rosenbad, and panic spreads throughout the once-happy palace. Ehrengard, upon hearing the news, shrieks and determines to go in hot pursuit of the stolen prince. Cazotte
smiles quietly to himself as the girl races off impetuously. He
has pieced two and two rather neatly together, and he is sure
that Ehrengard will not find Lispeth and the child. In a more
leisurely fashion, he reassures Lothar and Ludmilla that he
will be successful in his pursuit, and mounting his horse, he
heads for the Blue Boar.

Ehrengard, however—guided by who knows what instinct
—goes straight to the Blue Boar. She asks hotly whether a
woman and child have entered, and upon being directed to
Matthias' room, she goes there directly. Without a word she
grabs the wicked Matthias by the head and begins beating
him against the wall in merciless fury. It is upon this scene

that the startled Cazotte enters a few minutes later. Lispeth can only sit and watch dumbly as the enraged Ehrengard beats her husband.

The man's cries are heard, however, below, and one of the guards is sent upstairs to find out what causes the commotion. As luck would have it, the guard chosen is none other than Kurt von Blittersdorff, Ehrengard's betrothed.

So startled is Ehrengard by the sudden appearance of Kurt that she leaves off beating Matthias, who immediately begins protesting that Lispeth is his wife but that the infant she holds is not her child. He says, further, that none can deny it, and tells Kurt to ask the other there whose the child is.

Kurt has no choice. He asks Ehrengard, "Whose child is it?"

Without batting an eye, Ehrengard answers steadily, "It is mine."

Kurt is, of course, overwhelmed, and insists upon her revealing the identity of the father. Ehrengard wavers only a moment, and then points to Cazotte, who stands in the doorway, his mouth open.

Cazotte feels a slow, burning blush suffuse his body.

Happily, Kurt is prevented from challenging Cazotte to a duel through the intercession of Lothar and Ludmilla, who admit Kurt into their secret.

A week later Kurt and Ehrengard are present at the baptism of the newborn prince. It is mid-July, and the infant is clearly the biggest, halest child ever born to the Fugger-Babenhausen dynasty. Shortly thereafter Kurt and Ehrengard are married.

Herr Cazotte attends neither ceremony. Much to the court's surprise, he is suddenly called away. The Grand Duchess is deeply disappointed, for she has had high hopes for him.

INDEX OF AUTHORS AND TITLES